Library of
Davidson College

The Pivot of the Four Quarters

Weltgeschichte ist Stadtgeschichte.
Alle echte Stilgeschichte spielt sich in Städten ab.
Jede Frühzeit einer Kultur ist zugleich die Frühzeit
eines neuen Städtewesens.

OSWALD SPENGLER
Der Untergang des Abendlandes

The Pivot of the Four Quarters

A Preliminary Enquiry into the
Origins and Character of the
Ancient Chinese City

PAUL WHEATLEY

at the University Press
Edinburgh

© Paul Wheatley 1971
EDINBURGH UNIVERSITY PRESS
22 George Square, Edinburgh
ISBN 0 85224 174 7

North America
Aldine Publishing Company
529 South Wabash Avenue, Chicago

Library of Congress
Catalog Card Number 79-115059

Printed in Great Britain by
T. & A. Constable Ltd, Edinburgh

Dedicated to the memory of

**NUMA DENIS
FUSTEL DE COULANGES**

List of Contents

Preface (xiii)

PART ONE. THE CITY IN ANCIENT CHINA

Chapter 1. The Genesis of the City in China
- Introduction   *page* 3
- The Historicity of the Shang Dynasty   9
- Sources for the Study of Shang Urbanism   13
- The Genesis and Morphology of Shang Cities   20
  - Pre-urban North China (22)
    - The Yang-shao stage (22)
    - The Lung-shan stage (26)
  - The Earliest Urban Forms (30)
    - Cheng-Chou (31)
    - An-yang (36)
    - Other Shang cities (47)
- The Political Structure of the Shang State   52
  - The Grand Lineage of Shang (52)
  - The Practice of Government (55)
    - The extension of patrimonial authority (57)
    - The Nature of Shang patrimonialism (59)
    - The Extent of Shang Dominion (61)
- Class Differentiation in Shang Society   63
- Technological Change   67
- The Economic Organization of the Shang Territories   75
- Notes and References   78

Chapter 2. The Diffusion of Urban Life in Ancient China
- The Chou Dynasty   107
  - State and Government (112)
    - The question of feudalism (118)

LIST OF CONTENTS

    Society (122)
    Economy (128)
      Environment (128)
      Technology (130)
      Land Tenure (132)
      Commerce (134)
  The Archeological Record   135
    The Western Chou (135)
    The Ch'un-Ch'iu Period (136)
    The Chan-Kuo Period (141)
  Literary Sources   150
  Epigraphic Evidence   160
  The Spread of Urbanism in Chou Times   161
    The Western Chou (161)
    The Eastern Chou (170)
  The Nature of Chou Urbanism   173
    The Function of the Chou City (173)
      The origin of the hsien city (179)
    Morphology of the Chou City (182)
    Size of the Chou City (189)
  Notes and References   191

PART TWO. THE EARLY CHINESE CITY IN COMPARATIVE PERSPECTIVE

Chapter 3. The Nature of the Ceremonial Center
  The Earliest Urban Forms   225
    Ceremonial Centers in Regions of Primary
      Urban Generation (226)
    Mesopotamia (226)
    Egypt (229)
    The Indus valley (230)
    Mesoamerica (234)
    The Central Andes (235)
    Southwestern Nigeria (238)
    Some Ceremonial Centers in Regions of
      Secondary Urban Generation (244)
    Crete (244)
    Etruria (244)
    Japan (245)
    Southeast Asia (248)

LIST OF CONTENTS

The Centripetalizing Function of the Ceremonial Center	257
The Genesis of the Ceremonial Center	267
The Ecological Component (268)	
The Demographic Component (275)	
The Technological Component (278)	
Factors Inducing Social Differentiation (281)	
Trade and marketing (281)	
Irrigation (289)	
Warfare (298)	
Religion (302)	
The Morphology of the Ceremonial Center	305
The Secularization of the Ceremonial Center	311
The Ceremonial Center as an Ideal-type	316
Notes and References	331
Chapter 4. The Urban Character of the Ceremonial Complex	371
The Role of Corporate Kin Groups (374)	
The Significance of Writing (377)	
The Emergence of Exact and Predictive Sciences (383)	
Notes and References	400
Chapter 5. The Ancient Chinese City as a Cosmo-Magical Symbol	
The Cosmo-Magical Basis of the Traditional City	411
The Cosmo-Magical Element in Chinese City Planning	419
Geomantic Precautions (419)	
Cardinal Orientation and Axiality (423)	
The Symbolism of the Center (428)	
The Parallelism of Macrocosmos and Microcosmos (436)	
Notes and References	453
Conclusion	477
Notes	482
Glossary of Transcriptions of Foreign Names, Terms and Bibliographical References	485
Index	551

List of Figures

1. The ceremonial precinct at Cheng-Chou — 33
2. The ceremonial precinct at Hsiao-T'un — 37
3. Plan of the ceremonial precinct at Hsiao-T'un — 41
4. Land use in part of the southwestern sector of the ceremonial enclave of the Great City Shang — 42
5. A reconstruction of the ceremonial enclave of the Great City Shang — 45
6. Reconstruction of building A4 in the northern sector of the ceremonial enclave of the Great City Shang — 46
7. A tentative systematization of the archeological evidence for the earlier phases of the urbanization process in North China — 48-9
8. The nuclear region of Chinese urbanism — 51
9. Functional diagram of the ten-section system of the royal house of the Shang dynasty — 54
10. **Gi̯wang-d̪i̯ĕng (Wang-Ch'eng), royal city of the Eastern Chou — 137
11. **G'ân-tân (Han-tan), capital of the state of **D'i̯og (Chao) from 386 to 228 BC — 143
12. Plans of representative Chou cities on a uniform scale — 147-9
    I. **Mi̯wo-d̪i̯ĕng (Wu-Ch'eng), a city of **D'i̯og (Chao) during the period of the Contending States
    II. **G'ân-tân (Han-tan), capital of **D'i̯og (Chao) from 386 to 228 BC
    III. Remains of a capital of the Prince of **Tsi̯ĕn (Chin) in a late phase of the Spring-and-Autumn Period
    IV. **Gi̯wang-d̪i̯ĕng (Wang-Ch'eng), royal city of the Eastern Chou
    V. The **G'å (Hsia) capital in the state of **·Ian (Yen)
    VI. An ancient city at Lin-tzŭ, identified as a capital of **Dz'i̯ər (Ch'i)
13. Recorded urban settlement during the period of the Western Chou — 165
14. Recorded urban settlement during the Ch'un-Ch'iu period — 169

LIST OF FIGURES

15. The character denoting the outer wall of an early Chinese city as it appears in early epigraphy — 186
16. A Shang ceremonial complex compared with representative cult centers in other regions of nuclear urbanism — 241-3
    I. Hsiao-T'un
    II. Copán in Honduras
    III. Cempoala in Vera Cruz, Mexico
    IV. The ceremonial center at Teotihuacán in the Valley of Mexico
    V. Poḷonnaruva, chief ceremonial city of Ceylon from the ninth to the fourteenth century AD
    VI. Yaśodharapura in Cambodia as it was in the time of Jayavarman VII (AD 1181-c.1220)
    VII. Afin Ọyọ in 1937
17. Settlements traditionally providing services and corvée for the afins of Ọyọ and Ọwọ — 263
18. The relative chronology of urban genesis — 322-3
19. The course of urban genesis in selected regions of the Old World — 327
20. The course of urban genesis in selected regions of the New World — 327
21. The layout of T'ang Ch'ang-an — 412
22. A reconstruction of the probable ground plan of Mohenjo-daro — 413
23. **Gi̯wang-ḍi̯ĕng (Wang-Ch'eng) as it was traditionally supposed to have been laid out according to the canonical plan — 415
24. A late-Ch'ing depiction of the Great Protector selecting the site of the future city of **Glâk-di̯ang (Lo-yang) — 422
25. Chin-T'ang *hsien*-city as depicted by Hsieh Wei-chieh in *Chin-T'ang Hsien Chih* (1810) — 424
26. The City of the Dipper. The constellations of Ursa Major and Ursa Minor superimposed on the plan of Han Ch'ang-an — 443

In the Notes

I. The character for **B'âk (*Po*), a Shang ceremonial center, as it appears on an oracle bone — 99
II. The character for **·i̯ap (*i*), denoting a ceremonial center, as it appears on Shang oracle bones — 100
III. The character for **pi̯ung (*feng*) as it appears in a Chou bronze inscription — 197
IV. A reconstruction of the relationship between ancient settlements and the drainage pattern in the neighborhood of Ch'eng-tzŭ Yai — 209

Preface

This volume seeks in small measure to help redress the current imbalance between our knowledge of the contemporary Western-style city on the one hand, and of the urbanism characteristic of the traditional world on the other. Specifically, it is an attempt to elucidate the manner in which there emerged on one part of the North China plain during the second millennium BC hierarchically structured, functionally specialized social institutions organized on a political and territorial basis, and to describe the way in which, during subsequent centuries, they were diffused through much of the rest of north and central China. The exigent question as to whether all the multifarious groupings of population past and present that are conventionally designated as 'urban' do indeed constitute a unitary field of study is discussed but not assumed; and those aspects of urban theory which, though relevant to our topic, have been derived predominantly from the investigation of Western urbanism, are tested against, rather than applied to, the society of ancient China. Moreover, whereas the majority of previous investigations into the nature of the Chinese city have been undertaken from the standpoint of the humanist, in the following pages I have adopted a point of view closer to that of the social scientist. In other words, I have espoused a generalizing and comparative approach in contrast to the hitherto more commonly essayed discussion of the formal and specifically Sinic features of Shang and Chou cities. Instead of seeking to distil from the totality of their characteristics the uniqueness of the earliest Chinese cities, I have tried to isolate and analyze those cross-cultural regularities which they shared with urban forms in other cultures. In practice this has meant that I have measured a fragment of the Chinese urban experience against a generalized model of urban genesis, a procedure which has posed problems of both a conceptual and a technical nature. So far as the conceptual aspect is concerned, the construction of a model has been the logical outcome of a commitment to a broadly hypothetico-deductive methodology, a belief that advances in our understanding of urban genesis will result in the first instance from the generation of testable hypo-

PREFACE

theses, rather than from a Baconian inductivist approach which, in my opinion, is concerned more with proof than with discovery. Whatever the inadequacies of the model discussed in Chapter Three, it is at least testable against both existing evidence and that which is likely to become available in the future. In this way not only do theoretical considerations act as a check on the validity of historical reconstructions, but the empirical substantiation of particular sequences and circumstances is capable of inducing revision and qualification of even the most cherished generalizations. Furthermore, the comparative method would seem particularly appropriate to an examination of the emergence, in widely separated regions and at widely different times, of such an intricately interrelated set of institutions as the city, and this conclusion must surely be reinforced when the whole problem is bedevilled by appalling lacunae in the evidence. At the same time, I am aware that my analysis is conducted at such a broad level of conceptualization that it does little more than identify gross criteria for assigning the early Chinese city a role in the infinitely complex pattern of urban evolution, without specifying those idiomorphic features that made it distinctively Chinese. It goes without saying that a more truly explanatory schema would consider differences as well as similarities between urban forms in diverse cultures. However, this is perhaps the appropriate point at which to draw attention to the sub-title of this work, the purpose of which is to affirm the partial nature of the inquiry, the incipient stage of the investigation, and the proleptical character of the conclusions.

At the level of technique, the single tool indispensable for a study of this nature is that assemblage of cognizances and crafts which constitutes the discipline of Sinology. It is not, as participants in a recent symposium have been at pains to emphasize, an end in itself, but it is a prerequisite for any worthwhile comparative study involving ancient China, and I regret that my own technical competence in this field has not permitted me to pursue my arguments in greater depth and with greater subtlety. My excuse is the old one adduced by Hippocrates.

The evidence bearing on urban genesis, in China as elsewhere, is both direct and indirect in character. Direct evidence is almost entirely the product of archeological research, for only in the Western tracts of that realm of secondary urban generation (this term is defined on p. 9) which has recently come to be known as Southeast Asia *sensu stricto* is the process even partially documented in written records (as opposed to archetyped in literary tradition). That region is virtually unique in that divers Chinese histories, encyclopedias, and topographies preserve observations, both informal and official, relating to the period of city generation. Although fragmentary and ambivalent, these records are still capable of affording some degree of control over the more hypothetical constructs derived from investigations in other cultural realms. In China such contemporary literary evidence is entirely lacking.

PREFACE

Indirect or circumstantial evidence, by contrast, is of a more diversified character, comprising inferences from the morphology, symbolism, and functioning of later cities, especially the great capitals, urban archetypes *par excellence*, as well as information derived from folklore and mythology. This latter genre of source material always proves especially difficult to handle. The collective memory of traditional society is by no means unresponsive to happenings in the past but, unable to retain individual persons and specific events, transforms them respectively into archetypes and categories, heroes and heroic situations. And because myth is the ultimate, not the primal stage, in the creation of these archetypes, it is often hazardous to attempt to reverse the process and to isolate the paradigm at the core of the legend. Evaluating such evidence is rather like trying to grasp a fish at the bottom of a deep pool. As the intruding hand shatters the shadowy image, so the irruption of a 20th-century mind into the conceptual framework of the ancient world inevitably induces cultural refractions of such magnitude that the image of the quarry at best undergoes distortion, at worst is wholly lost from sight. But recognition of the limitations imposed by this anamorphosis is a condition of entry into the traditional world, and the social scientist who would concern himself with urban genesis must be resigned for the present to seeing his elusive fish disintegrate into a thousand glittering fragments as he reaches towards the bottom of what is a very deep pool indeed. It is not to be doubted that in the future the social scientist and the historian will be able to probe the nature of the traditional world with subtler instruments less destructive of its value systems than those at present available, but meanwhile the present study should be regarded as no more than a distant glimpse, refracted almost to unintelligibility, of one early cultural manifestation of the most complex artifact yet devised by man. On finishing this volume the reader will need no reminder of the manner in which that image, so comprehensible and definite at a distance of three thousand and more years, disintegrated when we sought to examine it more closely.

University of California, Berkeley
and University College London
February 1968

NOTE

Orthographical matters

The exact manner in which the Shang people pronounced their words is probably beyond recall, but it is generally presumed that they spoke an early version of what later became the Chinese language. They certainly wrote in a

NOTE

script which was subsequently recognized as distinctively Chinese. In any case, of one thing we can be certain: the Chou scholars who composed the few literary analecta purporting to relate to Shang times, and which may indeed have preserved some authentic Shang values, rendered personal names, place names, and technical terms in early Chinese forms. The phonetic garb of this Chou Chinese as it was pronounced in about 800 BC (technically known as Archaic Chinese) has been reconstructed largely by the labors of Bernhard Karlgren, and is employed in the present work for the transcription of names and terms prior to the Han. This expedient provides only imperfect renderings of words from the later part of the Chou period, but is even less satisfactory in the discussions of the Shang city in Chapter One. However, there is every reason to suppose that the versions of names and terms that result (signified in the text by a brace of asterisks) are a good deal closer to the Shang vocalizations than are the phonologically reduced forms of Modern Standard Chinese. The inelegance of the phonetic symbols, which may even appear forbidding to some readers, is in my opinion not too high a price to pay for the enhanced awareness of the richness of ancient Chinese culture that they reveal. By disclosing the more diversified sound structure of the so-called Archaic language, they help us to recover some of the sensuous texture of that ancient world, and enable us to give the ancient names something approaching, however imperfectly, their original sound. Nevertheless, had Professor Schafer published his simplified version of the Karlgren reconstructions before I had written this book, I should have been happy to have used it. As it is, so that readers accustomed to Modern Standard Chinese pronunciation may the more easily recognize the words in their Archaic dress, I have always added the standard Wade-Giles version in parenthesis when the word is first mentioned. Occasionally, when dealing with names as familiar as those of, say, the culture heroes Yao, Shun, Huang-Ti, and Yü the Great I have relied primarily on the Modern Standard Chinese forms, and relegated the Archaic reconstructions to parenthesis. Certain Han and T'ang names have been transcribed according to Karlgren's reconstruction of Ancient Chinese (denoted by a single asterisk), the dialect of *D'i̯ang-·ân (Ch'ang-an) in about AD 600. In the case of a few names which are so well known outside China that they have a claim to be regarded as a part of world, rather than Chinese, culture, I have retained the Modern Standard Chinese transcription alone. Such, for example, were the style of the founder of the Ch'in dynasty, Shih Huang-ti, and the names both of the historian Ssŭ-ma Ch'ien and of his great work, the *Shih-Chi*. The names of dynasties and provinces have usually been rendered in their Modern Standard Chinese form (e.g. Shang, Chou, T'ang, etc.), although the names of the individual Chou states have been Archaized. The conventional orthographic distinction between Shen-hsi and Shan-hsi has been retained for the sake of convenience, even though, as the pronunciations of the two characters differ

NOTE

only in tone, it has no basis in the Wade-Giles system.

The system of transcription employed by Bernhard Karlgren and followed in the present work is as follows.

	Voiceless consonants	Voiced consonants
Gutturals	k, kʻ, χ [X]	g, gʻ, ng, γ
Palatals	t̂, t̂ʻ, ś, tś, tśʻ	d̂, d̂ʻ, ń, j, ź, dź, ńź
Dentals	t, tʻ, s, ts, tsʻ	d, dʻ, n, l, r, z, dz, dzʻ
Supradentals	ṣ, tṣ, tṣʻ	dẓʻ
Labials	p, pʻ	b, bʻ, m, w
Laryngals	·(·i̯u)	O (i̯u)

Kʻ, gʻ, etc. are aspirates; χ=German *ach*, γ=North German *g* in *wagen* (fricative); t̂ etc. are formed like the Italian *c* in *città* with the predorsum against the alveoli; the laryngal · (·i̯u) is the 'Knacklaut' in German *Ecke*; no initial letter : O (i̯u) is a smooth vocalic ingress as in English *aim*.

Vowels
â   as in French *pâte*
a   as in French *patte*
â̯=short â
ə   as *e* in German *Knabe*
e   as in French *été*
ä   as in German *Bär*
ε=a still more open, slack ä-sound (English *man*)
ɒ   as in English *but*
i   as *ee* in English *bee*
o   as in German *Sommer*
ô   as in French *beau*
ô̯=short ô
å=an open *o* as in English *law*
ŭ   as in English *value*
u   as in English *rude*
ă, ĕ, ŏ=short *a, e, o*
i̯, ę, ə̯ =subordinate vowels in diphthongs or triphthongs

Reproduced from 'Grammata Serica Recensa,' *Bulletin of the Museum of Far Eastern Antiquities*, no.29 (Stockholm, 1957), pp.3–4.

Bibliographical matters

As a very high proportion of the sources and scholarly expositions consulted in the preparation of this volume are mentioned only once and have no continuing relevance to the work as a whole, a bibliography has not been considered necessary. However, full references are provided in the *Notes and References*

NOTE

which follow each chapter. On those occasions when references are repeated, they are usually given in abbreviated form. Some Chinese authors writing in Western languages adopt transcriptions other than those of the Wade-Giles system and, moreover, not infrequently transpose the order of their family (*hsing*) and personal (*ming*) names, while yet retaining the Chinese sequence when writing in that language. In such cases the author's preferred Western form has been preserved, with the Wade-Giles orthography and the Chinese order appended in parenthesis, e.g., Kwang-chih Chang (Chang Kuang-chih); Tjan Tjoe Som (Tseng Chu-sen). In citations of contemporary Chinese works in the Glossary the simplified (and sometimes unauthorized) characters now or recently in use in the People's Republic of China are reproduced exactly as in the original books and articles.

Matters of definition

City in this volume is used generically to denote any urban form, and carries none of the ancillary connotations of size, status, or origin implicit in contemporary, everyday American or English usage. *Urbanism* is used to denote that particular set of functionally integrated institutions which were first devised some five thousand years ago to mediate the transformation of relatively egalitarian, ascriptive, kin-structured groups into socially stratified, politically organized, territorially based societies, and which have since progressively extended both the scope and autonomy of their institutional spheres, so that today they mould the actions and aspirations of vastly the larger proportion of mankind. *Urbanization* refers to the ratio of urban dwellers to total population, and can be expressed algebraically as

$$u = \frac{Pc}{Pt}$$

where u = degree of urbanization,
Pc = the number of urban dwellers,
Pt = the total population.

It follows that the distribution of urbanization is not necessarily (and today is still a long way from) the same thing as the distribution of urbanism (number and spatial arrangement of cities) or the distribution of urban dwellers.

Acknowledgments

In constructing the model of urban genesis which constitutes Chapter Three I benefited greatly from reading Robert McC. Adams's *Lewis Henry Morgan Lectures* for 1965 under the title *The Evolution of urban society: early Mesopotamia and Prehispanic Mexico* (Aldine Publishing Company, Chicago 1966). In this imaginative comparison of structural change in 'two territorially extensive, complex, long-lived, innovative, characteristically "civilized" societies', Professor Adams has carried forward the methodology of cross-

NOTE

cultural analysis to a point where he can be said, in Thomas Kuhn's phrase, to have inaugurated a new paradigm of knowledge. I am grateful to Professor Adams for allowing me to read his book before publication. I am also indebted to Mrs T'ung Huang Yih of University College London not only for a great deal of meticulous assistance during the later stages in the preparation of this book, but also for the calligraphy which graces the *Glossary*. Finally, I would like to express my thanks to Mr A.R. Turnbull and his colleagues at the University of Edinburgh Press for the skill and care that they have brought to bear on the production of this book, and to Mr Peter McIntyre for the discernment with which he has compiled the analytical index.

References

The notes and references are printed at the end of each chapter, and the appropriate page-number for each note is printed at the top of each text page.

Part One

THE CITY IN ANCIENT CHINA

•

1

The Genesis of the City in China

INTRODUCTION

Writers on the general topic of urban origins have not usually given much consideration to the Chinese experience. With very few exceptions they have confined their attention to the climacteric events that took place at various times in Lower Mesopotamia, Egypt and Nuclear America.[1] Some, while acknowledging the essentially independent character of the earliest Chinese urban configurations, have excluded them from consideration on the grounds that the available evidence is both exiguous and unrepresentative. It is true that, in comparison with the archeological evidence that has accumulated over the span of a century or so in relation to the cities of Sumer, or over a somewhat shorter period in relation to those of Mesoamerica, the Chinese materials are meager in quantity. They are also fragmented and both spatially and temporally discontinuous, while the stages immediately prior to the emergence of urban forms are but poorly elucidated. However, only a small proportion of the total finds from Sumer and Mesoamerica bear directly on urban generation, so that the abundance of archeological materials should not be taken to imply vast resources for the study of city origins. Moreover, as has frequently been pointed out, excavation has been confined almost exclusively to the environs of monumental complexes at the expense of the territory which supported them, as well as to the levels of the monumental complexes at the expense of the antecedent formative phases in their development.

In China the foundations for the study of urban origins were laid during fifteen seasons of excavation at An-yang, undertaken by the Archeological Section of the former National Research Institute of History and Philology of the Academia Sinica between 1928 and 1937.[2] It is true that these excavations were concerned solely with a single city, and were performed under conditions of great difficulty, but they did reveal a fairly detailed and reliable plan of part of the last Shang capital, as well as bringing to light a considerable number of ancillary and other contemporary settlements and an oracular archive of more than 17,000 pieces of inscribed bones and shells. Almost equally important was the fact that these excavations established beyond doubt the historicity of the Shang dynasty, hitherto known only from literary sources, at the very moment when a new school of critical historians was questioning the authenticity of virtually all pre-Han texts, and by implication the existence of the early dynasties.[3] By revealing on oracle inscriptions the names of no less than twenty-three of the thirty Shang kings mentioned in literary sources, Tung Tso-pin and others reaffirmed the potential worth, though not necessarily the factual accuracy, of the literary tradition so far as the Shang was concerned.

After the end of World War II field work was resumed at An-yang by members of the Chung-Kuo K'e-hsüeh Yüan, but more recently interest has tended to focus on a group of sites in the neighborhood of the city of Cheng-Chou in northern Ho-nan.[4] Discovered in 1950, these remains have provided an uninterrupted chronological sequence beginning with the phase of Developed Village Farming and culminating in a clearly defined example of Shang urbanism. Subsequently, other urban and proto-urban Shang sites have been located in an arcuate zone curving across the North China Plain from Shan-Hsien in the southwest to Ch'ü-yang in the northeast. The four fully fledged ceremonial cities and half dozen or so proto-cities, incompletely excavated as they are, still provide information in considerably more detail than is available for, say, Archaic Egypt or the central Andes.

The reaffirmation of the latent value of certain literary sources which is a corollary of these excavations of Shang urban sites has significant implications in view of the limitations of archeological evidence for the purpose in hand. As Robert Adams has recently been at pains to point out, archeological interpretation tends, from the nature of the tools and techniques that it employs, as well as by reason of other disciplinary proclivities, to overweight the integrative purport of its cultural assemblages. 'Emphasis is given,' as he says, 'to objects and institutions evoking consensual patterns of behavior – art styles, cult objects, rituals – rather than to those which might suggest incipient patterns of differentiation and stratification.'[5] Moreover, the nature of the raw materials of archeology has not infrequently predisposed its scholars to pay greater attention to technological matters than to social and institutional change, a tendency that is clearly apparent in the theories of urban genesis proposed by the archeologists of a generation or two ago. And as the processes of urban development brought a great increase in the complexity of social, economic, and intellectual institutions, so archeological techniques have proved progressively less capable of elucidating these relationships in their entirety.

It is in this context that the written word becomes a useful adjunct to archeological materials in the achievement of a balanced interpretation. As we shall see subsequently, the earliest Chinese records, inscribed on bone and shell, were of restricted import, being concerned only with certain activities of a small, though influential, group of people. They are probably comparable in their utility to the so-called Protoliterate texts of Mesopotamia from the end of the fourth millennium BC, but are of much less use than the wealth of varied and detailed cuneiform documents available by the end of the Early Dynastic period (*c*. 2500 BC), selective and in other ways inadequate though these latter are as a basis for the reconstruction of contemporary urban life. However, although the oracle records are unsatisfactory for present purposes, they afford a good deal more information than, say, the Mayan inscriptions of the Classic period, of which only the calendrical information has so far been deciphered. In the New World the handful of documents that survived the Spanish conquest of Mesoamerica are largely irrelevant to the study of urban origins in either the Aztec or Mayan realms, but there are post-Conquest Spanish records which do provide accounts of contemporary indigenous urban life refracted through the prism of an alien culture, as well as traditional genealogies, recollections, and pseudo-annals compiled in a Spanish idiom by native authors soon after the Conquest. In some respects these last are analogous to the 'classical' literature of China that was reconstituted in Han times but which may preserve phenocrysts of Shang history embedded in a matrix of later material. The nature of these early Chinese literary sources will be discussed in subsequent sections.

It is, of course, true that in no region of nuclear urbanism does the evidence, whether archeological, literary, or mythological, afford an adequate base on which to erect a definitive account of urban origins. It is all a matter of degree. Few scholars would deny that early Mesopotamia and Prehispanic Mexico offer the most ample and most diversified documentation of this momentous transformation, but even there the source material falls far short of adequacy. In Archaic Egypt, on the other hand, direct evidence for the crucial transformation from village to city appears to be lost for ever, buried far below the surface of the Nile alluvium. As far as archeological exposures are concerned, the situation of the Indus valley is not too dissimilar from that of China. Both exhibit two or three partially excavated cities and a constellation of lesser sites, but in the case of Harappā and Mohenjo-daro the earlier excavations were subject to only poor stratigraphic controls, so that we are left with a picture of powerful and flourishing cities but with little idea as to their mode of origin, while the inscriptional resources, which are apparently of a restricted functional range in any case, have not yet been deciphered. In the central Andes relevant archeological investigation has, with very few exceptions, been little better than superficial, there are no Prehispanic literary sources, and between us and the origin of urban forms is interposed the screen of Inca domination which, even when it did not obliterate earlier cities, transformed them into its own cultural image. It is true that the Inca screen is not entirely opaque, but it is a much more powerful distorting instrument than are the reconstituted Han texts. Adams has also made the point that the territories in this culture realm which have received the most attention from archeologists have not been those about which Spanish ethnohistories have the most to say.[6]

In this ecumenical context the case for undertaking a study of urban origins in China appears not to be wholly devoid of merit. Several urban and proto-urban sites partially excavated, one of which provides a complete chronological sequence from a level of Developed Village Farming through to the emergence of a ceremonial city, coupled with a vast archive of 100,000 inscribed oracle bones and shells, a handful of texts that may preserve memories of actual Shang events, and a corpus of later mythology which may reflect authentic Shang values is an inadequate, but not negligible, basis on which to found an argument. This is even more to the point when the evidence available in each of the other realms of nuclear urbanism is so meager, fragmented, and ambiguous that a comparative approach alone appears likely to provide fruitful insights into the dynamics of urban genesis. The Chinese evidence alone would prove inconclusive even were it very much more abundant than is in fact the case, but it assumes a completely new significance when viewed in the light of the totality of materials available for a study of the early history of urbanism.

There is, however, another set of objections which seem to have weighed heavily against the Chinese experience with students of urban origins. Mindful of the fact that the earliest Chinese cities post-dated those of Sumer and Egypt by about a millennium and a half, and those of the Indus valley by approximately a thousand years, some scholars have regarded the process of city formation in China as in some way secondary, contaminated as it were by the presence of cultural traits diffused from Southwest Asia. It is certainly possible for primary diffusion of the set of integrated institutions that is the city to occur through the migration of a people into new territories, as happened so notably when the Spanish-style city was carried to Latin America, when the English-style city was transported to North America, Australasia and elsewhere, or when Russian-style cities were founded in Siberia. This mode of urban diffusion is virtually inseparable from the extension of empire and was, in fact, a necessary concomitant of such happenings in ancient days, no less than of European colonial expansion from the sixteenth to the nineteenth century. The foundation of such cities is usually associated with (1) the creation of an administrative organization moulded according to, and designed to sustain, the value system of the colonial homeland, (2) the imposition on the simpler society of the legal definitions of property current in the colonists' homeland, and (3) not infrequently the extension to embrace the newly colonized territories of certain sectors of the metropolitan economy. But since the time of Joseph de Guignes no one has seriously contended that the Chinese people themselves derived from the Middle East.[7] So-called secondary diffusion, the direct borrowing of culture traits, is out of the question in the second millennium BC so far as such a complicated artifact as the city is concerned. So, indeed, is stimulus diffusion, which is held to occur when the *idea* of some technical process proves sufficient to induce its reinvention. It is, of course, obvious that the likelihood of diffusion of a complex invention depends very greatly on the general level of technological attainment of the societies concerned. While it is possible that some of the more fundamental inventions may have emanated from one or more hearths, the contemporary world affords abundant evidence that even the most complex technological achievements can now spread from continent to continent virtually instantaneously through the media of secondary or stimulus diffusion. In the sphere of urban forms, for example, the contemporary planned city, originally devised according to Western values, can be found in one form or another on five of the six continents. But in ancient times, at the lower end of the scale of technological competence, it is inconceivable that any form of city could have spread by either secondary or stimulus diffusion. Consequently, I am at a loss to understand what Sir Mortimer Wheeler had in mind when he declared, 'So also, we may suppose, in the third millennium BC India (Pakistan) received from Mesopotamia the already-established *idea* of city-life or civilization, but transmuted that idea into a mode substantially new and congenial to her'.[8] Apart from the imposition by an already established political authority of urban foundations – usually for administrative or military purposes – in tributary or uninhabited territories (primary diffusion), cities formerly could come into being only where an appropriate conjunction of internal forces induced spontaneous readjustments of social, political and economic relationships. Mere knowledge of city life diffusing through a folk society could, and can, never be sufficient to induce the generation of urban forms.

Of course, this is not to deny that in numerous instances cities have arisen as a result of the secondary diffusion of nexuses of cultural traits which have stimulated the evolution of society towards the point where cities were generated. Just such a process seems to have preceded the emergence of urban forms on the peripheries of the core regions of urban genesis, especially in those sectors where political jurisdiction lagged behind cultural imperialism. In particular it would seem to have been characteristic of parts of the Levant, the shores of the Ægean, Etruria, the Sudan, Central Asia, South China and Southeast Asia. This last region is of especial interest from the point of view of urban origins and I shall examine it in detail in a separate publication. Suffice it here to point out that the adoption in the western territories of Southeast Asia of certain political institutions on the Indian model induced a sequence of socio-economic changes that culminated in the emergence of ceremonial cities on an impressive scale. By no stretching of terms could this process be characterized as primary, secondary or stimulus diffusion of urban forms. It is clearly *generation* of urban life with which we are concerned in this corner of Asia, and I think it must have been a process of this nature that Bronislaw Malinowski had in mind when he wrote, 'Diffusion . . . is not an act, but a process closely akin in its working to the evolutionary process. For evolution deals above all with the influence of any type of 'origins'; and origins do not differ fundamentally whether they occur by invention or by diffusion.'[9] More recently Julian Steward, presumably thinking along similar lines, has asked whether, '. . . each time a society accepts diffused culture, it is not an independent recurrence of cause and effect?'[10] Subsequently, Morton Fried has distinguished between what he calls pristine and secondary states,[11] the former denoting 'a state that has developed *sui generis* out of purely local conditions,' the latter 'dependent upon pressures, direct or indirect, from existing states.' Where such pressures exist, he notes correctly that the process of development may be accelerated, condensed or warped. The relationship of the formation of the state to the emergence of civilization on the one hand and to the generation of urban life on the other is not easily defined, and will be the subject of comment in a later chapter, but whatever form that relationship may prove to take, if 'city' is substituted for 'state' in the sentences quoted above, Fried's distinction between pristine and secondary remains valid. There are cities which are (1) pristine or, in our terminology, of primary generation, and there are those which are induced directly or indirectly by the presence and activities of other urban forms. Those which are (2) inspired directly are the result of the extension of empire, those (3) induced indirectly are of secondary generation. Of these classes both (1) and (3) exemplify processes of generation, as opposed to imposition, of urban forms.

The problem of genetic interconnection between the primary realms of nuclear urbanism is by no means completely resolved. Secondary diffusion of culture traits between Protoliterate Mesopotamia and Gerzean Egypt has been established beyond doubt, and Mesopotamian cultural influence was certainly not absent in the Indus valley during the third millennium BC. The civilization of the Huang valley would appear at this stage of archeological investigation to have absorbed relatively few traits directly from Southwest Asia, and virtually none of a specifically urban character, but the role of stimulus diffusion, though at the moment not easily evaluated, may nevertheless have been considerable. However, among the civilizational nuclei of the Old World, the Chinese seems to have been the one most effectively insulated from contact with other foci of high civilization, and despite the lateness of its flowering, to have enjoyed an unusual degree of autonomy in its development.

The major discontinuity in the continuum of culture is obviously that between the Old and New Worlds, but the rapidly accumulating body of literature relating to trans-Pacific cultural contacts bears eloquent testimony to the fact that secondary or stimulus diffusion cannot be completely excluded from any study of sociocultural change in Nuclear America. However, even the most ardent proponents of cultural diffusion between these realms have not claimed to discern any direct borrowings of specifically urban traits, and Gordon Willey spoke for the majority of American prehistorians when he characterized the higher civilizations of the pre-Columbian New World as standing, 'To the best of our knowledge ... clearly apart and essentially independent from the comparable culture core of the Old World.'[12] Within Nuclear America the Andean civilizations apparently owed little to the cultures of Mesoamerica, but this latter realm itself constituted one great web of culturally interrelated developments.

In these circumstances, and with a measure of diffidence appropriate to the current fragmentary state of the archeological record, I am proposing to treat Mesopotamia, Egypt, the Indus valley, the North China Plain, Mesoamerica, the central Andes, and the Yoruba territories of southwestern Nigeria as regions of primary urban generation. Whether or no this is justified as an operational expedient, empirical field research alone will ultimately decide. Cases such as that of western Southeast Asia, on the other hand, or the Sudan, Etruria, the shores of the Ægean and so forth, I shall consider as instances of secondary urban generation. Investigation of urban genesis on the North China plain, particularly at the present stage of its archeological exploration, will probably not yield conceptual tools of a calibre equal to those forged in the study of Mesopotamian or Nuclear American urban origins, but such an undertaking will be bound to provide materials for the comparative study on which will eventually be based a generalized hypothesis of city origins and, ultimately, a comprehensive theory of urbanism.

The Historicity of the Shang Dynasty

It is usually asserted that cities first appeared on the North China plain during the Shang dynasty, which flourished during the second half of the second millennium BC. This is certainly the impression to be derived from those literary sources which purport to recount the history of Shang, where we read of 'cities' being founded, prospering, being besieged, and being captured. Precisely what was implied by the term which we translate as 'city' will be discussed at a later stage.

According to the traditional version of Chinese history as preserved in the ancient literature of that country, the creation of the universe was followed by the rule of a series of culture heroes who devised the basic elements of civilized living. They in turn were succeeded by a line of dynasts who styled themselves the Hsia (**$G'\hat{a}$), and who were eventually deposed by the founder of the Shang dynasty. The precise dates of this latter dynasty have not yet been settled to the satisfaction of all concerned. Until the beginning of this century, Chinese scholars accepted the chronology set forth in historical works written long after the events which they purported to describe, and placed the beginning of the dynasty at 1766 BC and the end at 1122 BC. More recently Bernhard Karlgren[13] and Homer Dubs,[14] founding their opinions on analyses of the *Chu-shu Chi-nien* and of astronomical data respectively, have proposed a time span from 1523 to

1028 BC. Members of the Academia Sinica (as reconstituted on T'ai-wan), however, have adopted the estimates, based on a study of oracle bones, of Tung Tso-pin, namely 1751 to 1111 BC.[15] This in fact accords with Dr Noel Barnard's conclusion, based on a re-evaluation of the implications of the chronological information in the *Chu-shu Chi-nien* and *Han-Shu*, that the Chou dynasty could not – even on the evidence of traditional texts – have been inaugurated later than 1100 BC.[16] If this were so, then for the present study, which is concerned with developmental trends rather than with precise chronology, there is little advantage to be gained by departing from the traditional dating of the Shang dynasty. Perhaps it should be remarked parenthetically that traditional Chinese historiography has tended to reserve the style Shang (**$\acute{S}_i ang$) for the dynasty prior to the founding of the last capital at Yin (**·$I ə n$), after which this latter term has normally been used. This is also, generally speaking, the practice of members of the Academia Sinica at the present time, but some contemporary scholars have sought a compromise in adoption of the term Shang-Yin.[17] However, the Shang never referred to themselves by any term other than Shang, and Noel Barnard is inclined to believe that the Western Chou followed suit,[18] so that, outside quotations and titles where it is necessary to preserve the style Yin, in this work the dynasty which witnessed the earliest development of urban forms in China will be known as the Shang.

In the classical canon the Shang were accorded a supernatural origin, tracing their descent back, according to one account, to the legendary Yellow Emperor. They owed their emergence as an effective political organization to one of their culture heroes, **$S_i at$ (Hsieh), who allegedly served the emperors Yao (**$Ngiog$), Shun (**$\acute{S}_i wən$) and Yü (**$G_i wo$) with such devotion that he was granted the benefice of Shang, a territory which Chinese commentators have usually assigned, on no very strong grounds, to the neighborhood of Shang-Chou in Shan-hsi.[19] During a span of fourteen generations, with the aid of a succession of culture heroes who introduced, among other innovations, the concept of animal traction, invented the chariot, and devised new modes of economic organization, the clansmen of Shang consolidated their power to such a degree that, when the misconduct and oppressive rule of the emperor of Hsia, the first recorded Chinese dynasty, became insupportable, they were able, under the leadership of **T'âng (T'ang) the Successful, to overthrow the old dynasty and establish themselves as rulers of the Central State, the core region of higher culture which, together with peripherally located tribal groupings, constituted the Chinese ecumene.[20] The dynasty thus established endured for seventeen generations, not without vicissitudes, it is true, but nevertheless maintaining hegemony over a unified state which occupied the whole of the North China plain, together with a fringe of highland to the north, west and south.[21] Finally, towards the close of the second millennium BC, when early

Shang paternalism had degenerated into tyrannical oppression, the dynasty was itself overthrown by the Chou (**Ṯi̯ôg), one of its own feudatories.

This version of Shang history was substantially that accepted by all scholars of early Chinese culture, whether Chinese, Japanese or Western, until the second decade of the present century. Then a new school of critical historians arose to challenge the veracity of the canonical texts, which alone at that time underpinned the traditional interpretation of Chinese history. Not only did these iconoclasts succeed in showing that the classical histories had been moulded in response to disputes and theorizings of a much later period, but they were also able to demonstrate that the chronological order of the Culture-heroes, Sages and Ancestors was the reverse of the sequence in which their descendants came to power.[22] Early in the Chou period, for instance, Yü the Great featured as a god who, at an unspecified but remote time in the past, had conjured the dry land from out of the waters. By the end of the Chou he had assumed the role of a human king, and during the Chan-Kuo era he came to be regarded as the founder of the Hsia dynasty. The sage rulers Yao and Shun are both completely absent in the earliest extant Chinese literature and are but shadowy figures in the *Analects*, yet in the traditional chronology they precede Yü. Among the last to join the august circle, probably under Taoist patronage, was Huang-Ti (**G'wâng-Tieg), the Yellow Emperor, for whom there was no historical niche available later than the 27th century BC. And so he was, in the late Arthur Waley's words, 'put into this remote period by the chronologists merely in just the same way as someone arriving late at a crowded concert is put at the back of the room.'[23] P'an-ku (**B'wân-ko), from whom the universe was born, first appeared in Chinese literature at an even later date, although the nexus of ideas of which he is the focus certainly existed unrecorded at an earlier period. Furthermore, Ku Chieh-kang has pointed out that each school of thought in ancient China modified these legends so as to ensure that its own central doctrine was clearly exemplified in the Golden Age.[24] The Mohists, for example, in the interests of good government emphasized the abdication legends and the accession of virtuous and competent commoners,[25] the Taoists praised Huang-Ti for conforming to the cosmic process and not transgressing against the course of Nature, and so on. Not infrequently downright emendation of a text might take place for illustrative and didactic purposes, as when Shun persists in the *Tso-Chuan* as a descendant of Chuan-Hsü (**Ṯ'i̯wan-Si̯u), that is a member of an aristocratic lineage, whereas in every other source he has been ascribed a humble birth in accordance with the Confucian principle that moral qualities, not right of birth, should qualify for kingship.[26] Of course, this imaginative reconstruction of allegedly defective or deficient texts should not be judged by present-day standards of historiographical conduct, for in ancient China the annals were recorded predominantly for didactic and moralistic, not for analytical, purposes.

So destructive did textual criticism of this sort appear to be that for a time all records relating to the period prior to the Chou were considered spurious. In the last forty years, however, archeological excavation has amply confirmed the historicity of *a* Shang culture (even though politically it may not have been organized in the unitary state implied by the classical canon), and in so doing has raised again the issue of the still earlier Hsia dynasty. As Ssŭ-ma Ch'ien could rely on sources of sufficient accuracy for him to record the styles of Shang kings, some two-thirds of which have been verified on oracle bones, may he not also have had access to authentic historical records relating to the Hsia? So far no archeological finds have been connected with this dynasty, but the classical histories picture it as an era of high culture. This would certainly be possible if it had existed contemporaneously with the Shang and the dynastic annals of the two states had subsequently been fused into a unified tradition. Or possibly the Hsia was no more than a proto-Shang tribe whose memory was preserved in the official Shang records. I do not think it very likely that it can have been a purely preliterate, pre-urban, folk society existing wholly *prior* to the advent of the Shang, as Andersson suggested,[27] for in that case it would have lacked an instrument for perpetuating its past and would have been history-less. There would have been no written tradition to incorporate in a Shang, and later in a Chou, version of events. Recently Professor Kwang-chih Chang has shown that the genealogy of the Hsia kings, as preserved by Ssŭ-ma Ch'ien in the *Shih-Chi*, exemplifies the same alternation between two prominent lineage groups with the posthumous ritual designations of **tieng (*ting*) and **·*i̯et*(*i*) as characterized the Shang royal house; and moreover, according to the same source, at the change of dynasty the throne would have passed from a Hsia monarch of the *tieng* group to a Shang king of the ·*i̯et* group.[28] This observation provides support for a suggestion put forward as long ago as 1936 by Ch'en Meng-chia, whose researches into ancient mythology led him to the conclusion that the Hsia and Shang were chronologically successive segments of a single royal lineage.[29] The succession from **Li̯ər-ki̯wɛr (Lü-kuei) of Hsia to **T'âd-·i̯ɛt (T'ai-i) of Shang would then have had no more significance than any of the other transfers of power between the two politically dominant lineage groups beyond the fact that it subsequently became enshrined in the canonical texts as a change of dynasty. The reasons why such significance should have been ascribed to this particular articulation in the dualistic organization of the ruling lineage are unknown, but would almost certainly have concerned matters of political prestige. The four books in the *Shu-Ching* which were traditionally held to be of Hsia date, in the form in which we now know them, are Chou compilations, though certain of their astronomical data may have derived ultimately from the Shang period or even earlier.[30] Creel has proposed that the concept of the Hsia state as it has come down to us may have been a fiction devised by the Chou to provide a precedent for the doctrine by which they legitimized their overthrow of the Shang.³¹ Chang's tentative interpretation, even if confirmed subsequently, need not necessarily invalidate the suggestion for, had the Chou indeed fabricated the dynastic genealogy of the Hsia, they would surely have constructed it on the dualistic principles with which they were familiar. My own view is that, while there is no room to doubt that the form in which the traditional account of the Hsia dynasty is cast owes a great deal to editorial moralizing, the hazy divide between mythology and history should be drawn so as to include that dynasty in the latter category.

Sources for the Study of Shang Urbanism

Apart from oracle archives, whose significance will be discussed in a subsequent section, there are no contemporary Shang records still extant. There are, however, a few sections in early texts which may preserve, in edited form, either authentic Shang materials or, perhaps more probably, faint echoes of Shang happenings. In handling such records it is clearly of first importance – but also often very difficult – to distinguish genuine transmissions from those events and cultural features which later generations wished upon the Shang, either because they were incapable of piercing the screen of cultural relativity and so assumed that the Shang had espoused the cultural values and mores of, say, the Chou or Han, or perhaps from a conscious desire to enhance the prestige of particular ancestors. And always, between us and the reality of pre-Ch'in events, is interposed the murky screen that was drawn across the course of Chinese history by Han scholars in their reconstitution of the ancient texts, a screen sometimes rendered yet more opaque by the exegetes of Sung Neo-Confucianism.

Among the classical texts which have traditionally been supposed to record events under the Shang dynasty are five of the books of the *Shu-Ching* or *Book of Documents*, one of the Five Classics of Chinese literature. This work has been the subject of interminable philosophical and philological controversy ever since the emergence of two variant versions of the text in the 2nd century BC. The extant version preserves the essence of this distinction and, although it is now agreed that chapters deriving from the antique-script (*ku-wen*) text include post-Han forgeries, the status of all sections of the 'modern' [that is Han]-script (*chin-wen*) text has not been evaluated precisely.³² Of the sections which purport to preserve Shang material only that entitled ***B'wân-kăng* (*P'an-keng*) is of direct interest in connection with Shang urbanism. It consists of a collection of speeches allegedly made by B'wân-kăng, nineteenth ruler of the dynasty, in connection with the founding of a new capital, that one, in fact, which has been partially excavated at An-yang. This particular chapter is certainly not pre-Chou in date and at best can only be a rifacimento of fragments from earlier times. Creel has even charged that it was composed in the cause of Chou propaganda.³³

B'wân-kăng reigned during the middle years of the Shang. This is of some importance because Edouard Chavannes has demonstrated that the relatively detailed accounts of the first and last rulers of each dynasty as related in the *Shu-Ching* are late accretions to a basically genealogical text.[34] Even so it should be borne in mind that B'wân-kăng was the founder of the last capital of the dynasty, which, even without the attentions of Chou editors, would probably have accounted for the fact that his actions bear not a few of the archetypal imprints inseparable from the culture hero. All in all, I think it must be concluded that even the *B'wân-kăng* chapter reflects Chou conceptions of urbanism rather than those of Shang times. In fact, it has been suggested that it was concocted to provide a precedent for the transference of the capital to the east at the end of the Western Chou period.[35]

Another account of Shang times occurs in the *Chu-shu Chi-nien*, popularly rendered in English as the *Bamboo Annals*. This work purports to be an official chronicle of the state of Wei (**Ngįwər) from high antiquity to the end of the 3rd century BC. It was found in an early Wei tomb in AD 281, by which time the bamboo slips on which it was written were sufficiently unfamiliar to give rise to the name by which this work has been known ever since.[36] The extant text is demonstrably corrupt but Wang Kuo-wei has partially reconstructed the original from early quotations.[37] The chronology of this text agrees with orthodox dating subsequent to 827 BC, but prior to that date the two systems diverge considerably, and some scholars have seen reason to prefer that of the *Bamboo Annals*.

The third historical work to devote a substantial section to the Shang period is that which, since the 2nd century AD, has been known as *Shih-Chi*, that is *Records of the [Grand-]'Historian'*. Compiled by Ssŭ-ma Ch'ien under the inspiration of his father, Ssŭ-ma T'an, just after the beginning of the 1st century BC, this work was originally entitled *T'ai-shih Kung Shu*, which might be translated as *The writings of his Honor the Grand Historian*. Chapter III of this work preserves an outline of Shang history under the rubric *Yin Pen-chi*, which, together with a genealogy of the ruling house in another part of the same work, has provided the basis for the received view of Shang history until the present century. Closely associated with the *Shih-Chi* are three commentaries on it, by P'ei-Yin (5th century AD), Ssŭ-ma Cheng, and Chang Shou-chieh (both 8th century) respectively, which in most modern editions are combined with the text of the *Shih-Chi* itself. Ssŭ-ma Ch'ien is often held, by virtue of his analytical treatment of events, to have been the founder of Chinese historiography. Independent in his judgment, critical and prudent he certainly was within the framework of Han thought, but he was no more capable than any of his contemporaries of transcending the limits of Han culture, so that his chapter on the Shang transmits a distinctly Han view of events under that dynasty. Nevertheless, as mentioned above, the fact that he was able to compile a genealogy of Shang rulers which has since been in great measure verified proves that he must have had access to early records since lost.[38] Perhaps his account of Shang times may be characterized most aptly as echoes of Shang themes absorbed into the conceptual framework of the Han *Weltanschauung*.[39]

The last of the ancient texts which may preserve some genuine Shang materials of importance is the *Shih-Ching* or *Book of Odes*, which, since the 2nd century BC, has been considered one of the Five Classics. In its present form it consists of 305 early songs of varied origins. Some are folk songs in the broadest sense of the term, but strict patterns of meter, rhythm and rhyme betray the fact that even these have been transformed within the ambience of a sophisticated literary tradition. Others of the songs are ceremonial odes of one sort or another, some of which are important for present purposes because they incorporate legends of dynastic origins and exploits, including the founding of capital cities. Among these are the *Shang-Sung* (***Śi̯ang-Dz'i̯ung*), which were traditionally supposed to date from Shang times, even though Ssŭ-ma Ch'ien had ascribed them to a minister of the state of Sung (**Sông) living during the Eastern Chou. It now seems unlikely that even the earliest of the *Odes* can antedate the Chou dynasty, and the later parts of the *Shang-Sung* may be but little earlier than Confucius. However, the rulers of Sung were lineal descendants of the Shang royal house, so that the odes used at the Sung court may possibly have preserved authentic attitudes espoused in times past by ancestors of that house.[40] If we may believe a colophon to the *Yin Pen-chi*, Ssŭ-ma Ch'ien himself took his account of the early Shang from the *Shang-Sung*.[41] In the present work occasional recourse will be made to the *Shang-Sung* not for factual information but for material illustrative of an ancient value system.[42] Other items of Chou literature also include incidental references to allegedly Shang customs, but they are mostly of dubious authenticity and, in any case, do little to forward the study of urban origins in China. Some of these sources will be discussed subsequently in connection with Chou cities.

When literary sources are as exiguous as those mentioned above, to say nothing of the fact that they are ill-adapted to the purpose in hand, it is obvious that the burden of sustaining any hypothesis of urban origins will fall on archeology. The progress of this discipline in China since World War I has already been touched on, and it only remains to set the excavations of Shang cities in their historical context. The first Shang site to be explored was situated some two and a half miles northwest of the *hsien* city of An-yang, on the western edge of the North China plain at the foot of the T'ai-hang mountains. Actually it lay in a meander of the Huan river on the northern edge of the village of Hsiao-T'un (Fig. 2), in a locality known to both the compiler of the *Tso-Chuan* late in the Chou and Ssŭ-ma Ch'ien early in the 1st century BC as *Yin-hsü* or the Ruins of Yin, the location traditionally associated with the last Shang capital.[43] Oracle bones and scapulae had been turned up by the plough and eroded from the bank of the Huan river regularly since the closing decades of the 19th century and had already been the subject of study by Chinese scholars, one of whom, Tung Tso-pin[44], began excavations at Hsiao-T'un in the autumn of 1928, under the auspices of the Archeological Section of the Research Institute of History and Philology of the Academia Sinica (*Kuo-li Chung-yang Yen-chiu-yüan Li-shih Yü-yen Yen-chiu-so*). By reason of the hot summers and bitterly cold winters, digging was restricted virtually to the spring and autumn, but between 1928 and 1937 no less than fifteen seasons of field work were undertaken in and around Hsiao-T'un. Excavation had to be abandoned prematurely at the time of the Japanese invasion, but was resumed in 1949.

This was the first large-scale controlled excavation to be undertaken by Chinese (or for that matter in China, if one excludes the primarily paleontological investigations, excellent of their kind, at Chou-k'ou Tien in the early twenties), and it served as a training ground for virtually a whole generation of Chinese archeologists. The site at Hsiao-T'un had been greatly disturbed, 'more or less thoroughly dug up' in the words of Cheng Te-k'un,[45] before the archeologists from the Academia Sinica began their work, and the local folk subsequently continued to plunder oracle bones and bronzes illicitly between seasons. Moreover, the character and emphasis of the excavations underwent considerable change during the fifteen seasons of work. The excavators themselves discerned five stages in the development of their investigation.[46] During the first stage, which comprised three seasons' work, digging was exploratory and unsystematic, but the discovery of some 4,000 pieces of oracle bones and shells, in addition to the usual miscellaneous archeological bric-à-brac associated with a major site, served to emphasize the importance of Hsiao-T'un in the early history of China. The second stage (seasons four to seven) saw the development of systematic excavation and the division of the site into the sectors which have provided the framework for all subsequent digging. A start was also made on the investigation of architectural remains, and the significance of the distinction between the pit dwelling and the surface structure raised on a stamped-earth platform was recognized. The third stage (seasons eight to ten) was characterized by greater mastery of working techniques and the extension of the investigations to other sites in the vicinity of An-yang, notably the royal cemetery at Hsi-pei Kang to the northwest. The royal mausolea on this site also provided the main focus of interest during the fourth stage (seasons eleven and twelve), but in the fifth and final period (seasons thirteen to fifteen) excavation was again directed to the architectural features at Hsiao-T'un. When in 1937 work had to be discontinued owing to the Japanese invasion of North China, it had already become apparent that the archeological complex at An-yang was a magnificent representative of the urban sector of ancient Shang culture, a culture which already incorporated many of the traits which are customarily recognized as being distinctively

Chinese. How far that high culture had diffused through the countryside by the end of the second millennium BC is still a matter for debate, as indeed is the precise relation of the city to preceding cultures, though we do know that the site was inhabited before T'âng the Successful founded his new ceremonial center there.[47] During the period of hostilities the bulk of the archeological collections from An-yang was transported to southwest China for safe keeping, after which it was returned to Nan-ching at the end of the Sino-Japanese war, and finally brought to T'ai-wan in 1949. Under these circumstances it is not altogether surprising that the materials have, even at this time, not been published in their entirety, and currently there are two streams of information relating to An-yang to be tapped, one emanating from Pei-ching and reflecting the contemporary activities of the Chung-Kuo K'e-hsüeh-yüan, the other flowing out of T'ai-wan and bringing detailed reports on the work of the old Academia Sinica, now some thirty years in the past. Both of these, of course, are additional to the plethora of journal articles which, particularly during the interwar years, constituted a veritable An-yang genre of archeological literature. Since World War II, when An-yang has functioned as a training camp for young field archeologists, investigations have been mainly concerned with outlying sites such as Hsüeh-chia Chuang, whose exploration has brought an added awareness of the extent and complexity of this ancient center.

In the same period the investigation of Shang sites has spread far beyond the vicinity of An-yang, so that it is now possible to define a nuclear hearth of Shang urbanism within the broad zone of Shang culture, and to distinguish this latter from a peripheral belt of territory into which individual Shang culture traits had diffused in somewhat irregular fashion. The most important of the specifically Shang sites discovered since World War II, especially from our present point of view, is probably that at Cheng-Chou in northern Ho-nan. Excavations are still in progress, but enough has been published to show that this was another Shang urban complex comparable to that at An-yang. In fact, most students of ancient China are inclined to agree with the excavators that the remains at Cheng-Chou are probably those of **Ngog* (Ao),[48] a Shang capital of earlier date than dynastic An-yang, which, according to literary sources, was founded by **D'i̯ông-tieng* (Chung-ting), tenth king of the dynasty (1562–1549 BC in the traditional reckoning, about a century later in Tung Tso-pin's chronology). An extensive city wall has been traced, and some degree of social and economic differentiation is already apparent in the areal distribution of finds, but perhaps most important of all is the reasonably complete stratification from Yang-shao times to the period of high Shang culture. Unfortunately, this is so far the only example of such a chronological sequence that has come to light and there is no assurance that it is of general application to Shang urban development.

The immense energy and devotion with which the Chinese have tackled the problems of national reconstruction, coupled with the need to forge an historical identity in strong contrast to the deplorable self-image of the colonial period, have had repercussions in the field of archeology. Field surveyors move ahead of the developers and, whenever possible, archeological teams salvage remains which would otherwise be destroyed in the process of economic development. Needless to say, much of this rescue work is done hurriedly and occupies a great deal of skill that might otherwise be engaged in planned excavations directed towards the solution of specific problems in Chinese prehistory, but nevertheless the quantitative increase in archeological materials during the last two decades has been enormous.

The Shang period has received its share of attention, so that it will be possible later in this chapter to provide some account of two other ceremonial cities as well as of a number of proto-urban centers in northern and western Ho-nan and in southern Ho-pei. Altogether there are now more than 150 excavations of so-called Shang sites for which reports are available, but on examination not a few of these turn out to be concerned not so much with Shang culture *sensu stricto* as with isolated Shang traits in a primarily Neolithic context.

The deficiencies of archeological research in China have been the subject of frequent comment by scholars in that field and there is no call, especially for one who is not an archeologist, to repeat them here – though, of course, any evaluation of the implications of the archeological record must take account of the methods by which the record was obtained. Suffice it to point out that, as late as 1959, an American scholar could write that, 'In the whole of China there is simply *not one dependable stratigraphic excavation* of a site.'[49] Today, when field techniques have been greatly improved, Chinese archeology has still not freed itself entirely from the inheritance of its past. There is still a tendency among some scholars to use archeological materials to verify preconceived interpretations of the classical literary sources, and, despite the publication of a few interpretative studies in recent years, the typological classification of artifacts, often on the basis of single elements of form or composition, appears to be the primary concern of many authors. Refinement of the systematics of space and time distributions is receiving fairly continuous attention, but so far there has been virtually no attempt to apply the concept of developmental trends in the manner both advocated and demonstrated by, among others, Robert J. Braidwood in Southwest Asia, Gordon R. Willey in Nuclear America and Robert McC. Adams in his recent comparative study of urban origins in the Old and New Worlds.[50] There has been no sustained endeavor to reconstruct the culture and society of ancient China, to use the typologies and classifications proposed as tools for an examination of the direction of socio-cultural change, or to deduce the interplay of forces contributing to such change. In short Chinese archeology still awaits its first syncretistic evaluation of the secular trends in the nexus of institutional, social, political and economic change of which the archeological record is the material manifestation. From this generalization it is necessary to exclude one outstanding scholar, a Chinese working outside China, namely, Professor Chang Kuang-chih of Yale University. In a series of prescient publications [51] over the past decade, this author has essayed single-handedly to chart the configurations of cultural growth in pre-Ch'in China in terms of developmental trends transforming levels of sociocultural complexity, and the conceptual framework of this present chapter owes much to his labors.

There is one further category of evidence of importance for the present investigation which is archeological in the sense that it is usually acquired from the earth by means of the specialist skills of the trained excavator, but which constitutes a medium sufficiently recondite to have given rise to a discrete branch of study. This is the oracle archive, the link between mute archeological evidence *sensu stricto*, whose implications must be elucidated by a trained interpreter, and the literary record which to a much higher degree is capable of speaking for itself.[52] The earlier scholars in the field of Chinese epigraphy put great faith in the potentialities of the oracle bones, often believing that they would ultimately provide the basis for a definitive history of the Shang dynasty, but, as more and more of them were deciphered, it became increasingly obvious that their information was not of the anticipated level of comprehensiveness. Discussion of the nature of the information inscribed on the oracle bones and of the role of scapulimancy will be reserved for subsequent sections: here we shall concern ourselves only with the limitations of this corpus of evidence.

In the first place, the oracle records contain a vast body of information relating both directly and indirectly to the ceremonial rituals and religious beliefs of the royal lineage, but they disclose relatively little about other aspects of the activities of the royal house, either public or private. A little can be gleaned by the diligent student concerning the political and administrative structure of the Shang state[53], but virtually nothing about the peasantry and artisanry who constituted the broad base of the social pyramid. Even within this contextual framework, which is oriented exclusively towards élite status, and which within that focuses overwhelmingly on the royal house, the information is spread very unevenly. The vast bulk of the oracle bones have come from An-yang, either directly through excavation or indirectly from the hands of dealers in 'dragon-bones', while those from Cheng-Chou have seldom been deciphered. This means that, apart from questions concerning remote ancestors, they relate to only twelve of the thirty kings who are recorded in the *Shih-Chi* as comprising the Shang dynasty, which in turn implies that they relate to a period of city *founding* rather than to the earlier and climacteric phase of city generation. And not all Shang kings were equally committed to the ordering of their personal and public lives according to the principles of scapulimancy. Under **Tso-kap (Tsu-chia), for instance, divination was restricted almost entirely to routine enquiries concerning sacrifice, military campaigns, hunting, royal itineraries, and the king's safety during ritual periods, whereas **Mi̯wo-tieng (Wu-ting) was given to consulting the oracle on a host of personal and public problems, ranging from his own toothache and the illness of the crown prince to the choice of crops and the possibility of rain. Finally, of the 100,000 or so oracle bones, mostly fragmentary but occasionally complete, which have so far been discovered, less than 15,000 have been deciphered.[54] The rest are either in such poor condition that there is little or no hope of eliciting their information or else the characters have not been identified. It is not surprising, then, that Tung Tso-pin, one of the pioneer interpreters of these records, after a lifetime's study should have been led regretfully to conclude that no more than a hundredth part of the total spectrum of Shang culture could be deduced from the oracle bones.[55]

This is the negative aspect of the oracle archives. Possibly some of the vigor with which some scholars have stated this case reflects disappointment at the nonfulfilment of earlier hopes. Imperfect though the oracle record be, it is still a much more valuable resource than any that exists for a comparable phase of development in most of the other areas of primary – or of secondary, for that matter – urban generation. As remarked above, these inscribed bones have a utility for present purposes at least comparable to that of the Protoliterate texts of Mesopotamia, are superior to the inscriptions of Archaic Egypt and the glyptic materials of the Indus valley in that a much higher proportion can be deciphered, and have no analogues at all comparable in the New World. The following pages will make frequent reference to information from this source.

The Genesis and Morphology of Shang Cities

Urban forms first developed in China on the great northern plain, a vast embayment of alluvial deposits, enclosed by peripheral uplands on north, west, and south but open to the sea at two points on its eastern rim. Structurally this plain comprises an enormous composite alluvial fan to the west and a composite subaerial delta to the east, both built up by the Huang river, its distributaries, and other streams flowing from the western mountains. The hearth of Shang culture occupied the higher parts of the fan, stretching in an arc from the neighborhood of present-day Ch'ing-yüan in central Ho-pei to the vicinity of Po-Hsien in northern An-hui, and comprising the territory known to the Chinese in later times as the Chung-yüan or Middle Plain. The physiographic history of the plain has not been elucidated with any degree of precision, but it seems likely that the lower northern and southern fringes were still extensive marshlands in Shang times. At present the Huang river flows obliquely across the plain from southwest to northeast, but in the past it has followed a variety of other courses, some passing to the north and others to the south, of the Shan-tung peninsula. In Shang times there is evidence that it bifurcated soon after entering the plain, one channel reaching the sea in the vicinity of modern T'ien-chin, the other at a point where the ancient coastline intersected the course of the present Huang river.[56] I have been forced into using this last periphrasis by the existence of a great deal of doubt as to the precise run of the coast in Shang times. It is certain that the leading edge of the Huang delta then lay to the west of its present position, but in the absence of reliable literary records, archeological distributions, and certainty that the rate of advance of the delta front has been constant over the past three thousand years, it is impossible to locate the Shang coastline precisely.

Today the climate of the plain is extreme: hot in summer, bitterly cold in winter, with summer monthly rainfall means up to five or six times those of winter, and a mean annual variability of 20 to 30 per cent (extreme variations are, of course, much more severe). More will be said about some aspects of the environment in a later chapter, but the thorny question of climatic change must be raised forthwith. And equally early in our investigation it must be stated that no definite conclusion is at present possible. In the absence of that type of problem-oriented research which is beginning to yield important results in Mesopotamia and Mesoamerica, it is impossible in China to apply the strictly scientific tools of the paleoclimatologist, so that it becomes necessary to rely on inferences from conditions in Asia generally during the second millennium BC, on the ecological implications of faunal assemblages from the An-yang excavations, and especially on the evidence of the oracle archives.[57]

When the An-yang faunal remains were analyzed it became clear that certain species such as the elephant, water deer, tapir, and bamboo rat had since become extinct or were now found only in more southerly latitudes. This led Father Teilhard de Chardin and C.C. Young to suggest the possibility of a deterioration in climatic conditions since Shang times.[58] However, the argument is not quite that simple. Present knowledge of the ecological history of the North China plain is insufficient to enable us to distinguish the possible effects of climatic change from those of human occupance. As man came to mould the environment to suit his own needs, so he must inevitably have eliminated certain ecological niches and the animals that occupied them, and part of the discrepancy between the ancient and modern faunas may stem from this cause.[59] Dr J.G. Andersson, the pioneer investigator of the Chinese Stone Ages, after an ingenious attempt to combine both genres of evidence with later literary sources, hesitantly speculated that the climate of ancient China might have been slightly warmer than at present.[60] But he concluded with a caution that millennia of human occupance had gone far towards an irreparable obliteration of the evidence.

Subsequently Hu Hou-hsüan,[61] relying on an impressive corpus of data culled from ancient texts, was able to reinforce the idea that there were marked differences in the patterns of ecological adaptation in ancient and modern China, but he made virtually no attempt to distinguish between the effects of natural and human agency. Hu also touched on the evidence of oracle bones, but this was exploited more fully by Karl Wittfogel.[62] Analysis of 108 queries concerning the weather abstracted from some 14,500 pieces of bone and shell led this author to confirm Andersson's suggestion that during the later Shang the climate was somewhat warmer than at present. Almost immediately, Tung Tso-pin, excavator of some of the largest oracle archives at An-yang, denied that these records could at present be used to furnish reliable evidence of climatic change, though they might possibly be made to do so after more intensive research.[63] He was particularly critical of Wittfogel's techniques of analysis, especially in so far as they related to the structure of the archaic language. According to Tung, the oracle records, as they can be evaluated by presently available methods, do no more than confirm the existence of two seasons : a cold, drier (but not completely rainless) winter and spring (from the tenth to the third month), followed by a wetter, warm summer and autumn (from the fourth to the ninth month). This dichotomy was reflected in the form of the enquiries submitted to the oracle. During the drier season the questions relating to precipitation were usually cast in some such form as, 'Will there be rain [or snow or hail] ?' Sometimes the query was tied to a particular time period such as a month or five days. During the wetter season, however, the questions were usually framed on the lines of, 'Will the rain stop ?', 'Will the rain continue ?' or, perhaps, 'Will there be a fine day ?'. It is, of course, true that the weather sequence of the North China plain is not this simple, but, nevertheless, the oracle records on this interpretation afford no support for any theory of climatic change. However, it may be pointed out that Tung's interpretation is qualitative and leaves open the possibility of quantitative variation. The amount of rainfall and the relative warmth of the seasons may have been modified, even though the regimen of the seasons remained essentially unchanged.

In these circumstances we can take the enquiry no further at present, and it will be necessary to await the resolution of this problem by the paleoclimatologists of the People's Republic of China.

PRE-URBAN NORTH CHINA

The Yang-shao stage. It is necessary at this point to sketch in briefly the cultural and social milieu within which Shang cities were generated. Fortunately there is no need to carry our discussion back before the appearance of food production in North China. I say fortunately, for evidence of even the terminal food-gathering phase is exiguous, and there is no shred of evidence bearing on either the period or the place at which farming was initiated. In these circumstances no intellectual profit would accrue from our reopening the controversy as to the relative contributions of external versus indigenous stimuli, a debate which, in the context of China's search for a national identity, has recently been pursued with especial vigor.

As no modern dating techniques have been applied in Chinese archeological work, it is not possible to propose an absolute chronology for the sequence of pre-urban societies which is, nevertheless, clearly evident in the archeological record. Suffice it to say that, at some undetermined time in the past, the western sectors of the Chung-yüan witnessed a series of ecological adaptations which eventuated in the achievement of what Robert Braidwood has called Primary Village Farming Efficiency.[64] In China, a late phase of this level of development is known as the Yang-shao stage, after a village of that name in Mien-ch'ih Hsien in western Ho-nan, which was considered until recently to provide the type-site for this culture.[65] Now it has become evident that the Yang-shao excavations revealed a transition phase between representative Yang-shao and a succeeding culture, but the name has become securely attached to the former, and will be used as such in this work. The earlier phases of Yang-shao culture, on present evidence, appear to have developed in and around the middle Huang valley, specifically in the vicinity of the confluences with the Fen and Wei rivers. Subsequently the culture diffused eastward on to the western edge of the plain proper, and northward and westward along the valleys leading into central Shan-hsi and eastern Kan-su.

All our knowledge of North Chinese prehistory has been acquired in little more than three decades of investigation, and during the first half of this period – from 1920 when Andersson discovered the site at Yang-shao Ts'un until 1937 when Japanese armies overran the plain – excavation was sporadic and uncoordinated. During the war years it was virtually non-existent. Only since about 1950 has the tempo of archeological exploration and investigation quickened as a result of the salvage operations already referred to, but these have been by no means sufficient to resolve all the problems outstanding in any evaluation of Yang-shao culture. However, enough has been laid bare to provide the basis for a general discussion of this stage, and we are fortunate in being able to draw on the masterly synthesis of all currently available information by Professor Chang which has been mentioned above.[66]

There can be no doubt but that the Yang-shao culture was based on a fairly advanced paleotechnic ecotype which, dimly discernible though it is by reason of a paucity of evidence, appears to have taken the form of some sort of long-term fallowing system. At least this seems to be the implication of the discontinuity of occupation at most of the sites. The implements of cultivation, namely hoes, spades, possibly digging sticks,[67] and semi-lunar stone sickles, are not inconsistent with this interpretation, while the prevalence of stone axes of a round or lentoid cross section and symmetrical edge adapted for forest clearance would tend to confirm it. The staple crops of the Yang-shao farmers were millets (*Setaria italica*, Beauv. var. *germanica* Trin. and *Panicum miliaceum*, L.), supplemented by wheat and an alleged sorghum usually identified by Chinese authors as *kao-liang* (*Andropogon sorghum*, Brot.). However, this crop was unknown in China until Sung times and there is, indeed, some likelihood that this grain, which was indubitably of African origin,[68] was popularized by the Mongol conquerors late in the 13th century A D.[69] As sorghums were by all accounts relatively late introductions into China, presumably the grain discovered in Yang-shao excavations was one of the larger millets. Another attribution that is almost certainly erroneous, but which has become firmly established in the relevant literature, is the inclusion of rice (*Oryza sativa*, Linn.) in the Yang-shao crop inventory. This seems to have arisen when the site at Yang-shao Ts'un itself was considered to be representative of that stage, whereas it is now known to have derived from a late or even transitional phase of the culture. There is, however, a strong likelihood that hemp was cultivated.[70] Dogs and pigs were the most common of the domestic animals, with cattle and sheep rather less prominent in the economy. A half-cut cocoon (*Bombyx mori*, Linn.) found at Hsi-yin Ts'un proves that silkworms were raised at this time.[71] There is also abundant evidence that hunting and fishing contributed important supplements to the Yang-shao diet, and the preservation of a foxtail weed (*Setaria lutescens*, Beauv.) at Ching-Ts'un probably implies the gathering of wild grains.[72] Crafts were well developed and included, in addition to the manufacture of stone, bone and antler implements, a mature tradition of handmade and moulded domestic pottery, the red and grey wares that became famous almost from the moment when Andersson discovered the first presumed Yang-shao site in 1920. Silk may have been spun on stone and pottery spindle whorls, which are common on Yang-shao sites, and hemp was probably used with the eyed bone needles which have also been found fairly frequently.

Settlements took the form of compact, self-contained, economically autonomous villages comprising a dozen or so semi-subterranean dwellings often grouped around a communal long-house. The planned and segmented layout of some of these settlements has been held to suggest that they functioned on a lineage or clan basis. Areal differentiation within the village was often manifested not only in the distinction between individual dwelling and long-house but also in the presence of an incorporated or annexed sector occupied by pottery kilns, and in a cemetery adjacent to the settlement.[73] In fact the disposition of some settlements excavated in the Pan-Shan in eastern Kan-su,[74] coupled with the evidence of similar relationships discovered among a group of settlements in Hua-Hsien in eastern Shen-hsi, indicate that during later phases of the Yang-shao stage several neighboring villages sometimes shared a common cemetery. This conclusion in turn has led to the further inference that population pressure had already induced the fission of parent villages into smaller clusters which were engaged in the colonization of cultivable lands interstitial and peripheral to the nuclear hearth.[75] That some process of expansion such as this was at work is also implicit in the very marked stylistic uniformity of the Yang-shao horizon over a wide extent of territory. To Professor Chang's scholarly acumen we owe the observation that these settlements were characterized by discontinuous but repetitive occupance, a conclusion hitherto obscured by the preliminary and sometimes unsystematic character of the investigations at most of the larger Yang-shao sites. Presumably at least some of the Yang-shao farmers moved their residences as they rotated their fields on a selectively repetitive pattern.

Professor Chang believes, on the basis of the occurrence of deer burials, the frequency of female symbols in ceramic decoration, and on the evidence of two stylized heads wearing fish-shaped headdresses depicted on *p'an*-basins from Pan-p'o Ts'un, that the Yang-shao villagers probably performed some kind of fertility rites to ensure the growth of their crops and the success of their hunting and fishing.[76] It is not unlikely, moreover, that some of the more carefully executed pottery bowls and miniature vessels may have been employed in the same rites. Whether or not the shamans – if that is indeed what they were – depicted on the *p'an*-bowls were full- or part-time specialists cannot be determined at this point, but it is certainly significant that the decorative arts were concerned only with domestic activities to the exclusion of the preoccupations of a ritual or secular élite. Certainly the coarse mesh of our archeological sieve has retained no evidence of social distinctions other than those based upon age, sex and personal achievement; but the still incipient state of Chinese archeology makes it difficult to be sure whether Yang-shao society should be categorized as an egalitarian or as a rank society. The first of these is defined, in the terms of Morton Fried,[77] as a society in which there are as many positions of prestige in any given age-sex grade as there are persons capable of filling them. In a rank society, on the other hand, differences in prestige are structured in another way. Additional limitations having nothing to do with sex, age or personal attributes are placed on access to prestige, so that there are fewer positions of valued status than individuals capable of achieving them. Neither in egalitarian nor in rank society is there developed exploitative economic power or genuine political power. In typical rank societies only two kinds of authority can be invoked, familial and sacred, and there is no access to the privileged use of force in support of either. Yet despite the equalitarian character of their economic and political sectors, rank societies do exhibit certain status differences, manifested in sumptuary specialization and ceremonial function. Such differentiation appears on present evidence not to have progressed far in Yang-shao society, but it may have been already initiated in rudimentary form.

The Lung-shan stage. In 1928, at Ch'eng-tzŭ Yai near Lung-shan Chen in Shan-tung, Wu Gin-ding (Wu Chin-ting) brought to light a culture which has since been proved to be a successor to the Yang-shao stage.[78] For almost thirty years these two cultures were regarded as contemporary, the Yang-shao adapted to the environment of the western uplands, the Lung-shan to that of the eastern plains. The *renversement* of this interpretation came with the recognition, during excavations in 1956 and 1957 at Miao-ti Kou, near Shan-Hsien,[79] of a proto-Lung-shan cultural assemblage overlying remains of the Yang-shao stage. Subsequently, this transitional stage has been identified at several other sites, including some, among them Yang-shao Ts'un itself, which had been excavated previous to 1956. Even more recently the Lung-shan culture has been found to extend into the western uplands, a final reason for abandoning the mutually exclusive two-culture theory.

Lung-shan culture seems to have developed in the nuclear area about the zone of contact of the provinces of Ho-nan, Shan-hsi and Shen-hsi, in which the Yang-shao culture had previously emerged. From there it spread through all eastern and southeastern China, where strongly marked regional traditions evolved that have been characterized by Professor Chang as 'Lungshanoid'.[80] Here we shall be concerned only with those traditions which developed in the nuclear area and on the North China plain, that is with the classical Lung-shan culture.

It is clear from even a cursory inspection of the available evidence that between the Yang-shao and the Lung-shan there had supervened considerable structural readjustments within society, in the ecotype on which it was based, and in political organization.[81] In the first place, for reasons that can at present only be speculated about, selectively repetitive occupance had been replaced by relatively permanent, certainly long-term, settlement. On the other hand, the invention of the well now allowed a wider choice in the selection of settlement sites. Villages were on the whole larger than in Yang-shao times and frequently surrounded by permanent ramparts of stamped earth. Within these walls there can be discerned the same contrast between semi-subterranean dwellings and communal long-houses as was found in Yang-shao villages, with added importance accorded to pit granaries, a symbol of the greater degree of permanence of Lung-shan settlement.[82] As Lung-shan farmers gradually colonized the still swampy plains to the east of their cultural hearth, so they developed a tendency either to seek or to build earthen mounds on which to locate their villages.

This increased permanence of village life reflected a change from shifting to permanent cultivation. Presumably some system of short-term fallowing, that is a rotation of crops, had replaced the Yang-shao swidden system or rotation of fields. The crop staples in the nuclear area were still millets, possibly supplemented at this time by wheat, though this has so far been archeologically attested only in the Huai valley.[83] Rice had also been incorporated into the crop inventory of the eastern plains, and cattle and sheep now seem to have played a more important role, although pigs and dogs remained the most numerous of the domestic animals. Possibly the domesticated horse may also have had some significance at this time, and poultry had certainly gained in importance. But the remains of wild game and the presence of fishing gear on the archeological sites leave no doubt that both hunting and fishing made substantial contributions to the Lung-shan way of life.

Although farming methods had been improved, the actual tools of the farmer seem not to have changed significantly since Yang-shao times, and the principal implements were still the hoe, spade, digging stick, and sickle. It should be noted though that Chang has discerned in the stone assemblages of Lung-shan a shift in emphasis from cutting tools suitable for skinning to those better adapted to harvesting.[84] There had, however, been considerable advances in industrial technology. Stone tools were mostly polished and were characteristically of asymmetrical edge and rectangular cross-section, that is they were of the adze family and adapted to the needs of carpentry, in contrast to the wood-felling axes of the Yang-shao stage. Moreover, although tools and implements of bone, antler, and mollusc persisted into the Lung-shan stage, there are certain indications that bronze working may have begun at this time. It is claimed that traces of a metal saw can be discerned on some fragments of antler, and metal objects have allegedly come to light on Lung-shan sites in Kan-su and Ho-pei, but these records are not beyond dispute.[85] However, it is a fact that the abrupt curves of a good deal of Lungshanoid pottery give the impression of being skeuomorphs inspired by metallic prototypes. If such did exist it is virtually certain that they were used for ritual purposes, and there is no evidence at all (in fact there is a good deal to the contrary) that either implements or tools were made of metal. In the field of ceramics the potter's wheel had been introduced (although hand-made pieces still predominated), pastes had been standardized, and the old Yang-shao tradition had been enriched by a distinctive style and a great variety of forms, notably tripods (*li*, *ting*, *chia*, and *kuei*) and ring-footed vessels (*tsun*, *p'ou*, and *tou*) which are usually ascribed ritual associations. The evidence for textile manufacture is wholly inferential but the frequent finds of spindle whorls, bodkins and eyed needles would seem to indicate that, though there may have been no major advances since Yang-shao times, this complex of crafts was not ignored.

In the sphere of religion the Lung-shan remains are less equivocal than are those from Yang-shao sites, and there is a close association between religious activities and status differentiation among the villagers. For the first time there is unambiguous evidence, in the form of phallic images, ceremonial vessels, bird motifs and scapulimancy, of an institutionalized ancestor cult[86] which may, however, have originated in Yang-shao times, and which probably provided the stimulus for a shift in the application of the decorative arts from domestic utensils to ceremonial crafts. This shift is signally evident, as is remarked above, in the pottery tradition. It was almost certainly as a response to the need to communicate with ancestors who, after making their contribution to the life of the settlement, had returned to the bosom of the earth, that there arose the practice of scapulimancy, which is attested in excavations and surveys almost throughout the extent of the Lung-shan culture realm, from Kan-su to Shan-tung and from Liao-ning to An-hui.[87] It is difficult to avoid the conclusion, particularly in view of the subsequent status of this ritual pseudo-science, that it must have been the prerogative of a specialized priesthood. Another indication of status differentiation within the community comes from an excavation at Liang-ch'eng Chen in Jih-chao in Shang-tung, where a hoard of finely worked jade objects is presumed to represent very considerable private wealth. That such differences in status did in fact exist is confirmed by variations in burial postures and inequalities in the quantities and qualities of accompanying grave furniture.

Nor was societal differentiation only hierarchical. There are also clear indications of occupational specialization. In addition to the skills of the ritual experts mentioned above, pottery manufacture, making use of the wheel and producing some wares of extreme delicacy and refinement, was almost certainly in the hands of specialists, as was metal working if it was in fact in existence in Lung-shan times. It has often been pointed out that the massive walls which surrounded at least some Lung-shan settlements, together with the presence of a variety of offensive weapons in Lung-shan villages, and the fact that some of the skeletons unearthed at a site near Han-tan had obviously encountered violent deaths,[88] imply the development of organized warfare and the emergence of incipient political consciousness consequent upon a more precise definition of political groupings. This conclusion is in agreement with the integral character of the functional network of village life and institutions so far as they can be reconstructed from the archeological evidence. Each settlement constituted an essentially self-contained unit.

If Professor Chang Kuang-chih is correct in his contention that in the Lungshanoid settlements there were specialized craftsmen, full-time administrators, and priest-shamans, and that there were also a theocratic art and a theocratically vested ceremonial pattern, which, no longer the common property of the entire village, were the prerogatives of a selected portion of the villagers[89] – and this is certainly the direction in which the available evidence points and is a conclusion consonant with the overall Lung-shan cultural configuration – then this society must surely be classed as a stratified society in the strict sense in which that term is used by Morton Fried.[90] Like the rank society defined above, a stratified society has fewer positions of valued status than individuals capable of filling them, but it goes further than the rank society in associating various degrees of status with differentials in the means of access to strategic resources.[91] In a fully developed stratified society, high status persons are privileged to enjoy almost unimpeded access, low status folk have only impaired access, to the community resources and are hedged about by socially sanctioned restraints which can often be circumvented only by the payment of dues, rents, or taxes either in labor or in kind. In my reading of Chinese prehistory the Lung-shan society was of this type.

Although Lung-shan society may be classed as stratified in this specialized sense, and although the Lung-shan ecotype was probably a paleotechnic sectional fallowing system pursued at the level of (in Braidwood's phrase) Developed Village Farming Efficiency,[92] nevertheless the Lung-shan community was still to a very large extent a society based on kinship. In fact, to judge from conditions in the immediately succeeding Shang period, kinship probably provided the basis for the differential access to resources which we have remarked above as implicit in Lung-shan archeological assemblages. In the over-generalized terminology of a decade ago, it was still a folk society. I am using this term broadly in the sense in which Robert Redfield first introduced it: 'The folk society may be conceived as that imagined combination of societal elements which would characterize a long-established, homogeneous, isolated and non-literate integral (self-contained) community.'[93] Redfield was interested primarily in processes of social change, and it has been pointed out, by George Foster among others,[94] that the categories which he devised for this purpose are unsatisfactory tools for the classification of societies, subcultures or communities in terms of structure. This is probably true (though in his later works Redfield did modify his scheme to some extent to meet the desiderata of his critics[95]), but it is not a complete disqualification in a study such as this, which is concerned pre-eminently with a period of climacteric social change. Different problems demand the formulation of different categories as research tools. Moreover, in the following pages, I shall endeavor to take some account of the deficiencies in Redfield's formulations, in particular his failure to demonstrate adequately the relationship between folk society and social class.

As far as the archeological evidence allows us to visualize Lung-shan society, it appears to accord closely with the anthropologist's generalized model of the more advanced form of folk society. Small, relatively isolated communities of preliterate agriculturalists were engaged in sedentary subsistence farming in the context of an economy that was structured around status relationships rather than some form of exchange. At the Yang-shao stage the division of labor, apart from that necessitated by and appropriate to differences in sex and age, was restricted to the recognition that certain individuals were especially skilful at certain crafts which were, nevertheless, practised by all men, at the same time as a few members of the community devoted a proportion of their labor to the perfection of a specialized accomplishment not attainable by the majority of their fellows, namely the keeping open of channels of communication between the group and the realm of the supernatural. By the Lung-shan stage, both occupational and sacral distinctions had become more clearly defined, but social relationships were still essentially familial, with kinship as the basis of all groupings and the whole of society permeated by common understandings as to the nature and purpose of life.

Some scholars,[96] considering that Redfield placed too much emphasis on the isolation of folk societies and ignored the systematic economic and ritual exchanges into which most of them enter, have pointed out that it is not the degree of involvement with other groups but rather the nature of that involvement which is the distinguishing feature of folk societies. One of the most succinct of the characterizations of the social and economic aspects of such societies that take account of these relationships is that provided by Marshall Sahlins:

'In primitive economies, most production is geared to the use of the producers or to discharge of kinship obligations, rather than to exchange and gain. A corollary is that *de facto* control of the means of production is decentralized, local, and familial in primitive society. The following propositions are then implied : (1) economic relations of coercion and exploitation and the corresponding social relations of dependence and mastery are not created in the system of production; (2) in the absence of the incentive given by exchange of the product against a great quantity of goods on a market, there is a tendency to limit production to goods that can be directly utilized by the producers.'[97]

It will be our task in the next section to relate the manner in which the instruments of economic coercion and exploitation and the concomitant relations of dependency emerged on the North China plain, and in a subsequent chapter some effort will be made to elucidate the dynamics underlying these changes.

THE EARLIEST URBAN FORMS

It was in the social and cultural milieu just described that, probably early in the second millennium BC, there was initiated a series of structural changes which transformed the whole configuration of society. Professor Chang has justly termed this a quantum change,[98] for it not only established North China in the roster of civilizations, but also thrust it into the secular cycle of world urbanization whose consummation is only now to be anticipated. That the earliest Chinese urban forms arose in the Chung-yüan is clear enough, but the precise location in which the event first occurred still eludes us. The tacit assumption of some authors that Shang urbanism was generated by the Ho-nan phase of the Lungshanoid horizon is extremely probable but still unproven. So far, the earliest evidence of this transition derives from excavations in the vicinity of Cheng-Chou in northern Ho-nan. Although the investigations are

GENESIS AND MORPHOLOGY

still incomplete, they have already laid bare a long stratigraphical sequence from a lower phase on the very border between Lungshanoid and Shang to the floruit of that dynasty, and they reveal explicitly and unequivocally that, at Cheng-Chou at any rate, Shang urbanism developed directly out of the cultures of the North Chinese Neolithic. It is, nevertheless, still possible that this may have been a local phenomenon, and we must be wary of generalizing from the sole instance of such evidence so far uncovered.

Cheng-Chou.[99] The archeological investigations conducted in the vicinity of Cheng-Chou more or less continuously since the discovery of the site in 1950 have extended over an area of some forty square kilometers from Hsi-ch'eng Chuang in the west to Feng-huang T'ai in the east and from Tzŭ-ching Shan in the north to Erh-li Kang in the south. Altogether nearly thirty sites have been explored, of which about half a dozen lie within or close under the walls of an ancient ceremonial center.

Both Yang-shao and Lung-shan remains have been excavated at sites in the vicinity of Cheng-Chou such as Lin-shan Chai, Niu-Chai and Ko-ta-wang, and the earliest Shang phases stratigraphically attested appear to have evolved out of these stages. The following table summarizes Chang Kuang-chih's systematization of the five stratigraphical phases that have been discerned in the Cheng-Chou excavations.[100]

V	Jen-min Kung-yüan phase	Jen-min Kung-yüan III
		Ko-ta-wang III
IV	Upper Erh-li Kang phase	Erh-li Kang II
		Jen-min Kung-yüan II
		Pai-chia Chuang II
		Nan-kuan-wai III
		Tung-Chai III
III	Lower Erh-li Kang phase	Erh-li Kang I
		Jen-min Kung-yüan I
		Pai-chia Chuang I
		Nan-kuan-wai II
		Tung-Chai II
		Ko-ta-wang II
II	Lo-ta Miao phase	Lo-ta Miao
		Nan-kuan-wai I
		Tung-Chai I
		Ko-ta-wang I
I	Shang-chieh phase	Shang-chieh

The site at Shang-chieh appears to have been a Lungshanoid settlement on the threshold of the transformation to urban form. Nine floors of dwelling

THE GENESIS OF THE CITY IN CHINA [91

houses were excavated, together with fifteen subterranean storage chambers exhibiting the typically Lungshanoid pocket shape. The inventory of the stone industry is particularly Lungshanoid in expression but some of the ceramic forms, particularly the *li* tripods, *tou* ring-footed vessels, jugs, bowls, and wide-mouthed jars are characteristically Shang. No metal artifacts have been found. Pig bones which had been used for divination have come to light,[101] but none bears evidence of the elaborate preparation which was associated with later phases of the Shang. The Shang-chieh stratigraphy is not continued upward and at the moment the value of the site rests solely on its very evident transitional character between Lungshanoid and Shang proper.

At Ko-ta-wang an early Shang phase lies directly above and was presumably continuous with a Lungshanoid stratum. Grouped with this phase are others of similar configuration at Nan-kuan-wai, Lo-ta Miao, and Tung-Chai. At each site the remains of apparently permanent villages were found, together with pottery kilns at Ko-ta-wang. The large quantity of shell artifacts, the bone hairpins with awl-shaped heads, and the unprepared oracle bones were still strongly Lungshanoid, but pocket-shaped storage chambers were less prominent, and Shang-style traits were increasingly evident in the ceramic assemblages.[102]

It is with the Lower Erh-li Kang phase that a distinctively urban nucleus first appears in the archeological record,[103] and it persists through the two succeeding phases. No one feature can be diagnostic of urban life, but at Cheng-Chou the configuration of the total assemblage of remains is decidedly urban in the sense in which that term is defined in Chapter Four. The most impressive single feature, though not one necessarily indicative of urbanism,[104] is the trace of a massive earthen wall enclosing a rectangular, presumably ceremonial, enclave some 2 kilometers from north to south by 1·7 from east to west. It thus occupies approximately 3·2 square kilometers, an area more than twice as large as that of the present-day walled city of Cheng-Chou (Fig. 1). The fact that this modern city is located directly above the ancient enclave may be symbolic, though not necessarily illustrative, of the extreme permanence of some site values in traditional China, but it has seriously hampered archeological investigation of the Shang city. So far two sections of the wall have been investigated, one of 1,720 meters at Tzŭ-ching Shan to the north of the present-day city, the other of 2,217 meters at Erh-li Kang to the southeast. Both sections show that the wall was built by the *hang-t'u* or stamped-earth technique. *Hang-t'u* was the term applied by the pioneer field archeologists at Hsiao-T'un to the layers of rammed earth[105] of which the Shang builders had made their foundations and city walls. The technique consisted of piling earth into a caisson of wooden planks, and then pounding it until it was sufficiently compact to withstand the ramming of another layer above it. Successive layers were added in this manner, one above the other, until the desired height was attained. The

32

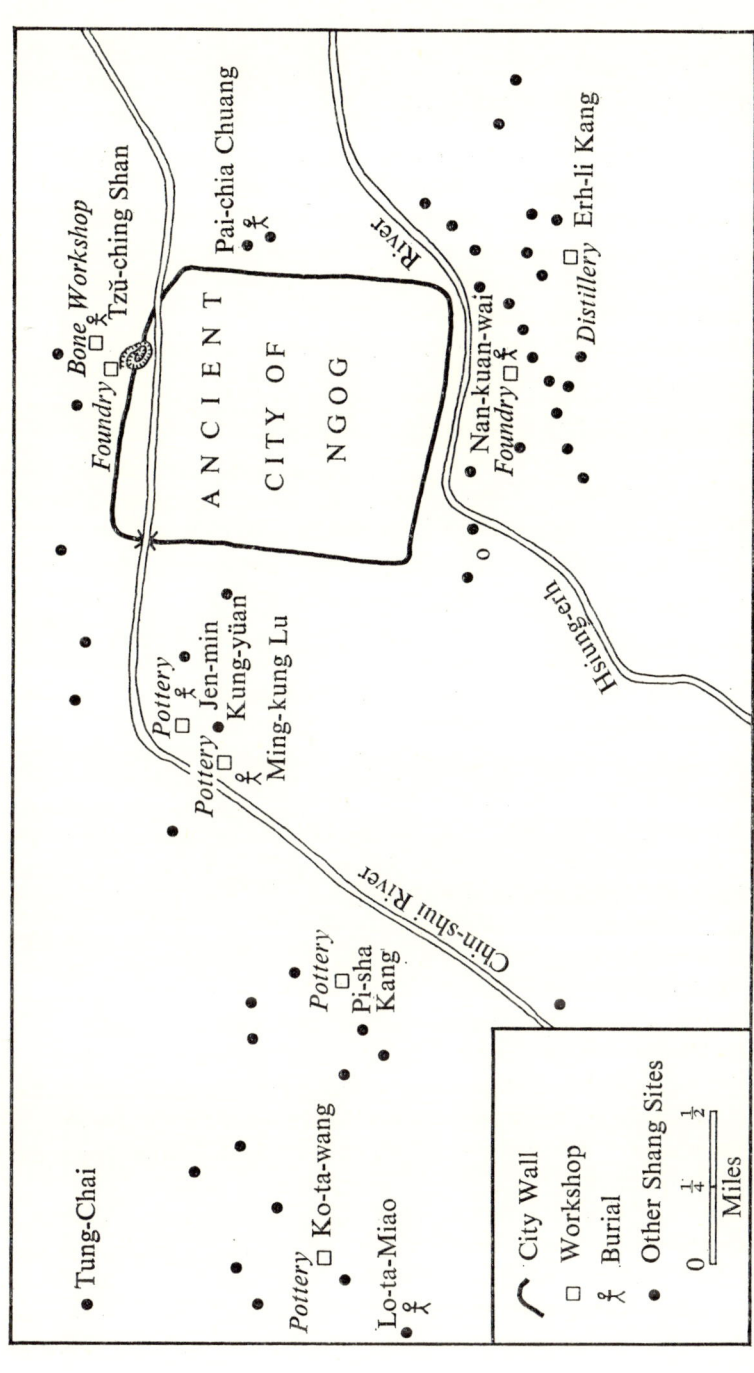

[1] The walled ceremonial precinct at Cheng-Chou which, together with its dependent settlements, may have constituted the city of **Ngog (Ao). Based on a plan in An Chin-huai, 'Shih-lun Cheng-Chou Shang-tai ch'eng-chih—Ao[**Ngog]-tu', *Wen-wu*, nos. 4 and 5 (1961), p. 73.

process, which was employed widely in China in subsequent ages and is used even today, was depicted vividly, not to say onomatopoeically, in the Ode **Mįan in Shih-Ching [Mao CCXXXVII]:

> And so [Duke **Tan-B'įwo : Tan-Fu] summoned the Master of Works,
> And so he summoned the Master of the Multitudes [that is the farmers called for corvée],
> And charged them with the construction of dwellings.
> They set their plumb-lines vertical,
> They lashed the boards to hold [the earth],
> And raised the Temple [of the Ancestors] on the cosmic pattern.[106]

> They collected [the earth] **ńiəng-ńiəng,
> They measured it out **Xmwəng-Xmwəng,
> They rammed it down **təng-təng,
> They scraped repeatedly **b'įəng-b'įəng;
> As the hundred **to-lengths [of wall] all rose upward
> The [rhythm-giving] drums could not keep pace.[107]

In The Ode **Sįĕg-kân [Szŭ-kan : Mao CLXXXIX] the same process is again depicted onomatopoeically:

> They are lashing [the frames for the earth] **klâk-klâk,
> They are ramming [the earth in them] **t'âk-t'âk.

Although, as noted already, the presence of the modern city has allowed only sporadic excavation within the enceinte delimited by the ancient wall so that its function can only be speculated about, the general configuration of the settlement and comparison with the apparently analogous sector at Hsiao-T'un (pp. 39–43 below), together with such remains as have been revealed in this central core, would seem to indicate that it constituted a ceremonial and administrative focus for a group of surrounding villages and hamlets. At least one of the buildings within the enceinte, even though incompletely excavated, was larger than any building so far discovered outside, and has been interpreted as a public edifice of some description. To the north of it was a large platform of rammed earth, which invites comparison with an altar in the center of the settlement at Hsiao-T'un, while from the northern edge of the enclave came a hoard of finely worked jade hairpins, which must establish beyond doubt the élite occupancy of the site.[108]

At distances ranging from a few hundred yards or less up to four or five miles from the enceinte there were located a variety of apparently ancillary settlements, a high proportion of which contained dwellings, both semi-subterranean and surface, often with a door in the southern wall. Subterranean storage chambers were distributed virtually throughout the settlement. At Erh-li Kang,

Pai-chia Chuang, Nan-kuan-wai, and to the west of the Ming-kung Lu drainage channels were interspersed among the dwelling sites.[109] One of these at Pai-chia Chuang still preserves the impressions of rounded posts which impliedly supported the sidewalls of the drain. The excavators concluded that these channels formed part of a drainage system, though whether it was designed merely to lead off rain water or functioned in the disposal of sewage as well is unknown. Burials have been unearthed at Erh-li Kang, Nan-kuan-wai, Pai-chia Chuang, Tzŭ-ching Shan, Lo-ta Miao, in the Jen-min Kung-yüan, and along the Ming-kung Lu, but the greater numbers, as well as the larger and more elaborate interments, have been found either within or close to the central enceinte, notably in the Jen-min Kung-yüan and at Pai-chia Chuang.[110] Full details have not yet been published but the excavators at this latter site refer to 'large tombs' with elaborate furnishings and, in two cases, to human sacrifices. These large tombs at Pai-chia Chuang apparently belong to the Upper Erh-li Kang phase, and similar graves in the Jen-min Kung-yüan to the final phase of that name. It is worth noting in connection with the development of the ceremonial enclave that, whereas the oracle archives associated with the Lower and Upper Erh-li Kang phases were largely unprepared bones, in the Jen-min Kung-yüan phase they consisted predominantly of elaborately prepared turtle carapaces.

Handicraft workshops appear to have been scattered through the settlements surrounding the ceremonial and administrative enclave. All those discovered so far have been assigned to the two Erh-li Kang phases. Nearly all the old Lungshanoid industrial traditions were still in existence, although some had undergone stylistic modifications. About 150 meters north of the enceinte, for example, there was a bone workshop from which has been recovered more than a thousand pieces of bone in all stages of preparation. The raw materials consisted mainly of bones of ox, pig, and deer, supplemented, somewhat surprisingly, by a proportion of human bones. The finished products comprised mainly arrow heads and hairpins.[111]

Somewhat farther afield, about 1,200 meters to the west of the central enclave, there was a pottery comprising no less than fourteen kilns, together with storage pits containing both fired and unfired pottery and tools of the trade, and the houses of the potters. It is noticeable that this particular site yielded only pottery of a fine clay texture, mainly *p'en* basins, *tseng* steamers, *kuei* bowls, and *kuan* jars, so that it could be argued that other kilns must have existed to manufacture both the sand-tempered domestic wares, such as *li*, *ting*, and *hsien* tripods, and the hard, glazed and white pottery which are attested at numerous sites throughout the city and its environs.

Other kilns have, in fact, been located, notably in the Jen-min Kung-yüan[112] and at Ko-ta-wang,[113] though none has yet provided evidence of such extensive operations as that just mentioned. Close to the Jen-min Kung-yüan were more potters' dwellings, still housing their tools and gear. Kilns dating from late in the Shang-chieh phase have been discovered at Pi-sha Kang and again at Ko-ta-wang.

Bone carving, ceramics, and jade working were already traditional crafts in Shang China, and there is abundant evidence that the lithic industry persisted to supply a wide range of tools and implements. What was wholly new and at the same time distinctively Shang in style and conception was bronze foundry, which first appeared in the Lower Erh-li Kang phase. Two foundries have been discovered so far, the one approximately 100 meters north of the ceremonial enclave, close to the Tzŭ-ching Shan,[114] and the other some 500 meters south of the enceinte, at Nan-kuan-wai.[115] The southern foundry was the larger, occupying 1,050 square meters, and was also the earlier, having been assigned to the Lower Erh-li Kang phase. The northern foundry was of Upper Erh-li Kang date and was associated with a residential sector for the craftsmen. It is significant that, both at the large kiln site described above and at the Tzŭ-ching Shan bronze foundry, the workmen's houses were provided with stamped-earth foundations, which presumably reflected a status somewhat above that of the common folk, who had to be content with semi-subterranean dwellings.

The last indication of spatial specialization in the technological complex of Cheng-Chou is provided by the tentative identification of a distillery at Erh-li Kang. It has been suggested that a white deposit on the inner surface of a collection of large, coarse-textured jars may have resulted from their having been used as containers for some sort of alcoholic drink.[116]

An-yang.† The stratigraphy of the Shang excavations northwest of An-yang has been much less fully elucidated than that at Cheng-Chou, partly because of the disturbance of the site by looters,[117] partly because of interruptions in the progress of excavation, and not least because this was the site where Chinese archeologists to a large extent effected their own training. Moreover, even today the results of the excavations undertaken between 1928 and 1937 have still not been published in their entirety. The absence from the published reports of Fascicle 1 of Volume I,[118] which will presumably deal with general considerations relating to the location and excavations, makes it especially difficult for anyone who has not been fortunate enough to visit An-yang to get a clear idea of the nature of the site and the work performed there, and forces all students of this aspect of Shang culture to rely on small-scale sketch maps in journals, such, for example, as that often reproduced from *K'ao-ku Hsüeh-pao* for 1947.[119] However, these disadvantages are to some degree mitigated by the greater intensity of excavation in the central sector of the city as compared with Cheng-

---

† An-yang is strictly the name of a *hsien*, the chief city of which is Chang-te Fu. However, like many other cities in similar positions, this *hsien* capital is often called by the name of its *hsien*.

GENESIS AND MORPHOLOGY

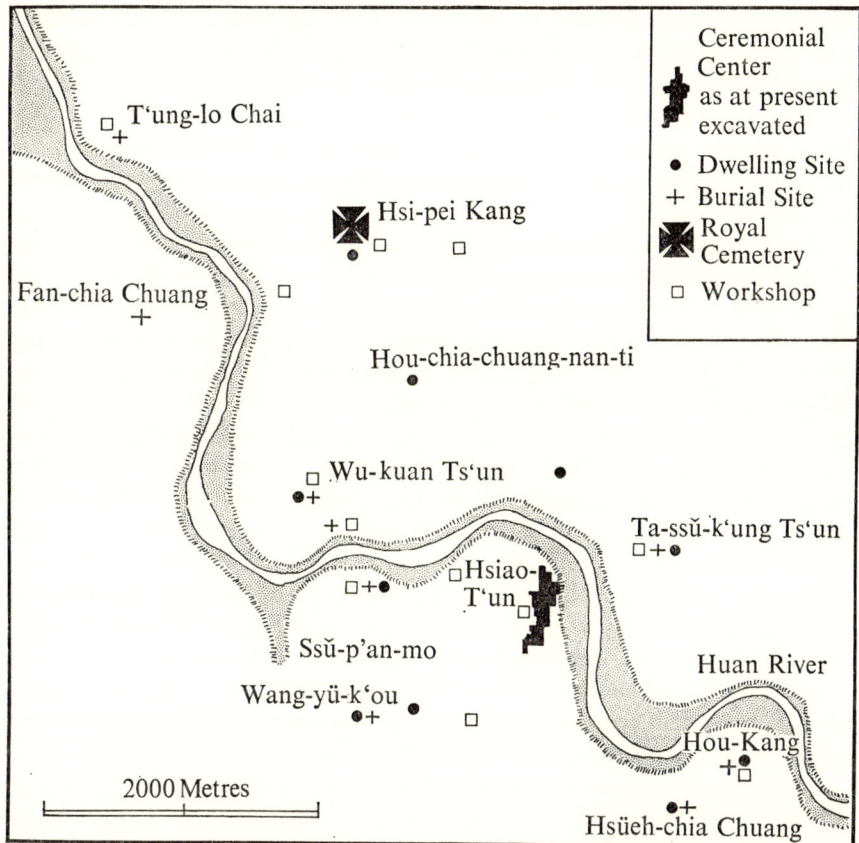

[2] The ceremonial precinct at Hsiao-T'un which, together with its dependent settlements, constituted the Great City Shang. Based on sketch maps in Shih Chang-ju, 'Yin-hsü tsui-chin-chih chung-yao fa-hsien; Fu: Lun Hsiao-T'un ti-ts'eng', *Chung-Kuo K'ao-ku Hsüeh-pao*, no 2 (1947), pp. 4 and 76.

Chou. It is clear from the evidence published to date that, as at Cheng-Chou, the settlement at An-yang consisted of a centrally situated ceremonial and administrative focus surrounded at varying distances by smaller dependent villages and hamlets. In this instance the core enclave was located in a loop of the Huan river immediately north of the village of Hsiao-T'un, and the attached settlements stretched along both sides of the river for a distance of some five kilometers (Fig. 2).

As soon as the stratigraphy of the Cheng-Chou site was published it became clear that the city at An-yang represented a somewhat later phase of Shang development. At Hsiao-T'un itself the excavators had already recognized three Shang levels, separated by a stratigraphical break from a Lungshanoid cultural stratum below.[120] The middle level, characterized by the adoption of the *hang-t'u* technique in the construction of architectural foundations, was held to have been initiated when B'wân-kăng established his capital at An-yang – in 1384 BC according to Tung Tso-pin's reckoning. The lower level, which consisted mainly of semi-subterranean dwellings and storage pits, would then have represented a pre-dynastic, but still Shang, occupation of the site, and the upper level could be considered to indicate a post-dynastic occupance, subsequent to 1111 BC in Tung's chronology. More recently Tsou Heng has claimed to distinguish two sub-stages in the dynastic phase, an initial one, presumably dating from the founding of the capital by B'wân-kăng, which was characterized by *hang-t'u* foundations in association with a system of drains, and a subsequent one in which *hang-t'u* structures were no longer accompanied by drainage channels.[121] The published evidence does not inevitably entail Tsou Heng's interpretation, but it is clearly prudent to refrain from dogmatic judgments until the reports of the excavations have been published in their entirety. In any case what is more relevant to present purposes is Tsou Heng's correlation of the *hang-t'u* phase at Hsiao-T'un with the Jen-min Kung-yüan phase at Cheng-Chou. The Hsiao-T'un phase prior to the *hang-t'u* he assigned a position earlier than the Jen-min Kung-yüan but later than the Upper Erh-li Kang. Subsequently more elaborate syntheses have been proposed, notably that of Cheng Te-k'un, who attempts a grand correlation of all Shang sites in five phases: Proto-Shang, Early Shang, Middle Shang, Late Shang, and Post Shang.[122] The present author is inclined to agree with Chang Kuang-chih that such syntheses are premature,[123] and in the following discussions archeologically based subdivisions in the progress of Shang urbanism will be restricted to the recognition of a distinctively earlier sequence of stages represented by the evolutionary forms at Cheng-Chou, followed, whether conformably or not, by a Late Shang floruit at An-yang. For practical purposes it will be accepted that the earlier phases of dynastic settlement at Hsiao-T'un were roughly contemporaneous with the decline and abandonment of Cheng-Chou (Fig. 7).

GENESIS AND MORPHOLOGY

So much for the stratigraphical underpinnings of the two main expressions of Shang urbanism. It is appropriate, however, to mention here a periodization devised by Tung Tso-pin which was based on information from the oracle archives.[124] Some 30,000 of these inscribed bones and shells were recovered *in situ* at Hsiao-T'un, of which 13,041 inscriptions have been published to date, and Tung used the style by which the court diviners addressed the royal ancestors to discriminate five periods in the dynastic occupancy of that site. In terms of his own chronology these were as follows:

- v 1209–1111 BC. Under the rule of two kings, ****Tieg-ˑi̯ɛt (Ti-i) and **Tieg-si̯ĕn (Ti-hsin).
- iv 1226–1210 BC. Under the rule of two kings, **Mi̯wo-ˑi̯ɛt (Wu-i) and **T'âd-tieng (T'ai-ting).
- iii 1240–1227 BC. Under the rule of two kings, **Bli̯əm-si̯ĕn (Lin-hsin) and **Kăng-tieng (Keng-ting).
- ii 1280–1241 BC. Under the rule of two kings, **Tso-kăng (Tsu-keng) and **Tso-kap (Tsu-chia).
- i 1384–1281 BC. Under the rule of four kings, **B'wân-kăng (P'an-keng), **Si̯og-si̯ĕn (Hsiao-hsin), **Si̯og-ˑi̯ɛt (Hsiao-i), and **Mi̯wo-tieng (Wu-ting).

Subsequently this schema has been modified to include only four periods of alternating conservatism and innovation.[125] Tso-kăng is then incorporated in period I and Tso-kap is assigned to the former period III, which has now been redesignated as period II. Tung also claimed to be able substantially to validate the objective reality of these periods by content analysis of the oracle archives. Using such categories as foreign ethnonyms and toponyms, personal names, and the special preoccupations of individual monarchs, combined with grammatical constructions, forms of the characters, and styles of calligraphy, he demonstrated a remarkable consistency in several aspects of the cultural morphology of each phase in his scheme. To a large extent, too, Tung's proposed periodization has been reflected in the changing spatial emphases brought to light by the field archeologists at An-yang. Oracle records from Tung's first phase (1384–1281 BC), for example, have come predominantly from the northern sectors of Hsiao-T'un, those from phase II (1280–1241) from the west-central sectors, those from phase III (1240–1227) from the southwest, those from phase IV (1226–1210) from the southeast, while those deriving from the last phase (1209–1111) have been found concentrated in a small sector of the northeast.

So far no wall has come to light to delimit the extent of the ceremonial and administrative enclave at Hsiao-T'un but, in view of the fact that *hang-t'u* ramparts featured in the earlier Cheng-Chou phase and in the Lungshanoid stage even before that, and continued into historical times long subsequent to the Shang, it is not unlikely that their absence is only apparent, a temporary consequence of the incompleteness of the excavations, perhaps helped by the unauthorized disturbances of the site. In any case, even if a wall had enclosed the eastern flank of the ceremonial center, it is doubtful if it would have survived the encroachment of the Huan river which has eroded away the edge of the settlement on that side. The surviving sectors of the ceremonial focus occupy about 10,000 square meters (Fig. 3).

On reading some of the earlier accounts of the excavations at Hsiao-T'un, one was left with the impression of a maze of *hang-t'u* foundations, semi-subterranean dwellings, storage pits, and burials of both men and animals in a wide range of attitudes and circumstances (Fig. 4). The Chinese archeologists expended a great deal of effort in fitting these various features into elaborate classifications, usually on a morphological basis,[126] but few of these schemes seemed to throw much light on the way in which the settlement as a whole functioned. More helpful for our present investigation are the spatial distinctions observed by Shih Chang-ju.[127] Although nothing has survived of the architecture of the city above foundation level Shih was able to distinguish a tripartite division into:

1. A northern sector containing fifteen rectangular, cardinally oriented structures raised on *hang-t'u* foundations. This he interpreted as the residential preserve of the ruling élite (A in Fig. 3 : cf. also Fig. 5).

2. A central sector, now partly eroded by the Huan river, but still containing twenty-one large halls, arranged in two longitudinally oriented rows on the south side of a square platform of *hang-t'u* construction (B in Fig. 3). These halls, also supported on *hang-t'u* foundations above a complicated system of underground drainage channels, and associated with a large number of human burials, are believed to have been the ancestral temples of the royal lineages, in which case Ling Ch'un-sheng may well be correct in his identification of the square *hang-t'u* platform (Y on Fig. 3) as the foundation of a *t'an* for the worship of ancestors.[128]

3. A southwestern sector, consisting of seventeen carefully ordered *hang-t'u* foundations, which Shih considers to have been the ceremonial heart of the central enclave (C in Fig. 3). A stepped *hang-t'u* structure (Z on Fig. 3) was almost certainly the foundation of a sacrificial altar.[129]

That this enclave at Hsiao-T'un was indeed the ceremonial and administrative focus of the (or a) Shang state is attested not only by mutilated and archetyped fragments of information preserved in the literature discussed in a previous section, by the presence of sacrificial and consecratory victims, both

---

[3] Plan of the ceremonial precinct at Hsiao-T'un. Based on a plan in Shih Chang-ju, *Hsiao-T'un: I-chih-ti Fa-hsien yü Fa-chüeh: Chien-chu I-ts'un* (T'ai-pei, 1959), fig. 4. For details of this complex see pp. 39–43 of the text.

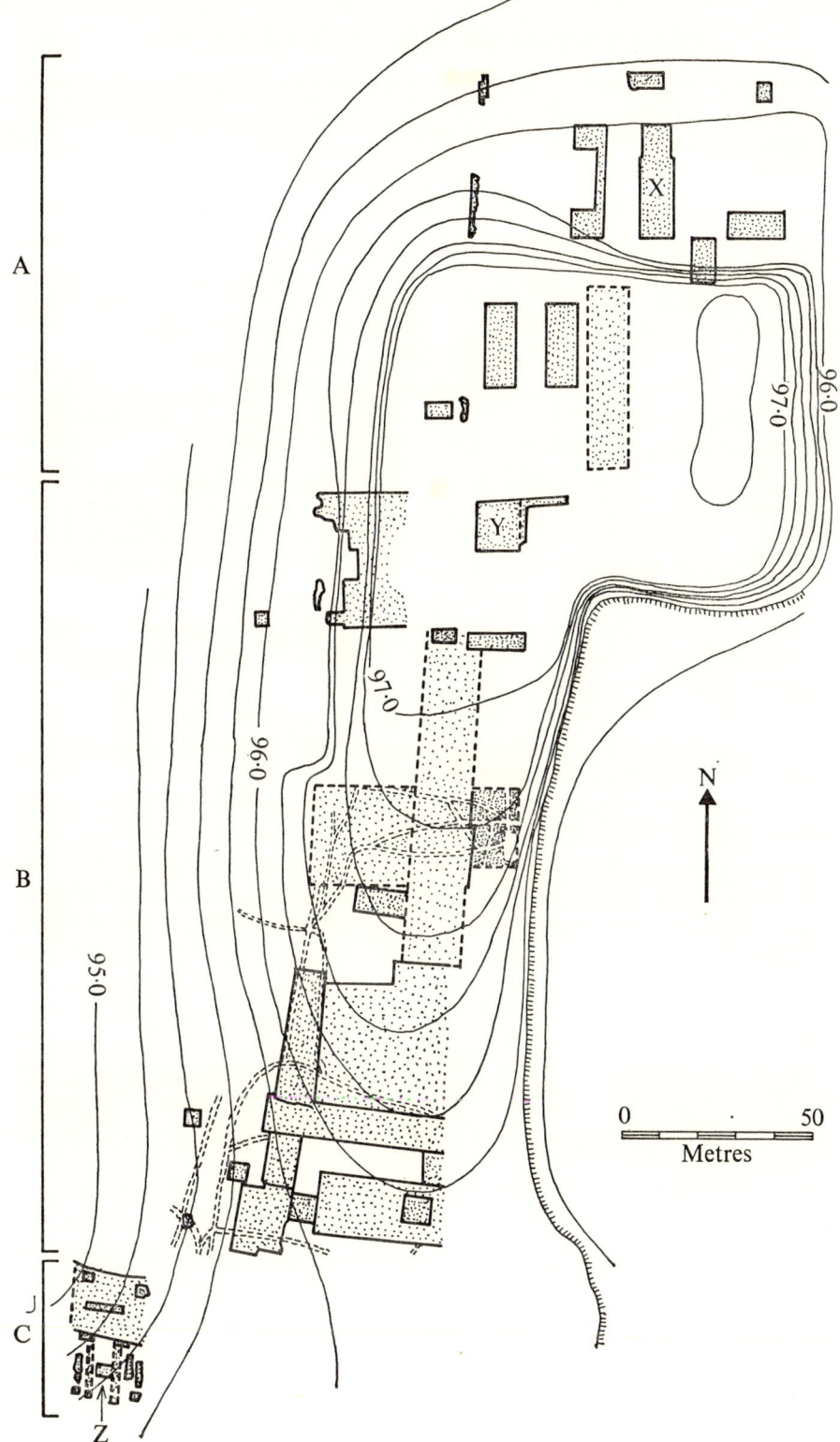

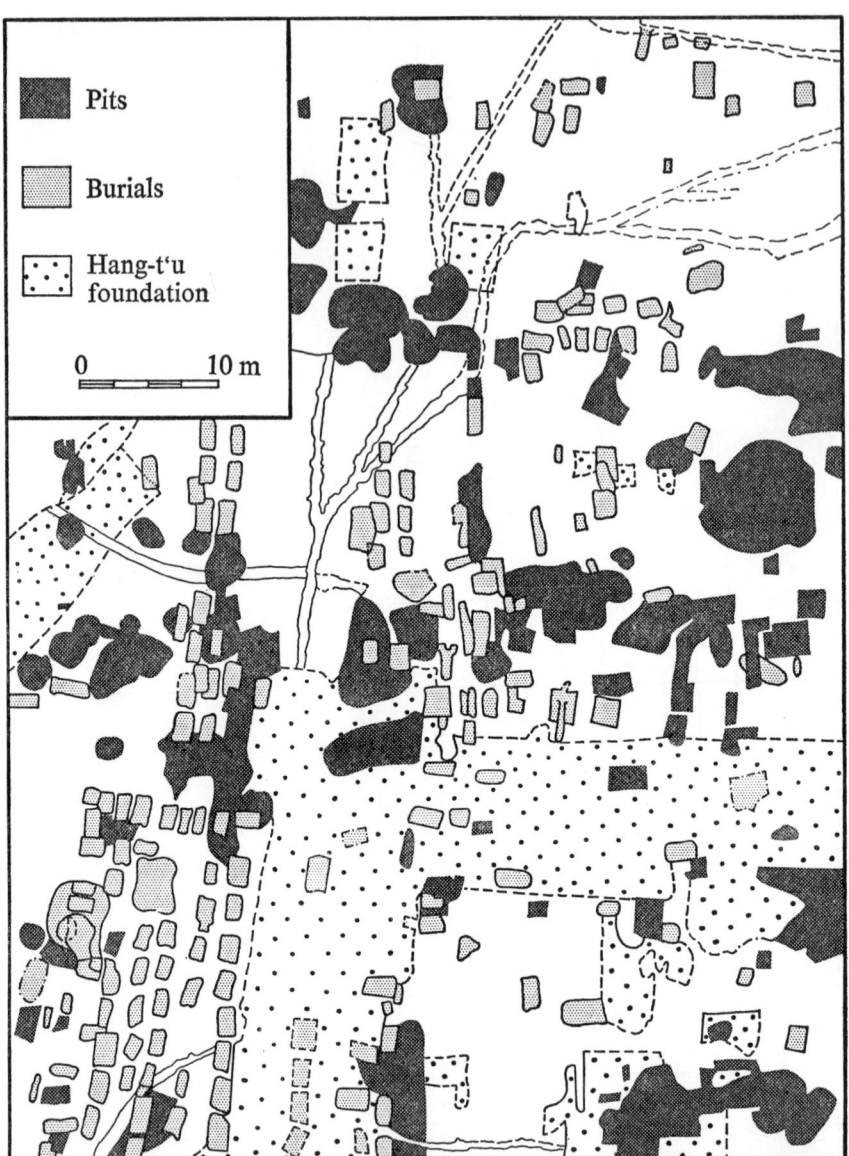

[4] Land use in part of the southwestern sector of the ceremonial enclave of the Great City Shang so far as it can be reconstructed from archeological excavation. Based on a plan in Shih Chang-ju, 'Yin-hsü tsui-chin-chih chung-yao fa-hsien; Fu: Lun Hsiao-T'un ti-ts'eng', *Chung-Kuo K'ao-ku Hsüeh-pao*, no. 2 (1947), fig. 20.

human and animal, which accompanied the construction of temple and altar, and by the finding (not always by archeologists) of an enormous number of bronze ritual vessels, but also by the huge quantity of oracle bones unearthed at the site. As these bones were associated exclusively with the royal court and the priesthood, their very numbers afford impressive testimony to the importance of Hsiao-T'un in the ceremonial organization of the state.

In one of the *hang-t'u* foundations excavated in the northern residential sector (X on Fig. 3) the pillar bases were still in their original positions, so that the archeologists of the Academia Sinica were able to reconstruct the general appearance of the building (Fig. 6).[130] The framework was of wood with outer walls of *hang-t'u* and a thatched gable roof, but with dimensions of twenty-four meters by eight, and an estimated overall height of six meters, it must have appeared as a reasonably imposing edifice. The position of a low platform, which has been interpreted as part of a flight of steps leading up to foundation level, suggests that the building faced the east. Shih Chang-ju has compared this structure to the royal palace allegedly erected by the first ruler of the Hsia dynasty, and described in the ancient Chou text *K'ao kung Chi*,[131] which was subsequently incorporated in the *Chou-Li* (*Chou Ritual*). Like so many other Chou texts, this latter work was given its present form in Han times, although it certainly incorporates materials from earlier periods.[132] The *K'ao-kung Chi* (*Record of Artificers*), which was substituted for a lost sixth book of the *Chou-Li* after that text had been recovered in Han times, is usually considered to be a work of considerable antiquity. In fact, it has been suggested that it may have been an official document of the state of ***Dz'iər* (*Ch'i*). Whatever its pedigree may be, it is not impossible that it preserved an architectural prescription from very ancient times which may have devolved ultimately from just such a building as that which we have been discussing. The fact of the preservation of this architectural prescription is itself a strong indication of the ceremonial purpose of its structural prototype. Its internal disposition is, in fact, consonant with habitation by just such an extended family as characterized the royal and aristocratic lineages of Shang.

In and around the more imposing dwellings of gods and their earthly mediators were what Tung Tso-pin has called service areas.[133] These included more than 600 semi-subterranean dwellings of servitors and menials, storage pits, some provided with round or rectangular bins, stone and bone workshops, pottery kilns, and bronze foundries (Fig. 4).

As at Cheng-Chou, the ceremonial enclave at Hsiao-T'un had its constellation of associated settlements. Among the most important of these was the cemetery at Hsi-pei Kang, near Hou-chia Chuang and some three kilometers to the northwest of Hsiao-T'un.[134] The report of the excavators of this site is scheduled for another of the volumes which is still unpublished, but from sundry information contained in papers oriented primarily to other topics, and from an early discussion by Paul Pelliot,[135] it can be ascertained that eleven massive mausolea were brought to light. Ten of these were excavated by Professor Kao Ch'ü-hsün and his associates in the nineteen-thirties, and one by the Chung-Kuo K'e-hsüeh Yüan in 1950. Apparently these mausolea were arranged in two lines, one of seven tombs and one of four, running from north to south and separated by an unoccupied strip of land about 100 meters wide. All were accompanied by sacrificial human burials. They have usually been interpreted as the resting places of the eleven Shang monarchs from B'wân-kăng, who established the capital at An-yang, to Tieg--jɛt, penultimate ruler of the dynasty, and thus reflected a time span of nearly two and a half centuries. Strictly speaking, it has not been proven that these tombs were those of the royal lineages. The field archeologists who excavated them called them simply 'large tombs' in 'a cemetery area', and it was Pelliot who, in a lecture at the Harvard Tercentenary Celebrations in 1937, first voiced the assumption that they were royal graves. However, it is unlikely that any group other than the royal clan would have commanded sufficient social power to undertake the excavation of these enormous pits, or have been able to muster sufficient wealth to furnish them with mortuary articles of the quantity and quality evidenced at Hsi-pei Kang. Professor Chang's elucidation of the dualistic arrangement of these tombs (to be discussed in a later section) is a powerful confirmation of Pelliot's assumption. This vast burial ground also contains, in addition to workshops and pit dwellings, literally thousands of humbler burials and sacrificial pits. Presumably some of these represented ordinary burials, but it is abundantly evident that many were of a sacrificial nature. From the records so far published it is impossible to distinguish the two types, but it is evident that the construction of the great mausolea at Hsi-pei Kang was accompanied by the same type of consecratory sacrifice as that which sanctified the palaces and temples at Hsiao-T'un. Cheng Te-k'un makes the pertinent point that, as elsewhere in East Asia, the residences of both the living and the dead were constructed on the same principles.[136] Two other large and richly furnished tombs (although on a smaller scale than those at Hsi-pei Kang) have been excavated at Hou-Kang,[137] about 1,500 meters downriver from Hsiao-T'un, and at Wu-kuan Ts'un, about the same distance to the northwest,[138] respectively. If these are to be described as royal tombs, then they are presumably those of the collateral, not of the main, lineages.

Other settlements associated with the ceremonial enclave at Hsiao-T'un

---

[5] A reconstruction of the ceremonial enclave of the Great City Shang at Hsiao-T'un as seen from the northeast. The workshops and semi-subterranean dwellings of the t̑i̯ông-ńi̯ěn (chung-jen) are interspersed among the more important structures raised on *hang-t'u* foundations only impressionistically.

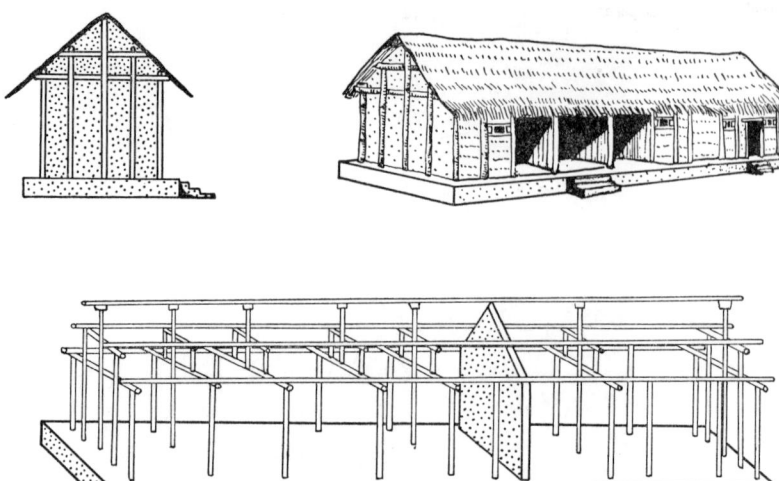

[6] Reconstruction of building A4 (X on fig. 3) in the northern sector of the ceremonial enclave of the Great City Shang. Redrawn from Shih Chang-ju, 'Yin-tai ti-shang-chien-chu fu-yüan-chih i-li', *Kuo-li Chung-Yang Yen-chiu-yüan Yüan-k'an*, vol. 1 (1954), p. 276.

have been discovered (but not fully reported on) at Hou-chia-chuang-nan-ti, Ta-ssŭ-k'ung Ts'un and Hsüeh-chia Chuang, as well as at a number of minor sites. Hou-chia-chuang-nan-ti, located midway between Hsiao-T'un and Hsi-pei Kang, appears to have been of special importance for, in addition to two foundations of *hang-t'u* construction (itself diagnostic of élite status), each furnished with subterranean storage chambers, there have also come to light caches of oracle bones.[139] As the enquiries inscribed on these particular bones were concerned primarily with the welfare of the royal family, the ordering of evening rituals, the weather and schedules for royal itineraries, it has been proposed that Hou-chia-chuang-nan-ti was the site of a resort palace of the Shang kings.[140]

At Ta-ssŭ-k'ung Ts'un both tombs and dwellings have been excavated. The former are of considerable interest in that, despite their relatively small size compared with those at Hsi-pei Kang and Hou-Kang, they were each provided with one or two human sacrifices, together with artifacts of bronze and jade.[141] The site at Hsüeh-chia Chuang is basically similar to that at Ta-ssŭ-k'ung Ts'un in that it has yielded dwellings, storage pits and graves, but human sacrifice appears to have been absent, being replaced in some of the larger tombs by dog sacrifices. There was also a fairly well-developed industrial aspect to the settlement, manifested in the presence of bone workshops, pottery kilns, and bronze foundries.[142]

Other Shang cities. Morphologically the ancient settlements at Cheng-Chou and An-yang appear to have had much in common. Each comprised a centrally situated ceremonial and administrative enclave, which can be safely presumed to have afforded a habitation only for members of the royal lineages, for a priesthood, and for a few selected craftsmen, together with, perhaps, something in the nature of a praetorian guard. Both the peasantry, who provided the material subsistence on which the ceremonial center depended, and the majority of the artisans who supplied it with ritual furniture, lived in villages dispersed through the surrounding countryside. Although the evidence is even more fragmentary than in these two instances, a similar settlement morphology, in which tributary villages surrounded a centrally located cult center, seems to be implied by Shang remains in the vicinity of both Lo-yang and Hui-Hsien.

In historical times Lo-yang was a prominent nodal center in the heart of the Chung-yüan, at a point where latitudinal routes across the North China plain were combined into a single strand prior to entering the passes through the western uplands, so that it is not altogether surprising to find it featuring among the more important Shang settlements so far discovered. Investigations at this site have been of a reconnaissance nature and the reports published so far have been preliminary in character,[143] but no less than twenty mausolea, complete with human and animal sacrifices, have been excavated in the neighborhood, together with, significantly, bronze foundries. The remains, which occur above Yang-shao and Lung-shan levels, apparently derive from all stages of Shang development, and it is possible that some of the tombs may date from a settlement of Shang survivors in the years after the Chou conquest.

For Hui-Hsien we are fortunate in being able to draw on the report of large-scale excavations undertaken by members of the Chung-Kuo K'e-hsüeh Yüan in 1950–51.[144] It is Kuo Pao-chün's conclusion that the settlement here was more or less contemporaneous with that at An-yang. Once again tombs with human and animal sacrifices occur, together with a bronze foundry, and Kuo has discerned a chronological sequence in the evolution of the burial customs as exemplified in the northern and southern sectors of the site.

The predominantly typological and classificatory point of view which pervades the reports of excavations at Lo-yang and Hui-Hsien is not particularly helpful in a study of more broadly conceived developmental trends, but the total cultural configurations of these two settlements would seem to indicate that their congeners are to be sought in the urbanized communities of Cheng-Chou and An-yang rather than in the population nuclei of pre-urbanized society. Chang Kuang-chih has, however, drawn attention to a possible variant

CHENG-CHOU					AN-YANG			
	Early Interpretation 1928-9	Post Dynastic	Later Interpretation 1930	Upper Level (*Burials*)	Shih Chang-ju	Post Dynastic	Li Chi	Post Hang-t'u
Jen-min Kung-yüan		Dynastic		Middle Level (*Hang-t'u*)		Dynastic	Dynastic	Tsou Heng	Hang-t'u
		Pre-Dynastic		Lower Level (*Subterranean dwellings and storage chambers*)		Pre-Dynastic	Pre-Dynastic		Pre Hang-t'u
Upper Erh-li Kang									
Lower Erh-li Kang									
Lo-ta Miao									
Shang-chieh									
Lungshanoid									

[7] A tentative systematization of the archeological evidence for the earlier phases of the urbanization process in North China.

	HSING-T'AI	LO-YANG	HUI-HSIEN

Tung Tso-pin:
1209 – 1111
1226 – 1210
1240 – 1227
1280 – 1241
1384 – 1281

HSING-T'AI	LO-YANG	HUI-HSIEN
	Chung-Chou Lu III *(Post Shang)*	
Upper Yin-kuo Ts'un *(Late Shang)*	Hsi-chiao II *(Late Shang)*	Liu-li-ke II *(Late Shang)*
	Hsi-chiao I *(Middle Shang)*	Liu-li-ke I *(Middle Shang)*
Middle Yin-kuo Ts'un *(Early Shang)*	Chung-Chou Lu II *(Early Shang)*	
Lower Yin-kuo Ts'un *(Proto-Shang)*	Chung-Chou Lu I *(Proto-Shang)*	
Lungshanoid	Lungshanoid	

of this type of settlement pattern in which similar administratively and ceremonially interdependent congeries of economically distinct settlements seem to have existed without benefit of centrally situated cult centers.[145] Such, for example, would appear to have existed in the vicinity of Shih-li Miao in Nan-yang Hsien,[146] Lu-wang Fen in Hsin-Hsiang,[147] Ch'ao-ko in T'ang-yin Hsien,[148] Shih-li P'u in Nan-yang Hsien,[149] Ta-hsin Chuang in Chi-nan Hsien,[150] Feng-chia An in Ch'ü-yang Hsien[151] and at Hsing-T'ai in southern Ho-pei. Most of these sites have received only cursory attention and have been inadequately reported for present purposes, but at Hsing-T'ai excavation has been of a somewhat more intensive, though still preliminary, character.[152] The lowest stratum revealed in any of the ten sites investigated, and found only at Yin-kuo Ts'un, has been correlated with the urban-threshold stage of Lo-ta Miao at Cheng-Chou, but other sites have yielded evidence of later Shang phases distinguished by such diagnostic horizon markers as oracle records, bone hairpins, and characteristic pottery forms. Pottery kilns occurred at several locations and a bone workshop at one, but *hang-t'u* foundations were completely absent and bronze artifacts were almost equally rare. At Ts'ao-yen Chuang only eight small bronzes (arrow heads, awls and ornaments) were found among some hundreds of bone and pottery objects. It is not impossible that the interdependence of the Hsing-T'ai settlements, which is implied by the irregular distribution of handicraft workshops, was organized from an administrative center as yet undiscovered. Alternatively, the cultural configuration of the network of settlements might be explained as the result of the secondary diffusion of culture traits from a Shang culture hearth, so that Hsing-T'ai, together with the other apparently proto-urban nexuses enumerated above, may have constituted examples of secondary urban generation (cf. p. 9 above) actually in progress during Shang times. In this connection it is pertinent to recall Chang Kuang-chih's attachment of a spatial significance to the typological classification of Shang sites that we have been discussing. An urbanized Shang society would appear to have been restricted to a zone in northern Ho-nan, running from the neighborhood of Lo-yang in the west (if the interpretation of this site proposed above should prove acceptable), through Cheng-Chou to An-yang in the north (Fig. 8). Round this core area there could then be said to exist a halo of territories, extending from Shan-Hsien in the southwest to Ch'ü-yang in the north and Chi-nan in the east, where diffusion of Shang culture traits had prepared the way for the initiation of the process of secondary urban generation as described above. Beyond that lay a much wider zone, reaching into northern Ho-pei, central Shan-hsi, Shen-hsi, Hu-pei, northern An-hui and eastern Shan-

[8] The nuclear region of Chinese urbanism. Sites plotted beyond the limits of developed Shang culture have yielded Shang culture traits only in primarily Lungshanoid contexts.

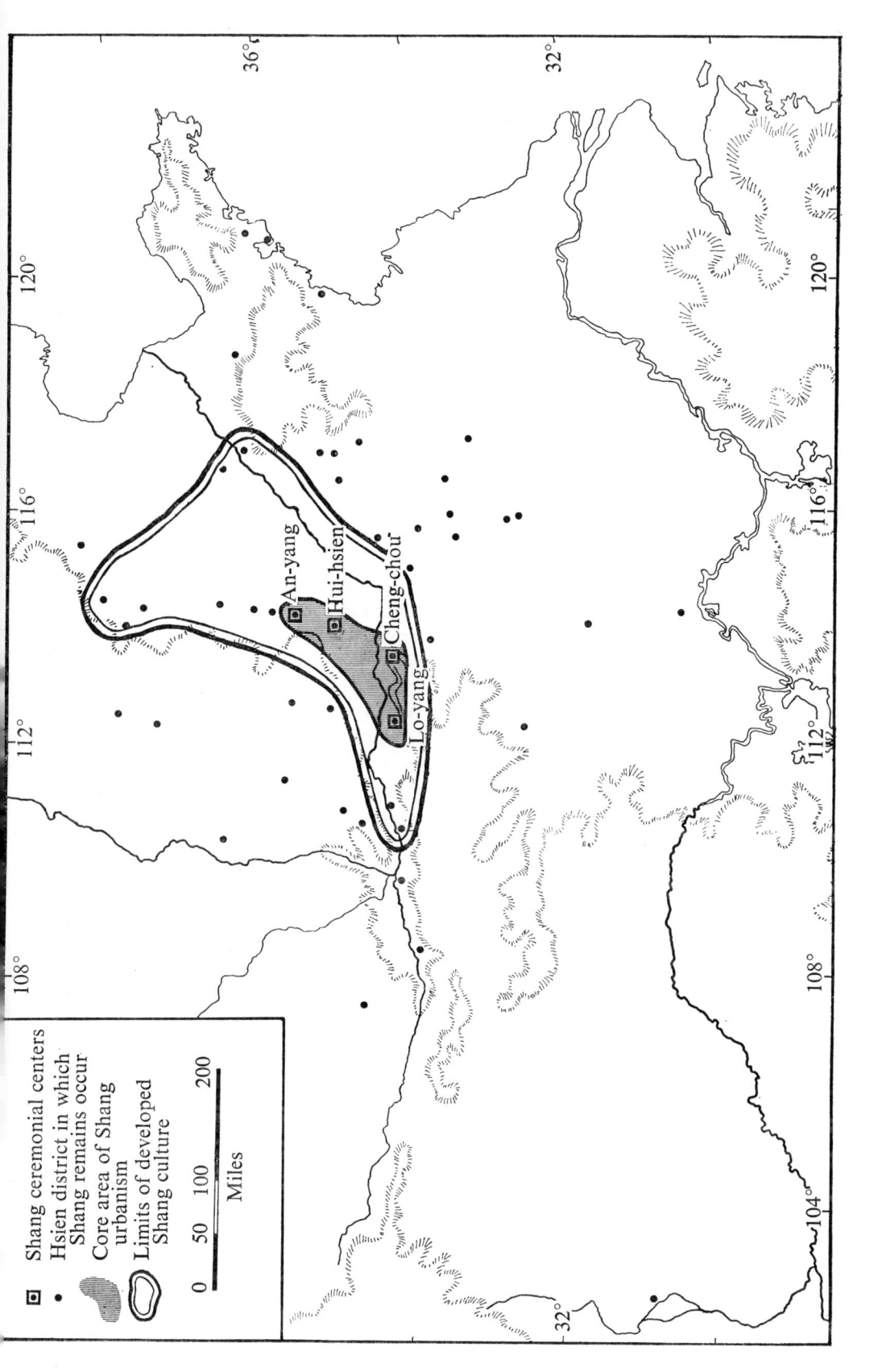

tung, in which selected Shang culture traits had diffused among pre-urban societies in a still predominantly Neolithic context.

THE POLITICAL STRUCTURE OF THE SHANG STATE

The political entity in Late Shang times appears to have partaken of the nature of patrimonial domain, a form of traditional rule which operates through a pervasive combination of traditionalism and arbitrariness.[153] It is characteristic of patrimonialism that the ruler treats all political administration as his personal affair, while the officials, appointed by the ruler on the basis of his personal confidence in them, in turn regard their administrative operations as a personal service to their ruler in a context of duty and respect. Provided they do not violate tradition or the interests of the ruler, their control over their subject populations is absolute, and as arbitrary as the ruler's is towards them. In Shang China this type of domain is not only implied by Chou writings of later times but is also attested directly by the oracle archives. At the pinnacle of the Shang political hierarchy was the king, referred to as ***gi̯wang* (wang) during his lifetime but posthumously as **tieg (*ti*). As the earthly instrument for the accomplishment of Heaven's (**Dʲi̯ang-Tieg : Shang-Ti) designs, the king was responsible for all government policies, and all decisions were officially attributed to him under his style of ***Di̯o i̯ĕt-ńi̯ĕn* (*Yü i-jen*), 'I, the Unique Person'. The affairs of the state were termed the king's affairs in official records, and appointments to government posts were reported, in the king's words, as 'to assist my affairs'.

THE GRAND LINEAGE OF SHANG

The royal branch of the ruling clan of the Shang was designated ***Tsi̯əg* (*Tzŭ*) in *Shih-Chi*, and its founding ancestor was accorded a miraculous birth in Chinese mythology. In the words of Ssŭ-ma Ch'ien,

'The mother of ***Si̯at* (Hsieh), [founder] of the Yin [dynasty], was called ***Kăn-d'iek* (Chien-ti). She was a daughter of the ***Ńi̯ông* (Sung) lineage and second consort of ***Tieg-K'ôk* (Ti-K'u). When, as with two companions she was going to bathe, she saw a dark bird let fall its egg, Kăn-d'iek picked it up and ate it. As a result she conceived and gave birth to Si̯at.'[154]

It is evident that the grand lineage occupied a position of supreme importance not only in the ceremonial activities of the state but also in its political structure, but the precise manner in which it functioned has been obscure. Recently Chang Kuang-chih has suggested that the ten Heavenly Stems which appeared in the posthumous styles of the Shang kings represented ten lineages which together formed the ruling branch.[155] He further concludes that the throne customarily alternated between two of the more important lineages, but occasionally passed to certain less politically influential affiliates. Royal marriages, according to Chang's hypothesis, were characterized by a patrisib endogamy after the manner of patrilateral cross-cousin marriage, and the throne passed from maternal uncles to sororal nephews in two generations, or from grandfathers to grandsons in three generations. When it was first published this hypothesis appeared to activate a good deal of hitherto latent speculation among Chinese litterateurs and anthropologists, some of whom were extremely critical of Chang's proposal.[156] However, in a later paper he was able to neutralize most of the adverse criticisms, and went on to amplify his theory by linking the dualism operative in the succession to the Shang throne with the well known but incompletely understood **$\overset{\circ}{d}iog$-$mi\hat{o}k$ (*chao-mu*) system that obtained during the earlier years of the Western Chou dynasty.[157] At the same time he suggested that the Shang lineages may have had something in common with the ramage system elucidated by Raymond Firth[158] and Marshall Sahlins,[159] or with the stratified lineages described by Morton Fried.[160] Subsequently Liu Pin-hsiung has used Chang's work as a basis for his own hypothesis that the kinship organization of the royal house of Shang was based on a ten-section double-descent system.[161] Characteristically such systems consist of five patrilineal descent groups which cross with two matrilineal moieties to produce ten marriage sections.[162] In the case of the royal house of Shang it appears that the rule was bilateral cross-cousin marriage between a man or woman and his or her second cousin once removed. Liu claims that the rearrangement of the genealogy of the Shang dynasts on this basis reveals the significance of certain classificatory characters in the posthumous styles. For instance, **$d\underset{\cdot}{i}ang$ (*shang*) was a style restricted to the founding ancestor of the grand lineage; **$d'\hat{a}d$ (*ta*) was assumed only by the founder of the dynasty and by the first king to be provided by each of the patrilineal descent groups; **$siog$ (*hsiao*) denoted the last king of a particular branch or one who had no successor within his branch; **$ngw\hat{a}d$ (*wai*) signified a king with no successor within his section; and **$ti\hat{o}ng$ (*chung*) occurred both in sections which contained a $d'\hat{a}d$ ruler but no $siog$ and in the style of the middle ruler in a section of three.

The evaluation of hypotheses such as these must remain a matter for the necessarily restricted number of scholars who are specialists in both Shang records and kinship organization, and even then their conclusions will be applicable only to the élite strata of society. About the kinship systems obtaining among the ordinary folk we know practically nothing. But even to the layman it is evident that the Shang lineages incorporated features of both kin and class. Power and authority always lay in close consanguineal proximity to the alleged main line of descent. In this respect the Shang kinship units would seem to have had much in common with the groups which Paul Kirchhoff has called conical clans,[163] that is 'kinship units which bind their members with common familial ties but which distribute wealth, social standing, and power most unequally among the members of the pseudo-family. Such kin units trace

THE GENESIS OF THE CITY IN CHINA

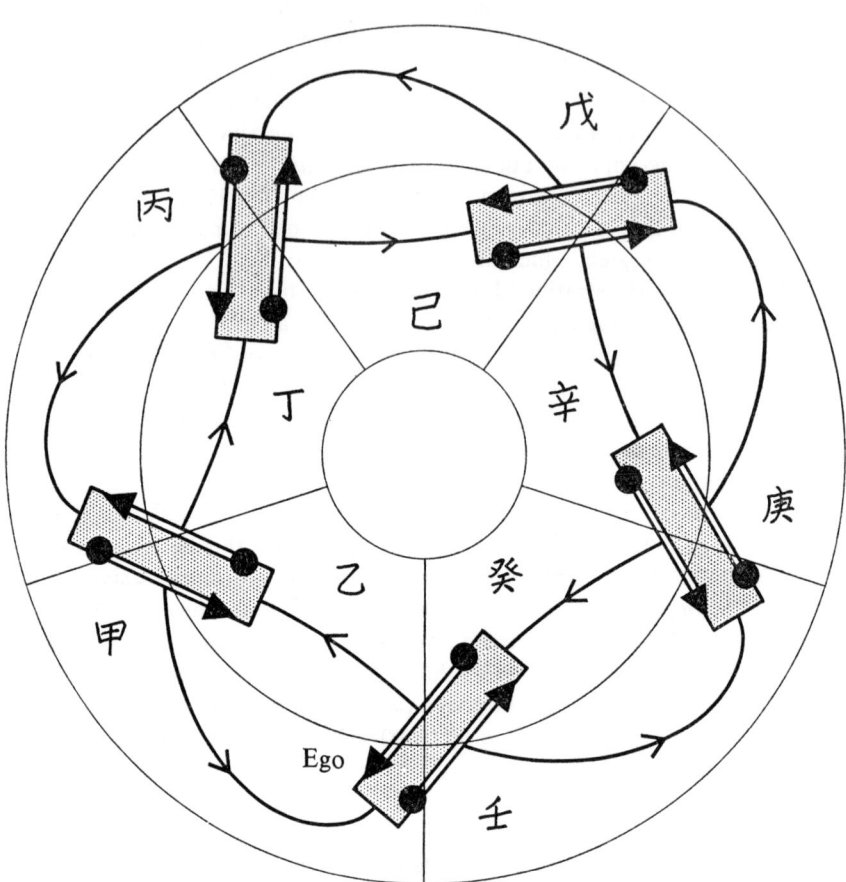

[9] Functional diagram of the ten-section system of the royal house of the Shang dynasty as reconstructed by Liu Pin-hsiung, 'Yin-Shang Wang-shih shih-fen-tsu-chih shih-lun', *Chung-yang Yen-chiu-yüan: Min-ts'u-hsüeh Yen-chiu-so Chi-k'an*, no. 19 (1965) p. 107.

98]   POLITICAL STRUCTURE

their descent back to an original ancestor, real or fictitious; but, at the same time, they regularly favor his lineal descendants over the junior or "cadet" lines in regulating access to social, economic, or political prerogatives.' Such conical units of fictional kin would have produced just such a close correlation of political status with kinship descent as does characterize the Shang sociopolitical system.

Presumably at Hsiao-T'un the palace was one among the cardinally oriented structures in the northernmost sector of the ceremonial enclave (cf. p. 40 above). Political custom, though, makes it unlikely that one building served as the palace of the monarch continuously for more than a single reign. Under the descent system described above it is probable that the architectural foundations which have been exposed in the northern sector at Hsiao-T'un represent a series of royal dwellings, at least one for each change in the ruling lineage. In this connection it is instructive to recall Chang Kuang-chih's suggestion that the arrangement of the supposedly royal tombs at Hsi-pei Kang, with seven mausolea in the western row and four in the eastern, may have reflected the dualism already evident in the posthumous styles of the dynasty.[164] Moreover, while it might be a coincidence that there were eleven mausolea and also eleven kings buried during the An-yang period,[165] other correspondences adduced by Professor Chang are less easily disposed of. In the first place he has made a strong case for regarding the **$tieng$ ($ting$) and **$·i̯et$ (i) groups within the Shang lineage system as the equivalents of the $d̯i̯og$ and $mi̯ôk$ generations of Chou times.[166] On this basis it can be said that, of the eleven Shang kings from B'wân-kăng to Tieg-·i̯ɛt, four were $d̯i̯og$ ($tieng$) and seven were $mi̯ôk$ ($·i̯et$); and – what would be an even more extraordinary coincidence – of the eleven mausolea at Hsi-pei Kang, four were in the $d̯i̯og$ row (east) and seven in the $mi̯ôk$ row (west) as those distinctions were set out in the Li-Chi.[167] Shih Chang-ju had already speculated on the resemblance between the layout of the cemetery at Hsi-pei Kang and that of the ancestral temples of the royal house in the central sector at Hsiao-T'un,[168] both of which were arranged in two rows running from north to south, and he also pointed to the human burials associated with both sites. This is in accord with the prescription for the arrangement of shrines within ancestral temples as described in the Li-Chi.[169]

THE PRACTICE OF GOVERNMENT[170]

Some authors have regarded the Shang state as virtually a theocracy. Wolfram Eberhard, for example, refers to the Shang ruler as the 'supreme lord and religious leader' and as 'a high priest'.[171] L. Carrington Goodrich speaks of the king as having 'a kind of priestly function',[172] and William Watson characterizes the Shang government as 'to some extent a theocracy'.[173] There is certainly considerable validity in this point of view, for the ruling monarch was a member of a lineage which coexisted ontologically on earth and in the heavens

55

above, and was the pivotal figure in all ritual procedures. The royal ancestors themselves were credited with supernatural power, and divination of their wishes was in the hands of a group of priestly augurs, experts in scapulimancy (**tiěng-ńiěn : chen-jen or **puk : pu), who were sufficiently important in the administrative hierarchy to have had their names recorded on the oracle scapulae and plastra.[174] So far no less than 117 of these tiěng-ńiěn have been counted, but this number certainly does not include all those who practised the art of divination during the two and a half centuries of dynastic An-yang.[175] The calendar of rituals for the glorification of, and communication with, the ancestors was elaborate and strictly controlled. Its performance was in the hands of specialists in ceremonial known as **ngio-sliəg (yü-shih), who might on occasion serve as envoys to neighboring territories.

It is characteristic of patrimonial domain that governmental and court administration coincide. Patrimonial rule is simply an extension to political subjects of the ruler's patriarchal control over his family. As Reinhard Bendix succinctly puts it, 'All political transactions that do not involve the [ruler's] household directly are nevertheless amalgamated with the corresponding function of the court.'[176] He goes on to cite the European instance of the supervision of cavalry, which might be put in the hands of the 'marshal' who supervised the royal stables.[177] Although the oracle records do not afford a comprehensive overview of all aspects of Shang government, this particular facet is clearly evident. A score or so official titles have been recognized so far, which may be functionally discriminated as secretarial, civil and military. The secretarial officials were closest to the seat of power and consequently highest in the hierarchy. Most important were the **·iěn (yin) councillors, among whom was numbered the great minister **·Iɛr-Iuěn (I-Yin). It seems that there were at any one time several court officers of ·iěn rank, who were in charge of agriculture, the management of palace affairs, the organization of feasts, and numerous similar matters. Collectively the corps was known as the **Tâ-·iěn (To-yin), and some of its members enjoyed great prestige. In fact Professor Chang Kuang-chih has suggested that some of the most influential among them may have been the heads of prominent lineages temporarily excluded from supreme power by the operation of a diôg-miôk style order of succession.[178] In this connection the position of ·Iɛr-Iuěn, chief minister under T'âng the Successful (posthumous style **T'âd-·iɛt : T'ai-i) and several succeeding kings, is particularly interesting. In the ritual cycle of the Tsiəg grand lineage he was accorded the same respect as were the ancestors of T'âd-·iɛt himself. Moreover, his cult was especially prominent during the reign of Miwo-tieng, the most powerful of all the *tieng* group of kings of the An-yang dynasty, which suggests to Professor Chang that ·Iɛr-Iuěn may have been the head of the *tieng* group of lineages during the reign of T'âd-·iɛt of the ·iɛt group.

Other offices within the secretariat were those of the diviners and ceremonial specialists mentioned previously, the court chroniclers (***tsâk-ts'ĕk* : *tso-ts'e*) who were entrusted with the drafting of the royal edicts and the superintendence of the court archives, the **kung (*kung*) or master artificers (whose province included the provision of music as well as the supervision of artisan crafts and welfare), and the ***li̯əg* (*li*) or general duties officials.

Further removed from the source of power, but still personal servants and personal representatives of the king, were the civil officers, known in the oracle records as ***d̥i̯ĕn* (*ch'en*) or ***t̂i̯ĕng* (*cheng*). Collectively they were called the ***tâ-d̥i̯ĕn* (*to-ch'en*) or corps of officials, but the use of such epithets as ***ngi̯wăn-d̥i̯ĕn* (*yüan-ch'en* : principal official), ***si̯og-d̥i̯ĕn* (*hsiao-ch'en* : subordinate official) and ***pi̯ĕk-d̥i̯ĕn* (*p'i-ch'en* : appointed official) would seem to imply that the various offices carried distinct differences in rank. Similar titles and offices occur subsequently both on bronzes and in literature dating from the Chou period.[179]

The third order of officials, the military, is also well represented in the oracle inscriptions. Those most frequently mentioned include the **må (*ma*) officers, possibly those charged with the responsibility of assembling, provisioning or equipping mounted warriors, the ***b'i̯ŭk* (*fu*) and the ***d̂'i̯ăg* (*she*) who were presumably connected in some way with archery, the ***·ăg* (*ya*), ***gi̯wad* (*wei*), and ***śi̯u* (*shu*) who appear to have functioned as various sorts of guards and garrison troops.

The extension of patrimonial authority. The situation described above approximates closely to the model of patrimonial rule as conceived by Max Weber, but it is also clear that by the Late Shang the acquisition of large extrapatrimonial territories which could not be governed on the basis of the ruler's personal resources and household management had induced an extension of the administrative staff, as well as the elaboration of a military force, to perform public duties beyond the scope of the royal household. There is abundant evidence that the Shang kings had been forced to delegate authority by granting benefices in return for services rendered to the throne. These benefices, which were often referred to as **kwək (*kuo*),[180] took several forms. A relatively small proportion were granted either to princes of the Shang, under the title *tsi̯əg*, or to queens (***b'i̯ŭg* : *fu*) who were no longer required to attend at court. Those in the vicinity of the ceremonial and administrative center were often designated ·*ăg* (*ya*) or ***ńźi̯uĕn* (*jun*); others, mainly on the fringes of the Shang polity, were known as **păk (*po*), a title usually rendered into English as 'earl'. Together with the ***g'u* (*hou*), or marquisate, the *păk* was a benefice customarily bestowed on members of the court who had, by meritorious service, given proof of both their loyalty and their administrative or military ability. **Nəm (*nan*) and ***d'ien* (*t'ien*) appear to have been benefices connected in some way with agricultural matters, possibly with reclamation of land: to judge from the oracle records they were conferred only infrequently. The total number of benefices in the gift of the Shang king is unknown, and doubtless it fluctuated from time to time, but merely incidental references in the oracle records of Mi̯wo-tieng (1339–1281 BC in Tung Tso-pin's chronology) and Tieg-si̯ĕn (1174–1111 BC) attest the existence of four *tsi̯əg*, three *b'i̯ŭg*, fifteen *păk*, twenty-seven *g'u*, two *nəm* and one *d'ien*. There is no reason to believe that these constituted more than a proportion of the total number of benefices during the periods concerned. From oracle and literary sources the more important benefices would appear to have included **B'âk* (*Po*), a former ceremonial center of the Shang dynasty,[181] and **D'i̯ĕng* (*Cheng*), both in the **Ti̯ông-Śi̯ang* (*Chung-Shang*) or metropolitan area; **Dz'i̯ər* (*Ch'i*) in the east; **Ts'i̯am* (*Ch'ien*), **K'i̯ang* (*Ch'iang*), **T̯i̯ôg* (*Chou*) and **Ḏi̯uk* (*Shu*) in the west; **Tsi̯ĕng* (*Ching*) and **G'wân* (*Huan*) in the north; and **G'wɐr* (*Huai*) and **Ñi̯ak* (*Jo*) in the south.[182] It appears that the organization and government of the individual benefices was patterned on that of the central government.

The chief duties of the benefice holders seem to have been concerned with the defence of the frontiers of Shang territory,[183] the supply of man-power for both military and construction purposes, and the collection of tribute for the court. Beneficed women assumed these obligations in the same way and on the same scale as their male counterparts, and the oracle archives record military expeditions under the command of two of Mi̯wo-tieng's superannuated queens against the K'i̯ang and **Li̯ung-pi̯wang (Lung-fang) barbarians respectively. The nature of the liturgical obligations[184] prescribed for each benefice not unexpectedly varied according to the natural resources of the territory, and ranged from, for example, 250 tortoise plastra from the marquisate of **Tsi̯ok (Ch'üeh) in the west, to sacrificial cattle from the benefice of Prince **G'wĕk (Hua) in the east.[184a] Especially meritorious service by a landholder was sometimes rewarded by a grant of the liturgical proceeds from his benefice for a period of years. Records of numerous such endowments have been found in the form of inscriptions on bronze ritual vessels cast specially for the occasion.

In addition to the benefices within the ambit of established and permanent Shang authority, there was an outer zone of **pi̯wang* (*fang*) territories. These were mostly the territories of tribal chieftains friendly to the Shang ruler whose authority over their own people had been confirmed by investiture according to Shang political theory. Such territories were sometimes known as **pŭng* (*pang*). That the process of proto-sinicization had already begun is attested by the fact that some of these chieftains figured in the oracle records as *păk* and *g'u*, presumably an indication of at least some adherence to Shang cultural norms and values on the part of the *pi̯wang*. The analysis of the oracle records of Mi̯wo-tieng and Tieg-si̯ĕn referred to above revealed the existence of at least twenty-six such *pi̯wang*. Among the more important of these territories were the **T'o-pi̯wang* (*T'u-fang*), **Kôg-pi̯wang* (*Kao-fang*), and **Ki̯wər-pi̯wang*

(*Kuei-fang*) on the northern margins of the Shang culture realm, and the *Ńi̯ĕn-pi̯wang* (*Jen-fang*) on the south.

The extension of the Shang patrimonial domain and the concomitant attenuation of the duties of the personal dependents of the monarch rendered necessary the maintenance of a military force competent to compel recalcitrant benefice holders to meet their obligations. The core of this force was the household guard, which was almost certainly accommodated close to the royal apartments in the ceremonial enclave. This was probably a carry-over from the early days of Shang patrimonialism when the polity had taken the form of a city-state, but by the later years of the dynasty such a praetorian guard had become wholly inadequate as an instrument for the enforcement of the royal will, so that a larger force had to be raised by conscription. According to the oracle records the numbers conscripted might range from 1,000 to 30,000 – although this last figure must be suspect when we read that the military expeditions conducted against some of the *pŭng* territories required only from 3,000 to 5,000 troops. On the other hand it is recorded that **B'i̯ŭg-Xôg (Fu-Hao), a queen of Mi̯wo-tieng with a benefice in the northwest, alone contributed no less than 10,000 troops to an expedition against a northern tribe, and on another occasion it was claimed that as many as 2,656 enemy soldiers were slain. The term used for conscription was ***təng-ńi̯ĕn* (*teng-jen*) or ***təng-ti̯ông-ńi̯ĕn* (*teng-chung-jen*), and recruits were known variously as ***ńi̯ĕn* (*jen* : men), ***si̯og-ńi̯ĕn* (*hsiao-jen* : common folk), ***gi̯wang-ńi̯ĕn* (*wang-jen* : king's men) and ***ti̯ông-ńi̯ĕn* (*chung-jen* : mustered men). The army seems to have comprised two main corps, one of infantry and one of chariots, each sub-divided into three sections that fought on the left, in the center, and on the right respectively. Shih Chang-ju believes that the war chariots constituted the spearhead of all attacks.[185] From the oracle records it would appear that, in later Shang times at least, the army was employed predominantly against *pi̯wang* raiders. Particularly was this true of the reigns of Mi̯wo-tieng, Tieg-i̯ɛt and Tieg-si̯ĕn. Concerning one such punitive expedition directed against the *Ńi̯ĕn-pi̯wang* to the south of the Huai river during the reign of the last of these kings, no less than seventy-eight entries have been counted on the oracle bones, and the extant information is sufficiently complete to allow the route of the army to be reconstructed in detail. On this particular occasion the troops were under arms for at least 260 days.

The nature of Shang patrimonialism. Whereas I have been describing the Shang polity as a patrimonial domain, not infrequently other scholars from both East and West have categorized it as a feudal system. Certainly both types of domain revolve about rulers who grant rights in return for military and administrative services, but beyond that the contractual character, social and legal aspects, and ideologies of the two systems are analytically distinct.

Whereas patrimonial government is an extension of the principles of paternal authority and filial dependence that obtain within the extended household of the royal family, feudal government is founded on a contractually ordered fealty, structured upon a basis of knightly militarism. 'Feudalism', in the words of one of Max Weber's American expositors, 'is domination by the few who are skilled in war; patrimonialism is domination by one who requires officials for the exercise of his authority.'[186] This having been said, it must be admitted that at the institutional level the two systems are not always entirely distinct. The extension of patrimonial rule over extrapatrimonial territories may induce the emergence of political structures which appear morphologically similar to, or even occasionally merge with, others arising from the centripetal orientation of independent status groups under stress of external factors, such as war. It may then be difficult to distinguish the personal obedience of a dependent from the public duties of a political subject. Patrimonial governments exhibit feudal aspects whenever such a ruler grants territorially based benefices on an hereditary basis, and feudal régimes equally exhibit patrimonial aspects whenever fiefs are subject to a strong central administration. In fact, Weber himself was constrained to admit that the differences between patrimonial and feudal governments were often distinct only after the personal positions of patrimonial officials and landed notables had been traced historically.[187] Whereas a patrimonial retainer is essentially a personal dependent, a knight entering the service of his ruler preserves his independence.

Although the materials available are inadequate for a complete analysis of the Shang system of government, it would seem clear enough that we are dealing with a matter of personal benefices granted to retainers rather than with an impersonal contractual relationship between ruler and vassal.[187a] It was the 'good king' of patrimonial ideology, the mediator on behalf of his people between heaven and earth, who occupied the position of supreme ruler, rather than a warrior-hero at the head of a free camaraderie of warriors of pledged loyalty to their leader. The patrimonial king legitimates his rule in terms of the welfare of his subjects and dependents, from among whom his servants and representatives are usually chosen. Their chances of preferment are almost entirely dependent on the confidence of the ruler in their abilities, and precipitate translations from the lowest to the highest orders of society and back again, often for wholly personal reasons, are a characteristic feature of patrimonial government. Under such a régime the ruler is by no means committed to maintaining a fixed distribution of property, and new landowners are usually not unwelcome as long as they do not assume the leadership of social groups capable of exercising authority independently of the arbitrary will of the supreme ruler. Royal favorites and rags-to-riches stories are characteristic of patrimonial domain. The tradition that ·Ἱɛr-Ἱuĕn, who held high office under the first four kings of the An-yang dynasty, had ingratiated himself with T'áng the Successful by skilfully exploiting his knowledge of the culinary arts[188] is probably apocryphal, but it is nonetheless true to the patrimonial mode. Moreover, Professor Chang has tentatively suggested that the conservative and innovative periods which Tung Tso-pin believes to have alternated during the An-yang period (p. 39 above) *may* have witnessed parallel changes in the personnel of the administration.[189] If so, such changes would have been wholly consonant with a patrimonial régime.

It is not difficult to define analytically other discrepancies between patrimonialism and feudalism : the social distinction between benefice holder and feudal vassal, even when the former has divested himself of much of his patrimonial dependence; the contrasting attitudes to property rights, to education, and particularly to legal matters, the patrimonial ethic tending to transform questions of law and adjudication into questions of administration, while the feudal order, concerned principally with contractual negotiation about rights and privileges, tends to transform problems of administration into problems of law and adjudication.[190] But the evidence for conditions relating to Shang times is too meager to permit of profitable discussion of these points. Suffice it to say that what evidence is available points to a patrimonial rather than a feudal style of government. The heavy reliance on military force towards the end of the dynasty, however, implies that some dependents at least were beginning to appropriate their benefices, though whether in response to a decline in central authority or as a result of the extension of Shang government beyond the limits imposed by distance and the communications media of the time is uncertain.

THE EXTENT OF SHANG DOMINION

We have spoken above of the areal extent of Shang culture but, despite the fact that more than 500 place-names have so far been identified in the oracle records, the boundaries of the territory subject to Shang dominion can only be a matter of speculation. A late gloss on a passage in the *Chu-shu Chi-nien* depicts the state under Mi̯wo-tieng, twenty-second of the Shang rulers and fourth in the An-yang period, as stretching far into west and south China. Under the rubric Mi̯wo-tieng we read:

'In his time the oecumene (*sc.* territory under Shang control) did not extend eastwards beyond the **Kŭng (*Chiang :* the Lower Yang-tzŭ) and the **Gʻwâng (the [Lower] Huang) [rivers], westwards beyond the ***Ti̯ər* (*Ti*) and ***Kʻi̯ang* (*Chʻiang* [tribes]) (usually located near the Wei-Huang confluence), southwards beyond the ***Ki̯ĕng* (*Ching*) and **Mlwan (*Man* [tribes] : referred vaguely to South China),[191] and northwards beyond ***Sâk-pi̯wang* (*Shuo-fang :* in Han times this was the name of a city on the Huang river in present-day Kan-su, but in this earlier context the graphs should certainly be read as "the northern regions generally").'

Despite the fact that this passage, or others of similar import, have formed the basis for most reconstructions of the Shang empire, the extent of territory it depicts is certainly an exaggeration, born no doubt of the anhistoricity of Han – or later – perceptions of the past. We have seen in a previous section (p. 50) that a fully urbanized Shang society (in the sense defined in Chapter Four) on present evidence existed only in northwest Ho-nan. Surrounding this core area in all directions but broadening to the east and north was a zone of territories that would seem to have been fully acculturated to Shang values, and, beyond that, occupying most of the rest of the North China plain, stretched the peripheral lands where individual Shang culture traits were only just beginning to penetrate.[192] It is tempting to see in this archeologically attested cultural zonation a reflection of the ternary world view of the Shang themselves. A metropolitan district on this view contained a royal seat and ceremonial-administrative center, known in the records as a **$d'âd$-$i̯əp$ (ta-i), and probably some of the chief settlements of the dependent benefices, for which the term ·$i̯əp$ (i) seems to have been used.[193] These would doubtless have boasted less imposing ceremonial complexes than that associated with the central government. This central area was surrounded by the benefices of $păk$ and $g'u$, these in turn being succeeded by an outer circle of incompletely assimilated $p\breve{u}ng$ territories.

Even if this interpretation were to prove correct in principle, the extent of the individual zones could be modified at any time – in fact, they certainly will be – by new archeological discoveries. More importantly, this view of the Shang ecumene raises again the problem of the nature of the literary records relating to the Shang state. How many states, and concomitant ceremonial centers, existed in the Shang culture realm at any one time is uncertain. The memory of one such polity has survived in the reconstituted literature of ancient China, and there is little reason to doubt that its last capital is represented by the ruins at Hsiao-T'un. But whether there were other similarly constituted polities within the ambit of developed Shang culture, and if so how many, cannot be known at this stage. The frequency with which the recorded Shang government was either at war with far from remote neighbors or repelling tribal raids at no great distance from the ceremonial center affords some indication that the effective political unit for which records survive was not large. In this case the inscribed oracle bones which have been brought to light outside the presumed capitals at Cheng-Chou and Hsiao-T'un may represent either earlier ceremonial foci of the recorded Shang state or, perhaps not less probably, rival capitals whose annals have been lost or suppressed. In this connection it is instructive to note that bone-text *Chia* 3510 (12) sought guidance as to whether a *śi̯u* (possibly a **$śi̯u$-$dzi̯əg$ $tsi̯əg$: cf. Note 183) should join forces with the king (**$g_{i}wang$) of a neighboring state, the name of which cannot be deciphered.[194] Moreover, it is no longer possible to overlook Noel Barnard's discrimination of two epigraphic traditions associated respectively with Shang and Chou polities. The former was identified with short and predominantly divinatory bronze inscriptions, the latter with longer secular texts designed for the instruction of posterity. It may well turn out, as Dr Barnard has indeed tentatively speculated, that the Chou, far from being the rude barbarians of traditional annalists, were in fact possessors of a more advanced culture than that of the Shang, and possibly therefore of a more complex political organization.[195] In any case, it is not at all impossible that the idea, which is implicit in later texts, of a unitary, maturely structured state dominating more or less the whole of the North China plain during Shang times was a Chou invention. If not, then it is unlikely to have materialized before the latter part of the so-called Shang period. In earlier times the Shang culture area probably comprised a number of competing ceremonial centers, each of which exercised direct control over a limited terrain in its immediate vicinity, and exacted tribute from other centers and surrounding tracts of territory to the extent that its ruler was powerful enough to do so.

CLASS DIFFERENTIATION IN SHANG SOCIETY[196]

On the stratified character of Shang society archeology, oracle bones, and later literary records are in agreement. Although the kinship oriented groupings of a folk-type society had not, as we have seen, been entirely eliminated, nevertheless a social system founded upon the physical expansion of a kin group within an established context of felt rights and obligations had been to a very large extent replaced by a politized social order. The incipient status differentiation that was already discernible in Lung-shan cultural assemblages had, by middle Shang times at latest, crystallized into a pyramidal society with the king and the royal lineages at the apex, a corps of officials, secretarial, civil and military, below and a broad stratum of *ṭịông-ńịěn* or peasantry at the base. We have already had a good deal to say about the upper echelons of this society and there is no need to recapitulate those remarks here. Suffice it to recall that political and social roles were related to ceremonial status through the medium of kinship, and that, through the real or fictional relationship of a proportion of benefice holders to the grand lineage of Shang, the settlement and tenurial hierarchies of the kingdom also received ritual sanction and were articulated with the central government.

The gulf between the peasant at one end of the social scale and the noble at the other, besides permeating the whole of later literature relating to the Shang, is only too apparent in the character of the dwellings inhabited by each. Whereas the peasant in the countryside and the servitor in the royal or aristocratic ceremonial enclave each lived in a semi-subterranean dwelling, normally some four meters or so in depth and about as wide, the noble occupied an imposing structure raised on a *hang-t'u* foundation at ground level. It is scarcely an exaggeration to equate nobility with *hang-t'u*, and commonalty with pit, dwellings.197 It is true that neither order used stone in the superstructure of its dwellings, but the gabled, pillar-supported roof and non-structural, screen-type walls of the aristocratic residence contrasted strongly with the wattle and daub lean-to of the peasantry.

The same disparity in degree of access to strategic resources is also apparent in the unequal treatment accorded to members of the two orders in death. So far at least 2,300 Shang graves have been excavated, of which more than 2,000 were in the vicinity of An-yang. The great majority of these have naturally been of a simple character. The extremely meager and simple grave goods associated with this type of burial are a world away from the 1,878 funerary articles, many of jade, bronze and marble, which remained in a supposedly royal tomb at Hou-Kang, despite it having been rifled twice.198 Customarily the peasant or mechanic was consigned to a grave that was little more than a hole in the ground and furnished with a few pottery vessels. Occasionally a jade or stone artifact was added but, on the other hand, burials with no trace of a pit and no grave furniture whatsoever were not rare. At the other end of the social scale were the royal mausolea at Hsi-pei Kang and some tombs of the nobility that were hardly less impressive. The excavators have detected an evolutionary sequence in élite burials from the simple interments of Proto-Shang times, through the somewhat larger and more elaborate tombs of the Cheng-Chou phase, to the massive mausolea of dynastic An-yang, a sequence that is accompanied by an ever greater disparity in the mortuary practices of the two main orders of society. By Middle and Late Shang times even a medium-sized tomb of the type which the excavators call 'regular', and which presumably was the grave of a member of one of the politically less prominent lineages comprising the royal branch of the ruling clan or of some non-royal member of the aristocracy, bears witness to the expenditure of considerable labor and skill, as well as to the preemption of personal service on a far from modest scale. The tomb itself usually took the form of a rectangular pit, in the floor of which a smaller *yao-k'eng* 199 was excavated. Over this latter was raised a wooden structure in the shape of a *kuo* or coffin chamber, and the space between this and the walls of the tomb was then filled with grey earth 200 or, in some cases, with pebbles and stone chips (presumably to minimize the ravages of damp), so as to form a platform surrounding the *kuo*.201 Both coffin and chamber were often painted with designs in black, white, red, and yellow, and mortuary objects, often in considerable quantity, were arranged on the platform. These included pottery vessels, especially *ting* and *li* tripods, *kuei*, *p'en*, *tou*, *kuan*, *chüeh* and *ku*, and, in the more elaborate burials, bronze vessels and weapons, and jade artifacts. Most such tombs also contained sacrificial victims, mainly animal but in a handful of cases human. Among the 166 tombs excavated at Ta-ssŭ-k'ung Ts'un, for example, five contained human victims.202 In one (Tomb 175) a chariot, complete with horses and charioteer, was brought to light. It is not unlikely that an earth tumulus was raised over the finished grave, but if so none has survived to the present.

The royal mausolea at Hsi-pei Kang were conceived on an even grander scale.[203] These great cruciform pits, some with ramps on all four sides, and with all the features of the 'regular' tomb incorporated in more elaborate form, were the scene of veritable holocausts of men and animals, and there is evidence that before they were rifled they contained enormous wealth in the form of mortuary furnishings. The largest of these royal tombs occupies an area of no less than 380 square meters. Similar large-scale immolations of men and animals, apparently a prerogative of the ruling lineage, were also associated with the ancestral temples in the central sector at Hsiao-T'un, though it is often impossible to be sure whether these had been sacrificed at the consecration of the buildings or during subsequent ceremonies of ancestral worship. Oracle records from the same site contain numerous references to the sacrifice to the ancestors of the royal lineage of prisoners obtained on raids among the tribal peoples of the west, notably the *K'iang* pastoralists. But Professor Shih Chang-ju has also shown that some of the burials exhibited a sequential arrangement consonant with the several stages of building construction, such as the consecration, chronologically, of *hang-t'u* foundations, of pillar bases, of entrances and, finally, of the completed building.[204] Seven of the structures in the central sector at Hsiao-T'un were apparently consecrated in this manner. As many as 852 human beings, 15 horses, 10 oxen, 18 sheep, 35 dogs, and 5 fully equipped chariots and charioteers were entombed at the dedication of these buildings, and 187 sacrificial pits excavated. In the southernmost or ceremonial sector at the same site a single building claimed 35 human sacrifices, and on another occasion some 300 animals constituted a single offering to the ancestors. Although disparities in quantity and quality of mortuary furniture do not necessarily reflect correlative distinctions in social status, ceremonial and ritual on a scale such as this cannot but have reflected a remarkable concentration of social power.

Such activities were a prerogative of the élite in their ceremonial centers, but the bulk of the Shang populace was made up of a peasantry living in villages and hamlets scattered through the countryside. Some of these rural folk could be described as free farmers, others should perhaps be more accurately designated serfs, defined in this context by Wolfram Eberhard as 'families in hereditary group dependence upon some noble families and working on land which the noble families regarded as theirs.'[205] One of the great controversies in recent Chinese historiography has concerned the precise nature of this rural component in Shang society, and the answers given to this problem have accorded closely with ideological conviction. In China the prevalent practice, derived largely from the writings of Kuo Mo-jo,[206] has been to designate it a slave society, thus bringing the Chinese experience within the schematic formularies of Engels, Morgan, and Marx. Most Western historians have rejected this interpretation in favor of a free or serf society. In actual fact the disagreement is really a matter of semantics. Both Kuo Mo-jo and his disciples on the one hand, and Western historians such as Eberhard on the other,[207] are substantially in agreement as to the implications of the evidence, but Kuo and his colleagues, holding preconceptions which predispose them to ascribe social change to economic factors rather than to internally generated fluctuations in the loci of power, use the term 'slave' with a broad connotation unacceptable to their opponents. It is certain that a small slave class – using this term in the restricted sense of Roman law as a creature virtually without rights – did exist in Shang China but, as it were, outside the structural dimensions of society, and it seems probably not to have been self-perpetuating. Although its numbers were continually being replenished by the raiding of peripherally situated tribes, no inconsiderable proportion of its total complement was expended in ritual and dedicatory immolations. Mao Hsieh-chün and Yen Yen have drawn attention to the fact that some of the sacrifices offered during the dedication ceremonies of important buildings were live slaves (or, the same thing, prisoners of war) suffering from malnutrition.[208] It would seem also that their bones were sometimes used in the manufacture of artifacts.

It has been the custom to group the craftsmen of Shang society together with the *ṭi̯ông-ńi̯ĕn* in a single class, but this may have had the effect of obscuring certain significant social distinctions between these two groups. It is true that, apart from a small number who resided within the precincts of the ceremonial centers, the craftsmen lived and worked in predominantly agricultural villages, but there is evidence that at least some of them enjoyed a status somewhat above that of the peasantry. Among the kilns of the pottery on the Ming-kung Lu near Cheng-Chou, for example, were found the houses of the potters, which were much superior to the semi-subterranean dwellings of the farming community in the vicinity.[209] Like those of the nobility, though on a smaller scale, these homes were surface houses erected on a foundation of *hang-t'u*, were furnished with a south-facing door and sometimes a window, and contained both a low platform at the rear and a corner fireplace with a chimney in the wall. The dwellings associated with the bronze foundry at Tzŭ-ching Shan, immediately north of Cheng-Chou,[210] indicate a standard of living comparable to, if not higher than, that of the potters, so there is ground for suggesting that craftsmen and artisans were sometimes socially distinguishable from the *ṭi̯ông-ńi̯ĕn*.

Both literary records and the disposition of archeological remains tend to imply that particular handicrafts were probably the prerogatives of individual kin groups, and possibly that certain branches of a particular handicraft were wholly within the hands of specific lineages. In the *Tso-Chuan*, under the fourth year of Duke **D'ieng (Ting : 505 B C) it is related that, when King **Ḋi̯ĕng (Ch'eng) was consolidating the Chou kingdom after the conquest of Shang,

Duke **Tĵôg (Chou) bestowed on **K'âng-śĵôk (K'ang-shu), the first Marquis of **Gịwad (*Wei*), seven lineages of **·Jən (*Yin*) people, five of which bore the name of products, presumably those which they themselves manufactured, namely the ***D'ôg* (*t'ao*=kiln) lineage, the **Śia (*shih* : ? = trappers) lineage, the ***B'wân* (*fan* : horse accoutrements) lineage, the ***G'ia* (*Ch'i* : cooking pot) lineage and the ***B'wân* (*fan* : harness) lineage.[211] Although this passage was not written down in its present form until relatively late in the Chou dynasty, has been subject to editing in later times, and relates to the last decade of the 6th century BC, yet there is a general consensus among classical scholars that some of the *Tso-Chuan* material is of considerable antiquity, so that it is not impossible that we have here a genuine recollection of a close relationship between kin groupings and handicraft organizations in the Late Shang. We have already noticed the fact that one of the potteries at Cheng-Chou appears to have specialized in a limited range of wares (p. 35), which implies that at least some of the other potteries in the area were equally specialized. There is no evidence that I know of to support the notion that these specialisms were expressions of kin affiliations, but it is not impossible that such was the case. The retention of specialist techniques as the prerogatives of particular kin groups is a phenomenon well known in other social and cultural contexts. Moreover, Professor Chang has drawn attention to the partitioned plan and regular arrangement of the houses of the bronzesmiths at Tzŭ-ching Shan, which may be held to indicate not only that these craftsmen's families were of the extended type, but that they all belonged to the same patrilineage.[212] This interpretation would tend to confirm the authenticity of the information contained in the *Tso-Chuan*. All in all, the implications of a close relationship between kin and craft in Shang times are not negligible, particularly when it is remembered that the archeological evidence, all of which derives from the Cheng-Chou complex, relates to the Middle Shang (Lower and Upper Erh-li Kang), while the literary record, if indeed it is of Shang provenance at all, throws light on the very last years of the An-yang dynasty.

Technological Change

Although the basis of life in the Shang state (or states) was agriculture, and although one of the chief preoccupations of the Shang kings was the promotion of agricultural prosperity through ritual intercession, it is noteworthy for the present study that this period saw no significant advance in field technology. There is no reason to believe that the short-term fallowing system practised in Lung-shan times had been improved upon to any degree, nor that the crop assemblages had been radically changed. The staples were still millets, with barley, wheat and rice (probably grown as a dry-field crop) somewhat less important.[213] Hu Hou-hsüan has stated that two crops of millet and rice were harvested each year,[214] but this would have been a virtual impossibility on the

North China plain in the absence of irrigation, and of this there is no evidence. Hu has claimed that it was probably practised in Shang times on the grounds that double-cropping would not have been feasible without it,[215] but this is a circular argument, whose conclusions are not compatible with what we know of Chou farming practice in subsequent centuries or can infer of Shang technological achievement. The water channels which have come to light at both Cheng-Chou and Hsiao-T'un, needless to say, were installed for purposes of urban and domestic drainage and, on all the evidence at present available, had nothing to do with irrigation. Much more credible is the evidence of the oracle bones that millet was grown in the first half of the year and wheat in the second, that is a summer crop was succeeded by a winter one, though, of course, they need not have been grown in the same field.[216]

Field preparation was still undertaken with the aid only of thick and heavy stone hoes hafted to wooden handles, and with a double-pronged levering instrument not dissimilar in principle to the *fumisuki* of later Japan, the caschrom of the Hebrides or the Irish *loy*. This implement seems to have developed out of the digging stick of Lung-shan times and to have been the forerunner of the **lįwər-dzįəg (lei-szŭ) of Chou times,[217] but it marked no new technological stage in the history of Chinese agriculture. At the end of the season the crops were harvested either with the semi-lunar knife which had been the common tool in the Lung-shan period or, increasingly frequently, with the *lien*-sickle.[218] This, an invention of the Shang period, was certainly a more efficient harvesting tool than the old semi-lunar knife, particularly on the North China plain where harvesting had to be fitted either into fine intervals during a rainy summer or into a short period between the end of that season and the onset of winter, but it signified no great change in the organization of the basic Sinic ecotype. The domestic animals that were raised were those of Lung-shan times, with the possible addition of the water buffalo, but there may have been some elaboration of the stock-breeding aspects of the economy in response to an augmented demand for cattle, sheep and dogs for sacrificial purposes.[219]

The remains of wild animals on archeological sites bear sufficient testimony to the importance of game as a supplement to agricultural produce in the Shang diet, but this subsistence activity should not be confused with the aristocratic pastime of the conventionalized hunt, which featured prominently in the oracle inscriptions, and which served the several purposes of simulating military training, inculcating qualities of character, and providing an acceptable outlet for the physical energies of the élite.[220] Possibly these two modes of hunting are reflected respectively in the finds of both stone and bronze arrow heads which have turned up in some quantity on archeological sites. The importance of fishing in Shang times is also revealed by the presence of fish bones and tackle of all sorts, ranging from hooks to tangles.

Among the handicrafts attested by, or inferred from, archeology, oracle bones, and literature, are shaping and carving in stone, jade, bone, shell and wood, bronze foundry, pottery manufacture, textile weaving and tailoring, and construction in earth and wood. Most of these crafts had their roots deep in the Neolithic past of North China. Carpentry and weaving, for example, had been practised by the earliest farmers of the Chung-yüan, lithic and bone industries at an even earlier date, and *hang-t'u* construction had been a Lungshanoid innovation; and in none of these crafts did the Shang period witness any radical improvement in technique, as opposed to elaboration of ornament, immediately prior to, or concomitantly with, the emergence of maturely developed ceremonial complexes.[221] The lithic assemblages, for instance, were all produced by the techniques of prehistoric times, namely sawing, chipping, pressure-flaking, hammering, pecking, polishing, and perforation, and, generally speaking, the tools manufactured in this way were of traditional patterns.[222] One innovation was the *lien*-sickle mentioned above. Another was the much less common *ch'i*-axe, a flat, more or less rectangular tool, with a straight or slightly curved cutting edge and with a series of tooth-shaped projections along each of the longer sides. Some of the more elaborate examples in jade were probably designed for ceremonial use, but striations on some stone specimens would seem to indicate that they at least had served a practical purpose. The primary use of the early stone prototype of the *ch'i*-axe is unknown, but it can hardly be regarded as marking a radical change in Shang technology.

A characteristic feature of the Late Shang stone industry is the unmistakable signs of decline in both the standard of craftsmanship and the use of many tool types, presumably as they were replaced by bone or, perhaps more probably, by wooden models. If this were so, though, none of the wooden forms has survived three millennia of inhumation. However, this apparent decline in the role of stone in technology was paralleled by a rise in the employment of more elaborate lithic artifacts for mortuary and ceremonial use. Associated with this trend was the carving of marble and jade, both in the Late Shang employed exclusively for ornamental purposes. We have already had occasion to notice the caches of jade artifacts accumulated in certain localities within Lungshanoid villages, and apparently implying some degree of status differentiation among the inhabitants, but Shang jades attained a much higher degree of sophistication in regard to both style and execution, particularly towards the close of the period.[223] Much of this advance appears to have derived from the application of some rotary apparatus, nothing of which has survived, needless to say, to the disk-knife, tube, and point which formed the essential items in the Shang jadesmith's technological equipment. Not only are jades from the earlier Shang occupational levels conceived and executed in a relatively crude fashion, but they are also directed preponderantly towards utilitarian purposes, whereas in the later period the vast majority of the articles produced by the jadesmith fall within the categories of ceremonial or mortuary objects (including *pi* disks, *tsung* squares and *kuei* scepters), ornaments of one sort or another and including numerous forms of pendants, and various types of decorative fittings for weapons and furniture.

Documentation for an account of the changes in Shang pottery technology is more adequate than for any of the other industrial traditions.[224] In addition to the quarter of a million sherds accumulated from the pre-World War II excavations in and around An-yang, substantial hoards have also subsequently been brought to light at Cheng-Chou, Lo-yang, Hui-Hsien, Hsing-T'ai, Ch'ü-yang and elsewhere, while evolutionary sequences of form and technology have been reconstructed without much difficulty. Although the wheel had been employed extensively in the manufacture of Lung-shan pottery, it appears to have been used, if anything, rather less frequently in Shang times.[225] Wheel marks tend to occur especially infrequently in the collections from Hsiao-T'un, that is, from Late Shang times, but are somewhat more common in sherds from Cheng-Chou, earlier Lo-yang (which has yielded a complete sequence from Late Neolithic to post-Shang), Hui-Hsien and Hsing-T'ai. In other words, it is the lateness of the Hsiao-T'un levels to which the paucity of wheel-turned pottery should be attributed. Why the Middle and Late Shang potters should have tended to reject wheel-shaping in favor of ring-building and beating and, to some extent, mould-building is unknown.

While the wheel-shaping of pottery was failing to advance in popularity or efficiency, it is clear that marked improvements were being introduced into the design of kilns. In fact Ma Ch'üan has been able to demonstrate an evolutionary typology in the remains of kilns from the potteries in the neighborhood of Cheng-Chou.[226] The earliest type was represented by two kilns which have been assigned to a proto-Shang level at Lo-ta Miao. Basically they preserved the Lung-shan traditions of firing. By the Middle Shang, however, several kilns in the potteries near the Ming-kung Lu, in the Jen-min Kung-yüan, and at Kang-tu and Ko-ta-wang Ts'un exhibited evidence of considerable improvement. The provision of heat vents in the floor of the baking chamber, for example, ensured better control of the fire in the Ming-kung Lu kilns, and some of those in the Jen-min Kung-yüan incorporated chimneys in the form of cylindrical tubes of baked clay. At Pi-sha Kang and Ko-ta-wang Ts'un a series of Late Shang kilns exhibited larger baking chambers, which necessitated more sophisticated systems of heat vents, together with thicker baking floors which obviated the need for supporting pillars in the fire pits. Berthold Laufer has suggested that contemporary developments in bronze foundry may not have been without influence in stimulating the more efficient application of heat in the pottery kilns of Shang.[227]

The effectiveness of the Late Shang kilns is evident in certain aspects of the pottery assemblages collected at Hsiao-T'un. There, in addition to the Grey and Red Wares, common on all Shang sites, which had devolved in the ceramic tradition of the North China plain, were invented two new types, a White Ware containing a high percentage of alumina,[228] and a Stoneware, sometimes glazed, which contained a high proportion of silica. The paste and glaze of this latter ware approached very closely indeed to what has been called the 'proto-porcelain' of the Han.[229] Only by means of a highly efficient kiln could the potters have ensured the constant hardness of 5 which characterizes this ware, as well as a porosity never in excess of 1 per cent for all sherds tested from Hsiao-T'un.[230] Such standardization of product suggests that this ware was designed to meet a specific demand, and it has been suggested that it may have served for the storage of water and wine, a function for which the porous Grey Ware was obviously unsuitable.[231] If such was the case, then it is not unrealistic to view the Stoneware as a response to the emergence of the great ceremonial centers of Shang, the palaces and temples of which would have posed problems of liquid storage never encountered in the agricultural villages of earlier times.

Shang ceramics, particularly the assemblage from Hsiao-T'un, exhibit great variety and richness of form. Li Chi has categorized six main classes, subdivided into no less than 143 types and 359 subtypes.[232] Many represented the continuation of Lung-shan traditions, but no inconsiderable proportion are Shang innovations. Among these latter are the cord-marked grey *li* tripods with short feet, round-bottomed cord-marked jugs with in-turned rims, large-mouthed beakers with exaggeratedly out-turned rims, flat-bottomed small-mouthed jars with rounded shoulders (*lui*), and ring-footed, round-bottomed, small-mouthed jars (*p'ou*). In addition Shang potters produced musical instruments in the form of ocarinas (*hsün*) and bells (*nao*), as well as industrial articles such as spindle whorls, pestles, net-sinkers, *k'an-kuo* crucibles and various types of moulds, and *tsu* figures and figurines.

The most dramatic advance in all the fields of Shang industrial technology was the development of bronze foundry, which provided us with what has become the most characteristic class of Shang artifacts.[233] It is just possible that the practice of metallurgy had been initiated at the very end of the Lung-shanoid phase (cf. p. 27 above), but in the earliest (Shang-chieh) phase of Shang culture at Cheng-Chou metal artifacts are completely lacking. The succeeding Lo-ta Miao phase has been only imperfectly explored, so that the absence of metal finds in these levels *may* imply no more than rarity. However, with the Erh-li Kang phase – which saw the building of the city wall of Cheng-Chou – there is revealed a vigorous, mature, bronze industry, adapting metallurgical techniques to pre-existing forms both of stone, bone, and horn implements, and of pottery and wooden vessels. By Late Shang times this industry had evolved into one of the world's great technological and artistic traditions.

If the term 'bronze' be restricted in connotation, as is customary, to an alloy with from 5 to 20 per cent of tin in copper, then the majority of Shang so-called bronzes are technically misnamed, for they do not conform to this chemical composition.[234] Moreover, in Late Shang times lead played an unusually large part in their composition, sometimes alloyed with both copper and tin, but occasionally in earlier times with copper alone. This was not because the foundrymen were intentionally seeking to produce a ternary alloy, but simply because they had no means of removing such impurities. Nor was this the only respect in which the Shang bronze founder's technical repertoire was severely limited. Whereas the Western (*au sens large*) founder had mastered annealing, smithy methods, and *cire-perdue*, the Shang craftsman was acquainted only with direct casting in piece-mould assemblies and the casting-on to the vessel body of pre-cast members such as handles and lugs. He knew nothing of sheet-metal working, riveting, annealing, tracing, engraving, stamping, or repoussé, and lacked anvils, fullers, swagers, tongs, flatters, and chisels. The Western craftsman, by contrast, was capable only of the most rudimentary achievements in direct casting. It is the distinctiveness of this metallurgical technology which has convinced Dr Noel Barnard, in the course of an intensive investigation of ancient Chinese bronze foundry,[235] that Shang foundrymen owed nothing directly to West Asian achievements in this field, even though these latter were long prior in time. The fact that the Shang bronzesmiths, in developing their new medium, drew on traditional artifactual forms affords confirmation of the independent development of the industry. But that Chinese bronze foundry was *sui generis*, both as regards industrial technology, plastic form, and ornamentation, there can be no doubt.

Once it had been initiated in North China the technology of bronze casting advanced with great rapidity. All three processes which came to constitute the casting repertoire of the Shang bronze founder were in use at Cheng-Chou, that is by Middle Shang times, namely single-mould casting, valve-mould casting, and multi-mould casting.[236] The composite valve-mould for the simultaneous casting of up to eight knives or arrow heads was also in use by this time, and the principle of the *k'an-kuo* crucible was known, although this instrument was considerably refined in later periods.[237] At first merely a pot adapted for the purpose by the addition of a layer of straw-tempered clay, then a specially designed vessel wholly of straw-tempered clay, the *k'an-kuo* finally evolved into a crucible in the shape of an inverted bell, but with a rod-like projection at the bottom to hold it upright in a charcoal fire. Made of a coarse gritty ware and with double-layered sand-filled walls, it was able both to withstand very high temperatures, and also the better to conserve heat when it was removed from the fire. Dr Barnard has pointed out that these crucibles, unlike those of the early West, show the effect of firing on the outside, and thus imply the use of a true reverberatory type of furnace. In fact, such a furnace would have developed naturally from the potter's kiln of Proto-Shang times, which illustrates another important difference between Western and Shang bronze technologies. Whereas the former exhibited little affinity with ceramic manufacture, the Shang bronze founder almost certainly derived not only the majority of his forms but also his furnace and, probably, the very principle of casting in moulds, from the pre-existing pottery industry.[238]

Although the basic technique of bronze foundry had been standardized by the Middle Shang, the skills of the smiths subsequently underwent noticeable changes in respect of both technology and esthetics. Bronze vessels from the lower levels at Cheng-Chou and Hui-Hsien, for example, are inferior on both counts to most of those from Hsiao-T'un. The plastic form of the earlier vessels was often cramped and inelegant, and set off with relatively ill-proportioned accessories, at the same time that the ornamentation tended to be crudely conceived and executed either in a single plane or in low relief. With the mastery of casting technique that characterized the later periods of the Shang, however, there came greater assurance and self-confidence in artistic matters, manifested in a series of new forms and styles. In addition to the traditional forms with which we are already familiar, the Late Shang offers a wide range of new types, including several versions of *yu* and *kuei* bowls, *chih* and *tsun* cups, *i* ewers and *yu* wine decanters, together with a suite of square (*fang*) vessels (*fang-i, fang-ch'i, fang-yu, fang-lei,* and so on), musical instruments, ceremonial apparatus, and fittings of all kinds. Few of these bronze artifacts, however, were designed for anything other than ceremonial use and the non-productive pursuits of the élite strata of society.[239]

It is important for our present investigation to notice that virtually all advances in Shang technology were directed towards conspicuous consumption. The three chief classes of demand stimulating this production were the ritual requirements of the ceremonial centers, the luxury and prestige items commissioned by the royal lineages and aristocracy, and the weapons needed to arm the corps of military retainers associated with both. The tradition of Shang bronze foundry, for example, attained its apogee in a varied array of vessels for ceremonial purposes, but also produced chariot fittings – though the bronze parts were decorative rather than functional – and a fairly wide range of weapons for both warfare and hunting.[240] Among these last, some items are certain to have been ceremonial weapons and tools used only in ritual. Such, for example, was the white-jade *lien*-sickle, inlaid with turquoise and hafted to a bronze handle, which is now in the Freer Gallery of Art in Washington. Clearly this weapon was too fragile, as well as too costly, for practical use. Moreover, the symbolism incorporated in its design is itself strong evidence of its ritual purpose. At the distal end of the shaft a *t'ao-t'ieh*, symbolizing the earth, spews forth the larva of a cricket, above which is a snake disgorging a bird into the air, its natural element, together with another *t'ao-t'ieh*. The famous *mao* spear-head, fitted into a socket of bronze inlaid with turquoise mosaic, which is now in the Fogg Museum of Art of Harvard University, was no less certainly designed for a ritual purpose, as indeed were numerous other highly ornate weapons and tools displayed in the museums and galleries of China, Japan and the Western world.

There was undoubtedly also a not inconsiderable private demand for bronzes, pottery, and carvings in several media to grace both the homes and the tombs of the nobility, and to a lesser extent those of minor functionaries as well. A *tao*-knife with tooth-shaped projections, an elongated adze with a minute perforation, and a thin-bladed axe with double perforation were probably all mortuary furniture. A high proportion of the rings and beads, head-dress ornaments, and figurines produced by the jade carvers were obviously destined for personal use by the more privileged sectors of the community, and numerous other jade artifacts were employed as funerary furnishings. Marble sculptures were commissioned for domestic and public architectural and ornamental purposes, and the same stone was used on a smaller scale for sacrificial vessels (apparently inspired by bronze prototypes),[241] furniture decoration and personal adornment. As for the ceramic industries, there can be no doubt that they made their contribution to both private and public display in the form of musical instruments and a wide range of containers.

In short, the overwhelming impression left by a survey of Shang technology is that its progress was a response to, not a determinant of, the emergence of a social class whose primary concerns were with ritual and ceremony, and with conspicuous display in the interests of political and social prestige. Contemporary farm implements and handicraft tools, by contrast, were almost exclusively of stone, shell, bone and, presumably, wood, and they exhibited no radical change in design or material throughout the Shang period. Writing in 1957, Huang Chan-yüeh pointed out that up to that time only three bronze spades and not more than ten bronze axes and adzes had come to light on Shang-dynasty sites.[242]

One further point is of interest for our present study, and that concerns the spatial distribution of the workshops in relation to the ceremonial centers. This has already been touched upon, so that it is only necessary to summarize the situation here. Some craftsmen certainly worked, at least temporarily, within the precincts of the sacred enclaves. At An-yang, for instance, bronze foundries, pottery kilns, and workshops engaging in the preparation of bone and stone artifacts occurred in close proximity to the palaces and temples of Hsiao-T'un, and more workshops were associated with the royal cemetery at Hsi-pei Kang. But the bulk of handicraft production was the work of artisans living in basically agricultural villages dispersed through the countryside. In the Cheng-Chou complex, for example, bronze foundries were located at Tzŭ-ching Shan and outside the south gate of the present-day city; a bone workshop had been established at Tzŭ-ching Shan; a pottery was sited about three-quarters of a mile to the west of the sacred enceinte; and what appears to have been a distillery at Erh-li Kang in the southeast. In the vicinity of An-yang, a bronze foundry, in addition to the one within the ceremonial precinct at Hsiao-T'un, was discovered among a group of dwellings at Hsüeh-chia Chuang. The site at Hsing-T'ai has so far been only partially excavated, but the same generally dispersed pattern of handicraft activity seems to be emerging, with pottery kilns located in several village clusters, and a bone workshop at another. Other Shang complexes where available archeological reports point towards the same conclusion have been mentioned on pp. 47 and 50 above.

The Economic Organization of the Shang Territories

There is a good deal of direct evidence which can be used to reconstruct the nexus of ecological adaptations and energy transfers that underpinned the evolving structure of Shang society, and its implications were summarized at the beginning of the previous section. For information about the precise manner in which the economy was organized, by contrast, we are dependent almost wholly on inference. It has already been emphasized that, although the Shang state (or perhaps states) was raised on an agricultural base, and although farming constituted one of the two major concerns of the Shang monarch, this period witnessed no significant improvements in agricultural practice. In the absence of any such technical advances, the ability of the Shang states to sustain a non-cultivating élite, at least a skeletal bureaucracy, a corps of military guards and functionaries, and a stratum of craftsmen and artisans must have derived from a reorganization of the forms of economic integration.

All that we know and have been able to infer about the village economy of North China during the Yang-shao and earlier Lung-shan phases indicates that it exhibited predominantly those 'movements between correlative points of symmetrical groupings' which have been succinctly categorized by Karl Polanyi as constituting an ideal-type system of reciprocity.[243] By Shang times, however, it is evident that an increasingly powerful centripetal force is remoulding the economy, with the allocative pressures of a ceremonial center generating appropriational movements primarily towards itself, though subsequently and secondarily centrifugally outwards. Testimony to this all-important transformation in the form of economic integration is inferential but, to my mind, conclusive. In the first place, the morphology of Shang settlements, in which agricultural villages and industrial quarters were dispersed through the countryside surrounding an elaborate ceremonial and administrative complex, is not easily explained on any other assumption. The implications of the irregular distribution of handicraft workshops are especially clear. By no means every settlement boasted one of each type, or even one at all, so that production could not have been solely for consumption within a particular village. In any case, we have already seen that the manufacture of bronze articles was almost entirely for the benefit of the élite who resided in the ceremonial centers, and it was this same class who created the demand for the more elaborate and finely executed products of the lithic, jade, and ceramic industries. Furthermore, the caches of stone sickles, often in large quantities, which are characteristic of Shang settlement sites have usually been held to indicate at least a degree of centralization in the management of agricultural labor. In one storage pit at Hsiao-T'un no less than 3,500 semi-lunar stone sickles, both used and unused, were found, and in another at the same site some 400, all of which bore signs of use. It is true that such sickles are not uncommon in Lungshanoid excavations, but it is only in the Shang period that they make up such a high proportion of the stone artifacts on any particular site. The presence of numerous storage pits in and about the ceremonial enclaves would seem to carry similar implications of centralized management. It is to be inferred that the harvest was stored in centrally located granaries, whence it was presumably distributed as required.[244] In fact, it has been suggested that it may have been such a centralization of activities as is here described, with a concomitant reliance on accurate timing and close regulation of field work, which stimulated the elaboration of the Shang calendar.[245]

Of course, centrally domiciled labor may not have been employed on all the royal domains and benefices. On particular fields controlled directly by the central administration some work may have been performed by slaves, or even by free men working for a specified number of days during the year. We know, for instance, that war captives were employed in this way, probably in many cases prior to their execution. This is, in effect, the contention of Amano Motonosuke,[246] who has suggested that the territory under the direct control of a cult center may have comprised two classes of land : a royal demesne cultivated by slaves under centralized management, and so-called clan fields farmed by a peasantry which consisted essentially of the less prestigious members of the great clans.

In any case, there can be little doubt that control of labor in one way or another had become highly centralized by Shang times: the massive constructions undertaken in the ceremonial centers are sufficient evidence of that. The wall encircling the ritual complex at Cheng-Chou affords an instructive illustration. An Chin-huai has calculated that this rampart, with a total length of 7,195 meters and an original height of 10 meters on a base 20 meters wide, could not have been raised by 10,000 workmen laboring for 330 days a year in less than 18 years.[247] How and in what quantities the labor force was disposed in time and place we cannot know, but the order of magnitude of the task is powerful testimony to the concentration of social and political power achieved by one group in North China no later than the Middle Shang. No wall has been discovered so far in connection with the An-yang complex, but Li Chi has estimated that the excavation of each of the eleven allegedly royal tombs at

Hsi-pei Kang would have required at least 7,000 man-days.[248] In a second calculation Professor Li has estimated that merely to dig the pit in Tomb HPKM 1001 at Hou-chia Chuang would have required 'no less than 4,200 day-labor units, if one labor unit at that time could have removed one cubic meter of dirt in a day, as the best of farm hands nowadays, with a much superior tool and better incentive, might occasionally be able to do.'[249]

The form of economic integration manifested in the organization implicit in the preceding paragraphs approximates closely to that which Polanyi has designated as redistribution *sensu stricto*.[250] Of course, reciprocity and redistribution are not mutually exclusive forms of economic integration. In fact, in non-market economies they customarily supplement one another.[251] Used in relation to the economy of the Shang state, the term redistribution signifies that the dominant and institutionalized movement of surplus products was away from the villages scattered through the countryside towards the ceremonial foci. In the case of some products this doubtless involved a physical relocation of goods, followed perhaps by storage and ultimately a partial return to the countryside; in other instances it was probably merely appropriational, involving only rights of disposal over the products. Side by side with this institutionalized integration of the, as it were, superordinate economy, the old forms of reciprocity persisted among villagers and nobility alike.

It is clear from what has been said above that, although Shang civilization had evolved uninterruptedly from the matrix of Lungshan culture, there had supervened between these two phases a major economic transformation, in which a predominantly reciprocal integration occurring spontaneously at village level had been subsumed into a superordinate, politically institutionalized, dominantly redistributive pattern. In Chapter Three we shall examine the possible relationships between this transformation and the emergence of urban life, and also attempt to isolate some of the factors which may have been involved in this change.

Notes and References

1. This term, which will appear frequently in subsequent sections of this book, has both a geographical and a cultural connotation. It was coined by Alfred L. Kroeber [*Anthropology*. Harcourt, Brace & Co., New York 1948, p.779] to designate the axis of aboriginal complex societies in the pre-Columbian Americas, namely central and southern Mexico, Central America, the northern Andes and Peru.

2. Summaries of the successive stages of these excavations are to be found in, *int. al.*, Li Chi et al., *An-yang Fa-chüeh Pao-kao*, 4 vols. Peking 1929–33; Shih Chang-ju, 'Yin-hsü tsui-chin-chih chung-yao fa-hsien. Fu : Lun Hsiao-T'un ti-ts'eng', *Chung-Kuo K'ao-ku Hsüeh-pao*, no.2 (1947), pp.1–81, and 'Hsiao-T'un C-ch'ü-ti mu-tsang ch'ün' *Kuo-li Chung-Yang Yen-chiu-yüan Li-shih Yü-yen Yen-chiu-so Chi-k'an*, vol.23 (1952), pp.447–87; Hu Hou-hsüan, *Yin-hsü Fa-chüeh*. Shanghai 1955; Tung Tso-pin, 'Chung-Kuo wen-tzŭ-ti ch'i-yüan', *Ta-lu Tsa-chih*, vol.5, no.10. T'ai-pei 1952; and *Chia-ku-hsüeh Wu-shih-nien*. T'ai-pei 1955; Ch'en Meng-chia, *Yin-hsü Pu-tz'ŭ Tsung-shu*. Peking 1956; Kuo Pao-chün, 'I-chiu-wu-ling-nien-ch'un Yin-hsü fa-chüeh pao-kao', *K'ao-ku Hsüeh-pao*, no.5 (1951), pp.1–61; Liu Hsiao-ch'un, 'I-chiu-wu-wu-nien-ch'iu An-yang Hsiao-T'un Yin-hsü-ti fa-chüeh' *K'ao-ku Hsüeh-pao*, no.3 (1958), pp.63–72; Ma Te-chih, Chou Yung-chen, Chang Yün-p'eng, 'I-chiu-wu-san-nien An-yang Ta-ssŭ-k'ung Ts'un fa-chüeh pao-kao', *K'ao-ku Hsüeh-pao*, no.9 (1955), pp.25–90; Chao Ch'ing-yün et al., '1958-nien-ch'un Ho-nan An-yang Shih Ta-ssŭ-k'ung Ts'un Yin-tai mu-tsang fa-chüeh chien-pao', *K'ao-ku T'ung-hsün*, no.10 (1958), pp.51–62; An Chih-min, Chiang Ping-hsin and Ch'en Chih-ta, '1958–1959-nien Yin-hsü fa-chüeh chien-pao', *K'ao-ku*, no.2 (1961), pp.63–76; and in definitive versions in the formal reports of the excavations issued under the auspices of the old Academia Sinica of the mainland and as reconstituted in T'ai-pei. The seriation of these last items is likely to be confusing to anyone who has not seen the volumes, so it may be as well to summarize the present situation. The reports were intended to be the second publication in the *Archeologia Sinica* series (of which the first was that dealing with the excavations at Ch'eng-tzŭ Yai : *vide* note 81 below). Of the first of the An-yang volumes, which was to include a general account of the excavations, only the fascicule dealing with architectural remains has so far been published. Vol.2, which constitutes a massive report on the oracle archives of An-yang, has appeared in four parts, the titles of which are as

NOTES AND REFERENCES

follows : Tung-Tso-pin, *Hsiao-T'un* : *Yin-hsü Wen-tzŭ*, vol.2, fasc.2. Shanghai and T'ai-pei 1948–54; Li Chi, *Hsiao-T'un*, vol.3 : *Ch'i-wu (Artifacts)* fasc.1 : *T'ao-ch'i (Pottery)*, pt.1. T'ai-pei 1956; Shih Chang-ju, *Hsiao-T'un : I-chih-ti Fa-hsien yü Fa-chüeh*, vol.1, fasc.2 : *Chien-chu i-ts'un (Architectural remains)*. T'ai-pei 1959. In addition there is a valuable book by Tung Tso-pin, *Yin Li P'u*. Li-chuang 1945; and a paper (one among many on the same subject) by the same author, 'Yin Li P'u hou-chi', *Kuo-li Chung-yang Yen-chiu-yüan Li-shih Yü-yen Yen-chiu-so Chi-k'an*, vol.13 (1948). Finally there are succinct but compendious accounts of the An-yang excavations in English in Cheng Te-k'un, *Archaeology in China*, vol.2 : *Shang China*. W. Heffer & Sons, Cambridge 1960; William Watson, *Archaeology in China*. Parrish, London 1960; and *China before the Han dynasty*. Ancient Peoples and Places Series, no.23. Thames and Hudson, London 1961; and Kwang-chih Chang [Chang Kuang-chih], *The archaeology of ancient China*. Yale University Press 1963, pp.154–62.

3. The views of this school of historical iconoclasts, led by Ku Chieh-kang, were set out in the volumes of *Ku-Shih Pien*, vols.1–7, 1926–41. All were edited by Ku Chieh-kang except vol.4 (1933) and vol.6 (1938) which were edited by Lo Ken-tse, and vol.7 which was edited by Lü Ssŭ-mien and T'ung Shu-yeh. Similar views were expressed at this time in the pages of *Shih-Huo* and *Yü-Kung*, both of which journals were published under Marxist auspices, and also informed the work of Kuo Mo-jo [e.g. *Chung-Kuo Ku-tai She-hui Yen-chiu*. Shanghai 1927] and T'ao Hsi-sheng [e.g. *Chung-Kuo She-hui-chih Shih-ti Fen-hsi*. Shanghai 1929]. There is a useful summary in English of the work of this school in Lin Mou-sheng, 'The revolution in the history of Chinese history', *China Institute Bulletin*, vol.3 (1938), New York. For a general account of Chinese historiography in this century see J. Gray, 'Historical writing in twentieth-century China : notes on its background and development', in W. G. Beasley and E. G. Pulleyblank (eds.), *Historians of China and Japan*. Oxford University Press 1961, pp.186–212. Ku Chieh-kang, in the autobiography (*tzŭ-hsü*) with which he prefaced the *Ku-Shih Pien* series, traced the origin of the new critical school of history to two works of K'ang Yu-wei (1856–1927): cf. A. W. Hummel (transl.), *The autobiography of a Chinese historian*. Sinica Leidensia edidit Institutum Sinologicum Lugduno-Batavum, vol. 1. E. J. Brill, Leyden 1931, p.152.

4. *Vide* An Chin-huai, 'Cheng-Chou ti-ch'ü-ti ku-tai i-ts'un chieh-shao', *Wen-wu Ts'an-k'ao Tzŭ-liao*, no.8. Peking 1957, pp.16–20 and 'Shih-lun Cheng-Chou Shang-tai ch'eng-chih – Ao-tu', *Wen-wu*, nos.4–5. (1961), pp.73–80; Tsou Heng, 'Shih-lun Cheng-Chou hsin-fa-hsien-ti Yin-Shang wen-hua i-chih', *K'ao-ku Hsüeh-pao*, no.3. Peking 1956, pp.77–103; An Chih-min, 'I-chiu-wu-erh-nien ch'iu-chi Cheng-Chou Erh-li Kang fa-chüeh chi', *K'ao-ku Hsüeh-pao*, no.8. (1954), pp.65–107, and 'Cheng-Chou Shih Jen-Min Kung-Yüan fu-chin-ti Yin-tai i-ts'un', *Wen-wu Ts'an-k'ao Tzŭ-liao*, no.6. (1954), pp.32–7; Chao

Ch'üan-ku et al., 'Cheng-Chou Shang-tai i-chih-ti fa-chüeh', *K'ao-ku Hsüeh-pao*, no.1. (1957), pp.53–73; Ch'en Chia-hsiang, 'Cheng-Chou Lo-ta Miao Shang-tai i-chih shih-chüeh chien-pao', *Wen-wu Ts'an-k'ao Tzŭ-liao*, no.10. (1957), pp.48–51; Chao Ch'ing-yün, '1957-nien Cheng-Chou hsi-chiao fa-chüeh chi-yao', *K'ao-ku T'ung-hsün*, no.9. (1958), pp.54–6; Chao Ch'ing-yün and Liu Tung-ya, 'Cheng-Chou Ko-ta-wang Ts'un i-chih fa-chüeh pao-k'ao', *K'ao-ku Hsüeh-pao*, no.3. (1958), pp.41–62; Chang Chien-chung, 'Cheng-Chou Shih Pai-chia Chuang Shang-tai mu-tsang fa-chüeh chien-pao', *Wen-wu Ts'an-k'ao Tzŭ-liao*, no.10. (1955), pp.24–42; Ma Ch'üan, 'Cheng-Chou Shih Ming-kung Lu hsi-ts'e-ti Shang-tai i-ts'un', *Wen-wu Ts'an-k'ao Tzŭ-liao*, no.10. (1956), pp.39 and 50–1; Ma Ch'üan and Mao Pao-liang, 'Cheng-Chou fa-hsien-ti chi-ko-shih-ch'i-ti ku-tai yao-chih', *Wen-wu Ts'an-k'ao Tzŭ-liao*, no.10. (1957), pp.58–9; Chao Hsia-kuang, 'Cheng-Chou Nan-kuan-wai Shang-tai i-chih fa-chüeh chien-pao', *K'ao-ku T'ung-hsün*, no.2. (1958), pp.6–9; Cheng-Chou Shih Wen-wu Kung-tso-tsu, 'Cheng-Chou Shih Jen-Min Kung-Yüan ti-erh-shih-wu-hao Shang-tai mu-tsang ch'ing-li chien-pao', *Wen-wu Ts'an-k'ao Tzŭ-liao*, no.12. (1954), pp.83–5, and Tung Hung, 'Cheng-Chou Pai-chia Chuang i-chih fa-chüeh chien-pao', *Wen-wu Ts'an-k'ao Tzŭ-liao*, no.4. (1956), pp.3–8; Yang Ch'i-ch'eng, 'Cheng-Chou ti-5-wen-wu-ch'ü ti-1-hsiao-ch'ü fa-chüeh chien-pao', *Wen-wu Ts'an-k'ao Tzŭ-liao*, no.5. (1956), pp.33–40; Yin Huan-chang, 'Pa-ko-yüeh-lai-ti Cheng-Chou wen-wu kung-tso kai-k'uang', *Wen-wu Ts'an-k'ao Tzŭ-liao*, no.9. (1955), pp.56–8. Cf. also the English-language works mentioned in footnote 2.

5. Robert McC. Adams, *The evolution of urban society. Early Mesopotamia and Prehispanic Mexico*. Aldine Publishing Company, Chicago 1966, p.28.

6. Adams, *Evolution*, pp.23–4.

7. Joseph de Guignes, *Mémoire dans lequel on prouve, que les Chinois sont une colonie égyptienne*. Desaint et Saillant, Paris 1760. Much the same idea had been propounded a century previously by Athanasius Kircher in his *Oedipus Ægyptiacus*. Romae, ex typographia V. Mascardi 1652–4. Colophon of vol.3 dated 1655.

8. R.E.M. (later Sir Mortimer) Wheeler, *Five thousand years of Pakistan. An archaeological outline*. Royal India and Pakistan Society, London 1950, p.30. Still less am I disposed to accept Hasmukh D. Sankalia's statement relating to the Indus cities: 'Some genius, who, it is believed, was under Mesopotamian influence where earlier cities existed, turned these rich agricultural villages into fine brick-built towns and cities' ['India', in Robert J. Braidwood and Gordon R. Willey, *Courses toward urban life*. Aldine Publishing Company. Chicago 1962, p.70].

9. Bronislaw Malinowski, *A scientific theory of culture*. University of North Carolina Press, Chapel Hill, 1944, pp.14–15.

10. Julian H. Steward, 'Cultural causality and law: a trial formulation of

NOTES AND REFERENCES

the development of early civilizations', *American Anthropologist*, vol.51, no.1. (1951), p.4; reprinted in the same author's *Theory of culture change*. University of Illinois Press, Urbana 1955, where the reference is to p.182. In this same connection the words of Leslie White are also worth quoting: 'To the evolutionist it made no difference whether a given people obtained a trait by diffusion or developed it indigenously; it was the evolution of the culture that they were concerned with, not the cultural experiences of this or that tribe. There is thus no incompatibility between diffusion and evolution of culture . . .' [Leslie A. White, 'Evolution and diffusion', *Antiquity*, no.124. (1957), p.218]. Nor is Robert F. Murphey's thesis that the acculturative situation is not only empirically the condition of, but is also structurally necessary to, almost all human societies, irrelevant to this discussion : 'Social change and acculturation', *Transactions of the New York Academy of Sciences*, series II, vol.26 (1963–4), pp.845–54.

11. Morton H. Fried, 'On the evolution of social stratification and the state', in Stanley Diamond [ed.], *Culture in History : essays in honor of Paul Radin*. Columbia University Press, New York 1960, pp.713 and 729–30.

12. Gordon R. Willey, 'The prehistoric civilizations of nuclear America', *American Anthropologist*, vol.57 (1955), p.571.

13. Bernhard Karlgren, 'Some weapons and tools of the Yin dynasty', *Bulletin of the Museum of Far Eastern Antiquities*, vol.17. Stockholm 1945, pp.114–21.

14. Homer H. Dubs, 'The date of the Shang period', *T'oung Pao*, vol.40. Leiden 1951, pp.322–35.

15. Tung Tso-pin, *Yin Li P'u*. Academia Sinica, Li-chuang, 1945; 'Wu-Wang fa Chou nien-yüeh-jih chin-k'ao', *Kuo-li T'ai-wan Ta-hsüeh Wen-shih-che hsüeh-pao*, vol.3. T'ai-pei 1951, pp.177–212; 'Kuan-yü ku-shih nien-tai-hsüeh-ti wen-t'i', *Ta-lu Tsa-chih*, vol.13, no.6. T'aipei 1956, pp.1–4; 'Chung-Kuo shang-ku-shih nien-tai', *Kuo-li T'ai-wan Ta-hsüeh K'ao-ku Jen-lei Hsüeh-k'an*, no.11. T'ai-pei 1958, pp.1–4. For a recent succinct statement of the current status of the question of Shang chronology see Noel Barnard's review of recent works on pre-Han archeology in *Monumenta Serica*, vol.22, fasc.1. Monumenta Serica Institute at the University of California at Los Angeles, Sumptibus Societatis Verbi Divini 1963, pp.213–55.

16. Noel Barnard, review (with postscript) of Chou Hung-hsiang's *Shang-Yin ti-wang pen-chi* in *Monumenta Serica*, vol.19 (1960), pp.486–515, especially p.515. It is interesting to recall that Herrlee Glessner Creel had come to much the same conclusion in 1937 [*Studies in early Chinese culture*. Waverly Press, Baltimore 1937, pp.xvi–xxii].

17. *Vide*, for example, the discussion of this question in Chou Hung-hsiang, *Shang-Yin Ti-wang Pen-chi*. Hong Kong 1958.

18. So far *Yin* has not been observed in *attested* (that is scientifically excav-

ated) Western Chou epigraphy, though this is not to deny the possibility that some Western Chou presently unattested inscriptions incorporating the term may eventually be validated or, perhaps more likely, materials scientifically excavated in the future may use the form *Yin*. Cf. also Creel, *Studies in early Chinese culture*, p.1, note 1, and pp.65–6.

19. I have been able to trace this tradition back to the *Kua-ti Chih* by Wei-Wang[Li] T'ai in the 7th century AD, where this original benefice of Shang is identified with the former sub-prefecture of Shang-lo, some 85 *li* east of present-day Shang-Chou; but the fact that this tradition was older even than the T'ang affords no guarantee of its authenticity.

20. This is substantially the story as related in *Shih-Chi*, chüan 3, ff.1–2. Other versions assembled in the *T'ung-chien Kang-mu* vary somewhat in detail but agree in the general tenor of their accounts.

21. This is the conception of the Shang state which is depicted, for example, in Albert Herrmann's *Historical and Commercial Atlas of China* [Harvard-Yenching Institute Monograph Series, vol.1. Harvard University Press 1935, Plate 9, II] and which has been reproduced in one form or another in numerous subsequent works.

22. Cf., e.g., Ku Chieh-kang, 'Yü Ch'ien Hsüan-t'ung hsien-sheng lun ku-shih-shu', *Ku-Shih Pien*, vol.1 (1926). As early as the 18th century the scholar Ts'ui Shu had remarked on the discrepancy between the alleged historical age of the culture-heroes and their actual literary age, but his work was virtually forgotten from that time until it was resurrected by Hu Shih in 1921.

23. Arthur Waley, *The way and its power. A study of the Tao Te Ching and its place in Chinese thought*. Evergreen Book E-84, Grove Press Reprint, New York, n.d., p.134.

24. Ku Chieh-kang, *Han-tai Hsüeh-shu Shih-lüeh*. Tung-fang, Ch'ung-ch'ing, 1944.

25. According to all Confucian sources and some Taoist texts, Yao abdicated and delivered the empire not to his son but to Shun, a virtuous farmer and fisherman. On the other hand the *Bamboo Annals* (*Kuang Hung-ming-chi*, chüan 11, f.13 verso) which, if the report of their late discovery is to be believed, presumably escaped the reconstructive efforts of Han scholars (see p.14), relate that Shun deposed Yao by force. Implications to the same effect are to be found in *Po-wu Chih* by Chang-Hua (*c.*AD 290), chüan 2, f.1 recto and in *Han-Fei-tzŭ*, chüan 13 (probably from early in the 3rd century BC).

26. As pointed out by Wolfram Eberhard, *Artibus Asiae*, vol.11, no.4 (1946), p.359 : review of Bernhard Karlgren's *Legends and cults in ancient China*.

27. J. G. Andersson, 'Researches into the prehistory of the Chinese', *Bulletin of the Museum of Far Eastern Antiquities*, vol.15 (1943), Stockholm, p.7.

NOTES AND REFERENCES

28. Kwang-chih Chang [Chang Kuang-chih], 'Some dualistic phenomena in Shang society', *The Journal of Asian Studies*, vol.24, no.1 (1964), p.51.

29. Ch'en Meng-chia, 'Shang-tai-ti shen-hua yü wu-shu', *Yen-ching Hsüeh-pao*, vol.20 (1936), pp.485–576.

30. Joseph Needham, *Science and civilisation in China*, vol.3. Cambridge 1959, pp.245–6.

31. H.G.Creel, *Studies in early Chinese culture*, p.105. Some thirty years after it was written, Creel's chapter entitled 'Was there a Hsia dynasty?' is still the most thorough and lucid analysis of the Hsia problem.

32. See Paul Pelliot, 'Le Chou King en caractères anciens et le Chang chou che wen', *Mémoires concernant l'Asie Orientale, Académie des Inscriptions et Belles-Lettres*, vol.2. Paris 1916, pp.123–77. Cf. also K.Nagasawa, *Geschichte der Chinesischen Literatur, und ihrer gedanklichen Grundlage*. Transl. from the Japanese by E.Feifel. Fu-jen University Press, Pei-p'ing 1945, p.120.

33. H.G.Creel, *The birth of China*. London 1936, pp.55–95, and *Studies in early Chinese culture*, pp.64–9.

34. Edouard Chavannes, *Les mémoires historiques de Se-ma Ts'ien*, vol.1. Leroux, Paris 1895, pp.cxl–cxli.

35. Arthur Waley, *The Analects of Confucius*. George Allen and Unwin Ltd, London 1938, p.53.

36. *Vide* Chavannes, *Les mémoires historiques*, vol.5 (1905), pp.446–79, and Kanda Kiichirō, *Shinagaku setsurin* (1933), p.1039.

37. Wang Kuo-wei, 'Ku-pen Chu-shu Chi-nien chi-chiao, part III', in *Haining Wang Chung-ch'io Kung I-shu*. Commercial Press, Ch'angsha, 1940. See also Fan Hsiang-yung, *Ku-pen Chu-shu Chi-nien Chi-chiao Ting-pu*. Shanghai 1957; and Henri Maspero, 'La chronologie des rois de Ts'i au IVe siècle avant notre ère', *T'oung Pao*, vol.25 (1927–8), pp.367–386.

38. Other indications that Ssŭ-ma Ch'ien had access to sources no longer extant occur from time to time in the *Shih-Chi*. A good example is afforded by the reference to a short quotation from the ***T'âng t̡i̯ĕng* (*T'ang cheng* : *T'âng's subjugation* [of the Count of **K'ât : Ko]). This is reputedly the title of a lost section of the *Shu-Ching*, but one which is to be found in neither the *chin-wen* text of Fu-Sheng nor in the *ku-wen* version provided by K'ung An-kuo. We can only conclude, therefore, that Ssŭ-ma Ch'ien obtained it from a source completely unknown at the present time. Cf. Chou Hung-hsiang, *Shang-Yin Ti-wang Pen-chi*. Hong Kong 1959.

39. On Han historiography in general see A.F.P.Hulsewé, 'Notes on the historiography of the Han period', in Beasley and Pulleyblank, *Historians*, pp. 31–43. For a summary of opinions on the date and subsequent fate of the text of the *Shih-Chi* see F.Jäger, 'Der heutige Stand der Shi-ki-Forschung', *Asia Major* vol.9 (1933), pp.21–37.

40. Cf. Wang Kuo-wei, 'Yin pu-tz'ŭ-chung so-chien hsien-kung hsien-wang k'ao' in *Hai-ning Wang Chung-ch'io Kung I-shu.* Ch'angsha 1940. Creel [*Studies in early Chinese culture*, pp.49–54] regards these poems as giving us 'a most interesting picture of the people of the State of Sung when they were as yet only half assimilated to the Chou philosophy of history'.

41. *Shih-Chi*, chüan 3, f.13 recto.

42. During the Former Han dynasty at least four recensions of the *Odes*, each with its corpus of commentary, were all taught at the capital, but from the beginning of the Later Han a collation by Mao-Heng, perhaps with some assistance from Mao-Ch'ang, gradually displaced the other versions which are now known only through early citations. Cf. Bernhard Karlgren, 'The early history of the Chou li and Tso Chuan texts', *Bulletin of the Museum of Far Eastern Antiquities*, vol.3 (1931), pp.12–33. See also Fu Ssŭ-nien, 'Shih-Ching Chiang-i-kao', in *Fu Meng-chen Hsien-sheng Chi*, vol.2B. T'ai-wan University, T'ai-pei 1952, especially pp.94–5.

43. For references to the site in Chinese literature see Tung Tso-pin, ' *Yin-hsü yen-ke*', *Kuo-li Chung-yang Yen-chiu-yüan Li-shih Yü-yen Yen-chiu-so Chi-k'an*, vol.2, pt.2. Nan-ching 1930, pp.224–40.

44. The pioneer collectors of oracle bones were Wang I-yung and Liu E, the latter of whom published the first collection of oracle inscriptions in 1903. Subsequently Wang Kuo-wei and Lo Chen-yü took the lead in deciphering the inscriptions.

45. Cheng Te-k'un, *Archaeology in China*, vol.2, p.4.

46. *loc. cit.*, pp.4–16.

47. Liang Ssŭ-yung, 'Hsiao-T'un, Lung-shan yü Yang-shao', *Kuo-li Chung-yang Yen-chiu-yüan Li-shih Yü-yen Yen-chiu-so Ch'ing-chu Ts'ai Yüan-p'ei Hsien-sheng Liu-shih-wu-sui Lun-wen Chi*, pt.2. Peking 1933, pp.555–68.

48. In P'ei Yin's commentary on *Shih-Chi* (T'ai-pei reprint of the Ch'ien-lung edition, 1964, chüan 3, f.8a) this name occurs under the orthography **Ngog : compare the *Shih-Chi Cheng-i* of the 8th-century commentator Chang Shou-chieh, *ibid.*; but in *Chu-shu Chi-nien*, under **D'i̯ông-tieng (Chung-ting), in *Shu-Ching*, preface, and in the 12th-century *T'ung-Chien Kang-mu* the form **χi̯og (*Ao*) is used.

For the identification of the Cheng-Chou sites with ancient *Ngog* see Mizuno Seiichi, *Sekai Kōkogaku Taikei*, vol.6, pt.2. Tōkyō, 1958 edition, p.9; and An Chin-huai, 'Shih-lun Cheng-Chou Shang-tai ch'eng chih – Ao-tu', *Wen-wu*, nos.4–5. Peking 1961, p.73. However, Liu Chi-i has voiced reservations about this identification: '"Ao-tu" chih-i', *Wen-wu*, no.10 (1961), pp.39–40. It was traditionally believed that *Ngog* had been located in the vicinity of present-day Ying-che but reasonably thorough reconnaissances of this district during the 1950s revealed no evidence of Shang settlement. Cheng-Chou lies about 15 kilometres to the southwest.

NOTES AND REFERENCES

49. Walter A. Fairservis, Jr, *The origins of oriental civilization*. Mentor Book 251, the New American Library, New York 1959, p.133.

50. Robert J. Braidwood, 'Means towards an understanding of human behavior before the present', in Walter W. Taylor (ed.), *The identification of non-artifactual archaeological materials*. National Research Council Publication no.565. Washington, DC, 1957, pp.14–16, and 'Levels in prehistory : a model for the consideration of the evidence', in Sol Tax (ed.), *Evolution after Darwin: the evolution of man*, vol.2. University of Chicago Press 1960, pp.143–151; Robert M. Adams, 'Some hypotheses on the development of early civilizations', *American Antiquity*, vol.21, no.3 (1956), pp.227–32, 'The evolutionary process in early civilizations', in Tax, *op. cit.*, and *The evolution of urban society. Early Mesopotamia and Prehispanic Mexico*. Aldine Publishing Company, Chicago 1966; Gordon R. Willey, 'Growth trends in New World culture', in E. K. Reed and D. S. King (eds.), *For the Dean*. Santa Fe 1950, pp.223–47, 'The prehistoric civilizations of Nuclear America', *American Anthropologist*, vol.57 (1955), pp.571–93, and 'Historical patterns and evolution in native New World cultures', in Tax, *op. cit.*, pp.111–41; Carl H. Kraeling and Robert M. Adams (eds.), *City Invincible. A symposium on urbanization and cultural development in the ancient Near East*. University of Chicago Press 1960; Robert J. Braidwood and Gordon R. Willey, *Courses toward urban life*. Aldine Publishing Company, Chicago 1962.

51. Cf. especially Kwang-chih Chang [Chang Kuang-chih], 'China', in Braidwood and Willey, *Courses toward urban life*, pp.179–82, and *The archaeology of ancient China*. Yale University Press, New Haven and London 1963.

52. The study of *chia-ku hsüeh* has now attained the status of a sub-discipline, with its own nexus of distinctive skills and its own technical literature, within the general field of sinology. Since Liu E published his pioneering work *T'ieh-yün Ts'ang-kuei*, containing 1,058 rubbings, in October 1903 a vast mass of epigraphic material has become available in the form of dictionaries, catalogues and reports. Among the classics of the formative period of *chia-ku hsüeh* was *Ch'i-wen Chü-li*. Shanghai 1904, in which Sun I-jang formulated the basic principles of oracle-bone interpretation. By the time that Hu Hou-hsüan came to publish his quinquagenary summary of the achievements of the new discipline (*Wu-shih-nien Chia-ku-hsüeh Lun-chu-mu*) in 1952 he was able to include in it no less than 875 descriptive and expository works. Among these were several which could justifiably be described as landmarks in the progress of *chia-ku hsüeh*, notably Wang Kuo-wei's *Yin pu-tz'ŭ chung so-chien hsien-kung hsien-wang k'ao*, in *Kuan-T'ang Chi-Lin*, and reprinted in *Hai-ning Wang Ching-an Hsien-sheng I-shu*. Ch'ang-sha 1940; Wang Hsiang's *Fu-shih Yin-ch'i lei-tsuan*; Shang Ch'eng-ts'o's *Yin-hsü Wen-tzŭ Lei-pien*; Tung Tso-pin's *Chia-ku-wen tuan-tai yen-chiu-li, Kuo-li Chung-yang Yen-chiu Yüan Li-shih Yü-yen Yen-chiu-so Ch'ing-chu Ts'ai Yüan-p'ei Hsien-sheng Liu-shih-wu-sui Lun-wen*

Chi, Kuo Mo-jo's *Pu-tz'ŭ t'ung-tsuan*, and Sun Hai-po's *Chia-ku-wen Pien*. More recently some 9,000 attested oracle records from Hsiao-T'un, both complete and fragmentary, have been made available in four volumes by the Academia Sinica (cf. note 2 above) and scholars in China, Japan and the Western world have begun to treat this immense corpus of evidence not merely as an adjunct to the study of literary and archeological evidence but as a powerful tool in its own right. Notable among such scholars are Ch'en Meng-chia (*Yin-hsü Pu-tz'ŭ Tsung-shu* 1956), Jao Tsung-i (*Yin-tai Chen-pu Jen-wu T'ung-k'ao*, 2 vols. Hong Kong University Press 1959, Shima Kunio (*In-kyo bokuji kenkyū*), and Noel Barnard, who is the first oracle specialist to face squarely the problem of forgeries. In a series of papers and reviews in *Monumenta Serica* and elsewhere he has sought to establish the interpretation of both bone and bronze epigraphy on a scientific basis, making use only of rigorously attested (i.e. scientifically excavated) primary materials, and eschewing modern *character equivalents* in transcription in favor of *modern character forms*, which preserve the original structural combination of character elements.

53. When the titles of benefice holders appear in the oracle records there is reason to believe that they were usually members of the royal lineage.

54. Tung Tso-pin, 'Yin-tai-ti niao-shu', *Ta-lu Tsa-chih*, vol.6, no.11 (1953), pp.9–11.

55. Tung-Tso-pin, *An interpretation of the ancient Chinese civilization*, Chinese Association for the United Nations, T'ai-pei, T'ai-wan 1952, p.6.

56. Cf. Henri Maspero, 'Contribution à l'étude de la société chinoise à la fin des Chang et au début des Tcheou', *Bulletin de l'Ecole Française d'Extrême-Orient*, vol.46, no.2 (1954), pp.336–41. On the morphological evolution of the North China plain see Ting Su (William S.Ting), 'Hua-pei ti-hsing-shih yü Shang-Yin-ti li-shih', *Chung-yang Yen-Chiu-Yüan : Min-ts'u-hsüeh Yen-chiu-so Chi-k'an* no.20 (1965) pp.155–62.

57. There is a summary statement of the position in Cheng Te-k'un, *Shang China*, pp.83–7.

58. Pierre Teilhard de Chardin and C.C.Young, 'On the mammalian remains from the archaeological site of An-yang', *Palaeontologia Sinica*, C47. Peking 1936; C.C.Young *et al*, 'Further notes on the mammalian remains of Yin-hsü, An-yang,' *Chung-Kuo K'ao-ku Hsüeh-pao*, no.4 (1949), pp.145–52.

59. It is not impossible, for example, that the disappearance from North China of such animals as the racoon, tiger and sika deer might have been caused by human agency.

60. J.G.Andersson, 'Researches into the prehistory of the Chinese, *Bulletin of the Museum of Far Eastern Antiquities*, vol.15 (1943), pp.32–41. This conclusion has been repeated in numerous subsequent papers : cf. for example, Ting Su, 'Hua-pei ti-hsing shih', p.158.

NOTES AND REFERENCES

61. Hu Hou-hsüan, *Chia-ku-hsüeh Shang-shih Lun-ts'ung*, series I and II. Ch'eng-tu 1944, 1945.

62. Karl A. Wittfogel, 'Meteorological records from the divination inscriptions of Shang', *The Geographical Review*, vol.30. New York 1940, pp.110–33.

63. Tung Tso-pin, Review of Wittfogel's 'Meteorological records' in *Hua-hsi Hsieh-ho Ta-hsüeh Chung-Kuo Wen-hua Yen-chiu-so Chi-k'an*, vol.3. Ch'eng-tu 1942, pp.81–8; and 'Tsai-t'an Yin-tai ch'i-hou', *Hua-hsi Hsieh-ho Ta-hsüeh Chung-kuo Wen-hua Yen-chiu-so Chi-k'an*, vol.5. Ch'eng-tu 1946, pp. 1–17.

64. Robert J. Braidwood, 'Levels in prehistory', in Sol Tax (ed.), *Evolution of Man after Darwin*, vol.2. University of Chicago Press 1960, p. 149. For the application of this concept to Chinese prehistory see Chang Kwang [Kuang]-chih, 'Major problems in the culture history of Southeast Asia', *Chung-yang Yen-chiu-yüan : Min-ts'u-hsüeh Yen-chiu-so Chi-k'an*, no.13 (1962), pp.1–26.

65. J. G. Andersson, *An early Chinese culture*. Peking 1923.

66. The same material is treated descriptively and typologically in Cheng Te-k'un, *Archaeology in China* : vol.1, *Prehistoric China*. W. Heffer and Sons, Cambridge 1959, Chapter 7. Earlier attempts at synthesis in both Chinese and Western languages were vitiated by a misunderstanding of the stratigraphical position of the Yang-shao stage. Such, for example, were the works of J. Gunnar Andersson, *Children of the Yellow Earth*. Kegan Paul, Trench, Trübner & Co., London 1934; and 'Researches'; P. Teilhard de Chardin and Pei Wen-chung, *Le Néolithique de la Chine*. Institut de Géo-Biologie, Peking 1944; Li Chi *The beginnings of Chinese civilization*. University of Washington Press, Seattle 1957; P'ei Wen-chung, *Chung-Kuo Shih-ch'ien-shih-ch'i-chih Yen-chiu*. Shanghai, 1948; Max Loehr, 'Zur Ur- und Vorgeschichte Chinas', *Saeculum*, vol.3 (1952), pp.15–55; Yin Ta, *Chung-Kuo Hsin-shih-ch'i Shih-tai*. Pei-ching 1955; Hsia Nai, 'Our Neolithic ancestors', *Archaeology*, vol. 10 (1957), pp.181–7; An Chih-min, 'Shih-lun Huang-ho liu-yü Hsin-shih-ch'i shih-tai wen-hua', *K'ao-ku*, no.10 (1959), pp.559–65. Yet even though the conceptual framework of these interpretations has been superseded, a great deal of their factual content is still relevant to present purposes.

67. The use of these implements has been inferred from the common occurrence in Yang-shao excavations of perforated stone discs which are most easily interpreted as weights for digging sticks. Ethnological evidence points to the Chinese culture realm as a region where the digging stick was early in use : cf. Fritz L. Kramer, *Distributions of primitive tillage*, Ph.D. dissertation, University of California, Berkeley 1957, p.273 *et seq.*

68. N. I. Vavilov, 'The origin, variation, immunity and breeding of cultivated plants', transl. from the Russian by K. Starr Chester, *Chronica Botanica*, vol.13, nos.1–6 (1949–50). *Andropogon sorghum* was, indeed, the inclusive genus established by Hackel within which *Sorghum* was regarded as a subgenus. Sorghum taxonomy is in a fluid state and for the exact status of the kao-liangs,

which is still debatable, the reader is referred to a recent survey by H. Doggett, 'The development of the cultivated sorghums', in Sir Joseph Hutchinson, *Essays on crop plant evolution*. Cambridge 1965, pp.50–69. What is not in doubt is the African provenance of the cultivated sorghums and their relatively late arrival in China.

69. Michael J. Hagerty, 'Comments on writings concerning Chinese sorghums', *Harvard Journal of Asiatic Studies* (1940), pp.234–63, especially pp.259–60.

70. J. G. Andersson, 'An early Chinese culture' *Bulletin of the Geological Survey of China*, no.5 (Peking, 1923), p.26; Huang-ho Shui-k'u K'ao-ku-tui, Hua-Hsien-tui, 'Shan-hsi [Shensi] Hua-Hsien Liu-tzŭ Chen k'ao-ku fa-chüeh chien-pao', *K'ao-ku*, no.2 (1959), p.73.

71. Li Chi, *Hsi-yin Ts'un shih-ch'ien-ti i-ts'un*. Ching-hua Research Institute, Pei-p'ing and Shang-hai 1927, pp.22–3.

72. Carl Whiting Bishop, 'The Neolithic age in Northern China', *Antiquity*, vol.7 (1933), p.395.

73. Shih Hsing-pang, 'Hsin-shih-ch'i shih-tai ts'un-lo i-chih-ti fa-hsien – Hsi-an-Pan-p'o', *K'ao-ku T'ung-hsün*, no.3 (1955) pp.7–16; K'ao-ku Yen-chiu-so Hsi-an-Pan-p'o Kung-tso-tui, 'Hsi-an-Pan-p'o i-chih ti-erh-tz'ŭ fa-chüeh-ti chu-yao shou-huo', *loc. cit.*, no.2 (1956), pp.23–30; Hsia Nai, 'Our Neolithic ancestors', *Archaeology*, vol.10 (1957), pp.181–7; K'ao-ku-so Pao-chi Fa-chüeh-tui, 'Shan-hsi [Shensi] Pao-chi Hsin-shih-ch'i shih-tai i-chih fa-chüeh chi-yao', *K'ao-ku*, no.5 (1959), pp.222–30 and 241; Huang-ho Shui-k'u K'ao-ku-tui, Hua-Hsien-tui, 'Shan-hsi [Shensi] Hua-Hsien Liu-tzŭ Chen k'ao-ku fa-chüeh chien-pao', *loc. cit.*, no.2, (1959) pp.71–5 and no.11, pp.585–7 and 591; An Chin-huai, 'Cheng-Chou ti-ch'ü-ti ku-tai i-ts'un chieh-shao', *Wen-wu Ts'an-k'ao Tzŭ-liao*, no.8 (1957), pp.16–20; Chao Ch'ing-yün, '1957-nien Cheng-Chou hsi-chiao fa-chüeh chi-yao', *K'ao-ku T'ung-hsün*, no.9 (1958), pp.54–7; Mao Pao-liang, 'Cheng-Chou Hsi-chiao Yang-shao wen-hua i-chih fa-chüeh chien-pao' *K'ao-ku T'ung-hsün*, no.2 (1958), pp. 1–5, An Chih-min, Cheng Nai-wu and Hsieh Tuan-chü, *Miao-ti Kou yü San-li Ch'iao*. Science Press, Pei-p'ing 1959 [Reviewed in *K'ao-ku*, no.1 (1961), pp.22–8 and no.4 (1961), pp.222–6].

74. J. G. Andersson, 'Researches into the prehistory of the Chinese', *Bulletin of the Museum of Far Eastern Antiquities*, vol.15 (1943), pp.1–304.

75. Chang, *Archaeology*, pp.61–2.

76. Chang, *op. cit.*, pp.65–6, and 'Chung-Kuo yüan-ku-shih-tai i-shih sheng-huo-ti jo-kan tzŭ-liao', *Chung-yang Yen-chiu-yüan: Min-ts'u-hsüeh Yen-chiu-so Chi-k'an*, no.9 (1960), pp.254–62.

77. Morton H. Fried, 'On the evolution of social stratification and the state', in Stanley Diamond [ed.], *Culture in history : essays in honor of Paul Radin*. Columbia University Press, New York 1960, pp.713–31.

NOTES AND REFERENCES

78. Wu Gin-ding (Wu Chin-ting), 'P'ing-ling fang-ku chi', *Kuo-li Chung-yang Yen-chiu-yüan Li-shih Yü-yen Yen-chiu-so Chi-k'an*, vol.1 (1930), pp.471–86.

79. An Chih-min et al., *Miao-ti Kou yü San-li Ch'iao* (1959).

80. Chang Kuang-chih, 'Chung-Kuo Hsin-shih-ch'i shih-tai wen-hua tuan-tai', *Kuo-li Chung-yang Yen-chiu-yüan Li-shih Yü-yen Yen-chiu-so Chi-k'an*, vol.30 (1959), p.269.

81. Li Chi et al., *Ch'eng-tzŭ Yai*. Academia Sinica, Nan-ching 1934. English translation by Kenneth Starr, Yale University Publication in Anthropology, no.52. Yale University Press, New Haven, 1956; Liang Ssŭ-yung, 'Lung-shan Wen-hua – Chung-Kuo wen-ming-ti shih-ch'ien-ch'i-chih-i' *K'ao-ku Hsüeh-pao*, no.7 (1954), pp.5–14; Liu Yao, 'Lung-shan Wen-hua yü Yang-shao Wen-hua-chih fen-hsi', *Chung-Kuo K'ao-ku Hsüeh-pao*, no.2 (1947), pp.251–82; Yin Ta, *Chung-Kuo Hsin-shih-ch'i Shih-tai*. Peking, 1955, pp.44–66; An Chih-min, 'Shih lun Huang-ho liu-yü Hsin-shih-ch'i shih-tai wen-hua', *K'ao-ku*, no.10 (1959), pp.559–65, An Chih-min, 'I-chiu-wu-liu-nien-ch'iu Ho-nan Shan Hsien fa-chüeh chien-pao', *K'ao-ku T'ung-hsün*, no.4 (1957), p.4, and An Chih-min, 'Chung-Kuo Hsin-shih-ch'i shih-tai k'ao-ku-hsüeh-shang-ti chu-yao ch'eng-chiu', *Wen-wu*, no.10 (1959), pp.20–1; *K'ao-ku*, no.10 (1959), p.531; Mei Fu-ken, 'Hang-Chou Shui-t'ien Fan i-chih fa-chüeh pao-kao', *K'ao-ku Hsüeh-pao*, no.2 (1960), p.95.

82. Li Chien-yung, P'ei Chi and Chia Ngo[O], 'Lo-ning Hsien Lo-ho liang-an ku-i-chih tiao-ch'a chien-pao', *K'ao-ku T'ung-hsün*, no. 2 (1956), pp.52–3; Liu Yao, 'Ho-nan Chün-Hsien Ta-lai Tien shih-ch'ien i-chih' *T'ien-yeh K'ao-ku Pao-kao*, no.1 (1936), p. 75; Liang Ssŭ-yung, 'Hou-kang fa-chüeh hsiao-chi', *An-yang Fa-chüeh Pao-kao*, no.4 (1933), pp. 614–6.

83. Hu Yüeh-ch'ien, 'An-hui Hsin-shih-ch'i shih-tai i-chih-ti tiao-ch'a', *K'ao-ku Hsüeh-pao*, no.1 (1957), p.26; Yang Chien-fang, 'An-hui Tiao-yü T'ai ch'u-t'u hsiao-mai nien-tai shang-chüeh', *K'ao-ku*, no.11 (1963), pp. 630–1.

84. Chang, *Archaeology*, p.92.

85. Chang, *Archaeology*, p.96. Although certain metal implements discovered at Huang-niang-niang T'ai in Kan-su appear to have occurred in a Ch'i-chia (i.e. Lungshanoid) context, it would seem from the report so far published that they were contemporaneous with the Early or Middle Shang [Kuo Te-yung, 'Kan-su Wu-wei Huang-niang-niang T'ai i-chih fa-chüeh pao-kao', *K'ao-ku Hsüeh-pao*, no.2 (1960)].

86. Chang Kuang-chih, 'Chung-Kuo yüan-ku-shih-tai i-shih-sheng-huo-ti jo-kan tzŭ-liao', *Chung-yang Yen-chiu-yüan : Min-ts'u-hsüeh Yen-chiu-so Chi-k'an*, no.9 (1960), pp.264–8.

87. Shih Chang-ju, 'Ku-pu yü kuei-pu t'an-yüan', *Ta-lu Tsa-chih*, vol.8, no.9 (1954), pp.9–13; Chen Hui, T'ang Yün-ming and Sun Te-hai, 'Ho-pei

T'ang-shan Shih Ta-ch'eng-shan i-chih fa-chüeh pao-kao', *K'ao-ku Hsüeh-pao*, no.3 (1959), pp.32–3; Shou T'ien, 'T'ai-yüan Kuang-she Hsin-shih-ch'i shih-tai i-chih-ti fa-hsien yü tsao-yü', *Wen-wu Ts'an-k'ao Tzŭ-liao*, no.1 (1957); Chou Tao, *K'ao-ku*, no.9 (1959); Chao Ch'ing-fang, 'Nan-ching Shih Pei-yin-yang Ying ti-i, erh-tz'ŭ-ti fa-chüeh', *K'ao-ku Hsüeh-pao*, no.1 (1958), p.14.

88. Pei-ching Ta-hsüeh, Ho-pei Sheng Wen-hua-chü, Han-tan K'ao-ku Fa-chüeh-tui, '1957-nien Han-tan fa-chüeh chien-pao'. *K'ao-ku*, no.10 (1959), pp.531–2.

89. Kwang-chih Chang, 'China', in *Courses toward urban life*, p.184.

90. Fried, 'On the evolution of social stratification', pp.721–6.

91. By 'strategic resources' Fried means those things which, given the technological basis and environmental setting of the culture, maintain subsistence. *Vide* Fried, 'The classification of corporate unilineal descent groups', *Journal of the Royal Anthropological Institute*, vol.87 (1957), p.24.

92. Robert J. Braidwood, *The Near East and the foundations for civilization*. Condon Lectures, Oregon State System of Higher Education; Eugene, Oregon 1952, p.41, and 'Levels in prehistory', in Sol Tax, *Evolution of man after Darwin*, vol.2. University of Chicago Press 1960, p.149. In the Middle East the analogue of the Lung-shan stage would be the '*Ubaid-Warqa*; in terms applicable to the world at large *Late Formative* or *Early Florescent*. Cp., for example, Julian H. Steward et al., *Irrigation civilizations : a comparative study*. Pan American Union Social Science Monograph I. Washington, DC 1955; Gordon R. Willey, The prehistoric civilizations of nuclear America', *American Anthropologist*, vol.57, no.2, pt.1. Menasha, Wisconsin 1955, pp. 571–93.

93. Robert Redfield and Milton B. Singer, 'The cultural role of cities', *Economic development and cultural change*, vol.3 (1954), p.58. Cf. also Redfield 'The folk society', *The American Journal of Sociology*, vol.52 (1947), pp.293–308, 'The natural history of the folk society', *Social Forces*, vol.31 (1953), pp.224–8, and *The primitive world and its transformations*. Cornell University Press, Ithaca 1953, Chapter 1.

94. George M. Foster, 'What is folk culture?', *American Anthropologist*, vol.55 (1953), pp.159–73. For comments on this paper see Sidney W. Mintz, 'On Redfield and Foster', *loc. cit.*, vol.56 (1954), pp.87–92.

95. Cf. Redfield, *The little community. The Gottesman Lectures*, vol.5. Uppsala University, 1955, and *Peasant society and culture*. University of Chicago Press 1956.

96. Notably Eric R. Wolf, *Peasants*. Foundations of Modern Anthropology Series, Prentice Hall, Inc., Englewood Cliffs, New Jersey 1966, pp.2–3.

97. Marshall D. Sahlins, 'Political power and economy in primitive society', in Gertrude E. Dole and Robert L. Carneiro [eds.], *Essays in the science of culture. In honor of Leslie A. White*. Thomas Y. Crowell Company, New York 1960, p.408. One aspect of the distinction between folk and urban society was

NOTES AND REFERENCES

epitomized by Mencius when he said: 'In courts [that is urbanized society] nobility holds the first place, in villages age holds the first place' (II, ii. 3, 6).

98. Chang, *Archaeology*, p.137.

99. Information in this and subsequent paragraphs relating to the archeology of Shang ceremonial sites (of which the author has no first-hand experience) is drawn from the papers and reports cited in notes 2 and 4, as well as from a fairly wide range of interpretative writings. Full bibliographies of these latter works are readily available in the volumes of Kwang-chih Chang and Cheng Te-k'un mentioned in note 2, so that specific citations will be furnished only when points of unusual significance are not easily traceable there.

100. Chang, *Archaeology*, p.148. Cf. also Cheng-Chou Shih Wen-wu Kung-tso-tsu, 'Cheng-Chou Shih Yin-Shang i-chih ti-ts'eng kuan-hsi chieh-shao', *Wen-wu Ts'an-k'ao Tzŭ-liao*, no.12 (1954), pp.86–95.

101. Ho-nan-Sheng Wen-hua-chü Wen-wu Kung-tso-tui, 'Cheng-Chou Shang-chieh Shang-tai i-chih-ti fa-chüeh', *K'ao-ku*, no.6 (1960), pp.11–12.

102. Chao Ch'üan-ku *et al.*, 'Cheng-Chou Shang-tai i-chih-ti fa-chüeh', *K'ao-ku Hsüeh-pao*, no.1 (1957), pp.56–8; An Chin-huai, 'Cheng-Chou Shih ku-i-chih, mu-tsang-ti chung-yao fa-hsien', *K'ao-ku T'ung-hsün*, no.3 (1955), p.18; Chao Hsia-kuang, 'Cheng-Chou Nan-kuan-wai Shang-tai i-chih fa-chüeh chien-pao' *K'ao-ku T'ung-hsün*, no.2 (1958), pp.6–8; Ch'en Chia-hsiang, 'Cheng-Chou Lo-ta Miao Shang-tai i-chih shih-chüeh chien-pao', *Wen-wu Ts'an-k'ao Tzŭ-liao*, no.10 (1957), pp.48–51; Chao Ch'ing-yün, '1957-nien Cheng-Chou hsi-chiao fa-chüeh chi-yao' *K'ao-ku T'ung-hsün*, no.9 (1958), pp.54–7; Chao Ch'ing-yün and Liu Tung-ya, 'Cheng-Chou Ko-ta-wang Ts'un i-chih fa-chüeh pao-kao', *K'ao-ku Hsüeh-pao*, no.3 (1958), pp.41–62.

103. Cf. note 4 above; also Ho-nan Wen-hua-chü, *Cheng-Chou Erh-li Kang*.

104. Cf. the Lungshanoid settlements described above, and pp.386–99 below.

105. In European English usage, and predominantly in the English-language reports of the Chinese archeologists, *hang-t'u* is translated as 'stamped earth' (cf., for example, Chang, *Archaeology*, pp.55, 137, 143, 342, *et al.*), but in American usage the term is usually rendered as 'tamped earth'. In French archeological writing, and in some English-language journals, it is translated as 'terre pisée'.

106. Cp. note 167 to Chapter Five.

107. In the above translation I have borrowed eclectically from previous authors and am only too obviously indebted especially to Professor Bernhard Karlgren and Dr Arthur Waley. Nevertheless, my rendering of the second stanza may appear idiosyncratic to those accustomed to more orthodox versions, although an appreciation of the onomatopoeic nature of the lines surely underlay Dr Waley's translation:

They tilted in the earth with a rattling,
They pounded it with a dull thud,
They beat the walls with a loud clang,
They pared and chiselled them with a faint *p'ing p'ing* . . .
  [*The Book of Songs*. George Allen and Unwin, Ltd, 1937, p.249].
Professor Karlgren, on the other hand, essayed what I believe to be the impossible task of trying to ascribe a rational meaning to the onomatopoeic graphs: 'In long rows they collected it (sc. the earth for the buildings), in great crowds they measured it out, they pounded it, (the walls) rising high; they scraped and (repeated =) went over them again, (so they became) solid...'
[*The Book of Odes. Chinese text, transcription and translation*. A reprint of two papers in the *Bulletin of the Museum of Far Eastern Antiquities*, vols.16 and 17, 1944 and 1945 (The Museum of Far Eastern Antiquities, Stockholm 1950), p.190].

For a more prosaic account of the construction of *hang-t'u* walls, this time round the city of **Ngi̯ən (*Yin*) in 597 BC, see *Tso Chuan*, Duke **Si̯wan (Hsüan), 11th year.

108. According to Chang Kuang-chih, only two or three such hairpins have come to light outside the enceinte [*Archaeology of Ancient China*, p.151].

109. An Chin-huai, *Wen-wu Ts'an-k'ao Tzŭ-liao*, no.8 (1957), p.18; Chao Ch'üan-ku *et al.*, *K'ao-ku Hsüeh-pao*, no.1 (1957), p.58.

110. Chao Ch'üan-ku *et al.*, *K'ao-ku Hsüeh-pao*, no.1 (1957), pp.70–2; Ch'en Chia-hsiang, 'Cheng-Chou Lo-ta Miao Shang-tai i-chih shih-chüeh chien-pao', *Wen-wu Ts'an-k'ao Tzŭ-liao*, no.10 (1957), p.51; Ma Ch'üan, 'Cheng-Chou Shih Ming-kung Lu hsi-ts'e-ti Shang-tai i-ts'un', *Wen-wu Ts'an-k'ao Tzŭ-liao*, no.10 (1956), pp.50–1; An Chin-huai, *Wen-wu Ts'an-k'ao Tzŭ-liao*, no.8 (1957), p.19.

111. Chao Ch'üan-ku *et al.*, *K'ao-ku Hsüeh-pao*, no.1 (1957), p.58.

112. Chao Ch'üan-ku *et al., op. cit.*, p.57; Ma Ch'üan, *Wen-wu Ts'an-k'ao Tzŭ-liao*, no.10 (1956), pp.50–1; Chou Chao-lin and Mou Yung-hang, 'Cheng-Chou fa-hsien-ti Shang-tai chih-t'ao i-chi' *Wen-wu Ts'an-k'ao Tzŭ-liao*, no.9 (1955), pp.64–6.

113. An Chin-huai, *Wen-wu Ts'an-k'ao Tzŭ-liao*, no.8 (1957), pp.16–20; Yin Huan-chang, 'Pa-ko-yüeh-lai-ti Cheng-Chou wen-wu kung-tso kai-k'uang', *Wen-wu Ts'an-k'ao Tzŭ-liao*, no.9 (1955), pp.56–8.

114. Chao Ch'üan-ku *et al.*, *K'ao-ku Hsüeh-pao*, no.1 (1957), p.72.

115. Liao Yung-min, 'Cheng-Chou Shih fa-hsien-ti i-ch'u Shang-tai chü-chu yü chu-tsao-t'ung-ch'i i-chih chien-chieh', *Wen-wu Ts'an-k'ao Tzŭ-liao*, no.6 (1957), pp.73–4.

116. An Chin-huai, 'Shih-lun Cheng-Chou Shang-tai ch'eng-chih – Ao-tu', *Wen-wu*, nos.4–5 (1961), p.78; Li Yang-sung, 'Tui Wo-Kuo niang-chiu ch'i-yüan-ti t'an-t'ao', *K'ao-ku*, no.1 (1962), pp.41–4.

NOTES AND REFERENCES

117. Cf. Cheng Te-k'un, *Shang China*, p.19: 'The localities excavated had been so badly disturbed at the beginning of the excavation that the materials unearthed were treated together as remains of the later Shang period.' Also p.43.

118. Cf. note 2 above. Vol.1 of the reports is entitled *The site. Its discovery and excavations* (*I-chih-ti fa-hsien yü fa-chüeh*) and was published in 1959.

119. Kuo Pao-chün, 'I-chiu-wu-ling-nien-ch'un Yin-hsü fa-chüeh pao-kao', *K'ao-ku Hsüeh-pao*, no.5 (1951), p.2. Cf. also Shih Chang-ju, 'Yin-hsü tsui-chin-chih chung-yao fa-hsien. Fu : Lun Hsiao-T'un ti-ts'eng', *Chung-kuo K'ao-ku Hsüeh-pao*, no.2 (1947), p.76.

120. Li Chi, *Hsüeh-shu Hui-k'an*, no.1 (1944), pp.1–14, and *The beginnings of Chinese civilization*. University of Washington Press, Seattle 1957.

121. Tsou Heng, 'Shih-lun Cheng-Chou hsin-fa-hsien-ti Yin-Shang wen-hua i-chih', *K'ao-ku Hsüeh-pao*, no.3 (1956), pp.77–103.

122. Cheng Te-k'un, *Shang China*, pp.37–8.

123. Chang, *Archaeology*, pp.164–5.

124. Tung Tso-pin, *Kuo-li Chung-yang Yen-chiu Yüan Li-shih Yü-yen Yen-chiu-so Ch'ing-chu Ts'ai Yüan-p'ei Hsien-sheng liu-shih-wu-sui lun-wen chi*. Pei-ching, 1933, pp.323–424; 'Yin-tai li-chih-ti hsin-chiu liang-p'ai', *Ta-lu Tsa-chih*, vol.6, no.3 (1953), pp.1–6; and *Chia-ku-hsüeh Wu-shih-nien*. T'ai-pei, 1955. For dissenting views see Ch'en Meng-chia, *Yin-hsü Pu-tz'ŭ Tsung-shu*. Pei-ching, 1956); Kaizuka Shigeki and Ito Michiharu, *Tōhō Gakuhō*, vol.23. Kyōto, 1953; and, particularly, Noel Barnard's review of Jao Tsung-i's *Yin-tai cheng-pu jen-wu t'ung-k'ao* in *Monumenta Serica*, vol.19 (1960), pp.485–6.

125. Tung Tso-pin, *Ta-lu Tsa-chih*, vol.6, no.3 (1953).

126. This Linnaean-style manipulation of the vast quantities of data available from An-yang is well exemplified, for example, by Shih Chang-ju's classification of underground constructions ['Hsiao-T'un Yin-tai-ti chien-chu i-chi', *Kuo-li Chung-yang Yen-chiu-yüan Li-shih Yü-yen Yen-chiu-so Chi-k'an*, vol.26. T'ai-pei 1955, pp.131–88]. This classification is also reproduced in Cheng Te-k'un, *Shang China*, pp.44–8.

(1) *Hsüeh*

(a) Round pits with steps built against the wall.
(b) Round pits with steps leading down into the middle of the pit.
(c) Oval pits with a single flight of steps against the wall.
(d) Oval pits with two flights of steps against the wall on opposite sides of the pit.
(e) Oval pits with steps leading down into the middle of the pit.
(f) Square pits with steps against one of the walls.

(2) *Chiao*

(a) Pits without foot-holes.

(b) Pits with two flights of foot-holes in opposite walls.
(c) Pits with two flights of foot-holes in the same wall.
(d) Pits with two flights of foot-holes in the same corner.
(e) Pits with two flights of foot-holes, one in a wall, the other at a corner.
(f) Pits with a flight of steps and a series of foot-holes.

(3) *Tou*
(a) Holes with a flat bottom and no foot-holes.
(b) Holes with a convex bottom and no foot-holes.
(c) Holes of such a narrow width that no foot-holes were necessary.
(d) Holes with two series of foot-holes, one in each of two opposite walls.
(e) Holes with two series of foot-holes in the same wall.
(f) Gourd-shaped holes with two series of foot-holes.

(4) *Mu*
(a) Rectangular pits with a *kuo* chamber.
(b) Rectangular pits with a *yao-k'eng* pit.
(c) Rectangular pits with no coffin hole.
(d) Rectangular pits with a square bottom.
(e) Small rectangular pits about half the size of a normal *mu*.
(f) A round pit incorporating *hang-t'u*.

(5) *K'eng*
(a) Chariot pits.
(b) Horse pits.
(c) Ox pits.
(d) Sheep pits.
(e) Dog pits.
(f) Ox and sheep pits.
(g) Sheep and dog pits.
(h) Pig pits.
(i) Fowl pits.

(6) *K'an*
(a) Elongated caves with irregular sides.
(b) Irregularly shaped caves with four sides.
(c) Oval irregular caves.
(d) Crooked caves.

(7) *Kou*
(a) Broad channels with irregular walls.
(b) Channels with post impressions in the walls.
(c) Channels without post impressions but incorporating *hang-t'u* constructions.

127. Shih Chang-ju, *Yin-hsü chien-chu i-ts'un*, vol.1, fasc.2 (1959). Cf. also Tung Tso-pin, 'Chung-Kuo wen-tzŭ-ti ch'i-yüan', *Ta-lu Tsa-chih*, vol.5, no.10 T'ai-pei 1952.

NOTES AND REFERENCES

128. Ling Ch'un-sheng, 'Pu-tz'ŭ-chung she-chih yen-chiu', *Kuo-li T'ai-wan Ta-hsüeh K'ao-ku Jen-lei Hsüeh-k'an* nos.25–6 (1965), pp.1–15.

129. *Vide* Ling, *loc. cit.*

130. Shih Chang-ju, 'Yin-tai ti-shang-chien-chu fu-yüan-chih i-li', *Kuo-li Chung-yang Yen-chiu-yüan Yüan-k'an*, vol.1 (1954), pp.267–80.

131. Tai-Chen, *K'ao-kung chi t'u*, vol.2 (1746; reprinted Shanghai 1955), p.104.

132. *Vide* Bernhard Karlgren, 'The early history of the *Chou li* and *Tso chuan* texts', *Bulletin of the Museum of Far Eastern Antiquities*, vol.3 (1931), pp.2–8, 35–8, 50–7; K. Nagasawa, *Geschichte der Chinesischen Literatur, und ihrer gedanklichen Grundlage*. Transl. from the Japanese by E. Feifel. Fu-jen University Press, Pei-p'ing 1945, p.122.

133. Tung Tso-pin, 'Chung-Kuo wen-tzŭ-ti ch'i-yüan', *Ta-lu Tsa-chih*, vol.5, no.10. T'ai-pei 1952.

134. Liang Ssŭ-yung and Kao Ch'ü-hsün', *Chung-Kuo K'ao-ku Pao-kao Chi*, vol.3, pt.2. T'ai-pei, 1962; Kao Ch'ü-hsün, 'The royal cemetery of the Yin dynasty at Anyang', *Kuo-li T'ai-wan Ta-hsüeh K'ao-ku Jen-lei Hsüeh-k'an*, no.13. T'ai-pei 1959, pp. 1–9; Li Chi, *Kuo-li Chung-yang Yen-chiu-yüan Li-shih Yü-yen Yen-chiu-so Chi-k'an*, vol.29 (1958), pp.809–16.

135. Paul Pelliot, 'The royal tombs of An-yang', in *Independence, convergence and borrowing in institution, thought and art*. Harvard University Press 1937, pp. 265–72.

136. Cheng Te-k'un, *Shang China*, p.77.

137. Shih Chang-ju 'Ho-nan An-yang Hou-Kang-ti Yin-mu', *Kuo-li Chung-yang Yen-chiu-yüan Li-shih Yü-yen Yen-chiu-so Chi-k'an*, vol.13 (1948), pp.21–48.

138. Kuo Pao-chün, *K'ao-ku Hsüeh-pao*, no.5 (1951), pp.1–61.

139. Tung Tso-pin, 'An-yang Hou-chia Chuang ch'u-t'u-chih chia-ku wen-tzŭ', *T'ien-yeh K'ao-ku Pao-kao*, no.1 (1936), pp.91–166.

140. Tung Tso-pin, *ibid.*; Kwang-chih Chang, *The archaeology of ancient China*, p.166.

141. Ma Te-chih, Chou Yung-chen and Chang Yün-p'eng, 'I-chiu-wu-san-nien An-yang Ta-ssŭ-k'ung Ts'un fa-chüeh pao-kao', *K'ao-ku Hsüeh-pao*, no.9 (1955), pp.25–90.

142. Chao Hsia-kuang, 'An-yang Shih hsi-chiao-ti Yin-tai wen-hua i-chih' *Wen-wu Ts'an-k'ao Tzŭ-liao*, no.12 (1958), p.31; Liu Tung-ya, 'Ho-nan An-yang Hsüeh-chia Chuang Yin-tai i-chih, mu-tsang ho T'ang-mu fa-chüeh chien-pao' *K'ao-ku T'ung-hsün*, no.8 (1958), pp.23–6.

143. Kuo Pao-chün and Lin Shou-chin, 'I-chiu-wu-erh-nien ch'iu-chi Lo-yang tung-chiao fa-chüeh pao-kao', *K'ao-ku Hsüeh-pao*, no.9 (1955), pp.91–116; Kuo Pao-chün *et al.*, 'Lo-yang Chien-pin ku-wen-hua i-chih chi Han-mu', *ibid.*, no.1 (1956), pp.11–28; An Chih-min and Lin Shou-chin, 'I-chiu-wu-

ssŭ-nien ch'iu-chi Lo-yang hsi-chiao fa-chüeh chien-pao', *K'ao-ku T'ung-hsün*, no.5 (1955), p.26; Ho-nan Wen-wu Kung-tso-tui Ti-erh-tui Sun-ch'i T'un Ch'ing-li Hsiao-tsu, 'Lo-yang Chien-hsi Sun-ch'i T'un ku-i-chih', *Wen-wu Ts'an-k'ao Tzŭ-liao*, no.9 (1955), pp. 58–64.

144. Kuo Pao-chün, Hsia Nai *et al.*, *Hui-Hsien Fa-chüeh Pao-kao*. Science Press, Peking, 1956. See also Li Te-pao, 'Ho-nan Wei-ho Chih-hung kung-ch'eng-chung-ti k'ao-ku tiao-ch'a chien-pao', *K'ao-ku T'ung-hsün*, no. 2 (1957), pp.32–5.

145. Chang, *Archaeology*, pp.163–4.

146. Yang Chi-ch'ang, 'Ho-nan Shan-Hsien Ch'i-li P'u Shang-tai i-chih-ti fa-chüeh', *K'ao-ku Hsüeh-pao*, no.1 (1960), pp.25–47.

147. Wang Ming-jui and Chin Shih-hsin, 'Ho-nan Hsin-hsiang Lu-wang Fen Shang-tai i-chih fa-chüeh pao-kao', *K'ao-ku Hsüeh-pao*, no. 1 (1960), pp.51–60.

148. Wen-wu Kung-tso Pao-tao, Ho-nan Sheng 'T'ang-yin Chao-ko Chen fa-hsien Lung-shan ho Shang-tai-teng wen-hua i-chih' *Wen-wu Ts'an-k'ao Tzŭ-liao*, no.5 (1957), p.86.

149. Yu Ch'ing-han, 'Ho-nan Nan-yang Shih Shih-li Miao fa-hsien Shang-tai i-chih, *K'ao-ku*, no.7 (1959), p.370.

150. Yang Tzŭ-fan, 'Chi-nan Ta-hsin Chuang Shang-tai i-chih k'an-ch'a chi-yao', *Wen-wu Ts'an-k'ao Tzŭ-liao* no.11 (1959), pp.8–9; Li Pu-ch'ing, 'Chi-nan Ta-hsin Chuang i-chih shih-chüeh chien-pao', *K'ao-ku*, no.4 (1959), pp.185–7.

151. An Chih-min, 'Ho-pei Ch'ü-yang tiao-ch'a-chi', *K'ao-ku T'ung-hsün*, no.1 (1955), pp.39–44.

152. See Ho-pei Sheng Wen-hua-chü Fa-chüeh-tsu, 'Hsing-T'ai-shih fa-hsien Shang-tai i-chih', *Wen-wu Ts'an-k'ao Tzŭ-liao*, no.9 (1956), p.70; [T'ang] Yün-ming; Lo P'ing, and [Ch'eng] Ming-yüan, 'Hsing-T'ai Shang-tai i-chih-chung-ti t'ao-yao', *ibid.*, no.12 (1956), pp.53–4; T'ang Yün-ming, 'Hsing-T'ai Nan-ta-kuo Ts'un Shang-tai i-chih t'an-chüeh chien-pao', *ibid.*, no.3 (1957), pp.61–3; T'ang Yün-ming, 'Hsing-T'ai Ts'ao-yen Chuang i-chih fa-chüeh pao-kao', *K'ao-ku Hsüeh-pao*, no.4 (1958), pp.43–50; T'ang Yün-ming, 'K'ao-ku tung-t'ai : Ho-pei Hsing-T'ai Tung-hsien-hsien Ts'un Shang-tai i-chih tiao-ch'a', *K'ao-ku*, no.2 (1959), pp.108–9; T'ang Yün-ming, 'Hsing-T'ai Yin-kuo Ts'un Shang-tai i-chih chi Chan-Kuo mu-tsang shih-chüeh chien-pao', *Wen-wu*, no.4 (1960), pp.42–5 and 69.

153. *Vide* Max Weber, *Wirtschaft und Gesellschaft*, vol.2. Second edition, J.C.B.Mohr Tübingen, pp.679–752.

154. *Shih-Chi*, chüan 3, f.1 recto et verso. Cp. *Shih-Ching*, ***G'iwen-tiôg* (Hsüan-niao : Mao CCCIII):

Heaven commanded the black bird
To descend and give birth to Shang (***Śi̯ang*)

NOTES AND REFERENCES

Who dwelt in the vasty land of Yin (**·*I̯ən*).

Although *g'iwen-tiôg* (= dark or black bird) has traditionally been understood as a swallow, Kuo Mo-jo [*Ch'ing-t'ung Shih-tai*. Shanghai 1946, p.11] believed that the phrase denoted a phoenix and symbolized the male sex organ. In *Ch'u-Tz'ŭ* (**Lia-Sôg: Li-Sao* and **T'ien-Mi̯wən: T'ien-Wen*) it is **Tieg-K'ôk (Ti-K'u) who sends the mysterious bird. For a discussion of the implications of this myth see Chang Kuang-chih, 'Shang-Chou shen-hua-chih fen-lei', *Chung-yang Yen-chiu-yüan: Min-ts'u-hsüeh Yen-chiu-so Chi-k'an*, no.14 (1962), p.67. The **Śi̯ang-Dz'i̯ung (Shang-Sung), the section of the *Shih-Ching* from which *G'iwen-tiôg* is taken, is generally considered to preserve the dynastic odes of the state of **Sông (Sung), the territory ruled over by the descendants of the old house of Shang (cf. *Shih-Chi*, chüan 3, f.13 recto), while the culture of **Tṣ'i̯o (Ch'u), where the *Ch'u-Tz'ŭ* were composed, is also held to have incorporated numerous elements derived from Shang civilization. It is not unlikely, therefore, that both works, Eastern Chou rifacimentos though they be, reflect to some extent authentic Shang values.

155. Kwang-chih Chang, 'Some dualistic phenomena in Shang society', *The Journal of Asian Studies*, vol.24, no.1 (1964), pp.45–61. There is an earlier statement by the same author entitled 'Shang-wang miao-hao hsin-k'ao', in *Chung-yang Yen-chiu-yüan: Min-ts'u-hsüeh Yen-chiu-so Chi-k'an*, no.15 (1963), pp.65–95.

156. E.g. Ting Su, 'Lun Yin-wang-p'i shih-fa', *Chung-yang Yen-chiu-yüan: Min-ts'u-hsüeh Yen-chiu-so Chi-k'an*, no.19 (1965), pp.71–9; Hsü Cho-yün, Kuan-yü "Shang-wang miao-hao hsin-k'ao" i-wen-ti chi-tien i-chien', *loc. cit.* pp.81–7; Lin Heng-li, 'P'ing Chang Kuang-chih "Shang-wang miao-hao hsin-k'ao"-chung-ti lun-cheng-fa', *loc. cit.*, pp.115–19; Hsü Chin-hsiung, 'Tui Chang Kuang-chih Hsien-sheng-ti "Shang-wang miao-hao hsin-k'ao"-ti chi-tien i-chien', *loc. cit.*, pp.121–37.

157. Chang Kuang-chih, 'Kuan-yü "Shang-wang miao-hao hsin-k'ao" i-wen-ti pu-ch'ung i-chien', *Chung-yang Yen-chiu-yüan: Min-ts'u-hsüeh Yen-chiu-so Chi-k'an*, no.19 (1965), pp.53–70. The **di̯og-mi̯ôk system is described in the *Wang-Chih* section of the *Li-Chi* (*Record of Rites*), a Han-time compilation which nevertheless includes material from earlier times, some possibly from the 5th century BC (though even at that time it was no more than an imperfectly understood tradition).

158. Raymond Firth, *We, the Tikopia*. Allen and Unwin, London 1936.

159. Marshall D. Sahlins, *Social stratification in Polynesia*. American Ethnological Society, Seattle 1958.

160. Morton H. Fried, 'The classification of corporate unilineal descent groups', *Journal of the Royal Anthropological Institute*, vol.87 (1957), pp.1–29.

161. Liu Pin-hsiung, 'Yin-Shang wang-shih shih-fen-tsu-chih shih-lun',

Chung-yang Yen-chiu-yüan : Min-ts'u-hsüeh Yen-chiu-so Chi-k'an, no.19 (1965), pp.89–114.

162. The combinations of the ten Heavenly Stems in the five patrilineal descent groups would have been *Chia-i, ping-ting, wu-chi, keng-hsin* and *jen-kuei*, and the two matrilineal moieties *Chia-ping-wu-keng-jen* and *I-ting-chi-hsin-kuei* [*loc. cit.*, pp.106–8].

163. Paul Kirchhoff, 'The principles of clanship in human society', *Davidson Journal of Anthropology*, vol.1 (1955), pp.1–10. Also pp.374–7 below.

164. Kwang-chih Chang, 'Some dualistic phenomena', pp.46 and 52–3.

165. Twelve kings ruled during the An-yang period but the last, **Tiegsi̯ĕn, is supposed to have perished in the flames of his palace when the capital was captured by the Chou armies.

166. Chang, 'Some dualistic phenomena', p.52.

167. *Li-Chi, Wang-Chih* section. Cf. Ling Ch'un-sheng, 'Chung-Kuo tsu-miao-ti ch'i-yüan', *Chung-yang Yen-chiu-yüan : Min-ts'u-hsüeh Yen-chiu-so Chi-k'an*, no.7 (1959), pp.141–84.

168. Shih Chang-ju, *Yin-hsü chien-chu i-ts'un*.

169. *Li-Chi, Wang-Chih* section. This idealized arrangement of the ancestral shrines within the temple compound is depicted in a plan, based on an exposition by Chu-Hsi, in the great Ch'ien-lung edition of the *Li-Chi*.

170. A full account of the Shang system of government in so far as it can be reconstructed is conveniently accessible in Ch'en Meng-chia's *Yin-hsü Pu-tz'u Tsung-shu*. Pei-ching 1956, pp.249–332 and 503–22. See also Kaizuka Shigeki (ed.), *Kodai Inteikoku*. Misuzu Shobu, Tokyo 1957.

171. Wolfram Eberhard, *A history of China*. Second edition, University of California Press, Berkeley and Los Angeles 1960, p.24.

172. L. Carrington Goodrich, *A short history of the Chinese people*. Harper Torchbook 3015, New York 1963, p.14.

173. William Watson, 'A cycle of Cathay', in Stuart Piggott (ed.), *The dawn of civilization*. McGraw-Hill Book Co., Inc., New York 1961, p.271.

174. Jao Tsung-i, *Yin-tai Chen-pu Jen-wu T'ung-k'ao*, 2 vols. Hong Kong, 1959; Ch'en Meng-chia, *Yin-hsü Pu-tz'ŭ Tsung-shu*. Pei-ching 1956.

175. According to Tung Tso-pin, the Shang capital was located at Hsiao-T'un from 1384–1111 BC, a total of 273 years ['Chung-kuo shang-ku-shih nien-t'ai', *Kuo-li T'ai-wan Ta-hsüeh K'ao-ku Jen-lei Hsüeh-k'an*, no.11 (1958), pp.1–4].

176. Reinhard Bendix, *Max Weber. An intellectual portrait*. Doubleday Anchor Book A281, New York 1962, p.334.

177. *Ibid.* Cf. also Thomas F. Tout, *Chapters in the administrative history of medieval England*, 6 vols. Longmans, London 1920–33.

178. Chang, 'Some dualistic phenomena', p.51.

NOTES AND REFERENCES

179. Tung Tso-pin, 'Wu-teng Chüeh tsai Yin-Shang', *Kuo-li Chung-yang Yen-chiu-yüan Li-shih Yü-yen Yen-chiu-so Chi-k'an*, vol.6 (1936), pp.413–30.

180. The oldest form of this graph depicts a mouth and a dagger-axe (i.e. army and command) inside an enclosure. Cf. Karlgren, 929.

181. Its former role as a Shang capital may be epitomized in the Shang and Chou forms of the graph, which depict a high building of some sort (Karlgren 773).

 [1] The character for $**B'âk$ (*Po*), the name of a Shang ceremonial center, as it appears on an oracle bone.

182. Li Hsüeh-ch'in, *Yin-tai Ti-li Chien-lun*. Pei-ching 1959.

183. One such benefice apparently carried the title of $**Śi̯u$-$dzi̯əg$ $tsi̯əg$ (*Shu-szŭ tzŭ*) or Heritable Lordship of Frontier Defense [Bronze inscription 26.50: *vide* Kuo Mo-jo, 'An-yang yüan-k'eng-much-ung ting-ming k'ao-shih', *K'ao-ku Hsüeh-pao*, no.1 (1960), pp.1–5]. Noel Barnard [review article in *Monumenta Serica*, vol.22. fasc.1 (1963), p.219] has suggested that the form of this title implies that the benefice had become associated with a permanent office connected with the outer regions of Shang dominion, and draws attention [*ibid*] to an office of $**sli̯əg$-$śi̯u$ (*shih-shu*) mentioned on a bronze vessel (insc. 6.5) recently excavated near Ling-yüan in Jehol, a district remote from the metropolitan territory of Shang.

The oracle-bone graph for *śi̯u* depicts, appropriately enough, a man and a so-called dagger-axe.

184. 'Liturgical' was the term used by Max Weber to denote payments in kind made to a central authority [after the liturgies of the ancient city-states in which certain groups of the population were charged with the provision and maintenance of naval vessels or the furnishing of theatrical performances]. *Vide* Weber, *The Theory of social and economic organization*. Oxford University Press 1947, pp.310–15.

184a. Cf. Ting Shan, *Chia-ku-wen so-chien Shih-tsu chi-ch'i Chih-tu*. Pei-ching 1956.

185. Shih Chang-ju, 'Yin-hsü fa-chüeh tui-yü Chung-kuo ku-tai wen-hua-ti kung-hsien', *Hsüeh-shu Chi-k'an*, vol.2 (1954), pp.8–23. Cf. also Hayashi Minao, *Tōhō Gakuhō*, vol.29. Kyōto 1959, pp.155–284.

186. Bendix, *Max Weber*, p.365.

187. Max Weber, *Staatssoziologie*. Duncker and Humblot, Berlin 1956, p.103.

187a. If, as Creel contends [cf. note 40], the *Shang-Sung* does indeed preserve some remembrance of Shang government, then the following passage

THE GENESIS OF THE CITY IN CHINA

from the *Shih-Ching* [Mao CCCV] affords no support for the theory that that government was in any way feudal:

Heaven charged the many princes
To establish the capital where Yü (**Gi̯wo) had labored;
They came [to court] in connection with their yearly service,
[Saying] Do not punish or reprove us –
We have not neglected our husbandry.

There is no question of an impersonal contractual relationship here, but rather an implication of personal benefices held at the royal pleasure.

188. *Shih-Chi*, chüan 3, f.3 recto : cf. *Meng-tzŭ*, V, i, 7.

189. Chang Kuang-chih, 'Shang-wang miao-hao hsin-k'ao', pp.85–8 and 'Some dualistic phenomena', pp.53–5.

190. Cf. Bendix, *Max Weber*, pp.367–8.

191. In later times **Mlwan (*Mwan) was a generic name for a congeries of tribal peoples in the southwest. Cf. Fan Ch'o's *Man*(*Mwan)-*Shu*, written between AD 860 and 865.

192. Based primarily on an analysis by Kwang-chih Chang, *Archaeology*, pp.163–4. Chang's evaluation of the implications of the available archeological evidence is not incompatible with the geography of the Shang culture realm as partially reconstructed by Li Hsüeh-ch'in on the basis of information in the oracle archives : *Yin-tai Ti-li Chien-lun*. The Science Press, Pei-ching, 1959 Reviewed by Hsü I in *K'ao-ku*, no.5 (1959), pp.271–2.

[II] The character for **·i̯əp (*i*), denoting a ceremonial center, as it appears on Shang oracle bones.

193. In its oracle-bone form the graph for **·i̯əp depicted an enclosure above a man in the deep-kneel posture, implying presumably an enclosed place where men dwelt. By Chou times it had come to denote a walled city, a fortified burgh, or a seigniorial town, and still later, under the Han, it signified the seat of a subprefecture. No doubt it was used anhistorically in one or other of these senses by Chou and Han authors who wrote about Shang times.

194. Cf. Noel Barnard's review article in *Monumenta Serica*, vol.22 fasc.1 (1963), pp.218–20.

195. Noel Barnard, 'A recently excavated inscribed bronze of Western Chou date', *Monumenta Serica*, vol.17 (1958), pp.33–6.

196. For more detailed discussions of the materials in this and the following sections see Ch'en-Meng-chia, *Yin-hsü Pu-tz'ŭ Tsung-shu*. Pei-ching 1956; and Li Ya-nung, *Yin-tai She-hui Sheng-huo*. Jen-min Press, Shanghai 1955.

NOTES AND REFERENCES

197. Exceptions to this generalization which have so far been observed concern certain potters and bronzesmiths working in the neighborhood of the ceremonial enclave at Cheng-Chou : see p.66.

198. Shih Chang-ju, 'Ho-nan An-yang Hou-Kang-ti Yin-mu', *Kuo-li Chung-yang Yen-chiu-yüan Li-shih Yü-yen Yen-chiu-so Chi-k'an*, vol.13 (1948), pp.21–48.

199. The *yao-k'eng* was a small pit excavated in the floor of the coffin chamber to receive a sacrificial victim, usually a dog.

200. The soil layer in which Shang cultural remains are customarily found, and which is normally drier than other earths in the neighborhood.

201. In the literature relating to the An-yang excavations this platform is referred to as *erh-ts'eng t'ai*.

202. Ma Te-chih *et al.*, 'I-chiu-wu-san-nien An-yang Ta-ssŭ-k'ung Ts'un fa-chüeh pao-kao', *K'ao-ku Hsüeh-pao*, no.9 (1955), pp.25–90; Chao Ch'ing-yün *et al.*, *K'ao-ku T'ung-hsün*, no.10 (1958), pp.51–62.

203. Kao Ch'ü-hsün, 'The royal cemetery of the Yin dynasty at An-yang', *Kuo-li T'ai-wan Ta-hsüeh K'ao-ku Jen-lei Hsüeh-k'an*, no.13 (1959), pp.1–9; Liang Ssŭ-yung and Kao Ch'u-hsün, *Chung-kuo K'ao-ku Pao-kao Chi*, vol.2, pt.3 (1962).

204. Shih Chang-ju, 'Hsiao T'un C-ch'ü-ti mu-tsang ch'ün', *Kuo-li Chung-yang Yen-chiu-yüan Li-shih Yü-yen Yen-chiu-so Chi-k'an*, vol.23 (1952), pp.447–487. It is noteworthy that dog sacrifices in considerable numbers (up to 30 in a single pit and a total of 130 in 8 pits) were associated with the construction of the wall surrounding the ceremonial center at Cheng-Chou [An Chin-huai, 'Cheng-Chou ti-ch'ü-ti ku-tai i-ts'un chieh-shao', *Wen-wu Ts'an-k'ao Tzŭ-liao*, no.8 (1957), p.18].

205. Eberhard, *History of China* (second edition), p.26.

206. Kuo Mo-jo has expounded this point of view in numerous publications over the past forty years, but has perhaps developed his argument most fully in *Nu-li-chih Shih-tai*. Jen-min Press, Pei-ching, 1954. Cf. also Han Hang-soo, 'Die ökonomische Struktur der Gesellschaftsformen in Ostasien', *Archiv für Völkerkunde* (1947), p.166.

207. *Vide*, for example, the discussion of 'Feudalism and gentry society' in Wolfram Eberhard, *Conquerors and rulers. Social forces in Medieval China*. E.J.Brill, Leiden; Second edition 1965, pp.22–47; and Ch'en Meng-chia, *Yin-hsü Pu-tz'ŭ Tsung-shu*. Pei-ching; 1956, p.616.

208. Mao Hsieh-chün and Yen Yen have shown that live slaves suffering from malnutrition were sacrificed during dedication ceremonies for important buildings, that they were buried with their ruler in royal tombs, and that their bodies were used in the manufacture of artifacts ['Dental condition of the Shang dynasty skulls excavated from Anyang and Huü-Xian', *Vertebrata Palasiatica*, vol.3, Pei-ching 1959, pp.79–80].

209. Cf. note 109 above.

210. Cf. note 114 above, and Chou Chao-lin and Mou Yung-hang, 'Cheng-Chou fa-hsien-ti Shang-tai chih-t'ao i-chi', *Wen-wu Ts'an-k'ao Tzŭ-liao*, no.9 (1955), pp.64–6.

211. **Śia=spread out, set [as a net], etc. Some scholars, presumably reading śia as a loan for **g'iəg (ch'i), translate as 'pennant' or 'flag lineage' [e.g. Chang Kuang-chih, *Archaeology*, p.170]. The other two lineages mentioned in this connection, the **Ki̯ər (*Chi*) and **Ti̯ông-g'i̯wer (*Chung-k'uei*), do not seem to be connected with crafts in any way, but the vocabulary of Archaic Chinese has not survived in all its ramifications and these names may once have carried connotations now lost to us.

212. Chang, *Archaeology*, p.171.

213. Most Chinese archeologists concerned with this topic have included sorghums among the crops grown by Shang farmers, but see note 68 above. For a pioneer study of farm implements and tools in ancient China, based primarily on literary sources, see Hsü Chung-shu, 'Lei-ssŭ k'ao', *Kuo-li Chung-yang Yen-chiu-yüan Li-shih Yü-yen Yen-chiu-so Chi-k'an*, vol.2 (1930), pp.11–59.

214. Hu Hou-hsüan, *Chia-ku-hsüeh Shang-shih Lun-ts'ung*, series II. Ch'eng-tu 1945, p.134.

215. *Ibid.*

216. I know of no evidence that would bear out Hu Hou-hsüan's contention that fertilization was practised, other than by the burning-off of scrub and brush [Hu Hou-hsüan, *Li-shih Yen-chiu*. Pei-ching 1955, p.1].

217. Cf. Hsü Chung-shu, 'Lei-ssŭ k'ao'.

218. Described in An Chih-min, 'Chung-Kuo ku-tai-ti shih-tao', *K'ao-ku Hsüeh-pao*, no.10 (1955), pp.27–52 : also Li Chi, 'Yin-hsü yu-jen shih-ch'i t'u-shuo', *Kuo-li Chung-yang Yen-chiu-yüan Li-shih Yü-yen Yen-chiu-so Chi-k'an*, vol.23 (1952), pp.523–619.

219. The dimensions of this demand are illustrated by inscriptions which contemplate the sacrifice of as many as fifty sheep, or even three hundred cattle, at one time [Lo Chen-yü, *Yin-hsü Shu-ch'i, ch'ien-pien* (1912), III, xxiii, 6 and IV, viii, 4]. Cp. also p.65 above.

220. Cf. Bendix, *Max Weber*, p.364, where the conventionalized hunt is described as 'the natural medium in which the physical and psychological capacities of the human organism came alive and became supple. In this form of "training" the spontaneous drives of man found their outlet, irrespective of any division between "body" and "soul" and regardless of how conventionalized the games often became.'

221. A vast quantity of reportage relating to the industrial technology of Shang times has been compendiously synthesized by Cheng Te-k'un in *Shang China*, Chapters VI–X. For Shang bone technology (not discussed in the text)

NOTES AND REFERENCES

see Cheng, *op, cit.*, Chapter VIII, and William Charles White, *Bone culture of ancient China*. University of Toronto Press 1945.

222. Cheng, *loc. cit.*, pp.93–108.

223. *Ibid.*, pp.109–25; Cheng Te-k'un, 'The carving of jade in the Shang dynasty', *Transactions of the Oriental Ceramic Society*, vol.29 (1957), pp.13–30. Li Chi, 'Yen-chiu Chung-Kuo ku-yü wen-t'i-ti hsin-tzǔ-liao', *Kuo-li Chung-yang Yen-chiu-yüan Li-shih Yü-yen Yen-chiu-so Chi-k'an*, vol.13 (1948), pp.179–82.

224. Cp. Cheng Te-k'un, *Shang China*, pp.137–55.

225. T'ang Yün-ming, 'Lung-shan wen-hua yü Yin wen-hua t'ao-ch'i-chien-ti kuan-hsi', *Wen-wu Ts'an-k'ao Tzǔ-liao*, no.6 (1958), pp.67–8.

226. Ma Ch'üan and Mao Pao-liang, 'Cheng-Chou fa-hsien-ti chi-ko-shih-ch'i-ti ku-tai yao-chih', *Wen-wu Ts'an-k'ao Tzǔ-liao*, no.10 (1957), pp. 58–9.

227. Berthold Laufer, *The beginnings of porcelain in China*. Chicago 1917.

228. J. A. Pope, 'An analysis of Shang white pottery', *Far Eastern Ceramic Bulletin*, vol.6 (1949), pp.49–54, and S. Umehara, *Etude sur la poterie blanche dans les ruines de l'ancienne capitale des Yin*. Kyōtō 1932.

229. *Ibid*; Cheng, *Shang China*, p.147.

230. Li Chi, 'Hsiao-T'un t'ao-ch'i chih-liao-chih hua-hsüeh fen-hsi', *Kuo-li T'ai-wan Ta-hsüeh Fu Ku-hsiao-chang Ssǔ-nien Hsien-sheng Chi-nien Lun-wen-chi*. T'ai-pei, 1952, pp.123–38.

231. Cf. W. Hochstadter, 'Pottery and stonewares of Shang, Chou and Han', *Bulletin of the Museum of Far Eastern Antiquities*, vol.24 (1952), pp.81–108; Cheng, *Shang China*, pp. 147–8.

232. Li Chi, *Hsiao-T'un*, vol.3 : *Ch'i-wu*, fasc.1 : *T'ao-ch'i*, pt.1. T'ai-pei 1956.

233. Cheng, *Shang China*, pp.156–76; Mizuno Seiichi, *Chūgokuno chōkoku; sekibutsu, kindobutsu*. Nihon Keizai, Tōkyō 1960.

234. Ch'en Meng-chia, 'Yin-tai t'ung-ch'i', *K'ao-ku Hsüeh-pao*, no.7 (1954), pp.15–59; but for the limitations of analyses derived from unattested or poorly attested bronzes see Noel Barnard's comments in a review article in *Monumenta Serica*, vol.22, fasc.1 (1963), p.230. Cf. also Li Chi, *The beginnings of Chinese civilization*. University of Washington Press, Seattle 1957, p.47. It should be noted, too, that Dr Barnard, in the paper mentioned above, has pointed out that the alloys from which Western bronzes were cast do not appear to have conformed very much more closely to a standard formula than do those of Shang China [*loc. cit.*, pp.229–40].

235. Noel Barnard, *Bronze casting and bronze alloys in ancient China*. Monumenta Serica Monograph XIV. Monumenta Serica, the Catholic University of Nagoya and the Australian National University, Canberra 1961, p.108.

236. Shih Chang-ju, 'Yin-tai-ti chu-t'ung kung-i', *Kuo-li Chung-yang Yen-chiu-yüan Li-shih Yü-yen Yen-chiu-so Chi-k'an*, vol.26 (1955), pp.95–129.

237. Cheng Te-k'un, 'The origin and development of Shang culture', *Asia Major*, series 2, vol.6 (1957), pp.80–98, and *Shang China*, pp.32 and 162–3; Li Chi, *Hsiao T'un, T'ao-ch'i*, pt.1.

238. Like everyone else who writes about Shang bronze foundry, I am indebted in general to Dr Noel Barnard's systematization of the available information (*Bronze casting and bronze alloys in ancient China*), and in this particular instance to his perspicuity in discerning the implications of the type of crucible employed in Shang China. The crucible itself had already been described by Shih Chang-ju and Cheng Te-k'un. Barnard attributes the first notice of the influence of ceramic manufacture on Shang bronze casting to Mrs Wilma Fairbank [*Monumenta Serica*, vol.22, fasc.1, p.235], though Sekino Takeshi had made much the same point in regard to both bronze and iron technology in 1956 [*Chugaku Kōkogaku Kenkyu*. Tōkyō, pp.189–91].

239. See C. Hentze, *Bronzegerät, Kultbauten, Religion im ältesten China der Chang-Zeit*. Antwerpen 1951, and Max Loehr, *Chinese Bronze-Age weapons*. University of Michigan Press, Ann Arbor 1956.

240. Cheng Te-k'un has devised a functional classification of Shang bronzes as follows, which, whatever its other merits, at least illustrates the wealth of forms in the bronzesmith's repertoire, as well as the almost exclusive emphasis on luxury items [*Shang China*, pp.167–8].

(1) *Food vessels*
Li tripod
Ting tripod
Ch'i four-legged vessel
Ting tripod with stove
Hsien tripod
Kuei tripod
Tou bowl
P'ou jar
Kuei bowl
I box
Pi ladle
Tsu table

(2) *Wine vessels*
Ho pot
Chia tripod
Chüeh tripod
Chio tripod
Yu wine-can
Tsun jar

Chih cup
Hu jar
Ku cup
Kung ewer
Bird-and-animal *tsun* cup
Shao spoon

(3) *Water vessels*
Yu water vessel
P'an basin

(4) *Musical instruments*
Nao bell
Ling bell
Ku drum

(5) *Military weapons*
Tsu arrow-head
Pang bow fitting
Mao spear-head
Ko dagger-axe
Ch'u axe
Yüeh axe

NOTES AND REFERENCES

Ch'i axe
Tao knife
K'uei armor plate
Chou helmet
  (6) *Tools*
Pen socketed axe
Hsiao knife
K'e-tao incisor
Kou hook
Tsuan drill

  (7) *Miscellaneous*
Ching mirror
Chu chopsticks
Yin seal
Chariot and harness fittings
Pole finial
Mask
Color container
Architectural fittings

241. Kao Ch'ü-hsün, 'Hsiao-ch'en Hsi shih-kuei-ti ts'an-p'ien yü ming-wen', *Kuo-li Chung-yang Yen-chiu-yüan Li-shih Yü-yen Yen-chiu-so Chi-k'an*, vol.28 (1957), pp.593–610; O. Karlbeck, 'An-yang marble sculpture', *Bulletin of the Museum of Far Eastern Antiquities*, vol.7 (1935), pp.61–9; Li Chi, *The beginnings of Chinese civilization*, Fig. 6.

242. Huang Chan-yüeh, 'Chin-nien ch'u-t'u-ti Chan-Kuo Liang-Han t'ieh-ch'i', *K'ao-ku Hsüeh-pao*, no.3 (1957), p.106.

243. Karl Polanyi, 'The economy as instituted process', in Karl Polanyi, Conrad M. Arensberg and Harry W. Pearson, (eds.), *Trade and market in the early empires*. The Free Press of Glencoe, Illinois, and the Falcon's Wing Press 1957, pp.243–70. The quotation is from p.250. In recent years Polanyi's theses have been subjected to severe criticism, notably by Scott Cook ['The obsolete "anti-market" mentality : a critique of the substantive approach to economic anthropology', *American Anthropologist*, vol.68, no.2 (1966), pp.323–45], but for the most part the debate has centered on the epistemological implications of the semantic dichotomy between economics in the substantivist sense of the provision of material goods and in the formal sense of rationalizing calculation. But even if the ideological basis of the substantivist approach to economic problems should ultimately prove untenable, the distinction between symmetrically disposed reciprocal systems and centripetally arranged redistributive organizations still holds as a conceptual framework for analysis of the economic competition which Cook, among others, rightly attributes to so-called primitive societies.

244. *Vide* Tung Tso-pin, *Yin Li P'u*. Li-chuang 1945; and 'Yin-tai-chih li-fa nung-yeh yü ch'i-hsiang', *Hua-hsi Ta-hsüeh Wen-shih Chi-k'an*, vol.5 (1946); Cheng Te-k'un, *Archaeology in China*, vol.2, p.197.

245. Tung Tso-pin, *Yin Li P'u*.

246. Amano Motonosuke, 'Yintai no nogyo to shakai kozo', *Shigaku Kenkyu*, vol.62 (1956), p.11.

247. An Chin-huai, 'Shih-lun Cheng-Chou Shang-tai ch'eng chih – Ao-tu', *Wen-wu*, nos. 4 and 5 (1961), p.77.

248. Li Chi, Preface to Shih Chang-ju's *Yin-hsü chien-chu i-ts'un*, p. iii.
249. Li Chi, *The beginnings of Chinese civilization*, p.53, note 13.
250. Polanyi *et al.*, *Trade and market*, p.250.
251. Cp. Walter C. Neale, 'The market in theory and history' in Polanyi *et al.*, *Trade and market*, p.371.

2

The Diffusion of Urban Life in Ancient China

THE CHOU DYNASTY[1]

According to the traditionally received account of ancient Chinese history the Shang dynasty, corrupted by the exercise of absolute power over several centuries, was overthrown by a coalition of tribes under the leadership of one of its own feudatories which went under the style of Chou(**Ti̯ôg). According to these same sources the Chou were rude barbarian tribes whose harsh existence on the steppes and hills of the northwest both fitted them to preserve the virtues of ancient times and consequently to deserve the Mandate of Heaven, and endowed them with the martial qualities necessary to wrest supreme power from the effete and decadent Shang dynasty. In the traditional chronology this was achieved in 1122 BC when King **Mi̯wo (Wu), profiting from the absence of the Shang ruler on a military expedition, was able to seize the Shang capital. Much of the success with which the Chou consolidated their victory is attributed to the Duke of Chou, younger brother of King Mi̯wo and *de facto* ruler of the new Chou state during the minority of his nephew Ch'eng (**D̂i̯ĕng). He it was, according to the traditional account, who suppressed a Shang rebellion (or, in the language of bronze inscriptions, effected 'the second conquest of Shang'), pacified the state, and ensured the continuation of the Shang sacrifices by establishing members of the deposed royal lineage in the district of **Sông (Sung) in present-day eastern Ho-nan. In the light of Chinese beliefs in later times this superficially altruistic act can be construed as having been motivated by the desire to avoid retribution at the hands of the powerful Shang ancestors if their sacrifices were discontinued.

This version of the transference of power from Shang to Chou, including as it does the stereotypes of the depraved terminal representative of a dynasty[2] and the able founder of a new line of kings upon whom is conferred the Mandate of Heaven, and who, with the selfless assistance of a virtuous chief minister, establishes a great and glorious new dynasty, has only too obviously been subject to the archetyping process which ultimately produces myth. But in the absence of archeological evidence it has hitherto proved impossible to penetrate to the original events which are now cast in the form of heroic situations.

Recently, however, Dr Noel Barnard has used information in the *I Hou Nieh I* inscription (Inscription 121.3 in Barnard's systematization) to demonstrate, first, that the so-called Shang rebellion was in fact more likely to have been but one in a series of Chou attacks on the Shang polity, and second, that the conquest, which the classical texts attribute to the Duke of Chou, was in fact effected by King Ch'eng in person, presumably after he had attained his majority.³ There can be little doubt that other epigraphic evidence yet to be excavated, when evaluated on the strict principles of interpretation established by Dr Barnard, will introduce further modifications into the traditional history of the Chou conquest.

Both the origin and the ethnic composition of the Chou people are obscure. Their own traditions, as preserved in Chinese classical literature, trace their descent from **G'u-Tsi̯ək (Hou-Chi) or Prince Millet, a legendary ancestor who was also an agricultural deity. According to these same dynastic traditions it was G'u-Tsi̯ək's grandson, Duke **Li̯ôg (Liu), who welded the Chou tribes into a unitary people, and **Tân-B'i̯wo (Tan-Fu) who gave them a political identity, at the same time as he brought them from the district of **Pi̯ən (Pin), traditionally identified with present-day Pin-Hsien in Shen-hsi, to settle permanently at the foot of Mount **G'i̯ĕg (Ch'i), customarily equated with the neighborhood of Pao-chi in the Wei valley.⁴ Two generations later, under **T̂'i̯ang (Ch'ang), who subsequently adopted the regnal style of **Mi̯wən-Gi̯wang (Wen-Wang), the Chou had come to constitute the most powerful state in the Wei valley, with its cult center at **P'i̯ông (Feng), a site on the southern side of the Wei valley not far from present-day Hsi-an. It was Mi̯wən-Gi̯wang's son, **Mi̯wo-Gi̯wang (Wu-Wang), who proclaimed the independence of Chou and, from a capital at **G'og (Hao), also in the vicinity of Hsi-an, initiated the conquest of Shang.⁵

Of this archetyped pre-conquest history of Chou, archeology has very little to say, either in confirmation or denial. Although Western Chou artifacts had been discovered in the Wei valley before World War II,⁶ it was not until the 'fifties that Su Ping-chi and Wu Ju-tso documented a transition sequence from Lungshanoid (K'ai-jui Chuang II in the terminology of the excavators) to Chou.⁷ So far, although a dozen or so Chou sites have been investigated in the vicinity of Hsi-an, it has proved extremely difficult to distinguish pre-conquest from later remains. It is, for example, practically impossible from the published reports to decide whether Chou elements in association with Hsiao-T'un-type finds were indeed contemporary with the Shang or were introduced after the conquest. When the Chou cultural imprint is found together with Shang remains of the Erh-li Kang phase we are on stronger ground – uniquely so for these finds afford the only incontestable archeological evidence for the pre-conquest Chou – but such associations are few and still inadequately analyzed.⁸

In the absence of an established basis of archeologically attested facts, any interpretation of Chou origins must rest on the implications of epigraphic and literary evidence. In the first place the oracle bones leave us in no doubt that the Shang rulers regarded the Chou as constituting one of the benefices in the gift of the Shang king, and were prepared to use troops to enforce their will. Conceivably the Chou may have been one of the ***pi̯wang* (*fang*) tribes (p. 58 above) whose chieftain had had his authority confirmed and validated by a ceremony of investiture. Of course, this would afford no guarantee that the Chou regarded themselves as dependents of the Shang king and the point may never be settled, for the surviving record of the Chou point of view has passed through the hands of later scholars who have had an intellectual commitment to systematizing the ancient dynasties into a morally acceptable sequence.

According to the received version of Chou history before the conquest, the Chou people had been established in the middle and lower Wei valley for at least four generations before Mi̯wo-Gi̯wang asserted his independence of the Shang ruler. Some scholars have seen reason to believe that they had previously occupied territories either in the Ordos or at least north of the Wei river, but, however that may be, the late recensions of their annals – which are the only ones extant – intentionally create the impression of a semi-nomadic people who had adopted a sedentary mode of life at some time prior to their conquest of Shang. Ssŭ-ma Ch'ien, who may have drawn his information from an earlier recension of the annals, attributes this transformation specifically to the culture-hero Tân-B'i̯wo who, he says, 'rejecting the customs of the **Ńi̯ông (Jung) and **D'iek (Ti),[9] organized the construction of an inner and an outer wall, and of houses and chambers, [so that] the settlement (**·i̯əp : *i*) constituted a distinctive environment (*pieh-chü*).' [10] This is the language of Chou documents in later times, and it is more than doubtful if it was applicable to the period of Tân-B'i̯wo. However, Chou mythology was not entirely inconsistent in its picture of the pre-urban way of life, for there are sundry other hints that these tribes had developed the pastoral aspects of their economy in early times, and it may not be wholly fortuitous that the *Chu-shu Chi-nien* records that, after Duke **Ki̯wɛd-liek (Chi-li) of Chou had subdued the **Di̯o-mi̯wo (Yü-wu) tribes of the Ńi̯ông, King **T'âd-tieng (T'ai-ting) of Shang appointed him to be Chief of Herdsmen (***mi̯ôk-si̯ər* : *mu-shih*).[11] This is a situation very similar to that envisaged above in which a tribal chieftain was accorded a Shang title and absorbed, first into the Shang polity, and then into the Shang culture group.

Intimations such as these of a difference between the Shang and Chou ways of life have induced speculation by modern scholars as to the possibility of the two peoples representing distinct ethnic groups and even linguistic stocks. In the earlier years of this century, the Chou were regarded simply as the first of a succession of nomadic invaders from the steppelands of Central Asia. In 1942 Wolfram Eberhard concluded from an analysis of such information as was available on the tribal federations which made up the Chou armies that at the time of the conquest the ruling house was ethnically Turkish, while the tribesmen were, generally speaking, of mixed Turkish and Tibetan stock.[12] At just about the same time Owen Lattimore, interpreting the same evidence in the light of ecological rather than linguistic considerations, came to precisely the opposite conclusion, namely that the Chou were of the same ethnic group as the Shang.[13] It is perhaps necessary to explain at this point that, according to Lattimore's hypothesis, the emergence of Chinese civilization out of a relatively uniform Lungshanoid culture was associated with the development of improved farming techniques. Lattimore placed particular emphasis on the adoption of irrigation, for which there is, in fact, no evidence in prehistoric China (cf. p. 68 above), but this is not seriously detrimental to his theory, as practically any other innovation in agricultural technology, whether the introduction of new methods of tillage or new crops, could have brought about the same result, namely more certain harvests, heavier yields per man and perhaps per acre, and ultimately an intensification of population density and a higher degree of social solidarity. Lattimore does not spell out this process in detail, and neither does he analyse the social processes involved, but presumably he is envisaging some sort of transformation such as that reported by Ralph Linton and Abram Kardiner when the Tanala of Madagascar changed from dry to wet padi cultivation.[14] Those communities on the North China plain which experienced these changes developed a consciousness of shared understandings and common aims and values which would ultimately provide the foundations for Chinese civilization. Those groups, on the other hand, who, by reason of circumstance or inclination, failed to accept technical innovation, were gradually forced out of the proto-Chinese community and into still poorer peripheral and interstitial territories, where they had no option but to elaborate the pastoral sectors of their economies. In extreme cases this might lead to fully nomadic ways of life in which farming played only a vestigial role. On this view the age-long conflict between sedentary Chinese and nomadic 'barbarians' was initiated as much by Chinese expansion as by nomadic inroads. It is in the context of this interpretation of Chinese history that Lattimore places both the Shang and the Chou – and, incidentally, the Hsia as well – among the nuclear Sinic communities.

Only the progress of archeological investigation will ultimately decide the ethnic status of the pre-conquest Chou, and even then the evidence will not be easy to interpret. But the whole question is not so purely academic as it may at first appear, for on it depends our interpretation of the origin and nature of the Western Chou polity and, consequently, of the status of the city in the political system of the time (cf. pp. 112–14 below).

The idea that the Chou were nomadic intruders into the Chinese culture realm led on to the notion that their culture at the time of the conquest was inferior to the civilization of Shang, and during the first half of this century this disparity in the cultural attainments of the two groups was held as an article of faith by virtually all Western historians of China. The Chou have been envisaged most frequently as rugged 'defenders of the marches and pioneers of the highlands',[15] whose continual struggle against both a harsh environment and hostile neighbors had bred in them the martial skills which eventually enabled them to overcome the Shang. The four generations since the time of Tân-B'i̯wo, during which they had been established in the Wei valley, had been insufficient for their élite to acquire more than a veneer of Shang culture, so that when Mi̯wo-Gi̯wang acceded to control of the premier polity in East Asia he brought with him a band of battle-hardened retainers more familiar with the mores and values of the camp than with the niceties of ritual and protocol.[16] The texts provide no real basis for this interpretation – which is hardly surprising since they preserve the version of events authorized by the Chou themselves – and archeology offers little evidence beyond the presence of metal artifacts in the Wei valley in pre-conquest times. On present evidence it is still possible to argue either that the early Chou were only a Neolithic Lungshanoid group somewhat affected by the absorption of selected Shang culture traits, or that they had already developed one of the Lungshanoid regional traditions to the point where it should be classed as a civilization running on a course parallel to that of the Shang. However, this choice may not be open to us for much longer, for Dr Noel Barnard has recently voiced some pertinent observations in this connection. He has pointed out that, whereas the Shang restricted their bronze inscriptions – as far as can be ascertained from scientifically attested specimens – to two or three characters recording names or emblems, the Chou, even before they had finally completed the conquest of Shang, were engraving texts of considerable length. The *I Hou Nieh I* inscription is, of course, the prime example. On a matter on which I am far from expert I cannot do better than quote Dr Barnard's conclusion to his evaluation of this inscription:

'The facts which face us are simply these – the Shangs made short inscriptions in bronze of little historical value; the Chous, even before the Shang state was entirely vanquished, manufactured bronze texts that are truly historical documents of tremendous interest. It is tempting to suggest that the Chous were possibly possessors of a somewhat more advanced culture than that of the Shangs – the two civilizations, however, exhibiting much the same form of culture; for example, the written scripts were identical in most respects but the contents of the more permanent documents differed. Much of Shang writing was connected with divination – the Chous, however, were apparently more concerned with lay affairs and had practical reasons to record, in a permanent form, matters for the instruction of posterity.'[17]

It is possible that Barnard's investigations have not yet quite reached the point at which they can support unaided the edifice of interpretation which he has erected upon them. In any case his conclusion requires that he disregard a considerable number of Shang bronze inscriptions containing up to a score or so of characters [18] which he considers, probably correctly, to be not properly attested, a phrase which he construes in rigorous fashion to mean 'acquired through scientifically controlled excavation'. Nevertheless, his fundamental arguments are extremely persuasive and based on analysis of a much more austere and punctilious character than has usually been accorded the oracle texts. In some respects Barnard's suggestion – and it is only a suggestion – is not in conflict with the inescapable conclusion of archeology that the post-conquest Chou culture was a lineal descendant of that of the Shang 'and the Conquest involves no major discontinuity as far as the civilizational growth of the Yellow River valley is concerned.' [19] Such a conclusion surely implies that the two cultures were much of a muchness at the time of the conquest.

STATE AND GOVERNMENT

When the Chou rulers finally found themselves in control of the Shang kingdom, together probably with some other eastern districts which had been outside the sphere of Shang dominion, they were faced with the problem of extending their version of patrimonial government to territories beyond the reach of personal authority. In response to this need they apparently instituted a network of garrisons designed to assert their control over virtually the whole of the North China plain. Many, perhaps most of these garrisons, constituted islands of ethnically Chou composition in a sea of Shang and other indigenes, but occasionally former Shang benefice holders were allowed to retain their lands provided they transferred their allegiance to the new rulers. One of the traditional annals records that no less than 1,773 dependent territories were established in this manner by the Chou king.[20] There is no independent confirmation of this figure but the order of magnitude at least implies that most settlements of any size were placed under a Chou chieftain or a Chou adherent. The Chou themselves retained direct control of their homeland in the Wei valley.

A proportion of the Chou vassals were doubtless kinsmen of the royal house, but the system of classificatory kinship nomenclature[21] was extended to include benefice holders who, despite their propagation of fictitious genealogies,[22] are now known to have had no biological connection with the Chou royal clan. In addressing a territorial magnate bearing the same surname as that of the royal house the Chou king used the term 'paternal uncle', whereas a lord with a different surname was addressed as 'maternal uncle'. In this way familial relations were not only integrated into the political framework of the state but also provided a model for the conduct of government. The authority of the Chou court was sustained by a series of ceremonies and rituals in which political duties were conceived on the pattern of family loyalty, and both linked with religion in a manner which accorded divine sanction to the system of government. In these circumstances the Chou king was able to rely on the majority of his vassals favoring the divinely ordained *status quo,* as against the innovator who failed to conform to the sacrally validated pattern. Long after the Chou ruler had ceased to wield significant secular power, he continued to exercise ritual authority, adjudicating in claims of legitimacy and, by sanctioning innovations when the force of events rendered them inevitable, easing strains in a developing society. In this respect the Chou capital shared something in common with Sumerian Nippur, and perhaps to a lesser extent with the Greek Delphi and Yoruba Ile Ifẹ, all of which were cult centers from which emanated culturally unifying influences [23] although they themselves were not especially powerful politically. Particularly this is true of the situation in China after the middle of the 8th century when the royal Chou had lost most of its power to influence events outside its own territory.

Traditionally the Chou has been pictured as a largely static era characterized by a gradual decline of centralized power. In a sense this image can be traced back to the Chou dynasty itself, for the philosophers of the age had evolved the myth of a preceding era of unity, peace, and prosperity as offering a model for an alternative to the conflict and misery of their time. Some four or five centuries later the Han rulers propagated just such an idealized version of the past as a demonstration of the benefits to be derived from a unified kingdom under a strong paternalistic monarch, an interpretation which of necessity forced the expositors of this thesis to treat the barely forgotten strife of the later years of the Chou dynasty as civil war.[24] This is the version of events which has come down to the present and which is still current in numerous writings by Chinese, Japanese and Western scholars. However, from the second decade of the present century a group of Chinese scholars, among whom the most prominent has been Ku Chieh-kang, have penetrated behind the veil of Han exegesis and revealed the so-called Chou dynasty in a very different light, and their interpretation has subsequently been adopted in its essentials by most Western specialists in this field.[25]

How long the Chou royal family retained effective control over their conquered territories is unknown, but after some three centuries of rule external forces intervened to diminish whatever degree of power they still exercised. In 771 BC internal disturbances resulted in the loss of the Chou capital of *G'og* to non-Chinese tribes from the west, from whom it was eventually recovered not by the Chou king but by the ruler of the former dependency of ***Dz'i̯ĕn* (Ch'in). The seat of government of the Chou domain was transferred to ***Glâk-di̯ang* (*Lo-yang*), which had hitherto functioned as the eastern capital of the realm. The royal house of Chou never recovered from this reverse, and by the end of the century had sunk to the level of her former vassals. In fact, the Chou court maintained its existence only by exploiting its validatory and consecratory functions, and by allying itself with the most powerful of its neighbors.

The three centuries or so of Chou hegemony prior to 771 BC have been designated by Chinese historians as the period of the Western Chou. From then until the final extinction of the dynasty in 221 BC is an era now known as the Eastern Chou dynasty, which is customarily sub-divided into two periods designated by names drawn from the literature of their time. The earlier of these, the Ch'un-Ch'iu (**T'i̯wən-T̂s'i̯ôg) or Spring and Autumn period, denotes the epoch covered by a history of the same title, namely 772–481 BC; the later, also named after a collection of Chou annals, is known as the period of the Contending States (Chan-Kuo; **T̂i̯an-Kwək). Its beginning is variously assigned to 475, 468 or 403, but it has been found convenient in the present study to date the period from 463, the year following the last entry in the *Tso-Chuan*, the most important of several commentaries on the *Ch'un-Ch'iu*. As has been stated previously, precise dates are not a prime requisite in an evolutional study such as this, and in any case the Eastern Chou constitutes a period of continuous political development rather than two developmentally discrete epochs articulating at a major break in time.

That the Chou king was no longer master of the whole Chinese culture realm at the end of the 8th century is evident from one of the earliest glosses in the *Tso-Chuan*, which records the defeat of the royal troops in 707 BC by an army of **D'i̯ĕng (Cheng).[26] At that time there were about 170 states[27] which, far from feuding within the framework of a unified empire as the traditional annals imply, exercised *de facto* sovereignty over their individual territories. Naturally not all these states were of equal importance. In the old culture hearth of North China the leading contenders for power were **Lo (Lu) **D'i̯ĕng (Cheng), **Gi̯wad (Wei), **Sông (Sung), **K'i̯əg (Ch'i), **D'i̯ĕn (Ch'en), **Dz'ôg (Ts'ao), **Ts'âd (Ts'ai), **Dz'i̯ər (Ch'i) and, of course, Royal Chou itself.[28] At the beginning of the Ch'un-Ch'iu period these states were the most powerful of the polities, and had evolved among themselves ritually sanctioned instruments of formal communication within the framework of a political system in which the Chou domain was of supreme ceremonial significance. Second only to Chou in prestige, though less powerful than some of its neighbors, was the state of Lo, whose authority derived partly from its alleged foundation by the Duke of Chou, and partly from the related circumstance that its ceremonial ritual and protocol, its ***li̯ər (li)*, approximated very closely to those of the old Chou court.[29] Generally speaking, these central states – the Chung-Kuo – at the beginning of the Ch'un-Ch'iu period also possessed the most advanced technologies and the most highly developed economies.

Further removed from the ceremonial center of ancient China was a zone of peripheral states which had come within the ambience of Chinese culture in relatively recent times and which, during the 8th and even later centuries, still preserved some of the old barbarian culture traits. To the northwest, in present-day Shen-hsi and Shan-hsi, were the states of **Dzʻiĕn (Chʻin), **Tsi̯ĕn (Chin), **Ngi̯wo (Yü), **Kwăk (Kuo) and **Li̯ang (Liang), while in the northeast, in the vicinity of modern Pei-ching, was the state of **·Ian (Yen). In the south, extending in a belt along the Yang-tzŭ valley, were **Tṣʻi̯o (Chʻu), **Dzwia (Sui), **Śi̯ĕn (Shen), **Si̯ək (Hsi), **Dzi̯o (Hsü), **Dʻəng (Tʻeng), **Kŏg (Chiao), **Tɨ̯ôg (Chou)[30] and **På (Pa), and still further towards the southeast, in present-day Chiang-su and Che-chiang respectively, were the states of **Ngo (Wu) and **Gi̯wăt (Yüeh). Finally, a third and outer zone was inhabited by barbarian tribes known under the general terms of **Dʻiek (Ti) in the north, **Di̯ər (I) in the east, **Mlwan (Man) in the south, and **Ńi̯ông (Jung) in the west. Some of these latter groups appear to have possessed fairly substantial and permanent settlements. In fact a process of sinicization was continually changing the status not only of these peripheral tribal peoples but also of the states themselves. Tsi̯ĕn, for example, was admitted to the company of the Central States in fairly early times, and subsequently assumed the leadership of these states.

The degree of political consolidation achieved during the era of the Western Chou is uncertain,[31] but from the middle of the 8th century the process can be documented in considerable detail. By this time the city-states, the ·i̯əp, which had originally constituted the domains of the Chou vassal lords, had been transformed into fully fledged territorial states. Within the inner circle of these states expansion was, generally speaking, possible only at the expense of territories already pre-empted by members of the group[32] and, as we have seen, by the end of the 8th century the contemporary political ethos based on the fiction of a unified empire was at variance with the realities of chronic interstate conflict. Henceforward, Chou political evolution manifested itself in a continuous process of absorption of smaller political units by larger ones, and the Chou technical vocabulary for territorial appropriation and state extinction[33] became increasingly prominent in the annals of the time.

Interstate relations came to be conducted more and more in terms of the expediential dictates of a power struggle rather than according to a sacrally sanctioned moral law. Government by customary morality (*li̯ər*) and by individuals was subordinated to government by law (***pi̯wăp : fa*);[34] in Max Weber's terminology traditional had been replaced by rational-legal authority,[35] and the old ethical code was invoked only when it might add a semblance of legality to power politics. Moreover, as conflict tended to promote a concentration of power, so the more potent among the Chou territorial magnates began to arrogate to themselves some of the functions that had previously been royal prerogatives. A major step in this direction was the assumption in 679 BC by the ruler of the state of Dzʻi̯ər of the title of **Păg (*Pa*) or Hegemon, a role not too dissimilar from that of the Shogunate in 19th-century Japan. As president of the assembly of nobles in the imperial capital, and sure of the support of the most powerful of all the states, this Păg was able to impose some degree of directional unity on the foreign policies of the states, to restrain to some extent the antagonisms of competing factions, and to achieve a measure of relative peace over a span of nearly forty years. Between 681 and 644 BC, he convened assemblies of the nobles (**g'wâd : hui) on at least twenty-four occasions,[36] and these face-to-face confrontations doubtless contributed to a general easing of tensions at a difficult period of interstate rivalry. Subsequently the hegemony passed to Dukes of Dz'jĕn, Sông, and Tsjĕn, and significantly, ultimately to a king of Tṣ'i̯o in the Yang-tzŭ valley. The institution of the Hegemon finally lapsed in 591, when a rough parity of power among the states prevented any particular ruler exercising political control over the others.

Although it had provided some support for the later fiction of a unified political entity on the North China plain, the institution of Hegemon had protected rather than strengthened the Chou court, which had, if anything, declined in prestige during the 7th century. The erosion of the aura of charisma that had attended the royal Chou in the earlier years of the dynasty is reflected very clearly in the debasement of the royal style **Gi̯wang (Wang). Originally this had been a prerogative of the Son of Heaven (**T'ien-tsiəg : T'ien-tzŭ), who alone could offer to Heaven the supreme sacrifices and thus maintain the parallelism between the macrocosmos and the microcosmos without which no state could prosper. He it was who, in the words of Marcel Granet, was 'à la fois l'auteur de tout péché, l'émissaire de toute expiation, le bénéficiaire de toute grâce, le principe de toute puissance.' In the universe of the early Chou there could be only one filial mediator between heaven and earth, and gi̯wang, as his style, was sacrosanct. The exception was to be found in the Yang-tzŭ valley state of Tṣ'i̯o, in which aboriginal customs formed a much larger element in the élite culture than they did in North China. Here the ruler had styled himself gi̯wang since the beginning of the Eastern Chou, and he retained the title when, during the Ch'un-Ch'iu, Tṣ'i̯o forced acceptance of itself as a major power in the Chinese culture realm. Towards the end of the Ch'un-Ch'iu period the rulers of two other southern states, Ngo and Gi̯wăt, followed the example of the Duke of Tṣ'i̯o. Even though there was no precedent in their own past for the use of this designation, yet they, like Tṣ'i̯o, were of aboriginal, mainly Gi̯wăt and **T'âd (T'ai), culture and it is unlikely that the Chou religion of Heaven had ever made much appeal to their élites.[37] Adoption of the Chou royal style in these cases probably signifies no more than the adaptation of a prestigious honorific to an already existing institution. When the custom began to spread among the inner circle of Chou states, however, it implied a rejection of the divinely sanctioned system of universal order on which the authority of the Chou monarch ultimately rested, and as such marked an important stage in the evolution of Chinese political forms. By the end of the 4th century AD, the rulers of at least five, and perhaps six, of the more powerful states had assumed the style of *giwang*.[38]

During the Ch'un-Ch'iu period, then, the smaller polities at first found themselves acting as buffer-states between more powerful contending neighbors and, after vainly attempting to preserve their identities by means of alliances, were ultimately absorbed into the territories of their aggrandizing neighbors. By the beginning of the 5th century BC there were no more than thirteen states of any importance, of which five lay outside the specifically Chou culture sphere.[39] During the rest of the life of this alleged dynasty the remaining states engaged in a protracted conflict of mutual extermination. Finally the dialectic of power, working itself out in a manner not totally dissimilar from that of the dialectic of ideology in present-day China, resolved itself into two polarized entities, in this case the state of Dz'i̯ĕn in the north contending against the state of Tṣ'i̯o in the south. In a series of campaigns between 230 and 221 BC, the former overcame Tṣ'i̯o and its ruler re-established the unity of the Chinese polity, the outcome of more than half a millennium of political evolution. Discarding the discredited style of *Giwang*, which had symbolized the old concept of government according to a divinely ordained moral law, the ruler of Dz'i̯ĕn assumed the title of **Tieg which, because of its attachment during the Contending States period to some of the more recently created culture heroes of mythological antiquity, had acquired overtones of universality something after the manner of the concept of *cakravartin* adopted by the Mauryas. Had Shih Huang-ti, the first Emperor of Dz'i̯ĕn, known the term, he would certainly have claimed to be a *digvijayin*, a conqueror of the four quarters of the world.

It was not only in the sphere of interstate relations that conflict concentrated power: an analogous change was effected concomitantly within the individual states, and it is fortunate that this process has recently been analyzed with exemplary rigor and perspicacity by Professor Cho-yün Hsü.[40] The internal administrations of almost all the states were characterized by struggles between nobles and rulers as well as between noble and noble. It was to be expected that, under the familialistic type of government of Western Chou times, close relatives of a ruler would monopolize important political offices. Brothers of rulers, in particular, often played very important roles in state government.[41] One of the earliest political changes discernible during the Ch'un-Ch'iu period was the replacement of these brothers in seats of power by an oligarchical aristocracy,[42] which was in turn often ruined by interfamilial conflicts. By the beginning of the 5th century BC this class of noble ministers had been virtually eliminated, and the great ministerial families had become things of the past (apart, of course, from the few who had managed to acquire supreme rule within their states). By the beginning of the Contending States epoch a new type of political entity had emerged, in which a ruler exercised despotic power over a bureaucracy the selection of whose personnel was not wholly divorced from merit, although neither had ascriptive principles of appointment been entirely abandoned. Generally speaking, in Max Weber's conceptualization of the nature of state government, the bureaucracies of the Contending States should be classed with those in which the ruler's administrative staff are separated from the *means* of administration (whether these be money, building, war material, vehicles, horses or other things), in contrast to the administrative staffs of the Ch'un-Ch'iu period who had predominantly owned their own means of administration.[43] In the latter (Ch'un-Ch'iu) case the ruler had shared his domination with an autonomous aristocracy, whereas by Chan-Kuo times he had assumed direct control while yet delegating executive power to qualified officials, men whom Weber categorized as 'propertyless strata having no social honor of their own.'[44] We shall have more to say of this new class of administrators subsequently.

The question of feudalism. 'Le mot "féodal" est un terme expressif, commode, – et dangereux.'[45] It has been applied to several periods of Chinese history – sometimes to almost all periods prior to 1949 – and particularly to the decentralized rule of the Chou dynasty. Such broad interpretations stem from generalized definitions of feudalism such as that of Dubrowsky,[46] in which virtually the only requirement for a society to be deemed feudal appears to be the existence of a class of landowners who appropriate the unpaid products of the immediate producers. According to this definition not only Chinese society, but most other Asian societies as well, have remained feudal until well into the 20th century. This, in fact, is the way in which the word is customarily employed in the language of the press and in political propaganda,[47] but, defined thus broadly, it can hardly serve any analytical purpose. At the other extreme there are those who restrict the term to the socio-political systems of certain parts of Western Europe at certain times in the Middle Ages.[48] Among these latter are, first, those who use the word as a generic classifier for a particular dominant political and social organization at a particular time and, second, those who confine it to the description of technical arrangements by which a graded system of land rights comes to correspond to an extreme development of the mode of personal dependence, a state of society in which public rights and duties are inextricably interwoven with the tenure of land and in which 'the whole government system – financial, military, judicial – is part of the law of private property.'[49] In the first instance the institutional structure is defined within the framework of a preconceived time span and limited area,[50] in the second instance the time span is adjusted to correspond with the persistence of a particular institutional complex.[51] Both the institutionally and the chronologically restricted definitions have proved attractive to European historians, who have thus been able to pursue their analyses of the system in the light of their own historical experience.[52] The drawback to this method of inquiry is, of course, that it affords no guarantee that the system under discussion is unique, and not merely one manifestation of a structural uniformity recurring in a series of disparate cultures. Nor does it help us to distinguish incidental and specifically European characteristics from structurally recurrent features common to all cultures in which the institution is found. Defined thus narrowly, the term can hardly serve any comparative purpose, let alone throw light on socio-political conditions during the Chou dynasty.

It is necessary, I think, to remember that at best the idea of feudalism is a high-order abstraction, evolved originally in the minds of European historians to describe a category of institutional complex that had become defunct some half millennium before the term was coined.[53] It seems not unreasonable that other scholars should then seek to discover if the structural characteristics inherent in the abstraction recur in other cultures. Whether or not they find them depends on how they define the institutional complex. It cannot be denied that the texts relating to the Western Chou depict a basically agrarian society in which a supreme ruler delegated sovereign powers to members of a hierarchically structured aristocracy. From the same texts other scholars have cited additional features customarily, though by no means exclusively, associated with European feudalism, notably a personalized government exhibiting a comparatively weak separation of political functions, hereditability of office, regularization of the rights of the lord over the peasant, the maintenance of private armies, and a code of honor stressing military obligations.[54] This complex of features certainly constitutes part of the image projected by the classical literature of China, and has been accepted by most scholars in this field as reflecting more or less truthfully the general lineaments of the Western Chou governmental system. Ch'i Ssŭ-ho, for example, acknowledged it as such in his comparison of Chinese and European feudal institutions,[55] at the same time as he assumed that the *Ch'un-Ch'iu* witnessed the dissolution of a unitary kingdom into civil war. From that point of view he was able, without being guilty of any gross inconsistency, to recognize the more important structural features of Chou feudalism as persisting through the Ch'un-Ch'iu era and beginning to disappear only during the period of the Contending States.[56]

The fact that the Ch'un-Ch'iu can now be categorized as a period of expansion, consolidation and centralization of the power of sovereign states, and that the socio-political aspects of the idealized system can be defined with some degree of confidence, does not mean that the information available is anything like adequate – with the analytical tools presently to hand, at any rate – to permit an assured dynamic historical interpretation of the reality behind the Han image of the Chou era. It is still a matter of debate, for instance, how the Western Chou system of government evolved. Wolfram Eberhard,[57] on the one hand, interpreting the evidence in terms of Alexander Rüstow's theory of feudal societies,[58] sees the Western Chou as a classic exemplar of feudalism resulting from suprastratification, in this instance the imposition of a Chou aristocracy on a substratum of Shang agriculturalists. Eberhard's belief in an ethnic difference between Chou and Shang further leads him to the conclusion that Chou feudalism was the outcome not merely of suprastratification, but of an *ethnic* suprastratification. On the other hand, Owen Lattimore, as already mentioned, interprets the same evidence as indicating an internally generated social stratification.[59] Between these two extremes lies a wide variety of intermediate opinions, including those which derive Chou feudalism from the disintegration of a powerful Shang empire,[60] which only serve to accentuate our ignorance of the true relations between Shang and Chou both before and after the conquest. Neither is there a consensus as to the precise stage at which feudalism may be said to have been established. Whereas Eberhard seems to assume that a feudal situation was initiated at the time of the conquest, Derk Bodde believes that such a system could have evolved only after a gradual evolutionary process had run its course. Feudalism, he says on one occasion, 'means something more than the mere existence of vassalship ties between a single group of territorial nobles on the one hand and a single ruling house on the other. In order to constitute a true feudal system, it should include a network of similar ties linking these same territorial nobles with a descending hierarchy of lesser and more localized dignitaries beneath them, until, ideally, virtually the entire population is integrated into a complex pyramid of delegated powers and responsibilities.... One or even two centuries may have been required before a fairly crystallized and broadly inclusive system emerged.'[61] Bodde finds some support for this point of view in Maspero's thesis that sub-infeudation was not practised in early Chou times, although it became fairly common later on when lesser fief-holders had become assimilated into the hierarchy of state nobility.[62] This, together with the evident looseness with which aristocratic titles were used in the early Chou, would seem to imply that a process of political evolution had been taking place. However, both Noel Barnard and Cho-yün Hsü claim to have recognized instances of sub-infeudation under the Western Chou.[63]

Definitive statements on matters such as this must await the attention of specialists, as well as more rigorous definition of the technical terms employed. Meanwhile it is apparent, even through the archetyped glosses of later exegetes, that the Western Chou system of government did present points of comparison with feudal Europe, but the degree of structural similarity involved is a matter for future investigation. To the present author it appears that the complex contractual and legal concepts of European feudalism were either absent or but poorly developed under the Western Chou. There was certainly a hierarchical aristocracy whose members received landed estates and titles from the Chou sovereign. Collectively they were known as the ***ţi̯o-g'u* (*chu-hou*), and ranked for ceremonial purposes according to the precedence of the particular ***tsi̯ok* (*chüeh*) or patent granted to them by the Chou monarch.[64] In late and idealized Chou books of ritual the five degrees of nobility are each ascribed territorial fiefs (***kwək : kuo*) of fixed areal extent,[65] but Richard Walker has shown that, at conferences convened after the middle of the 7th century BC, the states ranked according to their power positions.[66] There were, in addition, ***b'i̯u-di̯ung* (*fu-yung*) or 'attached' territories, whose rulers were denied direct access to the Chou king but who rendered their services to neighboring lords. What is of primary interest in the present context is the ceremony of investiture at which the noble was confirmed in the possession of his lands, and which was held in the Royal Chou ancestral temple.[67] After a fairly extended acquaintance with the texts which prescribe the ritual forms for this ceremony (which, incidentally, are all relatively late in time) it seems to the present author that the investiture, in the idealized form in which it has been transmitted to us, signified not so much the assumption of contractually determined obligations on the part of the lord in return for a fief but rather a sacrally sanctioned induction into the hallowed community of the Chinese aristocracy. As Marcel Granet expressed it in his posthumously published work *La Féodalite chinoise*, 'En recevant l'investiture (*fong*) qui lui permettait d'élever sur sa terre un Autel du Sol à la chinoise, un chef devenait à la fois un Chinois et un Seigneur.'[68] Certain undertakings were indeed required of the candidates for investiture but they were, in my opinion, in the nature of adherence to sacred family loyalties rather than secular contractual arrangements. The terms of investiture, in so far as we can know them, seem to have partaken of the character of an *exequatur* rather than of the *commendatio* of medieval Europe – or so I believe.[69] Of course, when ambivalent texts have to be interpreted not merely through the refracting lens of an alien culture, but also through the dark glass of the purposed idealization of a later age, such conclusions are bound to incorporate a high degree of subjectivity, and consensus is not likely to be achieved easily.

John Hall has argued forcibly that a feudal society cannot be categorized under a single inclusive concept, and that feudalism as an ideal type need not be exemplified in its totality by any particular society which is alleged to be feudal.[70] A feudal society is to be viewed as a mode of social, political, and economic integration which subsumes a range of essential variables. In defining such a system it is particularly necessary to pay attention to the limits of variability of these elements. The essential variables as isolated by Hall in his thought-provoking paper are : a lord-and-vassal relationship the crux of which 'is not a specific form of contract but rather the personal nature of the association ... and its military origin'; arms-bearing as a class-defining profession; a distribution of goods and services closely integrated with the hierarchy of social statuses; a landed, or locally self-sufficient, economic base 'with the merchant community essentially outside the feudal nexus'; a long-term restriction on the mobility of the bulk of the population; and a direct personal relationship of land manager to cultivator which, as Hall phrases it, 'places the cultivator under feudalism somewhere between slavery on one side and free tenancy on the other.'[71] I agree with the general structure of this model with one reservation. Whereas *a particular* form of contract may not be specific to feudalism, a strongly contractual basis is, in my opinion, essential to the feudal condition: otherwise how can it be distinguished from the patrimonial mode of sociopolitical integration? A final conclusion on the question of feudalism under the Western Chou and early Ch'un-Ch'iu – or rather on the question of varieties of feudalism in the different political entities of Chou China : Tṣ'io appears to have been an autonomous state from the earliest times until 223 BC – must await the outcome of a great deal of scholarly investigation of the degree of variability of the essential elements, both in the generalized model of feudalism and in the particular Chinese experience. Until comparative historians have provided a more refined structural definition of the phenomenon of feudalism in general, and not just a description of English or French or Russian or Japanese feudalism, it will be unprofitable to argue determinedly for or against feudalism in Chou China. Nevertheless, I cannot but express my belief that the evidence available for the Western Chou and earlier Ch'un-Ch'iu periods can, in the present unsatisfactory stage of historical analysis, be construed as testimony to a continuation of the patrimonial style of Shang government more readily than as proof of a feudal system of vassalage.[72] In any case, by Ch'un-Ch'iu times the Western Chou empire – if indeed such an entity had ever existed – had been replaced by a congeries of states which, even though they shared certain cultural understandings and acknowledged the supremacy of a common ritual center, enjoyed *de facto* political sovereignty.

SOCIETY

As literacy was a prerogative of the ruling élites, it was inevitable that the literature of the Chou period should reflect almost exclusively the actions, values and attitudes of those groups. But the extant writings of the Chou do not preserve simple statements about these matters : the actions have been archetyped, the values idealized, and the characters heroized. For the Western Chou even this genre of record is exiguous, and it is a matter of great difficulty to ascertain precisely how the various social groups actually functioned, as opposed to how later annalists and exegetes said they functioned. The idealized texts, for example, describe five grades of nobility in a fixed hierarchy of descending rank, but there is no shortage of evidence that in early Chou times the terms denoted types of benefice rather than ranks.[73] Moreover, the very early *I Hou Nieh I* inscription mentions three classes of people, King's men, counts and serfs, without reference to the traditional five noble ranks.[74] The King's men clearly enjoyed the highest status among these three groups and alone are accorded the enumerator ***sĕng : sheng* (for ***si̯ĕng : hsing* = family name), while the counts and serfs are merely listed under the general category of husbandmen. What the relation was between these three classes and the traditional rankings we have no means of knowing.

Turning from these negative aspects of the study of Chou society to matters about which it is possible to speak more positively, it can be stated with certainty that in the time of the Western Chou, society was disposed in a pyramidal form, with the king and a virtually closed aristocracy as an apex, supported by a broad base of peasant agriculturalists. In the early post-conquest period the king may well have been the supreme ruler that he always claimed to be, but by the end of the 8th century the royal clan of Chou had lost virtually all political power outside its own domain, and had in fact sunk to the level of its former vassals. Only the superior charisma associated with the king's ritual role as Son of Heaven distinguished the royal family from other minor rulers' courts situated at strategic points on the North China plain. Not that charisma was solely a prerogative of the royal Chou. In later times all the state rulers also believed that they were different from other men. In fact they all traced their descent from ancient culture heroes, adapted genealogies to prove it – a process which in the case of lords of other than imperial descent involved the transformation of not a few unpretentious local deities into emperors and dukes[75] – and undertook an annual schedule of sacrifices to ensure the welfare of their realms.

Associated with the ruler's role as the chosen instrument for communication with the ancestors was an elaborate, but in early times apparently unwritten, code of ceremony and etiquette subsumed under the Chinese term *liər* (*li*). As in the case of the Chou king himself, it was the punctilious attention of the ruler to *liər* which, combined with his personal **tək (*te*) or *virtus*, ensured the prosperity of the state. Marcel Granet has delineated the role of the ruler in evocative terms which express clearly the close association of religious ritual and legitimate sovereignty.[76]

> 'Le seigneur est donc, partout, le principle de toute fécondité, de toute fertilité. Il est, dans chaque domaine, un principe universel de fructification, de stabilité, de santé. Les joncs, les chrysanthèmes poussent vigoureusement tant que sont vigoureux la vertu, le *tao-tö*,[77] le *mana* princiers; le plantain a des milliers de graines et le peuple des enfants en foule, tant que ce *tao-tö* ne s'épuise point; tant que le seigneur a assez de *mana* pour vivre vieux, nul, parmi le peuple, ne meurt prématurément. Ni l'eau, ni la chaleur ne manquent en temps voulu, et les chevaux courent vite et les chevaux courent droit, et aucune invasion de sauterelles n'ose pénétrer, et aucun brigand n'ose lever la tête, ou aucun démon faire des siennes dans un pays où le prince conserve, entière, sa Vertu.'

During the Ch'un-Ch'iu period the ruling houses, from the genealogical point of view, fell into three groups, the **Tsi̯əg (Tzŭ) lineage, which had provided rulers for the old kingdom of Shang but which now ruled only in Sông; the descendants of Chou princes who were considered to have received their fiefs from King Mi̯wo at the time of the conquest, and who consequently bore the clan name of **Ki̯əg (Chi); and those who ruled over states which had joined the Chinese community subsequently as a result of a process of sinicization.[78] Both the Shang and Chou rulers claimed descent from gods, but the others traced their origins to ancient emperors, most of whom were eventually systematized into dynasties which today constitute an important part of the mythology of ancient China.

During the Western Chou the rank next below the rulers was filled by ministers of the government, whose relation to their rulers was functionally analogous to that of the Chou king to his dukes (using this latter term in the general sense of *ti̯o-gʻu* (cf. p. 120 above). There were two grades of ministers, the ***kʻi̯ăng* (*chʻing*), the higher rank, whose offices were hereditary and who were relatively few in number, and the ***tʻâd-pi̯wo* (*tai-fu*), who were more numerous and who functioned as assistants to the *kʻi̯ăng*. There were, in fact, several grades of *tʻâd-pi̯wo*, some of which seem also to have been hereditary. Together a ruler and his ministers constituted the power group in a state and, at least in the idealized texts of later times, were classificatory kin to one another. On the lower fringes of the power group, in some instances overlapping with it but in others falling far below it, was a class of ***dẓʻi̯əg* (*shih*), men who were descendants of rulers or ministers and trained in the six arts of propriety, music, archery, chariot driving, writing, and arithmetic, but who were often, perhaps predominantly, unlanded. Although ranked among the ***ki̯wən-tsi̯əg* (*chün-tzŭ*)[79] or gentlemen of good birth, such *dẓʻi̯əg* might be no more than officials in the bureaucracy or in a noble household. Others, who were fortunate enough to possess small estates, might have a few tenants to till their fields or might even work the land themselves. It was the code of behavior that had developed among the *dẓʻi̯əg* which was formalized and infused with additional moral content by Confucius in the period of the Contending States.

Apart from a few of the *dẓʻi̯əg*, none of the ruling classes engaged in agricultural or artisan activities, so that virtually the whole structure of society was supported by the labors of the peasantry, who were referred to variously as ***mi̯ən* (*min:* = people), or ***si̯ag-ńi̯ĕn* (*shu-jen :* = the masses), or ***dzʻi̯an* (*chien :* plebeians), or simply as ***si̯og-ńi̯ĕn* (*hsiao-jen :* = the mean people). In contrast to the aristocracy, these people possessed no family names, and therefore had no need of genealogies; they participated in no ancestral cult and had little understanding of the nature and formalities of *li̯ər*. They did not own the land they cultivated but were transferred with it whenever it changed hands. Whether the lord exercised formally recognized rights, inherent in the granting of his benefice, over the lives of the *si̯ag-ńi̯ĕn*, or whether the conditions of the time simply afforded no opportunity for the peasant to change his master, is uncertain, though Maspero tends to prefer the latter interpretation.[80] In any case, for all practical purposes the peasant was effectively *adscriptus glebae* and obliged to surrender a portion of his harvest to his overlord, at the same time as he was subject to corvée for construction work and sometimes to conscription into the lord's private army. Indeed, in this largely self-sufficient manorial type of economy there was little to distinguish official state business from the private affairs of a lord. Eberhard is certainly correct in applying the term 'serfs' to these 'men of few rights, few opportunities and few pleasures'.[81]

Included among the *śi̯ag-ńi̯ĕn* were artisans and merchants, both of whom seem to have been attached to manorial-style communities, probably as retainers of noble households. There is no evidence of even partially autonomous associations comparable to the guilds of medieval Europe, though there are some not wholly unambiguous indications that in the Ch'un-Ch'iu period both merchants and craftsmen were sometimes treated as collective entities.[82] Finally, at the very bottom of the social scale was a class of menials and true slaves.[83] The latter were mainly captives and criminals, and could be purchased; the prevailing price was low.[84] There are, too, a few records of slaves being interred in the tomb of their master.[85] Generally speaking, slaves seem not to have been very numerous and, indeed, appear to have occupied a position external to the main structure of Chou society.[86]

The preceding remarks apply primarily to conditions in the earlier centuries of the Chou era, but it will be apparent that, when social and political stratification coincide as closely as they did in ancient China, political transformations of the magnitude of those described above must have been accompanied by equally momentous social changes. These changes have recently been studied in considerable detail by Professor Hsü Cho-yün, and it is his researches which provide the basis for the following remarks.

Already by the middle of the Ch'un-Ch'iu period, say by 600 BC, there were unmistakable signs that the old social order of the Western Chou was crumbling. We have already seen that members of rulers' families had become progressively less powerful during the 7th century, and had sunk in the social scale at the same time as a new class of hereditary ministers had arisen. During the 6th century this ministerial class in turn lost power to a more impersonal bureaucracy, which offered opportunities of advancement to able men who yet lacked the advantages of powerful family influence. Thus the second half of the Ch'un-Ch'iu witnessed the disintegration of the higher social strata of Chinese society, and the upward rise of individuals on the basis of ability. And it was not only the civil bureaucracy which was able to make use of technical skills dissociated from noble birth : the high incidence of warfare during the Chan-Kuo also facilitated the rise of able commoners to positions of military command. At the same time the population base from which they were selected was broadened when infantry were substituted for the ritualized chariot warfare and archery of earlier centuries and a formalized system of military conscription reached deep into the villages.

Concomitant with these political and social changes was another series associated with economic changes to be discussed in a later section. When, towards the end of the Ch'un-Ch'iu, the use of serf labor was replaced by a system of taxes and rents and the old patrimonial relationship of lord and serf gave way to that between landlord and tenant, the way was opened for the emergence of a class of men who owned land but not rank. As these investors increased their holdings and with them their wealth, so, at the other end of the scale there began to appear a class of landless peasants. Thus these opposing, yet complementary, spirals induced an economic stratification, which in time hardened into class distinction and transformed the very basis of society. Meanwhile, the development of commercial activity was effecting a parallel trend within the framework of urban society. By the 5th century there had appeared a class of urban merchants who were using their wealth to acquire political influence. By investing their surplus wealth in land, this group also contributed to the formation of a landless peasantry and furthered the crystallization of class distinctions. These were the types of entrepreneurs who served as models for Ssŭ-ma Ch'ien's generalizations in the chapter of his history entitled *Huo-Chih*.[87] Among them were the members of the **Tŏk (Cho) family, originally from **D'i̯og (Chao) state,[88] the **K'ung (K'ung) family of **·I̯wăn (Yüan),[89] **D'i̯ĕng-D'i̯ĕng (Ch'eng-Cheng), from **Bli̯əm-g'i̯ung (Lin-ch'iung),[90] **Kwâk-Tsi̯ung (Kuo-Tsung) of G'ân-tân,[91] and the **Pi̯ăng (Ping) family of Dz'ôg (Ts'ao), all of whom made fortunes in the iron-smelting business during the closing decades of the Chan-Kuo period. **·Ia-Twən (I-Tun) achieved equal success in salt production, and was bracketed with Kwâk-Tsi̯ung as a man whose wealth could be compared with that of a ruler of a kingdom.[92] In the district known as Within the Pass, the **D'ien (T'ien), **Li̯ĕt (Li) and **D'o (Tu) were the dominant merchant families.[93] By the final years of the Chou dynasty the widow **Ts'i̯ĕng (Ch'ing) had amassed such wealth by skilful manipulation of the profits on the sale of cinnabar cakes in På (Pa) and **Dj̑uk (Shu) that the first emperor of Dz'i̯ĕn entertained her and built the **Ni̯o-g'wɛr-ts'i̯ĕng (Nü-huai-ch'ing) terrace in her honor.[94] A not inconsiderable proportion of the successful entrepreneurs whose achievements are described by Ssŭ-ma Ch'ien were of humble, sometimes picaresque, origins. **Dz'i̯ĕn-Di̯ang (Ch'in-Yang) was a ploughman, **K'i̯uk-Śi̯ôk (Ch'ü-Shu)[94a] was a grave robber, **G'wân-Pi̯wăt (Huan-Fa) was a gambler, **·I̯ung Glåk-d̑i̯ĕng (Yung Lo-ch'eng) was a peddler, **·I̯ung-Păk (Yung-Po) began as a purveyor of fats, the **T̑i̯ang (Chang) family as vendors of syrups, the **T̑i̯ĕd (Chih) family as knife sharpeners, the **Tŭk (Cho) family as dealers in dried sheep stomachs, and **Ti̯ang-Li̯əg

(Chang-Li) as a horse doctor. But the prince of all Chan-Kuo businessmen, and exemplar of the new age, was **B'ăk-Kiweg (Po-Kuei), a native of Chou in the time of Marquis **Mi̯wən (Wen) of Ngi̯wər. His story, as told by Ssŭ-ma Ch'ien and felicitously translated by Dr Burton Watson,[95] is reproduced below and can stand as symbolic of the entrepreneurial spirit of the times.

'... Po Kuei delighted in watching for opportunities presented by the changes of the times.

> What others throw away, I take;
> What others take, I give away,

he said. "When the year is good and the harvest plentiful, I buy up grain and sell silk and lacquer; when cocoons are on the market, I buy up raw silk and sell grain. When the reverse marker of Jupiter is in the sign *mao*, the harvest will be good, but the following year the crops will do much worse. When it reaches the sign *wu*, there will be drought, but the next year will be fine. When it reaches the sign *yu*, there will be good harvests, followed the next year by a falling off. When it reaches the sign *tzŭ*, there will be a great drought. The next year will be fine and later there will be floods. Thus the cycle revolves again to the sign *mao*."

By observing these laws, he was able to approximately double his stores of grain each year. When he wanted to increase his money supply, he bought cheap grain, and when he wanted to increase his stock, he bought up high-grade grain. He ate and drank the simplest fare, controlled his appetites and desires, economized on clothing, and shared the same hardships as his servants and slaves, and when he saw a good opportunity, he pounced on it like a fierce animal or a bird of prey. "As you see," he said, "I manage my business affairs in the same way that the statesmen I-Yin and Lü-Shang planned their policies, the military experts Sun-Tzŭ and Wu-Tzŭ deployed their troops, and the Legalist philosopher Shang-Yang carried out his laws. Therefore, if a man does not have wisdom enough to change with the times, courage enough to make decisions, benevolence enough to know how to give and take, and strength enough to stand his ground, though he may wish to learn my methods, I will never teach them to him!"

Hence, when the world talks of managing a business it acknowledges Po-Kuei as the ancestor of the art.'

Of this new breed of men in general Ssŭ-ma Ch'ien has this to say:

'None of them enjoyed any titles or fiefs, gifts, or salaries from the government, nor did they play tricks with the law or commit any crimes to acquire their fortunes. They simply guessed what course conditions were going to take and acted accordingly, kept a sharp eye out for the opportunities of the times, and so were able to capture a fat profit. They gained their wealth in the secondary occupations and held on to it by investing in agriculture; they seized hold of it in times of crisis and maintained it in times of stability. There was a special aptness in the way they adapted to the times. . . .'[96]

In short, the Eastern Chou can be characterized as a period when the power élites of a congeries of *de facto* sovereign states were reconstituted, when political influence ceased to be wholly ascriptive and came to be based to a large extent on achievement, and when new political and economic stratifications congealed into social classes. At the same time there was an increase in vertical social mobility, as the upper strata of society lost a good deal of their former kin-based cohesiveness and allowed a proportion of their members to sink in the scale, while the development of bureaucratic institutions, by introducing competition for high positions, facilitated the rise of able individuals on merit alone.

ECONOMY

As compared with that of the Shang period, the economy of Chou China was influenced by significant changes in both environmental and technological considerations. Let us look at the environment first.

Environment. The Chou period witnessed a marked enlargement of the *Lebensraum* of the Chinese, but even more important was the increased diversity of the resource base which accompanied this extension of territory. The original Chou benefices or fiefs (according to whether the government is considered patrimonial or feudal) occupied an area not greatly in excess of that of the old Shang kingdom – or perhaps more accurately of the Shang culture realm as revealed by archeology (cf. Fig. 8). There were, in fact, only two significant additions to those territories, one in the west and one in the east. Chou itself had built up its power in the Wei valley in central Shen-hsi and maintained its capital and the royal domain there until 771 BC, after which the region became the territory of Dz'jĕn. This valley, together with the lower reaches of the Ching, Lo and other tributaries of the Huang, is essentially a sheltered extension of the North China plain protruding into the more rigorous environment of the löss uplands, but in Chinese history it has fulfilled a dual role. By reason of the potential fertility of its lössic soils wherever water could be made available, it has afforded a productive agricultural base for political and military activity,[97] and by reason of its location and physiography it has provided the entrance to the main routeway from the Chinese heartland to Central, and ultimately to Western, Asia. On the eastern marches of the North China plain the Western Chou conquests brought firmly within the Chinese culture realm a fringe of territories that had apparently resisted Shang encroachments until the very end of the dynasty. In this direction the early Chou probably extended their political control to the shores of the Po-Hai and the edges of both the Shantung highlands and the Huai marshes.

By the beginning of the Ch'un-Ch'iu period the Chung-Kuo or Central States (as defined on p. 114) still occupied this territory which had constituted the original kingdom of the Chou, but they were now surrounded by a zone of peripheral states which, during the Western Chou, had become acculturated – though sometimes imperfectly – to the Chinese way of life. In the far north, in the embayment of the North China plain which now constitutes the environs of Peking, was the state of ·Ian; to the northwest, in present-day southern Shan-hsi, was Tsi̯ĕn, which subsequently disintegrated into the three smaller states of **D'i̯og (Chao), **Ngi̯wər (Wei), and **G'ân (Han)[98]; in the west Dz'i̯ĕn ruled the former Chou homeland in the Wei valley; and in the south the Han and Yang-tzŭ lowlands afforded territorial bases for at least eight states, of which Tṣ'i̯o and Ngo were both territorially the most extensive and politically the most powerful. Somewhat later Gi̯wăt, in the present province of Che-chiang, forced itself into the Chinese comity of states. In the north this expansion of the Chinese culture realm effected no great changes, though it did establish the Chinese mode of ecological adaptation on the löss upland of Shan-hsi. In the south, however, Tṣ'i̯o, Ngo, and Gi̯wăt constituted a bridge between North China, a climatically rigorous land of limited and uncertain rainfall, and South China, a land of benign climate and abundant moisture; between predominantly level, dust-blown plains and dissected, verdure-clothed hills; between growing seasons of seven or eight months and year-round continuous growth; between wheat and millet on the one hand and rice on the other; in short between precarious livelihood and potentialities for prodigal abundance.[99] Tṣ'i̯o extended particularly far south, reaching deep into Hu-nan in the vicinity of the Tung-t'ing lake. When, towards the close of the 3rd century BC, Shih Huang-ti welded the last survivors of the Contending States into a unitary polity, his empire reached from the löss uplands in the west to the Yellow Sea in the east, and from the north of present-day Ho-pei to northern Hu-nan.

The diversity of this environmental base is explicitly evident in two of the oldest Chinese geographical documents extant, and is implicit in numerous other writings from the Chou period. The oldest of these accounts is the **Gi̯wo-Kung or Tribute of Gi̯wo [Yü], which now constitutes a chapter in the Shu-Ching. Gi̯wo was a culture hero, probably of central Chinese origin, who, during the period of the Contending States,[100] was incorporated into the systematized dynasties of ancient times as founder of the Hsia. For this reason, and also because it includes information about the Yang-tzŭ valley, the Gi̯wo-Kung is itself today usually ascribed to the Chan-Kuo period. This is undoubtedly true of the text, but may be less than the truth so far as the substantive material which it contains is concerned. In the first place the schedule of tribute products is arranged on the basis of natural regions, with no allusion to the political structure of the Contending States. The organizational framework is that of another, and presumably much older, age. In the second place the inventory of natural resources and products is fuller for the three inner provinces, which occupied approximately the territories of the old Chung-yüan, than for the six outer provinces, which may be held to imply that the text was originally compiled in this metropolitan area. In the light of these considerations it would appear not unlikely that the *Giwo-Kung* is a cumulative text, cast in its present form during the era of the Contending States, but incorporating material from one or more earlier periods. In later times it exercised great influence on the thinking of Chinese scholars, and it may well be that some of the material was already old, perhaps almost sacrosanct, when the present recension was made. Possibly the hallowed name of Giwo, in view of that culture-hero's achievements and the legends associated with his bronze cauldrons, was likely to become attached to any serious compendium of geographical information, and an original nucleus of matter may have been repeatedly augmented as it was transmitted across the centuries under his name. The Ptolemaic corpus provides an interesting parallel in the Western world. What is of interest in the present context is the evidence of this document for a tribute system which reflected a natural environment of considerable diversity.

The second work which attests the regional diversity of the Chou realm is the chapter entitled **Tiək-piwang-diĕg (*Chih-fang-shih*) in the *Chou-Li*. This work, in the form in which it now exists, may well be of Han date, and is certainly not earlier than the Chan-Kuo, but its contents are equally certainly cast in an antique mould. The attribution of 'profitable items', that is natural products, accords fairly well with that of the *Giwo-Kung*, and both works may in fact derive from a common, but ancient, tradition.

Of greater significance than the mere fact of diversity is the implication of scattered fragments of evidence of an incipient regional specialization in handicrafts,[101] but apart from the production of salt on the coast and various forms of mining in the interior, this could hardly have gone farther than the fabrication of exotic luxuries. And, according to the *K'ao-kung Chi*, a primitive lack of craft specialization still prevailed in Giwăt, ·Ian, and Dz'iĕn, where every man was, respectively, his own blacksmith, armourer, and spear maker.

Technology. Throughout the Chou period the basis of the economy was agriculture, but there is little evidence of technical innovation during the first half of the dynasty. During the Western Chou, cultivation seems to have been effected by men working in pairs and using caschrom-like, wooden implements known as **liwər-dziəg (*lei-szŭ*).[102] At least some of the fields were cultivated on a swidden cycle, and the crops were those of Shang times, although rice became of vastly greater importance as the Yang-tzŭ valley states were absorbed into the Chinese culture realm. Iron hoe blades and sickles began to appear towards the end of the Ch'un-Ch'iu,[103] though it is doubtful if they became at all common until another century or two had passed, and had certainly not wholly supplanted bronze and stone tools even at the close of that era. More significant was the introduction of the ox-drawn plough and more efficient methods of fertilization in the period of the Contending States. At the same time there was a great expansion in the practice of hydraulic engineering, both for irrigation of crops and for transport of commodities, a development which is partially documented in the latter, and therefore non-mythical, part of the chapter on 'The Yellow River and its canals' in *Shih-Chi* (chüan 29). Early in the Contending States an irrigation system based on the **Tįang (Chang) river brought prosperity to the district of **G'â-nəp (Ho-nei) in Ngįwər.[104] At the end of the 4th century BC a scheme was initiated for the control of the waters of the Ch'eng-tu plain[105] and the completed system, only slightly modified, is still functioning today. In the north a vast area of Dz'įĕn territory was rendered productive when a giant canal, over 300 *li* in length, was constructed between the Ching and Lo rivers in Shen-hsi.[106] It was claimed that on the completion of this project the Lands-within-the-Passes were converted into fertile fields, yields were raised five-fold,[107] and the people of Dz'įĕn no longer suffered from lean years.[108] Contemporaneously there was an improvement in the efficiency of water-lifting devices, notably the introduction of the counter-balanced bailing bucket (*chieh-kao*), first mentioned in a well-known passage of the *Chuang-tzŭ*.[109] Yet, despite these innovations, Chan-Kuo farming was still relatively primitive, with few safeguards against the vagaries of the weather. Li-K'uei, a jurist and minister at the court of Gįwad in about 400 BC, is alleged to have reckoned the variation in yields as oscillating between a fifth of, and four times, the average.[110]

The diffusion of iron technology during the Contending States period has already been mentioned in connection with the introduction of hoes and plough-shares. The Chinese had been familiar with techniques of iron casting since the end of the 6th century[111] – which is not surprising in view of their splendid tradition of bronze foundry. It is usually accepted that the first literary reference to the use of iron refers to the 29th year of Duke **D'įog (Chao), that is 513 BC, but the earliest tools so far excavated date only from the 5th century BC. From late in the 4th century iron began to be forged,[112] but this innovation seems to have had a greater effect on the form of weapons than on that of agricultural implements. It was at just about this time that long iron swords came into use, first it would seem in the armies of Tṣ'įo and later in those of Dz'įĕn. In the 3rd century long single-edged blades, which occur in some quantity on archeological sites, may have been instrumental in establishing the supremacy of the Dz'įĕn armies.

Meanwhile the old Shang traditions of ceramic manufacture, jade carving, lacquering, and bronze foundry continued into the early Chou, together with the working of stone, bone and shell. These last three industries remained in the

Shang tradition, but pottery and jade craftsmanship achieved major advances from the point of view of both technology and aesthetics. Bronze working, too, underwent technological improvement, chiefly in the process of the casting-on of accessories, although there was a decline in general quality during the Contending States. Each of these traditions is worthy of, and indeed is a subject of, study in its own right, and the fact that they are not discussed in the present instance reflects only their lack of direct relevance to the study of urban origins and diffusion.

Land Tenure. A comparison has frequently been made between the economic institutions of the Western Chou and those of the manorial system of Western Europe. Certainly the early Chou economy was based on predominantly self-sufficient agricultural units in the form of fiefs of noble households, within which neither exchange nor labor specialization was very important. A peasant worked both the fields allotted to his family and, probably, part of his lord's demesne land as well. We need only note in passing the long-standing controversy over the precise nature of the ****tsiĕng-dʻien** (*ching-tʻien*) or well-field system of land settlement which is described in the *Mencius*[113] and, derivatively, in the *Chou-Li*.[114] In this system, it is alleged, eight peasant families each cultivated its own holding (****siər-dʻien : ssŭ-tʻien**), at the same time as all joined together to cultivate a centrally located demesne tract belonging to the lord (****kung-dʻien : kung-tʻien**).[115] It is extremely unlikely that such a checkerboard pattern of landholdings could have been established as rigorously as Mencius implies over any considerable area, and certainly not even the territory of a single benefice, let alone the whole of the Chou kingdom, could have been carved up in this fashion. Beyond that there is little agreement among scholars as to the implications of the texts. There are those who regard the whole system as an idealization conceived in the minds of later writers purely for didactic purposes,[116] and there are those, Kʻang Yu-wei among them,[117] who have accepted it as a practical mode of agricultural colonization devised by sages in some socialist millennium of antiquity. Between these two polar views is ranged a spectrum of opinions which between them take account of almost all possible interpretations. One of the most interesting of these is Wolfram Eberhard's suggestion that the *tsiĕng-dʻien* units arose as semi-military *colonia*-style settlements of Chou tribesmen under the direction of their clan leaders, and amid an initially hostile Shang population.[118] In this case the system would have been a prerogative of the Chou conquerors. Probably a majority of Chou scholars today concede that the notion of *tsiĕng-dʻien* does perpetuate some kind of social and economic land system of Western Chou times in which both agricultural land and its produce were communally shared, with the fief holder pre-empting a ninth part of the harvest. If this were so Chʻi Ssŭ-ho does not exaggerate unwarrantably when he compares the *kung-dʻien* with the demesne land of the European manor and the *sįər-dʻien* with the land held in villeinage.[119] Whether the name *tsįĕng-dʻien* implies that the nine units of cultivation did in fact share a common well, or whether the term arose because of a graphic resemblance of the idealized Mencian layout to the character for well, is still a topic of contention which need not, however, delay us at this time.

During the Chʻun-Chʻiu period it is possible, ambivalent though the evidence proves to be, to discern a change in the relationship between lord and cultivator. There are increasingly frequent indications that taxes in kind were being substituted for labor services. The *Tso-Chuan*, for example, ascribes the imposition of the first tax of this kind in the state of Lo to the year 594 BC,[120] and it is implied in the *Lun-Yü* that the rate was customarily a tenth of the harvest,[121] a figure that is almost certainly too low. When the cultivator paid such a tax to a member of the landholding nobility he had become virtually a rent-paying tenant, but with the elimination of the less powerful noble houses and the concentration of political power in the hands of progressively fewer territorial magnates, the peasant not infrequently found himself the tenant of a landowner who occupied the supreme position in the state, of the ruler in fact. It is unknown if the figment of Royal Chou suzerainty subsumed a claim to personal ownership of all the territory of the Chinese culture realm, but it is evident that in practice land was annexed, ceded and exchanged without reference to the wishes of the Chou monarch. As Hsü Cho-yün remarks, what mattered was not the ritually sanctioned claim to territory by a universal ruler, but the control which a member of the power élite could exercise over it,[122] and 'possession' is consequently a more apt term than 'ownership'. In any case, what is certain is that the tenant who paid a tax to a state – or, in other terms, a rent to a ruler – had freed himself from the bonds of serfdom. He was in essentially the same position as those other farmers who, during the Chʻun-Chʻiu and the Chan-Kuo periods, had brought waste land into cultivation or reclaimed fields abandoned during the ever-recurring wars, and not greatly different, so far as tenure was concerned, from those who were awarded grants of land in return for signal services to their ruler. All were virtually private landowners.

But if land was now often in private ownership, it had also become a purchasable commodity and the way was open for its concentration in the hands of the economically powerful. There is abundant evidence that this process was accelerated during the Chan-Kuo period, when a new class of merchant-capitalists turned the profits of trade towards the acquisition of land, the only form of investment, given the insecurity of the times and the relatively primitive character of economic instruments, available to them. But the lands which went to make up the estates of this new class of 'nobles without rank and lords without scepters'[123] were acquired at the expense of a peasantry poorly equipped to weather the storms of economic change. The social and political tracts of the time emphasized two mutually interacting factors as operating especially powerfully to prise land out of peasant hands, namely a combination of heavy taxation and unseasonable labor service bearing on the cultivator on the one hand, and the ready availability of concentrations of capital in the hands of merchants on the other. And to mediate the interaction between these two groups there was evolved the instrument of usury, the oppressive character of which is described graphically enough in the *Kuan-tzŭ*.[124] The final outcome was that, by the end of the Chan-Kuo, in most of the states for which information is available, there had emerged a class of landless laborers owning 'not an inch of soil', as the saying went. The cycle did not everywhere run its course with the same rapidity, but the trend was universal during the later years of the Contending States, always involving an apparently inevitable progression from a familial lord-and-subject bond, through the contractual lien of creditor and debtor, to the impersonal relationship of master and hired hand.

Commerce. In the Spring-and-Autumn period, and presumably in earlier centuries, merchants figured among the retainers of noble households but, in a context of self-sufficient manorial-style socio-economic units, and in view of the concomitant absence of an active market and a developed monetary system, their role in the conduct of exchanges could have been of only relatively small significance. The commodities which passed through their hands were probably restricted to salt, metals and a fairly narrow range of luxury items. On the dissolution of the Chou kingdom into politically autonomous states, a multiplication of toll stations further hampered the development of commerce, though the Ch'un-Ch'iu era did witness the negotiation of some mutual agreements on border tariffs.[125] Not until the latter half of this period is there evidence of the emergence of a powerful merchant class, presumably encouraged at that time by the establishment of centralized governments over larger and larger tracts of territory, the improvement of roads and the construction of waterways, and the incipient delineation of a regional specialization and interdependence in natural products and craft goods consequent upon the extension of Chinese culture into new and varied environments.[126] *Pari passu* with this expansion of commerce bronze money came into general use. Strings of cowries seem to have been used as media of transaction, and therefore fulfilled some of the functions of money, during Shang times, and metals and cloth were both used in the same way in later centuries, when salaries were also paid in grain. In fact commodities were used to make payments throughout the Chou era, but a metallic currency of fixed value was introduced in either the 4th or 3rd century BC,[127] thus fostering more complex modes of exchange and facilitating capital accumulation.

The instruments of exchange employed by Chan-Kuo merchants are not readily apparent from the archetyped texts of classical China, but it can be inferred with confidence that they attained only a low degree of economic

The Archeological Record

sophistication. The volume of trade is attested less by direct references in the texts than by the resources commanded by some parvenu merchants, as evidenced by their ability to acquire large landed estates.

The Archeological Record

It cannot be doubted today that the only material which can be regarded as of primary character for the study of urbanism during the Western Chou – possibly for the whole of the Chou period – is properly attested archeological evidence, while the transmitted texts must be considered as of only secondary importance. In these circumstances it is doubly unfortunate that archeological discoveries pertaining to the Western Chou period are exiguous in the extreme, often of doubtful scientific validity, and restricted largely to tombs. We have seen already that evidence relating to the Chou before the conquest is of even smaller quantity and poorer quality, and it will be demonstrated subsequently that material is by no means abundant for the era of the Eastern Chou. Numerous of the Chou settlement sites are occupied by present-day cities, so that archeological investigation is often limited to chance exposures revealed during construction work. Other sites have been ploughed so frequently during the last twenty centuries that the imprint of urban life has been wholly obliterated, while many ancient cities remain as yet unlocated. Although the ruins of nearly a score of Chou cities are known, not one has been subjected to thorough investigation. Indeed, most have been surveyed rather than excavated. And although a proportion can be identified as foundations of ancient times, only rarely can they be ascribed dates accurate to within a century or so.

THE WESTERN CHOU

Although literary sources refer to the founding of cities in pre-conquest times, so far no archeological evidence of urban life at that time has been brought to light. Before World War II Shih Chang-ju carried out a preliminary survey of those districts in which the pre-conquest capitals were traditionally supposed to have been located, but he apparently failed to find any remains of indisputably urban forms.[128] However, both Shih and subsequent investigators[129] have established with certainty that pre-conquest Chou culture developed out of a Lungshanoid regional tradition strongly influenced by secondary diffusion from – and, if the traditional literary texts are to be trusted, political domination by – the Shang metropolitan territory. It should be noted that, although no distinctively urban features have been demonstrated at pre-conquest archeological sites, yet one of the settlements constituted a more or less fully occupied area of some 480,000 square meters.[130]

Several settlement sites of Western Chou date have been excavated, notably those at Chang-chia-p'o[131] near Hsi-an, at Hsi-kuan-wai[132] near Hsing-T'ai, at Tung-Chai in Cheng-Chou,[133] at Wang-wan in Lo-yang,[134] at San-li T'un in Chiang-su,[135] and at Chin-p'en in Hung-an in the middle Yang-tzŭ valley,[136] but the only investigations which have revealed indications of urban form are those of Ch'eng-tzŭ Yai, near Chi-nan in Shan-tung.[137] This was the site in ancient times of the capital of the small state of **D'əm (T'an), allegedly founded by a Shang benefice holder whose descendant featured in Eastern Chou times as a *tsi̯ag*.[138] An examination of the relevant literary sources led Tung Tso-pin[139] to conclude that this ceremonial center was established in about 1200 BC, and was still in existence as late as 200 BC, even though the Ch'un-Ch'iu recorded its destruction (***mi̯at* : mieh) by Dz'i̯ər in 684 BC.[140] Indeed, the excavators of the city have claimed to see evidence of this event in two mass burials, both devoid of funerary furniture, which were found close under the north wall of the city. Probably the walls were razed at that time but, if so, they appear to have been subsequently restored.

The city had been built on a site long occupied by a Lungshanoid people. The walls, which formed a more or less rectangular enclosure of approximately 450 × 390 meters, were of a composite character. The Chou – or, if Tung Tso-pin is correct in his conclusions, perhaps the Shang – builders had incorporated into their new structures old Lungshanoid walls that were already in an advanced state of dilapidation. Both elements were of *hang-t'u* construction. Near the wall were four pottery kilns manufacturing typical Chou grey ware.

THE CH'UN-CH'IU PERIOD

Lo-yang. In Chou times there were two cities in the neighborhood of present-day Lo-yang. According to transmitted texts **D̂i̯ĕng-T̂i̯ôg (Ch'eng-Chou), built to house the population of the old Shang capital, lay to the east of the modern city, with the Ch'an river to its west and the Lo river on its southern flank, while **Gi̯wang-D̂i̯ĕng (Wang-Ch'eng) or the Royal City, also known as **Kap-ńi̯uk (Chia-ju), was situated to the west of present-day Lo-yang, in an angle between the Chien and Lo rivers (Fig. 10). Both cities were mentioned in literary and bronze epigraphic texts, but the *Ch'un-Ch'iu* leaves us in no doubt that, during most of the 7th and 6th centuries at any rate, Gi̯wang-D̂i̯ĕng, the city where King Mi̯wo (Wu) was believed to have deposited Gi̯wo (Yü) the Great's nine cauldrons, was considered the more important. This is not surprising in view of the fact that the city, as its name implies, became the capital of the Royal Chou when the court was transferred from G'og in the Wei valley to the east in 771 BC. It retained this status for twelve generations, but in about 509 **Kli̯ăng-Gi̯wang (Ching-Wang) chose D̂i̯ĕng-T̂i̯ôg, which had meanwhile attracted to itself the sobriquet of **G'å-to or Lesser Capital, as his metropolis. Towards the end of the Chan-Kuo, however, the honor was restored to Gi̯wang-D̂i̯ĕng by **Nan-Gi̯wang (Nan-Wang), penultimate ruler of the Chou dynasty. Archeological investigation has been focused exclusively

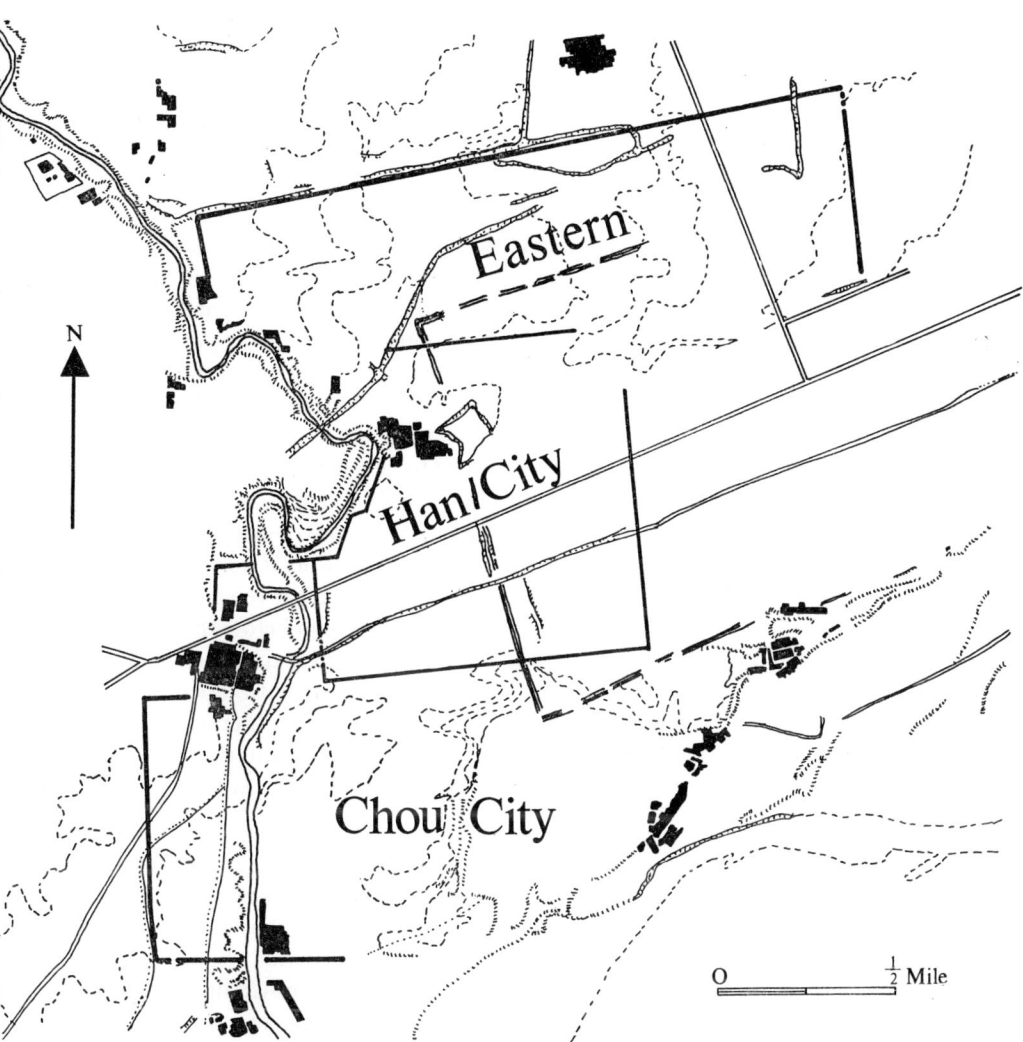

[10] **Gi̯wang-dḭĕng (Wang-Ch'eng), royal city of the Eastern Chou. Based on Ch'en Kung-jou, 'Lo-yang Chien-pin Tung-Chou ch'eng-chih fa-chüeh pao-kao', *K'ao-ku Hsüeh-pao*, no. 2 (1959), fig. 1. This record of excavation can be contrasted with the stylized symbolism that was attributed to Gi̯wang-dḭĕng in the Chinese literary canon and which is depicted in fig. 23 on p. 415.

on the Royal City but, even though work began more than a decade ago, to date only preliminary reports have been published.141

Sections of walls of *hang-t'u* construction which have been traced imply that the city was in the form of a rough square with sides of about 3,000 meters and an area of no less than 8,000,000 square meters. So far only the northern wall, the northern section of the eastern wall, both northern and southern sections of the western wall, and a part of the southern wall where it forms the southwestern corner, have been traced, but these are sufficient to show that the thickness of the walls varied considerably. At their narrowest in the west they barely exceeded five meters, whereas at their widest in the east they attained a thickness of fifteen meters. More than two and a half millennia after their construction the surviving portions range from one-and-a-half to four meters in height. To date no traces of the street plan or of the gates have been uncovered, but it has been suggested that quantities of pottery tiles bearing *t'ao-t'ieh* and cloud-scroll patterns may point to the central and southern sectors of the city as the former sites of the Chou royal palace and other important buildings. A pottery kiln was excavated in the northwestern sector of the enceinte, together with an adjacent house foundation presumed to be the dwelling of a craftsman, and workshops for the manufacture of bone tools and stone ornaments have been brought to light in the same general area. At various points water channels have been uncovered, but there is so far no way of knowing if they formed part of an integrated drainage system. Analysis of the cultural remains found in different parts of the city indicates that the walls were built before the middle of the Ch'un-Ch'iu period and were already undergoing repairs as early as the Chan-Kuo, and that the site was occupied continuously until late in Former Han times, a conclusion which is fully in accord with the literary evidence. Subsequently a much smaller city was constructed within the crumbling walls of Gi̯wang-D̂i̯ĕng and served as the seat of government for Ho-nan county.142

Hou-ma Chen. The choice in 1955 of the historic locality in southern Shan-hsi, known in Chou times as the **Si̯ĕn-D'ien (Hsin-T'ien) or New Fields, for the site of the planned industrial town of Hou-ma Shih led to the mounting of an archeological salvage operation which revealed two partially superimposed cities (Fig. 12, III), dating from the second half of the Ch'un-Ch'iu. These were identified as capitals of Tsi̯ĕn state during the rule of no less than thirteen princes.143

The earlier of the two cities appears to have been that which is situated close to the present-day village of Niu. Its stamped earth walls, now only about one meter high, formed a quadrangular enclosure with sides of 1,340, 1,100, 1,740 and 1,400 meters respectively. Despite this irregularity in the lengths of the sides, the fact that the western and southern walls meet in a right angle imparts a general impression of cardinal orientation to the plan of the city. A section of ditch six meters wide and three or four deep on the outer side of the south wall is probably all that remains of a former defensive moat. Somewhat to the north of the geometrical center of the enceinte is a square, cardinally oriented platform of *hang-t'u* construction, which has sides of 52·5 meters and a height of 6·5. Whereas the northern edge is bounded by a vertical face, the southern is constructed in the form of a ramp. Sherds of pots and tiles would seem to indicate that the platform was surmounted by an architectural structure of some sort. Within the enceinte the excavators have revealed a section of road running from north to south and, in its excavated sector at least, wide enough for two or three chariots to advance abreast. Another road apparently ran round the inner face of the wall.

The second, and later, city is known by the name of the neighboring village of P'ing-wang. It was intruded into the northwest corner of the Niu-Ts'un settlement and it is, in fact, only this intrusive sector of its enceinte which has so far been traced. It is also clear that there was a cardinally oriented, triple-terraced platform of *hang-t'u* somewhere towards the center of the enclosure, though its precise geometrical relationship to the overall plan of the city will be determined only when the line of the rest of the walls has been traced. The excavators' reports leave the impression that this platform, with its three stages, was of more complex construction than that at Niu-Ts'un. It was certainly larger, measuring 75 meters at the base of each side and rising to a height of 8·5 meters. Like the platform at Niu-Ts'un, it was provided with a ramp on the southern side but descended vertically to ground level on the north. And, also like the Niu-Ts'un structure, it carried on its upper level a building of imposing dimensions. The excavators of these sites refer to both the platforms as 'palace foundations', though it seems more likely that they were the mounds on which were raised successive ancestral temples of the Tsjěn ruling family. Certainly they were impressive structures, facing over the city and approached by long ramps.

Remains of dwellings have been discovered both within the city enceinte and grouped in villages to the south and east of the Niu-Ts'un settlement. The dwellings were all semi-subterranean in character, and a high proportion had tiled roofs. Their doorways invariably faced south. Interspersed among them were subterranean and semi-subterranean storage pits, some of unusually large capacity and measuring several meters in both width and depth, together with a number of wells. Not infrequently a storage chamber was linked with a living space to form one habitation complex.

The excavators leave us in no doubt that craft activities were not restricted to the environs of the city but were dispersed through the surrounding countryside. For example, two bronze foundries were located near the southernmost of the villages mentioned in the preceding paragraph, and it is significant that there is good evidence that they engaged in specialized production. Whereas at one site the moulds were designed exclusively for the manufacture of spades, chisels and *pu*-type coinage, at the other emphasis was equally strongly directed towards the manufacture of belt hooks and chariot fittings. In the same neighborhood as these foundries were two workshops, for bone and antler respectively, while a third was found a kilometer and a half to the southeast of Niu-Ts'un. Finally, not far distant from this last site was a craft settlement devoted solely to potting, where kilns and their ancillary apparatus occupied an area of half a square kilometer. Kwang-chih Chang has justly remarked on the similarity of this settlement morphology to that of some Shang urban forms, in which dispersed agricultural and craft villages were integrated into a political, social and economic nexus organized for the support of a ceremonial center. Presumably the groups of animal burials discovered half a kilometer south and three kilometers east of Niu-Ts'un constituted yet another element in this functional unity. The animals – chiefly horses, together with some sheep and a few cattle – had been placed, alive but with their feet tied, upside down in a series of pits arranged regularly in groups of either two or four. One of the pits contained an elephant which had been entombed in the same manner. Bronze and jade ornaments accompanied most of the burials and, although the precise purpose of these entombments is unknown, the excavators are surely right in suggesting that they were associated with important rituals conducted at the Tsjĕn court during Ch'un-Ch'iu times.

A third city has been discovered about ten kilometers to the east of the Sjĕn-D'ien.144 The remains explored so far consist of a double enclosure oriented a few degrees east of north. The original form of the inner enceinte was probably that of a square with a side of 1,100 meters, but the K'uai river has eroded the southern edge of the city so that now only 600 and 1,000 meters of eastern and western wall respectively remain. The surviving walls now reach a maximum height of only three meters and are usually considerably less, but the foundations show that they were originally about twelve meters wide. The outer enceinte was of similar construction, though only the northern and western walls remain, respectively somewhat more than 3,100 and 2,600 meters in length, up to four meters high and nine thick. Some idea of the extent of this city can be gained from the fact that the distance between the two enceintes on the northern side is 1,400 meters, and about the same on the west. The space between the two eastern walls, though, is only a quarter as far, so that the inner city is not centrally placed in relation to the outer. The situation on the south has been irretrievably obscured by the encroachment of the K'uai river. Traditionally this locality was believed to be the site of the capital of **·Ok (Wo), a small independent territory which was occupied by a marquis of Tsjĕn in the 8th century BC. Subsequently it became the seat of the Tsjĕn rulers until they transferred their capital to the New Fields. The excavators seem inclined to follow literary tradition by equating these remains with ·Ok, but the ruins and associated cultural relics appear to be of rather later date. Certainly the city was occupied right through Chan-Kuo and into Han times, though this is not to deny that there may have been a continuity of occupance from earlier periods.

Chao-k'ang Chen. In 1959 a brief report was published recording the discovery of an ancient rectangular enceinte at Chao-k'ang Chen in Hsiang-fen, Shan-hsi, and in 1963 the meager information in this notice was amplified in a somewhat longer article.[145] Apparently the sections of *hang-t'u* wall remaining were sufficient to imply dimensions of five kilometers from north to south and four from east to west. A broad avenue connected opposing gaps, presumably denoting former gates, in the eastern and western walls. A similar opening was observed in the northern wall, but the southern was so poorly preserved that no positive evidence could be adduced for such a gate on that side of the city, although it is to be presumed that such a one did exist. Another section of wall also came to light inside the southeastern corner of the enceinte, but cannot at present be satisfactorily related to the overall plan of the city. Conceivably it could have been part of an inner city such as we have seen existed at ·Ok. The dating of the foundation of this city cannot be precise, but early Eastern Chou potsherds recovered from the *hang-t'u* of the wall imply that it cannot have been established later than the Ch'un-Ch'iu period.

Wu-chi Chen. Two ruined cities have been observed as still existing in districts to the southwest of Wu-an Hsien in southern Ho-pei, territory which formed part of the ancient state of D'i̯og.[146] The more westerly, at Wu-chi Chen, was investigated in 1956 and reported to be unusually well preserved. It comprised a roughly rectangular enceinte 889 meters from east to west, 768 from north to south, and enclosing some 680,000 square meters of land. The walls varied from eight to thirteen meters in width and are still between three and six meters high. There was a gate in each wall after the manner of the site at Chao-k'ang Chen, but in the present case there were also the remains of paved roads leading into the city. Most attention in the preliminary survey – which has been the only investigation undertaken so far – was directed to a series of pottery kilns producing vessels, tiles and bricks, but semi-subterranean dwellings, burials and wells were also noted in the western sectors of the city. The remains in their totality indicate a period of occupation extending from the Eastern Chou through the Former Han.

No information is yet available about the second city in this neighborhood.

THE CHAN-KUO PERIOD

Altogether thirteen cities of Chan-Kuo date have been investigated at least cursorily.

**G'ân-tân (*Han-tan*). It has long been recognized in traditional literature that the ruins situated some four kilometers to the southwest of the present city of Han-tan in southern Ho-pei are those of the ancient capital of D'i̯og state. The city itself was in the form of a cardinally oriented and only slightly irregular square, with two sides each of 1,475 meters, one of 1,456 and one of 1,387 (Fig. 11).[147] The Japanese excavators of the site provided us with one of the very few estimates of the original dimensions of a city wall : they accorded it a reconstructed height of no less than fifteen meters and a reconstructed width at the base of more than twenty meters. They also discovered gaps in the wall which were associated with debris of brick and tile, and consequently interpreted as gates, but their occurrence was irregular. Whereas there was only one in the east and two in both south and west, there were three in the north, which, given the predominantly southerly orientation of Chinese town planning, is a somewhat singular arrangement.

Within the city the north-south axis of the enceinte was delineated by four *hang-t'u* platforms. The most southerly, known locally as Lung T'ai or Dragon Terrace, was the largest : 13·5 meters high, and with sides of 210 × 288 meters at the base. Surprisingly no cultural remains of any significance were discovered on its summit. By contrast, the next platform to the north, 4·5 meters high and with basal dimensions of 49 × 51 meters, apparently supported a two-storey structure, for two parallel rows of stone pillar foundations were found *in situ*, together with flanking rows of bricks. The third platform, three meters high and 60 × 70 meters at the base, yielded tiles, pottery, knife-money and a few bronze and iron implements, but no stone foundations. Finally, the fourth and northernmost platform differed from the others in being circular, with a diameter of 62 meters and a height of 7·5.

This then is the city proper, but this simple plan which has formed the basis for numerous subsequent Chinese cities is, in this instance, complicated by the addition of an eastern annex. This consists of an enclosure about half the size of that of the main city, the eastern wall of which forms the western wall of the annex. The southern and northern walls of the annex are each 875 meters in length, and the eastern and western walls exceed those of the city proper by a few meters only. The annex also contains two square, cardinally oriented platforms arranged along a line parallel to, and to the west of, the north-south axis. There is, too, an as yet unexplained section of wall, more than 520 meters in length, running due north from the northern wall of the city proper, which it joins slightly to the east of the mid-point. Finally, both inside and outside the enceintes there are ten additional *hang-t'u* platforms, all square or rectangular apart from one which is circular, and all bearing bricks and tiles on their summits.

The cultural debris associated with this city points unequivocally to the Chan-Kuo period, which is why it is being discussed at this point, but G'ân-tân

THE ARCHEOLOGICAL RECORD

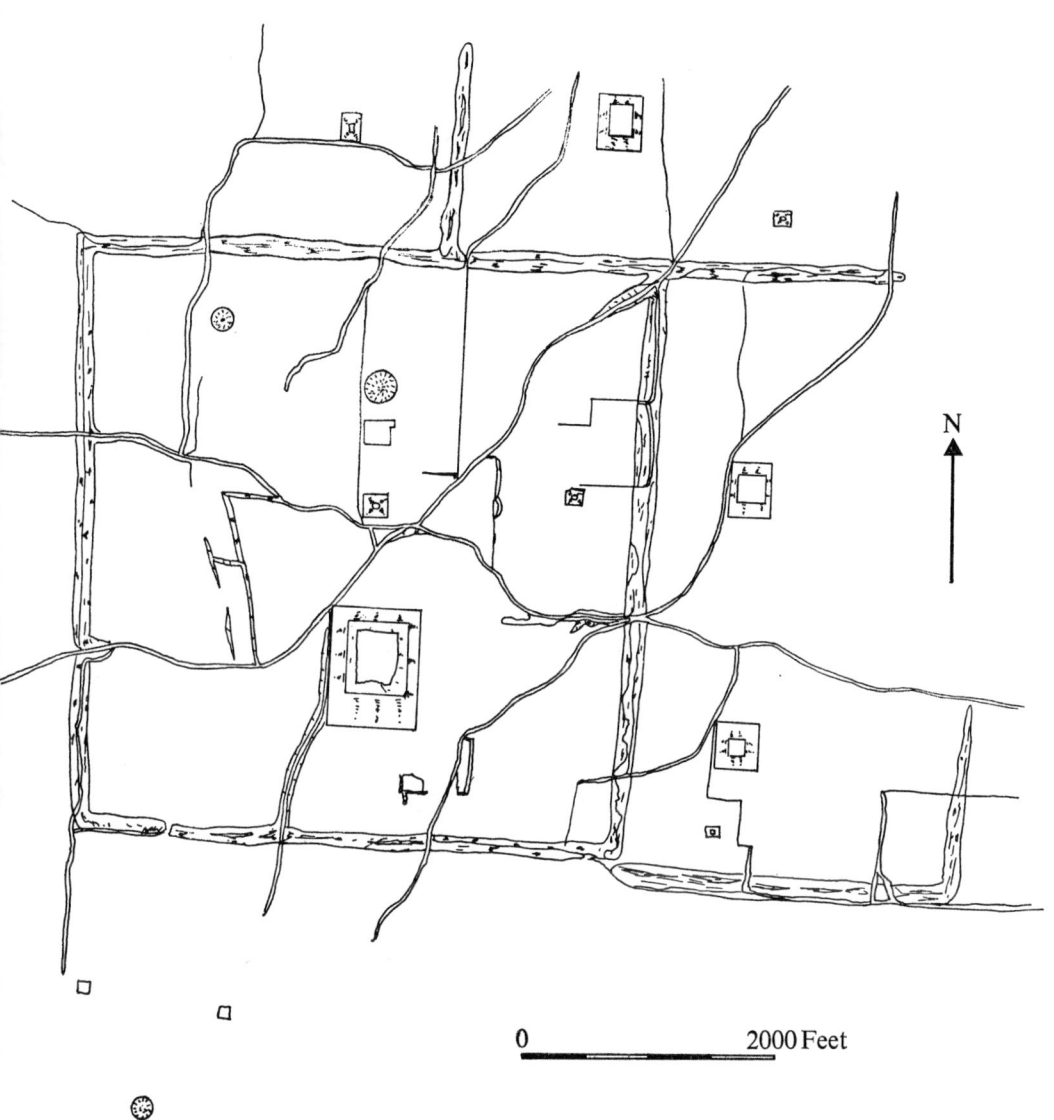

[11] **G'ân-tân (Han-tan), capital of the state of *D'i̯og (Chao) from 386 to 228 BC. Redrawn from Komai Kazuchika and Sekino Takeshi, 'Han-tan', *Archaeologia Orientalis*, series B, vol. 7 (1954), fig. 2.

was first mentioned as a city of Tsi̯ĕn in reference to the year 500 B C.[148] However, it was not until 386 B C that it was chosen as the capital of the succession state of Dʻi̯og. It continued in that role until Dʻi̯og was extinguished (mi̯at) by the armies of Dzʻi̯ĕn in 228 B C.

**Gʻå-to (= *the Lesser Capital*). Excavations were carried out on the site of this ancient city of the state of ·Ian, near I-Hsien in Ho-pei, as early as 1930, and were resumed in 1958.[149] As it exists today the enceinte takes the form of an irregular figure with maximum measurements of 8,300 meters from east to west and 3,930 from north to south (Fig. 12, V). However, this curiously shaped enclosure gives all the indications of having been built up through time from a more or less regularly ordered nucleus, perhaps a square or rectangular enceinte, by the addition of sundry extensions and annexes. Indeed, excavations have already revealed that the southeastern sector was at one time separated from the rest of the city by a wall so that it constituted a smaller enclosure of 4,500 × 3,200 meters. Even today the average height of the walls exceeds five meters.

A distinctive feature of this settlement as it exists at present is a scatter of more than fifty *hang-tʻu* platforms. They occur both inside and outside the enceinte but are particularly numerous in the northern sectors. Most are believed to have been burial mounds, but several in the northeastern parts of the city may have served as raised foundations for temples, much in the manner that similar structures in Gʻân-tân did. The largest of these platforms, which attains a height of more than eight meters and which is known to the local people as Lao-lao Tʻai (the Old Dame's Terrace), is actually outside the northern wall. It is square in shape with three terraces carved from its southern face, and it is surmounted by a circular mound, an arrangement which is reminiscent of the two parts of the diviner's board (*shih*), in which a discoidal plate representing the heavens (*tʻien-pʻan*) was superimposed on a square earth plate (*ti-pʻan*).[150] Architectural remains, pottery, bronze and iron weapons, ornaments, and coins were found on the upper terrace of this structure in some quantity.

It is thought that the inner enclosure was the site of the more important buildings in the city when Gʻå-to was the capital of ·Ian. It is in the northern part of this area that the excavators found most of the more imposing platforms, together with a row of *hang-tʻu* foundations arranged symmetrically in relation to the platforms and perpendicular to the inner northern wall, a pattern of construction which led them to infer that this was the palace precinct. Immediately to the southwest of this enclave are the remains of iron and bronze foundries, and in the southern part of the inner enclosure are relics of what has been interpreted as *śi̯ag-ńi̯ĕn* quarters, perhaps those of artisans or retainers. The city was probably occupied more or less continuously from 697 to 226 B C, but the cultural remains so far revealed relate exclusively to the Chan-Kuo period.

**Mįwo-Dįĕng (*Wu-Chʻeng*). The ruins of this city, which at one time formed part of the state of Dʻjog, are enclosed within a cardinally oriented enceinte approximately square in shape and with sides of 1·1 kilometers. The walls are twelve meters in thickness at the base, and five openings have been uncovered in each of the northern and western sides. Although the enceinte has been traced on the other two sides, the walls are in such poor condition that it has not been possible to elicit the arrangement of their gates. A ditch some 20–30 meters in length, below the outer edge of the northern wall, would appear to have formed part of a moat. Within the enclosure tiles, potsherds, *pu* coins, spindle whorls and bronze arrowheads indicate a floruit during the period of the Contending States.[151]

Tsʻai-Chuang. This locality, situated to the southwest of Chou-kʻou Tien in Ho-pei, is the site of the remains of another, but much smaller, city of ancient ·Ian. The walls can be traced on three sides, being in places still as much as three meters high, but evidence is lacking for the northern boundary. However, it is believed that the enceinte was originally square with sides of about 300 meters. A protruding section adjacent to the western wall may indicate the existence of a former annex or merely a reinforcement of a city gate.[152]

Lin-tzŭ. The ruins of an ancient city at Lin-tzŭ in northern Shan-tung, which has been identified as the capital of Dzʻiər state during the Chan-Kuo period, was investigated by Japanese archeologists in 1940–1 and again by Chinese in 1958.[153] The *hang-tʻu* walls formed a roughly rectangular shape, with approximate cardinal orientation and overall dimensions of 3,000 meters from east to west and 4,000 from north to south. The southeastern corner, which disturbs the regularity of the rectangular shape (Fig. 12, VI), may have been an addition to an essentially regular figure. Moreover, a smaller enceinte in the form of a square of about 1,350 meters side has been constructed over the southwestern corner of the main enclosure. Sekino Takeshi, the archeologist who excavated at this site in 1940, suggested that the smaller enclosure was the palace precinct of the prince of Dzʻiər. If so, an oval-shaped *hang-tʻu* platform, some 65 × 73 meters in size at ground level and situated just to the west of the center of this enclosure, may have been the supremely sacred spot of the Dzʻiər territories, the altar to the Dzʻiər god of the soil. A wide range of cultural remains have been found at sites scattered through the rest of the city, including tiles, bricks, potsherds, knife-money, bronze arrow heads and, allegedly, cowry shells, a clay mould for the making of bronze mirrors and a clay seal – though these last were obtained by purchase from present-day inhabitants rather than by excavation.

Ch'ü-fu. To the northeast of Ch'ü-fu in central Shan-tung are the ruins of a capital of the old state of Lo.[154] Its walls enclose an irregularly bounded oval measuring some 3·5 kilometers from west to east and about 2·5 from north to south. There is evidence of a single gate in the east, of two in the south and, curiously enough, of three in the north, but no trace has so far been uncovered of any entrances in the western side.

T'eng-Hsien. The ruins of two ancient cities have been discovered in T'eng-Hsien in southern Shan-tung.[155] The first, lying about twenty kilometers to the southeast of the present-day hsien city, are the remains of the capital of the former state of **Sjat (Hsüeh). They are enclosed in a rectangular enceinte of 3·6 × 2·8 kilometers, the walls of which still in places reach up to ten meters in height. There are the remains of one gate on the eastern side, and of two on both north and south, but again no evidence of an entrance on the west.

The second cluster of ruins in the vicinity of T'eng-Hsien are those of the ancient city of **D'əng (T'eng).[156] The general plan of the settlement is reminiscent of that of ·Ok, for it consists of a rectangular inner precinct of 900 × 600 meters, surrounded by an outer enceinte of 1,500 × 1,000 meters. The inner wall averages about three meters in height and its thickness varies from six to nine meters. There are traces of four gates, one on each side of the city.

Ch'ang-Chou. South of Ch'ang-Chou (Wu-chin) in Chiang-su are the ruins of the former capital of the ethnically Gi̯wăt state of **·Jam. The layout of this capital is more complex than any discussed previously.[157] At the heart of the settlement is a roughly square enceinte oriented a few degrees east of north and measuring about a kilometer in circumference. It is known today as the Tzŭ-Ch'eng or Prince's City. Surrounding this innermost enclosure is another, also roughly square and of similar orientation, which is known as the Inner Wall. It is about three kilometers in circumference and was formerly bordered on its outer side by a moat. Finally, both these enceintes are set eccentrically within a third some six kilometers in circumference and known, appropriately enough, as the Outer Wall. This third wall was roughly circular rather than square, and was also moated on its outer side. Today both Outer and Inner Walls are razed almost to ground level, but the boundary of the Tzŭ-Ch'eng is even yet a prominent feature in the landscape. Between the Outer and Inner Walls in the western sector of the city is still to be seen a row of three earthen mounds bearing evidence of former buildings on their summits. Cultural remains associated with this settlement consist predominantly of pottery, stone tools, bronze vessels and, in the moat surrounding the Inner Wall, three dugout canoes, representing a mode of transport appropriate to the water-threaded terrain of the Yang-tzŭ delta.

Figure 12 (on the two pages following)

Plans of representative Chou cities on a uniform scale.

I. **Mi̯wo-di̯ĕng (Wu-Ch'eng), a city of **D'i̯og (Chao) during the period of the Contending States. Based on Ao Ch'eng-lung, 'Ho-pei Tz'ŭ-Hsien Chiang-wu Ch'eng tiao-ch'a chien-pao,' *K'ao-ku*, no. 7 (1959), fig. 3.

II. **G'ân-tân (Han-tan), capital of **D'i̯og (Chao) from 386 to 228 B C. Redrawn from Komai Kazuchika and Sekino Takeshi, 'Han-tan,' *Archaeologia Orientalis*, series B, vol. 7 (1954), fig. 2.

III. Remains of a capital of the Prince of **Tsi̯ĕn (Chin) in a late phase of the Spring-and-Autumn period. Based on Ch'ang Wen-chai, 'Hou-ma ti-ch'ü ku-ch'eng-chih-ti hsin-fa-hsien' *Wen-wu Ts'an-k'ao Tzŭ-liao*. no. 12 (1958), fig. 1.

IV. **Gi̯wang-di̯ĕng (Wang-Ch'eng), royal city of the Eastern Chou. Based on Ch'en Kung-jou, 'Lo-yang Chien-pin Tung-Chou ch'eng-chih fa-chüeh pao-kao,' *K'ao-ku Hsüeh-pao*, no. 2 (1959), fig. 1.

V. The **G'å (Hsia) capital in the state of **·Ian (Yen). Based on Hsieh Hsi-i, 'Yen Hsia-tu i-chih so-chi,' *Wen-wu Ts'an-k'ao Tzŭ-liao*, no. 9 (1957), p. 61, and Huang Ching-lüeh, 'Yen Hsia-tu ch'eng-chih tiao-ch'a pao-kao,' *K'ao-ku*, no. 1 (1962) fig. 1.

VI. An ancient city at Lin-tzŭ which has been identified as a capital of **Dz'i̯ər (Ch'i). Based on Shan-tung Sheng Wen-wu Kuan-li-ch'u, 'Shan-tung Lin-tzŭ Ch'i-ku-ch'eng shih-chüeh chien-pao,' *K'ao-ku*, no. 6 (1961), fig. 1.

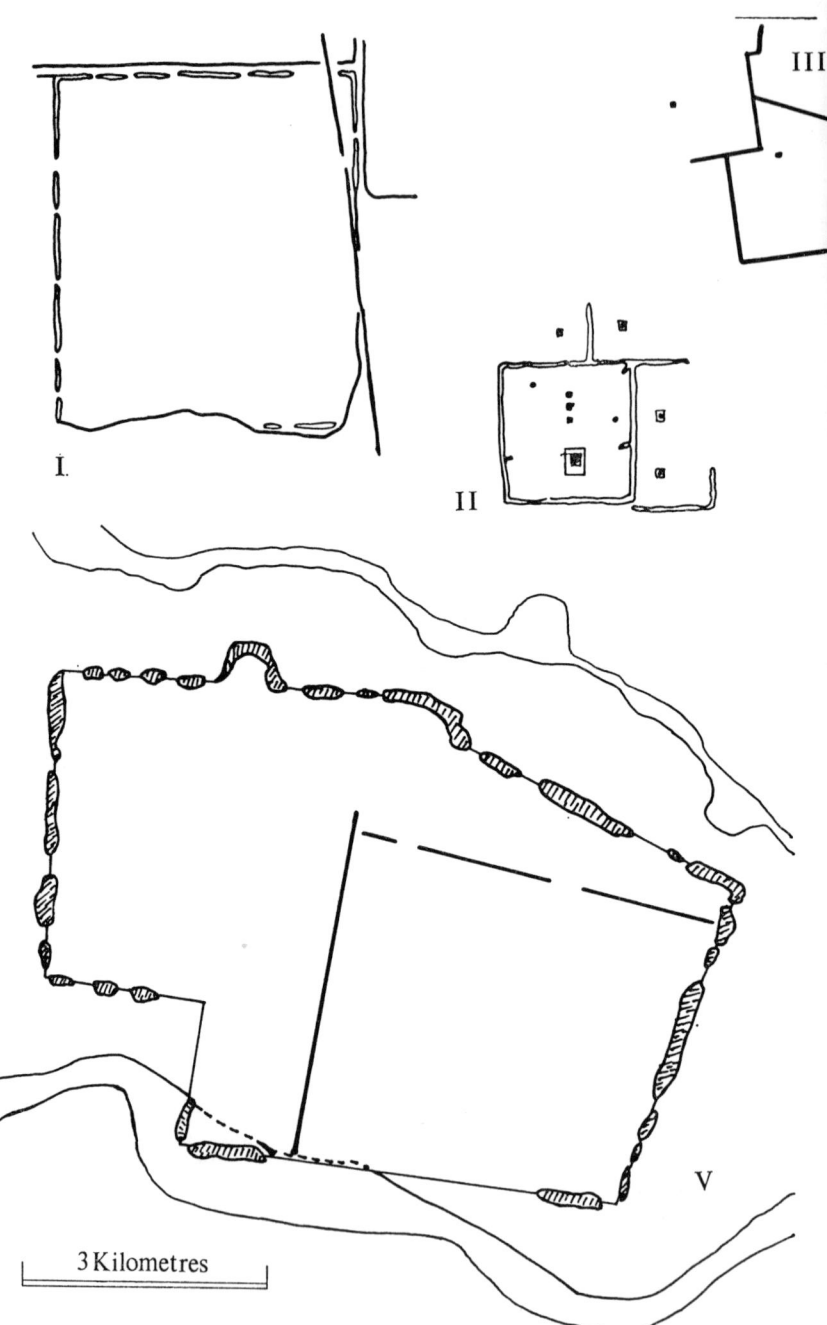

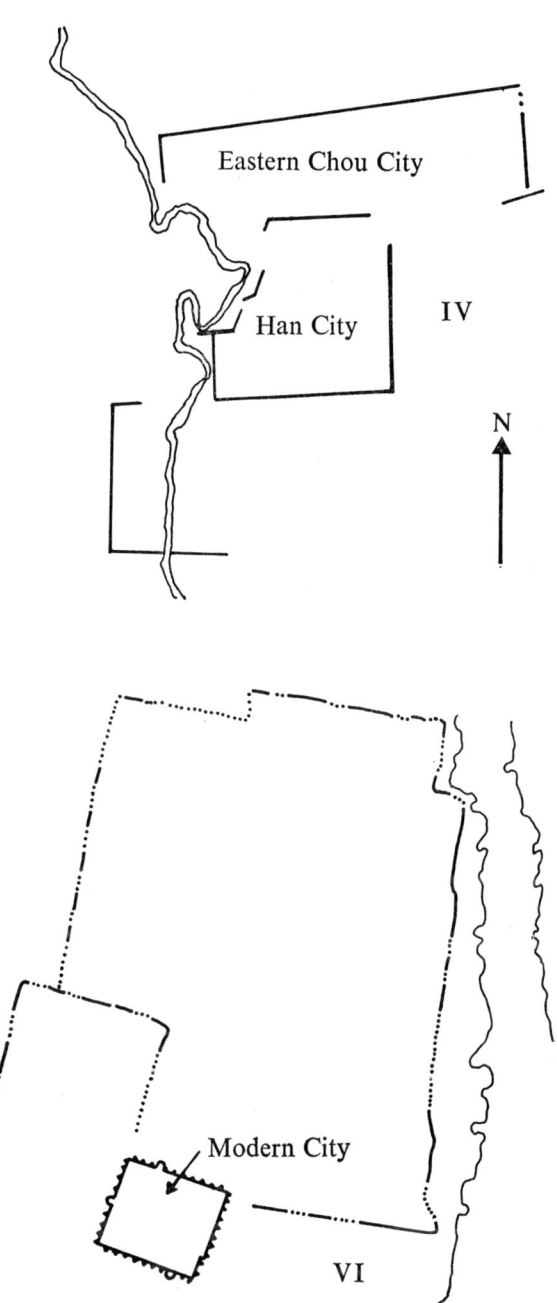

Hsi-Shan Hsien. The ruins of an ancient city have been discovered about a kilometer and a half northeast of present-day Hsi-Shan in southwestern Honan.[158] It was much smaller than most of the examples we have discussed, being roughly in the form of a rectangle only 800 meters from east to west and 850 from north to south. There can be no doubt that the settlement was constructed with the needs of defence in mind, for both its eastern and western flanks are set atop of sheer precipices, while the northern and southern walls are protected by moats.

Nan-yang Hsien. The present *hsien* city of Nan-yang occupies a part of an earlier and much larger enceinte on the same site. So far no excavation has been undertaken and the site has received only cursory notice.[159] The northeastern corner of the ancient enclosure is more than two kilometers to the northeast of the present city, and its *hang-t'u* walls have been traced for a kilometer and a half in roughly western and southern directions. At their base they were formerly about seven meters thick.

Hua-yin Hsien. At Yüeh-Chen in Hua-yin Hsien in Shen-hsi ruins have been found[160] which are thought to have been those of **·Iəm-tsi̯ĕn (Yin-chin), a fortress city built by the Gi̯wad rulers close to their frontier with Tsi̯ĕn and constituting an important node in a defensive system of which the great wall of Gi̯wad was perhaps the most impressive feature. The ancient city was roughly oval in shape, with its longer axis running approximately north-south. Sections of wall survive only in the north and west, the other two sides having been razed to the ground. The walls were 7·4 meters wide at the base, but were reinforced by an additional thickness of 5·6 meters where they adjoined a gate, and the gate itself revealed traces of additional fortification.

There has also been a cursory survey of a walled city of Ho-nan which is thought to have formed part of ancient G'ân, one of the succession states of Tsi̯ĕn. So far no more than a short note on the morphology of the site has appeared in print, and it is impossible to evaluate the significance of the city beyond pointing out that it appears to have some pretensions to cardinal orientation and axiality.[161]

Literary Sources

The fact that only scientifically acquired archeological evidence can be considered primary for the study of Western, and perhaps later, Chou urbanism does not mean that the transmitted texts are completely worthless, but it is true that their value is different from that accorded them by traditional Chinese scholarship. They are not so much records of events as vehicles for the aspirations and values of subsequent ages. In a word, they have been archetyped, partly through an unconscious process natural to the passage of time and partly through consciously undertaken historiographical editing and exegesis at least from Ch'un-Ch'iu times onwards.

There is a relatively extensive literature relating to the Chou dynasty but none of it is devoted specifically to the character of cities, so that materials for a history of Chou urbanism have to be abstracted from a large corpus of texts dealing with Chou civilization in general. They include works of an annalistic and genealogical character, prescriptions for rituals and ceremonies, folk lore and folk songs, dynastic hymns, philosophical treatises, moral tracts, and divination texts. The vast bulk of this material stems from the Eastern Chou and later, so much so in fact that reliable written records of Western Chou times are scarcely more numerous than are those for the Shang era. Indeed, the same literary sources often serve for both periods. The more important of these, such as the *Shu-Ching*, *Chu-shu Chi-nien*, *Shih-Chi* and *Shih-Ching* have already been discussed in connection with Shang urbanism in Chapter One.

As the activities of editors have been so pervasive, it is a matter of great difficulty to distinguish those texts which contain authentic accounts of genuine events from those which have been intentionally amended to afford support for later value systems and moral judgments. So intractable does this problem appear at first sight that some scholars, among whom Lou Kan-jou is fairly representative,[162] have eschewed the use of all texts other than the *Ch'un-Ch'iu*, *Tso-Chuan* and *Kuo-Yü*. Just after World War II Professor Bernhard Karlgren made an attempt to evaluate the available texts from the standpoint of their historical reliability. From a combined philological and historical point of view he distinguished what he called 'free' pre-Han texts from 'systematizing' or 'reconstructive' pre-Han texts, and both from Earlier and Later Han systematized texts.[163] Free texts are those in which, in his own words, 'accounts of ancient men, happenings and cults are given *en passant*, either as occasional records of events or inserted in speeches of politicians and philosophers, who refer to current traditions in elucidating some moral or political theme.'[164] Such, for example, are the *Shu-Ching*, *Shih-Ching*, *Tso-Chuan*, *Kuo-yü*, *Chan-kuo Ts'e*, *Lun-yü*, *Meng-tzŭ*, *Mo-tzŭ*, *Chuang-tzŭ*, *Li-Sao*, and *T'ien-Wen*. Systematizing texts, on the other hand, 'are the products of scholars who deliberately tried to lay down laws or make a consistent whole of the ancient traditions and ritual ideas. Their goal was to work up and compile a diffuse and heterogeneous material, to create a system.'[165] To this class belong, say, the major part of the *Li-Chi* and the whole of both the *I-Li* and *Chou-Li*, together with numerous later texts. Karlgren, by reason of his long familiarity with the texts and immense sinological erudition, was confident that he could distinguish between them. However, not all sinologists have been so confident. Wolfram Eberhard, in particular, has argued strongly that the distinction between these two classes of texts is not made anything like so easily as Karlgren supposed.[166] As an example of one of Karlgren's free texts which does in fact contain interpolations from Han times we may cite the *Tso-Chuan*, in which were inserted passages designed to validate the legitimacy of the usurper Wang-Mang's newly established dynasty.[167] If this is true of the *Tso-Chuan*, then, as the texts are closely related from the point of view of filiation, the same must also hold for the *Kuo-Yü*. On the other hand, what formerly appeared to be imaginative glosses on the genealogy of the Shang kings in Ssŭ-ma Ch'ien's *Shih-Chi* have since been confirmed by fully attested inscriptions from the oracle archives of that dynasty, a situation which can only be explained by hypothesizing that Ssŭ-ma Ch'ien had access to some treatise now lost, possibly, as Karlgren himself suggests, a genealogical list preserved by the ruling house of Sông.[168]

According to Eberhard, the consistency with which legends and beliefs are presented in the free texts, even in those of the most opposed schools, stems not, as Karlgren believed, from the preservation of their pristine form and freedom from corruption but from the unity of the *Weltanschauung* of the men who transmitted, and only too frequently amended and edited, them. In short, Eberhard denies the validity, and even in many instances the possibility, of assigning a particular text to one of Karlgren's categories, and argues that each section and aspect of a work should be examined on its intrinsic merits, in terms – as he puts it – of its structural matrix.[169] From this standpoint all texts are in a manner of speaking authentic in that all preserve versions of events presented in the context of their respective authors' ideological predilections. Some will have emphasized an aspect of which they approved, others will have suppressed it in the interests of denigration or, possibly, have selected an entirely different episode with which to press their point, but none of this was a prerogative of Han exegetes : Chou authors were no less prone to view the past in terms of their own present. What makes the Han glosses so prominent in our thought is that they frequently provide the form in which the text has been preserved until our own time. But even these glossifiers sometimes had access to texts no longer available to us, and an apparently late (because not confirmed by an extant earlier mention) version of events may sometimes be more reliable than that preserved in an earlier, but no less severely amended, recension. This is not to deny the immensity of the problems associated with the transmission of Chou texts or, in many instances, the opacity of Han glosses, but rather to question the absolute validity of a dichotomy into free and systematized texts in the sense in which Karlgren used those terms.

It would clearly be impracticable at this juncture to attempt a critical evaluation of all the literature relevant to urban evolution in Chou times, for that would encompass virtually all the literature relevant to Chou political, social, and economic development. The following notes are, therefore, restricted to a few of the texts of more than usual importance for present purposes. The most valuable corpus of written evidence for the period of the Eastern Chou is without doubt that incorporated in the *Ch'un-Ch'iu* and its associated commentaries. *Ch'un-Ch'iu*, meaning literally 'Springs and Autumns', was a generic name applied in Middle Chou times to the archival records of at least some of the Chou states,[170] but all have been lost, perhaps destroyed during the proscription of 213 BC, except a condensed and apparently garbled recension of the chronicles of the state of Lo from 722 to 481 BC. This is the *Ch'un-Ch'iu* which we have today, and which owes its preservation in no small measure to the fact that it was supposed to have undergone some unspecified form of editing by Confucius.[171] It has traditionally been held that in the process of redaction the Sage passed moral judgments on the actors, and thus handed on to posterity a grammar of political ethics. The difficulty resides in the fact that he expressed his judgments not by explicit statements but by a discriminatory use of terminology, a device which encouraged the rise of competing schools of exegesis. Confucius did, it is alleged, expound some of his judgments orally to his disciples, and these explanations were supposedly incorporated in explicatory traditions (*chuan*), of which three are still extant. Two of these, the *Kung-yang Chuan* (*The Tradition according to Kung-Yang*) and the *Ku-liang Chuan* (*The Tradition according to Ku-liang*),[172] are concerned principally to expatiate on the principles allegedly informing Confucius's moral judgments, but the third, the *Tso-Chuan* (*The Tradition according to Tso*[173]) confines itself mainly to elaborating the background to events which the Master had chronicled in terse, often elliptical, phrases. Towards the close of the Chou dynasty Tso's chronicle was arbitrarily combined with the annals of Tsjĕn, Tṣ'jo, and Gjwad, and the whole subsequently distributed as a fragmented commentary on the separate sections of the *Ch'un-Ch'iu*. It is, consequently, quite proper to regard it as an historical compendium sectionalized so as to fit into the framework of a condensed version of the annals of Lo, and it is this combination of documentarily attested historical fact and supplementary oral tradition which constitutes the single most important literary source for the history of the Ch'un-Ch'iu period. In its present form it is said to comprise 170,000 Chinese characters, which would be the equivalent of at least 300,000 words in translation into any European language.

As we now reject the traditional view that the *Tso-Chuan* was solely Confucius's exposition of the esoteric implications of the *Ch'un-Ch'iu*, so we can equally disregard the belief which was espoused by the *avant-garde* historians of the sceptical movement at the beginning of this century that it was deliberately forged by Liu-Hsin (or by one of his associates) for political ends.[174] Analyses by Karlgren, Maspero and Ojima have disposed of any basis for such an argument. As early as 1926 Karlgren concluded that the Tso Tradition exhibited a homogeneous grammar consonant with a 4th-century date.[175] Subsequently, he was able to demonstrate that the text was known to Mao-Heng and Mao-Ch'ang when they wrote their famous commentary on the

Shih-Ching at some time prior to the middle of the 2nd century BC.[176] Meanwhile, Maspero,[177] utilizing some previous investigations by Ojima,[178] had succeeded in establishing that the ritual and ethical tradition contained erroneous references to winter solstices and eclipses which must have been calculated between 352 and 238 BC, while the chronicle sections incorporated exact prophecies of events which actually occurred as late as 327 BC, so that their redaction must have taken place after that date. Analysis of the same prophecies led Liu Ju-lin to conclude that the chronicle sections were compiled between 375 and 340 BC.[179] These scholars are by no means in complete agreement among themselves, but their combined efforts point uncompromisingly towards a date in the 4th century, and probably in the second half of that century, for the compilation of the *Tso-Chuan*. However, William Hung has also shown that several passages contain ideas which first entered into the amalgam of Chinese thought in later centuries, notably in Han times when Liu-Hsin set his imprint upon the work.[180] There is also reason to believe that sections of commentary were incorporated into the text at different times so that, although the *Tso-Chuan* demonstrably preserves a great deal of ancient material, it is prudent to adopt a sceptical attitude to the moralizings which occur from time to time. Such passages are easily concocted, and were the favorite media of redactors who wished to use a classical text for propaganda purposes. As early as Sung times, scholars such as Lin-Li questioned the authenticity of numerous of the paragraphs beginning with the phrase 'The superior man says . . .' and Legge passed the warning on to the modern world, together with a list of passages which he considered dubious.[181] And, clearly, passages which successfully predict events whose outcome could not have been known to their authors have been tampered with at some time or other. In the present work I have eschewed such passages as sources of factual information about events in ancient times but, even so, the *Tso-Chuan* remains a massive repository of material for any scholar concerned with Chou society.

Much the same situation obtains with regard to the voluminous *Kuo-Yü* (*Discourses on the States*), for long believed to have been fashioned from the materials on the Chou states other than *Lo* which were accumulated by Tso-ch'iu Ming during his preparation of the *Tso-Chuan*. As such it has traditionally been classified as an External Tradition (*Wai-Chuan*), while the *Tso*, *Kung-yang* and *Ku-liang* have been designated Internal Traditions (*Nei-Chuan*). Since Sung times, however, doubt has increasingly been cast on the common authorship of the *Tso-Chuan* and *Kuo-Yü*. Bernhard Karlgren in recent times, for instance, has, on grammatical and linguistic grounds, attributed these works to different authors working contemporaneously in the same school.[182] William Hung, on the other hand, has concluded that the *Kuo-Yü* is older than the *Tso-Chuan* and has attributed it to the very end of the Chan-Kuo period.[183] Hung's thesis is, in fact, a more sophisticated version of an interpretation put forward in 1891 by K'ang Yu-wei, who maintained that the *Tso-Chuan* was excised from a truly massive recension of the *Kuo-Yü* by Liu-Hsin.[184] Whatever view be taken in this matter, it is evident that this text must be used with caution.

Two other works which partake of the same general character as those we have been discussing also require discriminating attention. The *Lü-Shih Ch'un-Ch'iu* (*Master Lü's Springs and Autumns*), in twenty-six chüan, is an apparently eclectic collection of moral and political essays, compiled under the patronage of the Dz'jĕn chancellor Lü Pu-wei.[185] According to a codicil which has found its way into the middle of the book, it was completed in 239 BC. A great deal of the material which goes to make up this work has been traced back by Li Chün-chih and Liu Ju-lin[186] to its origins in the lore of the competing schools of the Chan-Kuo period so that, although subject to redaction in Ch'in times, it does preserve a reasonably faithful record of some aspects of Chan-Kuo thought. It appears virtually certain that a numerological symbolism underlies the form of this work. It is divided into three main sections symbolizing the Chinese trinity of Heaven, Earth and Man. The first of these sections is subdivided into twelve chapters, each of which begins with a schedule of the rites and functions appropriate to a particular month of the year. The number associated with Heaven is, of course, twelve, but each of these chapters is further sub-divided into five sub-sections, representing the five elements which govern the workings of Heaven. The second main section is composed of eight chapters, each of eight sub-sections, eight being the figure numerologically assigned to the Earth. Man, symbolized by the third main section, is represented by six chapters, each with six sub-sections.

The second of these works is the *Chan-Kuo Ts'e* (*Intrigues of the Contending States*), one of the earliest of a class of writings known to the Chinese since Sui times as *Tsa-Shih* or *Miscellaneous Histories*. The authors of the patently discrete sections of this work are unknown, but the materials seem to have been selected from the records of Chan-Kuo diplomats, strategists and politicians which had been preserved in the Han Imperial Library, and the resulting collectaneum edited either then, or later by the scholar Liu-Hsiang. Since that time the book has undergone extensive alteration, chiefly at the hands of Sung exegetes, who attempted to replace lacunae in the text with imaginative glosses. The *Chan-Kuo Ts'e* in its present form contains numerous anachronisms, duplications and inconsistencies, which reveal only too clearly its composite, and even cumulative, character, but nevertheless the society, institutions and values which it portrays are essentially those of Chan-Kuo times.[187]

The books of ritual which at first sight appear to convey so much information about ancient China, and which have provided the material for numerous expository accounts of Chou institutions, are in fact nearly all later compilations. It was these works to which Karlgren pointed as prime exemplars of his class of systematizing texts (p. 151), and there is no doubt that they are, as he said, 'the products of scholars who deliberately tried to lay down laws or make a consistent whole of the ancient traditions and ritual ideas'. Nevertheless, it can also be shown that some at least of their information is based on fact deriving from even as early as the Western Chou period. The records of investiture ceremonies preserved on bronze ritual vessels, for example, bear out in a general way the prescriptions of the *Li-Chi*, and the arrangement of the tablets in the ancestral temples as detailed in the same work [188] has been partially confirmed by archeological investigation. Of the fifty-five investiture ceremonies described in Western Chou epigraphy and published by Kuo Mo-jo,[189] forty-four took place, as the *Li-Chi* prescribes, in the royal ancestral temple. For nine no locality was mentioned, and only two were definitely performed outside the capital. One of these was carried out at D'jěng (Cheng), a site which possessed considerable ritual significance in the early years of the dynasty and which was itself to become the Chou capital in 509 BC, while the other took place at **G'ân-ts'jěg (Han-tz'ŭ) when the king was undertaking a ceremonial progress through the realm.[190] In this particular instance the investiture was still carried out in the presence of the royal court. There is, of course, the possibility that bronze inscriptions similar to those studied by Kuo Mo-jo may have been used by Han systematizers as a model for an idealized ceremony, but, if so, this only serves as a guarantee of the accuracy of their reconstruction of the event. Of a more disruptive character are the warnings of Noel Barnard against epigraphic forgery, possibly on a considerable scale.[191] But on the whole it would seem that the testimony of epigraphy affords no inconsiderable support for the authenticity of certain sections of the ritual books.

A nucleus of what was later to be constituted as the *Chou-Li* (*Chou Ritual*) seems to have been in existence in some form late in the Chou era, because it featured among the works most actively suppressed by Shih Huang-ti in 213 BC. In the middle of the 2nd century BC a copy in archaic script, which had somehow escaped the proscription, was presented to the imperial library, where in about 40 BC it came to the notice of Liu-Hsiang. Unfortunately the last section of this copy was missing, and it was as a replacement for it that Liu-Hsiang substituted the *K'ao-kung Chi* (*Record of Artificers*), a work itself of some antiquity, possibly originally an official document of the state of Dz'iər. During the Han the whole work was known as the *Chou-Kuan* (*Officers of Chou*), a name which was changed during the *Tsjěn (Chin) dynasty to *Chou Kuan-li* (*Official ritual of the Chou*). Only in the T'ang did *Chou-Li* become the official title. During the Sung, scholars in general tended to discredit the work as a source for the study of Chou institutions, and Hu An-kuo went so far as to brand it a forgery of Liu-Hsin. However, Chu-Hsi's researches did much to re-establish the authenticity of the *Chou-Li*, which was not again questioned until K'ang Yu-wei mounted his attack on the veracity of the classics at the end of the 19th century. K'ang's allegations were in turn refuted by Ojima, Maspero, and Karlgren (cp. p. 151).¹⁹² But none of this debate has done much to elucidate the crux that faces all researchers into Chou government and society, namely to what extent does the elaborately structured hierarchy described in the *Chou-Li* reflect actual conditions during the Western Chou period ? After a recent re-evaluation of the evidence, Dr Sven Broman concluded that the Chou-Li 'depicts a governing system which, in all its essentials, prevailed in middle and late feudal Chou in the various states and has its roots in the system pertaining to late Yin and early Chou.'¹⁹³ If this were so, then Western Chou administration was of a rigidity unparalleled in any other known governmental system. My own reading of inscriptional materials and of the available 'unsystematizing' (Karlgren's 'free') texts does not lead me to the same conclusion, and, although Broman has adduced an impressive quantity of evidence, I am not convinced that it really implies such an involuted and inflexible system of government as that which the ritual texts portray. Nevertheless, faced with Broman's closely reasoned arguments, I am no little encouraged to find that Professor Creel shares my opinion.¹⁹⁴ His interpretation seems to accord closely with the general implications of the little that we know or can infer about Western Chou government from other sources. Briefly, he believes that the *Chou-Li* preserves a late Chan-Kuo elaboration of a system of government which did actually exist at one time, but that the relative contributions of Western Chou ritualists and later systematizers is still unsettled.

The *Li-Chi* (*Record of Rituals*) and *I-Li* (*Ceremonies and Rituals*) are less pertinent to present purposes and need not be discussed here. Both are essentially similar in character to the *Chou-Li*, that is they are 2nd-century compilations, systematizations in Karlgren's phrase, of earlier materials, which subsequently underwent further modification.¹⁹⁵

The *Kuan-tzŭ*, in twenty-four chüan, is another of those ancient works which would be a valuable source for the background of Chou urbanism if its text could be dated with any degree of certainty. Although best known for its discussion of early economic theory, in particular an application of the quantity theory of money, this series of treatises contains a great deal of material relating to the ideologies of Chou China, political and administrative organization, etiquette, logic, natural phenomena, and even a chüan of what should perhaps be described as wisdom literature. Already by the 2nd century BC there was in existence a corpus of materials attributed to Kuan-Chung, chief minister of Duke Huan of Dz'iər during part of the 7th century BC. Late in the 1st century BC these materials were reconstituted by Liu-Hsiang, and it is essentially this recension which we have today.¹⁹⁶

As early as the 3rd century AD Fu-Hsüan recognized that the then current version of the *Kuan-tzŭ* could not have come from the hand of Kuan-Chung.¹⁹⁷ Since that time there has developed a large exegetical literature dealing with the character, origin and transmission of the work, but only recently has there been any sustained attempt to evaluate the status of the text on a chapter-by-chapter basis. The first scholar to adopt this method of approach was Lo Ken-tse in 1931,[198] but the most successful use of this technique has been achieved by Professor Rickett.[199] In a work published only very recently he has been able to ascribe positive datings to twelve of the chüan, and even to parts of certain chüan. He has shown, for example, that the *Ta-K'uang* (***D'âd-K'iwang*) chüan is composed of two discrete sections, an historical romance and a fragment of a philosophical treatise. Both were, on internal evidence, written in about the middle of the 3rd century BC, and probably combined by Liu-Hsiang more than two centuries later. The chüan entitled *Nei-Yeh* (***Nəp-Ngi̯ăp*), by contrast, may have been written as early as the end of the 4th century BC and certainly not later than the beginning of the third. The *Fa-Fa* (***Pi̯wăp-Pi̯wăp*) chüan is another composite chapter, consisting this time of three separate sections which may have been the work of one man or of three men belonging to the same school. All three sections should probably be dated to the end of the 3rd century BC. And each of the other chapters is of a similar nature and must be judged independently. Rickett has also endorsed the widely accepted theory that the nucleus of writings around which the *Kuan-tzŭ* crystallized was produced in the famous Chi-hsia (***Tsi̯ək-g'å*) Academy, founded by King Hsüan (***Si̯wan*) of Dz'iər in about 302 BC. Probably the collection began to take shape towards the middle of the 3rd century BC, was added to for another couple of centuries or so and finally stabilized by Liu-Hsiang perhaps between 230 and 220 BC.[200]

Numerous other works can be made to contribute fragments of information to the study of Chou urbanism, among them the *I-Ching* (*The Book of Changes*), the Taoist classics *Chuang-tzŭ* (*The Book of Master Chuang*) and *Tao-Te Ching* (*The Canon of the Way and its Power*), the *Hsün-tzŭ* (*The Book of Master Hsün*), the *Han-Fei-tzŭ* (*The Book of Master Han-Fei*), the *Meng-tzŭ* (*The Book of Master Meng*), and the *Lun-Yü* of Confucius (usually rendered into English as *The Analects*), but the exiguous quantity of material that can be extracted from their pages does not justify extended discussion of their authenticity. Suffice it to say that they are all composite and, what renders them the more difficult to handle from our present point of view, cumulative texts. Each of them – indeed, each fragment extracted from them – must be evaluated on its own merits and from the standpoint of the argument to which it is directed. In the present work I have been at pains to use these sources with discretion. This does not imply a simple process of acceptance or rejection, but rather of selection according to circumstance. A chance remark in, say, one of the Confucian classics may have no value in the documentation of an historical happening in the Western Chou period to which it purports to relate, but may yet be an authentic record of a Chan-Kuo belief. More often than not, however, even this kernel of truth will be enveloped in a cocoon of Han and later editing, which must be carefully peeled away before the Chan-Kuo evidence is ready for use. Consequently the analysis of Chou institutions only too often becomes an exercise in the penetration of layers of interpretation and value judgments from later centuries. And, not infrequently, deep in the heart of the cocoon there lies not a record of a Western Chou event, perhaps not even an echo, but only the faint memory of an echo smothered in the resonant sounds of subsequent exegesis. Needless to say, only very rarely can this earliest memory be isolated from the web of values and ideas in which it has been encapsulated. Neither is it always possible to discriminate between the results of the process of archetyping which accompanies the passage of time and the deliberate emendation of texts in the interests of ideology. All of which helps to explain why literary sources relating to Chou urbanism must be used with extreme care.

Even though it has been mentioned in Chapter One it is perhaps necessary, in conclusion, to say a further word or two about the post-Chou *Shih-Chi*, for it is the earliest extant example of systematic Chinese historiography and is the only major source (secondary though it be in the sense defined on p. 135) for Chou history which belongs to that genre. Moreover, it is, among the works with which we are presently concerned, the one that has suffered least at the hands of redactors. Text and subsequent commentaries have been kept rigorously separate and, although at least one chapter is now missing in its entirety and several others appear to be incomplete or even fragmentary, the *Shih-Chi* is the best preserved among the works that we have consulted.

Collection of the material for, and apparently the conception of, a history of the Chinese people were initiated by Ssŭ-ma T'an, Grand-'Historian' at the court of Emperor Wu of Han, shortly after that ruler's accession in 141 BC. But the working out of the design, most of the actual writing, and certainly the general flavor of the history we owe to his son Ssŭ-ma Ch'ien. He it was who labored for more than twenty years to produce a monumental history, in 130 chüan, of the Chinese culture realm from the earliest times down to his own lifetime, say the end of the 2nd century BC, and in so doing forged a new medium for the transmission of political and social experience. Here, of course, we are concerned only with those sections of his work which relate to the Chou dynasty.

The *Shih-Chi* consists of five major sections, respectively *Pen-Chi* (*Basic Annals*), *Nien-Piao* (*Chronological Tables*), a series of Treatises (*Shu*) on rituals, music, astronomy, religious affairs and economics, thirty chapters entitled *Shih-Chia* (*Hereditary Houses*) which deal mainly with the pre-Dz'iĕn states, and finally seventy chapters of *Lieh-Chuan* (*Organized Traditions* or *Biographies*). Of these sections the *Annals* and the *Hereditary Houses* are both cast in the old annalistic mould which had characterized the historiography of Chou times, but Ssŭ-ma Ch'ien extended both the scope of the enquiry and the quantity of information handled. Most of the improvements, however, came with the later chapters relating to the Han dynasty, and for the earlier periods

Ssŭ-ma Ch'ien did little more than string together extracts from ancient works. As already mentioned, he appears to have had access to sources now lost which preserved in secondary form genealogical materials going back as far as the Shang dynasty. The *Tables*, in fact, are largely a systematization of such materials, but the attempt at a synchronization of events related in the old annals was new. The technical treatises are also innovations, as are the biographies. They represent new means of organizing material, around institutions and persons respectively, and mark the beginnings of an analytical study of the past. However, not a little of the biographical section is of an anecdotal or romantic character, which betrays its origins in the ancient tradition of historical romance, of which the first part of the *Ta-K'uang* chüan of the *Kuan-tzŭ* is a good example.[201]

For Karlgren, who apparently believed that no pre-Ch'in texts extant in the Han era had been lost since that time,[202] Ssŭ-ma Ch'ien was often no better than a forger. It is certainly true that the historian selected evidence to suit his purpose and fitted it into a framework in which it would do just that, namely render justice to the virtuous and cast reproach upon the unworthy, but I am aware of no specific instance in which it can be positively asserted that he manufactured the evidence. Where, as in the paragraphs relating to Huang-Ti, he is the earliest author to provide extant material, it may be hypothesized that he had access to texts now lost or that the record had been preserved orally, either among the Little Traditions of China (using that term in the technical sense advocated by Robert Redfield) through the centuries or, perhaps for a much shorter period of about four generations since the proscription of 213 BC, by individual families. Our conclusion is that, although Ssŭ-ma Ch'ien was by no means an objective historian, he was not a counterfeiter.[203]

Epigraphic Evidence

Inscriptions on bronze vessels are of such importance, both actual and potential, for the history of the Western Chou that it is proper that they should receive brief mention here. However, for most of that period they derive from bronzes of the Royal Chou, and only towards the end of the era do vessels of other than Chou states begin to appear. The inscriptions are also restricted to a narrow sector of the total spectrum of Chou life, chiefly that concerned with ritual and ceremonial. Although this has implications for institutions not specifically of a religious nature, notably those of a political and social character, it is of only indirect relevance to the study of urbanism. During the Ch'un-Ch'iu, bronze inscriptions were still connected preponderantly with state functions, but it is observable that some powerful ministers were also beginning to use them in their private ceremonies. Finally, by Chan-Kuo times inscriptions were appearing on a wider range of vessels as well as on weapons, coins and a variety of other objects. It is one of the minor ironies of

THE SPREAD OF URBANISM

Chinese history that, in the period when the secularization of epigraphy began to introduce a wider range of topics into inscriptions, the significance of those very inscriptions was greatly reduced by the preservation of much longer texts written in other media. Nevertheless, the bronze inscriptions do afford direct, if limited, access to the ideas of the time in a way that archetyped and edited texts do not, and as such provide an important check on the classical literature of the Chou era. They make a particularly valuable contribution to the study of the Western Chou, when other evidence, both literary and archeological, is exiguous.

THE SPREAD OF URBANISM IN CHOU TIMES

THE WESTERN CHOU

It has been shown in Chapter One that urban development in Shang times was, on present archeological evidence, restricted to an arcuate zone of the Chung-Yüan. On the outer edge of this zone was a fringe of territory apparently characterized by incipient urbanism. Literary records of dubious reliability refer to contemporary urban forms in the middle Wei valley, but such have not so far been attested archeologically.

During the early decades of Chou hegemony there is no reason to think that the situation was radically different. Presumably the spatial pattern of urbanism at that time comprised two main elements: Shang cities persisting into the later age, and the new foundations of the Chou conquerors. There is no way of knowing how many of the Shang cities survived into the new era, and speculation on this point will depend largely on the view taken of the Shang polity. If political complexity, despite the demonstrable cultural unity of the Shang people, had not advanced beyond the level of the city-state, for instance, then there is probably less likelihood of the pattern of Shang urbanism having persisted for long under Chou domination; for, when city and state are one, reorganization of the political framework tends to eliminate the *raison d'être* of a proportion of the urban foci. Cities with developed specialist functions outside the sphere of politics and administration are those which stand the best chance of survival. On the other hand if, as the transmitted texts would lead us to believe, there was indeed a Shang territorial state controlling a sizable tract of North China, within which cities enjoyed a degree of administrative (though not political) autonomy, then the old urban pattern would be more likely to have persisted under the new dynasty. The assumption of power by the Chou conquerors need not have precipitated a major dislocation of the urban network. But all this is supposition and serves little purpose beyond directing attention to a matter requiring further investigation. There were, in any case, ritual and cosmological aspects of urban life which have to be taken into account in this connection, and which are discussed in Chapter Five.

THE DIFFUSION OF URBAN LIFE   [215

It is more profitable to turn to a discussion of the pattern of urban distribution during the Western Chou dynasty. After the conquest, the Chou king established his benefice holders in fiefs scattered strategically throughout the old Shang culture realm and, apparently, even farther afield, particularly in the east, on lands that had never been brought wholly within the Shang dominion and certainly not under Shang political control. Whereas some of these fief seats were entirely new foundations in the shape of garrison establishments created *de novo* by Chou aristocrats in both Shang and tribal territories, others may have been old Shang settlements adapted to new purposes. In any case they constituted a network of garrison posts, which were at the same time cult centers for members of the nobility. The number of such settlements is, as already mentioned, reported very differently in different texts, the figures ranging from 1,773 to considerably fewer than a hundred (p. 112 above and Note 20). No more than twenty-six of these seats are mentioned by name in any text, and that of a much later date. It is, in fact, the *Tso-Chuan*, under the 24th year of Duke **Xi̯əg (Hsi : 635 BC), which enumerates the benefices established after the conquest.

'The King was incensed [at happenings which need not concern us here] and wished to invade D'i̯ĕng with the help of the D'iek. **Pi̯ŭg-D̑i̯ən (Fu-Ch'en) remonstrated with him, saying "Forbear to do this. Your servant has heard that in high antiquity the populace was kept in tranquillity by virtue. In later times it was customary to show favor to relatives. Formerly the Duke of Ti̯ôg, grieved by a lack of accord with the two younger brothers [of King Mi̯wo], beneficed his relatives as fences and screens [to protect] Ti̯ôg. The [princes of] **Kwân (Kuan), **Ts'âd (Ts'ai), **D̑i̯ĕng (Ch'eng), **Xwâk (Huo), **Lo (Lu), **Gi̯wad (Wei), **Mog (Mao), **T'nâm (T'an), **Kôg (Kao), **·I̯ung (Yung), **Dz'ôg (Ts'ao), **D'əng (T'eng), **Pi̯ĕt (Pi), **Ngi̯wăn (Yüan), **P'i̯ông (Feng), and **Dzi̯wĕn (Hsün) were descendants of [King] Mi̯wən in the d̑i̯og (chao) generation.[204] Those of **Gi̯wo (Yü), **Tsi̯ĕn (Chin), **·I̯əng (Ying), and **G'ân (Han) were descendants of [King] Mi̯wo in the *mi̯ôk* (*mu*) generation. Those of **B'i̯wăm (Fan), **Tsi̯ang (Chiang), **G'ieng (Hsing), **Môg (Mao), **Dz'âg (Tsu) and **Ki̯wər (Kuei) were descendants of the Duke of Ti̯ôg (Chou).'

These benefices were identified by Ch'i Ssŭ-ho in a paper in 1946,[205] and subsequently plotted on a map by Chang Sen-dou, who took them as 'roughly representing the walled cities at that time'.[206] There are, I think, five, and possibly six, reasons why it is unlikely that this map presents an accurate – or even an impressionistic – picture of urban development in North China in about 1100 BC. First, the passage in which the schedule of benefices occurs is incorporated in a work compiled probably between seven and eight hundred years after the event, and fashioned into its present form some three centuries after that. Thus, at least a millennium elapsed between the alleged apportionment of the benefices and the final redaction of the record, during which time the epic of the Chou accession to power had been archetyped, sanctioned by the invention of the theory of the mandate of Heaven, and integrated into a scheme of genealogies designed to validate the power exercised by the principal ducal houses of North China and the Yang-tzŭ valley. That this particular paragraph is not to be relied upon is confirmed by the implications of the *I Hou Nieh I* inscription with regard to the role of the Duke of T̂i̯ôg, which have been discussed in an earlier section of the present work (p. 108).

In the second place the notice in question is one of the moralizing passages which, we have already seen, are likely to be later interpolations. It purports to recount the remonstrance of a perspicacious and virtuous minister to a ruler about to embark on a course of action of dubious morality, and the schedule of names has all the hallmarks of a literary device rather than the similitude of an actual debate. I think there is every chance that the coupling of the reference to the Duke of T̂i̯ôg and the early days of the dynasty with the tale of Fu-Ch'en represents the fusion of a literary with an oral tradition in a manner that is only too characteristic of the *Tso-Chuan*.

Third, the genealogies on which this apportionment of benefices is based are more than dubious, but – and this is the fourth point – even were they reliable, it would appear that the schedule is incomplete, for additional territories are listed in a passage in the *Shih-Chi* (chüan 4), where **Tsi̯og (Chiao) was allegedly granted by King Mi̯wo to a descendant of Shen-Nung (**D̂'i̯ĕn-Nông), **T̂i̯ok (Chu) to a descendant of Huang-Ti (**G'wâng-Tieg), **G'i̯ĕg (Chi) to a descendant of Yao (**Ngiog), **D'i̯ĕn (Ch'en) to a descendant of Shun (**Śi̯wən), and **K'i̯əg (Ch'i) to a descendant of Yü (Gi̯wo [the Great]). In a second part of the same passage Mi̯wo is recorded as bestowing other benefices on ministers (mostly relatives) who had rendered distinguished service or sage counsel in the Chou cause. Some of the later territories are those which appear in the passage translated above, but one, **·Ian (Yen), is an additional name. I do not mean by this to imply that the map would be rendered accurate simply by combining these two lists of benefices. Clearly both are part of the lore of ancient Chinese genealogy, which embodies kernels of garbled fact [207] enmeshed in a tissue of imaginative glosses, and which can be accepted at its face value only at the scholar's peril. Were a third list still extant, no doubt it would afford yet a third variation on the theme.

Fifth, Ch'i Ssŭ-ho's identifications of the names in the passage from the *Tso-Chuan* are based not on research in the tangled thickets of toponymy in early Chou times but on the glosses of a long line of scholars, who in turn have relied predominantly on local tradition and, failing that, on standards of toponymic analysis which are presently unacceptable. Of course, there is no real doubt as to the position of the territory of Lo (although its boundaries cannot be delimited with anything approaching precision), or of Gi̯wad or even Ts'âd, but the locations of others of these benefices are by no means so certain. Karlgren expressed the very strongest doubts as to the traditional identifications of place names proposed by Chinese commentators.[208] Perhaps he was, as Eberhard contends,[209] a little too pessimistic, but the difficulties of relating names, which are not infrequently *hapax legomenon*, to localities in early Chou times are often insuperable. Certainly not all Ch'i Ssŭ-ho's identifications can be accepted.

About the sixth reason I am prepared to be less dogmatic. But a cursory check through the literary texts – by no means reliable sources, as I have been at pains to emphasize – leads me to conclude that, although they mention only twenty-six aristocratic seats by name, they imply a rather higher number. Furthermore, a total of twenty-six holdings, together with the domain of the Royal Chou, scattered through some 350,000 square miles of North and Central China, would imply benefices of a massive size compared with the inferred territories of the pre-conquest Shang city-states. This last is not a strong argument, but its deficiencies do not weaken my main contention that the notice in the *Tso-Chuan* is an inadequate basis for a map of early Chou urbanism.

Under the circumstances I can see no alternative but to abandon the attempt to map the distribution of urban centers at the beginning of the Western Chou dynasty. The most that can be said is that urban foundations either persisted or were established throughout the nuclear area of Shang culture, that is throughout the Chung-Yüan, and, within a relatively short space of time, were disseminated eastwards into the hitherto tribal territories of present-day Shantung, which came to constitute the state of Dz'iər. There seems also to have been a significant early development of urban forms in the valleys of the Wei river and its tributaries, which were the old Chou domain, but to what extent this had been initiated in pre-conquest times is still uncertain.

So exiguous is the archeological evidence, and so ambivalent and intractable are the literary sources available even for later periods of the Western Chou, that it is debatable whether it is worth trying to map the information that can be gleaned from them. However, Fig. 13, for what it is worth, is just such an attempt. On it are depicted all the Western Chou urban forms to which I have found reference in pre-Han texts, together with those which I have culled from Ssŭ-ma Ch'ien's *Shih-Chi* (completed at the beginning of the 1st century BC) and from the *Chu-shu Chi-nien*. The basis of the distribution derives from the *Shih-Chi*, but I am not unaware that in the relevant sections of that work Ssŭ-ma Ch'ien was reproducing older archetyped material. When abstracting references to urban forms from the *Shu-Ching* I have used only the orthodox

---

[13] Recorded urban settlement during the period of the Western Chou. For the limitations of this distribution see pp. 164–8 of the text. Note: the river systems shown on this map are no more than skeletal approximations based on very inadequate evidence.

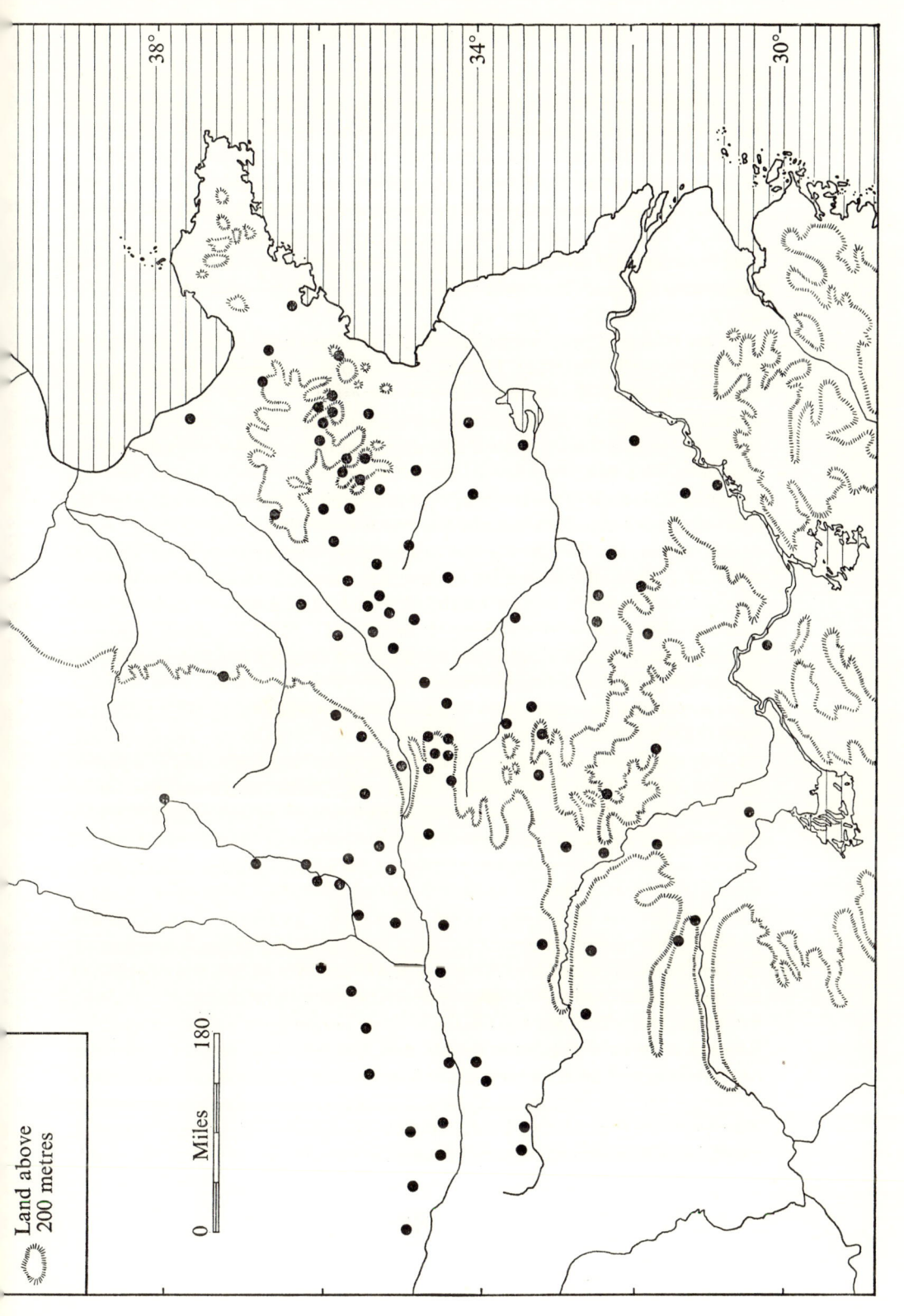

ku-wen text (cf. p. 13). With regard to the *Chu-shu Chi-nien*, I have drawn only upon those references occurring in Wang Kuo-wei's reconstitution of the early text.[210] I am by no means convinced that the so-called modern text is valueless for present purposes[211] but, compared with that of the *Shih-Chi*, the contribution of the *Chu-shu Chi-nien* is relatively minor in any case, while the quantity of additional materials to be extracted from the 'modern' text (as opposed to those provided by the reconstructed version) does not justify the long excursus that would be necessary to evaluate their reliability. Scraps of information quarried from other Chou sources have been used with the caution advocated in previous pages.

In the matter of place-name identification I have perforce had to settle for a wide range of probability. I have followed to their sources, with Karlgren's strictures in mind, the correspondences suggested in Chavanne's magnificent *apparatus criticus* to his translation of the Chou chapters of the *Shih-Chi*,[212] and have rejected them wherever they appeared to be based on unduly suspect traditions. However, very few of the traditions are firmly based, so that the exercise became one of selecting the least unreliable from among predominantly equivocal traditions. This was not quite such a profitless undertaking as might at first appear, for the aim was not to attain absolute accuracy so much as to arrive at a regional location for a name. Of course, a handful of toponyms, chiefly ducal capitals, can be identified with a high degree of certainty and occasionally located with considerable accuracy (it should be noted in passing that identification and location are not the same thing), but a high proportion can be assigned only an approximate locality. Perhaps, for example, a settlement is recorded as having been in the vicinity of, close to, or not far from, the capital. Or it may have been described as midway between two known points. Or, only too frequently, it may be implied only that it was situated in a particular part of a state. All such identifications are, I think, worth plotting. States in the inner group (cf. p. 114 above), which are those with which Western Chou records are mainly concerned, were not large and, on the scale at which Fig. 13 is reproduced, a symbol plotted on the eastern border of, say, Kwân would be only an eighth of an inch from one plotted on the western border. Although Lo was apparently wider latitudinally, its northern and southern frontiers were no farther apart than were those of Kwân. When it is recorded, for example, that the army of Sông invaded **Dzʻôg in 489 BC and established five ·jəp on the frontier,[213] it is not introducing any significant error to locate five urban symbols along the relatively short border zone between those two states. It must be remembered though that, whereas the capital of a state can often be fixed with a fair measure of confidence, only very rarely can the frontiers be located with any degree of accuracy. Yet, even so, in this case the error of the placement on Fig. 13 can hardly exceed one-quarter of an inch. There is inevitably a large element of subjectiveness in the selection of toponyms on this principle, and I can only say in justification of this enterprise that I have, generally speaking, plotted only those names which seemed to be both identified and located by traditions that stood a reasonable chance of being genuine. In one or two instances I have plotted a settlement which could be located but not identified.

Subjectiveness was not restricted to the plotting of place names: it also lay at the basis of the decision as to what constituted an urban settlement. **$Kwək$ (kuo), a word which was sometimes used metonymically to denote the fortified cult center of a noble as well as his territory, and **to (tu), capitals of states and benefices, were accepted as urban forms, and the justification for this will be presented in the next chapter, but **·$i̯əp$ (i) is more difficult to evaluate. It, too, could, and often did, denote a ceremonial center, usually surrounded by a $hang$-$t'u$ wall, but difficulties arise when we try to estimate to what extent it exercised urban functions as those are defined in Chapter Four. The texts are seldom explicit on this point. Sometimes the word ·$i̯əp$, for example, seems to carry no implication beyond that of 'place', or 'locality' or 'district', or 'settlement'. Whereas in the *Lun-Yü* (V, 27), Confucius is alleged to have alluded to 'a ·$i̯əp$ of ten households', the *Appended Judgment* (*Hsi-Tz'ŭ*) to the **$Dzi̯ung$ (*Sung*) hexagram in the *I-Ching* apparently implies that 300 households constituted a representative size of ·$i̯əp$.[214] I have had to make my judgments in the general context of the source concerned, in the light of the events being described and, not least important, with due consideration of the nature of the narrative. After acquiring some familiarity with the texts I have come to sense that highly archetyped passages, particularly those fragments of folklore incorporated in a literary tradition, tend to upgrade settlements in the urban hierarchy. ·$I̯əp$ in such contexts was certainly intended to denote a city but, contrariwise, because virtually all settlements in such contexts had been archetyped as cities, was regarded with suspicion when I came to plot the map. Once again I can only say that I included in the distribution solely those settlements which seemed to be something more than villages with their inhabitants working the surrounding fields. To be classified as urban (in the sense defined in Chapter Four) a settlement had to appear to be an instrument for the organization of the surrounding territories, not merely the locus of a labor force. That the method of categorization is unsatisfactory I do not deny, but the attempt may be justified by the purpose for which the map was constructed. It was, in fact, designed simply to provide a visual impression of the broad pattern of urban development under the Western Chou. Hopefully, it will be the first in a series of distributions tracing the evolution of the spatial pattern of urban development in China from the earliest times to the present. The nature of the sources dictated that the pattern be cumulative throughout the era of the Western Chou, but the fact that cities were destroyed or moved to new sites during the three centuries of that dynasty means that it does not depict conditions at the end of that period. It is a record of those settlements mentioned in classical texts which are believed to have manifested urban characteristics at any time during the dynasty, together with the sole archeologically attested and indisputably urban capital of the state of D'əm (p. 136 above). The qualifications to this statement should be noted. The classical texts are concerned predominantly with the central states, so that there may have been more urban foundations in the larger outer states (where incidentally it was more hazardous locating a toponym whose position was specified only in general terms) than appear on the map. This is, I think, particularly true of Tṣ'i̯o, which may have developed urban foci at a relatively early date but whose cities are at any time only sparsely represented in the records. It will be recalled that Duke **Sni̯ang (Hsiang) of Lo in 541 incurred the opprobrium of his ministers and subjects when he had a palace built for himself in the style of those of Tṣ'i̯o.[215] Presumably this act by the ruler of one of the technologically most advanced of the central states reflects the existence of a developed urban architectural style in contemporary Tṣ'i̯o. There is, of course, no reason to think that the record of urban centers is complete for the central states, but neither is there any reason to suppose that it does not afford a more or less representative sample of Chou cities in those states.

Despite its inadequacies, Fig. 13 does show that the three centuries of the Western Chou had witnessed a significant areal extension of urban society. Even allowing for the inchoate state of the archeological investigation of Shang remains and the consequent deficiencies of Fig. 13, there can be no doubt but that urban settlements had both become more numerous in the central states and had extended far beyond the borders of the Shang culture realm. The highest incidence of cities appears from the map to have occurred in the old states of Lo, Sông, Gi̯wad, D'i̯ĕng and the Chou domain, though there was already a fairly dense scatter in Tsi̯ĕn, Dz'i̯ĕn and southern Dz'i̯ər; but, as mentioned above, this distribution may reflect the character of the sources rather than the pattern of urbanism in Chou China. There seems a strong likelihood, however, that the center of gravity of urban development was shifting from the Shang hearth in northern Ho-nan eastwards towards a point in Lo or Gi̯wad. To the south distinctively urban settlements were to be found in the Han valley and along the middle Yang-tzŭ, where they signified the introduction of new modes of social organization into hitherto tribal territories.

---

[14] Recorded urban settlement during the Ch'un-Ch'iu period. For the limitations of this map see pp. 170–2 of the text. Note especially that the pattern of distribution is cumulative over some two and a half centuries, so that more than one capital may occur within the territory of any particular state. The river systems shown on this map are no better than skeletal approximations based on very inadequate evidence.

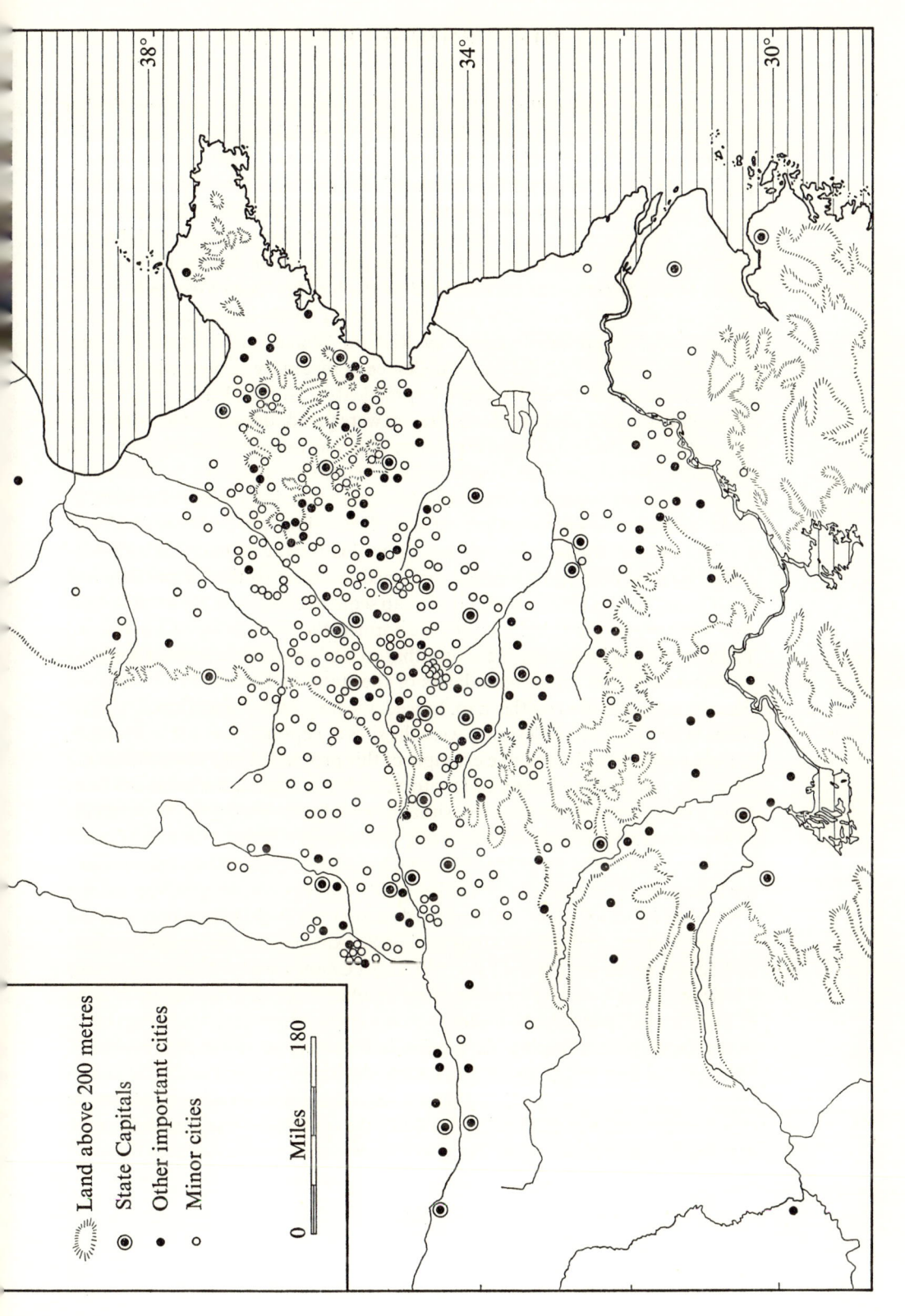

THE EASTERN CHOU

Fig. 14 is based essentially on the *Tso-Chuan*, augmented by a variety of other sources discussed on pp. 150–160 and by a sprinkling of archeologically attested sites, some of which are in any case mentioned in the relevant texts. It depicts, therefore, those settlements mentioned in classical sources and archeological reports which are believed to have exercised urban functions (again as defined in Chapter Four) during the Spring and Autumn period. Originally I had toyed with the idea of analyzing this pattern of urban distribution in terms of the twelve twenty-year periods used by the late Professor George Kennedy in his seminal paper on the process of historical development depicted in the *Ch'un-Ch'iu*[216] and subsequently by Richard Walker in his study of Chou political systems,[217] but the doubtful degree of reliability of the evidence available rendered such an undertaking impracticable. Not the least intractable of the problems which sabotaged my attempt were the continual, and often abrupt, fluctuations in the frontiers of the states. This was important because many of the urban centers could be located only in relation to frontiers, or even more frequently, with respect to one particular tract of territory within the state. In some instances the broad outlines of such fluctuations can be determined with confidence, and Richard Walker has done this for the state of Dz'iər.[218] By connecting the outermost localities assigned to Dz'iər by the *Ch'un-Ch'iu* and *Tso-Chuan*, he was able to depict on a map sequent changes in the extent of the core territory of the state. I myself performed the same exercise for Lo and Tsi̯ĕn but in all instances, including that of Dz'iər, there remained a strong likelihood that the actual boundaries of the states had extended well beyond the core area delimited on the map. Indeed, the texts seldom mentioned frontier zones in precise terms unless they were the sites of captured cities or battlefields.

Dz'iər affords an instructive example of this problem. Until about 660 BC the state was restricted to a tract of territory, with maximum dimensions of from 300 to 350 miles by from 60 to 70, situated principally among the western hills of Shan-tung. By 600 BC, mainly under the hegemon Duke **G'wân (Huan) and his advisor **Kwân-D'i̯ông (Kuan-Chung), the frontiers had been pushed northwestwards across the **Dz'iər (Ch'i) or eastern distributary of the **G'wâng (Huang) river, and eastwards across the Wei-Hsien valley into the eastern uplands of the Shan-tung peninsula. Already the Dz'iər government had 'imposed terms' (*g'ộng*) on **T̑i̯ang (Chang) and 'removed' (*ts'i̯an*) **Di̯ang (Yang), as well as persuading a noble of the principality of **Ki̯əg (Chi) voluntarily to agree to the incorporation of his territory, **G'iweg (Hsi), in the Dz'iər polity. During the ensuing half century or so the small states of **Ləg (Lai) and **D'âng (T'ang) were 'destroyed' (*mi̯at*) and **Kăd-kən (Chieh-ken) 'annexed' (*ts'i̯u*), thereby extending the boundaries of Dz'iər significantly southwards. Finally, by 480 BC the state had come to include some of the valleys and plains of the Tung-wen river system on the southern flanks of the western highlands. This five-fold increase in the area of the state, during which altogether fourteen neighboring territories were absorbed into Dzʻiər, can be documented in broad terms, but only seldom can a border be determined with precision. It is more than probable, for example, that by the close of the Chʻun-Chʻiu period the Dzʻiər writ ran throughout most of the seaward tracts of the Gʻwâng delta and eastward to the tip of the Shan-tung peninsula, but, as no written references to these territories survive, they can be included in the Dzʻiər kingdom only by inference.[219] It follows that to plot the cities of this one state during twenty-year periods would, on the imprecise evidence available, be extremely difficult, not to say hazardous, but to plot the urban development of all the Chinese states on the same principle would be an impossibility.

For these reasons, Fig. 14 represents the cumulative pattern of urban distribution for the whole of the Chʻun-Chʻiu period. From even a cursory glance at the map it is evident that the extent of territory supporting urbanized societies had not changed greatly since the time of the Western Chou. The rise of ·Ian in the embayment of present-day Pei-ching, and the emergence of Ngo and Gi̯wăt in the Yang-tzŭ delta and modern Che-chiang, had introduced urban forms somewhat farther north and among the very definitely non-Chinese peoples of the southeast, but elsewhere the spatial frontiers of urban society at the end of the Chʻun-Chʻiu were essentially those of the Western Chou. Apparently, during the intervening two and a half centuries, the social and economic changes adumbrated above had induced an intensification of urbanism both within the old core of central states and in some of the outer polities such as Tṣʻi̯o. To what extent the apparent increase in density of urban foundations reflects the greater detail of the *Chʻun-Chʻiu* and related texts, as compared with the rather meager sources for the Western Chou period, is uncertain. Certainly nothing like 367 cities (the difference in the number of symbols on Figs. 13 and 14) are recorded as having been founded during those two and a half centuries. In fact, by collating information from the *Tso-Chuan* and the *Kung-yang Chuan*, Oshima Riichi was able to find mention of the foundation of only seventy-eight cities during this period,[220] usually expressed in some such phrase as, 'In the summer [of 713] **Lâng (Lang) was walled', 'In the winter [of 695] **Xi̯ang (Hsiang) was walled', or on one occasion, 'The Marquis [of Tsi̯ĕn in 660] walled **Kʻi̯uk-·ok (Chʻü-wo) for his son'.[221] If the distribution of Fig. 14 approximates to, or understates, the actual distribution of cities during the Chʻun-Chʻiu, then either the vast proportion of instances of city founding are indeed unrecorded or the number of Western Chou cities is underrepresented on Fig. 13. My own feeling is that both factors are operative. I have emphasized already that Fig. 13 depicts only those Western Chou cities which happened to play a more or less decisive role in the history of a handful of states; and, as for the Chʻun-Chʻiu distribution, on perusing the texts one does in fact get the impression that, generally speaking, only cities established by the state governments were considered worthy of mention. This would not be altogether unexpected in view of the fact that the basic annalistic materials around which the framework of the *Tso-Chuan* and *Ch'un-Ch'iu* was constructed were originally court archives. In any case the *Tso-Chuan* deals primarily with the conflict between the northern states of Dz'iər and Tsjĕn on the one hand and the southern state of Tṣ'i̯o on the other, so it should come as no surprise that the former two kingdoms accounted for one-sixth of the cities mentioned and Tṣ'i̯o for nearly a quarter.

Sen-dou Chang, drawing his materials from Ch'en P'an's revision of Ku Tung-kao's *Ch'un-Ch'iu Ta-shih Piao*,[222] has published a map showing ninety-seven walled cities of the Ch'un-Ch'iu period.[223] It is not clear why Chang used this secondary source, published between 1957 and 1959, in preference to the original texts, but in any case there can be no dispute about the fact that his map depicts only a fraction of the number of cities in existence in Ch'un-Ch'iu times. If, as Oshima claims, there are references to the actual founding of seventy-eight cities during that era (and these, it is to be remembered, are only the *recorded* foundings), then Chang's figure would imply that there were less than a score of urban settlements in the whole of the Chinese culture realm at the end of the Western Chou. Such was certainly not the case.

All the limitations and inadequacies discussed in relation to the distribution of Western Chou cities apply with equal cogency to Fig. 14. Subjectivism, illation, relativism, even compromise, all played their part in the construction of the map, and will doubtless render it liable to modification in the future as more sophisticated techniques become available for the analysis of ancient Chinese society.

The reader who has persisted this far may well expect to find at this point a map depicting the distribution of cities during the era of the Contending States. The reason such a map is not included is that the sources for the spatial study of Chan-Kuo urbanism are less satisfactory from the point of view of both quantity and quality than are those relating to the Ch'un-Ch'iu period, and the only map that can be compiled from them simulates a less detailed version of Fig. 14. In other respects, though, the Chan-Kuo sources are more informative. In fact, they reveal the advent of important changes in the nature of the city at that time, which will be touched upon in subsequent sections of this work.

It may be of interest before closing this section to interpolate a few comments on the results of an inquiry into the city-building activities of the Chou Chinese published by Dr Li Chi as long ago as 1928.[224] This author based his study on materials in the *Ch'in-ting Ku-chin T'u-shu Chi-ch'eng*, an encyclopedia prepared – as the title says – by imperial order, under the general editorship of Ch'en Meng-lei. It was completed in 1726.[225] Section VI of this work contains the dates at which walled cities were established in the various provinces of China, the information having been extracted from the great tradition of local gazetteers that form such an important strand in the web of Chinese historical and geographical writing.[226] The provincial scholars who produced these local histories and topographies through the centuries without significant exception drew their information on ancient times from the archetyped and edited classical texts discussed above. It follows, therefore, that they, followed by the scholars who labored on the *Ch'in-ting Ku-chin T'u-shu Chi-ch'eng*, and ultimately by Li Chi, made use of a great deal of information which we have found it necessary to reject. Consequently it is not surprising that Li Chi's estimates of the number of cities in Chou China are higher than the number of symbols on Figs. 13 and 14. For the period prior to 722 B C, the beginning of the Ch'un-Ch'iu, he had discovered references to the building of 163 cities, and for the period from 722 to 207 B C, that is for the remainder of the Chou dynasty, he had counted no less than 585. In addition 233 of uncertain age were mentioned for the first time during the latter period. These figures are to be compared with the 91 for the Western Chou on Fig. 13, and 466 plotted on Fig. 14, which relates to the Ch'un-Ch'iu (722–481 B C). While maintaining that Li Chi's estimates are based on unacceptable evidence, we must admit that our own figures are too low, because there is absolutely no reason to suppose that anything like all the cities in Chou China were mentioned in the sources that we judge reliable – or in any other sources for that matter. This is, in fact, merely an oblique way of drawing attention to the ironic situation in which Li Chi's estimates may be nearer the truth than our own, but for reasons that are unacceptable to us. Both are, in any case, too low. In the matter of relative, as opposed to absolute, incidence of building activity, by contrast, we are in substantial agreement with Li Chi. He finds that prior to 722 B C, urban life was restricted to the five provinces of Kan-su, Ho-nan, Shen-hsi, Chih-li and Shan-hsi (he uses the old Manchu provincial names appropriate to the source of his materials), from which it extended during the Eastern Chou into Shan-tung, Hu-pei, and Chiang-su. We have drawn the limits of urban development somewhat more narrowly during both periods, chiefly as a result of having adopted more stringent criteria of source evaluation. It is more than doubtful, for example, if Kan-su, Chih-li, and Chiang-su should figure as prominently in the history of Shang and Chou urbanism as Li Chi contended.[227] But he was certainly correct in postulating a shift in the focus of building activity from the Chung-yüan, hearth of the Shang culture, out into the eastern parts of the plain and the foothills of Shan-tung.

The Nature of Chou Urbanism

THE FUNCTION OF THE CHOU CITY

The mosaic of settlements spread over the North China plain early in the

Western Chou comprised old Shang foundations dating from before the conquest, tribal villages which had existed outside the framework of an organized polity until the advent of Chou overlords, and, perhaps most important of all, the garrison establishments of the new dynasty. Each of these settlement forms was integrated into the political structure of the Chou kingdom, and each sooner or later, despite its distinctive origins, assumed a role in the emergence of a hierarchy of cities, each unit of which at each level of the system combined ceremonial, military, and agricultural functions. At the apex of the hierarchy was the imperial capital at G'og in the Wei valley, the style center whence diffused the intellectual, religious, social, and aesthetic values of Western Chou culture. At various levels in the hierarchy the seats of benefice holders reproduced a proportion of these functions and, finally, in interstitial and peripheral locations were to be found the lowest levels of urban development, the seats of ministers, members of ruling families, and even of tribal chieftains in process of assimilation to the Chinese way of life. The level at which an urban center articulated with the political and administrative structures of the state was reflected, at least in the phraseology of later texts, in the term used to describe it: **$t\underset{\cdot}{i}\hat{o}ng$-$to$ ($chung$-tu) for the capital of the Son of Heaven, **to (tu) for the seat of a powerful aristocrat, and **·$i\underset{\cdot}{\partial}p$ (i) for that of a lesser landholder or the chief of a $b'\underset{\cdot}{i}u$-$d\underset{\cdot}{i}ung$ (fu-$yung$). In some of these later texts the several ranks within the hierarchy were rationalized as representing an evolutionary sequence. In the $Shih$-Chi, for example, we read that, 'On the first occasion when Shun (Śi̯ən, one of the legendary model emperors) migrated he built a ·$i\underset{\cdot}{\partial}p$; on the second occasion he founded a to; and on the third occasion he established a **$kw\partial k$ (kuo : = city-state), to which he attracted nobles from the four directions.' Similar statements occur in the $L\ddot{u}$-$Shih$ $Ch'un$-$Ch'iu$, the $Kuan$-$tz\breve{u}$ and the $Chuang$-$tz\breve{u}$, but we shall see in Chapter Three that the actual process of urban genesis was probably somewhat different from that postulated by systematizing Chinese editors.

That some hierarchical distinction was also recognized by the compiler of the Tso-$Chuan$ is evident in a gloss on a passage in the $Ch'un$-$Ch'iu$ dealing with the enclosing of a settlement at **Mi̯ər (Mei). 'Mi̯ər', he wrote, 'was not a to. All ·$i\underset{\cdot}{\partial}p$ having ancestral temples providing a lodging for their former rulers were designated to, those without such a temple were termed ·$i\underset{\cdot}{\partial}p$. A ·$i\underset{\cdot}{\partial}p$ is said to be enclosed (**$t\underset{\cdot}{i}\breve{o}k$: chu), a to is said to be fortified (**$d\underset{\cdot}{i}\breve{e}ng$: $ch'eng$).'[228] It is implicit in the second sentence of the passage just quoted that ·$i\underset{\cdot}{\partial}p$ denoted all urban foci other than state or benefice capitals. In the wider context of Chou literature it seems in fact to have included settlements that were hardly more than hamlets. We have, for example, already mentioned the reference in the Lun-$Y\ddot{u}$ (V, 27) to a ·$i\underset{\cdot}{\partial}p$ of only ten households. It is important, therefore, that each reference to a ·$i\underset{\cdot}{\partial}p$ be evaluated in the light of its context and not assumed uncritically to have been urban in character.

NATURE OF CHOU URBANISM

One of the two essential features of the Western Chou city, at whichever level of the hierarchy it occurred, was the altar to the god of the soil (*she* : ***ḍi̯å*), which, like the *apadana* of Xerxes (p. 439 below), was always kept open 'to receive the hoar frost, dew, wind, and rain, and to allow free access by the influences of Heaven and Earth' (*Li-Chi*). The roofing-over of this altar signified the extinction both of the ruler's line and of the state and the city. The state might subsequently be reconstituted and the city rebuilt or resuscitated, but for the time being both were extinguished. As the Son of Heaven received his mandate from Heaven, so the noble received his territory, his city, and his people from the Chou king, and piled his altar to the god of the soil around a clod of earth from the great national altar in G'og – or later in the Gi̯wang-Ḍi̯ĕng at Lo-yang. The other essential feature of the city at this time was the temple of the ancestors (***mi̯og* : *miao*), wherein rested the tablets of the agnatic ancestors and their wives in *di̯og-mi̯ôk* order. No state could hope to survive without the favor and intercession of its former rulers who, in turn, traced their lineage back to sage emperors or culture heroes of antiquity. When the ancestral sacrifices were discontinued, then also both ruler and state had become extinct. It was this temple of the ancestors which served as the focus for all important state functions, whether religious, political, diplomatic or military. A third feature which – as there was no overlord without a city and, with very few and temporary exceptions, no city without an overlord [229] – was an inevitable (though not essential) concomitant of all urban development, was the ruler's palace. And moving between these ternions of cityhood was the ruler, the animating force of state, city, and temple, whose *d'ôg-tək* [230] caused nature and men to be what they were, who, in Granet's phrase, 'dispensed to men and things their destiny'.[231] As the *Li-Chi* has it : 'When [the former Emperors] presented their offerings to Shang-ti in the outskirts [of the capital], wind and rain were duly regulated, and cold and warmth came each in its appointed season, so that the Sage [Emperor] had only to stand with his face to the south for order to prevail throughout the world.'

The agricultural and military functions of Western Chou cities were closely related. Discussion of the Chou settlement of the North China plain has customarily focused on a nexus of ideas involving the relations between the martial Chou conquerors, 'the hundred lineages', established in fortified settlements, and the food-producing Shang and tribal peoples, 'the black-haired folk'; and the argument has then usually hinged on the nature of the instruments devised by the Chou leaders to ensure the peace of the countryside, and ultimately their own food supply. The most elaborate of the available expositions, and also that which is most hypothetical, was put forward by Wolfram Eberhard a few years ago.[232] This author points out that the Chou were probably often unable, by reason of disaffection or perhaps inability to produce a surplus, to rely on the local populace for their rations, and consequently were obliged to devise alternative arrangements. In the event Eberhard believes, following hints provided in the earlier work of Hsü Chung-shu, that the Chou benefice holders organized their followers in semi-military cadres, each of eight families. These groups, who must have found themselves in much the same situation as the early British settlers among the forest Indians of North America, are held to have gone out from the fortress at the beginning of spring, cultivated parcels of land on a swidden cycle, and returned to the protection of the fortress at the onset of winter. This, according to Eberhard, was probably the origin of the well-field system discussed on p. 132 above. The clearings of the eight families in each cadre, together with an alleged ninth section the produce of which went for the maintenance of the non-cultivating élites in the fortress community, were subsequently idealized by systematizing editors into the regularly shaped and spaced, communally worked, land-settlement scheme which, torn from its contextual setting in Mencius and the *Chou-Li,* has been taken by some more recent but no less systematizing authors as a prototype of 'natural socialism' or 'primitive communism' achieved in the innocence of the world. Contrasting strongly with these agro-military settlements were the villages of the indigenous folk, paying tribute to their new masters but, in the earlier days of the Western Chou, still self-contained and tribally organized. Only with the passage of time were the Chou *colonia* and the Shang or tribal populace fused into the unity of the Chou city. Perhaps this came about through the socially consolidatory medium of markets established under the fortress walls; possibly – as Eberhard suggests – it came about through intermarriage; and most probably through the initiation of a symbiotic process of mutual interdependence, as when the Chou needed to augment their labor force for construction work in the fortress, or when the indigenous folk sought to obtain the implements, tools and ornaments produced in city workshops. In other words the native and tribal territories are to be envisaged as being drawn into the ambit of the fortress through a combined process of political absorption and cultural diffusion. When the tribute of the indigenes was no longer distinguished from the tithe (or rather the ninth part of the harvest, if we accept the well-field as a working system) of the Chou bondsman, then the process was virtually complete. Not all scholars accept Professor Eberhard's interpretation in its entirety, particularly so far as it concerns the well-field system, but that something after this fashion took place in North China during the early years of the Western Chou is beyond dispute.

It is clear that these early Chou cities were primarily administrative and military foundations. Such industrial activities as they generated were restricted to crafts producing prestige items in bronze, jade, lacquer, pottery, and bone for the Chou nobility, while village workshops continued to manufacture the stone and bone implements used by the peasantry in farm and field. It has already been pointed out on p. 134 that in this almost wholly self-contained, manorial-style economy commerce played only an insignificant role. With the political, social and economic transformations of the Ch'un-Ch'iu period, however, the city often became a locus for the enterprises of the new merchant class. The representative Eastern Chou capital never lost its ceremonial functions, but not a few cities developed their commercial activities to a high level. In the ritualized schema of the *K'ao-kung Chi* the market was located behind, that is to the north of, the royal palace.233 Ssŭ-ma Ch'ien had no doubts about the contribution of trade to the prosperity of certain Chou cities. He reported, for example, that during the Ch'un-Ch'iu period **·I̯ung (Yung), the capital of Dz'i̯ĕn, had derived no inconsiderable benefit from its situation in the middle Wei valley, at a point where commodities from **Li̯ung (Lung), a district lying astride the approaches to the desert road to Central Asia, converged on those moving northeastwards from **D̂i̯uk (Shu), the region of present-day Ssŭ-ch'uan234. Later, under Dukes **Xi̯ăn (Hsien) and Xŏg (Hsiao) [384–338 BC], the capital had been relocated farther downstream at **Gliok (Li), where its merchants were able, while still retaining command of western and southern trade, to engage in commercial transactions with the succession states of Tsi̯ĕn to the east.235 In the Ho-tung, **Di̯ang (Yang) and **B'i̯ĕng-di̯ang (P'ing-yang) exploited their nodal position with relation to the **Dz'i̯ĕn (Ch'in) and **D'iok (Ti) barbarians of the west and the **T̂i̯ung (Chung) and **D'əg (Tai) of the north.236 G'ân-tân, the capital of D'i̯og, had profited from its ability to tap the trade of ·Ian (Yen) and **Tŭk (Cho) from the north at the same time as it had attracted to itself the commodities of Gi̯wad and D'i̯ĕng.237 Merchants in the Chou capital itself traded with Dz'i̯ər and Lo in the east and with **Li̯ang (Liang) and Tṣ'i̯o to the south.238 ·Ian, too, enjoyed an especially advantageous commercial location, situated as it was in the angle between the **·O-g'wân (Wu-huan) and **Pi̯wo-di̯o (Fu-yü) tribes on the north and the **·I̯wăd-g'lâk (Wei-ho), **D'i̯og-si̯an (Ch'ao-hsien), and **T̂i̯ĕn-p'i̯wăn (Chen-p'an) peoples of the east, at the same time as it had unobstructed lines of communication to the metropolitan heart of China to the south.239 All this and more was apparent to Ssŭ-ma Ch'ien when he came to compose his *Huo-Chih*,240 and in modern times Miyazaki Ichisada has collated a great deal of information from sources such as the *Tso-Chuan*, *Kuo-Yü* and *Chan-Kuo Ts'e* showing that during Ch'un-Ch'iu and Chan-Kuo times trade and commerce played no insignificant role in numerous Chinese cities.241 This was an age when, as Ssŭ-ma Ch'ien tells us, the 'secondary occupations', that is trade, and to a lesser extent handicrafts, were the best source of wealth for a poor man. Anyone in the ·i̯əp or *to* of late Chan-Kuo or early Han China, he says, who managed to sell 1,000 brewings of liquor, 1,000 jars of pickles and sauces, 1,000 jars of syrup, 1,000 carcases of cattle, sheep or swine, 1,000 *chung*242 of grain, 1,000 cart- or boat-loads of firewood and kindling stubble, 1,000 logs of timber, 10,000 bamboo poles, 100 horse carriages, 1,000 two-wheeled ox carts, 1,000 lacquered wooden vessels, brass utensils weighing 1,000 *chün*,[243] 1,000 *tan*[244] of plain wooden or iron vessels, gardenia and madder dyes, 200 horses, 500 cattle, 2,000 sheep or swine, 100 slaves of either sex, 1,000 *chin*[245] of tendons, horns, or cinnabar, 1,000 *chün* of silk cloth, raw silk, or other fine fabrics, 1,000 rolls of embroidered or patterned silk, 1,000 *shih* of vegetable-fiber fabrics or raw or tanned hides, 1,000 *tou*[246] of lacquer, 1,000 jars of leaven or salted bean relish, 1,000 *chin* of globefish or mullet, 1,000 *shih* of dried fish, 1,000 *chün* of salted fish, 3,000 *shih* of jujubes or chestnuts, 1,000 fox or sable pelts, 1,000 *shih* of lamb or sheep skins, 1,000 felt rugs, or 1,000 *chung* of fruits or vegetables, anyone who could do any of these things 'might live as well as the proprietor of an estate of 1,000 chariots'.[247]

With the passage of time the market quarter became a venue not only for commercial but also for social exchange, a place where the businessman, the stallholder, the teamster, the housewife, the casual passer-by, the idler, and the countryman in town for a few hours could pass the time of day. It combined, in fact, the economic and social functions of the *agora* of the Greek *polis* and the *forum* of the Roman city, and there remained only a tenuous distinction between these facets of its activities. (In China, however, there was – as far as is known – no Aristotle to advocate the separation of these functions on the Thessalian pattern : *Politics*, VII, ii, 2).

In the immediately preceding paragraphs we have traced the evolution of the representative Chou city from its inception as a fortified ceremonial enclave established in an essentially colonial context to its mature development in Chan-Kuo times as a focus of centralized facilities serving a spatially integrated hinterland. Throughout the near millennium of this period there were grafted on to the ceremonial and agro-military roles of the city certain industrial and tertiary economic activities, a process which recalls Max Weber's view of the medieval European city as resulting from the fusion of fortress and market. However, whatever applicability such an interpretation may have to European urbanism, it would be an inadequate conceptualization of the Chinese experience. In the first place, despite the relative space which we have accorded commercial activities, these were but poorly developed by any absolute standard, and the vast majority of city dwellers, not only in Chou times but even in Han and later periods, were cultivators who, in summer at any rate, went out daily through the city gates to work in their fields. In this mass of agrarian labor which constituted the urban population, the craftsmen and merchants generated only a small leavening influence and, more important for urban theory, never constituted an autonomous group able to undertake the collective exercise of power. The cities of Chou China from first to last afforded no locus of countervailing power directed against central authority, but were themselves instruments for the exercise of that power, governed, if not by the ruler of a polity, then by one of his officials. In the second place Weber's concept of European urban origins found no place for the role of the ceremonial center, the axis of the kingdom, where alone the ruler could seek counsel and intercession from the ancestors who had served the state in the past and who now watched over its future, where alone he could preside over the universal harmony that, under a virtuous monarch, manifested itself in the spontaneous co-operation of animate and inanimate nature, and where alone, at the pivot of the universe, he could ensure the continuance of the cosmic process.

The origin of the hsien city. One legacy which the Chou bequeathed to later dynasties was the governmental instrument of the *hsien* (**g'ian*), which subsequently became the basic administrative unit of the empire. Until modern times the capital of the *hsien* has constituted the lowest level of the urban hierarchy through which the central government has exercised its authority directly. As such it has generated a low-order degree of centrality, probably approximately comparable to that assigned to the *Kreisstadt* in Christaller's hierarchy.[248]

It has long been recognized that the creation of the *hsien* was a response to the need for a degree of impersonality and categorization in the developing bureaucracies of the states of Chou China, but the first attempt to localize and date this process had to await the publication in 1938 of Professor Bodde's study of the life and work of Li-Ssŭ (**Lįəg-Sįĕg*).[249] Bodde saw the origin of the *hsien* in two situations: when land was conquered from tribal peoples along the margins of the Chinese culture realm, and when territory was annexed from another state. In either case the ruler of the polity, being under no obligation to delegate sovereign rights or apportion benefices within the newly acquired territory, tended to retain it under his direct control. Government was then carried out by non-hereditary, state-appointed officials. If, as is often asserted, the graph for *hsien* was originally composed of a pictograph of a severed human head, together with the post and cord with which to display it in a public place, the whole character signifying 'to suspend' or 'attach', then the postulated mode of origin of the term as a designation for recently annexed territory may receive some support from etymology.[250] Bodde believed that administrative units on this pattern were first established in Dzʻįĕn, where four such are mentioned in extant records as being instituted in a restricted territory in 688 B.C.[251] The fact that this erosion of the political privilege of the **$d\underset{\sim}{i}ĕg$ (*shih*) kin group in favor of bureaucratic control was ascribed to Dzʻįĕn, a state which even at the end of the Chʻun-Chʻiu was considered by the literati of the central states as being at least semi-barbarian,[252] was held to give added plausibility to Bodde's interpretation. Certainly it was in that state in 350 B C that the *hsien* was made the basis of a new and more highly centralized system of government.253 Concurrently the institution had been diffusing among the other states, so that by Chan-Kuo times *hsien* were to be found in each of the seven great states, D'įog, Ngįwər, G'ân, Dz'įĕn, Tṣ'įo, ·Ian, and Dz'iər. This has also been the point of view adopted by most subsequent scholars, including Sen-dou Chang in his exposition of the urban geography of the *hsien* city.254

More recently, however, this thesis has been considerably revised by Professor H. G. Creel.255 In the first place Creel questions whether the *Shih-Chi* reference to *hsien* in Dz'įĕn in 688 and 687 BC was in fact concerned with administrative districts. The phrase ***g'ian-t̂įəg* (*hsien-chih*) could – indeed probably does – mean simply that the territories in question were annexed, without any corollary implications as to the manner in which they were integrated into the Dz'įĕn polity. In the whole of the extant corpus of Chou literature there is only one other reference, and that almost certainly a late interpolation, which mentions *hsien* in connection with Dz'įĕn during the Ch'un-Ch'iu.256 Creel has also pointed out that what little evidence is available would indicate that in Dz'įĕn governmental institutions tended to lag behind those in some other states, notably Tṣ'įo. Dz'įĕn, he says, was a borrower rather than an innovator, and, a factor of some importance so far as diffusion of its institutions was concerned, was held in low esteem by its neighbors.257 He is certainly correct when he denies the existence of conclusive evidence for the existence of *hsien* administrative units in Dz'įĕn in the 7th century, and probably so when he casts doubt on the innovatory proclivities of the Dz'įĕn government.258

Hsien are reliably reported during Ch'un-Ch'iu times in only two other states, Tsįĕn and Tṣ'įo.259 So far as Tsįĕn is concerned, the earliest mention relates to the year 627 BC,260 and Creel has argued that by 543 the whole state was apportioned in *hsien* under administrative officials.261 It appears also that *hsien* soon became hereditable,262 which allowed powerful *dįĕg*, kin-based corporate groups as Creel defined them, to treat their *hsien* as normal benefices, and thus to retain a great deal of their political privilege at the expense of the development of centralized government. During the 6th and 5th centuries, in fact, Tsįĕn administration exhibited increasingly powerful centrifugal tendencies, which culminated in its disintegration into three separate states in 453. In other words *hsien* administration seems neither to have been particularly congenial to the Tsįĕn political ethos, nor to have persisted in the bureaucratic form in which it was originally conceived. It consequently seems unlikely that it originated in that state.

The only other state in which the *hsien* functioned as an administrative institution during the Ch'un-Ch'iu was Tṣ'įo, and it is here that Creel looks for its beginnings.263 In a detailed excursus he shows that during the Ch'un-Ch'iu and Chan-Kuo periods central authority was much more strongly developed in Tṣ'įo than in the northern states, that tenure of office depended to a greater extent on merit, and that hereditary office was almost non-existent. It is possible that a factor contributing powerfully to this situation was the different kinship system obtaining in Tṣʻi̯o, possibly even to the exclusion of the *di̯ĕg* until that institution was adopted into the Tṣʻi̯o cultural inventory during the Chʻun-Chʻiu.264

Creel has elicited the further fact that, not only is the *hsien* likely to have existed earlier in Tṣʻi̯o than in any of the northern states, but also that evidence of a system of *hsien* government existed earlier there than elsewhere. The early existence of *hsien* in Tṣʻi̯o is to be inferred from a somewhat cryptic passage in the *Tso-Chuan*. In a statement made in 478 BC 265 a Tṣʻi̯o official recalls that King **Mi̯wən (Wen), who reigned from 689 to 675, converted the states of **Śi̯ĕn (Shen) and **Si̯ək (Hsi) into *hsien*, presumably after the attack which both the *Tso-Chuan* and the *Shih-Chi* 266 record as having been mounted in 688. A subsequent reference to a Tṣʻi̯o *hsien* officer in 664, and the presence of a Śi̯ĕn army under Tṣʻi̯o command in 635, afford some support for Creel's interpretation of the evidence,267 but even more significant is a report in the *Tso-Chuan* 268 of two districts which were put under **i̯uĕn (*yin*) administration by King **Mi̯wo (Wu) of Tṣʻi̯o, who reigned from 740 to 690 BC. *I̯uĕn* was a title of *hsien* administrators regularly used in Tṣʻi̯o in later years, so it is not unlikely that the institution of the *hsien* existed in that state even as early as the beginning of the 7th century BC. In any case, whether or not this inference proves acceptable, Creel has been able to demonstrate beyond doubt that, well before the beginning of the 6th century, Tṣʻi̯o had an established system of government in which the *hsien* was an important unit.269

We have already seen that, whereas in Tṣʻi̯o the *hsien* had been established as an instrument for centralized control, in Tsi̯ĕn it functioned in that way only for a short time, before being subverted in the interests of powerful kin associations. This would seem to presuppose that the *hsien* had not been devised in Tsi̯ĕn, but merely represented an abortive attempt to adopt a political instrument which, in the event, proved not readily assimilable to the structure of Tsi̯ĕn society and politics. Creel is probably correct in his conjecture that the institution of the *di̯ĕg* was significant in this connection. This point of view inevitably raises the question as to how Tsi̯ĕn came to undertake the experiment of *hsien* government, and Creel has also provided a considerable quantity of circumstantial evidence bearing on this problem. In 635, for example, a son of the Tsi̯ĕn ruler returned from an exile spent partly in Tṣʻi̯o to become Duke **Mi̯wən (Wen).270 According to the *Tso-Chuan*, he had become well acquainted with the role of career officials in the Tṣʻi̯o government. During the reigns of Duke **Mi̯wən and his successors the government of Tsi̯ĕn underwent extensive remodelling, and welcomed into the administration a number of able officials from Tṣʻi̯o.271 In the *Tso-Chuan*, under the 26th year of Duke **Sni̯ang (Hsiang), there occurs the following passage:

THE DIFFUSION OF URBAN LIFE

"The high ministers of Tsi̯ĕn," said **Śi̯ĕng-tsi̯əg (Sheng-tzŭ), "are not the equal of those of Tṣ'i̯o . . . and like the wood of the medlar and the catalpa, like skins and leather, [administrative talent] is exported from Tṣ'i̯o. Although Tṣ'i̯o possesses the raw material, it is Tsi̯ĕn which puts it to use." It is surely not stretching the bounds of probability to attribute some of the Tṣ'i̯o-style features which appeared in Tsi̯ĕn administration during the 7th and 6th centuries to this influx of talent from the great Yang-tzŭ valley state, and among these features there is good reason to include the institution of the *hsien,* and with it the *hsien* city, which was to play such an important role in later Chinese imperial administration.

MORPHOLOGY OF THE CHOU CITY

For our account of the functioning of Chou cities we have had to depend almost wholly on materials of a secondary character, namely the transmitted texts. When we turn our attention to the morphology of these cities we shall find that the literary sources are still important but that, for the period of the Eastern Chou at least, they are supplemented by a body of archeological evidence which is of considerable value from two points of view. Not only is it a primary source in its own right, but it can also be used as a check on conclusions derived from textual information. Even with this additional increment of primary information, however, it is still not easy to formulate generalizations which hold for the whole of the Chou territories at any one time, and it is not to be expected that urban forms would have undergone no change during the nine centuries or so of Chou hegemony. There are barely a score of known urban sites spread, unequally, through the whole of that period, and there is no reason to doubt that states as far apart as ·Ian and Gi̯wăt, Dz'i̯ĕn and Dz'i̯ər developed distinctive regional traditions of urbanism which have so far escaped the eye of the archeologist. Moreover, the remains relate to settlements at different levels in the urban hierarchy. Some were capitals of major states, others of minor polities, and the rest were apparently provincial towns. It follows that such structural uniformities as can be elicited are of a most general order, and the presumed variety of cultural expression has to be almost entirely ignored. There is reason to think that this may be especially deleterious to our concept of the Tṣ'i̯o city, which shared in the architectural traditions of the Yang-tzŭ valley rather than in those of the North China plain. Yet, although the archeological material is exiguous in relation to the territorial and chronological extent of Chou China, its confirmation of certain categories of literary evidence gives it a value out of all proportion to its bulk.

Through the whole Chou period cities were walled, and the importance of this wall is reflected in the fact, which has been frequently remarked, that the same character was used to denote both city and wall. According to the ***Ngi̯wăt-Li̯ĕng* (*Yüeh-Ling*) of the *Li-Chi,* the ritually sanctioned season for the *construction* of city walls was the second month of autumn, which was incidentally a relatively slack season in the farming year. The *repair* of walls and gates was winter work. All the walls investigated so far have proved to be of *hang-t'u* construction though, as was to be expected, their dimensions varied widely not only between different cities but between different sections of wall within the same city. In the Royal City in the neighborhood of present-day Lo-yang, for example, some sections of the western wall are only five meters in width, while certain lengths of the eastern wall are as much as fifteen meters wide. The inner walls of ·Ok, with a width of twelve meters, and the outer with a width of nine, fall between the two extremes encountered in the walls of the Royal City. At one of the ruined cities near Wu-an the thickness of the wall varied between eight and thirteen meters. The most massive of the walls recorded in the archeological literature are those of G'ân-tân, which exceeded twenty meters at the base. The Japanese archeologists who investigated this site have also provided the only estimate that I have come across of the original height of a city wall. Their figure for the reconstructed height was fifteen meters, which must have made the city an impressive feature in the flat landscape of southern Ho-pei. On the evidence available I have not been able to discern any correlation between the areal extent of a city and the size of its walls. In at least two instances, the Tsi̯ĕn capital at Niu-Ts'un and the ·I̯am capital near Ch'ang-Chou, the walls were flanked on their outer sides by moats, and literary references indicate that this was a common occurrence.[272]

The areas enclosed within the walls also varied enormously: from the square enceinte of 300 meter sides of the ancient ·Ian city at Ts'ai-Chuang, to the very large site of G'å-to with maximum dimensions of 8,300 × 3,930 meters. Among other areally extensive enclaves were those at Lin-tzŭ (3,000 × 4,000 meters), Chao-k'ang Chen (5,000 × 4,000 meters), Lo-yang (3,000 × 3,000 meters), T'eng-Hsien (3,600 × 2,800 meters), Hou-ma Chen (probably approximately 3,000 meters square, though erosion has destroyed the possibility of accurate measurement), and Ch'ü-fu (3,500 × 2,500 meters). Apart from the city at Chao-k'ang, whose status has not been determined, these were the state capitals of, in order, Dz'i̯ər, Royal Chou, Si̯at, ·Ok, and Lo. The dimensions of the other capital cities which have been investigated so far are that of Tsi̯ĕn at Niu-Ts'un, the sides of whose quadrangular enceinte varied between 1,340 and 1,740 meters; of D'i̯og near Han-tan, with a maximum extent of 1,387 × 1,475 meters; and of the small state of D'əng in modern T'eng-Hsien, whose outer rampart measured some 1,000 meters by 1,500. The outer circular enceinte of the old state of ·I̯am is best measured in terms of its circumference, which was about 600 meters in length. There is no reason to think that the areal extent of cities was larger at the end of the Chou period than at its beginning. And neither is there any reason to assume that a correlation of size with rank in the urban hierarchy which is adduced in the *Tso-Chuan* was anything more than a late systematization. The passage in question runs, 'The walls of any state capital (*to*) which exceed a hundred **d'i̯ər (chih) [in circumference] constitute a danger to the state. According to the institutions (**ti̯ad, chih) of the former kings, the walls of a city of the first order must not exceed one-third the length of that of the capital, that of a second-order city one-fifth, and that of a third-order city one-ninth.'[273] That this archetyped notion of the urban hierarchy was indeed a piece of literary furniture brought out to grace a certain type of occasion is rendered the more likely by the inclusion of another passage, expressing very similar sentiments, in a patently moralizing context.

'The King [of *Tṣ'i̯o*] asked **Śi̯ĕn Mi̯wo-gi̯wo (Shen Wu-yü) what was likely to happen if a state contained great cities [in addition to the capital. Śi̯ĕn] replied that in [the state of] **D'i̯ĕng [the existence of] **Kli̯ăng (Ching) and **Gliok (Li) was the real cause of the death of **Mwân păk (Man-pe); [the existence of] **Siôg (Hsiao) and **B'âk (Po) in Sông led to the murder of **Tsi̯əg-Di̯ôg (Tzŭ-Yu); in Dz'i̯ər [the existence of] **G'i̯o-k'i̯ŭg (Ch'ü-ch'iu) was directly responsible for the slaying of **Mi̯wo-Ti̯ĕg (Wu-Chih); in Gi̯wad [the existence of] **B'wo (P'u) and **Ts'iôk (Ch'i) brought about the expulsion of Duke **Xi̯ăn (Hsien). In the light of these examples it must be concluded that [such cities] are injurious to the state. Large branches are sure to break, a large tail cannot be wagged.'[274]

It would be premature to deny that, at the ceremonies by which benefice capitals were established in the early centuries of the Chou, the formal layouts may not have been conceived according to some descending order of size based on the rulers' positions in the social and political hierarchies (though I know of no independent evidence to support such a contention), but it is inconceivable that such a graded ranking of urban size should have persisted as the pressures of developing tertiary economic activities (modest in scale though these were) began to interact with the ever-present strains of political conflict. In any case, beyond confirming the truism that the more important cities of ancient China had larger enceintes, such archeological evidence as we have affords no confirmation of any such rigorously ordered hierarchy of size.

The shape of Chou urban enclaves is sufficiently significant to merit separate discussion in Chapter Five. Suffice it to note here that there was a strong tendency to regularity in the layout, a regularity which was expressed predominantly in the form of a square, or at least of a rectangle. On several of the occasions on which city plans at first appear to be fortuitously irregular, closer inspection leads to the inference that they were in fact built up by the accretion of individually regular units. Such appears to have happened, for example, in the evolution of the G'â-to. That such a process of accretion did indeed operate from time to time to modify the layouts of Chou cities is attested by the remark in the *Tso-Chuan* that 'in summer [of 667 BC] **Dẓ'i̯əg-Gwia (Shih-Wei), Grand Minister of Works (**D'âd-si̯əg-k'ung : Ta-szŭ-k'ung), walled [presumably implying in this context that he enlarged the walls of] **Kộng (Chiang) in order to secure a greater depth for the palace.'[275] The archeological reports also reveal a tendency to both cardinal orientation and cardinal axiality of city enceintes. This latter feature is perhaps suggested by the central location of the presumably ceremonial platform in the Tsi̯ĕn capital at Niu, is implied by the arrangement of the gates leading into the enclosure at Chao-k'ang, and is partly traced out in paved roads at the D'i̯og city near Wu-an. In G'ân-tân it is explicit in the arrangement of the *hang-t'u* platforms along north-south axes. The number and arrangement of city gates were also important elements of city morphology, but are best discussed in connection with the topic of symbolism included in Chapter Five.

A prominent feature of urban design throughout the whole Chou period was the raising of important buildings on platforms of *hang-t'u* construction. At Niu-Ts'un such a platform was located at the geometrical center of the city enceinte; at P'ing-wang one appears to have been similarly located; at G'ân-tân two series were arranged along meridional axes, and an additional ten were scattered both within and without the city; at Lin-tzŭ one was located in a small enclave in the southwest of the main enclosure; at the site of ·I̯am three very large examples, situated between the so-called Inner and Outer Walls, were aligned parallel to the western sector of the former; and more than fifty were dispersed in and around the enceinte of the G'å-to. In this latter case a proportion of these small tumuli are believed to have been burial mounds, but elsewhere the platforms have usually been construed as the foundations of palaces and temples, and the localities in which they occur consequently interpreted as palace precincts and ceremonial centers. In plan these platforms were predominantly square and circular, though the one at Lin-tzŭ was oval, and those at ·I̯am (Yen) of irregular shape. Of the sixteen platforms at G'ân-tân, fourteen were square and only two circular. Just outside the northern wall of the G'å-to a large square platform, the Lao-lao T'ai, provided a base from which rose a circular mound. This platform was also diversified by three terraces cut in its southern face, a feature which had occurred earlier in the P'ing-wang platform. At both P'ing-wang and Niu-Ts'un the southern edges of the platforms were constructed in the form of ramps. It is tempting to ponder on the different purposes reflected in the varying forms of these *hang-t'u* mounds, but so far archeology has provided no basis for such speculation beyond the presence of architectural remains on the summits of numerous of them.

At several of the earlier urban sites archeologists have reported the existence of workshops not only within the walled enclaves but also dispersed through the surrounding countryside on the old Shang pattern. This dispersed morphology was especially prominent in the Royal City of Chou and in the Tsi̯ĕn capitals in the vicinity of Hou-ma Chen, and, as in Shang times, presumably implies a redistributive mode of economic integration. During the Eastern Chou, however, this dispersed morphology seems to have undergone a major transformation when outer walls were constructed to enclose previously extramural settlements and workshops. Miyazaki Ichisada was apparently the first to notice indications of this process in Chou literary sources,[276] and during the past twenty years his observations have been confirmed by archeological investigation. This scholar seems to have regarded the original enceinte as having at one time provided a site for virtually all urban activities, and to have assumed the role of administrative and ceremonial enclave only after the building of the outer wall. We take a slightly different view, and visualize the inner enclosure as having from the beginning constituted the ceremonial focus, the outer wall being added subsequently to afford protection to the populace and handicrafts that had been attracted to the neighborhood of the cult center. That such a spatial expression of the dichotomy between the two main sectors of society, the $k_iwən\text{-}ts_iəg$ and the $di\mathring{a}\text{-}ńi\breve{e}n$, the sacrally ordained élite and the mass of the populace, did exist in Chou times is attested by fragmentary references in ancient literature which divide the representative city into two sectors. One, termed alternatively the **to (*tu*) or **kwâk (*kuo*), contained the sacred structures without which a state could not come into, or remain in, being, together with the palace of the ruler, and accommodation, usually in early times in the form of semi-subterranean dwellings, for retainers, servitors and some craftsmen. The other sector, known as the ***p̣iəg* (*pi*), housed the rest of the community and provided sites for most of the handicraft workshops serving it. Occasionally the names attached to some of the discrete quarters of these cities have been recorded in Chou literature, chiefly in the *Tso-Chuan*. One quarter of the capital of D'i̯ĕng, for example, was known straightforwardly as the Central District (**Ti̯ông-Pi̯wən : Chung-Fen),[277] and another within the capital of Sông went by the name of the Southern Neighborhood (**Nəm-Li̯əg : Nan-Li).[278] In the suburbs the dwellings were partly of *hang-tʻu* and partly of thatch, and in the dry and dusty winter months fire was an ever-threatening hazard. As early as 563 BC precautionary measures were

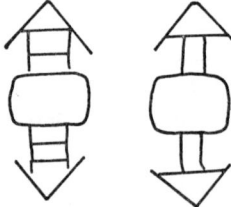

[15] The character denoting the outer wall of an early Chinese city as it appears (right) on Shang oracle bones and (left) on an early Chou bronze [Karlgren, 774b and c].

initiated in the capital of Sông after the city had been devastated by fire. Although the conflagration was denoted in the *Tso-Chuan* by the graph for a calamity sent by Heaven (**tsəg* : tsai),[279] the government nevertheless made every effort to prevent the divine will manifesting itself in the same form on a subsequent occasion. **Nglŏk-Xi̯əg (Yüeh-Hsi), the equivalent of a Minister of Works, appointed an official to supervise preventative measures in those parts of the city which the flames had not reached. Small houses were to be removed altogether and large ones to be rough-cast. Baskets and barrows were to be placed at strategic spots, well-ropes, buckets and water-jars were to be provided, and supplies of earth and mud held in readiness. A fire-watch was to be maintained within the city, and reserve forces were to be summoned from the countryside. Particular attention was to be paid to the safety of the state records in their several repositories, and to the precincts of the palace. This is the only instance of preventative action to have been recorded in such detail, but we may be certain that the problem was one common to all cities of the time.

The fundamental role of the inner wall enclosing the administrative and ceremonial focus of the territory, the axis about which revolved the microcosm of the state, is reflected in the etymology of the word **ḍi̯ĕng (ch'eng), which came to denote both 'city' and '[the] wall', whereas **kwâk (kuo), the outer wall, acquired overtones associated with fortification and subsequently developed the secondary meaning of 'suburb'.[280] That the two enceintes were not always constructed simultaneously is attested by an account of the founding of **Tṣ'i̯o-k'i̯ŭg (Ch'u-ch'iu), the new Gi̯wad capital, after the previous city had been razed by the D'iek barbarians. The neighboring states sent contingents to assist in the raising of the inner wall surrounding the ceremonial center in the spring of 657,[281] but the suburbs (**p'i̯ug* : fu) were not walled until the spring of 647, when a D'iek attack appeared to be imminent.[282] The royal capital of Ḍi̯ĕng-Ti̯ôg (cf. p. 136 above) affords another example. The suburb of **D'iek-dz'i̯wan (Ti-ch'üan), site of the royal tombs outside the eastern wall, had certainly come into existence by 517 B C,[283] but was not brought within the wall until 508.[284] In Lo the suburbs of the city of **Ḍi̯ĕng, which appears to have been mentioned first in 705,[285] were not walled until 557 in the face of an attack by the forces of the Marquis of Dz'i̯ər.[286] And, as a final example, we may point to a brief notice in the *Tso-Chuan* which records the walling of the already existing suburbs of **Dz'ŏg (Ch'ao) and **Ki̯wɛd-ńi̯an (Chi-jan) in Tṣ'i̯o.[287]

The *Kuo-Yü* expressed the spatial and functional dichotomy of the city rather differently in opposing an administrative enclave (**kwân-pi̯u* : kuan-fu) to a market place (**ḍi̯əg-tsi̯ĕng*), and realistically also included within the urban sphere the fields that lay beyond its walls (**d'i̯en-di̯â*). It would seem that Mencius had a similar pattern of land use in mind when he wrote that, if the King were to establish a government of perfect virtue, then 'the officials of the kingdom would all be anxious to establish themselves at Your Majesty's court, the farmers would all be anxious to cultivate Your Majesty's lands, and the merchants would all be anxious to store their goods in Your Majesty's market-places.'[288]

Although it is clear that these changes in urban form took place during the Chou dynasty, because of the relative paucity of archeological evidence and the difficulty of dating the information contained in cumulative and systematizing texts, it is not yet possible to define the stages by which they came about. In any case, there is no reason to suppose that the transformation proceeded contemporaneously in all states. Certainly the old dispersed pattern of urban integration appears to have persisted in the settlements of the New Fields well into the second half of the Ch'un-Ch'iu period, whereas the newer compact urban forms, with their double enceintes, seem to have become common during Chan-Kuo times, with the rise of cities such as the Dz'iər capital at Lin-tzŭ and the D'əng, ·I̯am, and ·Ok[289] capitals. Precisely which point of view one adopts in this matter will depend very largely on how one interprets the urban annexes that feature in the plans of some of these cities, notably that of G'ân-tân. Wolfram Eberhard has proposed to group such cities into a class which he calls appropriately 'double cities', each sector of which he regards as inhabited by ethnically distinct populations.[290] In his view most of the Chou *colonia* established after the conquest would have taken this form. It is true that the *I Chou-shu*, which probably preserves material from the beginning of the 3rd century BC, attributes just such a formal dichotomy to **Glâk-·i̯əp (Lo-i, later known as Dji̯ĕng-Ti̯ôg: cf. p. 136 above),[291] and similar divisions are mentioned in connection with the old Chou capitals of P'i̯ông and G'og, but only archeological investigation will ultimately decide if the ancient texts are to be relied upon in this respect. Even if they are, it still remains an open question as to whether the ethnic division of the early Chou *colonia* was the precursor of the class division apparent in later times. All that can be said at present is that such an ethnically based duality does not appear to us to have been a prerequisite for the development of the double enclaves of Chan-Kuo times.

In the idealized city of the Western Chou the ruler's palace was raised exactly in the center of the enceinte, and itself constituted a city within a city. At its very center the hall of audience fronted southwards on to the axial avenue which ran between the altar to the god of the soil and the temple of the ancestors. At the next lower level in the social hierarchy the dwellings of the more powerful families, each grouped round its own great hall, reproduced on a smaller scale the residence of the ruler. As in all classical, which is synonymous with archetyped, literatures, the cities of the Western Chou are represented as splendid creations of Chinese architectural genius. That they were something less, indeed – although they contained the seeds which would later flower into the glories of Ch'ang-an and Pei-ching – often mean and cluttered settlements, has

NATURE OF CHOU URBANISM

been stated so persuasively by Marcel Granet that I can do no better than quote his description of these ancient cities.[292]

'It appears however that in every country the princely residences were usually humble dwellings, quickly built and rapidly demolished. In 502, for example, a highly placed personage had a house of beaten earth made for his son, at the side of his own palace.[a] There was no hesitation in throwing down entire houses to make way for a funeral.[b] An old ritual rule (which is explained by the constitution of the family) required that sons should not have the same abode as their father: fathers and sons resided (in alternate generations) on the right or left of a building which was supposed to have been the house of the founder of their line. The same disposition held good for the chapels of the ancestral Temple which were consecrated to the most recent ancestors. All these ephemeral dwellings, enclosed within low little walls and separated by narrow alleys, were crowded around a sort of fortress. In time of revolts and vendettas (for example at Chin [$Tsi\check{e}n$] in 549 BC) attackers are seen to leap over the low walls. When they have hoisted themselves upon the gate of the palace, they can rain arrows into the prince's chamber: but a fortified tower serves as an entrenchment for the defenders. At Ch'i [$Dz'i\partial r$], in 538 BC, under a prince famous for his ostentation, the chief minister resides in a low quarter containing the market. He inhabits "a low and narrow house, exposed to the dust". The prince is alone in possessing "a piece of ground which is well lighted, high and dry". Built upon an eminence and flanked by towers, the seigniorial residence looks like a fortified village dominating the low-lying outskirts of a market.[c]'

[Granet's footnotes refer to Séraphin Couvreur's French translation of the *Ch'un-Ch'iu* and *Tso-Chuan* in 3 volumes (Mission Press, Hochienfu, 1914): (*a*) vol. 3, p. 547; (*b*) vol. 3, p. 291; (*c*) vol. 2, p. 293, and vol. 3, pp. 59, 60, 736.]

SIZE OF THE CHOU CITY

The level of intensity of archeological excavation of Chou urban sites does not permit us to use the dimensions of the enceintes described in the preceding section to estimate the populations of these cities in the manner in which, say, Henri Frankfort was able to calculate early urban densities for Lower Mesopotamia.[293] Of the density of dwellings within either or both enceintes we have practically no idea. The problem is especially intractable in the case of the dispersed settlement form associated with the Shang and earlier centuries of the Chou. To judge from analogous developmental stages of urban evolution in other parts of East Asia and Nuclear America, by no means all the space within the city walls was under structures of any kind, let alone residential buildings (cf. also p. 436 below). In default of a sound archeological basis for calculation, we can only fall back on the few population estimates which occur in Chou literature. The *Chan-Kuo Ts'e* (chüan 8), for example, credits the Dz'iər capital at Lin-tzŭ with 210,000 inhabitants. In view of what we have said about such texts in a previous section, it is doubtful if this figure can be relied upon. When the Gi̯wad capital was re-established at **Tṣ'i̯o-k'i̯ŭg (Ch'u-ch'iu) after its sack at the hands of the D'iek barbarians in 659 BC, it was reputed to have had a mere 5,000 inhabitants,[294] including the people of two smaller settlements, **Ki̯ung (Kung) and **D'əng (T'eng), who had been brought into it. Presumably the population of the earlier capital had been somewhat larger. That many, perhaps most, Ch'un-Ch'iu urban settlements were much less populous than this is implicit in numerous passages in the literature of the time. It was proposed, for example, to invest a single Gi̯wad minister with as many as sixty ·i̯əp,[295] which surely implies that each was a relatively small settlement; and we have already drawn attention to the implication in an appendix to the *I-Ching* that some three hundred households constituted a reasonable population for a representative ·i̯əp (p. 167). It must be remembered, of course, that, whatever its pretentions, this particular appendix was composed, at the earliest, towards the end of the Chou period, and its assumptions are those of the era of the Contending States or later.

Notes and References

1. I have made no attempt to furnish primary documentation for this introductory section, but these notes do provide a skeleton bibliography of secondary and exegetical writings which should help a student of urbanism to acquire an appreciation of the background against which Chou cities evolved.

2. For pertinent comments on this stereotype see Arthur F. Wright, 'Sui Yang-ti: personality and stereotype', in Wright [ed.], *The Confucian persuasion*. Stanford University Press, Stanford, California 1960. Reprinted in Wright [ed.], *Confucianism and Chinese civilization*. Atheneum Paperback no.64, 1964.

3. Noel Barnard, 'A recently excavated inscribed bronze of Western Chou date', *Monumenta Serica*, vol.17 (1958), pp.12–46, and review article in vol.22, fasc.1 of the same journal (1963), pp.223–4. In any case, the canonical view of the role of the Duke of Chou was probably only an elaboration of events by genealogists of the ducal house of **Lo (Lu), who claimed him as their ancestor. Confucians would naturally be well disposed towards the progenitor of the royal house whose early rulers were revered by their master. On the other hand, the Duke of Chou is mentioned only twice in the *Shih-Ching*, and not at all in the *Shang-Sung* section.

4. There are indications that **Tân-B'i̯wo (Tan-Fu) may have been a culture-hero who at one time rivalled the Chou progenitor **G'u-Tsi̯ək (Hou-Chi). It is possible, for example, that one of the **D'âd-Ngâ (*Ta-Ya*) Odes [Mao 237] associates him with the gourd seeds from which, in certain East Asian mythologies, germinated the human race [cf. Arthur Waley, *The Book of Songs*. George Allen and Unwin Ltd, London 1937, pp.246–7], whereas G'u-Tsi̯ək was traditionally associated with domesticated plants : 'he understood the ways of the earth [so that] appropriate grains were planted and the harvest gathered in' [*Shih-Chi*, chüan 4, f.1 verso]. The fact that Tân-B'i̯wo was eventually assigned to a later period than G'u-Tsi̯ək is no guarantee of the chronological priority of the latter's myth : indeed, such is the nature of early Chinese historiography, it may well be held to imply an earlier date for the Tân-B'i̯wo legend.

5. This is the pre-conquest history of the Chou people as it is recorded in *Shih-Chi* : in other ancient sources the detail varies but the general tenor of the account remains substantially the same.

6. Shih Chang-ju, 'Kuan-chung k'ao-ku tiao-ch'a pao-kao', *Kuo-li Chung-yang Yen-chiu-yüan Li-shih Yü-yen Yen-chiu-so Chi-k'an*, vol.27 (1956),

pp.205–323; Su Ping-chi, *Tou-chi T'ai Kou-tung-ch'ü Mu-tsang*. National Academy of Pei-p'ing 1948.

7. Su Ping-chi and Wu Ju-tso, 'Hsi-an fu-chin ku-wen-hua i-ts'un-ti lei-hsing ho fen-pu', *K'ao-ku T'ung-hsün*, no.2 (1956), pp.32–8.

8. For discussions of these materials, and particularly the *T'ien-wang Kuei*, an inscribed bronze vessel which may date from the pre-conquest period of Chou history, see Sun Tso-yün, 'Shuo "T'ien-wang Kuei" wei Wu-wang mieh Shang i-ch'ien t'ung-ch'i' *Wen-wu Ts'an-k'ao Tzŭ-liao*, no.1 (1958), pp.29–31, and "Tsai lun 'T'ien-wang Kuei' erh-san-shih," *Wen-wu*, no.5 (1960), pp.50–52; Ch'ien Po-ch'üan, "'Shuo T'ien-wang Kuei wei Wu-wang mieh Shang i-ch'ien t'ung-ch'i'" i-wen-ti chi-tien shang-ch'üeh', *Wen-wu Ts'an-k'ao Tzŭ-liao*, no.12 (1958), pp.56–7; Yin Ti-fei, 'Shih-lun "T'ien-feng Kuei"-ti nien-tai', *Wen-wu*, no.5 (1960), pp.53–4.

9. Generic names for the tribes of the western and northern frontiers respectively. In the *Kuo-Yü* [*chüan* 1, f.2 verso], a ministerial descendant of the Duke of Chou (t̯i̯ôg) found it more expedient to claim that during the Hsia dynasty the ancestors of the Chou kings 'had hidden themselves among the **Ñi̯ông (Jung) and **D'iek (Ti)', while yet retaining their Chinese culture.

10. *Shih-Chi*, chüan 4, f.3 recto.

11. *Chu-shu Chi-nien*, Shang dynasty, *sub* Wen-ting (**Mi̯wən-tieng).

12. Wolfram Eberhard, *Kultur und Siedlung der Randvölker Chinas*. Supplement to *T'oung Pao*, vol.36, E.J. Brill, Leiden 1942; *A history of China*. University of California Press, Berkeley and Los Angeles, second edition, 1960, p.29; and *Conquerors and rulers. Social forces in medieval China*. E.J. Brill, Leiden, second edition, 1965, p.28. Cf. also Gustav Haloun, 'Beiträge zur Siedlungsgeschichte chinesischer Clans', *Hirth-Festschrift der Asia Major*. Leipzig 1922; 'Contributions to the history of clan settlement', *Asia Major*, vol.1. Leipzig, 1924; and 'Die Rekonstruktion der chinesischen Urgeschichte durch die Chinesen', *Japanisch-deutsche Zeitschrift für Wissenschaft und Technik*, vol.3, pt.7 (1925).

13. Owen Lattimore, *Inner Asian frontiers of China*. American Geographical Society, New York 1940, parts II and III. Reprint by the Beacon Press, Boston 1962. Cf. also Lattimore, *Studies in frontier history*. Oxford University Press 1962, p.547 [This paper is a reprint of a review article which first appeared in *Past and Present*, vol.12 (1957)].

14. Ralph Linton and Abram Kardiner, 'The change from dry to wet rice cultivation in Tanala-Betsileo', in *The individual and his society*. Columbia University Press, New York 1939. Reprinted in *Readings in social psychology*. New York 1952, pp.222–31. After the Tanala had adopted the techniques of wet padi cultivation from their Betsileo neighbors Linton was able to document the following concomitant changes in the structure of their society: the gradual emergence of a group of landowners; the disruption of the joint family, endo-

NOTES AND REFERENCES

gamy and self-sufficiency; the establishment of permanent settlements; modifications in the patterns of warfare; the attachment of an economic value to slaves and an associated formulation of ransom procedures; and the institutionalization of kingship. Linton further pointed out that the situation to be expected when this transformation – which had been initiated by a change in methods of production – should be consolidated and institutionalized was already apparent in Betsileo society, which he characterized as 'a feudal system of a kind' (*ibid.*, p.227).

15. René Grousset, *The rise and splendour of the Chinese empire*. University of California Press, Berkeley and Los Angeles 1958, p.22. This work is a translation by Anthony Watson-Gandy and Terence Gordon of *Histoire de la Chine*. Fayard, Paris 1942.

16. Herrlee Glessner Creel's evaluation is entirely representative of this school of thought : '... we know that the Chou were relatively rude barbarians who overran their more cultivated Shang neighbors and consolidated a large portion of North China under a rule that was necessarily rather harsh.... The chiefs of the Chou tribe had neither the experience nor the facilities (communications and a monetary system) necessary for highly centralized government...' [*Confucius : the man and the myth*. John Day Company, New York 1949, p.157 : p.146 of the reprinted edition under the title *Confucius and the Chinese way*. Harper Torchbook no.63, New York 1960].

17. Noel Barnard, 'A recently excavated inscribed bronze of Western Chou date', *Monumenta Serica*, vol.17 (1958), pp.35–6, and 'A recently excavated inscribed bronze of the reign of King Mu of Chou', *Monumenta Serica*, vol.19 (1960), p.75, note 8.

18. Barnard regards inscriptions of this kind included in Lo Chen-yü's well known compendia as either spurious or of non-Shang origin (*loc. cit.* p.36, note 21).

19. Kwang-chih Chang, *The archaeology of ancient China*. Yale University Press, New Haven 1963, p.180.

20. Another tradition, neither more nor less reliable than the one quoted, alleges that the Chou ruler destroyed some fifty or so [city-]states and founded seventy, while the *Hsün-tzŭ* (4, i and 8, xii) mentions a figure of seventy-one, of which fifty-three were granted to royal kinsmen. The *I Chou-Shu*, possibly compiled in the 3rd or 4th century BC, states that the Chou armies conquered ninety-nine [city-]states and imposed their authority on 652 others [Chu Yu-tseng's edition, Han-k'ou, 1911, chüan 4, f.7 recto], while the late-Chou *Lü-Shih Ch'un-Ch'iu* mentions figures of 400 and 800 for the two categories respectively.

21. This term is used in the sense advocated by Lewis Henry Morgan, 'The systems of consanguinity and affinity,' *Smithsonian Institution contributions to knowledge*, vol.17 (1877). Cf. also A. R. Radcliffe-Brown, *Structure and function*

in primitive society. The Free Press edition, New York 1965, p.64 : 'A nomenclature is classificatory when it uses terms which apply to lineal relatives, such as "father", to refer also to collateral relatives.'

22. Genealogical tables of rulers and their chief ministers are to be found in the Sung scholar Ch'eng Kung-shuo's *Ch'un-Ch'iu Fen-chi* (in the *Ssŭ-k'u Ch'üan-shu*), Book I, chüan 1–18 : cf. also Sun Yao, *Ch'un-Ch'iu Shih-tai-chih Shih-tsu.* China Book Co., Shanghai 1931. On the spurious nature of, for example, the genealogies of the rulers of **·*Ian (Yen)* and ***Ngo (Wu)* see Ch'i Ssŭ-ho, 'Yen-Wu fei Chou feng-kuo shuo', *Yen-ching Hsüeh-pao,* no.28 (1940), pp.175–96. Cf. also Lou Kan-jou, *Histoire sociale de l'époque Tcheou.* Paris 1935, p.42.

23. The comparison with Nippur is apt in another respect, for there is good evidence that *Kengir,* the only term known to have been used for Sumer as a political unit, originally denoted Nippur itself, and consequently affords a parallel with the term Chou (**t̯i̯ôg) : *vide* Thorkild Jacobsen, *Journal of the American Oriental Society,* vol.59 (1939), p.487, note 11, and 'Early political developments in Mesopotamia', *Zeitschrift für Assyriologie,* vol.52 (1957), pp.91–140.

24. *Vide* Ku Chieh-kang (ed.), *Ku-shih Pien,* vols.1 and 2, *passim,* and Tjan Tjoe Som [Tseng Chu-sen], *Po-hu T'ung,* vol.1. Brill, Leiden 1949.

25. The first full-scale study of the political structure of pre-Ch'in China in this new idiom was that by Richard Louis Walker, *The multi-state system of ancient China.* The Shoe String Press, Hamden, Connecticut 1953, which presented essentially the interpretation adopted in the present work. Earlier authors who had moved in the same direction but somewhat more hesitantly included Ch'en Shih-ts'ai, *A fragment on the equality of states.* A doctoral dissertation submitted to Harvard College, 1945; and 'The equality of states in ancient China', *American Journal of International Law,* vol.35 (1941), pp.641–650. Hung Chün-p'ei [*Ch'un-Ch'iu Kuo-chi Kung-fa.* China Book Company, Shanghai 1937, Chapter I, pp.1–9] summarizes a variety of previous works in this vein. The first Western author to apply the analytical techniques of modern political science to the multi-state system of the Ch'un-Ch'iu was Roswell Britton, 'Chinese Interstate Intercourse before 700 BC', *American Journal of International Law,* vol.29 (1935).

26. *Tso-Chuan,* Duke **·I̯ən (Yin), 3rd year and Duke **G'wân (Huan), 5th year.

27. This figure has been computed by modern scholars on the basis of information in the *Ch'un-Ch'iu,* its commentaries, and other relevant texts relating to the early years of the Eastern Chou. Cf. Li Tung-fang, *Ch'un-Ch'iu Chan-Kuo P'ien. Chung-Kuo Li-shih T'ung-lun* series. Commercial Press Ch'ung-ch'ing 1944, p.65. Ku Tung-kao, in his meticulous chronological systematization of events recorded in the Ch'un-Ch'iu, *Ch'un-Ch'iu Ta-shih*

NOTES AND REFERENCES

Piao (preface dated 1748), table 5, pp.1a–15a [in *Huang-Ch'ing Ching-chieh Hsü-p'ien*, ts'e 17–34], lists 209 states which are mentioned in the *Ch'un-Ch'iu* and *Tso-Chuan*, but a proportion of these were drawn into the Chinese culture-realm during, rather than before, the period and consequently were not counted by Li Tung-fang. Cf. also Ch'eng Te-hsü, 'International law in early China (1122–249 BC)', *Chinese Social and Political Science Review*, vol.11 (1927), p.42.

28. The most detailed map of the boundaries of the Ch'un-Ch'iu states is probably that at the end of vol.1 of Otto Franke's *Geschichte des chinesischen Reiches*. Walter de Gruyter, Berlin 1930.

29. In this connection we are reminded that when a **Tsi̯ĕn envoy investigated the **Lo archives in 540 BC, he is reported to have exclaimed, 'The institutes (**li̯ər) of T̂i̯ôg (Chou) are all in Lo. Now, indeed, I recognize the virtue of the Duke of T̂i̯ôg and understand how [the Duke of] T̂i̯ôg attained royal status.'

30. Not to be confused with the Royal T̂i̯ôg (Chou), which is denoted by a different character.

31. But see Hou Wai-lu, *Chung-Kuo Ku-tai She-hui-shih*. Shanghai 1948.

32. The exception was the state of Dz'i̯ər, which was able to extend its territory at the expense of non-Chinese peoples on the Shan-tung peninsula, a process which has been analyzed and mapped by Walker, *The multi-state system*, pp.29–30. Eberhard has argued that the peripheral states were also better placed, being farther from the focus of power, to develop their own effective systems of local administration [*Conquerors and rulers*, pp.29–30].

33. E.g. ***mi̯at* (*mieh*)=extinguish, exterminate, destroy; ***ts'i̯u* (*ch'ü*)=take, seize; ***g'ộng*/*ʔg'lông* (*hsiang*)=bring to terms, submit; ***ts'i̯an* (*ch'ien*)=remove, be removed.

34. Fung Yu-lan, *A history of Chinese philosophy*. Transl. from the Chinese by Derk Bodde, second edition, Princeton University Press 1952, p.312.

35. Max Weber, *The theory of social and economic organization*. Transl. from the German by A.M. Henderson and Talcott Parsons, The Free Press of Glencoe, Illinois 1947, pp.136–8, 329 *et seq.* and 341 *et seq.*

36. A schedule of these *g'wâd* (*hui*) has been prepared by Li Tung-fang, *Ch'un-Ch'iu Chan-Kuo P'ien*, Chapter I, note 49.

37. Marcel Granet, *La féodalité chinoise*. Instituttet for Sammenlignende Kulturforskning. H. Aschehoug, Oslo 1952, p.66.

38. These were Tṣ'i̯o, Dz'i̯ər, Dz'i̯ĕn, **G'ân (Han, a succession state which emerged on the dissolution of Tsi̯ĕn at the end of the 5th century) and ·Ian. **D'i̯og (Chao), another succession state, followed suit at about this time but the precise year is uncertain.

39. Ssŭ-ma Ch'ien (*Shih-Chi*, chüan 14 and 15) refers to twelve states but enumerates thirteen. This apparent anomaly is usually explained either by

assuming that Ngo was still counted as barbarian, un-Chinese, or that the term 'Twelve Rulers' had become a synecdochic synonym for the whole Chinese culture-realm before Ngo was admitted to the group, and was retained subsequently.

40. Cho-yün Hsü [Hsü Cho-yün], *Ancient China in transition. An analysis of social mobility, 722–222 BC*. Stanford University Press 1965, Chapter 4.

41. Cf. the genealogy of the *Lo* ducal house on p.79 of Hsü's work, and the commentary which accompanies it on pp.78–9.

42. Cf. Table 2, p.30 in Hsü's *Ancient China*.

43. Cf. Max Weber, 'Politik als Beruf', *Gesammelte Politische Schriften*. München 1921, pp.396–450. According to Gerth and Mills this paper was originally presented as a speech at München University in 1918, and published by Duncker and Humblot in the following year. There is an English translation in H.H. Gerth and C. Wright Mills, *From Max Weber*. Galaxy Book no.13, Oxford University Press, New York 1958, pp.77–128. This change in the nature of Chou administration has already been noted by Professor Cho-yün Hsü, *Ancient China*, p.92.

It must be emphasized that direct evidence of Western Chou government is extremely meager, so that there is an unavoidable tendency to regard changes such as those discussed in the present instance as having been initiated in the Ch'an-Ch'iu period. However, it is worthy of note that Professor H.G. Creel has recently drawn attention to the existence under the Western Chou of officials who might reasonably be called proto-bureaucrats (although it is difficult to say to what extent they functioned in the domains of vassals as well as in those of the king). 'It appears quite possible,' he writes, 'that there was [early in the Western Chou] ... a more effective and centralized administration than critical scholars have usually been willing to suppose'. ['The beginnings of bureaucracy in China: the origin of the *Hsien*', *The Journal of Asian Studies*, vol.23, no.2 (1964), p.169, note 75].

44. Gerth and Mills, *From Max Weber*, p.82.

45. Granet, *La féodalité chinoise*, p.20.

46. S. Dubrowsky, 'Über das Wesen des Feudalismus', *Agrar-Probleme*. Moscow and Munich 1929, p.214. The relevant passage has been translated into English by Wolfram Eberhard in *Conquerors and rulers*, p.24, which also contains a discussion of several theories of feudalism as applied to China.

47. In contemporary Chinese historiography 'feudalism' is the only permitted epithet for some three millennia of the Chinese past, a truth revealed, if not discovered, by Chairman Mao himself in the famous phrase 'feudal from Chou and Ch'in': Mao Tse-tung, *Chung-Kuo Ke-ming ho Chung-Kuo Kung-ch'an-tang*. Hong Kong 1949.

48. This attitude is typified by the remark of Joseph Calmette [*La société féodale*, Third edition, Paris 1925, p.1: 'En réalité, la féodalité est proprement

NOTES AND REFERENCES

occidentale et mediévale'], and is very close to that of Bryce Lyon, *The Middle Ages*, p.13.

49. F. W. Maitland, *The constitutional history of England*. Cambridge University Press 1908, pp.22–3.

50. This is the class of definition which John W. Hall has termed 'particularistic' ['Feudalism in Japan – a reassessment', *Comparative Studies in Society and History*, vol.5, no.1 (1962), p.21].

51. This is Hall's 'linear or developmental conception of feudalism', *loc. cit.*, p.23.

52. Attempts to define feudalism in ethnocentric terms have certainly not been confined to Western Europe. S. B. Veselovsky, for example, spent a lifetime in study of the political and manorial aspects of feudalism in northeastern Russia from the 14th to the 16th century, and, although methodologically he relied on Seebohm, Maitland and Fustel de Coulanges, his conclusions, so far as they were published, related only to one part of Russia. Cf. *Feodal'noe zemlev-ladenie v Severo-Vostochnoï Rusi*. On the other hand, S. Yushkov [*Voprosy Istorii*, vol.7 (1946)] adduced interesting parallels between societies as diverse as those of Kievan Russia prior to the 11th century, the Mongol realm prior to Činggis Khan, and the Anglo-Saxon kingdoms before the 9th century AD.

53. It appears that the term 'feudalism' was first coined by the Comte de Boulainvilliers and given wider currency by Montesquieu. Cf. Marc Bloch, *Feudal Society*, transl. from the French by L. A. Manyon. Chicago University Press 1961, pp.xvii–xviii. Learning of this abstraction, Chinese historians rendered it by a term which subsumed a rich store of associations from classical times, namely *feng-chien chih-tu*. According to the Chin philologist Chang-I, both *feng* and *chien* meant 'to establish', and either could be used alone to

 [III] The character for **$p\!\!\!_\iota ung$ (*feng*), signifying 'a mound' or 'to raise a mound', as it appears in a Chou bronze inscription.

denote enfeoffment [*Vide* Chang-I, *Kuang-Ya*, with commentary by Wang Nien-sun (1879), chüan 4, f.22 verso]. Moreover, *feng* (**$p\!\!\!_\iota ung$) had in early Chou times signified a mound, the raising of a mound, and to earth up a plant. In fact, in Chou bronze inscriptions the character depicts a hand beside a plant rooted in soil, and presumably implies the act of piling earth around a plant. According to books of ritual composed in much later times, the Western Chou ceremony of investiture involved the implanting, in the capital of the new benefice, of a clod of earth from the altar of the national God of the Soil. The new altar mound (*feng*) was then raised around the clod, whence the use of the term (*feng*) to signify enfeoffment. This was the word, with its aura of mellow, half-hallowed classical associations, which Chinese historians used to translate the European concept of feudalism, but many of them, often less familiar with the specialist studies of medieval European history than with Japanese translations of works of Marxian socialism, perceived the lineaments of feudalism as permeating all Chinese history prior to the 20th century, with the exception, of course, of a pre-feudal period lost in the mists of prehistory. For others feudalism developed out of a slave society, and the exigent problem then was to devise a periodization appropriate to these two societies. Cf., for example, Lü Chen-yü, *Chung-Kuo Cheng-chih Ssŭ-hsiang-shih*. Shanghai 1937; and *Chung-Kuo She-hui Shih-kang*, 2 vols. Shanghai 1947; Chien Po-tsan, *Chung-Kuo Shih-kang*, 2 vols. Shanghai 1946. The more sophisticated approach to the study of Chinese feudalism by Ch'i Ssŭ-ho is mentioned below.

54. These are the additional features cited by Derk Bodde in a paper in which he evaluated previous studies of the Chinese experience in the light of the findings of an interdisciplinary conference on comparative feudalism, held at Princeton University in 1950. *Vide* Bodde in Rushton Coulborn (ed.), *Feudalism in History*. Princeton University Press 1956, p.90. Granet [*La féodalité chinoise*, pp.24–8], who considered that the institutional parallels between ancient Chinese and medieval European society were sufficiently close for the former justly to be termed 'feudal', cited as the distinctive characteristic of both societies the dichotomy between a noble warrior class living according to an elaborate code of honor and performing military service in return for enfeoffment on the one hand, and a peasantry who lacked the code, possessed no rights to the land they worked, and served in war only as conscripted levies on the other.

55. Ch'i Ssŭ-ho, 'A comparison between Chinese and European feudal institutions', *Yenching Journal of Social Studies*, vol.4 (1948), pp.1–13, 'Feng-chien-chih-tu yü Ju-chia ssŭ-hsiang', *Yen-ching Hsüeh-pao*, no.22 (1937), pp.175–223, and 'Chan-Kuo chih-tu k'ao', *Yen-ching Hsüeh-pao*, no.24 (1938), pp.159–219.

56. Ch'i Ssŭ-ho, 'A comparison', p.2.

57. Eberhard, *Conquerors and rulers*, pp.27–8, and *Collected papers, vol.1 : Settlement and Social Change in Asia*. Hong Kong University Press, Hong Kong and Oxford University Press, London 1967, p.25.

58. Alexander Rüstow, *Ortsbestimmung der Gegenwart*, vol.1. Zürich, 1949.

59. Lattimore, *Inner Asian frontiers of China*, Chapters IX and XI.

60. An antecedent empire in process of disintegration is one of the dynamic criteria of feudalism proposed in Coulborn, *Feudalism in history*, *passim* and, especially, A. L. Kroeber's preface, p.viii: 'Coulborn sees feudalism as a socio-political aid in the revival of civilization when this, following the death of creativity in intellectual endeavor, begins to dry rot . . . its political and

NOTES AND REFERENCES

economic fabric disintegrates . . . Feudalism may or may not develop; if it does . . . it is as a rude but healthy reconstructive device from the low point of disintegration and decline and as an instrument of the reconstructing civilisation.' For Owen Lattimore feudalism 'is a complex of economic, social, military, and administrative methods of organisation . . . [which] . . . emerges in periods when, in the relationship between these aspects of society, military striking power has quite wide geographical range, but transport is so cumbrous and expensive that the exchange of food and goods of daily consumption cannot be organized within a common market as wide as the periphery to which military operations can reach' [*Studies in frontier history*, pp.543–4]. Lattimore, together with Joseph Levenson [review of Coulborn's *Feudalism in history* in *Far Eastern Quarterly*, vol.15, no.4 (1956), pp.569–72] and Etienne Balazs [*Far Eastern Quarterly*, vol.16, no.2 (1957), pp.329–32], are among the few China specialists who have considered feudalism as a developmental (and, according to Lattimore and Balazs, a devolutional) stage.

61. Bodde in Coulborn's *Feudalism in history*, pp.53–4.

62. Henri Maspero, 'Le régime féodal et la propriété foncière dans la Chine antique', *Mélanges posthumes sur les religions et l'histoire de la Chine* vol.3. Paris 1950, pp.133, 143–4. Cf. also the same author's 'Les régimes fonciers en Chine, des origines aux temps modernes', *ibid.*, pp.147–92, and 'Les termes désignant la propriété foncière en Chine', *ibid.*, pp.193–208.

63. Barnard [*Monumenta Serica*, vol.17 (1958), p. 32, note 18] writes: '. . . subinfeudation, too, was characteristic and numerous examples may be observed in unattested sources – both bronze texts and traditional literature [I think that Barnard must be using the term in a somewhat different sense from Maspero, at least in so far as literary sources are concerned – Author]. The fully attested Inscription 23.9 excavated at Chün-Hsien in 1936 (see *T'ien-yeh K'ao-ku Pao-kao*, 1936 for details and rubbing) reliably indicates the practice.' Cho-yün Hsü [*Ancient China in Transition*, p.5, note ǂ] draws his example from a bronze inscription published by Kuo Mo-jo in *Liang-Chou Chin-wen-tz'ŭ Ta-hsi K'ao-shih*. Bunkyodo, Tokyo 1935, p.85.

64. The ***tsi̯ok* (*chüeh*) were of five degrees of nobility, all of which are also mentioned in Shang inscriptions [*vide* Hu Hou-hsüan, 'Yin-tai feng-chien-chih-tu k'ao' in *Chia-ku-hsüeh Shang-shih Lun-ts'ung*, first series, vol.1. Ch'eng-tu 1944, pp.32 *et seq.*] : **kung (*kung*), ***g'u* (*hou*), **păk (*po*), ***tsi̯əg* (*tzŭ*), and **nəm (*nan*). The ceremonies and precedences associated with each of these ranks are recounted with great elaboration in *Chou-Li* : cf. p. 156–7.

Hu has gone further and attempted the difficult task of assigning etymologies to these titles, e.g. *kung* originally signified 'patriarch', the ancestral head of a family; *g'u*, depicting an arrow striking a target, was a military title; *păk* denoted 'senior' or 'elder'; *tsi̯əg* meant 'a son', of the king presumably;

and *nəm* meant 'male', possibly with the implication of a warrior age-grade. Cf. Bodde in Coulborn, *Feudalism in China*, pp.55–6.

65. Cf. *int. al.*, *Chou-Li*, and Ma Tuan-lin, *Wen-hsien T'ung-k'ao*, pp.2059 et seq.

66. Walker, *The multi-state system of ancient China*, p.26. By Ch'un-Ch'iu times all the rulers of the Chou states were accorded the posthumous rank of duke, irrespective of their ranks in life.

67. The Ch'ing scholar Chu Yu-fu composed no less than seven treatises on Chou investiture ceremonies, but it is only too evident in retrospect that – as was inevitable given the time at which he was writing – he was concerned more to expound the formulations of the classical texts than to penetrate to the reality underlying these relatively late systematizations (cf. pp.150–160 below). For a detailed description of the ceremony of investiture (first mentioned under the term **siek-miăng* [hsi-ming] in the *I-Ching*, but in other texts referring to the Chou – though not necessarily given their final form during that dynasty – as **si̯ĕg-mi̯ăng* [tz'ŭ-ming]), based on contemporary, though not always scientifically attested, bronze inscriptions and idealized literary texts of later times, see Ch'i Ssŭ-ho, 'Chou-tai hsi-ming-li k'ao', *Yen-ching Hsüeh-pao*, no.32 (1947), pp.197–226; also Eduard Chavannes, *Le T'ai Chan : essai de monographie d'un culte chinois*. Bibliothèque d'Etudes : Annales du Musée Guimet, Paris 1910, Appendix entitled 'Le Dieu du Sol dans la Chine antique'; and Marcel Granet, *La féodalité chinoise*, pp.112–13.

68. Granet, *loc. cit.*, p.112. *Fong* = a French transcription of MSC *feng* < **pi̯ung*, a word which is etymologically connected with the idea of the piling up of earth round a plant. Cf. note 53 above.

69. I am not the first to gain this impression from the ritual texts. Marcel Granet has already written, 'Il [the candidate for investiture] ne recevait pas un domaine contre une promesse de fidélité, il ne remettait point des droits éminents sur son domaine contre une garantie de protection, il ne s'inféodait pas au Fils du Ciel. Il déclarait entrer, lui et sa terre, dans la discipline et la civilisation chinoises' [*La féodalité chinoise*, pp.112–13].

The ceremony of investiture of a high official of the Western Chou is related in considerable detail on both the Large K'o and the Mao-kung tripods. The inscription on the former reads as follows:

> The king was at the ancestral capital of Chou. At dawn the king arrived at the Mu temple and took his seat. Shan-fu K'o, accompanied by Tung[?] Chi, entered the gate and stood in the middle of the court, facing north. The king commanded Yin-shih to invest Shan-fu K'o, and said, "K'o, formerly I had ordered you to promulgate Our decrees; now I shall [. . .] invest you with a title. I grant you [. . .] land at Yeh and at Pei. I grant you farm households cultivating the land at Yung to serve as your subjects and subordinates. I grant you land at K'ang, at Yen, and at Fu-yüan. I grant

NOTES AND REFERENCES

you servitors, drums, bells [. . .]. Be diligent by day and by night, and do not disregard Our order. K'o bowed and made obeisance, and humbly praised the virtues of the king [. . .].
[Ch'i Ssŭ-ho, *Yen-ching Hsüeh-pao* (1947)].
There is an English version in E-tu Zen Sun and John de Francis, *Chinese Social History*. American Council of Learned Societies, Washington, DC 1956, p.45. It is difficult to discern anything exclusively feudal about the investiture ceremony described above.

70. Hall, 'Japanese feudalism', pp.26–7.

71. *loc. cit.*, pp.31–2.

72. Several scholars define feudalism in such broad terms that it subsumes the concept of patrimonialism. Among them is H. G. Creel, for example, who, in a most perspicacious paper, has offered a minimal definition as '. . . a system of government in which a ruler personally delegates limited sovereignty over portions of his domain to vassals' ['The beginnings of bureaucracy in China: the origin of the *Hsien*', *The Journal of Asian Studies*, vol.23, no.2 (1964), p. 163]. For Creel's purpose at the time, namely to contrast feudalism and bureaucracy, this definition may have been entirely adequate, but I personally find it constitutes feudalism as too broad a category for it to prove a useful tool for analyzing the pre- or non-bureaucratic governments and societies of China. It does not, for instance, help to differentiate the Shang from the Ch'un-Ch'iu mode of government, or that of Dz'iər from that of Tṣ'i̯o. Creel does indeed illuminate our idea of the nature of Tṣ'i̯o government, but he does not use this particular tool to help him do it. In fact, unless 'vassal' be understood in a highly restricted technical sense (and it is apparent from Creel's subsequent discussion of his definition [p.164, note 50] that he did not use it in this way), the definition does not distinguish between feudalism and patrimonialism.

73. Cf. note 64 above.

74. Barnard, *Monumenta Serica*, vol.17 (1958), pp.14 and 35.

75. Students of Chinese mythology commonly denote this process by the term 'euhemerization', even though this word customarily signifies the creation of myth by the archetyping of human actions and situations. Cf. Derk Bodde, 'Myths of ancient China' in Samuel Noah Kramer (ed.), *Mythologies of the ancient world*. Anchor Book 229, Doubleday & Co., Inc. New York 1961, pp.372–6.

76. Granet, *La féodalité chinoise*, pp.122–3.

77. *Tao-tö* is a French transcription of the MSC phrase which is rendered in the Wade-Giles system as *tao-te* < ***d'ôg-tək*. This is a term difficult, perhaps impossible, to define in English. Marcel Granet has an interesting discussion of it in his *Chinese civilization*. Meridian Books No.14, New York 1958: transl. of *La civilisation chinoise*, second edition, Albin Michel, Paris 1948: *Evolution de l'Humanité* series no.25; pp.250–1, in which he defines it as

'an animating force of universal essence ... the characteristic of a Chief whose way (tao) is opened by Heaven and who is invested with it (*ming*) with a specific genius (*tô*) while it bestows upon him the destiny (*ming*) suitable for an overlord' (p.250). This is very close to the quality which Max Weber denoted by 'charisma': '"Charisma" soll eine als ausseralltäglich (ursprünglich, sowohl bei Propheten wie bei therapeutischen wie bei Rechts-Weisen wie bei Jagdführern wir bei Kriegshelden : als magisch bedingt) geltende Qualität einer Persönlichkeit heissen, um derentwillen sie als mit übernatürlichen oder übermenschlichen oder mindestens spezifisch ausseralltäglichen, nicht jedem andern zugänglichen Kräften oder Eigenschaften oder als gottgesendet oder als vorbildlich und deshalb als "Führer" gewertet wird. Wie die betreffende Qualität von irgendeinem ethischen, ästhetischen oder sonstigen Standpunkt aus "objektiv" richtig zu bewerten sein würde, ist natürlich dabei begrifflich völlig gleichgültig : darauf, wallein ie sie tatsächlich von den charismatisch Beherrschten, den "Anhängern", bewertet wird, kommt es an' [*Wirtschaft und Gesellschaft*, vol.3 of the collaborative work *Grundriss der Sozialökonomik*, pt.2, second edition, J.C.B. Mohr, Tübingen 1925, pp.133–4]. Elsewhere on the page cited above Granet defines the terms separately : $d^‘ôg$ as 'indicating pure efficacy, concentrated, so to speak, and quite indeterminate', and $tək$ as 'the same efficacy in the act of spending itself and becoming particularized'. In these two terms there is something of the complementary opposition of the concepts of power (the production of intended effects : $tək$) and authority (the expected and legitimate possession of power : $d^‘ôg$). In a sense $d^‘ôg$ is a potential, $tək$ a kinetic, quality. In later centuries, of course, different philosophical schools attached different, and in some cases more restricted, meanings to these terms.

78. *Vide* Haloun, *Asia Major*, vol.1 (1924), especially pp.76 *et seq.* and 84 *et seq.*

79. The term $k_iwən\text{-}ts_iəg$ (*chün-tzŭ*) is composed of two graphs signifying 'lord' and 'son' respectively, and may originally have denoted sons of rulers, possibly undergoing a subsequent extension of meaning to include all classificatory kin of the ruling houses, by which time it had become a virtual synonym for 'nobility'. This is the basic sense in which the word was used in the *Shih-Ching*, although it had by then already acquired the extended connotation of 'husband'. However, during the later Ch'un-Ch'iu and Chan-Kuo periods the implications of this term were so modified that it came to denote a person of high moral stature, a member of a moral rather than a social élite. Cf. Cho-yün Hsü, *Ancient China in transition*, pp.158–74.

80. Maspero, 'Le régime féodal', p.126.

81. Eberhard, *Conquerors and rulers*, pp.22–3. The quotation is from Hsü, *Ancient China in transition*, p.11.

82. References in Hsü, *Ancient China*, p.11.

NOTES AND REFERENCES

83. The general term for slaves in ancient times was ****liei* (*li*). Male slaves were also known as ****ḍi̯ĕn* (*ch'en*) and females as ****ts'i̯ap* (*ch'ieh*).

84. Cho-yün Hsü cites an occasion [*Ch'un-Ch'iu Tso-Chuan Cheng-i*, 12/9 (Hsi 5)] when a slave was ordered to taste some meat suspected of containing poison after a dog had died from eating it, which may indicate that a slave was valued rather below a dog. A bronze inscription probably from the 9th century records that five male slaves were purchased for 100 pieces of metal (****li̯uĕt : lieh*), but the value of these units is unknown. *Vide* Kuo Mo-jo, *Liang-Chou Chin-wen-tz'ŭ Ta-hsi K'ao-shih*. Bunkyodo, Tokyo 1935, p.97.

85. In 679 BC, 66 slaves were interred with Duke Mi̯wo (Wu), and just over half a century later no less than 177 accompanied Duke ****Mi̯ôk* (Mu) to the grave [Cited in Lou Kan-jou, *Histoire sociale de l'époque Tcheou*, p.112].

86. On slavery in ancient China see E.G.Pulleyblank, 'The origins and nature of chattel slavery in China', *Journal of the Economic and Social History of the Orient*, vol.1, pt.2 (1958), pp.185–220.

87. Chüan 129. *Huo-Chih* (=Augmentation of wealth) is an allusion to Confucius's remark, in an almost certainly corrupt passage of the *Lun-Yü*, to the effect that ****Si̯ĕg* (Tz'ŭ) was discontented with his lot and was setting out to enrich himself [XI, viii].

88. *Shih-Chi*, chüan 129, f.16 verso.

89. *loc. cit.*, f.17 recto.

90. *loc. cit.*, f.16 verso.

91. *loc. cit.*, f.6 recto.

92. *loc. cit.*, ff.5 verso – 6 recto. The So-yin and Cheng-i commentaries provide much fuller accounts of both ****·Ia-Twən* (I-Tun) and Kwâk-Tsi̯ung (Kuo-Tsung) than does the *Shih-Chi* itself (*ibid*).

93. *loc. cit.*, f.18 verso.

94. *loc. cit.*, f.6 verso.

94a. Several recensions read ****D'ien-Śi̯ôk* (T'ien-Shu).

95. *loc. cit.*, ff.5 recto et verso; Burton Watson, *Records of the Grand Historian of China*, vol.2. Columbia University Press, New York and London 1961, pp.482–3.

96. *Shih-Chi*, chüan 129, f.19 recto; Watson, *Records*, pp.498–9.

97. Cf. *Ch'ien-Han Shu*, chüan 28B, ff.6 verso – 7 recto : 'Although the territory of Dz'i̯ĕn comprised [only] one-third of the empire, and although the number of its inhabitants did not exceed three-tenths, yet, if its wealth were to be estimated, it would be found to amount to six-tenths.'

98. The dismemberment of Tsi̯ĕn began in 453 BC, and was formally recognized exactly fifty years later.

99. The contrasting environments of the Huang plains and the Yang-tzŭ valley are very much apparent in the literature of Ch'un-Ch'iu and Chan-Kuo times. In the *Kuo-Yü* [chüan 20, f.20 recto], for example, we read of an

THE DIFFUSION OF URBAN LIFE

official of Ngo in the Yang-tzŭ delta advising his king not to undertake a military expedition against the northern states : 'Landsmen must live on land and men of the waters near water. If we attack and conquer the Chinese states we still shall not be able to live in their territories nor ride in their chariots. If, on the other hand, we attack and conquer the [southern, non-Chinese state of] Gi̯wăt, we shall be able to occupy its territories and travel in its boats.' The same theme occurs again in a deposition by a Tṣ'i̯o envoy protesting against an invasion by Dz'i̯ər in 655 BC [4th year of Duke Xi̯əg (Hsi)] : 'Your Grace's territory is by the northern sea, mine by the southern. [So far apart are they that] our very horses and cattle cannot interbreed.'

100. Ku Chieh-kang, 'Yü Ch'ien Hsüan-t'ung Hsien-sheng lun ku-shih-shu', *Ku-Shih Pien*, vol.1 (1926), pp.106–34, 165–86, and 207–10.

101. E.g., swords and other iron weapons from G'ân, Ngo and Gi̯wăt, sabers from D'i̯ĕng, axes from Sông, blades from Lo, daggers from D'i̯og- and purple cloth from Dz'i̯ər. Cf. extended remarks on this topic by Hsü, *Ancient China in transition*, pp.120–2.

102. Henri Maspero, 'Contribution à l'étude de la société chinoise à la fin des Chang et au début des Tcheou', *Bulletin de l'Ecole française d'Extrême-Orient*, vol.46, pt.2 (1952–4), pp.349–56. Hsü Chung-shu ['Lei-ssŭ k'ao', *Kuo-li Chung-yang Yen-chiu-yüan Li-shih Yü-yen Yen-chiu-so Chi-k'an*, vol.2, pt.1] has found little support for his contention that the *lei* and *ssŭ* were separate and distinct implements.

103. Hua Chüeh-ming, Yang Ken and Liu En-chu, 'Chan-Kuo Liang-Han t'ieh-ch'i-ti chin-hsiang-hsüeh k'ao-ch'a ch'u-pu pao-kao,' *K'ao-ku Hsüeh pao*, no.1 (1960), pp.82–3.

104. *Shih-Chi*, chüan 29, f.3 recto.

105. *Shih-Chi*, chüan 29, f.2 verso.

106. *Shih-Chi*, chüan 29, f.3 recto et verso.

107. An estimate arrived at by comparing Ssŭ-ma Ch'ien's reported yield with the average quoted in *Kuan-tzŭ*.

108. *Shih-Chi*, chüan 29, f.3 verso.

109. *Chuang-tzŭ*, chüan 12. Cf. also Liu-Hsiang, *Shuo-Yüan* (c.20 BC), chüan 20. There is a study of Chan-Kuo irrigation works by Weng Wen-hao, 'Ku-tai kuan-kai kung-ch'eng fa-chan-shih-chih i-chieh', in *Kuo-li Chung-yang Yen-chiu Yüan Li-shih Yü-yen Yen-chiu-so Ch'ing-chu Ts'ai Yüan-p'ei Hsien-sheng Liu-shih-wu-sui Lun-wen Chi*, vol.2. Academia Sinica, Pei-p'ing, 1935, pp.709–12.

110. Wang Hsien-ch'ien, *Han-Shu Pu-chu*. Ch'ang-sha, 1900, chüan 24A, pp.7–8.

111. Joseph Needham, *The development of iron and steel technology in China*. Second Biennial Dickinson Memorial Lecture, Newcomen Society. London 1958.

NOTES AND REFERENCES

112. Sekino Takeshi, *Chugaku Kōkogaku Kenkyu*. University of Tokyo Institute for Oriental Culture 1956, pp.187–8.

113. *Meng-tzŭ*, III A, iii, 19.

114. *Chou-Li*, ts'e 6, chüan 12, f.18 verso (*Ssŭ-pu Ts'ung-k'an* ed., Shanghai 1942).

115. The system as set out in *Chou-Li* is somewhat more complicated than that described in the *Mencius*. According to the former the boundaries between fields and between *tsiěng* were marked by **ku (*kou*=drains) and **χiwĕt (*hsü*=ditches) of sizes varying according to their place in the hierarchy of territorial units. On the outer edges of this *ku-χiwĕt* system the channels must have been very broad and deep indeed. Some scholars have regarded the *tsiěng-d'ien* and the *ku-χiwĕt* as separate systems [e.g. Chu-Hsi, 'Li-i : Chou-li,' *Chu-tzŭ ch'üan-shu*, ed. Li Kuang-ti (1714), ts'e 15, chüan 37, f.12 verso; Tazaki Masayuki, *Shina kōdai keizai shisō oyobi seido*. Tokyo 1925, pp.495–511], but most have treated them as different versions of one underlying reality.

116. E.g., Hu Shih, 'Ching-t'ien pien', *Hu Shih Wen-ts'un*. Shanghai, 1927. This essay had originally been published in 1920. In 1935 Kao Yün-hui remarked that *tsiěng-d'ien* had no existence in reality : it was simply a category of social thought, an idealization in the mind ['Chou-tai t'u-ti-chih-tu yü ching-t'ien', *Shih-huo*, vol.1, no.7 (1935), p.12].

117. *Vide* Laurence G. Thompson (transl.), *Ta T'ung Shu : the One-World Philosophy of K'ang Yu-wei*. London 1958, pp.137 and 211. From time to time during Chinese history there had been attempts to use *tsiěng-d'ien* as a basis for agrarian colonization and social reform [e.g. by Wang-Mang in AD 9, by Wang An-shih in Sung times, and under the Manchu in 1724, when a form of *tsiěng-d'ien* was established in two counties of Chih-li], but none ever proved successful. For the deployment of *tsiěng-d'ien* as an instrument of social reform in modern times see Joseph R. Levenson, 'Ill wind in the well-field : the erosion of the Confucian ground of controversy', in *Confucian China and its Modern Fate*, vol.3, *The problem of historical significance*. University of California Press, Berkeley and Los Angeles 1965, pp.16–43. There are general discussions of *tsiěng-d'ien* in Hsü Chung-shu, 'Ching-t'ien chih-tu t'an-yüan', *Chung-Kuo Wen-hua Yen-chiu Hui-k'an*, vol.4 (1944), pp.121–56; Kuo Mo-jo, *Shih P'i-p'an Shu*. Ch'ung-ch'ing, 1945, pp.1–62; Li Chien-nung, 'Ch'e chu kung', *Ch'ing-hua Ta-hsüeh She-hui K'o-hsüeh Chi-k'an*, vol.9 (1948), pp.25–44, and *Chung-Kuo Ching-chi Shih-kao*, vol.1 (ND), pp.122–38; Lien-sheng Yang, 'Notes on Dr Swann's *Food and Money in Ancient China*', in Yang, *Studies in Chinese Institutional History*. Harvard University Press 1963, pp.85–118.

118. Eberhard, *Conquerors and rulers*, pp.35–6.

119. Ch'i Ssŭ-ho, 'Meng-tzŭ ching-t'ien shuo pien', *Yen-ching Hsüeh-pao*,

no.35 (1948), pp.101–27, especially 124–6. Cf. also Chʻao-ting Chi, *Key economic areas in Chinese history as revealed in the development of public works for water-control*. George Allen and Unwin Ltd, London 1936, p.58.

120. *Tso-Chuan*, Duke **Sįwan (Hsüan), 15th year.

121. *Lun-Yü*, XII, 9. The precise nature of this tax has elicited a good deal of comment from modern scholars, particularly with regard to its apparent regional and chronological variations. Kato Shigeshi thought he was able to discern both spatial and developmental differences involving labor service, tax on annual yield, and tax at a fixed rate [*Studies in Chinese economic history*, vol.1. Toyo Bunko, Tokyo 1952, pp.555–86]. Cho-yün Hsü, on the other hand, considered 'that this tax was more a developmental phenomenon than a regional difference, since labor service involves both direct control by the landlord over the peasant and annual shifting of fields. The latter practice is necessary for any type of technologically undeveloped agriculture, such as that of the early Chʻun-Chʻiu, whereas a land tax is possible only when the peasants can use their land permanently. The purpose of tax reformation is not merely to increase the burden on the tiller'. [*Ancient China in transition*, p.108]. Miyazaki Ichisada has suggested that the introduction of a so-called tax could more profitably be regarded simply as an extension of the tribute system, hitherto restricted to the nobility, to the peasantry [*Shirin*, vol.18, nos.2 and 3 (1933), pp.1–18]. In any case, whatever the nature of this tax, the outcome of its introduction was as described in the text. Cf. also Maspero, 'Le régime féodal', pp.124 and 138, and Amano Motonosuke, *Toho Gakuho*, vol.30 (1959), pp.141–4.

122. Hsü, *Ancient China in transition*, p.110.

123. *loc. cit.*, p.178.

124. *Kuan-tzŭ*, XV, 11–12 (*Ssŭ-pu Tsʻung-kʻan* edition, annotated by Fang Hsüan-ling). One of the best-known instances of unseasonable labor service was the corvée imposed at harvest time by **Gʻwâng Kwək-bʻįwo (Huang Kuo-fu), **Tʻâd-Tsəg (Tʻai-Tsai) under Duke **Bʻįĕng (Pʻing) of Sông, for the purpose of building a terraced platform [*Tso-Chuan*, Duke **Snįang (Hsiang), 18th year].

125. E.g. *Chʻun-Chʻiu*, Duke **Dʻįĕng (Cheng), 12th year.

126. For the role of merchants and the development of trade see Ku Chi-kuang, 'Chan-Kuo Chʻin-Han-chien chung-nung-chʻing-shang-chih li-lun yü shih-chi' *Chung-Kuo She-hui Ching-chi-shih Chi-kʻan*, vol.7, no.1 (1944), pp.1–22.

127. Yang Lien-sheng, *Money and credit in China*. Harvard University Press 1952, pp.1–2. There is an interesting passage in the *Kuo-Yü* which reports discussions on the possibility of issuing 'heavy coins' in Chou in 524 BC. However, the passage is probably a later interpolation: it is evaluated by Yang, *loc. cit.*, p.33.

NOTES AND REFERENCES

128. Shih Chang-ju, 'Chou-tu i-chi yü Ts'ai-t'ao i-ts'un', *Ta-lu Tsa-c* supplement no.1 (1952), pp.357–85.

129. Notes 6 and 7 above.

130. Chang Hsüeh-cheng, 'Wei-ho shang-yu T'ien-shui, Kan-ku liang-hsien k'ao-ku tiao-ch'a chien-pao', *K'ao-ku T'ung-hsün*, no.5 (1958), pp.1–5; Jen Pu-yün, 'Kan-su Ch'in-an Hsien Hsin-shih-ch'i shih-tai chü-chu i-chih', *loc. cit.*, pp.6–11; Kuo Te-yung, 'Kan-su Wei-ho shang-yu Wei-yüan, Lung-hsi, Wu-shan san-hsien k'ao-ku tiao-ch'a', *K'ao-ku T'ung-hsün*, no.7 (1958), pp.6–16.

131. Shan-hsi [Shensi] Sheng Wen-wu Kuan-li Wei-yüan-hui, 'Ch'ang-an Chang-chia-p'o Ts'un Hsi-Chou i-chih-ti chung-yao fa-hsien', *Wen-wu Ts'an-k'ao Tzŭ-liao*, no.3 (1956), p.58; Wang Po-hung, Chung shao-lin and Chang Ch'ang-shou, '1955–57-nien Shan-hsi [Shensi] Ch'ang-an Feng-hsi fa-chüeh chien-pao', *K'ao-ku*, no.10 (1959), pp.516–30.

132. T'ang Yün-ming, 'Hsing-T'ai Hsi-kuan-wai i-chih shih-chüeh', *Wen-wu*, no.7 (1960), pp.69–70.

133. Chao Ch'ing-yün, '1957-nien Cheng-Chou hsi-chiao fa-chüeh chi-yao : 4 : Tung-Chai Shang-tai yü Chou-tai wen-hua i-chih-ti fa-chüeh, '*K'ao-ku T'ung-hsün*, no.9 (1958), p.56.

134. Li Yang-sung and Yen Wen-ming, 'Lo-yang Wang-wan i-chih fa-chüeh chien-pao', *K'ao-ku*, no.4 (1961), pp.175–78.

135. Yin Huan-chang *et al.*, 'Chiang-su Hsin-i Hsien San-li Tun ku-wen-hua i-chih', *K'ao-ku*, no.7 (1960), pp.20–2.

136. Wang Ching, 'Hu-pei Hung-an Chin-p'en i-chih-ti t'an-chüeh', *K'ao-ku*, no.4 (1960), pp.38–40.

137. Li Chi *et al.*, *Ch'eng-tzŭ Yai* : Tung Tso-pin, 'Ch'eng-tzŭ Yai yü Lung-shan Chen'. Academia Sinica, Nan-ching 1934, pp.96–8.

138. Cf. Tsang Li-ho *et al.*, *Chung-Kuo Ku-chin Ti-ming Ta-tz'ŭ-tien.* Shanghai 1933, p.1355.

139. Tung Tso-pin, 'T'an "T'an",' *Kuo-li Chung-yang Yen-chiu-yüan Li-shih Yü-yen Yen-chiu-so Chi-k'an*, vol.4, pt.2 (1933), pp.159–74. As early as the middle of the 18th century Ku Tung-kao (1679–1759) had included D'əm (T'an), by implication, among those territories which he believed to have been enfeoffed in pre-Chou times [*Ch'un-Ch'iu Ta-shih Piao* (Wan-chüan-lou edition, Wu-hsi, 1748)]. Ku also relied on Sung authors of somewhat dubious reliability in an attempt to show that the clan name of the ruling house of D'əm could be traced back to Shang times, but we now know that such genealogies were manufactured in much later times by rulers of small (and, indeed, often of large) states as instruments of political validation [*Vide* Liang Lü-sheng (1748–93), *Tso-t'ung Pu-shih* in Wang Hsien-ch'ien, *Huang-Ch'ing Ching-chieh Hsü-pien*. Canton 1888; Lo-Pi, *Lu-Shih*. Tun-hua T'ang edition 1611]. There are, indeed, works which state explicitly that D'əm was a Shang foundation.

Yü-Ch'in, for example, arguing against the statement of an otherwise unknown source, the *San-Ch'i Chi*, to the effect that P'ing-ling was the capital of **Tieg--i̯ɛt (Ti-i) of Shang, insists that, 'as P'ing-ling was not then in existence, then the site of the capital must have been at Ch'eng-tzŭ Yai'. Needless to say, arguments such as this are based on illusory premises as to the nature of their source materials.

The earliest extant reference to the state of D'əm is to be found in the **Gi̯wad-Pi̯ŭm (*Wei-Feng*) section of the *Mao Shih*, and the preface to that recension of the *Odes* attributed the ode *Ta-Tung* to a high official of D'əm living at the end of the Western Chou period. A Duke of D'əm also appeared in the genealogical section **Gi̯wad Si̯ad-kå (*Wei Shih-chia*) of the *Shih-Chi*, under the 5th year of Duke Chuang of Wei (753 BC), and another is mentioned in a later work, the *Feng-su t'ung-i* of Ying-Shao, who lived from AD 140–206. Ssŭ-pu Ts'ung-k'an edition, Shanghai 1929.

140. Duke **Tṣi̯ang (Chuang), 10th year. The Han scholar Tu-Lin elaborated this statement with the further information that D'əm 'was southwest of P'ing-ling Hsien in Chi-nan' [Quoted in Tsang, *Chung-kuo Ku-chin Ti-ming Ta-tz'ŭ-tien*, p.1355], and Yü-Ch'in (1284–1333) noted that 'Eastern P'ing-ling is 75 *li* east of Chi-nan. As for the state of *D'əm* mentioned in the Ch'un-Ch'iu, Duke Huan [of *Dz'i̯ər*] destroyed it. The old city was in the southwest, opposite Lung-shan Chen' [*Ch'i-Ch'eng* AD 1781]. Li Tao-yüan [*Shui-Ching Chu* : Northern Wei, late 5th or early 6th century AD] adds : 'The Kuan-lu river rises in the Ma-erh mountains. To the north it flows on the west side of Po-t'ing Ch'eng and continues northwestwards, where it joins the Wu-yüan river at P'ing-ling Ch'eng. This river [the Wu-yüan] issues from low-lying marshland to the south of the city of T'an [D'əm], where it is always known as the Wu-yüan Spring. [Thence] it flows northwards and passes to the east of the city of T'an, which is commonly held to be an ancient foundation. Once more this river flows northwards and passes to the west of the old city of Eastern P'ing-ling . . . farther north it passes to the east of Chü-ho Ch'eng . . . [and eventually] unites with the Kuan-lu river to form the Chü-ho river'. A reconstruction of the course of these rivers in ancient times and the locations of the cities mentioned above is presented in Fig.IV.

141. Ch'en Kung-jou, 'Lo-yang Chien-pin Tung-Chou ch'eng-chih fa-chüeh pao-kao', *K'ao-ku Hsüeh-pao*, no.2 (1959), pp.15–34.

142. Kuo Pao-chün, 'Lo-yang ku-ch'eng k'an-ch'a chien-pao', *K'ao-ku T'ung-hsün*, no.1 (1955), pp.9–21. Pan-Ku, the author of *Ch'ien-Han Shu*, the celebrated commentator Cheng-Hsüan, and Li Tao-yüan, author of *Shui-*

[IV] A reconstruction of the relationship between ancient settlements and the drainage pattern in the neighborhood of Ch'eng-tzŭ Yai. Redrawn from Li Chi *et al.*, *Ch'eng-tzŭ Yai* (Nan-ching, 1934), fig.10, p.103.

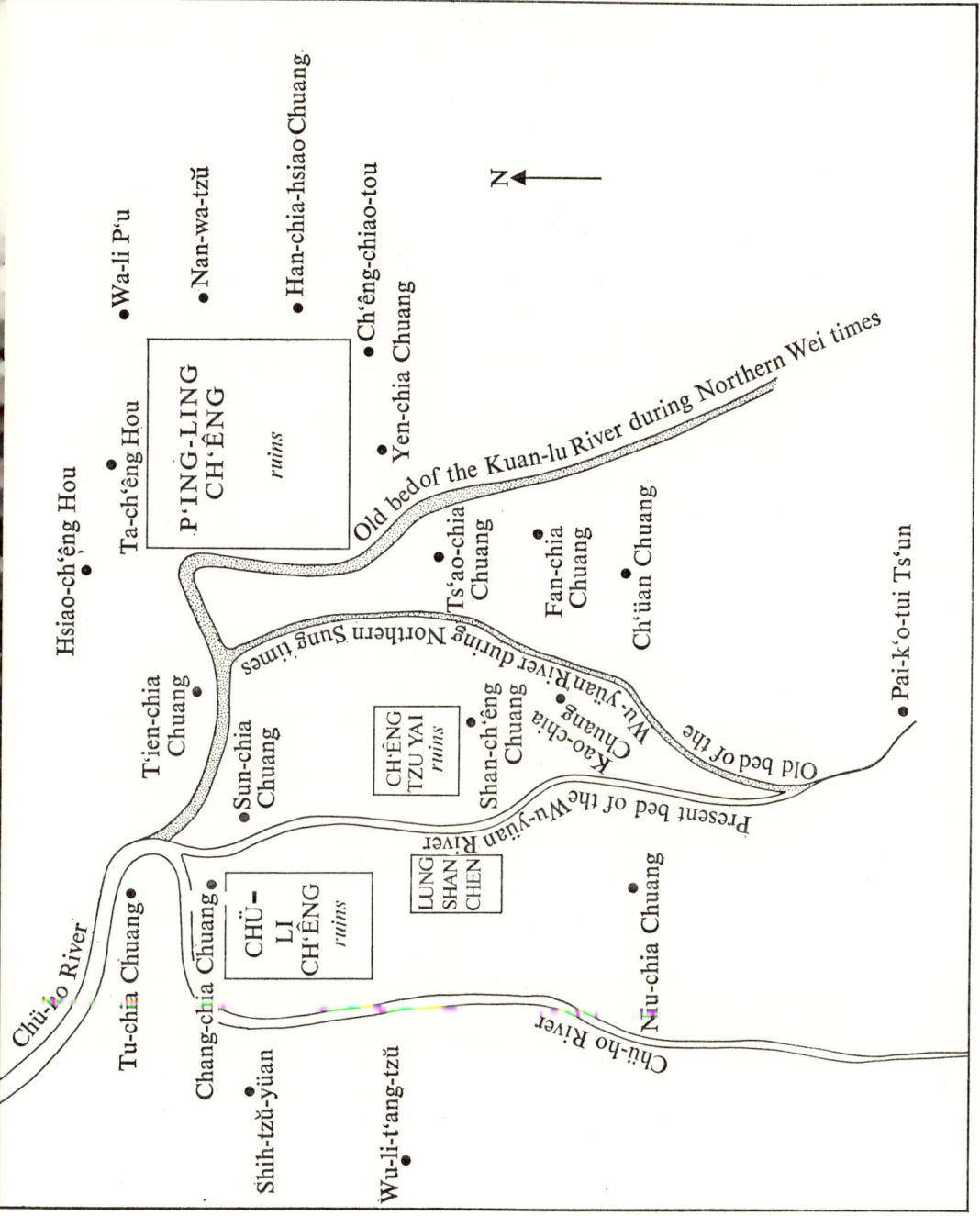

Ching Chu, each in his day confirmed the association of Ho-nan *hsien*-city of the Later Han with the ruins of the old Royal City of Chou, and there can be no doubt that the modern excavators have identified the former correctly.

143. Chang Shou-chung, '1959-nien Hou-ma "Niu-Ts'un ku-ch'eng"-nan Tung-Chou i-chih fa-chüeh chien-pao', *Wen-wu*, nos.8–9 (1960), pp.11–14; Yang Fu-tou, 'Hou-ma-hsi hsin-fa-hsien i-tso ku-ch'eng i-chih', *Wen-wu Ts'an-k'ao Tzŭ-liao*, no.10 (1957), pp.55–6; Ch'ang Wen-chai, 'Hou-ma ti-ch'ü ku-ch'eng-chih-ti hsin-fa-hsien', *loc. cit.*, no.12 (1958), pp.32–3; Ch'ang Wen-chai, Chang Shou-chung and Yang Fu-tou, 'Hou-ma Pei-hsi Chuang Tung-Chou i-chih-ti ch'ing-li', *Wen-wu*, no.6 (1959), pp.42–4; and several continuing anonymous notes in subsequent issues of *Wen-wu*.

144. Shan-hsi Sheng Wen-wu Kuan-li Wei-yüan-hui, 'Shan-hsi Sheng Wen-kuan-hui Hou-ma Kung-tso-chan kung-tso-ti tsung-shou-huo', *K'ao-ku*, no.5 (1959), pp.222–8.

145. Yang Fu-tou, 'K'ao-ku Tung-t'ai : Shan-hsi Hsiang-fen Hsien fa-hsien-ti liang-ch'u i-chih : 2 : Chao-k'ang-Chen-ti Tung-Chou ku-ch'eng-chih', *K'ao-ku*, no.2 (1959), p.107; Ch'ang Wen-chai, 'Shan-hsi Hsiang-fen Chao-k'ang fu-chin ku-ch'eng-chih tiao-ch'a', *K'ao-ku*, no.10 (1963), pp.544–6.

146. Meng Hao, Ch'en Hui, and Liu Lai-ch'eng, 'Ho-pei Wu-an Wu-chi ku-ch'eng fa-chüeh-chi', *K'ao-ku T'ung-hsün*, no.4 (1957), pp.43–7; Meng Hao, 'Ho-pei Wu-an Hsien Wu-chi ku-ch'eng-chung-ti yao-chih', *K'ao-ku*, no.7 (1959), pp.338–42; Ch'en Hui, 'Ho-pei Wu-an Hsien Wu-chi ku-ch'eng-ti Chou, Han mu-tsang fa-chüeh chien-pao', *K'ao-ku*, no.7 (1959), pp.343–5.

147. Komai Kazuchika and Sekino Takeshi, 'Han-tan', *Archaeologia Orientalis*, series B, vol.7 (1954); Sekino Takeshi, *Chūgaku Kōkogaku Kenkyu* (Tokyo, 1956), pp.295–302; Pei-ching Ta-hsüeh and Ho-pei Sheng Wen-hua-chü Han-tan K'ao-ku Fa-chüeh-tui, '1957-nien Han-tan fa-chüeh chien-pao', *K'ao-ku*, no.10 (1959), pp.531–6.

148. *Tso-Chuan*, 10th year of Duke **D'ieng (Ting-Kung).

149. Fu Chen-lun, 'Yen-Hsia-tu fa-chüeh pao-kao', *Kuo-Hsüeh Chi-k'an*, vol.3. Peking University 1932, pp.175–82, and 'Yen-Hsia-tu fa-chüeh-p'in-ti ch'u-pu cheng-li yü yen-chiu', *K'ao-ku T'ung-hsün*, no.4 (1955), pp.18–26; Hsieh Hsi-i, 'Yen-Hsia-tu i-chih so-chi', *Wen-wu Ts'an-k'ao Tzŭ-liao*, no.9 (1957), pp.61–3; Huang Ching-lüeh, 'Yen-Hsia-tu-ch'eng-chih tiao-ch'a pao-kao', *K'ao-ku*, no.1 (1962), pp.10–19 and 54. This 'Lesser Capital' should not be confused with the city with the same sobriquet in the vicinity of Lo-yang (cp. p.136).

150. Diagrammatic reconstructions by Wang Chen-to, 'Ssŭ-nan chih-nan-chen yü lo-ching p'an, I', *Chung-Kuo K'ao-ku Hsüeh-pao*, vol.3 (1948) [Reproduced by Joseph Needham, *Science and civilization in China*, vol.4, pt.1. Cambridge 1962, p.263], and Harada Yoshito and Tazawa Kingo, *Rakurō Gokan-en Ō Ku no Fumbo*. Tokyo 1930 [Reproduced by W.C. Rufus, 'Astro-

NOTES AND REFERENCES

nomy in Korea', *Journal of the Korean Branch of the Royal Asiatic Society*, vol. 26, pt.1 (1936) and by Needham, *loc. cit.*, vol.3 (1959), plate LXXX].

151. Ao Ch'eng-lung, 'Ho-pei Tz'ŭ-Hsien Chiang-wu Ch'eng tiao-ch'a chien-pao', *K'ao-ku*, no.7 (1959), pp.354–7.

152. Wang Han-yen, 'Pei-ching Shih : Chou-k'ou Tien Ch'ü Ts'ai-Chuang ku-ch'eng i-chih', *Wen-wu*, no.5 (1959), p.73.

153. Sekino Takeshi, *Chugaku Kōkogaku Kenkyu*. Tokyo 1956, pp.241–94; Shan-tung Sheng Wen-wu Kuan-li-ch'u, 'Shan-tung Lin-tzŭ Ch'i-ku-ch'eng shih-chüeh chien-pao', *K'ao-ku*, no.6 (1961), pp.289–97.

154. Sekino, *Chugaku Kōkogaku Kenkyu*, pp.303–25.

155. Sekino, *Chugaku Kōkogaku Kenkyu*, pp.313–23; Chuang Tung-ming, 'T'eng-Hsien Lin-Ch'eng ch'a-te ku-i-chih i-ch'u', and 'T'eng-Hsien Ku-Hsüeh-Ch'eng fa-hsien Chan-Kuo-shih-tai yeh-t'ieh i-chih', *Wen-wu Ts'an-k'ao Tzŭ-liao*, no.5 (1957), p.82.

156. Sekino, *Chugaku Kōkogaku Kenkyu*, pp.305–12.

157. Ni Chen-kuei, 'Yen-Ch'eng ch'u-t'u-ti t'ung-ch'i', *Wen-wu*, no.4 (1959), pp.3–5; Wei Chü-hsien, *Chung-Kuo K'ao-ku-hsüeh-shih*. Commercial Press, Shanghai 1937, p.255; Tseng Chao-yü and Yin Huan-chang, 'Shih-lun "Hu-shu wen-hua",' *K'ao-ku Hsüeh-pao*, no.4 (1959), p.54; Hsieh Chun-chu, 'Yen-Ch'eng fa-hsien Chan-Kuo-shih-ch'i-ti tu-mu-ch'uan', *Wen-wu*, no.11 (1958), p.80.

158. Han Wei-chou and Wang Ju-lin, 'Ho-nan Hsi-hsia Hsien chi Nan-yang Shih liang-ku-ch'eng tiao-ch'a-chi', *K'ao-ku T'ung-hsün*, no.2 (1956), pp.47–8.

159. *loc. cit.*, pp.49–50.

160. Li Yü-ch'un, 'Shen-hsi [Shensi] Hua-yin Yüeh-Chen Chan-Kuo ku-ch'eng k'an-ch'a-chi', *K'ao-ku*, no.11 (1959), pp.604–5.

161. Chung-Kuo K'e-hsüeh Yüan K'ao-ku Yen-chiu-so Lo-yang Fa-chüeh-tui, '1959-nien Yü-hsi liu-hsien tiao-ch'a chien-pao', *K'ao-ku*, no.1 (1961), p.32.

162. Lou Kan-jou, *Histoire sociale de l'époque Tcheou*. Paris 1935, p.25.

163. Bernhard Karlgren, 'Legends and cults in ancient China', *Bulletin of the Museum of Far Eastern Antiquities*, no.18 (1946), pp.199–366.

164. *loc. cit.*, p.201. On p.351 Karlgren refers to these texts as 'free, narrative texts'.

165. *ibid.*

166. Wolfram Eberhard, Review article in *Artibus Asiae*, vol.9, pt.4 (1946), pp.355–64.

167. *loc. cit.*, p.357.

168. It is true, though, that there are discrepancies between the list of Shang kings provided by Ssŭ-ma Ch'ien and that attested by oracle inscriptions. For example, Ssŭ-ma has confused the sequence by placing **Pôg-tieng (Pao-ting) before, instead of after, **Pôg-ịet (Pao-i) and **Pôg-pi̯ăng (Pao-ping),

has omitted **Tsjĕt and his two sons who are mentioned in both the *Songs of Ch'u* (*T'ien-Wen*) and oracle inscriptions, and, possibly on good grounds, has included a King **T̂i̯ən (Chen), who has not so far been identified in the oracle archives.

169. Eberhard, *Artibus Asiae*, vol.9, p.362. Eberhard also criticizes Karlgren's methodology from the point of view of the sociologist and folklorist : *vide loc. cit.*, p.360.

170. Mo-Ti mentions *Ch'un-Ch'iu* of Chou (T̂i̯ôg) itself, Sông, Dz'i̯ər and ·Ian, but the precise date of Chapter 31 of the *Mo-tzŭ*, in which this reference occurs, is uncertain. Probably it was composed shortly after 400 BC. *Ch'un-Ch'iu* was, of course, an abbreviation of 'spring, summer, autumn and winter', signifying 'years'.

171. This tradition was first voiced, in extant literature, by Mencius some three or four generations after the death of Confucius : 'When the world fell into decay and principles were unimportant... Confucius was afraid and put together [*tso*] the *Springs and Autumns*. This work comprises matters proper to the Son of Heaven, wherefore Confucius remarked, 'It is the *Springs and Autumns* by which men will know me, and it is the *Springs and Autumns* by which they will condemn me" ' [*Meng-tzŭ*, III, ii, IX, 8]. There is, however, no certainty that Mencius was referring to the same text as the one which is extant today.

172. The merits of these rival Traditions were debated in the presence of the Emperor Wu (141–87 BC) by Tung Chung-shu (supporting the *Kung-yang Chuan*) and Chiang-Sheng (espousing the *Ku-liang Chuang*) respectively. For general comments on these Traditions see Wu K'ang, *Les trois théories politiques du Tch'ouen Ts'ieou interprétées par Tong Tchong-chou d'après les principes de l'école de Kong-yang*. Leroux, Paris, 1932, *passim*, but especially pp.172–81.

173. The Tso in question has traditionally been identified as Tso-ch'iu Ming (or perhaps Tso Ch'iu-ming : the precise form is uncertain), who was supposed to have been a disciple of Confucius, but modern scholarship has shown that the *Tso-Chuan* in its present form is a composite work : see below.

174. This notion was first proposed by K'ang Yu-wei, *Hsin-hsüeh Wei-ching k'ao* (Block print edition 1891; Wang-yün Lou lithographic edition, 1891; book and typeset ordered to be destroyed in 1894; presented to the throne in 1898; book and typeset destroyed in 1898 and 1900; Wan-mu ts'ao-t'ang ts'ung shu edition in vermilion, 1917; several subsequent editions, among them the Wen-hua Hsüeh-she edition, Pei-p'ing 1931, in which the reference is to ts'e 3A, pp.29–35).

175. Bernhard Karlgren, 'On the authenticity and nature of the Tso chuan', *Göteborgs Högskolas Årsskrift*, vol.32, no.3 (1926), pp.1–65.

176. Bernhard Karlgren, 'The early history of the Chou li and Tso chuan

texts', *Bulletin of the Museum of Far Eastern Antiquities*, vol.3 (1931), pp.1–59.

177. Henri Maspero, 'La composition et la date du Tso tchouan', *Mélanges Chinois et Bouddhiques, Institut Belge des Hautes Etudes Chinoises*, vol.1. Bruxelles 1931-2, pp.137–215; *La Chine antique*. Boccard, Paris 1927 : vol.4 of E. Cavaignac [ed.] *Histoire du Monde*, pp.592–5, and review of Karlgren's 'On the authenticity and nature of the Tso chuan', *Journal Asiatique*, vol.212 (1928), pp.159–65.

178. Ojima, *Shinagaku*, vol.3 (1923), pp.50–61, 127–39 and 452–68.

179. Chang Hsin-cheng, *Wei-Shu Tʻung-kʻao*, vol.1. Commercial Press, Chʻang-sha 1939, pp.408–9.

180. Hung Yeh (William Hung) *et al.*, *Chʻun-Chʻiu Ching-chuan Yin-te*, vol.1. Harvard-Yenching Institute Sinological Index Series, Supplement no.11. Pei-pʻing 1937, pp.1–106. Hung's further conclusion that the *Tso-Chuan* was assembled by Chang-Chʻang early in Former Han times has not received general assent. Cf. also Chʻi Ssŭ-ho, 'Professor Hung on the Chʻun-chʻiu', *The Yenching Journal of Social Studies*, vol.1, no.1 (1938), pp.50–71. Studies bearing on the nature of the *Tso-Chuan* which have not been mentioned in previous notes include that by Wolfram Eberhard, R. Müller and R. Henseling, 'Beiträge zur Astronomie der Han-Zeit : II', *Sitzungsberichte der preussischen Akademie der Wissenschaften*, philosophisch-historische Klasse, vol.23 (1933), and a magnificent contribution by George A. Kennedy, 'Interpretation of the Chʻun-chʻiu', *Journal of the American Oriental Society*, vol.62, no.1 (1942), pp.40–8.

181. James Legge (transl.), *The Chinese Classics : vol.5, The Chʻun Tsʻew with The Tso Chuen*. Lane Crawford, Hong Kong and Trübner, London 1872 : photolitho reissue, Hong Kong University Press, 1960, pp.34–5.

182. Karlgren, 'On the authenticity and nature of the Tso Chuan', pp.58–9 and 64–5.

183. Hung, *Chʻun-Chʻiu Ching-chuan Yin-te*, p.lxxxv.

184. Kʻang Yu-wei, *Hsin-hsüeh Wei-ching Kʻao*, tsʻe 4, pp.6–7.

185. Cf. *Lü-Shih Chʻun-Chʻiu*, annotated by Kao-Yu. Ssŭ-pu Tsʻung-kʻan edition; Liang Chʻi-chʻao, *Chu-tzŭ Kʻao-shih*. Chung-hua, Shanghai 1936; Tʻai-pei reprint 1957, p.104. As this work is not a chronicle of court events, the phrase *Chʻun-Chʻiu* in the title must be used in a metaphorical sense to denote a work of moral and political principle such as the *Chʻun-Chʻiu*, attributed to Confucius at the end of the 3rd century, was conceived to be. Cf. Burton Watson, *Ssŭ-ma Chʻien, Grand Historian of China*. Columbia University Press 1958, p.103.

186. Li Chün-chih, 'Lü-Shih Chʻun-Chʻiu-chung ku-shu chi-i', *Ku-shih Pien*, vol.6 (1938), pp.321–40; Liu Ju-lin, 'Lü-Shih-Chʻun-Chʻiu-chih Fen-hsi', *loc. cit.*, pp.340–58.

187. *Vide* Ch'i Ssŭ-ho, 'Chan-Kuo Ts'e chu-tso shih-tai k'ao', *Yen-ching Hsüeh-pao*, vol.34 (1948), pp.257–78.

188. *Li-Chi*, Wang-Chih section.

189. Kuo Mo-jo, *Liang-Chou Chin-wen-tz'ŭ Ta-hsi K'ao-shih*. Tokyo. 1935, p.202.

190. Ch'i Ssŭ-ho, 'Chou-tai hsi-ming-li k'ao', p.202.

191. Cf. pp.111–12 above.

192. See particularly Karlgren, 'The early history of the Chou li and Tso chuan texts', pp.2–8, 35–8, 50–7.

193. Sven Broman, 'Studies on the Chou Li', *Bulletin of the Museum of Far Eastern Antiquities*, vol.33 (1961), p.73.

194. Creel, 'The beginnings of bureaucracy in China', p.169, note 75.

195. The history of these texts is summarized succinctly by Charles S. Gardner, *Chinese traditional historiography*. Harvard University Press 1938, pp.56–7, note 69.

196. On the pedigree of this text see Piet van der Loon, 'On the transmission of the *Kuan-tzu*', *T'oung Pao*, vol.41 (1952), pp.357–93. Cf. also Gustav Haloun, 'Legalist fragments: Part I: Kuan-tsï 55 and related texts', *Asia Major*, new series, vol.2, pt.1 (1951), pp.85–120, and 'Das Ti-tsï-tṣï, Frühkonfuzianische Fragmente II', *Asia Major*, vol.9 (1933), pp.467–502.

197. Fu-Hsüan (AD 217–278), quoted by Liu-Shu (1032–1078) in the *T'ung-chien Wai-chi*. Subsequently K'ung Ying-ta (574–648), Tu-Yu (735–812), Su-Ch'e (1039–1112), Yeh-Shih (1150–1223), Chu-Hsi (1130–1200) and Huang-Chen (fl. *c.*1270) were all of the same opinion.

198. Lo Ken-tse, *Kuan-tzŭ t'an-yüan* (Chung-hua Shu-chü 1931).

199. W. Allyn Rickett, *Kuan-tzu. A repository of early Chinese thought*, vol.1. Hong Kong University Press 1965.

200. *loc. cit.*, pp.12–13. Rickett's whole book is a confirmation of Karlgren's ['On the authenticity of ancient Chinese texts', pp.173–6] and van der Loon's ['On the transmission of the Kuan-tzu'] rejection of Maspero's [*La Chine antique*, pp.485–6, and review of Gustav Haloun's *Seit wann kannten Chinesen die Tocharer oder Indo-germanen überhaupt?* in *Journal Asiatique*, vol.210 (1927), pp.144–52] thesis that Liu-Hsiang's edition of the *Kuan-tzŭ* was lost and replaced by a modern forgery perpetrated during the 4th and 5th centuries AD.

201. The best introduction to Ssŭ-ma Ch'ien and his work in a Western language is Burton Watson's *Ssŭ-ma Ch'ien, Grand Historian of China*. Columbia University Press 1958. Chapter IV deals specifically with the form of the *Shih-Chi*.

202. Karlgren, 'Legends and cults in ancient China', p.231.

203. For works offering critical analyses of the *Shih-Chi* see Chapter One notes 37, 38, and 39.

NOTES AND REFERENCES

204. For the significance of *d̦iog* and *mi̯ôk* generations see pp.53 and 55.

205. Chi'i Ssŭ-ho, 'Hsi-Chou ti-li-k'ao', *Yen-ching Hsüeh-pao*, no.30 (1946), pp.96–7.

206. Sen-dou Chang, 'The historical trend of Chinese urbanization', *Annals of the Association of American Geographers*, vol.53, no.2 (1963), p.113.

207. The testimony of the *I Hou Nieh I* inscription must now cast doubt on such apparently established events as the beneficing by the Duke of Chou (ți̯ôg) of his son with the territory of Lo (cf. p.108 above).

208. Karlgren, 'Legends and cults', p.302.

209. Eberhard, *Artibus Asiae*, vol.9 (1946), p.360.

210. Wang Kuo-wei, 'Ku-pen Chu-shu Chi-nien chi-chiao', *Hai-ning Wang Chung-ch'io Kung I-shu* (Ch'ang-sha, 1940), with refinements in Fan Hsiang-yung, *Ku-pen Chu-shu Chi-nien Chi-chiao Ting-pu*. Shanghai 1957.

211. This was also the opinion of Henri Maspero, 'La chronologie des rois de Ts'i au IVᵉ siecle avant notre ère', *T'oung Pao*, vol.25 (1927–8), pp.367–86.

212. Edouard Chavannes, *Les mémoires historiques de Se-Ma Ts'ien*, 5 vols. Leroux, Paris 1895.

213. *Tso-Chuan*, Duke **·ər (Ai), 7th year.

214. It is generally agreed that, apart from certain spurious chapters, (of which v is not one), the *Lun-Yü* (which is usually rendered into English as *The Analects*) is an authentic treasury of maxims assembled by students of the Confucian school a generation or so after the Master's death [Cf. Ts'ui Shu, 'Chu-Ssŭ k'ao-hsin yü-lu', in Ku Chieh-kang (ed.), *Ts'ui Tung-pi I-shu*, vol.3 (Shanghai 1936), chüan 2, p.17, and 'Lun-Yü yü-shuo', *loc. cit.*, vol.5, pp.24–35; also Herrlee Glessner Creel, *Confucius and the Chinese Way*. Harper Torchbook, New York 1960, pp.291–4.

The *I-Ching* seems to be an amalgam of peasant superstitions and sophisticated divinatory texts [*Vide* Arthur Waley, 'The Book of Changes', *Bulletin of the Museum of Far Eastern Antiquities*, vol.5 (1933), pp.121–42, and Li Ching-ch'ih, 'Chou-I shih-tz'ŭ hsü-k'ao', *Ling-nan Hsüeh-pao*, vol.8, no.1 (1947), pp.1–66 and 169–73]. Li Ching-ch'ih (*ibid.*) believes that some of the omen texts in this compendium might go back to the 7th or 8th century BC, but that the *T'uan* and *Hsi-Tz'ŭ* did not receive their present form until very late in the Chou dynasty. Other commentaries which now form part of the *I-Ching* were appended in Ch'in and Han times. There is an extremely lucid introduction to this book in Joseph Needham, *Science and civilisation in China*, vol.2 : *History of Scientific Thought*. Cambridge 1956, pp.304 *et seq.*

215. *Tso-Chuan*, Duke **Sni̯ang (Hsiang), 31st year.

216. Kennedy, 'Interpretation of the Ch'un-Ch'iu'.

217. Walker, *The multi-state system of ancient China*, *passim*, but especially p.14.

218. *loc. cit.*, p.30.

219. The sequence of extensions of the Dzʻiər borders are conveniently listed in Ku Tung-kao's *Ch'un-Ch'iu Ta-shih Piao*, table 4, ff.7 recto–8 recto.

220. Oshima Riichi, 'Chugaku kodai no shiro ni tsuite', *Tohogakuho*, vol.30 (1959), pp.39–66.

221. These notices occur respectively in *Tso-Chuan*, Duke **·I̯ən (Yin), 9th year, Duke **Gʻwân (Huan), 16th year, and Duke **Mi̯wɛn (Min), 1st year.

222. Ch'en P'an, 'Ch'un-Ch'iu Ta-shih-piao, Lieh-kuo chüeh-hsing chi tsʻun-mieh-piao chuan-i [A]', *Kuo-li Chung-yang Yen-chiu-yüan Li-shih Yü-yen Yen-chiu-so Chi-kʻan*, vol.26 (1955), pp.59–93; 'Chʻun-Chʻiu Ta-shih-piao, Lieh-kuo chüeh-hsing chi tsʻun-mieh-piao chuan-i [B]', *loc. cit.*, vol.27 (1956), pp.325–64, together with 'Chuan-i chung-pʻien pa' (with comments by Lao Kan), pp.365–70; 'Chʻun-Chiʻiu Ta-shih-piao, Lieh-kuo chüeh-hsing chi tsʻun-mieh-piao chuan-i [C, pt.1]', *loc. cit.*, vol.28 (1956), pp.393–440 and [C, pt.2], *loc. cit.*, vol.29 (1957), pp.513–44.

223. Chang, 'The historical trend of Chinese urbanism', p.114.

224. Chi Li [Li Chi], *The formation of the Chinese people. An anthropological inquiry*. Harvard University Press 1928.

225. This monumental work comprises 10,000 chüan (The Table of Contents alone occupying 40), which, according to Giles's calculation, contain 144 million characters, or from three to four times as much matter as the Eleventh Edition of the *Encyclopaedia Britannica* : Lionel Giles, *An alphabetical index to the Chinese encyclopaedia (Chʻin Ting Ku Chin Tʻu Shu Chi Chʻeng)*. British Museum, London 1911, pp.8–9.

226. These gazetteers are termed in general *fang-chih*. If they are concerned with a province they are known as *tʻung-chih*, and variously as *fu-chih*, *chou-chih* and *hsien-chih* if they deal with smaller units in the administrative hierarchy. There is a brief evaluation of the character of these works in Joseph Needham, *Science and civilisation in China* : vol.3, *Mathematics and the sciences of the heavens and the earth*. Cambridge, at the University Press 1959, pp.517–20. For an excellent introduction in Chinese see Wang Pao-hsin, *Tʻung-chih Tʻiao-i*. Chi Sheng Book Co., Kowloon, 1958. *Vide* also Cheng-siang Chen (Chʻen Cheng-hsiang), *Chung-Kuo Fang-chih-ti Ti-li-hsüeh Chia-chih*. An inaugural address in the Chinese University of Hong Kong (1965).

227. Chi Li (Li Chi], *The formation of the Chinese people*, pp.94 and 100–1.

228. *Chʻun-Chʻiu* and *Tso-Chuan*, 28th year of Duke **Tsi̯ang (Chuang). Although this gloss has all the hallmarks of later systematization, it does show that the compiler of that particular paragraph in the *Tso-Chuan* was able to recognize the basic distinction between these two types of urban settlement in the sources at his disposal, in the same way as we can discern it from the sources available to us.

229. A representative exposition of this belief – one among many – occurs

NOTES AND REFERENCES

in the *Tso-Chuan*, Duke **Tsi̯ang (Chuang), 28th year. Two officers of the Tsi̯ĕn court are addressing the Duke : '**K'i̯uk-·ok (Ch'ü-wo) is [the precinct of] Your Grace's ancestral temple, **B'wo (P'u) and **Ńi̯ər-k'i̯wət (Erh-ch'ü) mark your frontiers. They cannot be without overlords. If your ancestral city be without its overlord, the populace will not stand in awe; if the border mounds are not watched over the Ńi̯ông will be induced to encroach . . .'

230. Cf. p.123 and note 77.
231. Granet, *Chinese civilisation*, p.250.
232. Eberhard, *Conquerors and rulers*, pp.33–40.
233. *Chou-Li*, chüan 12, f.14 recto (1886 edition).
234. *Shih-Chi*, chüan 129, f.7 recto. Ssŭ-ma Ch'ien does, indeed, imply that Duke **Mi̯wən (Wen) had deliberately located his capital on this site in order to take advantage of the opportunities for trade which it offered. This, I think, is rationalization after the event.
235. *ibid.*
236. *Shih-Chi*, chüan 129, f.8 recto. The text also includes the name **D'i̯ĕn (Ch'en) as one of the places engaging in this trade, but it appears to be an anomalous interpolation. However, the combination **Di̯ang (with radical 75 instead of the 163 of the previous folio) B'i̯ĕng Di̯ang D'i̯ĕn recurs on the succeeding folio, from which it appears that a copyist or commentator had at some time read the names as Di̯ang-b'i̯ĕng (Yang-p'ing) and Di̯ang-d'i̯ĕn (Yang-ch'en).
237. *loc. cit.*, f.8 verso.
238. *loc. cit.*, f.9 recto.
239. *ibid.*
240. Cf. note 87 above.
241. Miyazaki Ichisada, Eastern Studies Fifteenth Anniversary Volume, *Toho Gakkai* (1962). There is also useful information in the same author's paper on what he calls the age of the city-states in China in *Shirin*, vol.33, no.1, (1950), pp.144–63, and 'Les villes en Chine à l'époque des Han', *T'oung Pao*, vol.48, pts.4–5 (1960), pp.376–92.
242. An ancient measure equivalent to 4 *tou*, *q.v.* in note 246 below.
243. A weight of 300 *chin*, *q.v.* in note 245 below.
244. Both a liquid and a dry measure; a weight of 100 *chün*, *q.v.* in note 243.
245. 16 *liang* (oz.) on the Chinese scale. Often translated as 'catty' and stipulated in modern times as $21\frac{1}{3}$ oz. avoirdupois (604·53 grammes).
246. A dry measure. Often translated as 'peck' and standardized in modern times as containing 316 cubic inches.
247. Watson, *Records of the Grand Historian*, vol.2, p.495 [transl. from *Shih-Chi*, chüan 129, f.16 recto].
248. Walter Christaller, *Die zentralen Orte in Süddeutschland : Eine*

ökonomisch-geographische Untersuchung über die Gesetzmässigkeit der Verbreitung und Entwicklung der Siedlungen mit städtischen Funktionen. Gustav Fischer Verlag, Jena 1933).

249. Derk Bodde, *China's first unifier. A study of the Ch'in dynasty as seen in the life of Li Ssŭ (280?–208 BC)*. E.J.Brill, Leiden 1938. See especially pp.135–9 and Appendix, pp.238–43.

250. Ting Fu-pao, *Shuo-wen Chieh-tzŭ Ku-lin* (1928), pp.3970a–1b. Cf. also Kuo Mo-jo, *Liang-Chou Chin-wen-tz'ŭ Ta-hsi K'ao-shih*, p.203a; Chang Yin-lin, 'Chou-tai-ti feng-chien she-hui', *Ch'ing-hua Hsüeh-pao*, vol.10, no.4 (1935), p.826; and Ku Chieh-kang, 'Ch'un-Ch'iu-shih-tai-ti hsien', *Yü-Kung*, vol.7, nos.6–7 (1937), p.179.

251. Something similar had indeed been hinted at by Chinese scholars somewhat earlier (though Bodde's was the first formal and adequately documented statement): Chao-I, 'Kai-yü ts'ung-k'ao', *Ou-pei Ch'üan-chi* (1877), chüan 16, ff.8 verso–10 recto; Yao-Nai, *Hsi-pao Hsüan Wen-chi* (Ssŭ-pu Pei-yao edition), chüan 2, f.1 recto. Cf. also Ch'i Ssŭ-ho, 'Chan-Kuo chih-tu k'ao', p.214, note 369.

252. In 361 BC Dz'iĕn was not represented at the conferences of rulers, who regarded its government as not greatly superior to that of the Diər and D'iek tribal peoples: *Shih-Chi*, chüan 5, f.17 verso. Even as late as 266 a noble of the state of Ngiwər warned his king that, 'Dz'iĕn has the customs of the Ñiông and the D'iek. Its heart is that of the tiger or the wolf. It is avaricious, perverse, desirous of [nothing but] profit, and lacks sincerity. It knows nothing of customary public morality (*liər*), proper relationships (**ngia) or virtuous conduct (***tək-g'ăng*)...' [*loc. cit.*, chüan 44, ff.12 verso–13 recto]. Cf. also *Chan-Kuo Ts'e*, Wei section, chüan 26, f.4 recto. Hsün-tzŭ said much the same thing when he observed that the people of Dz'iĕn failed in large measure to practise proper family relationships because they did not observe *liər* and *ngia* [chüan 23].

253. *Shih-Chi*, chüan 5, ff.16–17.

254. Sen-dou Chang (Chang Sheng-tao), 'Some aspects of the urban geography of the Chinese hsien capital', *Annals of the Association of American Geographers*, vol.51, no.1 (1961), p.25. Cf. also W.Allyn Rickett, *Kuan-tzu. A repository of early Chinese thought*, vol.1. Hong Kong University Press, 1965, p.65, note 138.

255. H.G.Creel, 'The beginnings of bureaucracy in China: the origin of the Hsien', *Journal of Asian Studies*, vol.23, no.2 (1964), pp.155–83.

256. The passage in question occurs in a conversation between a Tsiĕn pretender and a Dz'iĕn envoy, as reported in the *Kuo-Yü* under the year 651 BC [Ssŭ-pu Pei-yao edition, chüan 8, f.10 verso], but the *Kuo-Yü* is not free from fanciful literary embellishment, and Professor Bodde is doubtless correct in stigmatizing this paragraph as an interpolation [*China's first unifier*, p.243].

NOTES AND REFERENCES

257. Creel, 'The beginnings of bureaucracy', p.172. Cf. also note 252 above.

258. *loc. cit.*, pp.172–3.

259. Creel has shown that references to *hsien* in other states during the Ch'un-Ch'iu are either of highly questionable authenticity or afford no confirmation that they connote an administrative institution [*loc. cit.*, p.173, note 97]. Kuo Mo-jo has published an inscription on a bronze vessel ascribed to the reign of Duke **Lieng (Ling) of *Dz'iər* (581–554 BC), which records a grant of 300 *hsien* to a retainer [*Liang-Chou Chin-wen-tz'ŭ Ta-hsi K'ao-shih*, pp.202b–205b] in that state, but both Bodde [*China's first unifier*, p.241] and Creel ['The beginnings of bureaucracy', p.172, note 88] have rejected this inscription as evidence of institutionalized *hsien* administration. The former questioned the authenticity of the inscription on the grounds that the number of *hsien* was impossibly large: according to the *Tso-Chuan* there were only 49 in the whole of the state of Tsi̯ĕn (We may recall here Dr Noel Barnard's warnings against epigraphic forgeries, cf. p.111 above). Creel passed no judgment on the authenticity of the inscription but maintained that *hsien* in this context referred 'only to small "suburban" areas associated with towns'. It is not surprising to find *hsien* attributed to very early times by late systematizing texts, but such testimony is of no more value in a study of Ch'un-Ch'iu times than is Shakespeare's *Coriolanus* for the study of the costume of ancient Rome. The *Huai-nan-tzŭ*, for example, which was put together in the middle of the 2nd century BC, even went so far as to ascribe a *hsien* administration to the kingdom of **G'i̯at (Chieh), traditionally dated as 1818–1766 BC, [Ssŭ-pu Pei-yao edition, chüan 13, f.9 verso].

260. *Tso-Chuan*, 33rd year of Duke **Xi̯əg (Hsi).

261. 'The beginnings of bureaucracy', p.173. Creel relies partly on the testimony of the *Tso-Chuan*, 30th year of Duke **Sni̯ang (Hsiang), where the chancellor questions an old man as to his **g'i̯an d'âd-pi̯wo (*hsien tai-fu*), thus implying that such an official must have existed, no matter which district the old man hailed from. However, Ku Chieh-kang ['Ch'un-Ch'iu-shih-tai-ti hsien', pp.190–3] had categorized this passage as a forgery of Liu-Hsin and, though not necessarily espousing all Ku's argument, Creel also draws in support of this view on a later passage from the *Tso-Chuan*, 5th year of Duke **T̂i̯og (Chao). This states that in 537 (i.e. only six years after the date of the disputed reference) Tsi̯ĕn had 49 *hsien* able to furnish 4,900 war chariots, an immense force which is possibly the largest attributed to any state in the Ch'un-Ch'iu, and one which must imply that virtually the whole of Tsi̯ĕn territory was apportioned in *hsien*: only eight years later, in 529 [13th year of Duke T̂i̯og], the whole state was apparently able to assemble only a round figure of 4,000 chariots.

262. The evidence for the hereditability of *hsien* in Tsi̯ĕn is complex, obscure and, of course, fragmented so that discussion of apparent individual instances

is hardly, if ever, conclusive, and Creel bases his conclusion on the cumulative impression left by his detailed studies of the Tsi̯ĕn *hsien* in the *Tso-Chuan*. He discusses a selection of the relevant references in 'The beginnings of bureaucracy,' p.173, note 96.

263. Creel himself ['The beginnings of bureaucracy', p.174, note 98] pays tribute to the perspicacity of Hung Liang-Chi (1746–1809), who attributed the creation of *hsien* to Tṣ'i̯o, but without citing his evidence or discussing the problems that inevitably accompany such an interpretation ['Ch'un-Ch'iu-shih i ta-i wei hsien shih-yü Ch'u lun', *Keng-sheng-chai Wen Chia-chi* (1802), chüan 2, ff.1–2].

264. Creel, 'The beginnings of bureaucracy', pp.174–9.

265. *Tso-Chuan*, Duke **·ər (Ai), 17th year.

266. *loc. cit.*, Duke **Tṣi̯ang (Chuang), 6th year; *Shih-Chi*, chüan 40, f.4.

267. Creel, 'The beginnings of bureaucracy', p.178, note 15.

268. *Tso-Chuan*, Duke Tṣi̯ang, 18th year.

269. Creel, 'The beginnings of bureaucracy', p.181, note 124.

270. *Tso-Chuan*, Duke **Xi̯əg (Hsi), years 23 and 28; *Shih-Chi*, chüan 39 ff.43–5.

271. Cf. also *Tso-Chuan*, Duke **Si̯wan (Hsüan), 17th year; Duke **Ḓi̯ĕng (Ch'eng), years 2, 7, 8 and 16; *Kuo-Yü*, chüan 17, ff.3 verso–5 verso.

272. Cf., *int. al.*, *Li-Chi*, *Li-Yün* section: 'It is the purpose [of great men] to make the walls of their cities and suburbs strong, and their ditches and moats secure.'

273. *Tso-Chuan*, Duke **·I̯ən (Yin), 1st year. It is immaterial, in view of our imprecise knowledge of early Chou measurements, whether 100 d'i̯ər be translated as 3,000 cubits [James Legge, *The Chinese Classics*, vol.5: *The Ch'un Ts'ew with the Tso Chuen*. Hong Kong University Press reprint 1960, p.5] or 4,600 meters [Cho-yün Hsü, *Ancient China in Transition*, p.134]. It would be unrealistic to attempt to match information in a text of this nature with data from present-day archeological investigation. In our opinion the passage in the *Tso-Chuan* is nothing more than a systematization of the simple observation that the more prestigious cities of ancient China tended to have the longer perimeters. Neither, in our opinion and for the same reason, should any significance be attached to the fact that such areal dimensions as archeological research has so far made available are not conspicuously accordant with those of Mencius's representative city, one with a *di̯ĕng* of 3 *li* and a *kwâk* of 7 *li* (Bk. II, pt.2, Chapter i).

274. *Tso-Chuan*, Duke **Ḓi̯og (Ch'ao), 11th year.

275. *Tso-Chuan*, Duke **Tṣi̯ang (Chuang), 26th year.

276. Miyazaki Ichisada, *Rekishi To Chiri*, vol.32 (1933).

277. *Tso-Chuan*, Duke **Sni̯ang (Hsiang), 9th year.

278. *Tso-Chuan*, Duke **Ḓi̯og (Ch'ao), 21st year.

NOTES AND REFERENCES

279. *Tso-Chuan*, Duke **Sni̯ang (Hsiang), 9th year. In the *Kung-yang Chuan* the character for 'fire' (**χwâr : huo) is used instead of that for 'calamity'.

280. Shang and early Chou graphs for *kwâk* (*kuo*) depict a wall with gate towers [Karlgren no.774b,c,d. Cf. Fig.15].

281. *Tso-Chuan*, Duke **Xi̯əg (Hsi), 2nd year.

282. *Tso-Chuan*, Duke **Xi̯əg, 12th year.

283. *Ch'un-Ch'iu* and *Tso-Chuan*, Duke **D̂i̯og (Ch'ao), 23rd year. According to the traditional commentators, D'iek-dz'i̯wan was so named after the D'iek spring and pool on the east of D̂i̯ĕng-ti̯ôg – a good example of folk etymology if ever there was one.

284. *Tso-Chuan*, Duke D'ieng (Ting), 1st year.

285. *Ch'un-Ch'iu* and *Tso-Chuan*, Duke **G'wân (Huan), 6th year.

286. *Ch'un-Ch'iu* and *Tso-Chuan*, Duke **Sni̯ang (Hsiang), 15th year.

287. *Tso-Chuan*, Duke **D̂i̯og (Ch'ao), 25th year.

288. *Meng-tzŭ*, Bk. I, pt.1, Chapter VII. Mencius draws the same distinctions again in Bk.II, pt.1, Chapter V.

289. Although literary traditions equate this site with that of the capital of independent ·Ok prior to its absorption by Tsi̯ĕn in the 8th century BC, the remains which have been brought to light so far appear to date from the Chan-Kuo (cf. pp.140–1).

290. Wolfram Eberhard, 'Data on the structure of the Chinese city in the pre-industrial period', *Economic Development and cultural change*, vol.3 (1957), pp.258–9.

291. The *I Chou-shu* is the earliest of the *Pieh-Shih* or 'Separate Histories'. It was alleged to have been found, together with the *Chu-shu Chi-nien* (cf. notes 36 and 37 to Chapter One) in an ancient **Ngi̯wər tomb during the 3rd century AD. If any of its contents are genuine they will date from the end of the 4th and beginning of the 3rd century BC, so that they will almost certainly already have undergone a great deal of systematization before that time, and ideas about urban morphology will be just as likely to relate to the later as the earlier centuries of the Chou. The author of the work is unknown.

292. Marcel Granet, *Chinese civilization*. Transl. from the French by Kathleen E. Innes and Mabel R. Brailsford. Meridian Books Inc., New York, 1958, p.242.

293. Henri Frankfort, *Kingship and the gods*. University of Chicago Press 1947, p.396, note 23.

294. *Tso-Chuan*, Duke **Mi̯wɛn (Min), 2nd year.

295. *Tso-Chuan*, Duke **Sni̯ang (Hsiang), 27th year.

Part Two

THE EARLY CHINESE CITY IN COMPARATIVE PERSPECTIVE

•

3

The Nature of the Ceremonial Center

THE EARLIEST URBAN FORMS

Whenever, in any of the seven regions of primary urban generation (as proposed on p. 9 above), we trace back the characteristic urban form to its beginnings we arrive not at a settlement that is dominated by commercial relations, a primordial market, or at one that is focused on a citadel, an archetypal fortress, but rather at a ceremonial complex. Of course, the modes of religious expression are often more stylized and repetitive than are those of, say, petty commerce or political organization, and are consequently likely to be more readily discernible in archeological assemblages. It is also true that the material manifestations of cult and ritual are likely to be cast in a durable form capable of surviving the vicissitudes of time. Indeed some of the most ancient are of striking impressiveness even today. Moreover, writing and representational art, on which we are dependent for a large part of our knowledge of these centers, but which were both intimately associated with, and were perhaps born of, ritual, may induce us to exaggerate the role of religious ceremonial. But even allowing for the biases in interpretation thus induced by the nature of the evidence, and discounting the number and visual preponderance of religiously prescribed elements in the morphology of these complexes, the predominantly religious focus to the schedule of social activities associated with them leaves no room to doubt that we are dealing primarily with centers of ritual and ceremonial. Naturally this does not imply that the ceremonial centers did not exercise secular functions as well, but rather that these were subsumed into an all-pervading religious context. Beginning as little more than tribal shrines, in what may be regarded as their classic phases these centers were elaborated into complexes of public ceremonial structures, usually massive and often extensive, and including assemblages of such architectural items as pyramids, platform mounds, temples, palaces, terraces, staircases, courts, and stelae. Operationally they were instruments for the creation of political, social, economic, and sacred space, at the same time as they were symbols of cosmic, social, and moral order. Under the religious authority of organized priesthoods and divine monarchs, they elaborated the redistributive aspects of the economy to a position of institutionalized regional dominance, functioned as nodes in a web of administered (gift or treaty) trade, served as foci of craft specialization, and promoted the development of the exact and predictive sciences. Above all, they embodied the aspirations of brittle, pyramidal societies in which, typically, a sacerdotal élite, controlling a corps of officials and perhaps a praetorian guard, ruled over a broad understratum of peasantry.[1]

CEREMONIAL CENTERS in regions of primary urban generation

Mesopotamia. In the regions of primary urban generation the existence of such ceremonial centers has long been recognized as a prelude to full urban development. The most amply (though still wholly inadequately) documented, as well as the most thoroughly (though still, by all desirable standards, only meagerly) investigated, of these regions of nuclear urbanism occupied the plains of Lower Mesopotamia from the neighborhood of present-day Baghdād roughly to the confluence of the Tigris and Euphrates, some fifty or so miles north of modern Baṣrah.[2] Within this region the earliest cult centers developed in the extreme south, and are typified by such well-known names as Eridug, Ur, Uruk, Girshu, and probably Lagash, Ninā, and Umma. From 'Ubaid times, when these ceremonial foci first appeared in the archeological record, through the Warqa and early Protoliterate periods such developments were apparently restricted to a narrow zone of territory, not much more than fifty miles long, lying between the latitudes of present-day Tell Abū Shaḥrain and Fara. In the second half of the fourth millennium, however, with the emergence, if not the actual founding, of Shuruppak, Nippur, Kish, and Eshnunnak,[3] it is possible to discern the spread of such cult centers northwards to approximately the latitude of Baghdād, and even on to the plains of the lower Diyālā, at the same time as there seems to have been a decline in the prosperity of the south. Eridug was virtually abandoned at the end of the 'Ubaid period, and Ninā and Lagash in Early Dynastic I and II. It has been suggested that this shift in the center of gravity of Sumerian civilization may have been induced by salinization of the soil under protracted cultivation with only imperfect drainage techniques.[4]

There is no basis on which to reconstruct a city plan prior to those of the Early Dynastic period (*c.* 2900 – *c.* 2370 BC) in the Diyālā basin, and the complete picture, in so far as archeological research allows, has to be assembled from fragmentary, and perhaps unrepresentative, evidence. However, the predilection of archeologists for excavation within ceremonial precincts has provided us with a sequence of temple evolution reaching back to the earliest occupation levels at Eridug. The first significant development preserved in the archeological record was the conversion of the small village or domestic shrine into a temple, a transformation that took place during the first half of the fourth millennium BC. At Tell Abū Shaḥrain, the ancient Eridug, no less than thirteen such temples have been discovered in 'Ubaid levels (*c.* 4000 – 3500 BC). The earliest of which a ground plan has been preserved was found in Level XVI. It consisted of a small, roughly square room, with a single door in the southeastern side, and two short screens suggesting a division of the interior. An altar was placed in a recess in the rear wall, and signs of burning revealed the existence of an offering-place in the center. By the end of the 'Ubaid period a tripartite arrangement had been evolved, in which a central cella was flanked on either side by rows of small rooms.[5] The architectural form thus established was sustained, with increasing complexity, for something like a thousand years, until by the middle of the third millennium it had crystallized into a massive complex of traditionally arranged cult chambers surrounded by dwellings, workshops, granaries, and storehouses. During the second half of the fourth millennium, for example, this building tradition was exemplified in a series of temple precincts laid out on a magnificent scale, and located not only at Warqa itself but also at Tell 'Uqair, at Khafājah in the Diyalā, and even as far north as Tell Brak in the Khabūr valley. One of the most remarkable of these structures is the complex known today as the Pillar Temple at Warqa (Sumerian *Uruk*, Biblical *Erech*, Greek *Orchoe*). It is still incompletely excavated so that its plan is unknown, but its columned portico is impressive enough. Set on a raised platform entirely decorated with the characteristic Sumerian cone mosaic, it consists of a hall with a double row of eight free-standing, mosaic columns, supplemented by a row of engaged columns along one of the side walls. Some of the columns are as much as 2·62 meters in diameter, and the portico constitutes the earliest known example of large-scale columnar architecture. More completely excavated is the White Temple, also at Warqa, and dated to about 3100 BC. This building, constructed on the 'Ubaid tripartite plan that was already ancient in Warqa times, is of mud-brick with whitewashed walls, and its façade and nave are decorated with elaborate buttresses and recesses. The temple itself measured 22·3 × 17·5 meters, but it was raised on a platform 70 meters long by 66 wide and some 13 meters high. This platform, or *ziggurat*, incorporated the remains of many earlier sanctuaries. Because the god of the temple was considered to be the landowner in perpetuity of the ground that had been consecrated to him, his shrine could not easily be transferred to a new site. Consequently, when the temple had to be renewed, the old structure was filled solid with brickwork and the new building raised on the summit of the terrace thus formed. Not infrequently some of the possessions of the god were also buried inside the abandoned temple. In later centuries both temples and their supporting ziggurats, the 'mountains' where the natural potency of the earth and therefore of all life was concentrated, became still larger and more elaborate, and well into the Early Dynastic period the temple far exceeded any other building in both size and complexity.[6] It is uncertain when full-time priests first appeared, but they were depicted on seals and stone carvings from about 3000 BC, and almost certainly existed in earlier times. On the basis of comparative studies, it has been inferred that they were probably the first persons to be released from the stultifying routine of direct subsistence labor. Ration lists found in temples[7] would seem to indicate that in Early Dynastic times, at least, these priests were not concerned exclusively with spiritual matters but also participated actively in the administration of earthly affairs – in so far, that is, as these two categories of activities could ever at this time have been deemed distinct.

From a study of Sumerian mythology as written down in the dynastic period but preserving the social and political institutions of an earlier age, Thorkild Jacobsen has argued that, during the closing centuries of the fourth millennium BC, political authority resided in an assembly of the adult male members of the community.[8] Archeological evidence for the concentration of power in the hands of a secular personage or class does not occur until the beginning of the third millennium. Then the rise of kingship is attested by the presence of monumental palaces[9] and royal tombs. The term for 'king' also appears in Sumerian epigraphy at this time. Equally significant is the differentiation of classes that was taking place, as witnessed both by grave furniture in successively later cemeteries and by Early Dynastic texts. By 2750 BC there had developed a social and economic stratification that, royalty apart, ranged from grand palace dignitaries controlling estates of no mean order, through minor officials, artisans, and cultivators to a small but not unimportant slave class.

Contemporaneously defensive walls began to be built around the settlements[10] and, from about 3000 BC at latest, there began to develop a distinctive morphological pattern within the enceintes. Straight streets wide enough for wheeled vehicles radiated outwards from a nexus of public buildings, both sacred and secular. The residences of the wealthier members of the community were located along these thoroughfares, with those of the poor dispersed on no apparent plan in the maze of alleys that filled the interstices between the main avenues. So far nothing corresponding to a market-place or bazaar for private trade has been discovered, but several of the larger settlements that had developed in Lower Mesopotamia by about 2500 BC encompassed as many as 250 acres within their walls and one of them, Uruk, occupied all of 1,100 acres with, according to an informed estimate, a population of the order of 50,000 persons.[11]

Naturally these decisive changes in the social structure and settlement pattern of Lower Mesopotamia stimulated new types of economic demand, which were in turn reflected in the realm of technology. As late as 3500 BC full-time craftsmen were very few[12] and their output was consigned almost wholly to the temples for cult purposes. A millennium later, however, the need for weapons and other military equipment generated by the chronic raiding and warfare that accompanied the rise of the city-states, the commissioning of luxury and status products for both palace and temple display, as well as the private needs of a small middle class, had induced a burgeoning of production. But it is significant that this was a change in quantity of production rather than in style or technology.

Egypt. Apart from North China, which has been discussed in detail in Chapter One, there are two other regions of primary urban generation in the Ancient World, namely the Nile and Indus valleys. About these it is not possible to be so specific, in the case of Egypt because the evidence is still (and perhaps for all time) buried beneath Nile mud, in the case of the Indus because archeological investigation has barely turned its attention to the problem with which we are concerned in this study, namely the transformation from folk to urban society. The meagerness of the evidence at our disposal makes it very difficult to say anything worthwhile about the social, political and economic conditions of pre-dynastic Egypt. Prior to the unification of Upper and Lower Egypt, by which is meant not the historic units known by those names but the territories lying between some point north of the First Cataract and some point within the Delta, the basic unit of settlement, as indeed of government, appears to have been the village, under the leadership of a chieftain and the protection of a local incarnation of one of the universal deities.[13] At least some of these villages were walled, as is apparent both from excavations at Marimdah beni Salamah and from a survey at Hierakonpolis,[14] and this has led several authors to refer to them as 'towns', though the published records afford no evidence of urban status, as far as I can see. Rather they seem to indicate a Lung-shan type of walled village, associated, as far as can be deduced from not wholly satisfactory evidence, with a Lung-shan type of stratified society (cf. p. 28 above).

So far incipient cult centers have not been recognized among these villages, but there is no doubt that, with the unification of the Two Lands, monumental mortuary complexes and royal ceremonial centers began to feature among the more dramatic elements in the cultural landscape of the Nile valley, and it is most unlikely that such ritual instruments had no evolutionary development behind them. The importance of Memphis, allegedly the first of these sacred enceintes, is reflected in the text known today as the *Memphite Theology*, which deals in large part with the cosmological roles of Memphis and of the Memphite god Ptah, and with the ceremonies which took place at that city.[15] According to an account which persisted into Greek times, this ceremonial center was founded, a little to the south of modern Cairo, on land newly reclaimed by diverting a branch of the Nile, and was called the White Walls, white being the color of the mother-goddess Nekhbet, protectress of Upper Egypt, whence came, according to these late sources, Menes, unifier of the kingdom. Although Memphis was thus established as the supremely sacred cult center of ancient Egypt (and indeed remained so for some fifteen hundred years), the Pharaohs of the First and Second Dynasties resided in palaces at Thinis and were buried in neighboring Abydos. This practice set a pattern for the development of royal ceremonial centers, in which individual Pharaohs each established their earthly palace enclaves conveniently near the great mortuary complexes which would be their more permanent residences. During the lifetime of the Pharaoh, work would continue on the pyramid and its temple, while government would be conducted from a neighboring ceremonial center but, on the king's death, the palace precinct would often be abandoned to the priests and officials charged with the management of the royal cult and the mortuary estate. Hence we find the royal cult center migrating from Memphis to Herakleopolis, to Thebes, to Lisht, to Avaris, back to Thebes, and then to Ramses. Each center in its turn consisted of a palace and one or more temple complexes, together with suites of structures ancillary to each and, near by, the royal tomb. It has been suggested, moreover, that the mortuary cities built by the Pharaohs may in some respects have reflected the layouts of the capitals. Professor Fairman writes,

'Just as in life the courtiers could seek houses close to the palace, so in death they desired their "houses of eternity", their tombs, to be near the resting place of their lord. This can be seen most clearly at Gizeh where a veritable city of the dead exists around the pyramids. In the center is the pyramid and around in neat and orderly rows, in streets and cross streets, are the mastabas of the nobles, sometimes having the external appearance of houses, and grouped and graded, moreover, according to the rank of their owners. It is hard to escape the conclusion that these pyramid cities do reflect to a certain extent the lay-out of the capital, though possibly the plan is an ideal one and the reality may not have been quite so orderly.'[16]

Available information relates almost wholly to the most splendid of these centers, those which served as the seat of a divine Pharaoh, so that it is difficult to say whether or not a hierarchy of lesser cult centers existed in the Nile valley at this time.

The Indus valley. When we turn our attention to the rise of ceremonial centers in the Indus valley the difficulty of evaluating the evidence is exacerbated by a variety of circumstances. Not least among them is the fact that the earlier excavators of the sites of Mohenjo-daro and Harappā were, generally speaking, concerned with different questions from those for which the present work is attempting to provide partial answers, so that for nearly forty years we were left with a description of an allegedly mature urban civilization whose antecedents were completely unknown. Not until comparatively recently has the work of Sir Mortimer Wheeler at Harappā, of Dr F. A. Khan at Kot Diji, and of Messrs B. B. Lal and B. K. Thapar at Kalibangan made reference to earlier stages in the development of the Indus civilization. And then, to add to our difficulties, this decade is witnessing an as yet incomplete re-evaluation of the available evidence, so that it would be a pleasant relief to be able to defer the writing of these paragraphs for a few years. However, the situation as it appears at the moment is as follows.

By about the middle of the third millennium BC there had come into being an urbanized culture best known from its two largest cities, Mohenjo-daro on the banks of the Indus in Sind, and Harappā beside a former course of the Rāvī, in the Panjab, some 400 miles to the northeast. However, in recent years it has been discovered that this culture stretched far beyond the Indus valley, reaching from the foot of the Simla hills to the neighborhood of Karachi, and from Sutkāgen-dor, just behind the Makran coast, through Kathiāwāḍ to the estuaries of the Narbadā and the Kim on the Gulf of Cambay.[17] The uniformity of this culture over an extensive area, and its stability over a millennium, have been subjects of comment since its first discovery. The idea that Mohenjo-daro and Harappā, both more than three miles in circumference, were densely populated urban foci with a more or less full range of urban functions has recently been disputed by Walter Fairservis, who regards them rather as ceremonial centers with functions 'similar to the centers of the Old Kingdom Egyptians and the Mayans'.[18] Fairservis has, in fact, sought to connect these Indus cult centers with much smaller shrines which have come to light in the Quetta valley, in Loralai, Zhob, Kalat and Las Bela.[19] In the Quetta valley, for example, Fairservis has himself traced an evolutionary sequence of settlement forms which, beginning with villages dependent on sheep and goat pastoralism combined with limited cultivation, culminated in an elaborate ceremonial complex replete with monumental buildings, fertility figures, and what he interprets as ablutional and sacrificial facilities. In his opinion there was in the third millennium BC a cultural continuum embracing both the Baluch hills and the Indus plains, the only important difference between these two major ecological zones being a quantitative one. In both regions the chief settlements shared features indicative of a ceremonial function. Fairservis summarizes his position as follows:

'This pre-Harappan evidence in Sind [provided by excavations at Amri[20] and Kot Diji] and our awareness of the increasing cultural complexities in pre-Harappan Baluchistan, where many prototypes of Harappan traits occur, suggest that the Harappan civilization is but the latest phase in a long development. . . . It would appear that the Harappan culture is the most Indianized, but I think that its essential roots are unquestionably Iranian. We can, in fact, envision two parallel, mutually influential developments occurring in the Indus valley and in Baluchistan. The Indus valley cultures became more and more Indianized, and this Indianization diffused to Baluchistan, both areas achieving greater cultural complexity as a result of these processes. Certainly the Indus valley with its soil and water resources must have encouraged and supported denser populations. There too, the native fauna and flora and the still hypothetical surviving forest cultures aided in the Indianization which is already apparent, for example, in pre-Harappan Kot Diji. The Harappan civilization as the last phase is the most complex of the Indianized cultures in the Indus valley.'[21]

By no means all specialists in the study of the Indus civilization have accepted this interpretation of the evidence. Fairservis is probably on firm ground when he describes some of the structures in settlements of the last major prehistoric phase in the Quetta valley as ceremonial buildings, and credits them with being centers for ritual bathing and sacrifice. On top of the mound of Damb Sadaat (Mian Ghundai), for example, was found a large mud-brick platform furnished with stone drains and providing evidence for the former existence of some sort of architectural structure on its surface, as well as for a massive wall enclosing the enceinte.[22] Associated with these remains were indications of a mother-goddess cult since discovered to be widespread in the Loralai and Fort Sandeman districts and in southern Afghanistan, together with numbers of bull figurines.[23] And Fairservis would seem justified in categorizing the Las Bela Complex A as 'a ceremonial hierarchy supported by farmers'. But that Mohenjo-daro and Harappā were exclusively ceremonial centers is a point of view that few other scholars have been prepared to adopt. The prevalent urban dispositions as revealed in these two great cities, and at the smaller sites of Kalibangan[24] and Lothal,[25] would seem to have taken the dual form of a monumental architectural complex raised on a natural or artificial mound and constituting something in the nature of an acropolis, and a lower city laid out on a fairly rigorously defined grid pattern. At Harappā and Kalibangan, cemeteries were located in close proximity to the acropolis. The precise role of this so-called 'acropolis' is not wholly clear. Whereas in a smaller settlement partially excavated at Chanhu-daro it was apparently lacking altogether, at Mohenjo-daro, Harappā, and particularly at Kalibangan, it exhibited signs of fortification. The prominence of facilities for ablution that must almost certainly have been of a ritual nature apparently define ceremonial roles for at least some of these settlements, at the same time as the presence of granaries at Mohenjo-daro, Harappā, and Lothal, and the construction of a dock at the last-named site, presumably imply an economic function. Clearly, ceremonial occupied a prominent place in the life of these cities, but whether it played such a dominant part that they deserved to be called ceremonial or cult centers awaits a great deal of further investigation. Possibly the roles of Mohenjo-daro and Harappā differed in this respect from those of the smaller settlements as, say, that of Pei-ching has customarily differed from those of lesser Chinese cities, or the function of Makka from that of Jidda. Nevertheless, the main difference between Fairservis's description of the layout of the Late Kullian Complex A, quoted below, and that of Mohenjo-daro as summarized in any of the works listed in Note 17 is evidently mainly one of scale.

'Initial observation revealed a consistent plan : large structures, on the bluffs overlooking the river, consisted of ascending stages receding as they rose in ziggurat fashion, and crowned at the top with platforms supporting brick buildings. These platforms were reached by ramps or steps. There are two good examples of drains let into the body or edge of a platform. Surrounding these high structures, some of which rose over 30 feet above the surrounding area, are complexes of structures with intervening lanes or streets, stone-paved floors and drains or cisterns located in these floors, apparently in small chambers. Beyond these structures groups of rectangular buildings some over 70 feet long and compartmented, present a formal appearance, suggesting hierarchical living quarters or perhaps tombs.'[26]

Of course, this gross morphological similarity between the cult centers of marginal hill peoples of Baluchistan and the civilizational nuclei of the Indus, even though they *may* reflect the operation of analogous but quantitatively disparate processes, cannot be held to imply lineal continuity. Speculation about the origins of the Indus cities is likely to be illusory until archeologists provide more evidence of pre-Harappān settlements. So far the most instructive of such materials for present purposes comes from the site of Kot Diji, about twenty-five miles northeast of Mohenjo-daro, where F. A. Khan has discovered a fortified village underlying an open Indus settlement. On the information presently available, this Kot Dijian settlement appears to have been morphologically not too dissimilar from those at Marimdah and Lung-shan.

The dating of the Harappān culture in its entirety, let alone of individual cities, is far from precise. Until recent years it depended entirely on the evidence of trade links with Mesopotamia, which implied dates ranging from about 2350 to some time in the 16th century B C. Contact between these two civilizations was especially strongly attested during the Sargonid period, which is now securely dated to 2370–2284. Somewhat more than a dozen radio-carbon analyses, and borings into the Indus floodplain at Mohenjo-daro carried out by G. F. Dales in 1965, have done little more than confirm the general validity of this time span. In any case it is not necessary that all the regional components of a civilization as widespread as the Harappān should have been terminated contemporaneously. Indeed, such evidence as we have indicates that they were not. Whereas in the Indus valley proper, particularly at Mohenjo-daro, there are sporadic and uncertain indications of a dramatic ending to cities already in economic decline, in Saurashṭra a late regional Indus cultural tradition apparently underwent a slow transformation into sub-Indus and successor cultures. The evident economic decline at Mohenjo-daro has been variously attributed to deforestation in the process of providing fuel for the brick kilns, over-grazing, a rising water-table, soil salination, interruption of trade with Mesopotamia, and what Sir Mortimer Wheeler has called 'the wearing out of the landscape'.[27] Among the instruments which may have administered the coup de grâce, catastrophic flooding and Aryan invaders have been invoked most frequently. Certainly there is evidence of a massacre in the closing years of Mohenjo-daro. But it is not necessarily — or even probably — to be extrapolated to the rest of the Harappān culture realm. It is true that the earlier investigators of the Indus cities considered Mohenjo-daro and Harappā as contemporary, sometimes even as twin capitals of a theocratic state, but recently Robert Raikes has suggested that Mohenjo-daro was in fact replaced by Harappā when uplift of the northern shores of the Arabian Sea ponded back the waters of the Indus and induced severe flooding in parts of Sind.[28] Some of Fairservis's conclusions as to the chronology of the Harappān civilization are not inimical to such an interpretation.[29]

Mesoamerica. In the New World ceremonial centers developed in two regions. The first of these was the culture realm that existed as a distinctive entity from the emergence of effective food production, in about the middle of the second millennium BC, until the Spanish conquest in the 16th century AD, and which Paul Kirchhoff has aptly denoted by the term Mesoamerica.[30] It comprised the southern two-thirds of mainland Mexico, Guatemala, British Honduras, the western half of Honduras, El Salvador, the Pacific coast of Nicaragua, and the northwestern sector of Costa Rica. The second New World nucleus of urban development comprised various tracts of territory in and adjoining the Central Andes which were bases for cultures that Wendell Bennett has compositely characterized as the Peruvian Co-tradition.[31] The area of particular concern in the present context includes the coast and highland of Peru, together with the adjoining Titicaca basin in Bolivia.

Let us turn first to the emergence and distribution of ceremonial centers in Mesoamerica. Here the earliest examples appear to have arisen in upland valleys, particularly in the basins of Guatemala, Oaxaca, and the Valley of Mexico. Temple mounds adjacent to sedentary village compounds, and dated as early as 1000 BC, have been reported from the neighborhood of Kaminaljuyú in the Guatemalan highlands,[32] and by about 300 BC this particular site had evolved into a major cult center, with huge adobe platform mounds containing richly furnished burials of priests or chiefs.[33] A fragmentary carved-stone altar bearing hieroglyphic inscriptions affords additional evidence of the ceremonial nature of this site. At much the same time temple enclaves began to appear in other parts of Mesoamerica. At Monte Albán in Oaxaca mound architecture occurred in association with hieroglyphics;[34] at La Venta in lowland Tabasco several groups of mounds were raised, including one no less than thirty-two meters in height, all in association with courtyards, stone cist graves covered by mounds, carved stelae and altars, and carved human heads;[35] in the Valley of Mexico plastered terraces and stairways[36] foreshadowed a slightly later development of large ceremonial mounds at Cuicuilco in the Pedregal of San

Angel,[37] at the same time as a platform mound and plaza were laid out at the site that was subsequently to witness the rise of Teotihuacán.[38] Simultaneously the practice of temple building was extended into the Maya lowlands, as is testified by the temple E-VII-sub at Uaxactún[39] and a mound of impressive dimensions at Yaxuná.[40]

In the succeeding Late pre-Classic and Classic periods (*c.* 300 BC – AD 900[41]) ceremonial centers, often of great size, were found in large numbers from Tamaulipas to Honduras and from Oaxaca to Yucatán. So far more than a hundred such architectural clusters have been discovered in the Maya territories alone, including such imposing cult complexes as Tikal, Copán, Uxmal, Uaxactún, Dzibilchaltún, Calakmul, Piedras Negras, and Palenque.[42] Typically these were distinguished by stone architecture of considerable pretensions and including large multi-chambered buildings, structures somewhat resembling cloisters, priestly dwellings and seminaries, storehouses, courts for the ritual ball game, stairways, and masonry platforms, all set round a plaza, and dominated by one or more temple-pyramids that may also on occasion have served as mausolea or cenotaphs. By the late pre-Classic period the ceremonial center at Kaminaljuyú had come to cover several square kilometers.[43] Even more extensive are the ruins of Teotihuacán (= House of the Gods) in the Valley of Mexico, a cult center which covered nearly thirty square kilometers early in the first millennium AD, and whose architectural structures fully merit the clichéd epithets 'massive' and 'monumental'.[44] The Pyramid of the Sun, which may have been built at the end of the pre-Classic, and which in any case is not younger than the early Classic period, is 689 feet square at the base, 210 feet high, and contains 1,300,000 cubic yards of earth. Beyond the watershed, to the southeast, in the Puebla valley, there was raised more or less contemporaneously the pyramid of Cholula which, with a height of 181 feet and covering an area of 40 acres, exceeds in magnitude the pyramid built by Cheops at Gizeh.

Some of the ceremonial complexes which flourished in Mesoamerica during the Classic phase fell victims to attacks by their neighbors, others failed in economic competition, a great many faded from the scene for reasons which cannot be known. Still others acquired a new range of functions which, while not suppressing their ceremonial role, greatly modified the character of the city; but not a few persisted – as far as can be deduced at this distance of time – purely as cult centers, until the Spanish conquest in the first half of the 16th century destroyed the religious foundations on which they had been raised, and brought to an end a Mesoamerican tradition of ceremonial architecture that had endured for more than 2,000 years.

The Central Andes. In Peru, the southernmost sector of Nuclear America,[45] religious ceremonialism can be traced back to about the beginning of the first millennium BC, when some of the earliest farmers in the vicinity of Aspero, in Supe, erected a rude structure of natural stones for purposes of worship. An equally crude contemporary temple has also been discovered in the Virú valley.[46] By the beginning of the latter half of the same millennium impressive ceremonial centers had made their appearance, among them the one at Chavín de Huántar, on a tributary of the Marañon river. This complex of raised platforms, a sunken court, terraces, mounds, plazas, and stone buildings honeycombed with galleries and chambers interconnected by stairways and ramps, the whole oriented to the cardinal points of the compass, occupies a space of more than 640,000 square feet. A triple-terraced pyramid crowning a hill crest at Kuntur Wasi, on the upper reaches of the Jequetepeque river, seems to have formed part of a similar complex; other examples are known from the Virú, Nepeña and Casma valleys; and possibly Pucara in the northern part of the Titicaca basin should be placed in a similar category. This last site has not been excavated, so that only three of the larger buildings, believed to be temples, have so far been distinguished.[47] John Rowe has drawn attention to what seems to have been an abrupt compaction, at a somewhat later date, of the population of the Ica valley into large settlements[48] which were certainly urban by his definition but may not have been by ours.[49] The most prominent of these settlements in the archeological record to date are those at Tajahuana, in the middle section of the valley, and at Media Luna, in the oasis of Callango far below. Presently existing mounds in both complexes are believed to have been the foundations of former temples. Ceremonial centers such as these, occurring over a wide area in the northern highlands and along the northern and central coastal tracts, exhibit considerable variety of detail, but all appear to have shared the common function of serving as administrative centers for surrounding tracts of territory.

Succeeding centuries witnessed the spread of functionally analogous complexes into southern Peru. Cahuachi, in the ravine of Nazca, for example, comprises shrines, plazas, cemeteries, and habitation sites which extend along the valley side for more than a kilometer,[50] and Tambo Viejo, in the Acarí valley, is equally large and, additionally, enclosed within walls of fieldstone and adobe. A site at Marango, between Lima and Callão, is distinguished by a cluster of impressive temple mounds, and Howe has written of contemporary large settlement sites in the vicinity of Ayacucho.[51] In the second half of the first millennium AD and in the first half of the second a whole series of massive complexes came into being, including Old Ica in the Pago de Tacaraca (where there is a large cluster of adobe temple mounds, but little habitation refuse), Patan-qotu and Qotu-qotu in central Peru,[52] Pachacámac on the central coast, Cajamarquilla in the Rimac valley, and, most impressive of all, Tiahuanaco, situated at an elevation of 13,000 feet on a treeless *puna*, some thirteen miles southeast of Lake Titicaca. Here are masonry structures occupying about a sixth of a square mile and including a stone-faced pyramid, stairways and enclosures, and a carved monolithic gateway. Little archeological investigation has been undertaken at this site, and no credible traditions serve to illuminate its sacred function, but there can be no doubt that, in this bleak environment, it cannot have been other than a ceremonial focus, probably visited by pilgrims from the lower valleys at certain seasons of the year. Building had taken place on the site of Tiahuanaco during much earlier periods but, in the absence of controlled excavation, it is virtually impossible to assign all the elements in the complex to their precise horizons.

The century and a half after about AD 1300 is known to some archeologists as the *Urbanist* or *City Builder* phase of Peruvian history,[53] which is an adequate epitomization of one form of social grouping characteristic of the period, the series of urban complexes along the length of the coastal lowland, which was at this time divided among three competing states. Most of the documentation for this period relates to these coastal tracts, and particularly to those of the Chimú, whose kingdom extended from the Lambayeque and Piura valleys in the north to the Casma valley in the south. It is apparent that the overall design of urban forms, manifested in a general rectangularity and a combination of pyramids, stairways, terraces and courts, was similar throughout all three territories. Virtually every valley leading from the highlands down to the coast had its city, but the grandest of those in the northern region was Chanchan, on the outskirts of the present-day city of Trujillo.[54] Alden Mason's description of the ruins of the city reads in part as follows:

> 'Chanchan is a stupendous site – and sight. The ruins cover over eight square miles, filled – the major part at least – with great tall boundary walls, smaller house walls, streets, reservoirs, pyramids, and other edifices and features expected of a great metropolitan center. All are built of large rectangular adobe bricks. The occasional torrential rains have eroded the tops of the great walls and covered their bases, but they still tower to a height of some thirty feet (9 m.) . . .
>
> The city was apparently composed of ten large units, generally rectangular, each, probably, the locale or ward of a clan or some other social group, and the domain of a sub-chief. Each unit is surrounded by one or more great high walls, within which is a gridiron of streets with many small houses, large pyramids – probably for temples – reservoirs, gardens, and cemeteries. In between the wards there were apparently irrigated and cultivated areas, marshes, cemeteries, and some isolated small structures. Some of the units are said to be as large as 1,100 by 1,600 ft (355 by 480 m.), or about forty acres.'[55]

In the central sector of the coast, Pachacamac and Cajamarquilla continued as massive ceremonial centers, but in the more restricted valleys of the south coast, settlements tended to be smaller. Despite the general resemblance of their layouts to those of the northern and central complexes, it is probable that none attained urban status in the manner in which it is defined in Chapter Four.

Meanwhile, from the beginning of the 13th century or thereabouts, there was consolidating in the highlands around Cuzco the militaristically inclined dynasty of the Inca. For many years Cuzco was a relatively small, and presumably compact, settlement, but it was rebuilt in the form of a ceremonial center by Pachakuti, the architect of Inca expansion who ruled probably from AD 1438 to about 1471. At the center were a group of palaces, temples, and government buildings, separated by open country from a circle of residential villages, a layout which became the pattern for the provincial administrative centers established by the Incas as they extended the boundaries of their empire throughout the Central Andean realm. Dorothy Menzel has distinguished this separation of commoners' dwellings from the religious and administrative enclave, for example, in the Inca foundation in Acarí.[56] The exceptions to this mode of planning may, according to Rowe,[57] have occurred in some of the provincial capitals of the north, such as Pumpun, Wanuku (Huánuco Viejo), and Tumipampa. In the fourth decade of the 16th century the Inca empire disintegrated before the onslaught of a handful of Spaniards, and the foundations were laid for a new pattern of settlements compounded of both indigenous and foreign elements.

Southwestern Nigeria. Finally there remain to be considered the ceremonial centers which developed in the Yoruba territories of Nigeria, possibly towards the end of the first millennium AD – though the evidence for this dating is far from satisfactory. The information available about these centers is derived from the accounts of European travellers from the 16th century onwards, from Yoruba traditions which have clearly undergone an archetyping process, and especially from observation of the examples extant today. This means that, although it is virtually impossible to say anything significant about the origins of these cult centers in antiquity, they are the only ones among those discussed in these pages which have survived into the 20th century and whose functioning, though greatly modified, can therefore be observed at first hand.[58]

At the heart of each of the major settlements of Yorubaland was an *afin*, the palace precinct of an ǫba, supreme ruler of one of the kingdoms which made up the Yoruba culture realm. The ǫba was, in the words of Afolabi Ojo, 'the visible symbol of the deity among the Yorubas . . . the High Priest of his kingdom',[59] and the afin was his seat, from which he brought power and prosperity to his territories. Sharing the afin with the ǫba were important national deities. The combined sacredness of the ǫba's person, the shrines dedicated to these deities, and a variety of other sacred places raised the sanctity of the afin far above that of any other shrine in the kingdom. It was, as Ojo says, a temple of temples. Whenever possible the afin was erected on rising ground, whence it could over-

THE EARLIEST URBAN FORMS

look the compounds of the surrounding settlement. It appears that in the past there was only one pattern of afin, but accidents of history, interacting with regional custom, have generated a diversification of form which to some extent expresses differences in functions. In recent times there existed a triple-ranked hierarchy of afins which reflected a parallel hierarchy of ọbas, in which authority descended from four who were traditionally pre-eminent through those of the second rank to a class of uncrowned ọbas, more properly termed *bales*. It followed that the status of any particular afin depended on the traditional ranking of its ruling ọba, rather than on the intrinsic character of the settlement with which it was associated. In fact, in earlier times the official residence of a bale did not qualify as an afin, and was known simply as *ilé ọlọja* or 'the house of the lord of the market' – even though Ibadan, now the largest indigenous city in tropical Africa, was such a settlement.

In ancient times it seems that there was only a single ọba, the Oduduwa Ọlọfin of Ifẹ, and consequently only a single afin, but subsequently three other supreme ọbas established claims over roughly the northern, western and southern sectors of the Yoruba culture realm, namely the Alafin of Ọyọ, the Alake of Abẹokuta, and the Awujalẹ of Ijẹbu-Ode. Each of these in turn delegated authority to ọbas of the second class, a majority of whom claimed historical – though probably in fact fictional – links with Ifẹ. The rest traced their origin to other powerful kingdoms such as Ọyọ and Ijẹbu-Ode, and even to Benin, a neighboring (but not a Yoruba) state. Previously, too, there was only one afin in a settlement, and even today there is still only a single afin in the whole of the Ọyọ major kingdom, and in the Ifẹ major kingdom only one to each city. In the Ijẹbu and Ẹgba kingdoms, however, there are pluralities of afins even within individual settlements. In all but one city of Ijẹbu, for example, where the office of ọba circulates among several grand lineages, there are as many afins as there are ruling houses, although the official palace at any particular time is that occupied by the currently ruling ọba. The exception to this rule is Ṣagamu, where four crowned ọbas rule simultaneously over separate quarters of the city, a situation which arose in the second half of the last century as a result of a process of synoecism involving thirteen separate settlements. The co-existence of sectional ọbas is also characteristic of the Ẹgba major kingdom, where existing afins are mostly of fairly recent date. The synoecism of 153 settlements to form the township of Abẹokuta in 1830 resulted in the establishment of five ọbaships and five afins, one in each of the more important quarters of the city. In Ilaro and Otta, by contrast, where formerly single ọbas each acceded to single afins, in recent times an inability to maintain the traditional afins has led each succeeding ọba to designate his family residence as the official afin. In these circumstances it is not surprising that afins vary widely in size, ranging from Ọwọ with a precinct of 108·5 acres down to Itaji, Iṣan, Ikere, Isẹ, and Emurẹ with less than three acres each. In the past the important afins seem often to have been on a grand scale. It was reported in 1829, for instance, that the afin of Old Ọyọ occupied a square mile of land.

The afin was the seat of the ọba, whence he issued forth only on rare ceremonial occasions, and even then his face was shielded from the gaze of the people by the fringes of a beaded crown. With him in the afin lived his, often numerous, wives, and some of his other relatives. In fact, the large size of some of the afins was the direct result of the size of the harem. Outside the ruling ọba's lineage, the inhabitants of the afin were restricted to eunuch servants and attendants, the most talented artists and craftsmen in the kingdom who were summoned from their homes to produce objects and materials for the personal use of the ọba, and people afflicted with natural deformities, who had the right to attach themselves to the afin. Uncastrated servants, and some craftsmen producing for the palace though not for the personal use of the ọba, generally returned to homes outside the afin at night. Among these were the drummers, trumpeters and flautists whose business it was to notify the ọba by means of signal-tunes of the sequence of his ritual activities. The drummers also had the responsibility of keeping the ọba informed of events beyond the walls of the afin. There was, too, another group who helped to bridge the gulf between the closed community of the afin and the world at large. This consisted of a clientele of visitors, dependents, and hangers-on who made their home in the afin, and whose presence was often regarded as an indication of the popularity of the ọba. However, the location of their apartments, usually on the side nearest to the main gate, signified quite clearly that these clients were functionally in, but not of, the afin. Apart from matters of accommodation and sustenance, their interests were directed outwards to the secular settlement rather than inwards to the sacred, ceremonial enclave.

Figure 16 (on the two following pages)

A Shang ceremonial complex compared with representative cult centers in other regions of nuclear urbanism.

I. Hsiao-T'un. Based on a plan in Shih Chang-ju, *Hsiao-T'un: I-chih-ti Fa-hsien yü Fa-chüeh: Chien-chu I-ts'un* (Academia Sinica, T'ai-pei, 1959), fig. 4. For details of this site see the text, pp. 39–43.

II. Copán in Honduras, a ceremonial precinct noted for the refined calendrical calculations which were carried out there during the Classic period of Mayan history (3rd century AD–c. 900). No less than sixteen dependent subgroups of ceremonial buildings were associated with this cult center, which itself consisted of a temple-complex and five adjoining plazas, together covering some seventy-five acres. The temple-complex includes two shrines dedicated in a year equivalent to AD 756, and a third which was consecrated to the planet Venus in 771. The plan has been redrawn from one in Sylvanus Griswold Morley's *The ancient Maya* (Stanford University Press: 3rd edition, revised by George W. Brainerd, 1956), p. 277.

III. Cempoala in Vera Cruz, Mexico. This walled ceremonial center was built by the Totonacs, tributaries to the Aztecs, and a description of it as it was in 1519, by Bernal Díaz del Castillo, has been published in both Spanish and English during this century. The plan is based on a reconstruction in Victor W. Von Hagen, *The Aztec: man and tribe* (Mentor Book No. 364, New York, 1958), fig. 45.

IV. The ceremonial center at Teotihuacán in the Valley of Mexico, which was apparently laid out at a period corresponding to the early years of the Christian era. Based on a plan in I. Marquina, *Arquitectura prehispánica*. Instituto Nacional de Antropología e Historia (México, 1951).

V. Poḷonnaruva, chief ceremonial city of Ceylon from the 9th to the 14th century AD. Redrawn from the official plan of the Archaeological Survey of Ceylon.

VI. Yaśodharapura in Cambodia as it was in the time of Jayavarman VII (AD 1181–c. 1220). Redrawn from the *Carte Archéologique d'Angkor*, Imprimerie du Ministère de l'Information (N.D.).

VII. Afin Ọyọ in 1937. Redrawn from a plan in G. J. Afolabi Ojo, *Yoruba palaces. A study of afins of Yorubaland* (University of London Press, Ltd, 1966), fig. 8, p. 47.

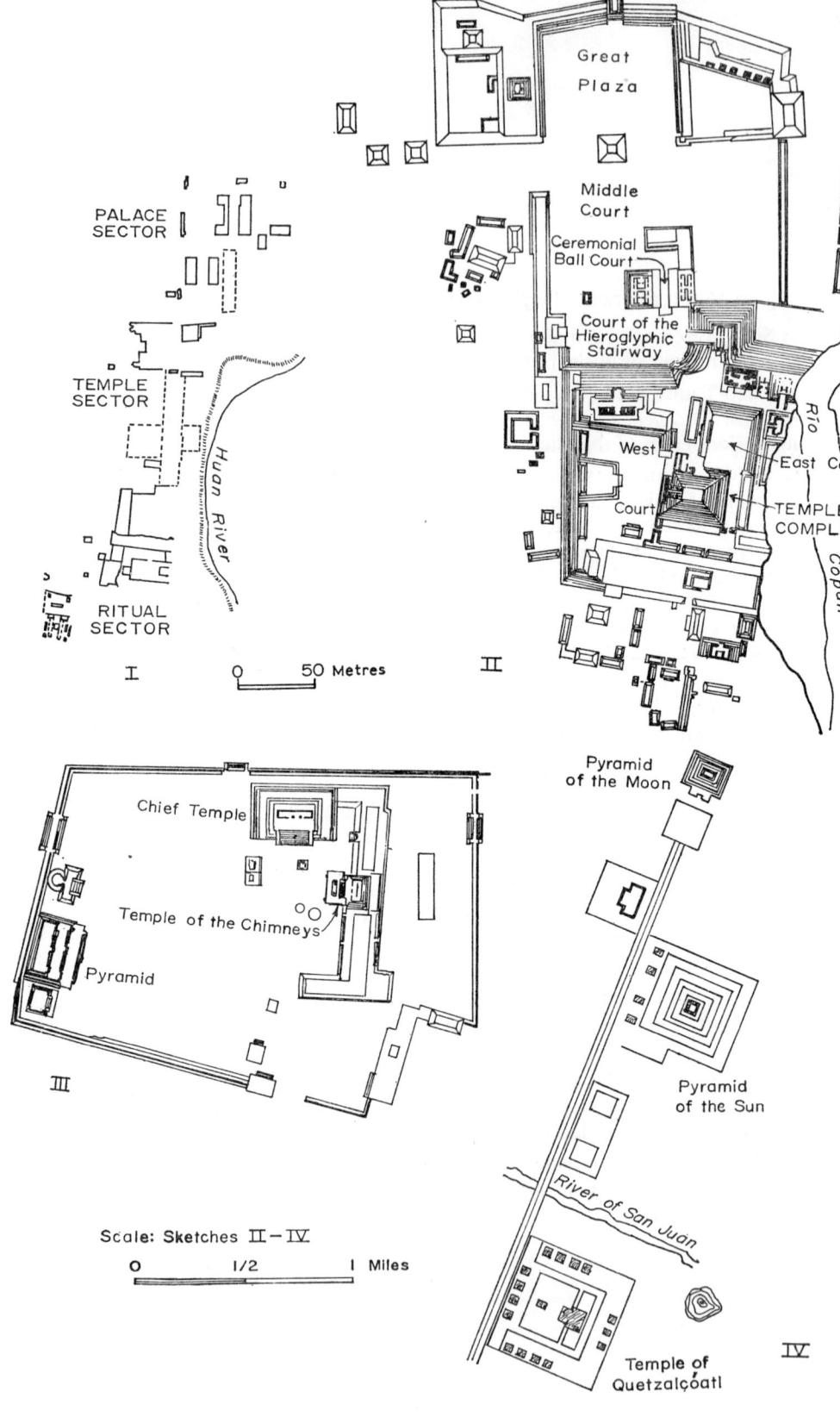

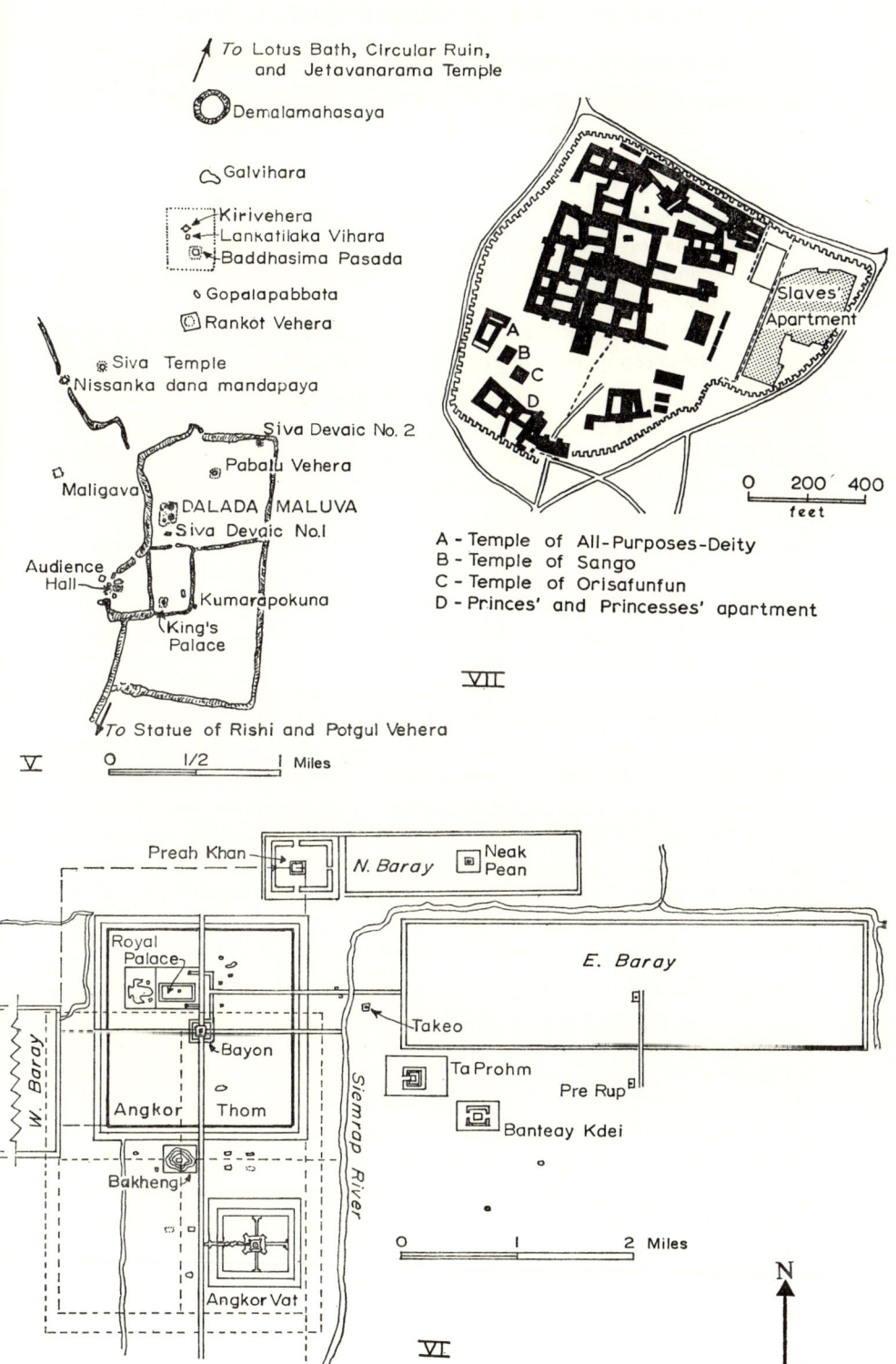

THE NATURE OF THE CEREMONIAL CENTER

SOME CEREMONIAL CENTERS in regions of secondary urban generation

The ceremonial centers which have just been described were all located in regions of primary urban generation, but cult foci of a similar pattern have also arisen in regions of secondary urban generation (cf. p. 9 above). These have all been situated on the margins of the primary regions, where secondary cultural diffusion has prepared the way for city generation. Although lack of precise information often makes it difficult in practice to distinguish cities of secondary generation from those associated with either the extension of empire or the expansion of a culture hearth, these several modes of origin are, as pointed out above, analytically distinct. Generally speaking, though, such secondary generation has been ignored by students of urban origins.

Crete. Among the areas which would repay investigation from this point of view is the island of Crete, where compact cities developed around palace complexes with apparent suddenness early in the second millennium BC.[60] It is not unlikely that palaces already existed in somewhat earlier times (the imposing construction at Vasiliki in eastern Crete, which has been assigned to the very beginning of the Bronze Age, may be such a one), but scholarly attention has concentrated on the maturely developed cities of the Middle Minoan period (c. 2000–1580 BC), such as Knossos, Phaistos, Mallia, and lately Zakro, to an extent that makes it virtually impossible to discuss their origins.[61] Nevertheless, there is no doubt that the ruler who sat in state in the so-called Throne Room of the palace at Knossos was a priest-king (or perhaps a priestess-queen), that political and religious authority were not significantly differentiated, and that the palace itself was a sanctuary as well as a seat of government. The sunken bath placed before the throne is most plausibly interpreted as in some way connected with ritual anointings or lustrations. It may also prove to be significant that, at the same time as cities emerged in the archeological record, there also appeared monumental sanctuaries on high places. Juktas to the south of Knossos, Prophetes Elias above Mallia, Petsophas above Palaikastro, Zakros, Khristos, Piskokephali, and probably the building on the summit of Edhikte, near Mokhos, are good examples of this type of structure.

Etruria. On the Italian peninsula this same mode of secondary urban generation may have obtained in Etruria and the Latin country to the south, though here the only satisfactory evidence to date relates to the ceremonial center of Rome during the 7th and 6th centuries BC.[62] The precise status accorded to early Rome will depend to a very large extent on the view taken of the origin of the Etruscans themselves, but students of this period are not yet in agreement as to whether this culture was introduced on to the peninsula by a vigorous immigrant minority from Asia Minor, or whether it represented a lineal development from the Villanovan of the Neolithic.[63] In any case urban life would seem to have been established in Etruria by the end of the 8th century BC, for some, if not all, of the cities of the Etruscan league were in existence at that time. However, the internal morphology of these cities is practically unknown, owing to the predilection of investigators for excavating cemeteries and public monuments. Only at Tarquinia has there been a methodical attempt to elicit the layout of the city, and that has so far been relatively unrewarding.

Japan. It is also possible to point to apparently similar instances of secondary urban generation in East and South Asia. In Japan, for example, Yamato clan seats seem to have functioned as ceremonial centers, possibly from as early as the 3rd century A.D.[64] Certainly from the 5th to the end of the 7th century the whole of the Yamato territories, which then stretched from the Kantō plain to South Korea, were organized about a hierarchy of cult centers. Information about this period is meager. Such as there is has to be sifted from later Japanese chronicles, and supplemented by reference to relict institutions which survived subsequent reform, and by wholly inadequate archeological evidence. Society appears to have consisted basically of semi-autonomous patriarchal units known as *uji*, communities comprising a number of households of the same ancestry, real or fictitious as the case might be. Each *uji* was under the leadership of a hierarch known as the *uji no kami*, who mediated between its members and the clan god, the *uji-gami*. Attached to the *uji*, moreover, were hereditary (though not blood-related) associations of workers, occupational groups termed *be* or *tomo,* which have sometimes been compared to the *corporati* of the later Roman empire. Such corporate groups were normally important items of property and sources of wealth for the clans or families which controlled them, but occasionally a corporation might enjoy substantial autonomy under its own hereditary leader. At the bottom of the social scale there was a small class of slaves, but they were of only limited economic importance.

In the heyday of the Yamato period a national association of kinship groups emerged which was integrated religiously, politically, and militaristically around the Yamato court. At the apex of this hierarchical structure was the head of the most powerful lineage, the so-called imperial clan. But the socio-economic functions of the individual *uji* were relatively poorly developed, levels of production were comparatively low, and the power commanded by the Yamato court was insufficient to effect the total political integration of society. Consequently the head of the imperial clan was unable to exercise direct rule over the land and people of clans other than his own, and had to rely on his religious authority to sustain the Yamato polity. He it was who alone could perform the ceremonies upon which the welfare of the Japanese culture realm depended. At lower levels of the hierarchy *uji no kami*, claiming descent from clan gods only a degree less powerful than those of the imperial clan, exercised virtually complete control within their own territories. As the head of the imperial lineage exercised hereditary rule over the totality of kinship groups, so the religious, political and military functions of an incipient bureaucracy were apportioned among the various *uji no kami*, who became the hereditary holders of offices of state of an importance more or less directly proportional to the power and prestige of their respective clans. The ranks of *ō-omi* or great ministers, for example, were prerogatives of clan hierarchs closely related to the imperial family; *ō-muraji*, territorial administrative officers of high rank, were appointed from among those who traced their descent from lineages of divine origin other than that of the emperor, and *omi* and *muraji* from those of still lower standing; while *kuni no miyatsuko* were little more than local chieftains. Finally, at the head of some of the more important corporations were officers known as *tomo no miyatsuko*. In this way the administrative and economic activities of the Yamato state were correlated with the kinship structure of *uji* society, and the whole sanctioned and validated by ritual and ceremony. The evolution of a bureaucracy was greatly facilitated at this time by the adoption of administrative institutions borrowed from the Chinese culture realm, particularly from the several states on the Korean peninsula.

Very little is known about the seats of individual *uji no kami* during the Yamato period, but something can be said about the location of the imperial capital.[65] It was moved freely from reign to reign, but always within a zone of south-central Honshu lying between Lake Biwa in the north and the eastern shores of the Inland Sea. It has been held traditionally by Japanese historians that from about AD 394 to possibly 427, that is during the reigns of Ojin and Nintoku Tennō, and again for a short period during the reign of Kōtoku Tennō (AD 645–654), the Yamato court was at Naniwa, on the site of present-day Ōsaka. During the last fifteen years Professor Yamane Tokutaro and his collaborators have excavated a palace precinct,[66] believed to be that laid out by Kōtoku Tennō, the principal part of which, the Chōdō-in, took the form of a symmetrically arranged group of sixteen buildings, one of which has been identified as the Daigoku-den, a term from ancient Japanese literature variously translated as 'imperial council hall', 'ceremonial hall' or 'hall of state'. There is no evidence of Naniwa ever having been walled, but the entrance gates were emphasized architecturally. During most of the 6th and 7th centuries the Yamato imperial court occupied a series of sites on the Āsuka plain, only infrequently moving outside that area. One such occasion was the period from AD 667 to 672, when it was transferred to Ōmi-no-Ōtsu-no-miya on the west shore of Lake Biwa. A few of the capitals during this so-called Āsuka period have been investigated by Japanese archeologists. For the most part they appear to have comprised a palace precinct, the seat of a divine emperor, surrounded by temples and shrines (particularly after the court adoption of the Buddhist faith in 587), and by an adventitious population attracted to the opportunities offered by proximity to the court. The first of the imperial palaces to be built as part of a planned city was that at Fujiwara-no-miya, on

THE EARLIEST URBAN FORMS

the northern edge of the Āsuka region. Constructed on the pattern of T'ang Ch'ang-an, or possibly on that of a Sillan capital near present-day Kyŏngju in Korea which was itself modelled on Ch'ang-an, Fujiwara was the material expression of a significant stage in the development of the Japanese polity. As a result of the Taika Reforms which were initiated in 645, the state was gradually transformed into a bureaucracy on the pattern of that of T'ang China. The great private landholdings were replaced by provincial administrations under appointees of the central government, and a uniform system of taxes introduced. The outcome of these changes was to divorce religion from secular administration, although the emperor exercised supreme authority in both spheres. Article II of the Reform Edict (*Kaishin no Chō*), among other things, inaugurated a metropolitan region known as the Kinai or Inner Province, and stipulated that the capital of the kingdom be 'regulated' by the establishment of a system of municipal government. In the event the new city was not built for nearly half a century, but in 690 the geomantic qualities of the proposed site were approved by imperial officials, the appropriate rituals carried out, and the court transferred to the new palace in 694. The city measured $1\frac{1}{2}$ miles from west to east by $2\frac{2}{5}$ from north to south. It served as the imperial capital only until 707, when the building of Heijokyō confirmed the institutionalization of the new style of city planning which had been inaugurated at Fujiwara.

The apogee of this tradition was attained in the building of Heian-kyō (Capital of Peace and Tranquillity), the capital from AD 794, which has been described by Sir George Sansom as follows:

'It was a rectangle measuring about three and a half miles from north to south and three miles from east to west, surrounded by a moat, and symmetrically divided by broad roads into squares, in their turn subdivided by narrow roads. Alongside each road was a moat and, as the city was on a gentle slope, all was running water. In the north centre of the city was an enclosure, about one mile by three-quarters, which contained the imperial residence, various residential apartments, ceremonial halls, and the great apartments of state. It had fourteen gates. Outside the enclosure, but mostly near it, were palaces used for various reasons by the emperors in preference to that within the enclosure; palaces where abdicated emperors resided; mansions belonging to great families; and certain government offices and institutions. Chief among the latter was the University, which adjoined the great southern gate. It comprised a number of buildings, small and large, including three great faculty halls, devoted respectively to Chinese studies, to mathematics, and to law. There was also a small temple devoted to Confucius.

When the capital was commenced there were already a number of shrines on or near the site, chief among them being the Kamo shrines; the Yasaka or Gion shrine of the god Susa-no-wo; and the Udzumasa temple or Kōryūji. The celebrated temple called Kiyomidzu was constructed from the materials of a great hall moved from the abandoned city of Nagaoka; and the first temple of Mount Hiei, the Komponchūdō, was built to guard the city against evil influences coming from the north-east, the malignant quarter. . . .

It was, of course, a city of wooden structures, great and small. Of the buildings in the great enclosure the most magnificent was the Daigoku-den, or Great Hall of State. It stood on a stone platform, guarded by red lacquered balustrades, and consisted of a hall about 170 feet long and 50 feet wide, under a roof supported by 52 pillars. The whole was painted red, and the roof was of emerald blue tiles. In the centre of the hall stood, on a raised platform under a canopy surmounted by golden phoenixes, the Imperial Throne. Other important buildings were the Hōgaku-den, or Hall of Rich Pleasures, where ceremonial banquets were held; and the Butoku-den, or Hall of Military Virtue (similar to Daigoku-den), near which were a parade ground and enclosures for equestrian games and archery. Within the great enclosure stood a group of buildings, surrounded by a wall thirteen feet high, of double red wooden pillars set in plaster and roofed with tiles. A further enclosure, within this wall, contained a block of connected buildings which formed the imperial residence. This smaller enclosure was bounded by a wall in the form of a double corridor, with a roof supported by pillars. The principle buildings within were the Shishin-den, or Purple Dragon Hall, a ceremonial pavilion, and the Seiryō-den, or Pure Cool Hall, which contained the emperor's living apartments and rooms for the use of his consort and concubines. Near the Seiryō-den was the Naishidokoro, a small apartment in which was enshrined the Sacred Mirror. At the north of the inner enclosure lay the "Forbidden Interior", where lived the empress and the imperial concubines, and close by their residences were apartments of ladies-in-waiting, styled, after the trees in their courtyards, the Pear Chamber, the Wistaria Chamber, the Plum Chamber, and so on.'[67]

Southeast Asia. The zones of secondary urban generation in Southeast Asia deserve especially close scrutiny, for this is virtually the only region of the world where the process of urban generation is even partially documented (as opposed to reflected) in written records. Normally the processual societal change of which literacy is born is not itself recorded in literature, but in this instance sundry Chinese histories, encyclopedias, and topographies preserve accounts of the area during the formative period of urban development. Although obscure and equivocal, these do yet serve in some small degree to substantiate the more hypothetical reconstructions based solely on archeological evidence from other realms of nuclear urbanism.

During the early centuries of the Christian era the process of brāhmaṇization, which through the centuries had been spreading eastward and southward from its hearth of origin in the northwestern part of the Indian subcontinent, finally reached across the ocean into the western territories of Southeast Asia. With it came the concept of divine kingship, a political instrument especially attractive to village chieftains in situations in which, as here, the egalitarian solidarity of tribal society – for reasons which are imperfectly understood but which in any case need not concern us here – was crumbling. But in Indian culture the spiritual and the temporal were so closely interwoven that the assumption of authority relationships on an Indian pattern was impossible without the adoption of an Indian cultural configuration in its entirety. The result was the burgeoning and elaboration in parts of Southeast Asia of a transplanted Indian culture, in which the gerontocracy or patriarchalism of the old tribal societies yielded to patrimonialism, occupational specialization hardened into something approaching caste, age-sets were subsumed into *āśrama*, the tribal meeting was transformed into an assembly on the model of the *sabhā*, adat or custom broadened into law within the framework of the *Dharmaśastra*, and economic reciprocity was transmuted into redistribution, the whole process signifying a transformation from culture to civilization. And one of the material manifestations of this civilization was the state temple, axis of the universe, the world, and the kingdom, and repository for the palladium of the state. In its sophisticated Cambodian form this latter often assumed the shape of a sacred *liṅga*, in which was embodied the eternal Subtle-Self or personality of the king. In later times the national temple also housed a statue of the king, invested with the attributes of a god, which had been animated by Indian religious rites so that it prefigured the final apotheosis that the monarch would undergo on the dissolution of his mortal body in death. Nor were these cult practices restricted to the king. Other members of the royal house and of the nobility, high officers of state, dignitaries of the priesthood, and successful commanders in war also sought to augment their *karma* by dedicating shrines to patron deities, and not infrequently they, too, took care to ensure the perpetual existence of their Subtle-Selves through the animation of their portrait statues. On their descendants devolved the duty of maintaining these shrines, which were apparently regarded as new architectural bodies for the Subtle-Self of the cosmicized man, much as the flesh had been during the man's lifetime. Many such shrines were, in fact, maintained for several generations. It follows that over the centuries the territory of ancient Kambujadeśa became apportioned among a hierarchy of cult centers. In the different subregions of Southeast Asia the process varied according to the prescriptions of pre-existing cultures, but, wherever Indian civilization penetrated, it set in motion a sequence of developments something after the pattern described above.[68]

On the mainland of Southeast Asia these early ceremonial centers were restricted almost exclusively to the lowland tracts, notably the Pyū country of Central and Upper Burma, the coastal plains of Arakan, the Mōn land around the lower courses of the Irawadi and Chao Phraya rivers, the pre- and proto-

Khmer territories in the middle and lower Mekong valley, and the coastal plains of east-central Vietnam. In the Pyū domain archeological finds do not go back before the end of the 5th century, and the ruins of the alleged Pyū capital of Śrī Kṣetra at modern Hmawza have not been dated specifically to the Pyū era, although it is reasonably certain that they represent a Pyū foundation, and probably a capital.[69] Whereas the walls demarcate a roughly circular perimeter some eight and a half miles in length, one Chinese source ascribes to the walls the length of a day's march[70] and another of 160 *li*.[71] I can suggest no way in which this discrepancy might be resolved. The description of the Pyū capital in the *Chiu T'ang-Shu* (chüan 197, ff. 16 verso-17 recto) reads as follows:

> 'The entire length of the city wall is faced with glazed bricks. It is 160 *li* in circumference. The sides of the moat are also faced with brick.... Within the walls dwell several tens of thousands of families. There are more than a hundred Buddhist monasteries, whose courts and chambers are all decorated with gold and silver, coated with cinnabar and [other] bright colors, varnished with lac, and covered with embroidered rugs.'

The revised T'ang history adds that the king's palace was decked out after the pattern of Buddhist monasteries, that the city had twelve gates, and that tiles of lead and tin, and timber of *li-chih* wood (*Nephelium litchi*, Camb.) were employed in construction work.[72]

Another important Pyū ceremonial center has been located at Halingyi in Upper Burma, but its ruins have been subjected to only superficial investigation.[73] It is certain that there were other urban nuclei in the Pyū realm, for they are mentioned in a Chinese history which drew its information from the reports of Pyū embassies to the Chinese court in 802 and 807,[74] but it is not possible to suggest locations for more than one or two. In the later days of the Pyū hegemony one of their most important cult centers was Arimaddanapura or, popularly, Pagan. According to Burmese chronicles the city was established by a process of synoecism in AD 849,[75] but there is no epigraphic reference to the city earlier than a Cham inscription of *c*. 1000–1050,[76] and the first Mōn record relates only to 1093.[77] It is likely, though, that Arimaddanapura rose to prominence after the armies of *Nâm-Tśi̯äu (Nan-Chao) had sacked the Pyū capital in 832. In later times (AD 1044–1287) it became the focus of an extensive conglomeration of temples, the ruins of some five thousand being still visible in a zone five miles deep that stretches along the bank of the Irawadi for twenty miles.

On the Arakan coast the combined testimony of fragmentary archeological remains, dynastic lists preserved in late chronicles, and the *Geography* of Ptolemy is insufficient for anything other than the broadest of generalizations: namely that temple-cities appear to have existed at least as early as the middle of the 4th century AD, and possibly earlier. As late as the nineteen-thirties (and probably today) the brick walls of a large enceinte were still visible on the bank of a tidal creek some six miles from Mrohaung, and it has usually been considered that this was the site of Vaiśālī, an ancient Arakanese capital.[78] It may also have been the capital whose embellishment and fortification by the first king of an otherwise unknown Candra dynasty is mentioned in a *praśasti* of uncertain provenance but datable to the beginning of the 8th century AD.[79] Professor E.H.Johnston has assigned the founding of this dynasty to the middle of the 4th century AD, and it is possible that the same inscription contains less reliable information going back even as far as the last quarter of the 2nd century AD.[80] Just prior to the time at which the *praśasti* was inscribed a settlement of some sort, probably a shrine, had been constructed at a place called *Pīlakkavanaka*, 'formerly named Domagha [?]'.[81] Other ceremonial foci recognized by Professor Johnston in this inscription are *Pureppura*,[82] which apparently flourished in the 6th century AD, and *Śrī Tāmrapattana*.[83] *Somatirtha Ḍaṅkaṅgamargaṅgaḍuvāra* and *Bhūrokanaulakkalavāraka* were shrines which may also have been in process of developing incipient urban functions.

At the beginning of the Christian era the deltas of the Irawadi and Salween rivers, the plains of the lower Chao Phraya, and at least the northern parts of the isthmian tract of the Malay Peninsula were ethnically Mōn. So far as the westernmost of these territories are concerned there are serious discrepancies between both the written and oral traditions of the Thai, the Burmese, and the Mōn themselves on the one hand, and the archeological evidence on the other. According to the former the hearth of Mōn culture was situated in lower Burma, particularly in the neighborhood of the cities of Thatōn (*Sudhammapura*) and Pegu (*Haṃsāvati*), which might have been expected to yield a rich harvest of Mōn remains. The opposite is the case. Even allowing for a paucity of excavations, it is safe to say that archeology and epigraphy afford no confirmation whatever of a specifically Mōn occupation of Lower Burma prior to the 9th or 10th century AD. Moreover, whereas Mōn, Burmese, and Thai chronicles all depict a strongly Theravādin state in that area in early times, such meager archeological vestiges as have come to light are uncompromisingly Hindu.[84] In Central Thailand, by contrast, the elements of the paradox are reversed. The fairly abundant archeological remains available for study, and which bear witness to the existence of temple-cities of considerable sophistication during the period from the 6th to the 11th century AD, have left no discernible impress on the written and oral traditions of any ethnic group. It is not necessary here to enter into discussions which might resolve this paradox : suffice it to say that, although the Ptolemaic text locates several 'cities' (πόλις) and trade emporia (ἐμπόριον) in Lower Burma at an early date,[85] archeology has so far failed to provide significant material evidence of their existence.

Once across the mountain ridge into Thai territory the archeological record becomes more ample. Generally speaking, the early ceremonial centers are distributed in an arc round the outer edge of the Bangkok plain. Although systematic excavation has so far been restricted to the western sector of this arc, sufficient evidence has accumulated in the form of shrine foundations still protruding through the soil, enceintes still discernible as faint undulations on its surface, and statuary discovered fortuitously throughout the area, to support the notion of a Mōn-speaking state, or possibly a confederacy, in existence from the 6th to the 11th century. It has long been inferred that this was the region rendered in Chinese records as *D'uo-γuâ-lâ-puâ-tiei (Tu-ho-lo-po-ti), that is Dvāravatī.[86]

Along the western sector of the arc of ceremonial centers mentioned above, the most productive archeological sites have proved to be in the neighborhood of – from north to south – the present-day towns of U-Thong, Nakhon Pathom, Ratburi, and Phetchaburi, with Kanburi Kao also contributing remains possibly from this same period. An enceinte has been reported from Kampheng Sen,[87] and a former settlement at Nakhon Pathom, vestiges of which have been found scattered over an area of approximately seven kilometers by two, must certainly have fallen into the category of developed ceremonial center.[88] From the central tract of this complex a causeway leads to a former satellite sanctuary at Non Phra, some seven kilometers to the south. At Phong Tük, in the lower valley of the Maeklong, the extent of the remains, as yet only partially excavated, indicate that they represent an important ceremonial center rather than an isolated shrine.[89] On the northern edge of the Bangkok plain numerous but scattered surface finds in the vicinity of Lopburi represent the material remains of the city known to Pāli and Chinese chronicles alike as Lavapura.[90] The same Pāli chronicle attributes to a queen of Lavapura the founding of the city of Haripuñjaya (modern Lamphun) during the 8th century.[91]

The Thai archeological sites enumerated thus far, and particularly the important ones at Phong Tük, Nakhon Pathom and Lopburi, have afforded bases for later settlements, so that a great deal of the morphological evidence which would have been of interest in the present context has in fact been obliterated. The eastern fringe of the plain, by contrast, appears to have seen relatively few changes after the dissolution of Dvāravatī, with the result that the traces of at least three former settlements are still clearly visible on the surface of the ground. At Dong Si Maha Phot, close to Prachinburi, a double rampart enclosing a moat forms a roughly trapezoidal figure with a perimeter distance of about five kilometers.[92] At Phanat, immediately behind the coast of the Gulf of Bangkok and not far from the estuary of the Prachin river, is another curiously shaped enceinte, consisting of a moat and rampart some two and a half kilometers in length, and this time assuming the shape of a spear-head.[93] It may be significant that both these sites are today known as Mu'ang Phra Rot, or the City of the Sacred Chariot. Stronger evidence of some former association between them is provided by traces of an avenue linking the two enceintes. The third enclosure, at Dong Lakhon, differs from the two preceding in that its double enclosing walls, separated by a moat, form a cardinally oriented square of 500 meters side.[94]

Turning to the east coast of Indochina, we find that from the beginning of the 5th century A D, or possibly a little earlier, there began to appear in the provinces of Quảng-nam and Phú-yên inscriptions that indicate the existence at that time of a state organized on Hindu principles of polity. These inscriptions emanated from a King Bhadravarman, who founded a sanctuary dedicated to Śiva Bhadreśvara in a hollow of the hills at Mĩ-sơn.[95] It is not clear what were the relations between these groups in Quảng-nam, who had been strongly influenced by Indian culture, and those to the northward allegedly subject to Chinese colonial rule, and certainly within the Chinese cultural sphere, but both were referred to in Chinese annals as *Ljəm-·jəp (Lin-i).[96] It seems probable that during the 6th century the northern group extended its control over the Hinduized kingdom of Quảng-nam province, and shortly afterwards the name Campā began to appear in the epigraphy of both present-day South Vietnam and Cambodia. There is, unfortunately, no extant description of any of the Cham cult centers at this time, but later a whole series of such ceremonial foci emerged, including that of Amarāvatī on the site of present-day Mĩ-sơn, Vijaya near modern Binh-dinh, Kauṭhāra on the plain of Nha-trang, and Pāṇḍuraṅga on that of Phan-rang.[97]

The earliest putative evidence of urban development in the so-called Indianized realms of Southeast Asia relates to the lower reaches of the Mekong valley. Chinese records affirm the existence in this region, from the first half of the 3rd century A D to early in the 7th, of a kingdom which they rubricate as *B'i̯u-nậm (Fu-nan).[98] They also preserve a dynastic legend, cast in an Indian mould, that would seem to place the founding of this kingdom a century or two earlier. But the collective memory is invariably anhistorical, and archeology has so far failed to reveal any settlement site in the Lower Mekong valley which would have qualified as a city in the 1st century A D. The precise focus and frontiers of B'i̯u-nậm are known only by inference, but it has been deduced on fairly good grounds that its metropolitan territory – at least in its heyday during the 6th century – lay along the Mekong river between Châu-đốc and Phnom Penh, and there is evidence for the existence of a port with far-ranging trade relations at Oc-èo in the Transbassac, as well as for several other important settlements in the same area. From the 3rd century it is possible to discern first, the emergence of a federation of city-states, and ultimately, the consolidation of a patrimonially organized thalassocracy, whose frontiers reached from Nha-trang in the east at least to the isthmian tracts of the Malay Peninsula in the west, and possibly even to the Gulf of Martaban.

The relative contributions of indigenous and Indian cultures to the earliest cult centers in B'i̯u-nậm is a matter that would repay further investigation.

THE NATURE OF THE CEREMONIAL CENTER [345

There is reason to believe that the earlier settlements which appear in the reports of Chinese envoys as *·i̯əp, a term which in Han times and later denoted the seat of a subprefecture, and which would consequently seem to have carried the implications of at least incipient urbanism when applied to Indochinese settlements, may have been established before the effective beginnings of the Indianization process. Even as late as the 5th century the city of Oc-èo was, as far as can be deduced from the evidence currently available, completely devoid of the spatial symbolism associated both with the Indian temple-city and the cities of the Aṅkor period. Neither is there at Oc-èo any evidence of the powerful centripetality induced in these cities by the presence of a sacred mountain at the generating focus of their axes, though it is also true that in all other known pre-Khmer cities, such as Vyādhapura, Aṅkor Bórĕi and Vat Phu, the cosmic mountains were also located outside the city enceintes.

The fragmentary and equivocal evidence of city life in B'i̯u-nậm permits only the sort of broad generalization that we have come to associate with the formative phase of urban origins. It would seem that, from the 3rd century onwards, palisaded and moated settlements which could almost certainly be assigned urban status were located at focal points in an hydraulic system that consolidated the heartland of the Mekong delta into a political and economic unity.[99] Essentially these settlements consisted of agglomerations of dwellings, constructed of light materials such as wood, bamboo and nipa fronds and often raised on piles, clustered – in the only instance so far excavated – about a monumental complex of brick and granite, which is presumed on strong grounds to have served a religious purpose. Integrated into this layout in a manner at present unknown to us was the palace of the ruler, a double-storeyed timber building, apparently on the pattern of those customarily built by Southeast Asian rulers until quite recent times. The cultic role of one center is explicitly attested by a report on the state of B'i̯u-nậm preserved in the Chinese history of the Southern Ch'i dynasty:[100]

'[*Nâ-ka-si̯än (Na-chia-hsien : [the monk] Nagasena)] stated that it was the custom of that country to make offerings to the celestial god *Muâ-Xiei-śi̯ǝu-lâ [Mo-hsi-shou-lo : = Maheśvara]. This deity descends continuously on Mount *Muâ-tậm (Mo-tan) [so that] the climate there is constantly mild and herbs and trees do not wither.'

After the replacement of the B'i̯u-nậm state in the middle of the 6th century by that known to the Chinese as *Tśi̯ĕn-lâp (Chen-la), and ultimately at the beginning of the 9th century by Kambujadeśa, the role of the temple-city becomes ever more important. Indeed, I have elsewhere written that it is scarcely an exaggeration to regard the economy of the country in its entirety as one great oblation organized for the appeasement of the gods of the Indian pantheon, and thus designed to maintain that harmony between the macrocosmos and the microcosmos without which the state and its people could not prosper. Hardly was it possible to stand anywhere on the plains of the middle Mekong and the Tonlé Sap without seeing the towers of a shrine rising in the distance, the larger among them constituting some of the most impressive temple-cities that have been built at any time or in any place.[101] More will be said about these great ceremonial centers in a later chapter.

The information available about the origins of city life in the archipelagic Malaysian world is the least satisfactory of that for any realm of Southeast Asia. This is partly because the Archipelago is remote from China, so that notices relating to it in Chinese annals and encyclopedias are correspondingly late and indeterminate, and partly because archeology has been overwhelmingly concerned with either prehistoric investigation or the interpretation and preservation of the monumental architecture of the great shrines of later days. On the isthmian tracts of the Malay Peninsula city-states appear to have been in existence as early as the 3rd century AD, and, although at least one, which was known to the Chinese as *Tuən-suən (Tun-sun), was probably a Mōn foundation, the populations of some of the others may have been ethnically Malay.[102] It is not impossible that the absence of incipient urban nuclei among the islands to the south at this time may have been more apparent than real, as the Chinese texts have very little to say about that region. Most of the information which the Chinese have preserved about the Malay world at this period derives from an embassy to B'i̯u-nậm in about AD 245. Although well informed about peninsular territories, this embassy collected very little material relating to the archipelago. By the 5th century AD, however, kingdoms known by Sanskrit honorifics, and ruled by kings with Sanskrit styles, had made their appearance on the Malayan isthmus and in both Java and Sumatra. The earliest descriptions of urban settlements date from the next century, but the information tells us little more than that they were walled or palisaded communities, living in thatch-and-timber dwellings clustered about a ruler's timbered palace which, in some cases at least, was also a cult center. This role of the palace was particularly evident in the report of a Chinese mission to Siṃhapura (the Lion City), the capital of the Red Earth Country, a state probably located in the neighborhood of Pattani.[103]

Only in Java has archeological investigation contributed significantly to our knowledge of early urban developments in the archipelago, and even then the information tends to be relatively late in time. An inscription from the foot of Gunong Měrbabu, in the central part of the island, has been attributed to the 7th century, but attests little more than a knowledge of Indian mythology, and the possible existence of a Vaiśnavite shrine associated with the Tuk Mas, a spring whose purifying power was regarded as comparable to that of the Ganges.[104] Perhaps a 7th-century inscription from the Dieng plateau is witness to the beginnings of monumental architecture on that upland whose very name is evidence of its sacred character.[105] And in 732 a King Sanjaya erected a *śivaliṅga* in a sanctuary on the Wukir hill, bordering the Kĕḍu plain.[106] It is customary also to ascribe to the late 7th or early 8th century the exclusively Śaivite monuments that betoken the former existence of a temple complex on the Dieng plateau, though the earliest inscription dates only from 809. Here, at a height of 6,000 feet, set amid solfataras and sulphurous lakes in a sediment-filled volcanic crater, is all that remains of the earliest Javanese temple-city that has survived in the archeological record.[107] Today this amounts to eight small *caṇḍi*, together with the foundations of other temples and several *peṇḍapa* or wooden halls, the whole constituting the material expression of a political development that underlay authority relationships in many other parts of Southeast Asia, namely the fusion of an indigenous cult of mountain spirits with Indian conceptions of monarchy. Farther eastwards, in the upper Brantas valley, the same pattern was recurring at least as early as 760, when one of a dynasty of Śaivite kings ruling over Kañjuruhan styled himself protector of a *liṅga* called Pūtikeśvara, in which was concentrated the subtle essence and validation of royalty.[108] Meanwhile there was establishing itself in Central Java a new Mahāyāna Buddhist dynasty, which styled itself Śailendra or Kings of the Mountain, and it is to this dynasty that we owe the mature development of the temple-city in Java. In particular, the second half of the 8th century saw the building of the great monuments which still stand on the Kĕḍu plain.[109] Just south of Gunong Merapi, on the left bank of the Opak river, a temple was dedicated to the Buddhist goddess Tārā in 778,[110] while at much the same time the shrine of Caṇḍi Sari, with its attached monastery, was built near by. Somewhat later and to the northeast, Caṇḍi Sewu was laid out as a complex of two hundred and fifty temples symbolizing the cosmos. This cosmological emphasis was repeated in the most magnificent of all these shrines, that at Borobudur, also a representation in stone of the Mahāyāna cosmic system and, perhaps, the dynastic temple of the Śailendras. It took the form of an immense stupa built up of stone terraces running round the slopes of a natural hill. Its height was 150 feet, the total length of the galleries was more than three miles, and the progression from ground level to the summit symbolized successive phases in the attainment of spiritual enlightenment. Associated with this Borobudur complex, though rather later in date, were two other caṇḍi, Mendut and Pawon, both sited exactly on the east-west axis of the great stupa.

In this context it is not inappropriate to include in Southeast Asia the island of Ceylon, in the eastern drier zone of which imposing ceremonial centers emerged as the indirect result of the spread of the so-called process of Aryanization. The earliest of these centers of which an authentic record has been preserved was Anurādhapura, which is believed to have been founded in the later centuries of the pre-Christian period. After enduring numerous vicissitudes for something like a thousand years, this ritual city was abandoned in favor of another ceremonial capital at Poḷonnaruva.[111] In the middle of the 13th century the focus of the Siṅhalese kingdom shifted westwards into the hills of the wet zone, and the ceremonial capital at various times was at Dambadeniya, Kurunagala, Gampola, Kotte, Sitawaka, and Kandy, until the island passed under European control.

This is as far as it is necessary to carry this enumeration at the moment. There were proto-urban ceremonial centers in other realms of western Southeast Asia at different periods, but I am discussing the role of these and other Southeast Asian urban developments in a separate publication. One or two aspects of their symbolism will also be touched upon in a later section of the present work. Here it is sufficient to remark that the several regional traditions of the temple-city persisted in Southeast Asia until the colonial era and in – among other parts – Burma and Java well into that period. In Burma, indeed, just such a ceremonial capital was laid out as late as 1857,[112] and all the Thai capitals partook largely of a ceremonial nature.[113] In any case the several localities discussed in the preceding pages do not exhaust the roster of instances in which cities arose through secondary generation, although they are those in which the process is best documented and therefore most easily discernible.

THE CENTRIPETALIZING FUNCTION OF THE CEREMONIAL CENTER

Wherever a ceremonial center such as those described above evolved, it is evident that it played a dominant role in the political, social, and economic organization of its locality. Its pre-eminent function as a shrine, a sacred enclave often containing the palladium of the group inhabiting the district, has been amply illustrated in the preceding pages. Some of these ceremonial complexes, those of Lower Mesopotamia in Protoliterate times, for example, the great cult centers of the Indus valley and of classical Cambodia, Teotihuacán in the Valley of Mexico, and some of the later Mayan centers of Yucatán, had attracted permanent settlement to the fringes of their sacred enceintes; but other ceremonial sites, notably Tiahuanaco, perhaps Chavín de Huántar, some of the Maya shrines (particularly Monte Albán where no source of water has so far been discovered) and, say, those erected on the Dieng Plateau in Java during the 8th century, were either so remote or in such agriculturally unproductive locations that it is to be inferred they accommodated no permanent populations of any size. In fact, it would seem that, apart from a corps of priests and a limited number of resident craftsmen, such a ceremonial complex was in all probability starkly empty during most of the year. Only during seasonal festivals, when cultivators were presumably drawn in from the surrounding countryside, would it have sheltered a more numerous and less specialized population.

Inseparable from the religious authority exercised by the ritual experts who mediated between god and man was the political and social power that they controlled. This is abundantly evident in the massive constructions undertaken at the ceremonial centers, numerous of which still extend over many acres or even square miles. Not infrequently individual structures required the labor of thousands over a period of years. The equivalent of 10,000 workmen laboring for eighteen years at Cheng-Chou, the 7,000 man-days required to excavate only one of the eleven tombs at Hsi-pei Kang, and the 4,200 day-labor units consumed in the digging of a single pit at Hou-chia Chuang have been mentioned previously. To these estimates may be added Adam Falkenstein's calculation that the construction of the Anu ziggurat at Warqa could not have been achieved by less than 1,500 men working ten hours a day for five years.[114] In similar fashion Edmund Leach has estimated that each of two massive dagobas at Anurādhapura, the capital of ancient Ceylon, each containing more than 20 million cubic feet of solid brickwork (probably about 200 million bricks rough laid), could have been completed only by a corvée of some 600 men assembled for not less than 100 days in each year over a period of fifty years.[115] In ancient Japan it is said that at one time more than 300,000 men were at work, both by day and by night, on the new palace at Nagaoka, and construction of the surrounding city continued for a total period of ten years. All the provinces were ordered to render at once their taxes for the whole year, together with a levy of materials. Of the taxes thus collected, 680,000 sheaves of rice were to subsidize the building of new residences by the higher ranks of the nobility, and a further 43,000 were paid out to landowners as compensation for holdings that had been pre-empted for the site of the new capital. And, an example from Mexico, it has been calculated that the Pyramid of the Sun at Teothihuacán would have absorbed the equivalent of the labor of 10,000 workmen over twenty years.[116] But such estimates are rare and, when they can be found, probably not very reliable. Usually it is simply the unquantified magnitude of an undertaking, say the ten square miles of virtually uninterrupted temple architecture at Dzibilchaltún, which has to serve as testimony to the existence of developed loci of political and social power. The dimensions of many of these ceremonial complexes have been noticed in the preceding sections of this essay.

Despite the implications of these estimates, it is sometimes evident that the labor and materials required to build these massive structures were deployed in a relatively short period of time. One of the clearest instances of intense constructional activity comes from ancient Kambujadesá during the reign of King Jayavarman VII, who came to the throne in AD 1181 and died in about 1218. During these four decades a greater quantity of stone was hewn, transported, and raised into monumental edifices than had been employed by all Jayavarman's predecessors put together. Perhaps the earliest of these shrine-cities was the Pūrvatathāgata or 'Buddha of the East', now known as the Banteay Kdei.[117] In 1186 the great shrine of the Rājavihara (now the Ta Prohṃ), with an outer enceinte of 1,000 × 700 meters, was dedicated to the King's mother in her apotheosis as Prajnaparamita, 'the Perfection of Wisdom'.[118] Five years later Jayavarman dedicated the temple Jayaśrī (now the Práḥ Khắn[119]) to shelter a statue of his father in the likeness of the Bodhisattva Lokeśvara. Its outer enclosure measured 640 × 820 meters, and the central sanctuary housed a pantheon of 430 images. There were also attached temples such as those of Krol Ko and Ta Som, and the tower sanctuary of Rajyaśrī (now the Neak Pean[120]), described in its foundation stele as 'a famous island, glorying in its lakes which cleanse the mud of transgressions from those who visit it.'[121] A hundred miles away to the northwest, at the foot of the Dangrek mountains, Jayavarman established the city whose immense ruins are today known as Banteay Chhmar, to fulfil the dual role of frontier fortress and funerary temple dedicated to one of the King's sons. Its outermost enceinte enclosed an area of approximately 2,000 × 2,500 meters. On the bank of the Mekong river just above Phnoṃ Penḥ he raised the temple presently called the Vat Nokor, and in the province of Bati another shrine which has subsequently been dubbed the Ta Prohṃ.[122] While all this monumental building was taking place Jayavarman was also erecting 121 'houses with fire', that is rest-houses for pilgrims journeying along the main routes of his kingdom towards the great shrines at Aṅkor,[123] together with 102 hospitals for the sick distributed throughout the land.[124] But the most impressive of all this monarch's architectural undertakings was the remodelling of the capital at Yaśodharapura on such an extensive scale that it became virtually a new city, that one in fact whose remains are known to the modern Cambodian as Aṅkor Thom. The previous capital, laid out by King Udayādityavarman II so as to pivot on the temple-mountain of the Bàphûon, 'ornament of the three worlds', was almost completely overlaid by a new foundation focusing on the Bàyon, an *axis mundi* whose symbolism, touched upon in a later section of this work, made it a veritable reduced image of the Khmer kingdom.[125] Round the perimeter of the whole ceremonial enclave, a distance of more than ten miles, Jayavarman built a wall flanked on its outer side by a moat more than a hundred yards in width. Just north of the geometrically central Bàyon he erected his residence, which he connected with other parts of the precinct by a series of carved terraces. The Terrace of the Elephants, which served as a reviewing stand on the occasions of festivals and parades, alone exceeded 300 yards in length. Finally, it must be pointed out that Jayavarman excavated several artificial lakes and added the final adaptations to the hydraulic system of the Aṅkor region, so that it came to be the servant of both agronomy and symbolism.[126] At its maximum development it comprised a magnificent technological design, which combined with a scheme of transcendent cosmic symbolism to produce a mutual complementarity capable of ensuring the prosperity of the sacred city, an outcome which could be guaranteed by neither of the components operating alone. What made all this constructional activity still more remarkable was that it did not end with the erection of the buildings. Indeed that was only a prelude to the work of an army of craftsmen who carved gallery after gallery of reliefs depicting the worlds of the gods and of men. Nor does it take account of the previous foundations which Jayavarman added to or restored. And all this barely fifty years after a period of only slightly less frenzied construction, which had witnessed the building of, among other shrines, Aṅkor Wat, the Banteay Samrè, Beng Mealea, and a large part of the Preah Vihear.

The Cambodian ceremonial enclaves are unique in the abundance of documentation relating to their construction, and usually we can do no more than speculate about the period of time involved in the building of such centers. But in any case it may be a mistake to emphasize the sheer size of these monumental edifices, for it is not so much the quantitative aspects of an enterprise which attest the existence of focused political and social power as the complexity of the task. Monumental architecture exhibits a progression from relative simplicity, through increasing intricacy, to maximal complexity and, by definition, size is common to all sectors of this continuum. The building of immense flights of agricultural terraces such as is undertaken by the Ifugao of northern Luzon and the Angami Nagas does not necessarily demand either large-scale organization or its implied sophisticated political underpinnings, for the whole operation involves only the repetition of essentially simple procedures, namely the construction of technically undemanding terrace units and spillways. The execution of such conceptually intricate undertakings as we have already encountered in ancient Kambujadeśa, by contrast, would have been impossible in the absence of a developed political authority and competent bureaucracy. In the Valley of Mexico, the rigorously premeditated distribution of space and mass along the axis between the Pyramid of the Moon and the Temple of Quetzalcóatl at Teotihuacán presupposes a concentration of political power far in excess of that attainable in tribal society. So, too, do the so-called 'acropolis' and plaza at Copán, and the Middle Minoan palace at Knossos, with its complicated layout of *insulae* containing state and ritual apartments, residential quarters, workshops and storerooms, and intricate systems of drainage and lighting arrangements. No less impressive are the citadel precinct at Mohenjo-daro, the temple-complex at Mī-sơn (*Amarāvatī*), and that on the Kĕḍu plain, to name but three such sites. These massive complexes are all attested by epigraphy and existing monuments. Such is not the case with regard to some of the immense constructional undertakings recorded in the Siṅhalese chronicles. Parākrama Bāhu I, for example, who reigned in Poḷonnaruva from 1164 to 1197, is credited with, among other labors, the building of no less than 101 *dagobas*, 476 statues of the Buddha, 300 image chambers, 1,770 new tanks, the repair of 2,355 old ones, the construction of 534 water courses, and the repair of another 3,621.[127] Probably a high proportion of works from other reigns were fathered on to this ruler, who was also the most celebrated of all kings of Siṅhala, during the archetyping process which we have had occasion to mention so frequently in previous pages, and doubtless the King was credited, even during his lifetime, with a large number of constructions actually undertaken by his subjects; but, nevertheless, the version of his achievements which has been preserved in the chronicles is true to the spirit of the society which he represents. And the ruins at Poḷonnaruva today are impressive enough testimony to a cumulative building program which, from the 9th to the 13th century, made it one of the great ceremonial cities of the world.

The erection of such massive and intricate structures as we have been discussing was clearly beyond the power of local groups, particularly those in areas of low population density, but the mechanics of the process by which labor was drawn in from beyond the immediate locality are seldom apparent in the archeological and historical record. In the Yoruba country, however, because the cult centers have survived as operational entities into the modern world, the process of recruitment is well understood. The corvée was placed not only on the inhabitants of the metropolitan city where the afin was situated, but also on all those far and near who owed allegiance to that particular ọba. The Afin Ọyọ, for example, was the work of men from the settlements of Ọyọ itself, Ẹjigbo, Iwo, Ogbomọṣọ, Iseyin, Oke-Iho, Irawọ, Ṣẹpẹtẹri, Igana, Ijio, Igboho, and Ṣaki (Fig. 17).[128] On the occasion of the annual thatching during the Bẹẹrẹ festival, tributes of the rush *bẹẹrẹ* (*Anadelphia arrecta*) were sent up from the coastal plain where the plant grows, while settlements in other regions contributed such items as slaves (from Ibadan), and kola nuts and alligator pepper (from Ekiti and Ijẹṣaland). Work on the Afin Ọwọ was apportioned among two labor pools. Whereas maintenance and minor repairs were primarily the responsibility of men from an inner ring of nine settlements in fairly close proximity to the Afin, namely Ọwọ itself, Ipẹlẹ, Iyẹrẹ, Emure-Ile, Iṣọ, Amunrin, Ipinmi Iṣuada, and Idaṣin, building and structural repairs were undertaken by settlements throughout the territories subject to Ọwọ. At their maximum these stretched from Kabba in the north to Upafa in the south, and from Igbo Eleyewo in the west to Odighiri in the east (Fig. 17). Within this realm each settlement was assigned either a portion of the afin as its responsibility or the provision of particular materials.

This was also the situation obtaining in the 15th century with regard to the palace of Malaka known as the *Mahligai*, as described in the *Sějarah Mělayu*.[129] According to this account the men of Běntan Karangan collected the materials, the men of Ungaran and Tugal constructed the shell of the building, the men of Panchur Sěrapong and Buru decorated the audience hall, and the men of Suir the pavilion, while the waiting rooms were prepared by the men of Sudar and Sayong, the drum hall by the men of Apong, the outer buildings by the men of

Měrba, the bathing facilities by the men of Tungkal, and the mosque was erected by the men of Těntai; the entrance gate was the responsibility of the men from Muda, and the fortifications were in the hands of an unnamed group. Unfortunately the *Mahligai* was a palace that probably never was, or, if it did indeed exist, then it was at some earlier period in Mělakkan history. The whole passage has all the hallmarks of a literary conceit, and the palace it describes, which bears for title the Tamil word meaning 'bower of the princess', is more likely to have been a splendid figment of the Malay mind, based possibly on South Indian conceptions of palace architecture, rather than any earthly istana. Yet the apportionment of the corvée, even though only two or three of the district names can be identified with specific localities, is almost certainly a valid representation of the manner in which labor had been assembled for the construction of earlier, Hindu shrines both on the Malay Peninsula and elsewhere in Southeast Asia.

The centralized character of resource exploitation is implied by the evidence no less frequently than is the centralized direction of architectural construction, but in only two or three cases is it attested explicitly. We have already referred to the caches of stone sickles unearthed at Shang settlement sites, which appear to imply the centralized control of farming activities, or at least of some portion of them. We may also at this point recall Amano Motonosuke's suggestion that the territory of a Shang cult center may have comprised two classes of land : a royal demesne cultivated by 'slaves' (or does he mean serfs?) under centralized management, and clan fields on which a peasantry produced both its own subsistence and a surplus which it contributed to the support of the ceremonial complex.[130] Superficially analogous institutions apparently existed in early Mesopotamia, where agricultural labor was often under the centralized control of temple officials. In the Shuruppak texts of Early Dynastic times, for example, plowing appears to have been under centralized direction,[131] and references to plowing officials in Protoliterate texts would seem to imply that this form of centralization goes back at least to the second half of the fourth millennium BC. Later sources also indicate that large herds of cattle and other beasts pertained exclusively to palace or temple,[132] a single Early Dynastic administrative schedule on one occasion listing no less than 9,660 donkeys, while nearly a hundred members of the Bau community were registered as specialized herdsmen. Robert Adams has suggested that centralized management of livestock may have been partly a response to a chronic shortage of forage during the desiccation of the Mesopotamian summer and partly, in the case of sheep, to the importance of wool as raw material for the textiles upon which the long-distance import trade in such commodities as copper must have depended. The analogue of the Shang demesne holding was perhaps the *nigenna* land of the Sumerian temple, that is fields reserved for the god and cultivated by corvée labor under the direct control of the *sanga* or chief priest.

THE CENTRIPETALIZING FUNCTION

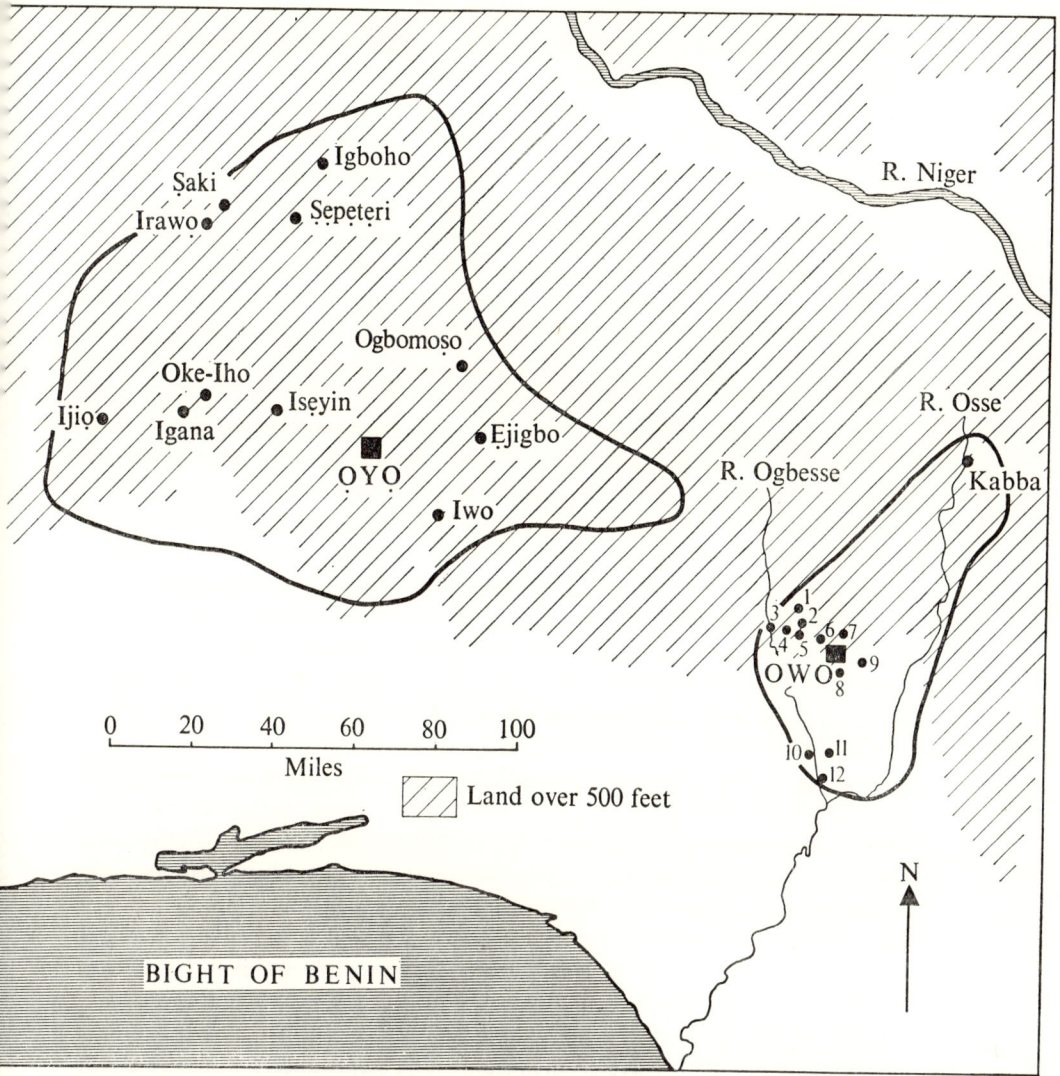

[17] Settlements traditionally providing services and corvée for the afins of Ọyọ and Ọwọ. Redrawn from G.J. Afolabi Ojo, *Yoruba palaces. A study of afins of Yorubaland* (University of London Press, Ltd, 1966), fig. 11, p. 64. The numbers represent the following settlements tributary to Ọwọ:
1. Eporo; 2. Emure-Ile; 3. Eleyewo; 4. Iṣo; 5. Amunrin; 6. Iṣuada;
7. Ipinmi; 8. Iyẹrẹ; 9. Ipẹlẹ; 10. Igbatoro; 11. Utẹ; 12. Okeluse.

Seed grain, draft animals, and agricultural implements for the working of this land were all supplied by the temple. The remainder of the temple lands, it would appear, were either held in fief by temple officials or leased to sharecroppers.[133] Father Anton Deimel's somewhat overgeneralized reconstruction, based mainly on the famous Bau archive from Lagash, of a pervasive *Tempelwirtschaft* has been subject to trenchant criticism during the last two decades, but his specific calculation of some 65 square kilometers of arable land cultivated under the unified direction of an official responsible to the consort of the ruler of Lagash is inherently reasonable. However, the Bau archive is relatively late from our present point of view, and perhaps greater importance should be accorded to a fragmentary tablet of Protoliterate date from Jemdet Naṣr, which lists more than 1,828 hectares of land in a single holding.

There is other evidence which, fragmentary and ambivalent though it is, tends to confirm the existence of centralized management of resource utilization in Protoliterate and Early Dynastic Sumer, but it is perhaps more profitable for one who is poorly versed in these matters to quote an expert rather than to try to elucidate the implications of these difficult records. Consequently I refer the reader to the comments on this topic in Robert Adams's *The Evolution of urban society*[134] and in Adam Falkenstein's study of the Sumerian city-temple.[135] Comparable centralized ownership of herds of milch cattle of up to 500 head is also recorded from medieval Cambodia,[136] and, though the evidence is less explicit, probably from other parts of Southeast Asia as well. Elsewhere it has to be inferred on more general grounds.

Economically the pre-eminent function of the ceremonial center resided in its role as an instrument of redistribution. In some instances this certainly implied a physical ingathering and storage of produce, with perhaps a subsequent partial re-apportionment to the countryside, but in other cases it seems to have been merely appropriational, involving only rights of disposal over certain goods. Testimony to the appropriative role of the ceremonial center is invariably implicit in the physical disposition, as well as in the organization, of the shrine and is not infrequently recorded in temple archives. Here is the paragraph in which Professor Adams summarizes the situation in Sumeria.

> 'In short, the subsistence patterns of late fourth and early third millennium BC Mesopotamia involve specialized groups of producers whose relations were characteristically mediated by the dominant urban institutions, including the palace and the temple. Although a quantitative summary has not yet been attempted (and indeed may be meaningless until a wider selection of contemporary Early Dynastic archives is available), the general outline of the system conforms strikingly well to the "redistributive" model that Polanyi and his collaborators have sketched; moreover, there are at least hints in the available data that the actual flow of goods and services was large in relation to the total available supply of such goods and services. Surely we see here

THE CENTRIPETALIZING FUNCTION

... not merely a complex pattern of subsistence but one in which the interdependence of its component features played a material part in shaping the institutions by which we identify the Urban Revolution itself.'[137]

Such a centrally administered redistributive pattern is perhaps most fully exemplified in the Bau archive, which comes late in the period with which we are concerned, but ration lists from the Eanna temple at Uruk carry it back well into Protoliterate times. Recently Professor Ignace Gelb has elucidated the manner in which rations of barley, oil, and wool were distributed, on a large scale and according to a graded schedule based on need, to dependents of some of the state institutions.[138] Nor was it only the products of the soil which were reallocated in this manner. The munificent 'offerings' of fish recorded in the so-called *mashdaria* texts from Lagash, for example, are now thought to have been items in a mode of ritualized exchange conducted under the aegis of the temple. Adams has recognized possible evidence of the prototype of this form of exchange in the large quantities of fish bones discovered in late 'Ubaid temple levels at Eridug.[139]

The wealth of documentation relating to the great temple-cities of ancient Cambodia makes them especially apt exemplars of redistributive institutions. A good example is afforded by the foundation stele of the temple of Ta Prohm, which was erected, as we noted above, by Jayavarman VII in the vicinity of his capital at Aṅkor in 1186.[140] As many as 3,140 settlements with a total population of 79,365 persons – among them 18 high priests, 2,740 officiants, 2,202 assistants, and 615 female dancers – were enfeoffed to this shrine, the recorded property of which included gold and silver dishes, 35 diamonds, 40,620 pearls, 4,540 precious stones, 876 Chinese veils, 512 sets of silk bedding, and 523 parasols. In addition substantial quantities of rice, *ghṛta* for lustration purposes, molasses, oil, cereals, wax, sandalwood, camphor, and 2,387 sets of ceremonial raiment for the holy images figured among the daily and seasonal schedules of this temple. The provisioning of the shrine now known as the Práḥ Khǎn was on an even more ample scale, requiring contributions in kind from no less than 97,840 persons, both male and female, in 5,324 settlements.[141] Equally impressive are the total quantities of drugs and provisions consumed annually by the 102 Buddhist hospitals established by Jayavarman throughout his kingdom, namely 11,192 tons of rice produced by 838 villages with a population of 81,640 persons, 2,124 kilograms of sesame, 105 kilograms of cardamom, 3,402 nutmegs, 48,000 febrifuges, and 1,960 boxes of salves. But perhaps the most compelling testimony to this appropriational movement of commodities in Cambodia is provided by the program inaugurated by Jayavarman VII in order to make of his kingdom one great offering to the gods of Mahāyāna Buddhism. According to the foundation stele of the Práḥ Khǎn, in 1191, some three decades before the program was finally terminated by the death of Jayavarman, there were more than 20,000 statues in gold, silver, bronze, and stone distributed in shrines throughout the realm, and 306,372 persons, living in 13,500 villages and consuming 38,000 tons of rice annually, were employed in their service.[142]

In ancient Mexico it is not indigenous records, but those of the Spanish conquerors, upon which we have to rely for information about redistributive institutions. Of course, they relate only to the close of the Aztec period, when the ceremonial role of the great city of Tenochtitlán had been fused with a wide range of activities characteristic of a more fully developed mode of urbanism. For earlier periods we are still dependent on inferences from archeological data. The following passage from Professor Adams's comparative study succinctly summarizes available knowledge of this mode of economic integration as it operated in the Mexico of Moctezuma II.

'For the same reason that territorial patterns of control were of such keen interest to the Spaniards, they also meticulously preserved Moctezuma's tribute lists. From them we learn, in a far more complete and accurate fashion than is possible for Mesopotamia in any period, of the organization of tribute as an economic system, including the demand for the delivery in the capital of specified types and quantities of goods at regulated intervals. The quantities are very impressive; the bulk foodstuffs alone are calculated to have amounted to perhaps 52,800 tons, or enough for more than 360,000 people at the estimated mean annual consumption. Moreover, the enormous flow of cacao beans, cloth mantles and other goods serving as media of exchange placed additional instruments of economic superiority not only in the hands of the palace but in those of the nobility and even of the capital population at large.

Centrally distributed through the palace, this wealth not only strengthened the autocratic features of the political structure but also heightened class stratification and urban-rural differences. Quantitative estimates of the patterns of distribution unfortunately depend on hotly debated assumptions about the size of the urban population and on the degree to which Tenochtitlán retained more than its stipulated share of tribute. However, it is suggestive of the power of the palace under these circumstances that, according to perhaps as reasonable an estimate as any, some 25 per cent of the cacao, 50 per cent of the salt, and 15–20 per cent of the maize was directly consumed within that institution. Thus it is only reasonable to conclude, as Friedrich Katz puts it, that "the whole economy of the city rested on tribute".'[143]

In other realms of nuclear urbanism the archeological evidence for the redistributive function of ceremonial centers is often scarcely less conclusive than the testimony of the literary and epigraphic sources available for Mesopotamia, Cambodia, and Mexico. In Shang China the frequent occurrence of storage pits in and around the ceremonial precincts must be held to imply a high degree of appropriational power on the part of the royal lineage and its retainers. The same conclusion must be drawn from the presence of large granaries at Mohenjo-daro, Harappā, and Lothal. The total floorspace of those at Harappā exceeded 9,000 square feet and, after enlargement, those at Mohenjo-daro covered an even larger area. The size of these buildings, and their situations in close proximity to the citadels of the cities, leave no room to doubt that grain collection was centrally organized and closely controlled, as would appear also to have been grain milling and, possibly, brick manufacture, the last of which may have led to the establishment of some sort of state-controlled forestry force to supply fuel for baking. The storerooms at Knossos and Phaistos, with their jars to hold grain or oil, tell the same tale, as indeed do those of some of the Andean palaces, which were described with awe by such 16th-century chroniclers as Francisco de Xerez, Pedro Cieza de Leon, and Pedro Pizarro. Analogous instances of such centripetal movements of commodities are implicit in the evidence from all the regions of nuclear urbanism, both primary and secondary, but suffice it here to say that some form of centralization of control over labor and land, as well as over the produce of the earth, whether plant, animal or mineral, was an invariable concomitant of the rise of ceremonial centers.

The Genesis of the Ceremonial Center

As archeological investigation probes more deeply into the realms of the traditional world, the evolution of tribal shrines into the ceremonial complexes of the 'classic' phase is becoming reasonably well documented, at least in certain localities, but we are still far from a full understanding of the processes involved. In gross terms we are seeking to identify those core elements in society which were concerned in the transformation variously categorized as from Status to Contract,[144] from *Societas* to *Civitas*,[145] from *Gemeinschaft* to *Gesellschaft*,[146] from mechanical to organic solidarity,[147] or from *Concordia* to *Justitia*, and which is invariably accompanied by the organization of 'effective space'[148] in the form of a tract of territory controlled from and oriented to (not merely exploited by) the cult center. Wherever this change is adequately recorded, it is seen to be sustained by the concurrent emergence of a redistributive superordinate economy[149] focused on the ceremonial complex. Such a change not only implies the generation of a centralizing power whose authority is validated by formalized sanctions of one sort or another, but also presupposes the development of new social institutions. Indeed, the questions it poses relate primarily to social differentiation, and it is this which, in formal terms, must be regarded as the dependent variable when we seek to elucidate the complex series of interrelated changes that eventuated in the emergence of the ceremonial city – though we recognize, of course, that it does not operate in isolation, and is inevitably associated with concomitant occupational and territorial differentiation. It means, too, that in the following analysis emphasis will be placed on sociological rather than cultural contexts, on the changing distribution and exercise of power rather than on inventories of technological and stylistic features.

It may be helpful at this point to interpolate a few comments on those other components which severally or in combination have attracted the attention of students of the process of urban genesis. Prominent among them have been a selection of environmental characteristics, a variety of demographic features, and the level of technological achievement involved. Let us consider the role of the ecological factor first.

THE ECOLOGICAL COMPONENT

In the more simplistic type of argument this has been invoked most frequently as a combination of benign climate and soil fertility (not infrequently supplemented by other natural resources) giving rise to an alleged surplus production which could be deployed for the support of non-cultivating élites, scribes, craftsmen, and warriors. Presumably it is not an absolute (biological) surplus that is intended here, but rather a socially derived, relative surplus; the type of surplus, in fact, which results from the re-allocation of goods or services from one use to another at least as often as (and in traditional society perhaps much more frequently than) from an increase in productive capacity or an accession of more abundant material means. A 'social' surplus, then, is designated as such by the society in question, and its realization depends on the existence of a locus of power capable of extracting products or services from the hands of its members. No primitive peoples have ever spent all their waking hours in eating, breeding and cultivating : even the most debilitated, by squandering some of their resources in non-utilitarian ways, have demonstrated the existence of a surplus. Those administrators charged with the mobilization of resources in redistributive economies long ago discovered that the human frame was almost infinitely extensible and that, consequently, it was almost always possible to wring from even the most wretched of cultivators yet another exaction for the support of the central bureaucracy. Moreover, it may be remarked – albeit supererogatively – that those authors who have postulated the existence of an absolute surplus as a prerequisite for urban development have invariably failed to isolate those cultural values or social contexts which have decreed that it should subsequently have been employed for the support of ceremonial complexes.[150]

Even a cursory review of environmental conditions in the realms of primary urban generation reveals that in the aggregate they subsumed a wide range of ecological zones, and that individually some of them comprised subregions of considerable diversity. The bald statement that, of the seven realms, only North China lay outside the tropics broadly defined, conceals the range of diversification induced in these regions by differences of aspect and elevation. Physiographically these environments ran the whole gamut of variation, from relatively undifferentiated potamic plains almost at sea level to dissected mountain slopes exceeding 10,000 feet in elevation, with all that that implies as to climate, drainage patterns, natural vegetation, soil types, and cropping patterns. Without pre-empting the score or so of pages which would be required for a meaningful enumeration of these diversities, it is abundantly evident that no fixed constellation of environmental conditions and resources could have constituted a precondition for the generation of ceremonial centers. Extending this statement to include the realms of secondary urban generation only provides additional confirmation of its validity. In recent years, however, several authors have carried out more sophisticated analyses of the role of ecological factors in urban origins. In particular W. T. Sanders[151] and Robert Adams,[152] have focused attention on the diversity of the subsistence base as an initial stimulus to reallocation, and as an inducement to the development of institutions capable of mediating exchanges between groups engaged in different modes of resource utilization.

Generally speaking, environmental diversity was more marked in the realms of the New World than in those of the Old, and was especially pronounced in the Central Andean territories, which included in a latitudinal traverse of barely 100 miles a catenary sequence from tropical desert, perhaps comparable to conditions in ancient Egypt or Sind, through a variety of intermediate zones rendered temperate by altitude, to the *puna* of the upper slopes of the sierra and the towering peaks above. The ecological responses of the Peruvian mountaineer, with his crop complex of roots, oca, and quinoa, and of the lowlander with his complex of maize, beans, squash, cotton, and fruit, were as dissimilar as were their respective environments; and both were far removed from the millet-based ecotype of Lung-shan China, the emphasis on wet-padi in Southeast Asia, on yams in the Yoruba territories, or on wheat, six-rowed barley, and field peas in conjunction with cattle husbandry on the Indus plains. It is possible – though the evidence for several of the realms is exiguous – that this diversity of crops does not reflect an equal diversity of agricultural techniques, and, despite the absence of domestic stock and the utilization of their products in the New World,[153] it certainly is not indicative of such a wide variance in ecotypes, but this is not to deny in any way the emergence in immediately pre-urban periods in different parts of the world of increasingly highly specialized eco-niches.

In the most comprehensive and acutely argued statement of this problem,[154] Professor Adams has demonstrated that even in such a superficially undifferentiated environment as the plains of Lower Mesopotamia there was already discernible a suite of specialized subsistence zones. Basic to the ecotype developed here was an extensive mode of winter cereal culture, with wheat predominant on the Assyrian uplands and barley, better able to withstand the effects of fluctuating salinity,[155] on the back-slopes of lêvées and the margins of swamps and other depressions within the Sumerian territories proper. Confined to low-lying areas adjacent to permanent watercourses were summer-ripening orchard and garden crops, among which the date was the most important. Not only was the yield of this crop less closely related to the height of the annual flood than that of most other irrigated crops, but its fall harvest was nicely complementary to the spring harvest of cereals. The third example of specialized adaptation was that of the herdsman, which itself assumed two modes: the pasturing of cattle by sedentary herdsmen on rough land and cereal stubble within the zone of permanent settlement, and the grazing of migratory herds by nomadic pastoralists on semi-arid steppe beyond the frontiers of settlement. A fourth source of subsistence was the swampland of Lower Mesopotamia, which provided both building material in the form of reeds and protein in the form of fish. The importance of this economic resource is clearly evident in the fact that, of the 1,200 members of the Bau community in Early Dynastic Lagash, over 100 were fishermen and 125 were sailors, oarsmen, pilots, or persons otherwise connected with boats and water. It is Adams's suggestion that the effective exploitation of these eco-niches was a predisposing factor in the evolution of a symbiotic interdependence between adjacent segments of society, and that the complementarity of these resources probably engendered occupational specializations which facilitated the emergence of redistributive institutions such as the temple and the palace.

Adams has also shown that much the same argument can be advanced with regard to adaptation in Mesoamerica, although here there were significant differences in the manner in which ecological interdependencies were organized. Whereas in Mesopotamia interdependencies were, owing to the small distances involved and the lack of restraining physical barriers, mainly intraregional, in Mesoamerica by contrast they tended to be interregional. Only the larger polities, established on an imperial basis, succeeded in transcending the limitations of a single ecological zone, so that the redistributive instruments developed in this realm tended to be more concerned with the promotion of external trade between states in different regions than with internal reallocations between different ecological zones within the same state. However, trade and tribute certainly did bring about a bulk movement of commodities between different zones, notably the exchange of chiles and maguey from the highlands for cotton and cacao beans from the lowlands and salt from the coastal pans.

For all other regions the evidence available is inadequate for the sort of analysis carried out by Adams into the ecological basis of the pre-urban cultures of Mesopotamia and Mesoamerica. This may seem surprising in the case of the Yoruba afins which exist even today and which were fairly carefully described in the 19th century. But the precise date at which these ceremonial

GENESIS OF THE CEREMONIAL CENTER

foci first appeared is unknown, so that the relative roles of the indigenous Sudanic crop complex, of the Malaysian crop complex (which arrived by overland transmission from the east probably at about the beginning of the Christian era), and of the American crop complex (which was introduced from Brazil and the West Indies after AD 1500) are to be disentangled only with difficulty. If, as is often claimed, the Yoruba cult centers were in existence by the end of the first millennium AD, then, although the staple yam and taro had been long established, the range of crop plants was considerably narrower than it would have been if the Yoruba cities had developed, as is possible, only at the beginning of the 17th century, when Ọyọ imperialism first became apparent. In any case the fact that Ifẹ, traditionally regarded as the earliest of the Yoruba states, lay on the northern fringes of the rain forest where it began to grade into savanna, and that the Ọyọ territories included extensive tracts of both ecological formations, are possible pointers to the sort of symbiotic interdependence which may well have obtained when the earliest Yoruba cult centers were formed.

In the Central Andean realm such agricultural specialization as is apparen in the archeological record was mainly on a regional basis, presumably a response to the rapid succession of ecological zones as one moved inland from the coast. As early as about 800 BC llamas from the sierra were ceremonially interred in a community shrine on the north coast of Peru and, in another roughly contemporary burial, were found in association with the skeleton of a person believed to be a priest.[156] Subsequently exchanges such as are implied by these burials became regularized on a considerable scale,[157] and it has been presumed that maritime products, cotton, peppers, fruits, and coca were among the commodities moving in the opposite direction. However, the Peruvian evidence for ecological specialization is meager in quantity and uncertain in implication. It is certainly not of the abundance or caliber necessary for the support of any major hypothesis in connection with urban origins. Neither is that from ancient Egypt, although tomb scenes of Old Kingdom officials indicate that vegetables and fruits, together with the yields of fowling, fishing, and animal husbandry, constituted substantial supplements to the grains which undoubtedly formed the main element in the peasant's caloric intake.[158] Least adequate in this respect is the evidence from the Indus valley, and it is possible to do no more than speculate about the specialized use made of hypothesized riverine marshes, forests of babul, tamarisk, kandi, sissu, and bahan farther away from the river banks, and the grasslands which graded into steppe and ultimately, in Sind and Baluchistan, into desert. This reconstruction of the immediately pre-urban environment of the Indus valley is bound up with the as yet unresolved problem of climatic change. Until that question is settled, all speculation about early Indus ecotypes is likely to be something less than profitable.[159]

THE NATURE OF THE CEREMONIAL CENTER [351

For North China, the realm with which we are especially concerned, the evidence is also unsatisfactory. During the Lung-shan era the crop staples were already millets and, possibly, wheat, and there is reason to believe that in Shang times summer millet and padi may have alternated with winter wheat, presumably on different categories of land. Pigs, dogs, cattle, and poultry contributed protein to the Shang diet, though some of the incentive for the breeding of these animals may have derived from a demand for them for sacrificial purposes. The importance of fishing in both Lung-shan and Shang times is attested by the excavation of fish bones and a wide range of tackle. Meager though the information is, it may not be overextending its implications to see here a shadowy parallel with the mosaic of specialized subsistence zones adumbrated by Adams for Lower Mesopotamia. In both realms adequate and balanced diets were available through the exchange of the products of distinctive eco-niches. In both areas the extensive cultivation of cereals provided the framework for the farming year, but it is possible that in China the availability of rice, a crop which, although possessing the roots of a dry-land plant, can yet grow and flourish in water, allowed the exploitation of damper low-lying tracts by means of a plant denied to the Sumerians. However, the Chinese had no crop comparable to the date in Mesopotamia, and paucity of information prevents any estimate as to the possible contributions made by gardens and orchards. There is, incidentally, no evidence of any such intensive mode of cultivation as that represented by the *chinampas* of the Mexican lakes, which supplied vegetables to the city of Tenochtitlán during Aztec times and probably at much earlier periods as well.[160] In the matter of pastoralism the parallel between Sumer and Shang China appears to have been close. What Adams has called 'the powerful ambivalence of relations between herdsman and farmer, involving both symbiosis and hostility, which has shaped the social life, tinctured the history, and enriched the literature of the civilizations of the Fertile Crescent'[161] has also for long been recognized as one of the major (though until recently least understood) themes of Chinese history and, as we have seen in Chapters One and Two, was clearly evident in the record of Shang and early Chou times. The graph **miôk,[162] meaning 'to herd cattle', occurs on bone inscriptions as early as the reign of **Mi̯wo-tieng (Wu-ting), and Creel has assembled a number of such epigraphs which appear to reflect conflict between herdsmen and sedentary farmers.[163] One of these, published by Lo Chen-yü, reads, 'It is stated that the [people of the] 凸 [164] country have come out to graze their cattle on our ... territory, seven men',[165] and another, 'It is stated that the [people of the] 凸 country also pastured their cattle on the lands of our western border settlements'.[166] Both these inscriptions have been dated by the diviner's name to the reign of Mi̯wo-tieng, and a third, which lacks this information, can be ascribed by reason of its paleography, syntax, and style, to roughly the same period: 'It is stated that the [people of the]

GENESIS OF THE CEREMONIAL CENTER

***T'o* country also graze their cattle on our land, ten men'.[167] It is surely significant that other oracle bones preserve questions which imply that both 𐎟 and *T'o* were about to suffer reprisals for the intrusion of their herdsmen on to Shang territory. On one occasion [168] both the incursion and the question of retaliation occur on the same bone. Finally, fishing was a source of significant quantities of protein in both early Mesopotamia and Shang China. The explicit evidence for the existence of institutional organs of centralization and reallocation in China is very much less than that which can be drawn upon in the case of Mesopotamia, but it is almost certainly significant that the overall ecological patterns in these two culture realms are remarkably similar. The suggestion that they may have been economically integrated along much the same lines is rendered the more likely by the existence of archeological evidence for the centralized management of craft production in both the Shang and the Sumerian ceremonial centers.

Even in Mesopotamia and Mesoamerica, the two regions of primary urban generation where it is possible to provide some documentation for the centralized organization of complementarily specialized units of production, the evidence relates to a period when the process was already well established. In Mesoamerica, indeed, the era of the cult centers had passed its zenith and was apparently about to evolve into a subsequent phase of urban development. In Mesopotamia the earliest explicit evidence can be pushed back to the later half of the Protoliterate era, but for earlier periods we are as much dependent on inferences from general archeological configurations as we are when reconstructing the ecological basis of urban development in the other nuclear realms. Thus, while there can be no doubt that symbiotic interdependencies arising from ecological diversity were integral parts of the organization of ceremonial centers at their *floruit*, there is no reason to suppose that they were preconditions for, or generative factors in, the emergence of these new settlement forms. It should be remembered, too, that a complex pattern of subsistence activity need not reflect a diversity of natural resources, but may itself be a product of social interaction. By the time that it becomes apparent in the archeological record, it may quite as plausibly have been induced by the structural changes occurring in society as have been a predisposing factor towards them. My own belief is that the integration of disparate ecological zones into a socio-politically definable unit was a necessary concomitant of the rise of ceremonial centers. After all, ecotypes based on a single crop are not too common in pre-urban (or any other) societies and, moreover, ecological zones characterized by a uniformity of plant forms are not usually extensive, so that a locus of centralized power was bound sooner or later to subsume a suite of them. At that point, as in all other societies, diversity would doubtless have been exploited as an assurance against natural calamity and, as such, in retrospect we can recognize it as an indispensable basis for long-term development, but this is not the same as saying that 'it must have been responsible for the development of trade, exchange and redistributive institutions which in turn enhanced the growth of some form of centralized authority.' At best it could but have facilitated such developments after the diffusely dispersed social and economic power of pre-urban society had already been concentrated in certain reallocative institutions. It is doubtful if the small-scale redistributive instruments of a pre-urban economy have ever been capable of both engendering and validating their own augmentation and subsequent institutionalization on a large scale. While it is certainly true that discrepancies in time between, say, harvest and consumption often do induce the emergence of relatively simple reallocative institutions in folk societies, it is not at all clear that these institutions actually generate a dynamic of expansion of the sort that could ultimately have produced the powerful redistributive instrument that was the ceremonial city. All this having been said, it must be admitted that diversities of environment and natural resources were exploited by, as far as the archeological record has been unravelled, ceremonial centers in virtually all the nuclear urban realms.

Professor Adams, as well as other scholars in this field, have also called attention to the significance of dependability of production as a guarantee of the continuity of nascent redistributive institutions and, indeed, of the political and social power with which they are associated. A degree of dependability could be achieved through the medium of diversification, as discussed above, but equally by plant and animal selection and the general improvement of agricultural techniques. Once again Adams has succeeded in documenting the beginnings of these trends in Mesopotamia and the Valley of Mexico, and once again the evidence is insufficient to do so in the other regions of primary urban generation. There are, of course, hints from time to time, but no basis on which to develop an argument. In any case dependability of production is as relative a concept as is that of social surplus discussed a few pages previously. Millet and wheat yields in the Shang culture hearth of North China were probably more reliable than in the marshes of the lower Huang river or on the uplands to the west, but they were equally probably less reliable than wet-padi yields in Cambodia (where ceremonial centers also attained a considerable degree of elaboration), or than maize yields in eastern North America (where cult centers never developed into temple-cities). And even in Cambodia crop yields were probably less reliable, at least in proto-Khmer times, which constituted the formative period of Cambodian urbanism, than in the maize-beans-squash realm of the Maya. There seems little reason to believe that unusual fertility was a precondition for the emergence of redistributive institutions, although it undoubtedly facilitated their subsequent development. For analytical purposes, it seems best regarded not as an independent (and certainly not as a causative) factor in the evolution of urban life, but as one component in a closely articu-

THE DEMOGRAPHIC COMPONENT

Writers on urban origins have frequently postulated the existence of some relationship between density of population and the emergence of urban life, but only rarely have they attempted to define this relationship in analytical terms. It is also only too evident that population density is itself related to agricultural productivity. In broad terms the primary distinction here (so far as ancient times are concerned) is between the delicate ecological equilibrium of swidden cultivation, with its inelastic and dispersive demographic tendencies, and the more stable equilibrium of permanent-field agriculture, characterized by tumescent and concentrative qualities.[169] Whereas swidden easily turns maladaptive under increasing population density, permanent-field agriculture is often better able to withstand such pressures. Unlike swidden, which is an attempt to manipulate a generalized ecosystem in the interests of food production, permanent-field farming has usually taken the form of a thoroughgoing remoulding of the environment, the transformation of a generalized into a more specialized ecosystem.[170] Consequently it has been on the whole more effective than swidden in extending the ecological niches capable of supporting food-producing cultigens, as a result of which it has throughout history enabled a higher aggregate number of settlement units in any given area to maintain roughly equivalent, and by no means negligible, outputs.[171] It is not surprising, therefore, that proto-urban forms have most frequently developed in regions of permanent-field agriculture. The significant exceptions to this generalization are the Maya settlements of Mesoamerica and the Yoruba afins of Southwestern Nigeria, in both of which regions swidden was the predominant ecotype. But there are at least partial explanations of this apparent aberration. In the first place both areas lie largely within the humid tropics (Köppen Af classification), where the natural climax association is rain forest and where the swidden ecosystem, because of its immense power of regeneration under conditions of maximal heat and moisture, is at its most stable. Second, the position is somewhat changed in Mesoamerica by the presence of maize, a cereal unique in its cultivational and nutritive characteristics. Whereas it has been variously estimated that swidden cultivation in different parts of Southeast Asia can support only between twenty and fifty persons per square kilometer, in lowland Mesoamerica it is thought that no more than between seven and fifteen hectares of cultivated land are required by a whole family at any one time.[172] Generally speaking, though, urban forms have arisen in areas of permanent-field agriculture. Yet although, as in the case of the physical environment, there have always been obvious limiting conditions, a dense population does not seem to have been a precondition for the institutionalization of a superordinate redistributive economy. That centralization of production and reallocation can take place in a milieu of relatively sparse population as well as in regions of high density is sufficiently evidenced by the presence of imposing ceremonial complexes in such forbidding localities (from the economic, though not necessarily from the spiritual, point of view) as those of Tiahuanaco and the Dieng Plateau. Whether or not the attainment of any specific population density, either absolute or in relation to other factors, was a prerequisite for the process of urban generation is unknown.

In this connection Professor Gordon Willey has proposed an interesting hypothesis as to the relation of ceremonial centers to changes in population density. He envisages a form of agricultural colonization having been initiated as families moved out of villages that had become too large for their available resources. In his own words, 'Certain villages then may have remained as the sacred centers of these expanding societies, and, in these, special constructions were put up as shrines, temples, and burial places. These temple or ceremonial centers eventually became the residences of priests and rulers, the seats of market places, and, as the resident leadership grew in power, the foci of art, crafts, and learning.'[173] This hypothesis clearly requires an increase in population relative to resources to induce a centrifugal movement outwards from the parent settlements. Presumably this could result from a deterioration of habitat equally as from an increase in the number of persons in the community. The difficulty is that both are difficult to document at the present stage of archeological research. Willey is confident that an absolute increase in population did occur at the appropriate time in Mesoamerica. 'It is also certain,' he writes, 'that the process of the change from village to villages-and-center was accompanied by a general population increase, probably over most of Mesoamerica.'[174] In both Mesoamerica and Peru ceremonial centers appeared very early in the archeological record, relatively earlier indeed than they have customarily been discerned in the Old World. They have been recognized in the southern part of Mesoamerica as early as 1500 BC, and some attained imposing dimensions just after 1000 BC. In Peru they apparently go back as far as the close of the period of incipient cultivation, and had attained an impressive size by about 500 BC. In other words, the increase in population with which Willey is concerned is essentially that which accompanied the period of momentous change from hunting and collecting to food production through the domestication of plants and animals. It is, I think, important to bear this point in mind when considering Professor Adams's remark that, 'Particularly in Mesopotamia, where the sedentary village pattern seems to have been stabilized for several millennia between the establishment of effective food production and the "take-off" into urbanism, it may be noted that there is simply no evidence for gradual population increases that might have helped to precipitate the Urban Revolution after reaching some undefined threshold.'[175] My own reading of the evidence – such as it is – relating to the other regions of primary urban generation, forces me into tentative agreement with Professor Adams, but this does not mean that I disagree with Professor Willey. These two scholars are writing about different stages in the process of urban generation. Whereas Adams is referring to the period when major monumental complexes had become sufficiently powerful instruments of centralization and redistribution so that they were the dominating features of the archeological record, in other words to the threshold of the development of urban forms, Willey is concerned with a much earlier evolutionary phase when village shrines were first beginning to exercise authority (rather than power) in localized communities. The whole tenor of available archeological evidence implies that the series of adaptations which brought about the shift from terminal food collection to incipient food production was accompanied by a substantial increase in absolute numbers of population, but the trend of the same evidence is equally opposed to the likelihood of there having been general population increases immediately prior to or during the periods (there were several in different parts of the world) of primary urban generation. This serves to draw attention to a point that will be emphasized subsequently, namely that the so-called urban revolution was a process and not an event, and that its roots must often be sought correspondingly deep in the past. In connection with this general line of thought, it is interesting to recall Chang Kuang-chih's suggestion that a fission of parent villages was taking place towards the end of Yang-shao times and resulting in a common cemetery being shared by a group of surrounding settlements (pp. 24–5 above).

The possibility that a deterioration in habitat in certain instances may have initiated the process leading to the emergence of ceremonial centers has received serious consideration, as far as I have been able to ascertain, from only one author. Walter Fairservis, in the course of developing a possible theory of urban origins in the Indus valley, has tentatively interpreted the rise of ceremonial centers both there and, on a less imposing scale, in Baluchistan as a response to anxiety engendered by food shortages resulting from population increases.[176] Even if Fairservis is correct in his interpretation of the Indus situation – and not all scholars are in agreement with him – we are so poorly informed about the factors which may have operated to render ancient subsistence practices maladaptive that it is difficult to estimate how generally such an argument might be applied. Climatic change, the migration of peoples from moist to drier habitats, the stability of certain ecosystems created by early man, in fact the whole complex of early agricultural practices, are among the topics which need investigation from this point of view before Fairservis's hypothesis can be fairly evaluated.

There is another point which arises in connection with the relation of population to urban genesis. Martin Orans has recently sought to shift the emphasis in discussions of the nature and function of social surpluses from the differential between *per capita* production and consumption, which has hitherto been the customary way of approaching this problem, to what he terms the gross amount of deployable wealth.[177] This conceptualization of the notion of surplus not only reinforces Harry Pearson's analysis of the mechanisms of surplus mobilization and focuses attention on the political instruments which make it possible, but also suggests that gross size of population, and indeed of the territorial unit, may be agents in the generation of a surplus equally as powerful as the more frequently cited efficiency of production. Adams shrewdly points out that, from this point of view, territorial aggrandizement and political unification can be regarded less as indirect consequences of urban genesis than as functionally interrelated processes at the very core of the transformation.[178]

Finally, it must be noted that no particular significance, so far as urban genesis is concerned, seems to have attached to the pattern on which the pre-urban populations in the several nuclear realms were disposed. Robert Adams has already commented on the contrast between the continuous zones of settlement arranged lineally along the banks of watercourses, which were characteristic of Sumer and ancient Egypt on the one hand, and the enclaves of relatively dense occupation separated from each other by tracts of inhospitable and virtually uninhabited terrain, which were the more common forms in Mesoamerica and Peru.[179] For the Indus valley, Walter Fairservis has reconstructed a settlement pattern in which farming villages radiated in diminishing numbers outwards across the plains from the precincts of massive monumental cult centers.[180] Unfortunately the evidence available for Shang China is inadequate for us to say more than that Lungshanoid settlements were found among the foothills of Shen-hsi and Shan-hsi and, apparently, on knolls raised above the level of the plains to the east. Of the *pattern* of settlement in this region in immediately pre-urban times we know nothing.

THE TECHNOLOGICAL COMPONENT

Technology, which in this analysis is regarded as an independent variable, has until recently been accorded a primary role in virtually all discussions of urban origins. Most writers on this topic have followed the late Professor Childe in regarding hypothesized advances in technology as the primary motivating force in the generation of those social surpluses upon which the rise of urbanism is believed to have depended. Childe apparently considered that early farming communities possessed an inherent proclivity to maximize production at whatever level of technological competence they found themselves, irrespective of their material needs, and also that in some unspecified way the appearance of surpluses not only made possible, but actually generated, new modes of appropriation and novel patterns of consumption.[181] Subsequent analyses of the concept of the surplus have tended to minimize – though, of course, not to wholly negate – the role of technology in the creation of surpluses, and to emphasize rather the importance of particular institutional contexts.[182] Concomitantly there has also developed an enhanced awareness of the fact that many of the most significant of the technological improvements involved in this nexus of changes may have played little direct part in production, but may have made their contribution in the sphere of transportation. Childe also paid little attention to the reciprocal influence exerted on technological development by the great centralizing institutions in the creation of which he believed technological innovation to have been a factor of prime importance. He has little to say, for example, about the effects on gross and *per capita* productivity of the rationalization, what Adams has called the organizational inputs, which must have accompanied the rise of the ceremonial centers.

More destructive of Childe's thesis, perhaps, are the criticisms directed against his basic but, so far as his published writings are concerned, unverified premise that the period of what he called the Urban Revolution was indeed characterized by an acceleration in the progress of technology. In fact, a survey of the archeological evidence currently available has revealed very little correlation between technological innovation and the emergence of ceremonial cities. It is true that such regionalizing instruments did not develop in hunting and gathering societies, or even among incipient cultivators, and that a level of agricultural attainment comparable to that of Braidwood's Developed Village Farming appears to have been a precondition of their formation; but during the phase of active generation of temple-cities technology can be said, in the light of present knowledge, more often than not to have evinced no significant advances – or perhaps we should say no changes which appear to have been significant from our present vantage point, significance itself being to a large extent conditioned by the manner in which the problem is viewed. It may well be that future refinements in our conceptualization of the enigma of urban origins will direct our attention to aspects of the process which currently seem to have only trivial significance. For the present, however, the generalization holds that technological advance seems not to have been a factor of primary importance in urban generation.

The situation in Sumer with regard to other than subsistence crafts has been described succinctly by Robert Adams, our constant cicerone in matters relating to incipient urbanism in Mesopotamia:

'While the development of different branches of the crafts naturally proceeded at different rates and in response to different stimuli, at least a few generalizations apply fairly uniformly. To begin with, rapid technological progress and greatly increased consumption of craft products seem to have occurred successively rather than contemporaneously. The earlier phase, consisting mainly of very small-scale production of cult objects within and largely for the temple establishments, apparently coincided roughly with the Protoliterate period. The Early Dynastic phase, on the other hand, is correlated with a burgeoning military demand for vehicles and weapons and with the growth of a private market economy alongside the normal redistributive mechanisms of the temple and palace. As best illustrated by metallurgy, the latter development produced little further technological advance but, instead, involved an important extension of administrative procedures (originally introduced by the temples for control of subsistence products) to provide for greatly expanded capitalization, training, production, and distribution of commodities not directly associated with primary subsistence. Tool and weapon designs were somewhat improved and bronze made its appearance during the Early Dynastic period, but the tremendously increased volume of available metal during the same period implies a whole series of far more striking organizational changes.* Probably it is justifiable to conclude from this sequence that the expansion of craft production and the market, and the simultaneous appearance of craftsmen and merchants as important (although still numerically small) social groups, occurred too late to be regarded as major precipitating factors behind the growth of cities, class stratification, and the emergence of dynastic authority.'[183]

To this we may add that agricultural technology in Mesopotamia also remained static during these crucial centuries. In so far as the evidence permits us to generalize, much the same conclusions hold for Nuclear America and Egypt, though in this latter region the evidence is desperately thin because, as mentioned earlier, there is so little material relating directly to the crucial phases of urban genesis. For the Yoruba territories and the Indus valley the evidence is so exiguous as not to warrant the drawing of conclusions. There is, however, a close parallel between the relative phases of technological and urban development in Mesopotamia and, for all the limitations of our sources, North China. The virtual absence of significant innovation in techniques of field cultivation

---

* [Adams's footnote: For example, metal objects occur in only one-sixth of the late 'Jamdat Nasr' Early Dynastic I graves at Ur but in four-fifths of those of Early Dynastic III date. Moreover, the average quantity of metal in the later graves increases substantially (C. Leonard Woolley, *Ur excavations* [London and Philadelphia]. II. *The Royal Cemetery* [1934]. IV. *The Early Periods* [1956]). In order to obtain these greatly increased supplies, a concomitant expansion was necessary in other industries whose products could be transported and exchanged for copper at its distant sources beyond the Persian Gulf and in Anatolia. The large labor force engaged in production of exportable textiles that is accounted for by the Baba temple archive (Deimel, *Sumerische Tempelwirtschaft* . . ., p. 108) thus may be a reflection of the increasing demand for metals.].

during the period of urban genesis, the main advances in craft technology occurring long prior to that period, the introduction of bronze metallurgy during dynastic times, and the proliferation of vessel, ornament, and ritual-weapon forms as a response to class differentiation and religious formalism, are features common to both regions. If the curves of some Lungshanoid pots are taken to be evidence of metallic prototypes (cf. p. 27 above), then these postulated bronze vessels could only have been for ritual use, so that the earliest Chinese production would have paralleled that of Mesopotamia in being on a small scale and for ceremonial purposes. There are, in fact, just enough more or less ambivalent fragments of evidence available in the other realms of primary urban generation to suggest that the pattern of technological emphasis here outlined will eventually prove, *mutatis mutandis*, to be that which obtained generally during the transition from folk to urban society. It can be characterized in brief as lack of change in the pattern of subsistence, and in handicrafts the elaboration of existing techniques to meet the expanded demand of a private (but still élite) section of the community and of the military.

Obviously a great deal more could be said about each of these components, but it is not the purpose of this chapter to advance a general theory of urban origins. Rather it aims to set the early Chinese city in comparative perspective. Enough has been said to show that the ecological, demographic, and technological factors were not independent agents in this transformation of society so much as components in a series of processual changes between what Julian Steward has felicitously termed levels of socio-cultural complexity. What cannot be doubted, however, is that the transmutation of these levels of systemic integration at all times and in all places involved changes in the structure and patterning of society. Social organization, in fact, is the dependent variable which constitutes the nub of the problem of urban origins, and the next step towards an understanding of this evolutionary process is an examination of the forces working to induce social differentiation.

FACTORS INDUCING SOCIAL DIFFERENTIATION

It goes without saying that an almost infinite number of factors are capable of interacting to bring about social differentiation, but analysis has tended to focus on four generalized activities as of primary importance in the social transformation which we have come to know – misleadingly, I believe – as the Urban Revolution. These are trade and/or marketing, irrigation, warfare, and religion, and I am proposing to add a few comments relevant to each.

Trade and marketing. Of these four activities trade and marketing have received far and away the most attention, probably a projection into the past of the very proper preoccupation of most present-day urbanists and location analysts with tertiary economic activity. From the point of view of the contemporary marketing approach – or, as Polanyi would say, under the sway of catallactic logic – trade and market are virtually inseparable, but in the experience of the ancients they were clearly distinguishable entities.[184] When and how they became conceptually fused is still imperfectly understood.

Despite the emphasis which has been placed on trade as a primary motivating force in the generation of urban forms, it has not yet been demonstrated clearly and unequivocally first, that a generalized desire for exchange is capable of concentrating political and social power to the extent attested by the archeological record, or second, that it can bring about the institutionalization of such power. There is, too, a basic anhistoricism in the argument *ex commercio*. Whereas its proponents have almost invariably assumed that the self-regulating market, even the self-regulating market system, was at least as old as sedentary agriculture, it has recently been demonstrated that such markets were the exceptions rather than the rule during historic time, in fact, until the 19th and 20th centuries according to an extreme opinion.[185] It has also been assumed in the making of this argument that the markets of antiquity were autonomous price-fixing markets. The contrary was probably nearer the truth. In the traditional world the economic process, because it has been embedded in non-economic institutions, has predominantly taken the form of an open system subject to pressures generated outside the sphere of demand, cost and price, which has meant in fact that it has been subordinated to a greater or lesser degree to the moral norms of society. Where price-fixing markets have occurred there can be little doubt that non-economic factors have played a significant role in their operation. In Polanyi's succinct phrases, 'In so far as exchange at a set rate is in question, the economy is integrated by the factors which fix that rate, not by the market mechanism.'[186] In other words the economic institutions of the traditional world have, generally speaking, been subordinated to a greater or lesser degree to the moral norms of society. By contrast, it is the self-regulating market which, deriving its dynamic from a set of circumstances independent of the cultural values that integrate society, is capable of imposing its own dictates on, and in certain cases of modifying, the structure of society.[187] It is often difficult to categorize specifically the fixed-price and non-regulating markets of the past, sometimes because of a paucity of textual evidence, but more often because the whole economic process is embedded in non-economic institutions, so that the occurrence of the term 'market' in an historical text can imply a whole range of set exchanges, but seldom the operation of an autonomous supply-demand-price mechanism.

Towards trade *sensu stricto* there was an ambivalent attitude. On the one hand there was administered trade in both its treaty and tribute forms. A classic example of the former is afforded by Assyria of the 17th century BC, where 'prices' – for want of a better word – took the form of equivalencies established under the authority of custom, statute, or proclamation, and there was no market in the sense of a free movement of prices.[188] Profit depended in this instance not on the maximization of return and the minimization of cost, but on turnover. There is also some evidence that in an earlier period a good deal of Sumerian intercity trade was either instigated or partially controlled from the royal palaces, and the *dam-gar* or factors engaged in it clearly enjoyed official status. The chief among the *dam-gar* seems to have had especially close relationships with the palace.[189] A corollary of this form of trade is the absence of a need for physical market places, a situation which, despite the ambivalence of arguments *ex silentio*, appears to have been partially confirmed in ancient Mesopotamia by recent archeological research.[190]

Karl Polanyi and his collaborators have demonstrated that this type of treaty trade was a dominant mode of exchange in the ancient Near East, in pre-Columbian Mesoamerica, and in pre-colonial West Africa, and have also speculated that it existed in ancient Egypt, the Indus valley, and Shang China. I know of no definite evidence that would support this contention so far as China is concerned, although there are indirect intimations that do not contradict such an interpretation. For example, the existence of long-distance trade can be inferred, and administered trade is invariably long-distance trade. Both the tin and turquoise which are attested on Shang archeological sites could have been obtained no nearer than South China. Nephrite could have come only from the neighborhood of Khotan and Yarkand, in present-day Hsin-Chiang.[191] Cowries and whale bones must have been brought from the Yellow Sea, if not from farther afield, and the larger tortoise carapaces used in divination were obtained from *Pseudocadia anyangensis*, a species indigenous to South China. Professor Shih Chang-ju has tentatively sketched out the routes over which long-distance trade commodities reached the Shang capital.[192] These were:

The northern route, possibly used for the transport of gold, copper and maritime products : An-yang – Pa-tai – Ching-ku-tui – Wang-she-jen-ch'ung – I-tu – Huang-Hsien – Lung-k'ou.

The central route, used possibly for the transport of copper, precious stones, and maritime products : An-yang – Pa-tai – Chin-Hsiang – Kao-huang Miao – Lien-yün Shih.

The southern route, over which may have passed copper and maritime products : An-yang – Cheng-Chou – Shang-chiu – Yung-Ch'eng – Kao-huang Miao – Lien-yün Shih.

The river route, possibly a major carrier of maritime products : from An-yang along the Huan river to join the Ch'i river, and entering the Gulf of Chih-li by way of the Ch'ing river.

What is of interest in the present context is that treaty trade was undertaken as a duty or public service, that is from a status rather than a profit motive, so that its personnel came almost exclusively from the upper echelons of the social scale : the *dam-gar* of Sumeria (p. 283 above), the *tamkarum* of ancient Assyria,[193] the *pochteca* of the Aztecs,[194] the chief interpreters attached to the 'Yellow Gate' (*I-chang shu Huang-Men*) of Han China,[195] and the hundred wives of the Alafin of Ọyọ whom the explorer Richard Lander encountered near Ilaro,[195a] were entirely representative of this class of élite traders. Treaty trade was, in fact, a highly structured occupation, and could only have been a result, rather than a cause, of the formation of ceremonial cities.

Gift trade, another form of administered trade, has not been unimportant in folk societies of the past and, in its more sophisticated form of the tribute system, has been institutionalized as one of the main instruments of interaction between hierarchically ordered states and empires. In this latter role it has been particularly effective in South and East Asia and in Mesoamerica, where it has taken the form of the tribute system. We have seen in Shang China the beginnings of such a system, which subsequently provided a framework for that enigmatic schedule of provincial products known as the *Tribute of Yü* (cf. pp. 129 above), and which remained a major instrument in the conduct of foreign relations until modern times.[196] Direct evidence is inevitably lacking for the earlier phases of Mesoamerican urbanism, but Spanish chroniclers have left fairly detailed accounts of the elaborate internal, labor-based tribute system which provided substantial, perhaps even primary, support for the Aztec polity. Alonso de Zurita's succinct reconstruction of that system is as follows.[197]

> 'Tribute commonly was paid in maize, peppers, beans and cotton, and fields were designated for this purpose by each town. The rulers kept a number of slaves, who guarded and cultivated these fields with the aid of the townspeople. People whose towns did not have tributary lands set aside also came and assisted in this task, but otherwise they cultivated their own lands and did not travel elsewhere. Firewood, water, and household service also were given to the lords as tribute. Craftsmen gave tribute in that which was their specialty. Tribute was never apportioned by heads, but instead each town and craft was told what it must give and then assigned this amount among its members and brought it at the appointed time....
>
> Tribute was not paid according to the value of either fields or estates, but in crops and other products. All was produced by communal labor, save the tribute of the craftsmen, fishermen, hunters, and those who gave fruit and pottery.'

In the 16th century Aztec political aggrandizement induced some modifications in this system, notably the emergence of an incipient bureaucracy in the form of officials specifically charged with the collection of tribute and a tendency to substitute exactions in kind for labor service.

In strong contrast to administered commerce, which was almost exclusively the preserve of élite groups, was the peddling trade, whose following came from the lower end of the social scale, 'floating scum' as Pirenne called them. Huge as the aggregate volume of such trade might be, it was made up of an infinitude of small-scale transactions, and its agents contributed to the great web of commerce predominantly labor in the form of carrying and ferrying rather than the capital by which the noble entrepreneur purchased his entry into the world of exchange. And it was the peddlers, whether trading on their own account or on *commenda*, whose peripatetic mode of life and consequent lack of allegiance to a single master caused them to be viewed by the *noblesse de robe* as a potential threat to the rigid and brittle structure of society in the ceremonial cities. In addition they were not infrequently foreigners, and therefore only too often, from the point of view of these authoritarian, conservative strata of society, intruders from beyond the frontiers of the sanctified territory of the we-group. There were, of course, intermediately situated groups whose presence served to blur somewhat this too sharply drawn antithesis : kṣatriyan entrepreneurs from Gupta India, for example, who may have personally undertaken the disposal of their wares in the ports of Southeast Asia, the Hellenistic merchant of metic ancestry, and factors who established themselves in ports alongside *commenda* investment in the peddling trade. Nevertheless, middle-class traders have been considerably less prominent in historical times than have the noble entrepreneur on the one hand and the peddler on the other, and it was the dramatic juxtaposition of these two opposed groups in the traditional city which evoked Polanyi's glittering paradox: Whereas he who trades for the sake of duty and honor grows rich, he who trades for filthy lucre remains poor.[198] Typical of the sentiments evoked by the low-class trader in the literatures of the Great Traditions is that which occurs in a Burmese etiological myth of the founding of Arimaddanapura. The Lord Buddha, seeing a *preta* (or ghost)[199] in the form of a monitor lizard with a double tongue, is held to have remarked that it signified 'that the people of that city shall not till the land but shall live by merchandise, selling and buying, and their speech shall not be the words of truth but of falsehood.'[200] A similar attitude to petty commerce is evident in the legendary tale of Mencius's mother, who moved her abode from a house overlooking the market place so that her son should not copy the demeanour and acquire the dubious values of the traders chaffering there. Comparable disparagements of small-scale traders could be cited from most of the other literary traditions of the Old World, but this almost universal execration of low-class merchants has not prevented them on occasion from exercising influence on the government of cities through a variety of informal channels.

The fact that information as to the nature and volume of trade in the formative phases of urban development is meager and ambiguous needs no emphasis. Administered trade obviously by its nature came into being at a somewhat later period of urban evolution, and there is no reason to think that small-scale commerce alone was capable of focusing diffuse authority and translating it into the sacrally oriented power that is reflected in the construction of the earliest ceremonial centers. At its most effective, commerce can hardly be regarded as more than a possible element in a core complex of functionally interrelated factors operating to modify a particular level of sociocultural integration. That it can play a significant part in stimulating both social differentiation and institutional development once loci of power and authority have been established is amply attested. The Ḥijāz in the later centuries of the Jāhilīya (immediately pre-Muslim times) provides a good example, and Eric Wolf has traced the transmutation of corporate kin groups in this region into politized units based on class divisions.[201] Muḥammad's own tribe, the Quraysh, for example, in the years immediately preceding the rise of Islam found themselves in a strategic situation in the valley of Mecca which allowed them to monopolize the trade of the Ḥijāz.[202] In the words of Wellhausen, they 'skimmed the fat off the fairs in neighboring localities. Mina, Maganna, Dhul Magaz, and not least 'Ukāẓ, were like outposts of Meccan trade. In all these places we find the Quraysh, attracting business into their own hands.'[203] Withal they developed credit institutions by means of which 'the most humble sums could be turned into capital down to the participation of a dinar or a piece of gold, or even . . . half a ducat of gold.'[204] The Quraysh best able to profit from the centralizing of the Arabian economy in Mecca appear to have been those *shuyukh* who held important positions in the religious hierarchy, particularly those of the Umayyad clan, and by the 6th or 7th century AD there was already apparent among the Quraysh a differentiation according to wealth not only between clans but also between clan-members. Whereas the powerful Makhzūm and Umayyad clans occupied those sectors of the city adjoining the supremely sacred sanctuary of the Ka'bah, and were designated Quraysh of the Center, the other less wealthy clans, known as the Quraysh of the Outskirts, were relegated to the suburbs of Mecca. This incipient stratification of society on the basis of restrictions on access to the wealth generated by trade was intensified when the ties of ritual kinship binding 'protected persons' or 'clients' (*mawāli*) to their patrons, although maintained fictionally, degenerated in practice into an exploitative relationship, often initially that between creditor and debtor, but ultimately that of one class over another. Credit, pricing (Byzantine and Persian coins in circulation were weighed rather than counted : that is they were treated as bullion),[205] and wages tended to consolidate class distinctions which had arisen in this way. Concomitantly, as the population of Mecca became increasingly diverse,[206] in the interests of trade the Quraysh purposively identified the sanctified enclave surrounding the Ka'bah (the *ḥarām*), the inviolable refuge where feuds were abated and where no blood could be shed, as the focus of their territory, and subsequently attempted to extend the sacred precinct. In this way they began to undermine the tribal notion of territory as belonging to a particular kinship group. Any Arab of any tribe born in the vicinity of the Ka'bah henceforth shared in the same social rights as were enjoyed by the Quraysh. Moreover, whereas the relation of god to worshipper had previously been seen, in terms of the ancient Arabian social system, as a relation between patron and client, henceforward there can be discerned the gradual ascendency of that particular god, Allāh, who was especially concerned with relationships lying outside the ethical motivations of the kin community. Julius Wellhausen has written:

> 'Allāh is the Zeus Xenios, the protector of *gar* and *daif*, of client and guest. Within the lineage and to a lesser degree within the tribe, *rahim*, the piety of family relationship, the holiness of the blood, exercises protection. But when rights and duties exist which go beyond the lineage, then Allāh is the one who imposes them and guarantees them. He is the promoter of the *giwar* by which the natural circle of the community is widened and supplemented in a fashion which benefits above all the client and the guest.'[207]

At the same time the shrine of the Ka'bah grew in importance proportionately with both the ascendancy of Allāh and the volume of commerce transacted in its precinct.

Other events at this time were also working towards the disenfranchisement of the clans. Muḥammad's doctrine of *islam* or voluntary surrender, by insisting on the spiritual equality of all men before the absolute majesty of God, only served to establish believers in the role of clients of the God of Clients. 'And warn therewith those who dread being gathered to their Lord,' says the *Qur'ān*, that patron or intercessor they shall have none but Allāh.'[208] The induction of a believer into the *Umma Muḥammadiyyah* or community of the faithful was equivalent in great measure to emancipating him from the pervasive bonds of kin. Not he of the most powerful lineage but 'he who fears Allāh the most is most worthy of honor in the sight of God,'[209] and 'they [believers] are one *umma* over against mankind.'[210] Al-Wāqidi (died 822/3) has Muḥammad declaring as he entered Mecca that, 'God has put an end to the pride in noble ancestry. You are all descended from Adam, and Adam from dust. The noblest among you is the man who is most pious.'[211] In other words, there had been created a theocracy in the form of the Muslim community. At one stroke ultimate political authority in Mecca had been transferred from the 'Union of the Quraysh', the oligarchy of wealthy merchants who headed the several lineages, and whose only means of effective social control had resided in the sanction of the blood feud, to Allāh and his Prophet. Although Muḥammad did not intend to abolish the old tribal framework of society but simply to adapt it to encompass the new and potentially world-wide community of Islam, and although he did attempt to impose a new and more functional mode of kinship on his followers,[212] yet the outcome was nothing less than the creation of an incipient state structure.[213] Its organization was haphazard and, of the machinery for carrying out the functions of government, only the legislative one was adequately provided for, and that only as long as Muḥammad remained alive, but it marked the first crucial steps along the road of political evolution, which in subsequent decades was to lead to the empire of the Caliphate.

The rest of the story need not concern us here. The point is that the transformation from a kin-based society to a rudimentary state organization was causally connected with the burgeoning of trade in the later years of the Jāhilīya. It was its virtual monopoly of Ḥijāz commerce which made of Mecca, in the words of the *Qur'ān*, 'a city secure and at peace, with provisions flowing in from every side'.[214] But all this is concerned with the expansion of the influence of a city which already existed. The name Mecca (strictly transliterated as *Makkah*) had been mentioned in the Ptolemaic corpus in the 2nd century AD under the orthography *Makoraba*,[215] which itself derived from the Sabaean *Makuraba*, meaning 'sanctuary'. Long before the time of Muḥammad the Ka'bah had served as the central shrine of a group of clans, each of whom had deposited its ritual stone, symbolizing its own god, in the sacred precinct. Already a council known as the *Mala* and drawn from the majlises of the clans had come to constitute a sort of oligarchy of clan elders, but it was an oligarchy which lacked direct legislative power and a central executive organ. It was the expansion of Quraysh-controlled commerce which introduced dysfunctions into this kin-based mechanism of social organization on such a scale that they necessitated a structural reorganization of society about new integrative and regulative institutions capable of absorbing and reintegrating the pressures of change.

In the western parts of Southeast Asia trade played a somewhat different role in urban genesis. There it was again the agent which induced dysfunctions into an essentially tribal society,[216] so that chieftains seeking to validate the exercise of power on a supra-village level were led to adopt the Indian institution of divine kingship, a concept easily assimilable to a Southeast Asian culture in which tribal chiefs were not uncommonly regarded as epiphanies of chthonic gods. This innovation in turn initiated a process of differentiation which eventuated in the emergence of the great cult centers of Cambodia, Campā, the Pyū and Mōn territories, and in the western tracts of the Malaysian world.

If I understand his argument correctly, Colin Renfrew is also suggesting the operation of an analogous process in the Ægean culture realm. In an attempt to relate an incipient urbanization to the stimulus of trade resulting from the local development of metallurgy towards the end of the third millennium BC, this author has adopted somewhat idiosyncratic criteria of urbanism,[217] so that, from the standpoint of the present study, his ascription of urban form to those particular Ægean settlements is premature by the best part of a millennium. However, Renfrew is not alone in attributing a primary causal role to trade in the emergence of city life in this realm. Walter Fairservis has previously characterized what he calls 'the intensifying factor' (elsewhere defined as 'the motivating factor' in a heightening of cultural activity) in Cretan civilization as commercial activity.[218] In this he was elaborating and codifying the hitherto unformulated implications of virtually all Cretan specialists. Nevertheless, it is difficult to see on what evidence this interpretation can be based, for the formative stages of Cretan urbanism are still completely obscure. It is, of course, true that trade played an important part in the later stages of the process of urban development, but what its precise role was in the beginning is to be inferred with the greatest possible caution. In any case, in each of the three regions of secondary urban generation that have been considered, trade was developed in association with, and to take advantage of, institutions already operative in neighboring states, and consequently these experiences cannot be readily invoked in a discussion of primary urban generation. Moreover, in Yamato Japan a functionally analogous urban form was the product of a process of secondary generation in circumstances where trade seems not to have played an especially significant part in the transformation from village to city.

Irrigation. The practice of irrigation has often been credited with the ability to mould the structure of societies engaging in it. The late Professor Childe, for example, regarded it as a uniquely integrative type of collective endeavor,[219] and Professor Karl Wittfogel more recently has sought to demonstrate that societies based on irrigation have in the past constituted a distinctive class of social phenomena, characterized by inordinately powerful political controls and incorporating structural restraints on their evolutionary development.[220] As Wittfogel's theory of what he calls 'oriental despotism' took its rise in the author's early studies of Chinese society, it has especial relevance for our present investigation, and deserves some comment. It will be necessary, however, to discuss only those aspects, both general and specific, of his elaborately developed model which relate to the *emergence* of specialized bureaucratic élites.

Briefly Wittfogel's thesis is that, in those parts of the world where farming was based on large-scale irrigation works, the development of centralized bureaucratic states was the only effective political response to the need for organization involved in the building of the required public works, and he argues his case on the following lines. In contrast to an industrial economy, in which 'preparatory labor' provides the ultimate producer with both raw and auxiliary materials and with tools, in an hydraulic economy – that is an agrarian economy based on large-scale irrigation and flood control : what Wittfogel calls hydraulic agriculture – preparatory labor is virtually restricted to the management of a single auxiliary commodity, namely water. Moreover, whereas in modern industry preparatory labor is carried out by full-time operatives, in an hydraulic economy it tends to be the part-time responsibility of the very farmers whose productivity it is designed to boost. It is therefore in the interests of both the agriculturalists and the government that the work should be completed as quickly as possible and the farmers released to their seasonal tasks, not to mention the probable need to adjust the labor schedule to the imperatives of a seasonal climatic rhythm. Consequently, whereas preparatory work in industry is undertaken with the minimum labor force, the exigencies of time exert a strong pressure on the organizers of the hydraulic corvée to mobilize the maximum force available. It is this mustering of labor in the mass, and its deployment according to a seasonal time-table, which involves the government in planning, record-keeping, communication, and supervision on a large scale, and which leads ultimately to the formation of a corps of permanent officials, to whom Wittfogel applied the term hydraulic bureaucracy, itself an adaptation of Max Weber's *Wasserbau-Bureaukratie*.[221] Furthermore, the increasingly rational approach to ecological adaptation necessitated by the creation and implementation of an hydraulic economy laid the foundations for advances in the sciences, at the same time as it induced a level of investment in capital equipment which was specific to hydraulic farming. But the forces which brought the hydraulic bureaucracy into being were also sufficiently powerful to inhibit its political evolution. Because the hydraulic state was, by definition, entirely a response to the needs of one particular mode of ecological adaptation, the only alternative to the highly centralized *Wasserbau-Bureaukratie* was the disintegration of political authority. There was no way in which countervailing power could be institutionalized in the hydraulic polity, so that, in Wittfogel's phrase, the state became stronger than society. Government was – also in Wittfogel's words – total and despotic. All internally generated development was stultified, and change could only take the form of cyclical decay and regeneration.

It is possible to point to several structural inadequacies in this theory. In the first place, irrigation and flood control, either singly or in combination, by no means constitute a constant, unitary factor but are rather a highly diverse set of responses to physiographic, technological, and sociocultural variables, so that it is difficult to see how all the manifold and widely-differing techniques of large-scale water management, with their diverse labor requirements, could have induced a common structure in society. If the Egyptian pharaoh, the Sumerian lugal, the Chinese emperor, the Cambodian god-king, the Russian czar, and the Sapa Inca were all, and at all times, despots, then they were certainly not making use of the same political and administrative instruments to maintain their several despotisms. And neither is 'managerial bureaucrats' a useful inclusive category for Middle Eastern slave officials on the one hand, and Chinese mandarins, recruited predominantly from the élite strata of society, and the princely ministers of Hindu, Cambodian and Nuclear American society on the other. It is difficult to envisage the analytical value of a theory which is so generalized that it tells us little more than that all these rulers were despotic (however that term be defined), and that they ruled with the aid of corps of bureaucrats. And it is simply not true that these societies remained static and changeless through the centuries. But the political, social, and economic evolution and vicissitudes which all of them experienced to a greater or lesser degree are obscured by the single external criterion of comparison imposed on them by Wittfogel, namely the evolution of Western-style institutions. In any case, absolute (or total) despotism [222] is a sociologically unacceptable concept. It is probably a functional impossibility and, indeed, in each of the societies discussed by Wittfogel, it is possible to point to institutions, groups, and circumstances which prescribed bounds to the exercise of unbridled power. Corporate bodies, such as craft and merchant guilds and religious groups, the bonds of kinship, and problems of communication become apparent on even a cursory reading in the history of these societies, but scarcely less important as restraining forces were the schisms that only too frequently divided far from homogeneous élites, as well as the paternalistic values that permeated most of the Great Traditions.

When we turn to the specific basis of the theory we find that it is raised on very insecure and shifting foundations. In no instance, not even for China which provided the initial stimulus for the conceptualization of an hydraulic society, does Wittfogel attempt a detailed analysis of the function of a particular localized irrigation system in the manner subsequently undertaken by Robert Fernea in an Iraqi tribal group. In the present context it is necessary only to review, first, the evidence for the existence of developed irrigation systems during the periods of city and state formation in the several nuclear regions of urban generation, and, second, the manner in which these systems – if they existed – were managed, the way in which they articulated with the central government. In the earlier versions of his theory [223] Wittfogel traced the formation of hydraulic society in China back to the absolutist and highly centralized state of **Dz'i̯ĕn (Ch'in). Subsequently, when, with the progress of research, it became evident that Dz'i̯ĕn also witnessed the appearance of private landownership, a feature which, in this schema, is associated with complex rather than simple hydraulic society, it became necessary to seek the roots of this society in an earlier period. By 1957, when Wittfogel published the definitive version of his theory, he had pushed the origins of the Chinese mode of hydraulic society back to Shang times. However, we have already seen that there is no evidence for the management of water *on a large scale* in Shang or even Western Chou times (other, of course, than the circular inferences of Hu Hou-hsüan which we have found cause to reject), and there is no need to repeat our remarks here. To some extent this is an argument *ex silentio*, for the archeological investigation of Shang China has been only sporadic and certainly not directed towards the uncovering of irrigation systems. But it is also true that what we know of the Shang state (or states) does not accord at all closely with Wittfogel's model of an hydraulic polity.

Eberhard has carried his criticism of the Chinese aspects of the theory somewhat farther.[224] He has shown that large-scale hydraulic constructions in China were designed primarily for purposes of transportation;[225] and that, with the exception of certain military undertakings on the frontier in connection with *t'un-t'ien* colonization, they resulted either from the co-operative action of local farmers or urban groups, or from the initiative of a district official. Furthermore, the allocation of water, the time-table for its distribution, and the supervision of repairs were all the responsibility of local committees, in whose decisions the central government played no part. Eberhard has also adduced a considerable amount of evidence to show that the Chinese government was usually a less centralized affair than Wittfogel appears to suppose, but this is not a matter of direct concern to us at the moment. What is relevant to our argument is the complete lack of evidence for the existence in Shang and Western Chou times of irrigation works sufficiently large in scale for their management to have induced the crystallization of a specialized, monopolistic bureaucracy. We have, indeed, already observed that such a bureaucracy developed in response to a very different complex of circumstances in much later times. In short, the Chinese experience affords no support for a Wittfogelian interpretation of irrigation as a stimulus to social and political differentiation in the formative phases of urban development.[226]

Much the same conclusions have been drawn by Robert Adams in his recent comparative survey of the role of irrigation in ancient Mesopotamia and the Valley of Mexico.[227] In Sumer, although Early Dynastic royal inscriptions do contain occasional references to fairly substantial hydraulic undertakings, the disposition of settlements along the banks of anastomosing stream channels would seem to imply that irrigation was, generally speaking, on a small scale, making use of the natural drainage network supplemented by only a minimal extension of artificial feeder channels. In Early Dynastic times the labor forces involved in the upkeep of these systems were provided and directed by individual temples, and the allocation of water was the responsibility of temple officials. Large-scale artificial canalization did not appear until the very end of the Early Dynastic or early in the Proto-imperial period. Adams is explicit in his conclusion that, 'there is nothing to suggest that the rise of dynastic authority in southern Mesopotamia was linked to the administrative requirements of a major canal system.'[228] Writing of the Diyālā region, where large-scale canalization was not undertaken until after the time of Hammurabi, he is even more explicit in respect of urban origins : '... there is nothing... to suggest that large-scale irrigation was being practised early enough to have been a factor in the formation of the walled city-states of the Early Dynastic period.'[229]

The situation in Mesoamerica is rather more complicated. Angel Palerm has evaluated nearly four hundred references to irrigation systems in the Aztec realm late in the Prehispanic period as showing concentrations of size and incidence in the areas characterized both by higher densities of population and urban centers and by foci of political and military power.[230] However, important though these systems undoubtedly were in maintaining the subsistence base in the valley of Mexico, there is little reason to suppose that they played any part in the formation of the earliest cities and states in the area. The relatively large-scale irrigation undertakings in both the Old Acolhua domain on the eastern edge of the valley (which has formed the subject of a special study by Eric Wolf and Angel Palerm[231]) and in the vicinity of Tenochtitlán itself, are known to have antedated the arrival of the Spaniards by less than a century. More crucial to our considerations are the circumstantial arguments advanced by William Sanders for the existence of irrigation in the valley of Teotihuacán a millennium or so before the beginning of the Hispanic period.[232] It is clear that an enormous ceremonial center of the dimensions recently revealed by René Millon[233] must have depended at least partly on more intensive farming practices than the swidden and sectorial fallowing which constituted the basis of subsistence in central Mexico. In fact, it is known that in immediately Prehispanic times agricultural terracing, the use of humid bottom land (*tierra de jugo*), and so-called 'floating gardens' or *chinampas* were all used to augment production in the Aztec territories, and it is not improbable that some of these techniques were of considerable antiquity. In this context of fairly intensive agricultural activity Sanders's inference, from the siting of settlements in relation to springs, watercourses, and alluvial fans, that irrigation was also pressed into service is not inherently unreasonable.[234] But, even so, the irrigated tract could not have exceeded 38 square kilometers, an area not significantly larger than the ceremonial center of Teotihuacán itself, and of a size which in many other parts of the world has been organized informally through intervillage cooperation. It is inconceivable that the managerial requirements of an irrigation system on this relatively modest scale should have induced the formation of the complex and strongly coercive political institutions which existed in immediately Prehispanic Mexico, and which had undoubtedly arisen at a much earlier period. This is also the conclusion of Professor Adams, who writes without reservation that, 'No more than in Mesopotamia, then, and in all probability less, can we look to the managerial requirements of irrigation as the major stimulus to the growth of the institutions of the state.'[235]

In the Mayan realm much the same argument holds. It is more than likely that Mayan farmers supplemented swidden agriculture with more intensive practices, possibly *chinampa* cultivation or the exploitation of the numerous lakes and swamps of the Petén. Indeed, Eric Wolf has suggested that the importance of these water resources in the Mayan ecosystem may have been responsible for the prevalence of the water-lily as a motif in their religious art.[236] But to characterize Mayan society, on the basis of its wells (*pozos* or *cenotes*), reservoirs (*aguadas*), and cisterns (*chultunes*), as a marginal hydraulic society – as Wittfogel does – is surely to over-extend a theory already stretched to breaking point.[237] Certainly there can be no question of according the management of such small-scale local undertakings primacy as an independent causative agency in the rise of the Mayan ceremonial centers.

Nor does the Central Andean culture realm afford evidence of any such process at work. Although canal construction on a small scale had probably begun in the Virú valley in the second half of the first millennium BC, large-scale hydraulic undertakings did not appear until about the beginning of the Christian era.[238] Five hundred years or so later, during the Early Florescent period, somewhat larger canals were being integrated into the layout of monumental complexes, the architectural features on present evidence appearing to antedate the hydraulic, and by about AD 750 valley-wide irrigation schemes were being constructed, though even the most extensive of these served rather less than 100 square kilometers of farm land. However, the canal of La Cumbre in the Chicama valley was as much as 113 kilometers in length. Subsequently some intervalley irrigation systems were constructed,[239] but this was long after the appearance of ceremonial centers. In the highlands irrigation, generally speaking, developed later than in the coastal tracts, and even the Early Inca systems were strictly localized, probably the work of individual family groups.[240] Once again Robert Adams speaks forthrightly on this topic: 'We seem to have evidence here of a very gradual evolution of irrigation practices beginning with local and small-scale terracing which emphatically did not require political organization embracing a large group of communities. Large-scale, integrated programs of canalization and terracing apparently were attempted only after the perfection of the Inca state as a political apparatus controlling the allocation of mass-labor resources. They are consequences, perhaps, of the attainment of a certain level of social development; we repeat that they cannot be invoked to explain the processes by which that level was attained.'[241] Professor John Rowe is no less explicit in his conclusions with regard to the Ica valley: '... large cities appear first and major irrigation canals were only built later. It would be difficult to argue that there was any relationship between irrigation and the development of cities in this area, unless it was that the growth of cities produced a pressure on the land which was met by irrigation projects on an unprecedented scale.'[242]

The three remaining regions of primary urban generation, all in the Old World, fail to provide evidence of any significance in the present context. Irrigation is not an issue in the Yoruba territories, and, although Walter Fairservis has discovered small, localized irrigation systems of Late Amri date in the upper Hab valley and elsewhere, investigations of the Indus civilization have so far produced no definite evidence of early water control. Neither is the Egyptian archeological record at all satisfactory in this respect. Although a royal architect of the Sixth Dynasty claimed to have excavated two canals for the king,[243] he did not state their purpose. Probably, like five other canals constructed at about this time to bypass the First Cataract on the Nile,[244] they were designed for the transport of building stone, or possibly they may have formed part of a scheme of swamp reclamation. It will be recalled that Egyptian tradition credited Menes, the unifier of the kingdom, with the drainage of the land on which Memphis was built. There is also a protodynastic mace-head which appears to represent a king taking part in the construction of a watercourse for an unspecified purpose,[245] and a charter of Pepi I not only exempts the priesthood of the two pyramids of Snefru from labor service on a presumed canal, but also prohibits the enumeration of their canals, lakes (? reservoirs), and wells for taxation purposes,[246] an injunction which surely suggests that water control was at that time a purely local affair. Let Robert Adams provide our conclusion yet again:

'In short, considering the number of known records of royal building activity in the Old Kingdom, it seems only fair to regard their silence on the construction of irrigation works as strange if the demands of large-scale irrigation had indeed been responsible for the initial emergence of a pharaoh at the head of a unified state. On the assumption of a centrally administered irrigation system, the failure of officials with long and varied careers of public service to refer to administrative posts connected with canal maintenance or water distribution is equally puzzling. To the degree that an *argumentum ex silentio* ever carries conviction, the Egyptian case parallels that of Mesopotamia.'[247]

Irrigation played a by no means unimportant role in two regions of secondary urban generation, namely ancient Kambujadeśa and Ceylon. In the former of these realms the Khmers integrated the complex irrigation systems necessary for the support of their temple-cities into the ritual compass of their urban layouts, subordinating their hydraulic science to the demands of cosmo-magical symbolism, and thus demonstrating beyond doubt the priority in time of urban forms and bureaucratic institutions over the development of irrigation systems. This phenomenon is particularly evident in the neighborhood of present-day Aṅkor,[248] where costly modifications in the disposition of hydraulic features were required to render the city a worthy likeness of Indra's capital of Sudarsana. Most of the information relating to water control in Cambodia dates from the later centuries of the Khmer hegemony, and the earlier stages in its development are obscure. However, hydraulic works on a considerable scale, although of uncertain purpose, were being undertaken in the Mekong delta nearly a thousand years earlier by a kingdom known to Chinese annalists as *B'i̯u-nậm. Pierre Paris was the first scholar to draw attention to the importance of ancient canals in the then provinces of Tà Kèo and Châu-đốc,[249] and his survey was subsequently refined and extended by Louis Malleret to cover the whole of the Transbassac.250 Virtually all of the network has been reconstructed from aerial photographs, so that most of the channels have not been dated, but the manner in which they focus on the chief sites of B'ịu-nậm settlement, combined with a striking absence of archeological finds from the Transbassac in later centuries, afford sure guarantees that at least the more important elements in the system date from the B'ịu-nậm period. At present this network of canals has been plotted over a distance of some sixty miles from north to south, but this is certainly not a complete reconstruction. Neither is there agreement as to the purpose of these waterways. In the context in which they occur drainage and transport are virtually certain, a ritual function is not unlikely in certain sectors of the network,251 desalinization of the soil has been proposed (though not explicitly defined),252 and irrigation is debatable, though to my mind not a necessary implication of the evidence. The whole history of B'ịu-nậm is at present so obscure that there is no way of knowing how this hydraulic system relates chronologically to the genesis of cities in the lower Mekong valley, but the area does have the distinction of being almost the only region of nuclear urbanism which does not specifically contradict Wittfogel's thesis.

On the fringes of the former Khmer dominion, on the Gio-Linh uplands in Quảng-Tri province, there are still to be seen the remnants of a series of integrated, but small-scale, hydraulic systems which formerly combined domestic and agricultural with ritual uses.253 The folk who constructed these suites of terraces and spillways not only conceived and planned each system as a whole, but also took care to ensure that the ritualistic aspects of the microcosm that they were creating received as much attention as the ecological. For them, as they sought to ensure the welfare of their settlement by propitiation of the earth god from whose soil they garnered the usufruct, the use of water for irrigation had no priority over its use for ritual lustration and bathing, and the upper terraces were probably as important for the cult of the mountain god as for the provisioning of the settlement. In these beliefs we see prefigured the underpinnings of the great Khmer agro-architectural complexes, in which technology and economics were subordinated to an all-pervading symbolism expressing the reciprocal relations between the deity and the state. But in the case of the prehistoric irrigators of Gio-Linh there was no state apparatus to effect an appropriate deployment of labor at the correct season.254 Precisely what was the sociopolitical status of these prehistoric hill men is a matter for speculation, but it is clear enough that their activities were sustained on an informal, *ad hoc* basis which never induced the development of a corps of permanent officials.

Edmund Leach has devoted a special study to the social and political effects of hydraulic engineering in Ceylon.255 Around the city of Anurādhapura, the capital of ancient Siṅhala from the end of the first millennium BC until the 8th century AD, and later in the neighborhood of Poḷonnaruva, there developed networks of major hydraulic undertakings. The Kalāwewa canal system alone extends over some fifty-five miles and includes giant tanks at both ends. But this impressive complex was not the planned product of an hydraulic bureaucracy – indeed there is no evidence that such an organization ever played a significant part in Siṅhala politics [256] – but rather the cumulative aggregation of small units over a millennium and a half. The original Tissewewa tank at the lower end of the system, for example, was first built in about 300 BC, the Kalāwewa tank at the upper end, with a circumference before silting of nearly forty miles, about 800 years later, and modifications and elaborations were undertaken for at least another six centuries. There is no question here of centralized planning of the system in its entirety, and, moreover, fairly firm implications that the system never functioned as a unity.[257] Certainly the physical plant survived, and even expanded, through several periods of internal dissension and foreign conquest which witnessed the repeated dissolution of centralized authority. Clearly the Ceylonese experience affords no support for a Wittfogelian interpretation.

In the preceding discussion I have relied more on the opinion of experts in the cultures concerned than on my own judgment, so that these paragraphs are impressive testimony to the consensus which obtains among scholars working independently in widely divergent fields as to the role of hydraulic activity in promoting social change. In the light of this consensus we have no choice but to deny irrigation the role of an autonomous causative factor in the emergence of primary urban forms. At best it can have been but a component in an extremely intricate network of cause and effect. As for the large-scale hydraulic systems to whose managerial requirements Wittfogel ascribed the power of generating coercive bureaucratic controls, they appear to have been more a result than a cause of the emergence of state and urban organizations. This is not to deny, however, that irrigation was often one of a group of functionally interrelated factors operating to augment agricultural productivity, and thus to facilitate the realization of a social surplus whenever a locus of power had crystallized out in society. In this connection I think that it is profitable to distinguish between small-scale localized irrigation, which does little more than modulate a given ecosystem, and large-scale, regional hydraulic schemes designed to transform a system of energy transfers by complete remodelling of the landscape, a reconstitution of the ecotype in fact. The first of these modes includes the construction of dams, reservoirs, flumes, wells, and short feeder canals, and often includes techniques for the manipulation of flood water. It requires no elaborate social organization, and demands no labor resources beyond those available to an individual community, kin group, or family through the reciprocal arrangements common to folk or pre-urban societies. At this level the potential effects of irrigation are on a par with those of any other technical innovation in farming practice : as mentioned already, it contributes to an intensification of cultivation, and, probably more important, by inducing a differentiation in the productivity, and hence inequalities in the value, of agricultural land, it is likely both to encourage the emergence of social stratification and – as some land increasingly assumes the nature of a potential capital asset – tends to stimulate competition for a scarce resource, which may ultimately lead to incipient militarism. Large-scale hydraulic activity, by contrast, does make many of the technical and social demands which Wittfogel claims for it. The mobilization of large quantities of labor for the construction and maintenance of such works, and the allocation of water on an equitable basis among competing communities, alike require the presence of a superordinate authority. But they presuppose such authority : they do not call it into existence. And, as such, they can make no contribution to our present enquiry.

Warfare. The notion of the early city as an archetypal fortress, the refuge within whose protecting walls the constraints of mutual proximity and the imperatives of war combined to restructure simple aggregations of tribesmen into class-oriented, territorially based polities, has been a favorite theme of urbanists in the past,[258] and even today has not received the quietus it deserves. This is undoubtedly partly because of the ambivalence of such archeological and mythological evidence as is available. It is often difficult, for example, to distinguish in the archeological record weapons of war from those of the hunt. On general grounds it would seem that organized and sustained conflict could have played only a limited, sporadic, and unrepresentative role so long as power and authority were diffused broadly through pre-urban society. Institutionalized warfare, like large-scale hydraulic undertakings, would seem to have been a result rather than a cause of the emergence of loci of social and political power. On present evidence the Classic phase in the evolution of ceremonial centers would appear, generally speaking, to have been relatively free of warfare, which became endemic only when the concentration of wealth in the hands of bureaucratic hierarchies, coupled with a diminution in the effectiveness of religious sanctions resulting from the increasing heterogeneity of society, induced the rise of raiding, the precursor of warfare. Not until this subsequent period, which often coincided with the beginning of dynastic rule, do we find evidence on the one hand of defensive works, and on the other of new instruments of authoritarianism, the most representative of which is the institution of kingship, with its archeological manifestations in the form of palaces and royal mausolea. It is this phase which has sometimes been recognized in the archeological terminology of the regions of nuclear urbanism as the Militaristic,[259] Dynastic,[260] or Expansionist era.[261] This is not to deny, of course, that warfare may often have made a significant contribution to the *intensification* of urban development by inducing a concentration of settlement for purposes of defence and by stimulating craft specialization.

As is almost inevitably the case in the study of the socio-political changes involved in urban genesis, the most fully documented record of the emergence of warfare derives from Mesopotamia. In the uplands bordering the Fertile Crescent walls, presumably, though not incontrovertibly, designed for defense, were erected as early as 'Ubaid times at Mersin, and not long afterwards at Tepe Gawra, but larger contemporary settlements in the alluvial lowland have so far revealed no trace of such works. The earliest direct archeological evidence for warfare in this latter region may be a seal impression from Uruk, of middle Protoliterate date and depicting captured prisoners in the presence of a leader (often described as a king) of the opposing forces.[262] Circumvallation does not become apparent in this area until the very end of the Protoliterate (Jemdet Naṣr) period, after which it is virtually ubiquitous. The earliest literary reference to a specifically military organization occurs in a tablet from Early Dynastic I, found at Ur, which lists a company (*un-sìr-ra*) of soldiers in the immediate charge of sergeants (*ugula*) and commanded by colonels (*nu-bánda*).[263] From this time onwards until the emergence of the Akkadian empire a state of chronic militarism is abundantly evidenced, explicitly by textual references and pictorial representations of warfare on funerary and other monuments of one kind and another, and circumstantially by an increasing emphasis on weapons and chariots in tombs. There can be little doubt that military considerations contributed substantially to the transformation which appears to have taken place at this time from dispersed ceremonial centers, *agglomérations centrales* as Falkenstein called them,[264] to compact cities.

In the other realms of nuclear urbanism the record is even less clear, and it is seldom possible to do more than hazard a few generalized remarks about the increasing incidence of warfare as the 'Classic' periods of ceremonial complexes draw to their close. Nothing significant can be said of the role of warfare in the formative periods of political authority in the Nile and Indus valleys, or in the Yoruba territories, and of events in Southeast Asia during the earliest phase of the transition from folk to urban society there remain only mythologized versions collected by Chinese envoys to B'i̯u-nậm in the 3rd century AD. According to one of these reports, in the second half of the 2nd century AD one among a number of rulers in the lower Mekong valley used force to establish his authority over an unspecified number of settlements,[265] and in the next century a dynast known to the Chinese as *B'i̯wɒn Ṣi-mi̯wɒn (Fan Shih-man) established an empire that stretched possibly from the Bay of Bengal to the China Sea.[266]

In Mesoamerica the militaristic proclivities of the Aztec bureaucracy and of its immediate predecessors are fairly reliably documented, but the instruments used to enforce political control in the area at the period of urban genesis, some fifteen hundred years earlier, can be glimpsed only fitfully. Adams is inclined to invoke the exercise of superordinate controls of 'a ... politico-military nature' to underpin the centripetalizing power of the cult city of Teotihuacán,[267] and there is a certain amount of representational evidence to support this interpretation. An Early Classic stele from the Mayan ceremonial center of Tikal in present-day Guatemala, for example, depicts an armed escort, presumably accompanying a trading mission, from Teotihuacán. Adams is also prepared to contemplate the possibility of Teotihuacán having achieved military control over Kaminaljuyú, in view of the enormous quantities of central Mexican pottery which have come to light there. At a rather later period weapons begin to appear in Teotihuacán murals, as well as representatives of military orders; and, finally, it is not unlikely that the destruction and looting which accompanied the partial abandonment of the great ceremonial complex at some time prior to AD 750 may have been the result of external military action rather than, or in conjunction with, an internal uprising. Towards the end of the Classic period the fortress city of Xochicalco was founded, probably by a Mixtec-speaking group, in the arid territory of southern Morelos, to the southward of present-day Mexico City. Built on a steep hillside only too evidently chosen for its defensive qualities, and further protected by a series of walls and moats, it was the forerunner of numerous other Militarist-period cities,[268] among which was Tula in Hidalgo, now believed to be the famous *Tollán*, capital of a Toltec group.[269]

In the Maya realm the earliest unequivocal evidence of warfare occurs, towards the close of the Classic period, in the Usumacinta valley on the western border of the Petén, indicating that it came in the form of external aggression rather than having been generated within Mayan society itself. The evidence takes the form of representations both of warrior figures on public monuments and of raids and the taking of captives in the Bonampak murals from Chiapas.[270] At the same time the inhabitants of certain lowland settlements transferred their abodes to more easily defended upland sites. Among famous cult centers abandoned at this time were Copán and Uaxactún. In Yucatán and the highlands militaristic immigrants from the north reorganized many of the populations into compact cities but, between these two axes of revival, the ceremonial centers of the Petén have mostly remained deserted until the present. It has been suggested that the Quiché legend, which tells how Hunahpu and Xbalemque descended into the underworld to defeat the rulers of Xibalba in a series of ceremonial ball games, may preserve an archetyped, mythologized version of the sequence of events in which the highlanders usurped the power of the old Petén theocracies.[271]

The Peruvian Co-tradition illustrates a feature common to several culture realms, namely the emergence, at certain times and in traditions of essentially open urban forms, of an emphasis on defense which was expressed in a deliber-

GENESIS OF THE CEREMONIAL CENTER

ate choice of protective terrain, often a mountain, crag, or commanding promontory. Such incidental, and often relatively shortlived, resorts to defensive measures, were quite distinct from the general and widespread construction of fortifications which characterized the Militaristic phase of urban development. In Peru organized warfare on a considerable scale first became evident in the earlier half of the first millennium AD,[272] although hilltop redoubts had been in use during the preceding five centuries. In the 4th or 5th century AD, however, so-called *castillos* began to appear on the north coast, presumably as a response to the Tiahuanacoid impact.[273]

In Middle America the earliest fortified site is Becán in Campeche, which probably dates from late in the Classic phase, say about AD 800. Here, a moat encircling the city provides evidence of a preoccupation with defense, but the case of Monte Albán in the valley of Oaxaca is more difficult to evaluate. At a height of 1,300 feet above the valley floor, the architects carved out of the rock a platform 3,117 feet long by 1,476 wide, on which to set a complex of courtyards, stairways, pyramids, and tombs, all arranged along a north-south axis. Any attempt to interpret the function of this ceremonial center has to balance its obvious defensive advantages against the large number of tombs which suggest that headmen of many surrounding districts were brought there to rest, and against – what must be borne in mind in any discussion of site values in Nuclear America – the desirability of raising temples as near to the heavens as possible. The fact that no source of water has been located within the precincts of the ceremonial center presumably implies the existence of a locus of power capable of organizing the delivery of a regular and reliable supply from the valley below.

Ceylon provides another ambivalent example of a ceremonial center on a site chosen for the best defensive advantage, though possibly influenced by other reasons as well. Towards the end of the 5th century AD King Kaśyapa I built himself a fortified palace on the crag known as the Sīgiriya or Lion Mountain. The fact that the site was virtually impregnable doubtless played an important part in its selection, but it is surely also significant that Kaśyapa modelled his palace on the celestial city, covering the rock face with apsarases and heavenly beings to signify that it was indeed the city of the gods. Who is to say at this distance of time which consideration weighed the more heavily with the King, defense or symbolism, particularly in view of the discussion to follow in Chapter Five? The most likely interpretation is that King Kaśyapa was in no way loth to utilize a site which achieved both aims at one and the same time.

It is only too evident that the materials that can be gleaned relative to the development of institutionalized warfare, meager as they are, afford no grounds for ascribing that activity a primary causative role in urban genesis. Like large-scale irrigation, it presupposes rather than generates superordinate authority. Tribal conflicts, by contrast, are endemic to non-urbanized societies at all levels of development, and are not necessarily self-augmenting. Indeed, only comparatively rarely, in the absence of sustaining institutions, have they been able to transgress the limitations as to duration and continuity imposed by the kinship-oriented value system of a folk society. There is some reason to think that warfare may have played a relatively more important part in stimulating social differentiation and inducing institutional development in regions of secondary urban generation, but in the realms of primary urban generation it appears, in the light of present knowledge, to have arisen only when emergent foci of power began to manipulate technological innovation to create gross inequalities in productivity. With this interpretation the Chinese evidence, exiguous and ambivalent though it be, is entirely consonant. Offensive weapons, together with settlement defenses in the form of *hang-t'u* walls, first appear in the archeological record during the Lung-shan period, and the massive circumvallation at Cheng-Chou would seem to imply an urgent need for protection against assault during the earlier years of the Shang era. During the later phase of this dynasty archeological, epigraphic, and perhaps literary, remains bear testimony to the endemic character of warfare, a situation which has already been the subject of comment in Chapter One.

Religion. As long ago as 1864 Fustel de Coulanges proposed that the cities of ancient Greece and Italy had taken their origins in the designation of certain tracts of territory as sanctuaries common to diverse tribes, and that citizenship had derived from a shared adherence to the cults of the gods of these sanctuaries.[274] Since that time the role of religion in urban genesis has been largely ignored in favor of commerce and warfare as supposed dependent causative agents. Although it is more than dubious if any single factor should be accorded this absolute primacy, there may be some validity in Fustel de Coulanges's interpretation, not only so far as it concerns the Classical world of the Mediterranean but also in relation to other realms of nuclear urbanism. Despite the possible bias inherent in the nature of the evidence, to which we have referred on p. 225, the combined testimony of archeology, epigraphy, mythology, literature, representational art, and either extant or recorded architecture leaves no room to doubt that religion provided the primary focus for social life in the immediately pre-urban period. In Fustel de Coulanges's straightforward phrasing, 'ce qui faisait le lien de toute société, c'était un culte.'[275] Indeed, the religious component is almost alone in having left in several of the realms of nuclear urbanism a more or less continuous succession of surviving material traces through from the phase of Developed Village Farming to fully evolved urban life.

In the archeological record of Nuclear America shrines are recognizable almost as early as settled village life itself.[276] In the Old World they are found in a comparable ecological situation at Jericho by about 7000 B C, and not much later at Çatal Hüyük, where it is alleged a special quarter of the settlement was devoted to religious purposes. In Mesopotamia proper shrines are first recognizable with certainty in a series of 'Ubaidian temples at Eridug, though the much earlier *tholoi*-like Halafian structures of the surrounding uplands were almost certainly also cultic in purpose. It should be remembered, though, that there is no guarantee that the relatively insignificant exposures of pre-'Ubaidian sites such as Sāmarrā, Hassuna, and Jarmo – where shrines have not been discerned – provide a representative picture of village morphology. So far village shrines have not been discovered in pre-dynastic Egypt, but this is the result of the settlement pattern of that time having been buried deep in Nile mud. In the Indus valley, too, the fact that such shrines have not been recognized must be considered less an indication of their absence than a reflection of the prevailing archeological preoccupation with the great cities of later days; though Fairservis has brought to light village cult centers in the Baluch hills and southern Afghanistan which may eventually prove to have been expressive of processes of social change analogous to those which operated on the Indus plains. In both these regions there is presumptive evidence that the limitations of archeological techniques and the idiosyncrasies of archeological practice make it less than certain that village shrines were wholly lacking in pre-urban contexts. Much the same is true of pre-dynastic North China, where such sanctuaries have not yet been discerned on Lung-shan sites. However, excavation has been so sporadic that it is by no means certain that they did not exist. In any case the quantity and variety of ceremonial vessels, combined with the practice of scapulimancy, leave no room to doubt the existence of a class of ritual specialists in Lung-shan society. It is, moreover, extremely unlikely, if not impossible, that the great ceremonial centers which distinguished each of these regions in subsequent centuries should have been born fully fledged and without a prior evolutionary development.

It is also more than probable that specialized priests were among the first persons to be released from the daily round of subsistence labor. Of course, the presence of such specialists is not always easily discernible in the archeological record and, even when their existence can be proved, it is not inevitably indicative of their status in society as a whole. This is particularly true of interpretations based on representational art, which does not always afford means of distinguishing between specific events and recurrent rituals. However, whatever may have been their antecedents, early in the process of urban generation priestly hierarchs came to assume the roles of economic administrators, and gathered into their hands control over emergent superordinate redistributive instruments.

It needs no further emphasis beyond that provided in previous sections of this chapter to establish that the earliest foci of power and authority took the form of ceremonial centers, with religious symbolism imprinted deeply on their physiognomy and their operation in the hands of organized priesthoods. This itself is powerful testimony to the role of religion in the complex of interacting factors involved in the process of urban genesis. It does not seem very probable, even if economic or technological factors had functioned as primary causative agents in the focusing of the predominantly diffuse authority of pre-urban society in the manner attested by both archeological-epigraphic and annalistic-literary evidence, that the material manifestation of that authority would have assumed the form of the ceremonial complex. Temporary fluctuations in the distribution of social and political power may, it is conceded, have arisen through the agencies of commerce, warfare or technology, but to achieve permanence such power had to be validated by some form of authority. This these factors, concerned primarily with the satisfaction of material needs, could not provide, whereas the shrine, which had from the beginning assuaged man's deepest anxieties by providing assurances of the continuity of the world as he knew it, was able to draw on supramundane sources of authority. In this connection it is pertinent to recall that Walter Fairservis has tentatively suggested that the rise of ceremonial centers in Baluchistan and the Indus valley was a response to anxieties engendered by food shortages resulting from population increase.[277] Moreover, Robert Adams has also pointed out that both Mesopotamia and Mesoamerica were characteristically regions of ecological instability, and that the earliest deities to make an appearance were those associated with the cycle of the seasons, of plant and animal regeneration, and of fertility in general.[278] Dumuzid or Ama-ušum-gal-an-ak (= Quickener of the [so-called] Date-cabbage) was held responsible for the date harvest, while the name of the goddess Inannak (< Nin-an-ak) signified 'the Lady of the Date Clusters'.[279] Enki, tutelary deity of Eridug, was the god of sweet waters, Ashnan bore a name that denoted grain, Lahar one that meant sheep, and Sumugan signified flocks of wild asses and gazelles.[280] In central Mexico Tlaloc (or rather the deity subsequently known as Tlaloc) was not only the god of rain but also of life itself. It would seem that a developing preoccupation with the seasonal cycles of plant and animal life was providing a new and more powerful integrative focus for group belief. Nor is it difficult to envisage how those persons associated with the shrine to one of these gods of fertility, and therefore closest to the fount of authority, should have come ultimately to mediate that authority and control the power derived from it. Cultivator and craftsman alike (and in pre-urban society these were predominantly but different aspects of the same individual), by submitting to the authority of the divine presence in the shrine, placed themselves within the economic power of the ritual experts who managed the affairs of the deity. But administration of production inevitably hardened into control, and the farmer who once brought his offerings as a sign to the gods that they should begin their great work of fructification, and who took part in the seasonal festivals that were for him nothing less than cosmic crises, eventually found himself caught up in a redistributive system whose re-allocative demands were sanctioned by divine authority. There had, in fact, been forged a new instrument for the organization of sacred, economic, social, and political space.

At the same time, as society developed cumulatively in scale and complexity, so it would have required an increasingly sophisticated set of ethical conceptions to give purpose and direction to life. This would have been especially necessary as there crystallized out new groups who directed their energies to the achievement of novel and unfamiliar goals. The old norms and customs, forged through time to sustain the solidarity of society, would have failed to provide both sanction for innovation and authority for new types of decisions. Only a greatly amplified ethical system would have been capable of sanctioning these unaccustomed goals, and of integrating into a coherent and viable synthesis the new values that resulted. This the ceremonial centers seem to have been able to achieve, as they assumed the role of chief innovative foci for both the restructuring of society and the advance of those branches of technology concerned with ritual display. They functioned as instruments for the dissemination through all levels of society of beliefs which, in turn, enabled the wielders of political power to justify their goals in terms of the basic values of that society, and to present the realization of class-directed aims as the implementation of collectively desirable policies. At the same time the rituals and ceremonies celebrated in the great cult centers would appear to have acted as mirrors to society at large, as reflectors of a sacrally sanctioned social order, as inculcators of the attitudes and values appropriate to that order, and, not least, as symbolic statements about the nature of society, which could serve as guides to action for its constituent individuals and groups. In other words they may be regarded as idealized structural models which, while giving ritual expression to the moral framework of social organization, defined the approved status relationships between groups and between 'social persons' (Radcliffe-Brown's term[281]) within those groups.

The Morphology of the Ceremonial Center

A cursory survey of the ground plans of ceremonial centers in the several realms of nuclear urbanism suggests that these complexes could assume either compact or dispersed form. In either case the focus of the settlement pattern was the sacred enceinte, wherein were grouped the habitations of the gods and of their ministrants, together with the dwelling places of the lesser servants and attendants of both. In the compact form of the ceremonial city the population density in the immediate neighborhood of the shrine was considerably higher than in the surrounding countryside, a pattern which is usually interpreted to mean both that a high proportion of the inhabitants were engaged in farming and that the artisanry of the district were concentrated in the ceremonial city. In the dispersed form the population density within the immediate environs of the cult center was not significantly higher than in the locality at large, a state of affairs which must surely imply that the permanent dwellers in the ceremonial center were restricted to, at most, the ruling élite, a priesthood, a selected group of craftsmen, and perhaps a praetorian guard.

Owing to the exiguous nature of the record in most of the regions of nuclear urbanism, and in view of the predilection of archeologists for excavating within the confines of the sacred enclaves, it is evident that the categorization of any particular ceremonial city as compact or dispersed must often be largely subjective. However, sufficient evidence has accumulated for us to be certain that such polar types as those described above did exist, and probably a fairly complete spectrum of intermediate forms as well. For Lower Mesopotamia in ancient times, for example, Henri Frankfort has calculated urban population densities which turn out to be roughly comparable with those of present-day Aleppo or Damascus.[282] That Tenochtitlán and the five Epigonal Toltec capitals were also compact settlements is attested by the writings of early Spanish chroniclers.[283] At Uaxactún in the Petén, by contrast, the Ricketsons calculated, allowing five persons for each house mound, that the density of population *in the immediate vicinity of the ceremonial precinct* probably did not exceed that of present-day New York state *as a whole*,[284] which was considerably less than the density estimated by Gordon Willey during his investigation of a *rural* area in the Belize valley of British Honduras, remote from any large ceremonial focus.[285] Moreover, the sacred enclaves of the Petén invariably yield little evidence of mass settlement, either in the form of dwelling mounds or middens. At Uaxactún, for example, despite a lengthy search only one significant midden could be discovered.[286] In the lowlands, at any rate, Maya house mounds seem to have been grouped in small clusters, often three sharing a single court, throughout the territory served by a ceremonial center, and showing a particular affinity for *bajo* fringes.[287] This pattern of scattered villages, hamlets, and even individual houses, grouped about a more or less centrally situated ceremonial complex is closely analogous to that reconstructed for Shang China. In classical Cambodia, at the early Mōn ceremonial seats such as Nakhon Pathom, and in early Java, it appears virtually certain (despite the superficiality of archeological investigation in the latter two regions) that the settlement pattern was also dispersed. Similarly there can be little doubt that in early Dynastic Egypt the mortuary cities of the Pharaohs housed no dense populations. The case of Teotihuacán is particularly interesting, as it illustrates the manner in which archeologists can differ among themselves in the interpretation of a site. Whereas the late George C. Vaillant regarded the complex as 'no residential city but a great ceremonial center given over to temples and houses for the people engaged in religious activity',[288] William T. Sanders is explicit in his view that it was the site of 'large, resident, non-food-producing, economically specialized populations'.[289] Finally and not unexpectedly, there appear to have been a large number of ceremonial complexes intermediate between the two extremes, cult centers in which, although the central enclave was set among the dwellings of the populace, the density of these latter was not significantly greater than that exemplified by neighboring villages. Among these were probably some Burmese temple-cities such as Ava, Amarapura, Sagaing, and Tagoung, Athens immediately prior to 431 BC, Etruscan Rome, and the great cult centers of the Indus valley. Still other ceremonial centers seem to have existed close to, but distinct from, populous cities. The Cham complex at Mĩ-sơn, not far distant from Trà-kiệu, possibly some of the Inca foundations, and the Tzacualli-period (c. 200 BC) settlement on the site of later Teotihuacán, would seem to have belonged to this class.

Although a considerable number of developed ceremonial centers were in their 'classic' period inhabited by compact aggregations of population, it is by no means certain that they had taken this form from the beginning. In Lower Mesopotamia, for example, we should perhaps be chary of projecting the Early Dynastic compact urban pattern too far into the past, for excavations at Protoliterate and Warqa levels have been restricted virtually to temple precincts.[290] Similar circumstances prohibit an informed evaluation of the Cretan evidence, for scholarly attention has again been directed to the maturely developed cities and palaces of the Middle Minoan period (c. 2000–1580 BC) to such an extent that it is impossible to discuss their origins. In the valley of Mexico, even if Sanders is correct in his contention that Teotihuacán was a compact city, evidence is accumulating, as noted above, which indicates the existence of a ceremonial center with dispersed population in the same locality as early as the Tzacualli phase,[291] to say nothing of the implications of the well-known site of Cuicuilco in the Pedregal of San Angel. It is, in short, still possible to argue either that temple-cities were initiated in both compact and dispersed forms, or that the dispersed condition was a functional stage in a lineal development towards the compact ceremonial complex. A great deal more work will have to be done before this problem can be settled with any degree of certainty, but it may be significant that not a few of the early dispersed temple-cities were subsequently transformed into, or at least superseded by, compact foci of population. In parts of Peru this may have come about with the rise of the Chimú kingdom in the first half of the 14th century AD, and in any case certainly with the advent of the Incas. In Egypt the compact city seems to have appeared for the first time at Tell el-Amarna in the 14th century BC, in North China possibly during the Ch'un-Ch'iu period, though it did not become the standard form until Chan-Kuo times. In Java compact concentrations of population in the *pasisir* existed contemporaneously with dispersed ceremonial complexes in the interior from some time in about the 10th century AD. In Cambodia the dispersed ceremonial city persisted until the fall of the classical Khmer empire in the earlier part of the 15th century, and among the lowland Maya until the abandonment of the cult centers by their priests and rulers in the 10th century, though the more northerly temple-cities in Yucatán were apparently subsequently transformed into compact settlements under Toltec influence.

Any evaluation of the situation on the Indian subcontinent in post-Harappān centuries is rendered extremely difficult by the obscurity which envelops all aspects of early South Asian history, and particularly the uncertainty as to whether we are dealing with a tradition of urbanism inherited from Harappān times or with a second, independently generated, cycle of urban life. Whereas most authors have tacitly assumed the latter to be true, G. R. Sharma, the excavator of Kauśāmbī, the site of a city with walls some four miles in circuit located not far from the Jumna-Ganges confluence, has stated the case, based largely on the stratification and Harappān-style layout and construction techniques employed in the Ganges valley, for the continuity of urban life.[292] In any case there was a remarkable burgeoning of urban forms on the northern plains of India during the second quarter of the first millennium BC. It is difficult to know how much weight to assign to the mention of urban forms in early Sanskrit literature, but it can hardly be doubted that descriptions of allegedly Vedic cities are, as in the case of references to Shang cities in Chou literature, projections into the past of concepts current in later ages. Moreover, the difficulty of dating early Hindu religious texts is so formidable as to have become proverbial. Most of them were written down for the first time only in the latter part of the 18th century or early decades of the 19th and, as Max Müller observed nearly a century ago, each constitutes an unvarying recension of a single standard text. It follows, therefore, that the principles of textual criticism and paleography are largely inapplicable. By the time of the *Taittirīya Araṇyaka*, however, when the term *nāgara* is first encountered in the sense of city, it does seem to be implied that the city was a compact focus of population.

In some instances it is possible to discern in the process of urban compaction an intermediate stage of synoecism, when a group of discrete settlements, hitherto subject only to the payment of tribute when the strongest among them was capable of exacting it, were brought under the direct rule of a dynast or religious oligarchy in a central settlement. Not infrequently this stage of urban development has been remembered – or perhaps sometimes ascribed – in etiological myth. The classic and eponymous example is that which attributes to the semi-legendary King Theseus of Athens an important extension of the power of the central cult center over the farmers of the surrounding countryside:

'... Most [of the Athenians] had been used to living in the country.
From very early times this had been more characteristic of the Athenians than of others. Under Kekrops and the first kings, down to the reign of Theseus, Attika had always consisted of a number of independent townships,

each with its own town-hall and magistrates. Except in times of danger the king at Athens was not consulted; in ordinary seasons they carried on their government and settled their affairs without his intervention; sometimes they even waged war against him as, for example, the Eleusinians, [leagued] with Eumolpus, did against Erechtheus. In Theseus, however, they had a king as prudent as he was powerful, who not only reorganized the state in other respects but also abolished the councils and magistracies of the minor settlements, and established them in the single council-chamber and town-hall of the present city. Individuals might still enjoy their private property as before, but they were henceforth compelled to use Athens as the sole capital, which thus counted all the inhabitants of Attika among her citizens, so that when Theseus died he left a great state behind him. And from his time even to this day the Athenians have celebrated at the public expense a festival called the Synoekia [Feast of Union] in honor of the goddess.'[293]

The religious aura that permeated the administrative role of the acropolis in the days before the synoecism was emphasized in Thukydides's concluding remarks:

'Before this the city consisted of the present citadel and the district beneath it looking rather toward the south. This is shown by the fact that the temples of other deities, besides that of Athene, are in the citadel; and even those that are outside it are mostly situated in this quarter of the city, as that of Olympian Zeus, of the Pythian Apollo, of Earth, and of Dionysus in the Marshes ... There are also other ancient temples in this quarter ...'[294]

Athens remained a dispersed ceremonial city long after the mythical age of Theseus. Possibly the final stage in the process of concentration was delayed until Pericles brought the countryfolk within the city walls on the outbreak of the Second Peloponnesian War in 431 B.C.[295] Prior to that date the permanent inhabitants of the city proper comprised only political and religious officials, together with a corps of artisans. Sparta provides an instructive contrast to Athens, for it retained its dispersed form until the end. In the words of Thukydides, 'The city is neither built in a compact form nor adorned with magnificent temples and public edifices, but is comprised of villages after the old fashion of Hellas.'[296]

The consolidation of the city of Rome apparently followed a similar pattern. For long the politico-religious community of the Quirites, established within a walled enceinte that enclosed the Palatine Hill and its environs, was quite distinct from both the peasantry of the surrounding countryside and the community of merchants on the Aventine Hill.[297] There is evidence that there was a tendency for these diverse elements to fuse into a unity through several centuries,[298] but the instrument which finally completed the consolidation of the city appears to have been the Icilian law *de Aventino publicando* as late as the middle of the 5th century B.C.[299]

A striking parallel to the archetypal synoecism of Athens can be drawn from Upper Burma. According to a legend preserved in the *Hman Nan Yazawin*, the ceremonial center of Arimaddana[pura] was formed from the union of nineteen villages.[300] Originally each village had its own *nat* or local guardian spirit, but in the course of time an especially efficacious *nat* who inhabited the summit of Mount Poppa came to dominate and, in some respects, to subsume the others, so that it acted as a centralizing principle for the surrounding territory in the manner that we have come to associate with the proto-urban cult center. According to Burmese chronicles the city was finally consolidated in AD 849, when King Pyinbya enclosed the still discrete settlements with a wall.

In ancient Mesopotamia the picture is less clear, but there are indications that at least some of the city-states of dynastic Sumer may have been formed through a process of synoecism.[301] Lagash, for example, was essentially an agglomeration of a score of shrines which appear to have been brought together in one polity, and there was also a plurality of temples even in that one section of the city of Khafājah which has been excavated. It has also been suggested that the settlements of Kulab and Eannak which, although mentioned in early records, subsequently disappeared as discrete political entities, were subsumed by a synoecic process into the city of Uruk during the reign of, and perhaps at the instigation of, Enmerkar.[302]

Although etiological myth often attributes the transformation from dispersed to compact city to a culture hero, a Theseus or a Pyinbya, and although there is sometimes reason to suspect a military motivation (cp. p. 299 above), I have been unable to correlate this structural development generally with changes in political or economic organization, or with innovations in technology as applied to agriculture, industry, transport, or warfare. It is worth emphasizing, however, that neither did the advent of the compact city invariably coincide with any distinctive change in social organization. Some authors have assumed somewhat gratuitously that it signalled a modulation from a society of mechanical solidarity to one of organic solidarity.[303] This does not, in fact, appear to have been invariably the case. As we shall argue in a subsequent section (pp. 390–1), mere compaction was not sufficient to induce an organic solidarity in society, though it was, of course, a prerequisite for that increase in social interaction which constitutes the basis of modern urbanism.

It follows from the fact that the ceremonial city represented only an initial stage in the transformation from mechanical to organic social solidarity that the great gulf between city and country, which has provided the conceptual framework for most urban investigation since the time of Louis Wirth,[304] was still incipient. Nor did the ceremonial city consist solely of an aggregation of distinct and discrete social universes, each dependent on its own liens with surrounding territories, such as Oscar Lewis has postulated for certain traditional-style cities in Latin America, and which is characteristic of urban forms in the more northerly Yoruba territories. There is reason to believe, though, that the craftsman or menial performing his tasks within the confines of the sacred city often maintained close relations with his family in the countryside. The countryfolk did not feel themselves to be disenfranchized or in any significant way different from those of their number who happened to have been selected for service within the temple-city. For all and each the ceremonial complex represented a reassurance of cosmic certainty; it was the sanctified terrain where were manifested those hierophanies that guaranteed the seasonal renewal of cyclic time, and where the splendor, potency, and wealth of their rulers symbolized the well-being of the whole community, potentate and peasant alike. The significant division in society came not between city and countryside, but rather between ruler and ruled.

The Secularization of the Ceremonial Center

From the preceding discussion it will have become evident that these ceremonial centers, both compact and dispersed, were pre-eminently instruments of orthogenetic transformation.[305] Economic institutions were subordinated to the religious and moral norms of society, which also provided sanction for a rigid social stratification. Change was mediated by literati in terms of a classical tradition, which they refined into a sacred canon that ensured the continuity of culture and constituted the basis of a future urban-based Great Tradition. These were temple-cities where, in the words of a Khmer monarch, resounded '... the chant of sacred texts recited by generations of teachers and disciples, and [where] the word of God, proclaimed by joyful crowds, muffled the staccato sounds of musical instruments.'[306]

It should be added that this orthogenetic role was invariably sustained long after the secularization of the ceremonial center, a fact, incidentally, which does nothing to facilitate our understanding of the process of secularization. In some instances the initial stages were undoubtedly associated with the rise of kingship, sometimes from within the sacral hierarchy, but more frequently from without, when a secular warrior was confirmed in his tenure of office by a series of military crises. In either case the office of kingship constituted a focus of power which constantly tended to expand the legitimate areas of secular authority at the expense of those of sacral jurisdiction. Once again Mesopotamia provides the most fully documented account of this change in the loci of power and authority, and Thorkild Jacobsen has been able to trace a shift in authority from that of sacerdotal hierarchs towards that of a militaristically oriented leadership.[307] Whereas the *en*, from his first mention in the earliest Protoliterate tablets, subsumed in his person both supreme administrative power and religious authority within the temple community,[308] from Early Dynastic II times onwards he retained only a religious responsibility. The erosion of his secular power appears to have been a result of the emergence of a new office, that of *lugal*, a term meaning literally 'great man', but usually translated as 'king' and certainly denoting paramount political authority during most of the Early Dynastic period.309 A third title, that of *ensik*, after alternating with lugal during the Early Dynastic period, eventually came to signify the appointed governor of a city.310 By analysis of a corpus of mythological and epic materials first recorded at a considerably later epoch, Jacobsen has also been able to infer the existence in Protoliterate, and possibly earlier, times of a popular assembly (*unkin*) of free males which, while leaving day-to-day policy in the hands of a council of elders (probably made up of the heads of corporate descent groups311), also rendered judgments and, in time of crisis, delegated power temporarily to a war leader. In other words the institution of kingship was introduced to meet the challenge of emergencies with which the primitive democracy of the assembly was unable to cope. Examples of this procedure can be found even as late as the Akkadian period, by which time the role of the assembly had become extremely circumscribed:

> In the 'Common of Enlil', a field
> belonging to Esabad, the temple of Gula,
> Kish assembled
> and Iphurkish, a man of Kish,
> . . .
> They raised to kingship.312

In the early days of the institution the lugal held office for a limited period and was scrupulously careful to obtain the consent of the assembly which had elected him before taking action, so that we find even the mighty Gilgamesh consulting both the council of elders and the assembly before making war. But it is also significant that the text adds the comment that when these two bodies announced their agreement 'his heart rejoiced, his liver was made bright'.313 Clearly Gilgamesh was not averse to assuming the responsibility inherent in his position. Nor were subsequent lugals reluctant to exploit the situation for their personal benefit. Marduk, for instance, is recorded as exacting the price of complete freedom of action before agreeing to deliver the gods from Ti'āmat:

> If I am to be your champion,
> vanquish Ti'āmat, and save you [lit. keep you alive],
> then assemble and proclaim my lot supreme.
> Sit down together joyfully in Ubshu-ukkinnak,
> and let me, like you, by word of mouth, determine destiny.
> So that whatever I shall decide shall not be altered,
> and my spoken command shall not [come] back [to me], shall not be changed.314

The result both of this tendency towards an extension of personal authority, and of the development of a state of chronic conflict as an increasingly large number of political units competed for limited resources, was the establishment of kingly rule in all the cities of Mesopotamia; but it was a rule which ultimately took the precaution of founding its authority on inherent divinity. The first Mesopotamian ruler known explicitly to have made such a claim was the Akkadian Naram-Sin (2291–2255 BC), but posthumous apotheosis had been accorded previous rulers, and still earlier references to divine parentage may not always have been intended metaphorically. At the same time the institution of kingship was further buttressed by the right of hereditary succession.

Robert Adams has demonstrated an analogous process of secularization of authority in the Valley of Mexico.[315] There, too, he discerned the resolution of an originally undifferentiated politico-religious authority into the two distinct components of a sacerdotal, predominantly peaceful, and a secular, militaristically inclined, leadership. In Teotihuacán the evident ceremonial character of the major architectural features, the general predominance of religious themes, and the manufacture of preponderantly ritual and cultic artifacts leave little doubt that government was essentially theocratic. During the lengthy period when hegemony was passing, probably first to Cholula and Xochicalco, but in any case ultimately to Tula, followers of new militaristic cults began to acquire power at the expense of the old theocratic leadership.[316] The tension that developed between these two loci of power seems to have been reflected in the legendary conflict between the gods Quetzalcóatl and Tezcatlipoca. In Paul Kirchhoff's reconstruction of events the former was the tutelary deity of a priestly hierarchy, whereas Tezcatlipoca was closely associated with a warrior élite, particularly with a temporal leadership which, as in Mesopotamia, became hereditary and finally succeeded to all intents and purposes in expelling Quetzalcóatl from the Mexican pantheon.[317] And, also on the Mesopotamian pattern, is the manner in which an Aztec ruler was, like Gilgamesh, forced to use a combination of personal charisma, persuasion, and cajolery in order to manipulate or circumvent the wishes of an assembly of elders and warriors. The following account was penned by the Spanish chronicler Alonso de Zurita:[318]

> 'The killing of a merchant or a royal messenger was regarded as a justification for war. The ruler would call together all of the elders and warriors to consider this course of action, informing them that it was desired to make war on a particular province and what the reason for it was. If it was for one of the indicated reasons, all said that this was justified and that the cause was sufficient. If it was for another, lesser reason, they indicated two or three times that war should not be declared, and on some occasions the rulers acceded to their wishes. But if the ruler persisted and they were called together repeatedly, they said that they would follow his wishes, that they

had now informed him of their opinions and would disclaim further responsibility.'

Adams has traced the several steps in the process which finally produced a fully constituted royal authority in the Aztec realm.[319] Probably it was initiated, or at least expedited, when Itzcóatl's victory over the Tepanecs of Azcapotzalco provided new territories which could serve as an independent economic base both for the monarchy and for the nobility. Soon afterwards the rules of succession, as reported in the *Codex Ramirez*, were revised so as to restrict the choice of a new ruler to the close relatives of his predecessor, at the same time as the picture histories which recorded past practices were burnt.[320] Subsequently, a further strengthening of the power of the king at the expense of that of the calpullec council, as the result of new military conquests, was reflected in the imposition of increasingly stringent criteria of distinction not only between nobility and commoners but also between the king and the nobility. Finally Moctezuma II (1502–1520) consummated the process when, with the aid of a purge, he substituted a patrimonial type of bureaucracy, with members chosen from the nobility, for the old calpulli-based corps of advisers.

In none of the other regions of primary nuclear urbanism can the process of secularization be traced with even the low degree of precision possible in Mesopotamia and Mesoamerica. In ancient Egypt the Pharaoh seems to have developed out of the conception of a chieftain endowed with power over natural forces, a 'rain-maker king' as Frankfort has it, who from the beginning laid claim to divine status; but of the process by which the institution of kingship evolved we know practically nothing.[321] Even less can be deduced about the situation in Peru, although it is possible that a reorganization of the government undertaken by the Inca may have reflected a desire on the part of secular elements to extend the reach of their authority – or, possibly more accurately, was a reaction to an attempt by sacerdotal groups to retain a power that was being steadily eroded by a militaristic and expansionist bureaucracy.[322] In South India and Southeast Asia the earliest kings appear to have been tribal chieftains who had sought to validate supra-village rule on the only adequately flexible pattern known to them, namely the Indian political model structured about divine kingship. It is, for example, this stage of the acculturation process which seems to be reflected in the well-known practice of Sanskritization of names in successive generations of indigenous dynasties. According to a sacrificial inscription from Muara Kanam in eastern Kalimantan, dated to about AD 400, the reigning king of a small principality bore the name Mulavarman, and was the son of 'the renowned Aśvavarman', founder of the dynasty (*vaṃśakartṛi*). Both these names are good Sanskrit, but an apparently predynastic ruler, father of Aśvavarman, was referred to as 'the famous prince Kuṇḍuṇga', which seems to be an Indonesian, or perhaps a Tamil, name.[323] Another and later inscription, this time from Javanese Mataräm and dated to

732, reveals that Sanjaya, founder of his dynasty and bearer of a Sanskrit name, was nephew and successor to Sannaha, a Javanese name Sanskritized.[324] In these dynastic styles we can surely discern the implication of an emergent political élite seeking to validate its authority on the Indian pattern. On the Indian subcontinent a continuing tension between sacred and secular authority was institutionalized in the roles of brāhmaṇ priest and kṣatriyan ruler. In Southeast Asia something of this dualism in the structure of authority is also discernible in, say, the institutions – in this case complementary rather than competitive – of *purohita* and king in ancient Kambujadeśa, where the king was not himself a god but was held to be incarnated as an aspect of a deity. Much more commonly, though, in the world at large kings ruled as vicegerents of gods. Even so, they do not seem to have been reluctant to extend the bounds of secular domain. As far as Shang China is concerned, nothing at all can be said about the evolution of the monarchy, although oracle bones, supported for what it is worth by literary texts of dubious authenticity, afford abundant testimony to the existence of a maturely established royal authority.

In all these instances it may be that use of the term 'secularization' is misleading, for kings no less than priesthoods subscribed to the all-pervading norms of religion. What distinguished the two power groups were their political goals, rather than the methods employed to attain them. Kings and corporate warrior groups tended to pursue aims not subsumed under, and indeed alien to, the values of kin-structured society. Whatever their precise relationship to the deity, they were prone to use religious authority not only as a means for consolidating their own social position, but also as a primary instrument for the achievement of autonomous political goals beyond the ethical conceptions of an ascriptively organized society, and for the validation of a concentration of power beyond that sanctioned by the moral order of a folk community. As such the importance of these groups lies not in a professed lesser intensity of religious conviction but in their willingness to extend the secular sphere of government operations, and to use their power in the prosecution of wholly secular aims. In these roles they were powerful agents in that climactic transformation from gentile to politized society which has come to be known as the Urban Revolution.

With the rise of secular, or rather secularly oriented, authority, there appeared also a new feature in the monumental architecture of the ceremonial city, namely the palace, a building which inevitably became the vehicle for conspicuous display, a distillation and projection of the glory and prestige of the territorially organized state over which the king ruled. The garish – and, if the truth be told, to modern eyes somewhat tawdry – splendors of these palaces have formed the subject of numerous travellers' tales, and figure prominently in the epigraphic records left by the dynasts themselves, so that there is no call to enumerate those which have either survived or been brought to

THE NATURE OF THE CEREMONIAL CENTER [367

light in the several realms of nuclear urbanism. So far as Shang China is concerned, Shih Chang-ju claims to have identified the palace precinct at An-yang, and his conclusions are incorporated in Chapter One. Concomitantly with the rise of kingship, there also appeared another feature, not infrequently even more impressive from the architectural point of view than the palace itself, and which, although often located outside the enceinte of the sacred city, yet nearly always constituted part of the ceremonial enclave in the wider sense. This was the royal tomb. The pyramids of Gizeh are perhaps the classic exemplar of architectural grandeur applied to tombs, but elaborate mausolea are a feature of numerous other ceremonial centers. Not least among them are those of the An-yang dynasty revealed by the archeologists of the Academia Sinica at Hsi-pei Kang. The funeral ceremonies which are implied by the holocausts of men and animals in these great cruciform pits (p. 44) obviously invite comparison with those whose physical remains were excavated by Sir Leonard Woolley in the so-called royal tombs of Sumerian Ur,[325] and with those of Moctezuma I in AD 1469, as described by the 16th-century Spanish author Diego Durán:

> 'Upon the death of this king he was accorded the appropriate obsequies for rulers of his station, and all the kings and lords of the region attended them with offerings and presents. According to their use and custom they killed many slaves and retainers in the belief that they might serve him in the afterlife, and they buried him with a great part of his treasures.'[326]

Each of these palaces and tombs, and many more besides, are eloquent testimony to the massive concentrations of social and political power commanded by monarchs invoking sacrally sanctioned authority in the pursuit of essentially secular goals.

THE CEREMONIAL CENTER AS AN IDEAL-TYPE

The progress of archeology, supplemented by various literary and epigraphic records, would seem to have established beyond dispute [327] the role of ceremonial centers as the precursors of fully urban forms. In the preceding pages emphasis has been placed on the recurrent institutional patterns exhibited by these ceremonial complexes, which appear to exist to a large extent independently of the cultural and historical settings in which they occur, and which point the way towards recognition of a widespread functional and developmental phase in the process of urban genesis. It is not claimed that the model of socio-economic transformation which is implicit in these discussions is the only one which could be constructed on the evidence available, nor that it is applicable to all types of generated (as contrasted with imposed) cities, but it would seem to have some potential value as a basis for further speculation. However, like all models, it is selective. In this instance a generalized statement of structural regularities has been abstracted at the expense of both the rich variety of cultural expression that is manifest in the several realms of nuclear urbanism, and the complex interplay of historical variables that gives to each its distinctive character.

The approach followed in the preceding pages is similar to that pioneered by Robert Adams in *The evolution of urban society*. Cultural evolution is viewed as a nexus of disjunctive processes by which one qualitatively distinct level of sociocultural integration is transformed into another with a higher degree of complexity, which in turn confers on it expanded potentialities for adaptation. The generalized integrative patterns with which the present study is concerned are, culturally, those of relatively egalitarian, ascriptive, kin-oriented societies on the one hand, and stratified, politically organized, territorially based societies on the other. Ecologically they are the levels respectively of reciprocally integrated, Developed Village Farming Efficiency and of superordinate redistributive integration about a ceremonial center (the degree to which such centers can be categorized as urban will be discussed in the next chapter). In North China, the region of nuclear urbanism with which we are especially concerned, these levels are denoted by Lungshanoid culture and Shang civilization respectively.

In analyzing the transformation between these two levels of sociocultural integration, resort has been had to a thesis formulated by Otis Duncan and Leo Schnore[328] on the basis of the argument in Emile Durkheim's *De la division du travail social*. These authors regard what they call the ecological complex (which appears to correspond closely to our generalized integrative pattern of functional relationships) as comprising four functionally interrelated basic components or dimensions, namely environment, population, technology, and social organization. Gideon Sjoberg has contended that this orientation is overly materialistic in the manner of the Marxian schema, and is deficient in that it rejects consideration of value systems.[329] As a matter of fact Duncan and Schnore do (and have been criticized for so doing),[330] apparently inadvertently, introduce into their model value orientations which it would seem formally designed to exclude. In the present work we have also attempted not only to introduce considerations of value into the Duncan and Schnore model (though this is less easily effected in the ancient world with which we deal than in the study of the contemporary city with which those authors are concerned), but also to define more rigorously each of the four components. Sjoberg finds the concept of social organization, which Duncan and Schnore appear to equate with division of labor, as especially ill-defined, 'particularly spongy' in his terminology. We have, generally speaking, preferred to speak of social differentiation rather than social organization, and we have followed mainly Eisenstadt's explication of the manner in which it is mediated.[331] As a classificatory concept differentiation

> 'describes the ways through which the main social functions or the major institutional spheres of society become dissociated from one another,

attached to specialized collectivities and roles, and organized in relatively specific and autonomous symbolic and organizational frameworks within the confines of the same institutionalized system.

Specialization is manifest first when each of the major institutional spheres develops, through the activities of people placed in strategic roles within it, its own organizational units and complexes, and its specific criteria of action. The latter tend to be more congruent with the basic orientations of a given sphere, facilitating the development of its potentialities – technological innovation, cultural and religious creativity, expansion of political power or participation, or development of complex personality structure.

Secondly, different levels or stages of differentiation denote the degree to which major social and cultural activities, as well as certain basic resources – manpower, economic resources, commitments – have been disembedded or freed from kinship, territorial and other ascriptive units. On the one hand, these "free-floating" resources pose new problems of integration, while on the other they may become the basis for a more differentiated social order which is, potentially at least, better adapted to deal with a more variegated environment.'

Of course, the social systems characteristic of a stated level of differentiation are not necessarily always expressed in the same institutional forms. Indeed, in extreme cases of failure to resolve institutionally the stresses of increasing differentiation there may remain only the alternatives of varying degrees of socio-political disintegration, clientage on the fringe of another society, or absorption by it. Examples of each of these developments can be cited early in the process of urban genesis. It is also possible to point to instances in which the processes of differentiation operated asymmetrically, with certain institutions developing relatively continuously and smoothly while others either failed to generate, or were for some reason insulated from, change, often developing in the process carapaces of ideology with which to resist external influences. Generally speaking, such asymmetrical socio-political change was more common in relatively advanced stages of differentiation than in those with which we are concerned in this study, although some instances can be discerned in the transition from city-state to empire.[332]

It has been posited in the preceding discussion of the emergence of ceremonial centers that, of the components in the ecological complex, environment, population, and technology should be regarded as independent variables,[333] but social organization as a dependent variable. Consequently a considerable portion of this chapter has been devoted to an analysis of the generalized activities which have been held to induce societal differentiation. It is doubtful if a single autonomous, causative factor will ever be identified in the nexus of social, economic, and political transformations which resulted in the emergence of urban forms, but one activity does seem in a sense to command a sort of priority. Whatever structural changes in social organization were induced by commerce, warfare, or technology, they needed to be validated by some instrument of authority if they were to achieve institutionalized permanence. This does not imply that religion (here defined for limited purposes as a set of symbolic forms and acts which relate man to the ultimate conditions of his existence[334]) was a primary causative factor, but rather that it permeated all activities, all institutional change, and afforded a consensual focus for social life. It was, moreover, manifested at a macrosocietal level in the presence of cult centers that were not only structurally differentiated from the major ascriptive groups in society, but which were also morphologically distinct from them in that they comprised predominantly closed, high-status communities. The emergence of such religio-political foci of society has been categorized by Eisenstadt as 'one of the most important breakthroughs of development from the relatively closed kinship-based primitive community.'[335] It signified for the first time in the history of the world the sundering of the populace at large from direct access to supernatural power, at the same time as it deprived the people *en masse* of participation in political decision-making. In other words the populace had been alienated from the loci of both sacred and secular power.

In the systems of *religious symbolism* that received concrete expression in these great ceremonial centers, the paradigmatic figures of tribal religion with whom men formerly identified in ritual had been accorded specific, and often characteristic, attributes. They had been objectified, and were conceived as actively involved in the ordering of both the material and human worlds, that is they had assumed the mantle of gods and, incidentally, had disposed themselves in a hierarchy which closely paralleled that of the ceremonial centers themselves. The prevailing world view was still monistic, but it was cast in terms of an increasingly more highly differentiated monism, in which a single all-embracing cosmology justified the existence and role of all things divine and natural. In this schema the high gods of the heavenly regions tended to hold supreme power.[336] *Religious action* in this classical phase of the ceremonial centers took the primary form of cult. This was a response to a growing distinction, in contrast with tribal religion, between gods and men, a distinction which necessitated the elaboration of a communication system mediated through worship and sacrifice.[337] While permitting a higher degree of conscious volition on the part of the human participants, this mode of communication also entailed some uncertainty as to the divine response, which possibly helps to explain the heavier burden of anxiety that some authors have associated with the rise of the cult centers. So far as *religious organization* was concerned, political and religious authority were poorly discriminated, with higher status groups usually laying claim to superior religious status as well. Priestly roles were often the prerogatives of noble families who asserted their divine descent. Bellah sees the most significant limitation on religious organization at this stage

319

to be the failure to develop differentiated religious collectivities which included adherents other than priests.[338] The cult centers, he points out, afforded facilities for sacrifice and worship for what were essentially transient groups, chiefly pilgrims and peasants at the seasonal festivals, who were not organized as coherent collectivities. Only the priesthood itself constituted such a closely knit group. The *social implications* of this phase of religious development have been the subject of frequent comment in the preceding pages. Traditional social structures and practices were subsumed within a divinely ordained cosmic scheme, so that there was little tension between religious prescription and social conformity. All social action was indeed reinforced by religious authority, a situation which nurtured the seeds of its own dissolution, for as society became yet further differentiated, so the problem of legitimizing the increased autonomy of each institutional sphere of society became more complex. Competing factions tended to espouse the cause of rival deities and to rend the fabric of the unitary cosmological world view, leading sometimes in periods subsequent to those with which we are mainly concerned to the inducement of messianic expectations.

The developing autonomy of the several institutional spheres, and the concomitant extension of their organizational scope, not only generated new and complex problems relating to the integration of specialized activities and incipient politized structures into a single coherent system, but also created new possibilities of development and creativity. Discussions of the technological, political, cultural, and religious aspects of these developments have occupied a substantial part of this chapter. At the same time a higher degree of differentiation enhanced systemic sensitivity to a wider spectrum of environmental resources. At least, that is the way we have interpreted the evidence. Julian Steward, on the other hand, basing his views on Robert Adams's analysis of urban genesis in Mesopotamia and Mesoamerica, seems prepared to accord technology virtually the role of an autonomous causative factor. In a review of Adams's book he writes: 'Primary importance need not be ascribed to population density, community size, potential surplus production, or any other single factor. But it seems to me that the author [i.e. Adams] has documented the incipiency of crop improvement, better utilization of microenvironments, and increased specialization and interdependency of local population segments as the new process or trends that led to state institutions.'[339] In the case of Mesopotamia and Mesoamerica this interpretation *may* be arguable, but it is less easily demonstrated in the other regions of nuclear urbanism and in some, such as the north coast of Peru or the Andean *puna*, would in any case appear difficult to sustain. We tend to view such changes from a slightly different standpoint, and to regard increasingly subtle ecological adaptations as merely one nexus of related factors involved in the transformation between levels of sociocultural integration. The recognition, sometimes even the realization, of the opportunities afforded by an expanded environmental perception does not inevitably guarantee the integration into the fabric of society of appropriate exploitative institutions. In fact such integration presupposes the validation of an amplified and diversified ethical system, such as was disseminated by the emergent ceremonial centers. It seems to have been cult centers, already of considerable antiquity in each of the realms of nuclear urbanism, which provided institutional foci capable of adapting to the pressures of social differentiation, as well as affording sanction for the requisite socio-political and administrative innovations. And not least in so far as the institutionalization of a superordinate redistributive mode of economic integration was concerned, they provided authority for the validation of the new social configuration, at the same time as they afforded symbolic statements about the nature of society, and in so doing defined the status relationships of its component parts.

It is this phase in the development of ceremonial centers which, largely on stylistic, religious, and esthetic grounds, has come to be regarded as 'classic'. What has been less adequately represented is the extent to which the institutions of this phase were by their very nature relatively transient. The increasing heterogeneity of society, although at first most evident in the elaboration of ceremonial and cultic hierarchies, tended increasingly to undermine the effectiveness of religious sanctions on the conduct of public affairs. Concomitantly the concentration of wealth in the hands of temple oligarchs on a scale quite alien to that of pre-urban society offered strong inducements to the substitution for localized and sporadic raiding of organized and sustained warfare, a development which has led to the recognition of a militaristic phase as representative of the next set of disjunctive processes in the evolution of urban society. The predominant characteristic of this phase is the progressive differentiation of political and religious authority, with the legitimation of political power coming to depend on a balance of forces between the secular and sacral leadership. Tensions between differentiated religious collectivities begin to be discernible, and the distinction between religious and secular élites tends to be reflected among the populace in the roles of believer and subject. At the same time the simple, though by no means absolute, social duality of the so-called classical phase in the evolution of ceremonial centers, which was manifested in the dichotomy between rulers and ruled, is replaced by a quadripartite division, in which cultural-religious and political-military élites are opposed to lower-status rural (that is peasant) and urban (predominantly artisan and merchant) groups. Robert Bellah has pointed out that the socio-political dualism of religious and secular authority is concurrently reflected in an increasingly clear-cut distinction between a sacred and a profane world.[340] In strong contrast to the cosmological monism of the earlier classical phase, these later religious systems tend to be to some extent transcendental, with the attainment of 'salvation' or 'enlightenment' or 'release' as a central preoccupation.

THE NATURE OF THE CEREMONIAL CENTER

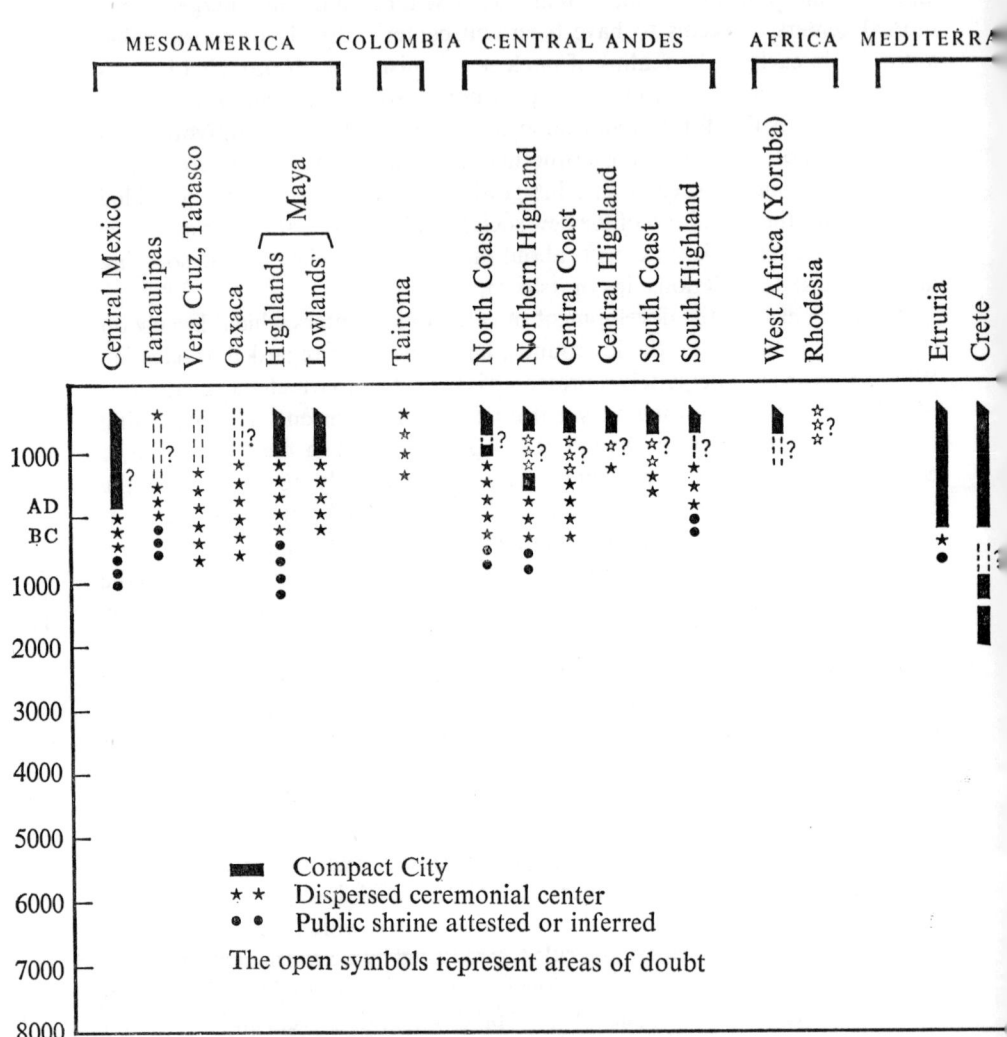

[18] The relative chronology of urban genesis.

CEREMONIAL CENTER AS IDEAL-TYPE

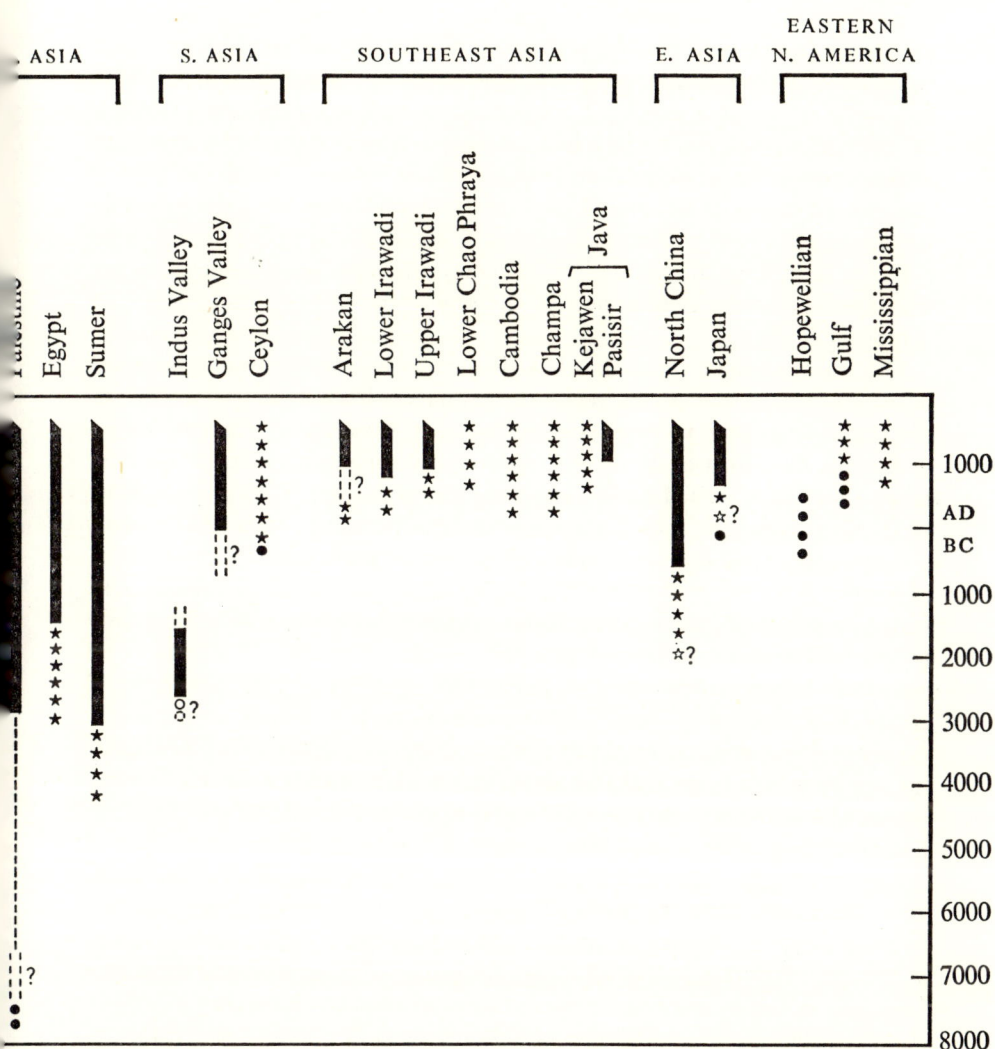

THE NATURE OF THE CEREMONIAL CENTER

A high proportion, possibly all, of these ceremonial complexes assumed a dispersed form at their inception, but subsequently the majority of them were transformed into compact aggregations of population. For a few of them there is record of a synoecic phase, the significance of which has not yet been fully evaluated. In any case, the old problem as to how the earliest cities managed to circumvent the diseconomies of agglomeration inseparable from their formation is seen in a new light, for it can now be argued that the evolution of interlocking roles in society had attained a critical degree of complexity before compaction of population began. In other words it would seem likely that the processes of social and territorial differentiation were not precisely synchronic during this phase of city genesis. Moreover, in no instance is there evidence to support the contention that compaction necessarily altered either the degree of solidarity of society or the role of the city as an instrument of orthogenetic change.

The information on which the above interpretation has been based has been drawn from the seven nuclear regions of primary urban generation, as defined in Chapter One of this volume. Two of these, early Mesopotamia and the Valley of Mexico, have formed the subject of a recent monograph by Robert Adams, to which we have made frequent reference in this chapter. We have sought to supplement Adams's detailed analysis of the transformation from folk to urban society in those two culture realms with somewhat more generalized accounts of parallel processes in the other five realms of primary urban generation, and with an especial emphasis on the Chinese experience. We have also, from time to time and whenever it seemed appropriate, utilized material from regions of secondary urban generation. It is hoped thereby to extend the principles of comparative analysis a stage further towards the formulation of a general theory of urban origins, aided in no small measure by the fact that, the larger the number of examples available for study, the more readily will the structural regularities in evolutionary process and institutional change be distinguished from the idiographic and stylistic content of culture in the several realms of nuclear urbanism. Against this must be weighed two substantial drawbacks. First, there is the certainty that both secondary and stimulus diffusion affected to some extent all regions of primary urban generation except Mesopotamia and Nuclear America, so that what appear superficially as evolutionary parallelisms may in fact be partly the result of cultural contacts. However, it is quite clear that the secondary diffusion of cultural traits was concerned with items of a complexity far below that of the city, man's most elaborate and complicated artifact, and that the process of city formation in each of the realms of nuclear urbanism was one of generation, as opposed to founding or imposition. This aspect of the relationship between these regions that have been of such crucial importance in the history of civilization has been discussed more fully in Chapter One. Secondly, we have been duly conscious of the risks inherent in any attempt to treat urban genesis on a world-wide basis: pre-eminently on the one hand such a high degree of generalization that no insights would have emerged, and comparisons could have been made only on a trite and trivial basis; and on the other hand a degree of particularization which would both have misrepresented my competence to handle the diverse corpora of evidence and extended this book beyond a reasonable length. In the event I have tried to steer a middle course between the Scylla of the gross cartoon and the Charybdis of a Pre-Raphaelite precision, the while seeking to elicit 'set characteristics' and recurrent phenomena in a multilinear evolutionary universe, rather than to illustrate the overwhelming abundance of particularistic data of cultural and historical import.

One of the most difficult problems encountered in structuring this study of urban genesis has been deciding precisely when the process can be said to have begun. In one sense, of course, the transformation can be regarded as having been initiated with the first emergence of a rank society, that is when prestige began to depend on factors unconnected with sex, age, or personal attributes (cp. p. 25); but the question then arises as to whether from that point onwards evolution took the form of a generalized (though not necessarily regular) increase in the autonomy of progressively differentiated institutional spheres, or whether it manifested itself in a series of phases of rapid socio-cultural change separated by periods of relative quiescence. Frankfort,[341] Childe,[342] and, rather more tentatively, Braidwood,[343] have interpreted the Mesopotamian evidence in terms of the latter paradigm, which Braidwood casts in the form of a 'step' metaphor. Willey, by contrast, regards the New World experience as more consonant with a gradualist model, which he characterizes by an evolutionary 'ramp' metaphor.[344] Braidwood admits that he may have been influenced in his evaluation by the nature of the evidence at his command. Whereas Willey was able to follow through the evolution of urban forms in Nuclear America wholly in terms of their archeological expression, Braidwood, an expert in the interpretation of the remains of pre-urban cultures in Southwest Asia, was confronted midway in the process by a change in the nature of the evidence from specifically archeological to predominantly epigraphic and literary, a mutation which may have predisposed him to postulate a step-like break in continuity at that point. More importantly, I think, both Braidwood and Willey relied primarily on the development of monumental architecture and related artistic achievements. While in Mesoamerica and Peru such characteristics appear to have been almost coeval with village agriculture, in Lower Mesopotamia they preceded compact urban forms by less than a millennium (although they are of somewhat greater antiquity in the surrounding uplands). In the other three Old World realms of primary urban generation the record is obscure. Particularly is this true of the Nile Valley, but in North China – on such evidence as is available – ceremonial centers seem to have

THE NATURE OF THE CEREMONIAL CENTER

[19] The course of urban genesis in selected regions of nuclear urbanism in the Old World. For the limitations inherent in these graphs see the text p.328.

[20] The course of urban genesis in selected regions of nuclear urbanism in the New World. For the limitations inherent in these graphs see the text p.328.

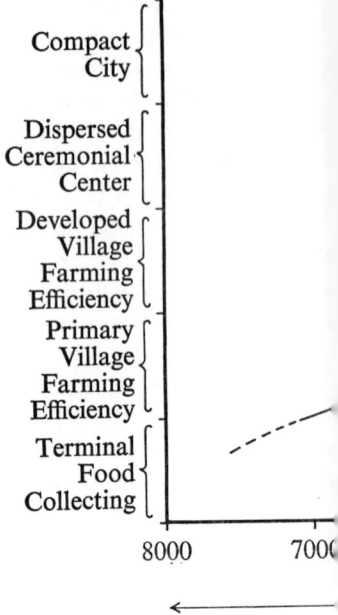

emerged with comparative abruptness. If the Baluch and Afghan shrines were indeed antecedent to the Indus valley cities, there is reason to think that the process there may have been somewhat less rapid. But the progressive differentiation of sectors of social, political, and economic activity was not necessarily expressed with equal succinctness in the archeological record throughout the whole process, nor equally for all institutional spheres. The truth is that we know extremely little of social differentiation during the era of Developed Village Farming, and it is by no means impossible that monumental architecture may have functioned as a material expression of certain socio-political nexuses only during the concluding phases of their evolution. Indeed, it appears *a priori* unlikely that the institutional evolution, crystallization of social classes, and emergence of new modes of economic integration developed wholly within the period spanned by the first appearance and subsequent elaboration of ceremonial art and architecture in Mesopotamia. Perhaps the implications of relative complexity in the societies recently revealed at Jericho and Çatal Hüyük in the Middle East, and at Haldas in northern Peru (discussed on pp.393–5), afford some support for this point of view. It is perhaps significant in this connection that Protoliterate Mesopotamia presents all the characteristics of a more transitory developmental phase than does its much longer Mesoamerican analogue, Classic Teotihuacán. Although functionally both

Mesopotamia
Indus valley
Egypt
North China
Rome
Japan
Inferred
Insufficient evidence
Insufficient evidence
Insufficient evidence
Ceylon
Cambodia
5000
4000
3000
2000
1000
1000
(1500)
BEFORE CHRIST
AD

ompact City
ispersed
emonial
Center
eveloped
Village
Farming
fficiency
Primary
Village
Farming
fficiency
erminal
Food
ollecting
Valley of Mexico
Vera Cruz/Tabasco
Maya Lowlands
Peru (N. Highlands)
Maya Highlands
Tairona
? Mississippi
5000
4000
3000
2000
1000
1000
(1500)
BEFORE CHRIST
AD

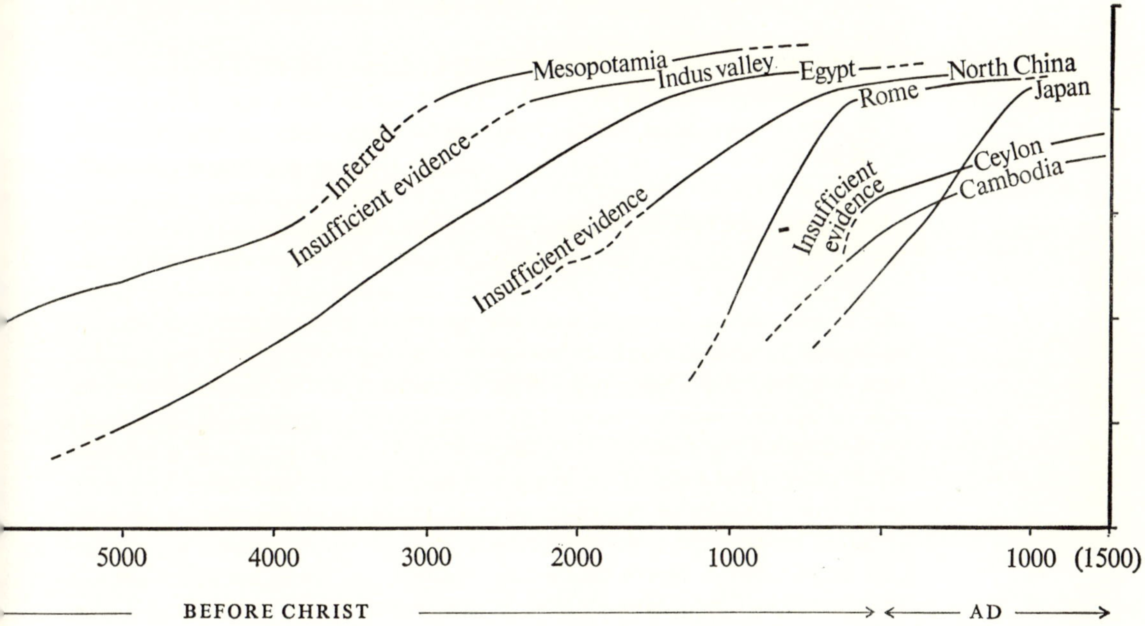

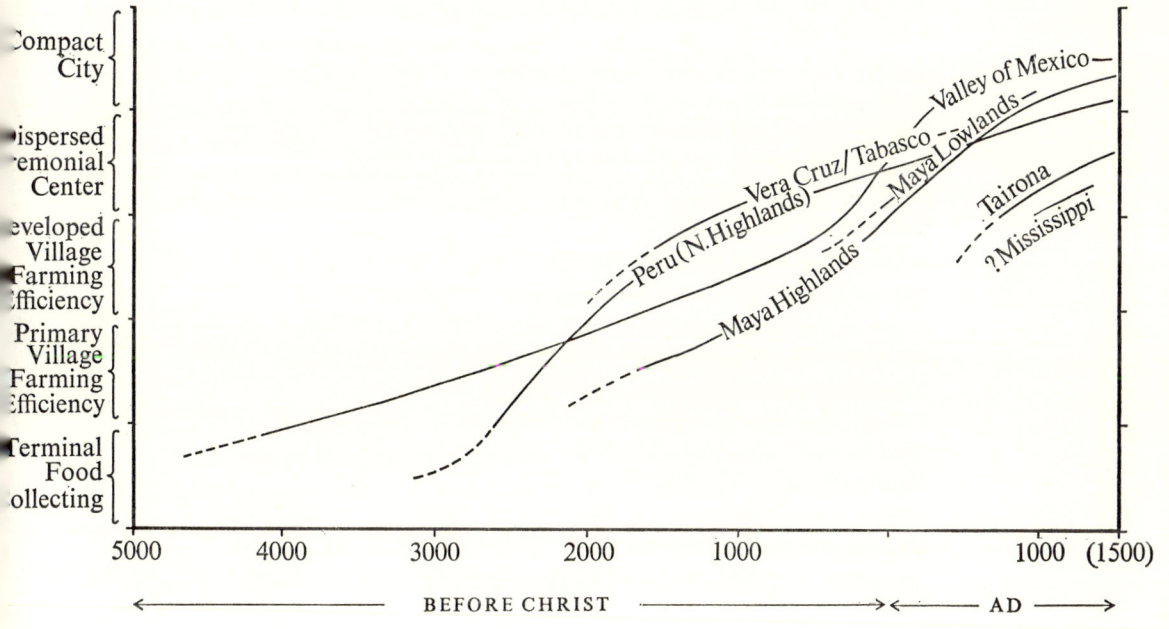

fulfilled transitional roles, there is clearly a vast difference in the time scales involved.

Figures 19 and 20 depict in gross terms the relative rates of transformation of ecotypes in the realms of primary urban generation and in certain of the regions of secondary generation. Within their very obvious limits the graphs tend to be more reliable in those sections relating to the eras of Primary and early Developed Village Farming Efficiency, when structural changes in both society and ecotype were limited in extent. The fact that the phase of Dispersed Ceremonial Centers appears as a step-like feature in an otherwise smooth and regular progression reflects less a scientifically established acceleration in the rate of socio-cultural change than our ignorance of the degree to which the socio-political and economic differentiation associated with that stage extended back into the era of Developed Village Farming. A matter of some interest in view of our discussion of cultural diffusion earlier in this work is the evident implication of the graphs that in the regions of secondary urban generation urban genesis proceeded at a rate much exceeding that in the realms of primary generation. To a lesser degree inequalities in the rates of evolution are also apparent between the regions of primary generation: the process was noticeably more rapid in North China and, probably, in the Indus valley than in Mesopotamia, Egypt, Mesoamerica, or the Central Andean realm. In any case, all the graphs represent generalized and cumulative tendencies towards an admittedly teleologically conceived level of socio-cultural complexity, which, in the next chapter, will be characterized as urban. The time when it will be possible to redraw them to take account of the temporary aberrations and reversals which it is proper to postulate as having occurred is still far into the future. Nor is there any reason, despite the striking similarities in the patterns and processes of urban development in the several nuclear realms, to suppose that in all social differentiation necessarily proceeded with the same regularity or at the same rate. In fact Robert Adams has already contrasted the Valley of Mexico with Mesopotamia from this point of view, the former exhibiting more distinctive interludes of political fragmentation, disjunctive occupation, and technological stagnation (or perhaps, subjectively, technological decline) than the latter.[345] Yet withal, the outstanding characteristic of the regions of both primary and secondary urban generation discussed in this chapter is the extent to which they shared both a core of recurrent institutional features and an essentially common pattern of evolution.

The preceding paragraphs have been devoted to a discussion of the genesis and formal characteristics of the ideal-type ceremonial center which, in our opinion, has strong claims to be considered as a functional and developmental stage in the evolution of city life. Recently, however, Dr Abdul Jalil Jawad has drawn attention to what he regards as a different course of urban development in northern Mesopotamia.[346] He finds that in the uplands bordering the Fertile

CEREMONIAL CENTER AS IDEAL-TYPE

Crescent the level of socio-cultural integration represented by the ceremonial center was lacking, a contrast in cultural evolution which, he says, justifies the construction of a different model of urban development from that which we have adopted, and which he agrees is applicable to the Sumerian experience.[347] He sees urban centers in the uplands crystallizing out as fortified, primarily secularly oriented settlements, rather than as ceremonial centers. Our reading of the evidence, by contrast, would shift the emphasis somewhat. But, before outlining our own interpretation, it is necessary to forestall certain possible confusions in terminology, for Dr Jalil Jawad's categories of urban form and function differ significantly from those used in the present work. The city he defines as 'a type of community in which the majority of the population are not necessarily non-agricultural in way of life, and which is featured by [*sic*] intensification of wealth and social stratification, walls, the multiplication of temples, the development of art, and the growth of polity.'[348] In addition, rather confusingly perhaps, he uses the term 'town' in a sense akin to its Old English connotation of 'a non-urban community in which the majority of the population are still dedicated to farming, and to which features such as fortifications, temples, fairly large settlements, not highly developed social stratifications, trade, cylinder seals, and sculptures are added.'[349] Transposed into our terminology, the admittedly meager evidence would seem to imply conclusions somewhat different from those reached by Dr Jalil Jawad, namely that the uplands of northern Mesopotamia did not constitute a region of primary or secondary urban *generation*, but one of primary *diffusion* associated with the extension of empire. Until the close of the Ninevite period (which was probably more or less contemporary with the Early Dynastic of the Mesopotamian lowlands, but chronology is not easily established in the highlands), that is until the establishment of the Akkadian empire early in the second half of the third millennium BC, the uplands were a region of villages which were increasingly, though always sporadically, affected by the secondary diffusion of culture traits from the lowlands. In this respect they were not too dissimilar from the zone of secondary diffusion surrounding the nuclear area of Shang urban development, with Brak and its famous 'Eye Temple'[350] at an incipient stage in the process of secondary urban generation, rather after the manner of, say, Hsing-T'ai in North China (cf. p.50). After that time sites such as Assur, Nineveh, Chagar Bazar, Tell Khoshi, Brak, Gasur, Tepe Gawra, Billa, and Jidle[351] all lay within the frontiers of the Akkadian empire, and such tendencies towards the development of urban forms as are discernible reflect the expansion of centers of power situated far to the south, notably that at Akkad, rather than locally generated transformations.[352] What is required for their understanding is not so much a new model as a completely new paradigm, designed to encompass not the progressive differentiation of autonomous sectors of social activity but rather the transference into the highlands of

THE NATURE OF THE CEREMONIAL CENTER

symbolic and organizational frameworks which had already been developed elsewhere, in this instance in the lowlands of Mesopotamia. In other words the history of urban settlement in northern Mesopotamia forms part of that field of study concerned with political unification and imperial aggrandizement, with urban imposition rather than with urban generation. To that extent its analogues are to be found in South rather than North China, on the mainland of Greece rather than on Crete, among the lowland Maya rather than in the Mesoamerican uplands.

Notes and References

1. 'Peasantry' is here used in the sense advocated by Robert Redfield: as the rural component in an urbanized society. 'It required the city to bring [the peasant] into existence. There were no peasants before the first cities. And those surviving primitive people who do not live in terms of the city are not peasants' [*The primitive world and its transformation*. Cornell University Press, Ithaca 1953, p.31]. If it is objected that the ceremonial complexes were only proto-cities, then I suppose that there would be no harm in terming these early agriculturalists proto-peasants. However, it will be argued subsequently that, in their classic phase at any rate, the ceremonial centers performed essentially urban functions. Eric R. Wolf [*Peasants*. Foundations of Modern Anthropology Series. Prentice-Hall, Inc., Englewood Cliffs, New Jersey 1966] has recently suggested that peasants should be defined in terms of their relationship to the state rather than the city. This shift in emphasis does not affect our definition significantly, as we shall show in a later chapter that the city was the instrument which brought the state into being, and that all generated cities were in their earlier phases city-states.

2. There is a vast technical literature relating to the temple complexes and city-states of early Mesopotamia. Fortunately this is also one of the regions with which Robert Adams is concerned in his *The evolution of urban society*, which includes a bibliography of those works bearing more directly on the subject of urban genesis. Generalized and descriptive but, within the limit of their compendiousness, accurate accounts of the emergence of cities during the Sumerian period are readily accessible in: Henri Frankfort, *The Birth of civilization in the Near East*. Williams and Norgate, London, and Indiana University Press, Bloomington 1951; Doubleday Anchor Book A89, Garden City, New York, n.d., Chapter III; Jean Perrot, *Civilisations préhistoriques et protohistoriques du Moyen Orient : co-ordination des recherches*. Centre National de la Recherche Scientifique 1964; André Parrot, *Archéologie Mésopotamienne*, 2 vols. Albin Michel, Paris 1946 and 1953; and especially *Sumer*. Librairie Gallimard, Paris 1960; Jacques Pirenne, 'Les institutions urbaines dans l'ancienne Egypte et dans le pays de Sumer', *Recueils de la Société Jean Bodin*, vol.6 : *La Ville*, première partie. La Librairie Encyclopédique, Bruxelles 1954, pp.27–48; Guillaume Cardascia, 'Les villes de Mésopotamie : leurs institutions économiques et sociales', *loc. cit.*, vol.7, deuxième partie (1955), pp.51–61. See also Robert J. Braidwood, *The Near East and the foundations for civilization*.

The Condon Lectures, Oregon State System of Higher Education. Eugene, Oregon 1952; Braidwood and Bruce Howe, 'Southwestern Asia beyond the lands of the Mediterranean littoral', in Braidwood and Gordon R. Willey (eds.), *Courses toward urban life*. Aldine Publishing Company, Chicago 1962, pp.132–146; Anton Moortgat, 'Die Entstehung der sumerischen Hochkultur', in *Der Alte Orient*, vol.43. J.C. Hinrichs, Leipzig 1945, and 'Grundlagen und Entfaltung der sumerisch-akkadischen Kultur', *Historia Mundi*, vol.2 (1953), pp.224–60.

3. Although final consonants were hardly ever lost in spoken Sumerian, they were, for reasons probably connected with the system of syllabification employed, indicated in writing only rarely prior to Ur III, and never at any time completely and consistently. In the sections of this work relating to ancient Mesopotamia I have followed Thorkild Jacobsen in using the complete forms of names as far as they can be ascertained, e.g., Eshnunnak, not Eshnunna.

4. Thorkild Jacobsen, 'Early political development in Mesopotamia', *Zeitschrift für Assyriologie und Vorderasiatische Archäologie*, Neue Folge, vol.18 (1957), p.98. Subsequently this argument has been worked out in detail by Jacobsen and Robert McC. Adams, 'Salt and silt in ancient Mesopotamian agriculture', *Science*, vol.128, no.3334 (1958), pp.1251–8, and with particular reference to the Diyala basin by Adams, *Land behind Baghdad. A history of settlement on the Diyala plains*. University of Chicago Press 1965.

5. This tripartite plan is found again in the two lowermost 'Ubaidian levels (XIX and XVIII) at Tepe Gawrah in Northern Mesopotamia, but in this region urban development took a rather different form. Cf. Arthur J. Tobler, *Excavations at Tepe Gawrah, II : Levels IX–XX*. University of Pennsylvania Press, Philadelphia 1950, and pp.329–30.

6. On Sumerian temples in general see, in addition to the references in note 2, P. Delougaz and Seton Lloyd, *Pre-Sargonid temples in the Diyala region*. Oriental Institute Publication no.LVIII. University of Chicago Press 1942; Delougaz, *The temple oval at Khafajah*. Oriental Institute Publication no.LIII. University of Chicago Press 1940; Heinrich Lenzen, 'Die Entwicklung der sumerischen Tempel', *Zeitschrift für Assyriologie und Vorderasiatische Archäologie*, Neue Folge, vol.17 (1954), pp.1–40; Adam Falkenstein, 'La cité-temple sumérienne', *Cahiers d'Histoire Mondiale*, vol.1 (1954), pp.784–814.

7. Cf. Ignace J. Gelb, 'The ancient Mesopotamian ration system', *Journal of Near Eastern Studies*, vol.24 (1965), pp.230–43.

8. Thorkild Jacobsen, 'Primitive democracy in ancient Mesopotamia', *Journal of Near Eastern Studies*, vol.2, no.3 (1943), pp.159–72, and 'Early political development in Mesopotamia', pp.91–140.

9. The earliest example of a palace so far excavated is that at Kish in northern Babylonia [Ernest Mackay, *A Sumerian palace and the 'A' cemetery at Kish*,

NOTES AND REFERENCES

Mesopotamia, II. Field Museum of Natural History, Anthropology Memoirs, vol.12. Chicago 1929], which dates from the first half of the third millennium BC. Another of not much later vintage has been investigated at Eridug [Fuad Safar, 'Eridu', *Sumer*, vol.6 (1956), pp.31–3].

10. Ring walls are first reported from the site at Jemdet Naṣr, dating from the very end of the Protoliterate period: *vide* Ernest Mackay, *Report on excavations at Jemdet Nasr, Iraq*, Field Museum of Natural History. Chicago 1931.

11. Robert M. Adams, 'The origins of cities', *Scientific American*, vol.203, no.48 (1960), p.10, and *The evolution of urban society*, pp.69–70.

12. Adams ['The origins of cities', p.10] has estimated that in 'Ubaid times only 5 per cent of the labor force was engaged in non-agricultural pursuits, with the proportion less than 20 per cent even at the end of the Protoliterate period.

13. There are readily accessible general introductions to the history of ancient Egypt in John A. Wilson, *The burden of Egypt*. University of Chicago Press 1951: republished as Phoenix Book no.11 under the title *The culture of ancient Egypt*, n.d.; Cyril Aldred, *The Egyptians*. Thames and Hudson, London 1961; Walter Bryan Emery, *Archaic Egypt*. Pelican Book A462, Harmondsworth 1961. Cf. also Frankfort, *The birth of civilization in the Near East*, Chapters II and IV.

14. Summarized in H. W. Fairman, 'Town planning in Pharaonic Egypt', *Town Planning Review*, vol.20, no.1 (1949), pp.34–5. It is not unlikely, though, that these villages were geographically marginal and consequently atypical: cf. John A. Wilson's remarks in Carl H. Kraeling and Robert M. Adams, *City Invincible. A symposium on urbanization and cultural development in the ancient Near East*. University of Chicago Press 1960, p.129. However, the existence of walls surrounding these early settlements may also be symbolized in the hieroglyph for 'city', which occurs in inscriptions from as early as the First Dynasty, and which comprises a circular enclosure divided into four parts by two supposedly intersecting roads (Griffith, *Hieroglyphs*, no.142).

15. The antiquity of the *Memphite Theology* is guaranteed not only by the early mould in which its language and textual construction are cast, but also by a good deal of internal evidence which places it at the very beginning of Egyptian history.

Herodotus (*c.* 480–429 BC) attributed the founding of Memphis to King Menes [*The History of Herodotus*. Transl. from the Greek by George Rawlinson. Everyman's Library, J. M. Dent & Sons, London 1910, II, 99], but it is still uncertain whether Menes should be identified with King Narmer or King Hor-aha, or possibly he may have been a composite personage embodying the achievements of both. For a succinct statement of the available evidence and its implications see Emery, *Archaic Egypt*, pp.32–7.

16. H. W. Fairman, 'Town planning in Pharaonic Egypt', *The Town Planning Review*, vol.20, no.1 (1949), p.36.

17. The progress of excavation at Indus valley sites is recounted in the following books and reports: Sir John [Hubert] Marshall, *Mohenjo-daro and the Indus civilization: being an official account of archaeological excavations at Mohenjo-daro carried out by the Government of India between 1922 and 1927*, 3 vols. A. Probsthain, London 1931; E. J. H. Mackay, *Further excavations at Mohenjo-daro: being an official account of archaeological excavations at Mohenjo-daro carried out by the Government of India between 1927 and 1931*, 2 vols. Delhi 1938; and *Early Indus civilizations*. Second edition, revised and enlarged by Dorothy Mackay. Luzac & Co., Ltd, London 1948; Mahdo Swarup Vats, *Excavations at Harappā: being an account of the archaeological excavations at Harappā carried out between 1920–21 and 1933–34*, 2 vols. Delhi 1940; Sir Mortimer Wheeler, *The Indus Valley civilization*. Second edition, Cambridge 1960; G. F. Dales, 'Harappan outposts on the Makran coast', *Antiquity*, vol.37 (1963), pp.111–15. There is a comprehensive bibliography of writings on the Indus valley civilization prior to 1951 in R. C. Majumdar (ed.), *The history and culture of the Indian people*, vol.1 : *The Vedic age*. George Allen and Unwin, Ltd, London 1951, pp.533–7.

18. Walter A. Fairservis, Jr, 'The Harappan civilization – new evidence and more theory', *American Museum Novitates*, no.2055. American Museum of Natural History, New York 1961, p.18.

19. *loc. cit.*, and Fairservis, 'Excavations in the Quetta valley, West Pakistan', *Anthropological Papers of the American Museum of Natural History*, vol.45, pt.2. New York 1956; and 'Archeological surveys in the Zhob and Loralai Districts, West Pakistan', *loc. cit.*, vol.47, pt.2 (1959). Cf. also the same author's 'The chronology of the Harappan civilization and the Aryan invasions', *Man*, vol.56 (1956), pp.153–6.

20. Jean-Marie Casal, *Fouilles d'Amri*. Paris 1964.

21. Fairservis, 'The Harappan civilization', pp.11–12.

22. Leslie Alcock in Fairservis, 'Excavations in the Quetta valley', pp.214–216.

23. Fairservis has since termed this religious complex the 'Zhob cult': *vide* 'Archeological surveys in the Zhob and Loralai districts', pp.308 and 330.

24. The site of Kalibangan overlooks the dry valley of the river Ghaggar (formerly the Sarasvatī) in the district of Ganganagar in Rajasthan, about 100 miles southeast of Harappā.

25. Lothal is situated on the Sabarmatī river on the plain of Kāthiāwaḍ, some 450 miles southeast of Mohenjo-daro.

26. Fairservis, 'The Harappan civilization', p.23.

27. Sir Mortimer Wheeler, *Civilizations of the Indus valley and beyond*. Library of Early Civilizations, Thames and Hudson, London 1966, p.77, and several previous works.

NOTES AND REFERENCES

28. Robert L. Raikes, 'The end of the ancient cities of the Indus', *American Anthropologist*, vol.66, no.2 (1964), pp.284–99, and 'The Mohenjo-daro floods', *Antiquity*, vol.39 (1965), pp.196–203. See also G. F. Dales, 'The decline of the Harappans', *Scientific American*, vol.214 (1966), pp.93–100. The concept of uplift of the Indus plain along an axis at right angles to that of the river has been severely criticized by H. T. Lambrick, 'The Indus flood-plain and the "Indus" civilization', *The Geographical Journal*, vol.133, pt.4 (1967), pp.483–495.

29. Fairservis, 'The chronology of the Harappan civilization', p.155.

30. Paul Kirchhoff, 'Mesoamerica', *Acta Americana*, vol.1 (1943), pp.92–107.

31. Wendell C. Bennett, 'The Peruvian Co-tradition', in Bennett (ed.), *A reappraisal of Peruvian archeology*. Society for American Archaeology, Memoir no.4. Menasha, Wisconsin 1948, pp.1–7.

32. E. M. Shook, 'The present status of research on the Preclassic horizon in Guatemala', in Sol Tax (ed.), *The civilizations of ancient America : Selected Papers of the 29th International Congress of Americanists*, vol.1. University of Chicago Press 1951. It is possible that temple mounds may have been constructed at an equally early date at Ocos on the Pacific coast of Guatemala: *vide* E. S. Deevey, L. J. Gralenski and V. Hoffren, 'Yale natural radiocarbon measurements IV', *American Journal of Science, Radiocarbon Supplement*. vol.1 (1959), pp.144–72.

33. E. M. Shook and A. V. Kidder, *Mound E-III-3, Kaminaljuyú, Guatemala*. Carnegie Institute, Contributions to American Anthropology and History, vol.11, no.53. Washington, DC 1952.

34. Alfonso Caso, *Exploraciones en Oaxaca, Quinta y Sexta Temporadas, 1936–37*. Instituto Panamericano de Geografía e Historia, Publication 34, Mexico City 1938.

35. Philip Drucker, R. F. Heizer and R. J. Squier, *Excavations at La Venta, Tabasco, 1955*. Smithsonian Institution, Bulletin of the Bureau of American Ethnology no.170. Washington, DC 1959.

36. M. N. Porter, *Tlatilco and the Pre-Classic cultures of the New World*. Viking Fund Publications in Anthropology no.19, New York 1953; Miguel Covarrubias, *Indian art of Mexico and Central America*. Alfred Knopf, New York 1957, pp.17–35.

37. Byron C. Cummings, 'Cuicuilco, the oldest temple discovered in North America', *Art and Archaeology*, vol.16, nos.1 and 2 (1923), pp.51–8; *Cuicuilco and the Archaic Culture of Mexico*. University of Arizona Bulletin, vol.4, no.8: Social Science Bulletin no.4. Tucson 1933; R. F. Heizer and J. A. Bennyhoff, 'Archaeological investigation of Cuicuilco, Valley of Mexico, 1957', *Science*, vol.127 (1958), pp.232–3.

38. Pedro Armillas, 'Teotihuacán, Tula, y los Toltecas : Las Culturas Post-

Arcaicas, y Pre-Aztecas del Centro de Mexico : Excavaciones y Estudios, 1922–50', *Runa*, vol.3 (1950), pp.37–70; René F. Millon, 'New data on Teotihuacán 1 in Teotihuacán', *Boletin del Centro de Investigaciones Antropologicas de Mexico*, no.4 (1957), pp.12–17.

39. O. G. Ricketson, Jr, E. B. Ricketson, *et al.*, *Uaxactun, Guatemala : Group E-1926–31*. Carnegie Institute, Publication no.477. Washington, DC 1937.

40. George W. Brainerd, 'Early ceramic horizons in Yucatan', in Tax, *The civilizations of ancient America*, vol.1, pp.72–8.

41. An informed opinion on the validity of the correlations that have been proposed between the Maya and Christian chronologies is possible only for the expert Americanist. Here I have followed the 11. 16. 0. 0. 0. (Goodman-Thompson) correlation, in which the earliest contemporaneous date in Maya hieroglyphic writing (8. 14. 3. 1. 12.) corresponds to AD 320. In the 12. 9. 0. 0. 0. (Spinden) correlation this would be the equivalent of a Christian date approximately 260 years earlier. Gordon R. Willey, no mean authority in this field, considers that 'the archeological sequences of Middle America as a whole seem to accord more closely with the 11. 16. 0. 0. 0. correlation than with the 12. 9. 0. 0. 0. ['The prehistoric civilizations of Nuclear America', *American Anthropologist*, vol.57, no.2, pt.1 (1955), pp.571–93]. This is true enough of both Classic Teotihuacán in the Valley of Mexico and the earlier phases of the Classic Maya in the Petén, but raises formidable problems of re-interpretation at the close of this latter period. However it would be unrealistic to expect a precise chronology at the very dawn of civilization. In fact, the absence of such a framework is inherent in the terms of reference set before the investigator of urban origins. On the other hand, as pointed out elsewhere in this volume, in a study concerned primarily with developmental forms rather than with particularist considerations, the lack of a precise and absolute chronology is not necessarily prohibitive of sound conclusions.

The Mayan Classic period is also known in various schools of thought as the Old Empire and as the Florescent Period.

42. There are general accounts of Mayan cities of the Classic period in J. Eric S. Thompson's *The rise and fall of Maya civilization*. University of Oklahoma Press, Norman, Oklahoma 1954, and in Sylvanus Griswold Morley's *The ancient Maya*. Third edition, revised by George W. Brainerd, Stanford University Press 1963. To cite adequately references to individual Maya ceremonial centers would grossly overburden the documentary sections of this volume, but I would refer the reader sceptical of statements made in this and subsequent sections to the bibliographies contained in both of the above works. Michael Coe has recently devised 'A model of ancient community structure in the Maya lowlands', in the *Southwestern Journal of Anthropology*, vol.21, no.2 (1965), pp.97–114, and William R. Coe reports on continuing investigations into the Pre-classic settlement at Tikal in 'Tikal, Guatemala, and

emergent Maya civilizations', *Science*, vol.147 (1965), pp.1401–19. Jeremy A. Sabloff and Gordon R. Willey have developed an apparently viable hypothesis to account for the collapse of Maya civilization in the Southern Lowlands in the *Southwestern Journal of Anthropology*, vol.23, no.4 (1967), pp.311–36. General discussions of developments in the Valley of Mexico and neighboring localities are readily accessible in Frederick A. Peterson, *Ancient Mexico. An introduction to the Pre-Hispanic Cultures*. Capricorn Book 221, New York 1962; Luis Aveleyra Arroyo de Anda, *Prehistoria de Mexico*. Ediciones Mexicanas, Mexico City 1950; Walter Krickeberg, *Altmexikanische Kulturen*. Safari-Verlag, Berlin 1956; and Eric R. Wolf, *Sons of the Shaking Earth*. University of Chicago Press 1959; reprinted as Phoenix Book no.90, 1962. George C. Vaillant's *The Aztecs of Mexico*. Pelican Book A200, Harmondsworth 1950, is a classic whose worth has not been wholly invalidated by the fact that it was first written over twenty years ago. There is a summary of progress towards the threshold of urbanism in Mesoamerica as a whole in Gordon R. Willey, 'Mesoamerica', in Robert J. Braidwood and Willey, *Courses toward urban life*. Aldine Publishing Company, Chicago 1962, pp.84–101.

43. E. M. Shook and Tatiana Proskouriakoff, 'Settlement patterns in Mesoamerica and the sequence in the Guatemalan highlands', in Gordon R. Willey (ed.), *Prehistoric settlement patterns in the New World*. Viking Fund Publications in Anthropology no.23. New York 1956, pp.93–100.

44. Armillas, 'Teotihuacán, Tula, y los Toltecas'; Millon, 'New data on Teotihuacán 1'.

45. There are general accounts of Peruvian archeology, including early ceremonial complexes, in Wendell C. Bennett and Junius B. Bird, *Andean Culture History*. American Museum of Natural History, New York 1949; J. Alden Mason, *The ancient civilizations of Peru*. Pelican Book A395, Harmondsworth 1957; and G. H. S. Bushnell, *Ancient peoples and places. Peru*. Revised edition, Frederick A. Praeger, New York 1963. Both contain bibliographies. Although it is now twenty years old, there is a wealth of useful information in Julian H. Steward, *Handbook of South American Indians*. Bulletin no.143 of the Bureau of American Ethnology, Smithsonian Institution, vol.2: *The Andean civilizations*. Washington, DC 1949, especially in the articles by Bennett, Larco Hoyle, Kubler, Rowe, and Valcárcel. See also Alfred Kidder II, 'Settlement patterns – Peru', in Gordon R. Willey (ed.), *Prehistoric settlement patterns in the New World*, pp.148–55. The following studies deal directly with the evolution of urban forms in the Central Andean culture realm: Richard P. Schaedel, 'The lost cities of Peru', *Scientific American*, vol.185, no.2 (1951), pp.18–23; 'Major ceremonial and population centers in northern Peru', in Tax, *The civilizations of ancient America*, pp.232–43, 'Incipient urbanization and secularization in Tiahuanacoid Peru', *American Antiquity*, vol.31, no.3, (1966), pp.338–44; and 'Urban growth and ekistics on the Peruvian coast',

THE NATURE OF THE CEREMONIAL CENTER

XXXVI Congreso Internacional de Americanistas. Sevilla 1966, pp.3–11; Louis Stumer, 'Population centers of the Rimac valley, Peru', *American Antiquity*, vol.20, no.2 (1954), pp.130–48; Donald Collier, 'The central Andes', in Braidwood and Willey, *Courses toward urban life*, pp.165–76; John Howland Rowe, 'Urban settlements in ancient Peru', *Ñawpa Pacha*, vol.1 (1963), pp.1–28. This last is the most detailed, as well as areally the most comprehensive, account of early Peruvian urbanism, but founds its interpretation on a definition of urbanism substantially different from that used in the present work (cf. pp.395–7). Consequently, it also differs from the statement of urban development presented here.

46. Gordon R. Willey, *Prehistoric settlement patterns in the Virú valley, Peru.* Bulletin no.155 of the Bureau of American Ethnology, Smithsonian Institution, Washington, DC 1953.

47. Photographs of the site in Alfred Kidder II, 'Some early sites in the northern Lake Titicaca basin', *Papers of the Peabody Museum of American Archaeology and Ethnology*, vol.27, no.1 (1943); and John Howland Rowe, 'The adventures of two Pucara statues', *Archaeology*, vol.11, no.4 (1958), pp.255–61.

48. Rowe, 'Urban settlements in ancient Peru', p.9.

49. For John Rowe's comments on the use of this category of settlement see pp.395–7 below.

50. William Duncan Strong, 'Paracas, Nazca, and Tiahuanacoid cultural relationships in south coastal Peru', *Memoirs of the Society for American Archaeology*, no.13 (1957).

51. Cited in Rowe, 'Urban settlements in ancient Peru', p.12.

52. Ishida Eiichiro et al., *Tōkyō Daigaku Andesu chitai gakujutsu chōsa dan 1958 nendo hōkokusho* [The report of the University of Tōkyō Scientific Expedition to the Andes in 1958]. Bijitsu Shuppan sha, Tokyo 1960.

53. Bennett and Bird, *Andean culture history*, pp.149–58; Mason, *The ancient civilizations of Peru*, pp.96–105; Bushnell, *Peru*, pp.110–20.

54. Otto Holstein, 'Chan-Chan: capital of the Great Chimu', *Geographical Review*, vol.27 (1927), pp.36–61.

55. Mason, *The ancient civilizations of Peru*, p.97.

56. Dorothy Menzel, 'The Inca occupation of the south coast of Peru', *Southwestern Journal of Anthropology*, vol.15, no.2 (1959), pp.125–42.

57. Rowe, 'Urban settlements in ancient Peru', p.18. In connection with Inca urbanism see also John V. Murra, 'On Inca political structure', in V.F. Ray (ed.), *Systems of political control and bureaucracy in human societies*. Proceedings of the 1958 Annual Spring Meeting of the American Ethnological Society. University of Washington Press 1958, pp.30–41.

58. Early European accounts of Yoruba ceremonial centers are to be found, *int. al.*, in J. Adams, *Remarks on the country extending from Cape Palmas to*

NOTES AND REFERENCES

the River Congo. G. & B.W. Whittaker, London 1823, and *Sketches taken during ten voyages to Africa, between the years 1786 and 1800*. Hurst, Robinson & Co. 1821; J. A. Barbot, *A description of the coasts of North and South Guinea*. No imprimatur, London 1732; João de Barros, *Ásia de João de Barros : dos feitos que os Portugueses fizeram no descobrimento e conquista dos mares e terras do Oriente*, 4 vols. (1553; sixth edition, Divisão de Publicações e Biblioteca, Agência General das Colónias, Ministério das Colónias, República Portuguesa, Lisboã 1945); W. Bosman, *A new and accurate description of Guinea*. J. Knapton, D. Midwinter, B. Lintot, G. Strahan, J. Round, and E. Bell, London 1705; R. Campbell, *A pilgrimage to my motherland : an account of a journey among the Egbas and Yorubas of Central Africa in 1859–1860*. W. J. Johnson, London 1860; H. Clapperton, *Journal of a second expedition into the interior of Africa, from the Bight of Benin to Soccatoo*. Carey, Lea and Carey, Philadelphia 1829; A. Hinderer, *Seventeen years in the Yoruba country*. Religious Tract Society, London, n.d., but c.1872; J. B. Labat, *Voyage du Chevalier des Marchais en Guinée, isles voisines, et à Cayenne, fait en 1725, 1726 and 1727*, 4 vols. La Compagnie, Amsterdam 1731; A. W. Millson, 'The Yoruba country, West Africa', *Proceedings of the Royal Geographical Society*, second series, vol. 13 (1891); Miss Tucker, *Abbeokuta; or, sunrise within the tropics : an outline of the origin and progress of the Yoruba mission*. James Nisbet & Co., London 1853. Cf. also S. O. Biobaku, *The Lugard Lectures*. Federal Information Service, Lagos 1955, and A. L. Mabogunje, *Yoruba towns*. Ibadan University Press 1962, pp. 4–5. The nature of Yoruba urbanism has been examined by William Bascom, 'Urbanization among the Yoruba', *The American Journal of Sociology*, vol. 60, no. 5 (1955), pp. 446–54. The following information is taken very largely from G. J. Afolabi Ojo, *Yoruba Palaces. A Study of àfins of Yorubaland*. University of London Press, Ltd 1966, and Peter C. Lloyd, 'The traditional political system of the Yoruba', *Southwestern Journal of Anthropology*, vol. 10 (1954), pp. 366–84, and 'Sacred kingship and government among the Yoruba', *Africa*, vol. 30, no. 3 (1960), pp. 221–37.

59. Ojo, *Yoruba Palaces*, p. 75.

60. There are general accounts of Cretan urbanism in J. D. S. Pendlebury, *The archaeology of Crete* (1939); republished in the Norton Library, no. 276, W. W. Norton & Co., Inc., New York 1965, and Richard Wyatt Hutchinson, *Prehistoric Crete*. Pelican Book A501, Harmondsworth 1962. The palace at Knossos is the subject of Sir Arthur Evans's great work *The palace of Minos*, 5 vols. Macmillan & Co., London 1921–35.

61. Cf., for example, the curious remark of R. W. Hutchinson: 'The immediate causes [of urban development in Crete] are obscure and doubtless bound up with local politics.' [*Prehistoric Crete*, p. 161].

62. A vast literature on the archeological and literary evidence relating to archaic Rome is summarized from various points of view in E. Gjerstad, *Early*

Rome, 3 vols., in *Acta Instituti Romani Regni Sueciae*. Lund 1953; Pietro de Francisci, *Primordia Civitatis*. Roma 1959; Hermann Müller-Karpe, *Vom Anfang Roms*. Heidelberg 1959; Raymond Bloch, *The origins of Rome*. Ancient Peoples and Places Series, no.15. Thames and Hudson, London 1960. Cf. also A. Momigliano, 'An interim report on the origins of Rome', *Journal of Roman Studies*, vol.53 (1963), pp.95–121.

The date of the founding (or perhaps more likely the emergence) of Rome has not been settled. The traditional authorities were themselves at variance: Timaeus put it in 814 BC, Fabius Pictor in 748, Cincius Alimentus in 728, and not until the 1st century BC did Varro give authority to the so-called traditional date of 753. Quite apart from the inadequacy of the sources at our disposal, there is the question as to what is implied by the phrase 'origins of Rome'. Does it refer to the establishment of the earliest cult-center on the Palatine Hill, to the union of the Latin tribes, to the walling of the city, or to any one of a variety of other possible dates? In the circumstances we can only note that Gjerstad concluded that the city was 'founded' in about 575 BC by the synoecism of a group of villages, and that Etruscan rule ended in the middle of the 5th century (Gjerstad believed, with K. Hanell [*Das altrömische eponyme Amt*, 1946], that 509 was the first year not of the Republic but of the new cult of Jupiter Capitolinus).

63. Different points of view about Etruscan origins, together with whatever can be deduced about the nature of Etruscan urbanism as manifested at such ancient sites as Caere, Tarquinia, Vulci, Vetulonia, and Populonia, are summarized in M. Pallottino, *Etruscologia*. Third edition, Milano 1955; L. Banti, *Il mondo degli Etruschi*. Roma 1960; and Raymond Bloch, *The Etruscans*. Ancient Peoples and Places Series, Thames and Hudson, London 1958. A more controversial interpretation is incorporated in O. W. von Vacano's *Die Etrusker: Werden und geistige Welt*. Stuttgart 1955. It is noteworthy that the two main views as to Etruscan origins which divide the scholarly community today were already in evidence in the ancient world, Herodotus (I, 94) believing that they arrived by sea from Asia Minor, Dionysius of Halicarnassus (I, xxv–xxx) regarding them as the aboriginal inhabitants of north-central Italy.

64. There is, needless to say, a vast quantity of material in Japanese on the cities of Japan. The implications, though not the substance, of a good deal of this are summarized by Takeo Yazaki in *Nihon Toshi no Hatten Katei*. Kōbundō, Tōkyō 1962, and less fully in the same author's *Nihon Toshi no Shakai Riron*. Gakuyōshobō, Tōkyō 1963: transl. into English by David L. Swain under the title *The Japanese city. A sociological analysis*. Japan Publications Trading Company, Rutland, Vt. and Tokyo 1963. Cf. also André Gonthier, 'Les villes japonaises. Histoire des institutions administratives et judiciaires', *La Ville*. Recueils de la Société Jean Bodin, vol.6. Editions de la Librairie

NOTES AND REFERENCES

Encyclopédique, Bruxelles 1954, pp.241-8. The background to the crucial period which saw the beginnings of Japanese urbanism is skilfully delineated in Sir George Sansom's *A history of Japan to 1334*. Stanford University Press 1958.

65. Woodbridge Bingham provides a summary of currently available information about the sites of Yamato imperial capitals in *Early Japanese palaces and capitals*. Paper presented to the Colloquium Orientologicum, University of California, Berkeley, 27 April 1966 (Mimeo).

66. Yamane Tokutaro *et al.*, *Reports of the historical investigation of the forbidden city of Naniwa*, 5 vols. Osaka 1956-65.

67. Sir George Sansom, *Japan. A short cultural history*. Appleton-Century-Crofts, Inc., New York; revised edition 1962, pp.191-3.

68. The most authoritative, yet succinct, account of the process of Indianization in Southeast Asia as it is at present understood is set out in two papers by George Coedès, 'Le substrat autochtone et la superstructure indienne au Cambodge et à Java', *Cahiers d'histoire mondiale*, vol.1, no.2 (1953), pp.368-377, and 'L'osmose indienne en Indochine et en Indonésie', *loc. cit.*, vol.1, no.4 (1954), pp.827-38. Cf. also the same author's *Les états hindouisés d'Indochine et d'Indonésie*. Third edition, E. de Boccard, Paris 1964, Chapter II, and L. de la Vallée Poussin, *Dynasties et histoire de l'Inde depuis Kanishka jusqu'aux invasions musulmanes*. E. de Boccard, Paris 1935, pp.360-1. For variant and, I believe, less happily conceived views of the Indianization process see J. C. van Leur, *Eenige beschouwingen betreffende den ouden Aziatischen handel*. Doctoral dissertation defended at Leiden on 5 October 1934. Since published in English translation in van Leur, *Indonesian trade and society*. W. van Hoeve, Ltd, The Hague & Bandung 1955; H. G. Quaritch Wales, *The making of Greater India : a study in South-East Asian culture change*. Bernard Quaritch, London 1951; R. C. Majumdar, *Ancient Indian colonisation in South-East Asia*. The Maharaja Sayajirao Gaekwad Honorarium Lectures 1953-4. Baroda 1955; and F. D. K. Bosch, 'The problem of the Hindu colonization of Indonesia'. Translation of an inaugural address delivered at the University of Leiden on 15 March 1946, in Bosch, *Selected Studies in Indonesian Archaeology*. The Hague 1961, pp.3-22. For information on the personal cult of ancient Cambodia see George Coedès, *Pour mieux comprendre Angkor*. Librairie d'Amérique et d'Orient, Adrien Maisonneuve, Paris 1947, Chapter III, and 'Le portrait dans l'art khmèr', *Arts Asiatiques*, vol.7, fasc.3 (1960), pp.179-198; Bernard-Philippe Groslier, *Angkor. Hommes et pierres*. Arthaud, Paris 1956, pp.22-7.

69. E. Forchhammer was the first to describe the visible remains at Hmawza in the *Reports of the Administration of British Burma*, pt.2 (1882-1883), p.155; (1883-1884), pp.94-5; (1884-1885), p.70. Subsequently the site was investigated by General L. de Beylié, who incorporated his findings in, among other

publications, *Prome et Samara*. Paris 1907 and *L'architecture hindoue en Extrême-Orient*. Paris 1907; and continued excavations were undertaken by Messrs Taw Sein Ko and Charles Duroiselle, whose reports appeared in the *Archaeological Survey of India* between 1926 and 1930, and in the *Archaeological Survey of Burma* during the same period. For a comprehensive bibliography of this topic see G. H. Luce, and Pe Maung Tin, 'Burma down to the fall of Pagan', *The Journal of the Burma Research Society*, vol.29, pt.3 (1939) : reprinted in the *Burma Research Society Fiftieth Anniversary Publication No.2*. Rangoon 1960; p.399, note 19 of the reprinted version.

70. Fan-Ch'o, *Man-Shu* (c.AD 865), chüan 10, p.45.

71. Liu-Hsü, *Chiu T'ang-Shu* (AD 974, but relating to the period 618–906), chüan 197, f.16 verso. In T'ang times the *li* appears to have approximated to 360 meters [*vide* Jen Nai-ch'iang in *K'ang-tao Yüeh-k'an*, vol.2, p.14], which cannot be equated with the extent of the walls of Śrī Kṣetra as they stand at present. The *Man-Shu* distance is a curious alternative to 160 *li*, as a day's march was usually reckoned at about 50 *li*: cf., for example, *T'ai-p'ing Huan-yü Chi*, chüan 171, f.7 recto where 10 days' journey is equated with 500 *li*, and *Ch'ien-Han Shu*, chüan 64B, f.7 recto where it is stated that the Chinese Emperor made 50 *li* a day when travelling with his entourage, but only 30 when leading his army.

72. Ou-yang Hsiu and Sung-Ch'i, *Hsin T'ang-Shu* (AD 1061), chüan 222C, f.9 recto *et seq*.

73. *Archaeological Survey of Burma* (1905), pp.7–10, (1906), p.7; Charles Duroiselle, 'Excavations at Halin', *Archaeological Survey of India* (*1929–1930*), pp.151–5. A legendary account of Halin is summarized in the *Shwebo District Gazetteer* (Rangoon) and Duroiselle, *Archaeological Survey of India, 1914–1915*, pp.44–5.

74. The reports are partially, and to some extent complementarily, preserved in both T'ang histories : cf. notes 71 and 72 above.

75. Pe Maung Tin and Gordon H. Luce (transl.), *The Glass Palace Chronicle of the Kings of Burma*. Oxford University Press 1923 : reprinted with identical pagination, Rangoon 1960, pp.28–9. Cf. also J.S.F.[John Sydenham Furnivall], 'The foundation of Pagan', *Journal of the Burma Research Society*, vol.1, pt.2 (1911), pp.6–9; Maung Htin Aung, 'The Lord of the Great Mountain', *loc. cit.*, vol.38, pt.1 (1955), pp.75–82.

76. Etienne Aymonier, 'Première étude sur les inscriptions tchames', *Journal Asiatique*, series 8, vol.17 (1891), p.29; and Louis Finot, 'Notes d'épigraphie', *Bulletin de l'Ecole Française d'Extrême-Orient*, vol.3 (1903), p.633.

77. *Epigraphia Birmanica*, plate VI, 1, 25. For Pagan in later times see Daw Thin Kyi, 'The old city of Pagan', in Ba Shin, Jean Boisselier, and A. B. Griswold, *Essays offered to G. H. Luce by his colleagues and friends in honour*

of his seventy-fifth birthday. Artibus Asiae, Supplementum XXII, vol.2. Ascona, Switzerland 1966, pp.179–88.

78. M.S.Collis and U San Shwe Bu, 'Arakan's place in the civilization of the Bay', *Journal of the Burma Research Society,* vol.15, pt.1 (1925), pp.34–52. Reprinted in *Burma Research Society Fiftieth Anniversary Publication no.2,* pp.485–504.

79. The *praśasti* has been described by Hiranandi Sastri in the *Annual Report of the Archaeological Survey of India (1925–1926)* and translated by the late Professor E.H.Johnston, 'Some Sanskrit inscriptions of Arakan', *Bulletin of the School of Oriental and African Studies,* vol.11, pt.2 (1944), pp.357–85.

80. *loc. cit.,* pp.359 and 368.

81. *loc. cit.,* p.382.

82. *loc. cit.,* pp.369 and 376.

83. *loc. cit.,* pp.372 and 379.

84. *Vide* Pierre Dupont, *L'archéologie mône de Dvāravatī.* Publications de *l'Ecole Française d'Extrême-Orient,* vol.41. Paris 1959, pp.7–11. Cf. also H. G. Quaritch Wales, 'Anuruddha and the Thaton tradition', *Journal of the Royal Asiatic Society* (1947), p.152.

85. The best edition of that part of Book VII of the *Geography* ($Γεωγραφικὴ$ $Ὑφήγησις$) which deals with Southeast Asia is that established by Louis Renou, *La Géographie de Ptolémée, l'Inde (VII, 1–4).* Librairie Ancienne Edouard Champion, Paris 1925. The date of the Ptolemaic corpus in its present form is still in dispute. Although Leo Bagrow probably overstated his case when he attributed the present version to a Byzantine author of the 10th or 11th century ['The origin of Ptolemy's Geographia', *Geografiska Annaler,* vol.27, pts.3–4 (1945), pp.318–87], there can be no doubt that it is a cumulative text, and each piece of information relating to Southeast Asia must be treated on its individual merits.

86. E.g., I-Ching, *Ta-T'ang Hsi-yü Ch'iu-fa Kao-seng Chuan.* In other works this state appears under a variety of orthographies. In any case it had been named after *Dvāravatī* [or *Dvāraka*]=the City of Gates, Kṛṣṇa's capital in Gujerat.

87. Pierre Dupont, 'Chronique : rapport de M.P.Dupont sur sa mission archéologique (18 janvier – 25 mai 1939)', *Bulletin de l'Ecole Française d'Extrême-Orient,* vol.39, pt.2 (1939), p.364.

88. Lucien Fournereau, *Le Siam ancien,* vol.1 (Paris 1895), pp.117 *et seq*; Dupont, *L'archéologie mône, passim.*

89. George Coedès,'The excavations at P'ong Tük and their importance for the ancient history of Siam', *The Journal of the Siam Society,* vol.21, pt.3 (1928), pp.195–209, and *Annual Bibliography of Indian Archaeology* (1927), pp.16–20; H. G. Quaritch Wales, 'Further excavations at P'ong Tük', *Indian*

Art and Letters, vol.10 (1936), pp.42–8; Dupont, *L'archéologie môme*, pp.102–114.

90. E.g., the *Jinakālamālini* of Ratanapañña (first composed in AD 1516) : cf. George Coedès, 'Documents sur l'histoire politique et religieuse du Laos occidental', *Bulletin de l'Ecole Française d'Extrême-Orient*, vol.25 (1925), *passim*. There are Chinese references to this city in *Sung-Shih*, chüan 489, f.23 recto and *Wen-hsien T'ung-k'ao*, chüan 332, p.2612.

91. Coedès, 'Documents', p.19.

92. R.P.Juglar, 'Note sur l'existence de ruines khmères dans la province siamoise de Mŭang Phanom Saraka', *Bulletin de l'Ecole Française d'Extrême-Orient*, vol.5 (1905), pp.415–16; Lunet de Lajonquière, 'Rapport sommaire sur une mission archéologique (Cambodge, Siam, Presqu'île malaisie, Inde, 1907–1908)', *Bulletin de la Commission Archéologique de l'Indochine*. Paris 1909, pp.212–15; E.A.Voretzsch, 'Über altbuddhistische Kunst in Siam', *Ostasiatische Zeitschrift*, vol.5, pt.2. Berlin 1916–17, fig.25; Dupont, *L'archéologie môme*, pp.118–20.

93. Lunet de Lajonquiere, 'Rapport sommaire', p.212, and 'Essai d'inventaire archéologique du Siam', *Bulletin de la Commission Archéologique de l'Indochine* (1912), pp.27–30.

94. Lajonquière, 'Rapport sommaire', pp.216–17 and 'Essai', pp.30–2.

95. *Vide* Louis Finot, 'Notes d'épigraphie', *Bulletin de l'Ecole Française d'Extrême-Orient*, vol.2 (1902), pp.185–91; R.[amesa] C.[haudra] Majumdar, *Ancient Indian colonies in the Far East*, vol.1 *Champa*. Lahore 1927, Inscriptions nos.2 and 4, pp.3–4 and 4–8 of pt. III; B.C.Chhabra, 'Expansion of Indo-Aryan culture during Pallava rule', *Journal of the Asiatic Society of Bengal, Letters*, vol.1 (1935), pp.47 and 50; Abel Bergaigne, *Inscriptions sanscrites du Campā. Académie des Inscriptions et Belles-Lettres : Notices et Extraits des Manuscrits*. Paris 1885, no.XXI, p.199.

96. Cf. Rolf A.Stein, 'Le Lin-yi, sa localisation, sa contribution à la formation du Champa et ses liens avec la Chine', *Han Hiue*, vol.2, pts.1–3. Pékin 947.

97. The only sustained treatment of the history of *Campā* is still that of Georges Maspero, 'Le royaume de Champa', *T'oung Pao*, series 2, vol.11 (1910), pp.125–36, 165–220, 319–50, 489–526, 547–66; vol.12 (1911), pp.53–87, 236–58, 291–315, 451–82, 589–626; vol.14 (1913), pp.153–201. Reprinted in book form by Les Editions G.van Œst, Paris 1928.

98. No one can write about *B'i̯u-nâm without acknowledging his indebtedness to Paul Pelliot, whose collation of the relevant Chinese texts first rendered their full implications apparent ['Le Fou-nan', *Bulletin de l'Ecole Française d'Extrême-Orient*, vol.3 (1903), pp.248–303]. Subsequently several other scholars, and notably Professor George Coedès, have made important contributions towards the refining of our knowledge of this ancient state as

NOTES AND REFERENCES

reflected in texts and epigraphy. For the archeological elucidation of the role of the Trans- and Cis-Bassac in the evolution of this culture we are beholden virtually to one man, Louis Malleret, whose investigations, although interrupted by hostilities in 1945 before their harvest could be fully gathered in, have yielded a mass of information on these two regions, and particularly on the ancient port of Oc-èo. Malleret's detailed reports and expositions appeared between 1959 and 1963 as Publication no.43 of *L'Ecole Française d'Extrême-Orient* under the general title *L'archéologie du delta du Mékong* : vol.1, *L'exploration archéologique et les fouilles d'Oc-èo*; vol.2, *La civilisation matérielle d'Oc-èo*; vol.3, *La culture du Fou-nan*; vol.4, *Le Cisbassac*. The two Chinese characters comprising the term *B'įu-nậm* have been identified as a transcription of Old Khmer [*Vraḥ*] *Vnaṃ*, meaning the [Sacred] Mountain.

99. Pierre Paris was the first scholar to draw attention to the ancient canals which seamed the surface of the (then) provinces of Tà Kèo and Châu-đôc ['Anciens canaux reconnus sur photographies aériennes dans les provinces de Tà Kèv et de Châu-đôc', *Bulletin de l'Ecole Française d'Extrême-Orient*, vol.31 (1931), pp.221–4, 'Notes et mélanges : anciens canaux reconnus sur photographies aériennes dans les provinces de Takeo, Chau-Đôc, Long-Xuyên et Rach-giá', *loc. cit.*, vol.41 (1941), pp.365–70, and 'Autres canaux reconnus à l'Est du Mékong par examen d'autres photographies aériennes', *loc. cit.*, pp.371–3], and his survey was subsequently refined and extended to cover the whole of the Transbassac by Louis Malleret [*L'archéologie*, vol.1, pp.117–24].

100. Hsiao Tzŭ-hsien, *Nan-Ch'i Shu* (AD 510, but relating to the period 479–501), chüan 58, ff.10 verso–11 recto. The embassy from which this information was obtained visited China in 484.

101. The history of the Khmer empire is dealt with fully by Lawrence Palmer Briggs, *The ancient Khmer empire*. Transactions of the American Philosophical Society, vol.41, pt.1. Philadelphia 1951, and Coedès, *Les états hindouisés*. The inscriptions on which the history of ancient Kambujadeśa is based have been published by Coedès, *Inscriptions du Cambodge*, 6 vols. Hanoi and Paris 1937–54. Generalized accounts of the temple-cities of Kambujadeśa are to be found in Coedès, *Pour mieux comprendre Angkor*; Groslier, *Angkor. Hommes et pierres*; Henri Parmentier, *Angkor. Guide Henri Parmentier*. Third edition, Phnom-Penh 1960; Victor Goloubew, 'Le Phnom Bakheń et la ville de Yaçovarman', *Bulletin de l'Ecole Française d'Extrême-Orient*, vol.33 (1933), pp.319–44, and 'Angkor in the ninth century', *Indian Art and Letters*, new series, vol.8 (1934–5), pp.123–9; Paul Mus, 'Angkor in the time of Jayavarman VII', *loc. cit.*, vol.11 (1937), pp.69–71.

102. For a summary of the evolution of urban life on the isthmus of the Malay Peninsula see Wheatley, *The Golden Khersonese*. University of Malaya Press, Kuala Lumpur 1961, and 'Desultory remarks on the ancient history of

the Malay Peninsula', in John Bastin and R. Roolvink, *Malayan and Indonesian Studies*. At the Clarendon Press, Oxford 1964, pp.33-75. H.L. Shorto is responsible for the suggestion that *Tuən-suən* was a Chinese transcription of a proto-Mōn *dun suŋ* = 'five cities', surely an early instance of the *pañcanagara* or five-unit system widely diffused through both mainland and archipelagic Southeast Asia. [Shorto, 'The 32 *myos* in the medieval Mon kingdom', *Bulletin of the School of Oriental and African Studies*, vol.26 (1963), p.583. Cf. also F.D.E. van Ossenbruggen, 'De oorsprong van het javaansche begrip Montjâ-pat in verband met primitieve classificaties', *Verslagen en Mededeelingen der Koninklijke Akademie van Wetenschappen*, Afdeeling Letterkunde, series 5, vol.3 (1918), pp.6-44; and A.W. Macdonald, 'Notes sur la claustration villageoise dans l'Asie du Sud-Est', *Journal Asiatique*, vol.245 (1957), pp.185-210.

103. There is a French translation of the relevant passage from the *Sui-Shu*, chüan 82, ff.3 recto-5 verso in Paul Pelliot, *Œuvres Posthumes : Mémoires sur les coutumes du Cambodge de Tcheou Ta-kouan*. Librairie d'Amérique et d'Orient, Adrien-Maisonneuve, Paris 1951, pp.150-2, and both text and an English rendering are incorporated, in *The Golden Khersonese*, pp.26-30.

104. H. Kern, *Verspreide Geschriften onder zijn Toesicht Verzameld*, vol.7 (1917), pp.199-204; N.J. Krom, *Hindoe-Javaansche Geschiedenis*, 's Graven-hage 1926, p.103; Bijan Raj Chatterjee, *India and Java*, pt.2. Calcutta 1933, pp.20-27; B. Ch. Chhabra, 'Expansion of Indo-Aryan culture during Pallava rule, as evidenced by inscriptions', *Journal of the Asiatic Society of Bengal*, Letters, vol.1 (1935), pp.33-4.

105. Dieng < *Di Hyang* = seat of the gods. Cp. Skt. *Devālaya* [L.C. Damais, *Bulletin de l'Ecole Française d'Extrême-Orient*, vol.48 (1957), p.627; Krom, *Hindoe-Javaansche Geschiedenis*, p.102; Chhabra, 'Expansion', p.33.

106. Kern, 'De Sanskrit-inscriptie van Canggal (Keḍu), uit 654 Cāka, *Verspreide Geschriften*, vol.7 (1917), pp.115-28; Chatterjee, *India and Java*, pp.29-34; Chhabra, 'Expansion'.

107. The remains on the Dieng plateau are described by N.J. Krom in *Inleiding tot de Hindoe-Javaansche Kunst*, vol.1. Second edition, The Hague 1926.

108. F.D.K. Bosch, 'Het Lingga-Heiligdom van Dinaja', *Tijdschrift voor Indische Taal-, Land- en Volkenkunde*, vol.64 (1924), pp.227-86.

109. An outline of the history of the Śailendra dynasty is to be found in Coedès, *Les états hindouisés*. An earlier account by Krom in *Hindoe-Javaansche Geschiedenis* is now rather severely dated. There is an excellent description of these monuments in A.J. Bernet Kempers, *Ancient Indonesian Art*. Harvard University Press 1959, and a shorter account in Frits A. Wagner, *Indonesia. The art of an island group*. Crown Publishers, Inc., New York 1959, Chapter IX. For the structure and symbolism of the Borobudur see N.J. Krom and T. van

NOTES AND REFERENCES

Erp, *Beschrijving van Borobudur*. La Haye 1920; W.F.Stutterheim, *Tjandi Bara-Boedoer, Naam, Vorm, Beteekenis*. Weltevreden 1929; and Paul Mus, *Bulletin de l'Ecole Française d'Extrême-Orient*, vols.32–35 (1932–5).

110. This shrine was not the Caṇḍi Kalasan which stands on the site today, but an earlier temple around which later structures were erected. Caṇḍi Kalasan as it is now known probably dates from the middle of the 9th century.

111. J.G.Smither, *Architectural remains, Anuradhapura*. Colombo 1894; G.E.Milton, *The lost cities of Ceylon*. John Murray, London 1928; Percy Brown, *Indian architecture*. D.B.Taraporevala Sons & Co. Private Ltd, Bombay 1959, Chapter XXXIV; *Annual Reports of the Archaeological Survey of Ceylon*, passim. Anurādhapura features prominently in the Singhalese chronicles *Mahāvaṃsa* [translated into English by Wilhelm Geiger. Pali Text Society, Oxford University Press 1912] and *Rājāvaliya* [translated into English by B.Guṇasēkhara. Government Printer, Colombo 1900. Reprinted 1954]. There is a general discussion of this period of Siṅhalese history in H.C.Ray, *History of Ceylon*, vol.1. Ceylon University Press 1959.

112. Cf. V.C.Scott O'Connor, *Mandalay and other cities of the past in Burma*. New York 1908, pp.4–7, and Robert von Heine-Geldern, 'Weltbild und Bauform in Sudöstasien', *Wiener Beiträge zur Kunst und Kultur Asiens*. Wien 1930.

113. H.H.Prince Dhani Nivat, 'The City of Thawarawadi Sri Ayudhya', *Selected Articles from the Siam Society Journal*, vol.3 : *Early History and the Ayudhya period*. The Siam Society, Bangkok 1959 : first published in 1939, pp.229–35; Larry Sternstein, ' "Krung Kao" : the old capital of Ayutthaya', *The Journal of the Siam Society*, vol.53, pt.1 (1965), pp.83–121; Rong Syamananda, 'The city of Bangkok', *Proceedings of the International Association of Historians of Asia, Second Biennial Conference, October 1962*. T'ai-pei 1963, pp.695–704.

114. Adam Falkenstein, *Zehnter Vorläufiger Bericht über die von der Notgemeinschaft der Deutschen Wissenschaft in Uruk-Warka unternommen Ausgrabungen*. Berlin 1939, p.24, note 2.

115. E.R.Leach, 'Hydraulic society in Ceylon', *Past and Present*, vol.15 (1959), pp.12 and 14.

116. Quoted at second-hand from Eric Wolf, *Sons of the Shaking Earth*. University of Chicago Press 1959, p.94.

117. I.e., the Citadel of the Cells. Georges Coedès, 'La stèle de Práḥ Khắn d'Aṅkor *Bulletin de l'Ecole Française d'Extrême-Orient*, vol.41 (1941), p.298, note 2.

118. George Coedès, 'La stèle de Ta Prohṃ', *Bulletin de l'Ecole Française d'Extrême-Orient*, vol.6 (1906), pp.44–81.

119. I.e., the Sacred Sword. The role of this shrine is elucidated by Coedès in 'La stèle de Práḥ Khắn'.

120. I.e., the Coiled Serpents.

121. Louis Finot and Victor Goloubew, 'Le symbolisme de Neak Peân', *Bulletin de l'Ecole Française d'Extrême-Orient*, vol.23 (1923), pp.401–5.

122. For descriptions of these temple-cities see Etienne Aymonier, *Le Cambodge*, vol.3. Ernest Leroux, Paris 1903; Lunet de Lajonquière, *Inventaire descriptif des monuments du Cambodge*, vol.3. Paris 1911; the *Guides archéologiques d'Angkor* by J. Commaille (1912), H. Marchal (1928), H. Parmentier (1936), and M. Glaize (1948); Philippe Stern, 'Le problème des monuments khmèrs du style du Bayon et Jayavarman VII', *Actes du XXIe Congrès des Orientalistes*. Paris 1948, p.252.

123. George Coedès, 'Les gîtes d'étape à la fin du XIIe siècle', *Bulletin de l'Ecole Française d'Extrême-Orient*, vol.40 (1940), pp.347–9.

124. George Coedès, 'L'assistance médicale au Cambodge à la fin du XIIe siècle', *Revue Médicale Française d'Extrême-Orient* (1941), and *Cahiers de l'Ecole Française d'Extrême-Orient*, vol.25 (1940), pp.8–11.

125. Paul Mus, 'Le symbolisme à Angkor Thom. Le "grand miracle" du Bayon', *Académie des Inscriptions et Belles-Lettres : Comptes-Rendus des Séances* (1936), pp.57–68.

126. Victor Goloubew, 'L'hydraulique urbaine et agricole à l'époque des rois d'Angkor', *Cahiers de l'Ecole Française d'Extrême-Orient*, vol.24 (1940), pp.16–19.

127. These are the figures extracted from the Singhalese chronicles by Sir James E. Tennent in *Ceylon*. Longmans, Green & Co., London 1859, vol.1, pt.3, Chapter 11 and vol.2, p.623.

128. Information about the corvée arrangements in the Yoruba territories is derived from Ojo, *Yoruba palaces*, Chapter 7.

129. *Sějarah Mělayu*. Raffles MS. 18, Library of the Royal Asiatic Society, pp.85–6. Romanized edition of the text by Sir Richard Winstedt, *Journal of the Malayan Branch of the Royal Asiatic Society*, vol.16, pt.3 (1938), p.116; English transl. by C. C. Brown, *loc. cit.*, vol.25, pts.2 and 3 (1952), p.88.

130. P.76 above.

131. Adam Falkenstein, 'Archaische Texte aus Uruk', *Ausgrabungen der Deutschen Forschungsgemeinschaft in Uruk-Warka*, vol.2. Berlin 1936, Zeichenliste no.24.

132. Anna Schneider, *Die Anfänge der Kulturwirtschaft : Die sumerische Tempelstadt*. G. D. Baedeker, Essen 1920.

133. Anton Deimel, 'Šumerische Tempelwirtschaft zur Zeit Urukaginas und seiner Vorgänger', *Analecta Orientalia : Commentationes Scientificae de Rebus Orientis Antiqui Cura Pontificii Instituti Biblici Editae*, vol.2. Pontificio Istituto Biblico, Roma 1931, pp.71–113; Schneider, *Die sumerische Tempelstadt*, p.21.

134. Cf. note 2 above.

NOTES AND REFERENCES

135. Cf. note 6 above.

136. Wheatley, 'A note on the extension of milking practices into Southeast Asia during the first millennium AD', *Anthropos*, vol.60 (1965), pp.577–90.

137. Adams, *The evolution of urban society*, p.51.

138. Ignace J. Gelb, 'The ancient Mesopotamian ration system', *Journal of Near Eastern Studies*, vol.24 (1965), pp.230–43.

139. Adams, *The evolution of urban society*, p.50.

140. George Coedès, 'La stèle de TaProhm', *Bulletin de l'Ecole Française d'Extrême-Orient*, vol.6 (1906), stanza XXXVIII.

141. George Coedès, 'La stèle du Práḥ Khắn d'Aṅkor', *Bulletin de l'Ecole Française d'Extrême-Orient*, vol.41 (1941), stanzas XLIV–CLXV.

142. Coedès, *loc. cit.*

143. Adams, *The evolution of urban society*, pp.164–5. The reference to Katz is to his 'Die sozialökonomischen Verhältnisse bei den Azteken im 15. und 16. Jahrhundert', *Ethnographisch-Archäologische Forschungen*, vol.3, pt.2. VEB Deutscher Verlag der Wissenschaften, Berlin 1956, p.106.

144. Sir Henry [Sumner] Maine, *Ancient Law. Its connection with the early history of society and its relation to modern ideas*. Murray, London 1861. Reprinted in 1916, with editorial notes by Frederick Pollock, and as Beacon Paperback no.155. Beacon Press, Boston 1963.

145. Lewis Henry Morgan, *Ancient Society, or, researches in the lines of human progress from savagery through barbarism to civilization*. Holt, New York 1877; reprinted as Meridian Book no.166, edited and with an introduction by Eleanor Burke Leacock. The World Publishing Company, New York 1963.

146. Ferdinand Tönnies, *Gemeinschaft und Gesellschaft*. Eighth revised edition, H. Buske, Leipzig 1935.

147. Emile Durkheim, *De la division du travail social : étude sur l'organisation des sociétés supérieures*. Alcan, Paris 1893. It should be emphasized that this transformation was only initiated by the rise of the ceremonial center and that, as will be made clear in the following pages, the society of the temple-city was neither fully *contractus, civitatis, Gesellschaft* nor organic.

148. John Friedmann's phrase : *vide* 'Cities in social transformation', *Comparative Studies in Society and History*, vol.4, no.1 (1961), p.92.

149. Robert Adams's phrase : *vide The evolution of urban society*, *passim*.

150. For discussions of the concept of surplus see Harry W. Pearson, 'The economy has no surplus : a critique of a theory of development', in Karl Polanyi, Conrad M. Arensberg and Harry W. Pearson, *Trade and market in the early empires*. The Free Press, Glencoe, Illinois 1957, pp.320–41, and Martin Orans, 'Surplus', *Human Organization*, vol.25, no.1 (1966), pp.24–32. The words of Karl Marx also bear repetition in this connection:

Favourable natural conditions alone, gave us only the possibility, never the reality, of surplus-labour, nor, consequently, of surplus-value and a surplus-product.... In the midst of our West European society, where the labourer purchases the right to work for his own livelihood only by paying for it in surplus-labour, the idea easily takes root that it is an inherent quality of human labour to furnish a surplus-product.... The productiveness of labour that serves as its foundation and starting point, is a gift, not of nature, but of a history embracing thousands of centuries [*Capital*, vol.1 (1867), Modern Library Edition, p.195].

151. William T. Sanders, 'The central Mexican symbiotic region : a study in prehistoric settlement patterns', in Gordon R. Willey (ed.), *Prehistoric settlement patterns in the New World*. Viking Fund Publications in Anthropology no.23. New York 1956, and *Tierra y agua : a study of the ecological factors in the development of Mesoamerican civilizations*. Harvard University Ph.D. dissertation 1957. Library of the Peabody Museum.

152. Robert M. Adams, 'Early civilizations, subsistence and environment', in Carl H. Kraeling and Adams, *City invincible*. A symposium on urbanization and cultural development in the Ancient Near East held at the University of Chicago, December 4–7, 1958. University of Chicago Press 1960, pp.269–95, and Chapter II of *The evolution of urban society*.

153. Certain Andean camelids were a partial but unimportant exception, for they were used almost exclusively for transport and were virtually restricted to the higher elevations.

154. Adams, *The evolution of urban society*, Chapter II; cf. also the same author's 'Early civilizations', in *City invincible*, and Kent V. Flannery, 'The ecology of early food production in Mesopotamia', *Science*, vol.147 (1965), pp.1247–56.

155. Thorkild Jacobsen and Robert M. Adams, 'Salt and silt in ancient Mesopotamian agriculture', *Science*, vol.128, no.3334 (1958),pp.1251–8.

156. Willey, *Prehistoric settlement patterns in the Virú valley, Peru*, p.56, and Willey and J. M. Corbett, *Early Ancón and early Supe culture*. Columbia Studies in Archaeology and Ethnology, IV. Columbia University Press, New York 1954, p.19.

157. W. D. Strong and C. Evans, *Cultural stratigraphy in the Virú valley, northern Peru*. Columbia Studies in Archaeology and Ethnology, IV. Columbia University Press, New York 1952, p.213.

158. Georg Steindorff, *Das Grab des Ti*. Leipzig 1913; Prentice Duell *et al.*, *The masataba of Mereruka, I-II*. Oriental Institute Publications, XXXI and, XXXIX. University of Chicago Press 1938. Robert Adams, who has provided a brief summary of the Egyptian evidence ['Early civilizations', pp.276–7], has suggested that the role of animal husbandry in ancient Egypt may have been underestimated by subconscious reference to its limited role in a very different ecotype at the present time. He quotes Kees to the effect that the concern of the

state with pastoralism is nevertheless evident in the emphasis on livestock in tribute lists, in the undertaking of periodic cattle counts, and in the appointment of officials charged with their care [cf. Hermann Kees, *Ägypten. Kulturgeschichte des alten Orients*, 3 Abt., 1 Teil, 3 Band, 1 Abschnitt. Handbuch der Altertumswissenschaft I. Munich 1933, pp.18 *et seq.*].

159. Broadly speaking, the earlier excavators of Mohenjo-daro, followed by Wheeler and Stuart Piggott [*Prehistoric India*. Pelican Book A205, Harmondsworth, Middlesex 1950, p.135], have invoked a progressive desiccation of the region in their discussions of the ecological basis of ancient Indus society. Subsequently Walter Fairservis, Jr argued that the available archeological evidence did not necessarily imply significant change ['The Harappan civilization', pp.3–4], but recently C. Ramaswamy has furnished strong paleometeorological evidence of damper conditions during the 3rd century BC: 'Monsoon over the Indus valley during the Harappan period', *Nature*, vol.217, no.5129 (1968), pp.628–9. The question is more likely to be resolved by field investigation and excavation than by additional theorizing with currently available evidence. Cf. also K. A. Chowdhury and S. S. Ghosh, 'Plant remains from Harappa, 1946', *Ancient India*, no.7 (1951).

160. For the ecology and economic significance of *chinampas*, often but inaccurately termed 'floating gardens', see Elisabeth Schilling, *Die 'schwimmenden Gärten' von Xochimilco*. Schriften des Geographischen Instituts der Universität Kiel, vol.9 (1939), and Robert C. West and Pedro Armillas, 'Les chinampas de México', *Cuadernos Americanos*, vol.50 (1950), pp.165–82.

161. Adams, 'Early civilizations', p.274.

162. On bone epigraphs this character is usually inscribed as a combination of the ox or cow radical (no.93) and the element denoting 'baton' or 'to beat', but a variant version also occurs in which the sheep radical (no.123) is joined to what appears to be a hand holding a crook [Lo Chen-yü, *Yin-hsü shu-ch'i, Ch'ien-pien* (1912), v, 45, 7–8].

163. Herrlee Glessner Creel, *Studies in early Chinese culture*. American Council of Learned Societies. Studies in Chinese and Related Civilizations, no.3. Kegan Paul, Trench, Trübner & Co., Ltd, London 1938, pp.183–4.

164. This graph has not been deciphered.

165. Lo Chen-yü, *Yin-hsü shu-ch'i Ching-hua* (1914), 2.

166. *Ibid.*

167. *loc. cit.*, 6.

168. *Yin-hsü shu-ch'i Ching-hua*, 2.

169. A recent shrewd analysis of agricultural practices along these lines constitutes the introductory chapter to Clifford Geertz, *Agricultural involution. The process of ecological change in Indonesia*. University of California Press, Berkeley and Los Angeles 1963.

170. A generalized ecosystem is one in which there exists a great variety of

THE NATURE OF THE CEREMONIAL CENTER

species, so that the energy produced by the system is distributed among a large number of different species, each of which is necessarily represented by only a small number of individuals. A specialized ecosystem is one in which a relatively small number of species is each represented by a large number of individuals.

171. Permanent-field agriculture also tended to insulate man's chosen plants from some of the pressures of natural selection to a higher degree than did swidden cultivation, thus facilitating the survival of a greater number of deviants from the normal phenotype. It also, as Adams has pointed out, created new opportunities for enhanced resource utilization in the form of manuring through the practice of stubble grazing [*The evolution of urban society*, p.40; cf. also Flannery, 'The ecology of early food production'].

172. J.A.van Beukering [*Het Ladangvraagstuk, een Bidrijfs- en Sociaal-Economische Probleem*. Mededeelingen v.h. Departement v. Economische Zaken in Nederlandsch-Indie, no.9. Batavia 1947] estimates an upper limit of 50 persons per square kilometer for swidden in Indonesia as a whole; J.D.Freeman estimates 20–25 as the maximum for the Iban territories of central Sarawak [*Iban agriculture*. Her Majesty's Stationery Office, London 1955, pp.134–5]; and Harold Conklin calculates that the Hanunóo territories on the island of Mindoro could carry 48 per square kilometer without deterioration [*Hanunóo agriculture in the Philippines*. Food and Agricultural Organization of the United Nations, Rome 1957, pp.146–7]. The Mesoamerican figure is from Adams, *The evolution of urban society*, p.43.

173. Willey, 'Mesoamerica', in Braidwood and Willey, *Courses toward urban life*, p.94.

174. *ibid.*

175. Adams, *The evolution of urban society*, pp.44–5.

176. Fairservis, 'The Harappan civilization', pp.29 and 32.

177. Cf. note 150 above.

178. Adams, *The evolution of urban society*, pp.46–7.

179. Adams, 'Early civilizations', p.273. Information about settlement patterns in ancient Mesopotamia relates almost wholly to the central and northern parts of the plain : *vide* Robert McC. Adams, *Land behind Baghdad. A history of settlement on the Diyala plains*. University of Chicago Press 1965. For the New World we are fortunate in being able to draw on the continent-wide survey edited by Gordon R.Willey, *Prehistoric settlement patterns in the New World*. Viking Fund Publications in Anthropology no.23. New York 1956. Cf. also W.R.Bullard, Jr, 'Maya settlement patterns in northeastern Peten, Guatemala', *American Antiquity*, vol.25, no.3 (1960), pp.355 *et seq.*

180. Fairservis, 'The Harappan civilization', pp.16–17.

181. V.Gordon Childe did not undertake a specific analysis of these issues but the general tenor of his argument is set out in a series of well-known works,

NOTES AND REFERENCES

including *Man makes himself*. Library of Science and Culture, London 1936; reprinted in slightly revised form in the Thinker's Library, London 1941; *What happened in history*. Penguin Book, Harmondsworth, Middlesex 1942; *New light on the most ancient East*. Routledge and Kegan Paul, London 1952; *Social evolution*. Watts & Co., London 1951. Cf. also 'The urban revolution', *Town Planning Review*, vol.21, no.1 (1950), pp.3–17, and 'The evolution of society', *Antiquity*, no.124 (1957), pp.210–13.

182. Cf. pp.277–8 above.

183. Adams, 'Factors influencing the rise of civilization in the alluvium: illustrated by Mesopotamia', in Kraeling and Adams, *City Invincible*, pp.32–3. Cf. also the same author's 'Developmental stages in ancient Mesopotamia', in Julian H. Steward *et al.*, *Irrigation civilizations : a comparative study*. Pan American Union Social Science Monographs no.1. Social Science Section, Department of Cultural Affairs, Washington, DC 1955, p.13.

184. For a statement of this problem see Polanyi, 'The economy as instituted process', in *Trade and market in the early empires*, Chapter XIII.

185. Walter C. Neale, 'The market in theory and history', in Polanyi *et al.*, *Trade and market in the early empires*, pp.365 and 371.

186. Polanyi, 'The economy as instituted process', in Polanyi *et al.*, *Trade and market*, p.255.

187. 'In a Self-Regulating Market System the whole complex of personal life is irrelevant. Religious faith, social status, political belief, family life, loving, hating, gossiping, do not decide what shall be done, except as they are part of the complex of motives and emotions creating demand for products' [Neale, The market in theory and history', p.364].

188. Polanyi, 'Marketless trading in Hammurabi's time', in Polanyi *et al.*, *Trade and market*, Chapter II, and A.L. Oppenheim, 'A bird's-eye view of Mesopotamian economic history', *loc. cit.*, Chapter III.

189. Adams, *The evolution of urban society*, pp.155–6; W. F. Leemans, *The Old Babylonian merchant : his business and social position*. E. J. Brill, Leiden 1950, p.41. But note that Adams [*ibid.*] reports an otherwise unpublished communication from Igor Diakonoff to the effect that at least some of the *damgar* were, by late in the Early Dynastic period, beginning to handle private trading accounts as adjuncts to their official responsibilities.

190. Cf. the communication from A. L. Oppenheim on p.17 of Polanyi, 'Marketless trading' : 'Archaeological evidence speaks against the existence of "market places" within the cities of the Ancient Near East'.

191. S. H. Hansford, *Chinese jade carving*. Lund Humphries, London 1950.

192. Shih Chang-ju, 'Traces of routes in the eastern part of the Yin-Shang empire'. Paper read at the International Conference on Asian History held at the University of Hong Kong, 30 August–5 September 1964.

193. Oppenheim, 'A bird's-eye view of Mesopotamian economic history', *passim*.

194. Anne M. Chapman, 'Port of trade enclaves in Aztec and Maya civilizations', in Polanyi *et al.*, *Trade and market in the early empires*, Chapter VII.

195. *Ch'ien-Han Shu*, chüan 28B, f.32 recto. *Vide* also Wheatley, 'Possible references to the Malay Peninsula in the Annals of the Former Han', *Journal of the Malayan Branch of the Royal Asiatic Society*, vol.30, pt.1 (1957), pp.115–121.

195a. Richard and John Lander, *Journal of an expedition to explore the course and termination of the Niger*, vol.1. John Murray, London 1832; Harper & Bros., New York 1854, pp.109–10. *Vide* also the Late Commander [Hugh] Clapperton, *Journal of a second expedition into the interior of Africa, from the Bight of Benin to Soccatoo*. John Murray, London and Carey, Lea & Carey, Philadelphia 1829, p.21.

196. Cf., for example, John K. Fairbank and Teng Ssŭ-yu, 'On the Ch'ing tributary system', *Harvard Journal of Asiatic Studies*, vol.6, pt.2 (1941), pp.135–246.

197. Alonso de Zurita, 'Breve y sumaria relación de los señores y maneras y diferencias que habia de ellos en Nueva España', in J. García Icazbalceta, *Nueva colección de documentos para la historia de México*. México 1941, pp.146 and 152. English translation by Adams, *The origins of urban society*, p.91.

198. Polanyi, 'The economy as instituted process', p.259.

199. A *preta* (Sanskrit; Pāli=*peta*) is the shade of a 'departed one', who is subject to continuous hunger and thirst.

200. Pe Maung Tin and G. H. Luce (transl.), *The Glass Palace Chronicle of the Kings of Burma*. Oxford University Press, London 1923, p.29.

201. Eric R. Wolf, 'The social organization of Mecca and the origins of Islam', *Southwestern Journal of Anthropology*, vol.7 (1951), pp.329–56.

202. A good deal of etymological interpretation of a popular character has collected around the tribal name Quraysh, most of it tracing the word to a root meaning 'to collect together'. Although none of it is soundly based, it is adjusted to the image of the tribe as it appeared to other Arabs. One interpretation derives the name from the fact that the Quraysh 'collected together' all their migratory kinship units around a sanctuary on the site of the Ka'bah; another – of interest in the present context – from their having 'collected together commodities from all sides for sale' [Ferdinand Wüstenfeld, *Geschichte der Stadt Mekka nach den arabischen Chroniken*, vol.4. Brockhaus, Leipzig 1864, pp.25 and 28]. Still another etymology, no better based than the former but reflecting even more explicitly the Arabian view of the Quraysh, derives their name from a word meaning 'to profit from trade' ['Abd al-Malik ibn Hishām,

NOTES AND REFERENCES

Das Leben Mohammeds nach Mohammed Ibn Ishak, vol.1, transl. by G. Weil. Metzler, Stuttgart 1864, p.46].

203. Julius Wellhausen, *Skizzen und Vorarbeiten*, vol.3. Reimer, Berlin 1894, p.88.

204. Henri Lammens, *La Mecque à la veille de l'hégire*, Mélanges de l'Université Saint Joseph, vol.9, fasc.3. Beyrouth 1924, p.233.

205. Aḥmad Ibn Yaḥya Ibn Jābir al-Balādhuri, *Futūḥ al-Buldān*, translated and annotated by Philip K. Hitti and F. C. Murgotten, *The origins of the Islamic state*. Studies in History, Economics, and Public Law, Faculty of Political Science of Columbia University, vol.68. Longmans Green, New York 1916, p.233.

206. Lammens [*La Mecque à la veille de l'hégire, passim*, but especially pp.12–32] mentions Syrian caravaneers, travelling monks and healers, Syrian merchants, foreign smiths, Copt carpenters, Negro sculptors, Christian doctors, surgeons, dentists and scribes, Christian women married into a Quraysh clan, and Abyssinian sailors and mercenaries, among the population of Mecca, as well as Abyssinian, Mesopotamian, Egyptian, Syrian, and Byzantine slaves for sale in the markets.

207. Wellhausen, *Skizzen und Vorarbeiten*, vol.3, p.190. English translation in Wolf, 'The social organization of Mecca', p.96. On these topics in general see also W. Montgomery Watt, *Muhammad at Mecca*. Oxford University Press 1953, and *Islam and the integration of society*. Routledge and Kegan Paul, London 1961.

208. *Qurʻān*, VI, 51.

209. *Qurʻān* XLIX,, 13.

210. Ibn Hishām, *Sīrat Saiyidnā Muḥammad*. Edition of Ferdinand Wüstenfeld, vol.1. Göttingen 1858, pp.341 *et seq*.

211. Muḥammad ibn ʻUmar al-Wāqidi: abridged translation by Julius Wellhausen, *Muhammad in Medina*. Reimer, Berlin 1882, p.338.

212. Muḥammad decreed that the Muhājirūn (his fellow refugees from Mecca) and the Anṣār (those of the Madinese who had helped him) should regard themselves as brethren and mutual heritors, and that the former should sever all relationships with their kin in Mecca. Cf. *Qurʻān*, VIII, 73 : 'Verily, they who have believed and fled their homes, and spent their substance in the cause of Allāh, and they who have taken in the Prophet and been helpful to him, shall be close kin one to another.'

213. This was not the first sign of incipient statehood to appear in the area. The most effective of the earlier clan federations to achieve this status had been that of the Kindah tribe which, late in the 5th and early in the 6th century, had established its control over an extensive tract of territory in north and central Arabia. However, this polity had failed to develop adequate institutional solutions to the problems which accompanied increasing social differentiation,

THE NATURE OF THE CEREMONIAL CENTER

so that it had crumbled away, leaving its only permanent impress on Arabic verse.

214. *Qurʾān*, XVI, 113.

215. *Geographike Huphegesis* (Γεωγραφική 'Υφήγησις), Book VI, Chapter 7, Section 32.

216. Various explanations have been proposed to account for the extension of Indian commercial activity into the waters of Southeast Asia during the early centuries of the Christian era. Among the most credible is that formulated by Professor George Coedès, who attributes the reorientation of Indian trade interests to changing political conditions in the Mediterranean and Central Asia. In the West the concentration of wealth that followed on the unification of the shores of the Mediterranean under the hegemony of Rome induced a demand for oriental luxuries which generated a commercial expansion along the whole length of the South Asian coastline, reaching ultimately to the archipelagic realms of gold, spices, and fragrant woods in the far southeast. At the same time, Vespasian's prohibition of the export of precious metals from the Roman empire aggravated a scarcity of gold that had existed in India since nomadic disturbances in Central Asia in the two centuries preceding the Christian era had interrupted India's supply of Siberian gold. In default of other more accessible sources of this metal, Indian merchants turned eastwards to the legendary regions beneath the sunrise, the region known to Indian literature as *Suvarṇadvīpa*, the Land of Gold.

217. Colin Renfrew, 'Trade and culture process in European prehistory'. Paper presented to the *Research Seminar on Archaeology and Related Subjects* at the Institute of Archaeology of the University of London, 7 November 1967. Renfrew does not explicitly define his concept of urbanism, but there are indications in his paper that he was probably influenced by Gordon Childe's criteria (cf. p.373 below).

218. Fairservis, 'The Harappan civilization', pp.13–14 and 18.

219. [V.] Gordon Childe, *What happened in history*. Pelican Book A108, Harmondsworth, Middlesex 1942; New York 1946, p.63.

220. Karl A. Wittfogel, *Oriental despotism : a comparative study of total power*. Yale University Press, New Haven 1957. Wittfogel also distilled the essence of this theory into a paper in William L. Thomas, Jr. (ed.), *Man's role in changing the face of the earth*. University of Chicago Press 1956, pp.152–164.

221. Max Weber, *Wirtschaft und Gesellschaft : Grundriss der Sozialökonomik*. J.C.B. Mohr, Tübingen 1921–2, p.117. Emile Durkheim [*De la division du travail social. Etude sur l'organisation des sociétés supérieures*. Alcan, Paris 1893] had also argued that an intensification in the division of labor required the presence of specialists to co-ordinate the activities of other specialists.

222. In *Oriental Despotism* and such other of his writings as are known to

NOTES AND REFERENCES

me Wittfogel has not clearly defined the implications of the term 'despotism'. It also becomes apparent from closer study of his book that he does not always distinguish between institutional and functional data. He often neglects, for example, to specify the precise period during which one of the oppressive laws or institutions which he is citing was in operation, or the sector of society or the locality to which it applied; and neither does he always state explicitly whether it was in general usage or merely a temporary aberration of an atypical ruler or bureaucrat.

223. During the past four decades Wittfogel has very properly both modified some of his basic assumptions and extended the scope of his theory. The formulations which I have in mind in the present instance are the ones adumbrated in 'Foundations and stages of Chinese economic history', *Zeitschrift für Sozialforschung*, vol.4, no.1 (1935), pp.26–60, and the fuller exposition in 'Die Theorie der orientalischen Gesellschaft', *Zeitschrift für Sozialforschung*, vol.7 (1938), pp.90–122.

It should also be noted in passing that Wittfogel has a habit of incorporating negative evidence into his theory as a morphological variant. The Classic lowland Maya, for example, despite their lack of large-scale irrigation, are characterized as a 'marginal hydraulic society'. Japan, on the other hand, which, because of its 'feudal' rather than 'oriental despotic' political system, is described as 'not hydraulic in terms of our enquiry', is still classified as belonging to the 'submarginal zone of the hydraulic world'.

224. Eberhard, *Conquerors and rulers*, Chapter III, section 3.

225. There is a, generally speaking, still acceptable outline of the history of water control in China in Ch'ao-ting Chi, *Key economic areas in Chinese history as revealed in the development of public works for water-control*. George Allen and Unwin Ltd, London 1936; Paragon Book Reprint Corp., New York 1963, although subsequent work has vitiated some of Chi's conclusions.

226. It may be significant that in the 1957 version of his theory Wittfogel tended to shift his emphasis somewhat away from the role of irrigation and to concentrate his attention on the organization of power.

227. In addition to the survey in *The evolution of urban society*, pp.68–76, see also Adams, 'Survey of ancient water courses and settlements in central Iraq', *Sumer*, vol.14, nos.1 and 2 (1958), pp.101–3; *City invincible*, pp.280–1; *Land behind Baghdad*, pp.40–1; and Thorkild Jacobsen and Adams, 'Salt and silt in ancient Mesopotamian agriculture', *Science*, vol.128, no.3334 (1958), pp.1251–8.

228. *City invincible*, p.281.

229. 'Survey of ancient water courses and settlements in central Iraq', p.103. Cf. also *Land behind Baghdad*, p.41 : '... it is difficult to see the emergence of the towns as a consequence of any monopolistic control of the water supply of surrounding villages, and still more difficult to imagine the growth of their

political institutions as a consequence of a need for a bureaucracy concerned with canal management.'

230. Angel Palerm, 'La distribucion del regadio en el area central de Mesoamerica', *Ciencias Sociales*, vol.5 (1954), p.71. Cf. also the same author's 'The agricultural basis of urban civilization in Mesoamerica', in *Irrigation civilizations : a comparative study. A symposium on method and result in cross-cultural regularities.* Social Science Monographs I, Social Science Section, Department of Cultural Affairs of the Pan American Union. Washington, DC 1955, pp.28–42.

231. Eric R. Wolf and Angel Palerm, 'Irrigation in the old Acolhua domain', *Southwestern Journal of Anthropology*, vol.11 (1955), pp.265–81.

232. I have not seen William T. Sanders's mimeographed preliminary report on his field seasons of 1960–3, but the evidence presented therein for irrigation in the valley of Teotihuacán early in the first millennium AD is summarized by Adams in *The evolution of urban society*, pp.75–6.

233. René Millon, *Teotihuacán* (n.d.). I have not seen this report, but again the substance is conveyed at second-hand by Adams (*ibid.*), from which it is evident that the presently known area of the settlement is several times as extensive as that previously revealed. In fact Millon's surveys indicate that it approaches a magnitude of thirty square kilometers in area.

234. Preliminary reports of surveys in the Tehuacán valley of southeastern Puebla afford some grounds for believing that canal irrigation may have been undertaken in that district at the beginning of the Christian era : evidence cited by Adams, *The evolution of urban society*, p.76. Pedro Armillas has also argued that cacao and fruit trees represented beside a watercourse in a mural from Teotihuacán imply irrigation practices, but the artificial nature of the water channels is not proved and the location of the scene is unknown [*Vide* 'Notas sobre sistemas de cultivo en Mesoamerica', *Instituto Nacional de Antropología e Historia. Anales*, vol.3 (1949), p.91].

235. *Ibid.*

236. Eric Wolf, *Sons of the Shaking Earth*. Phoenix Book 90, University of Chicago Press 1962, p.78.

237. Wittfogel, *Oriental despotism*, pp.184–8. It appears to have been the unsatisfactory position of Mesoamerica generally within the theory that induced Wolf and Palerm ['Irrigation in the old Acolhua domain', p.275] to propose a distinction between 'theocratic irrigation states' such as those of Protoliterate Sumer and Florescent Peru on the one hand, and 'ceremonial trade states' such as those of Classic Mesoamerica on the other [cf. also Steward, *Irrigation civilizations*, p.63]. But, as we are at pains to show, the role of irrigation was not substantially different in Classic Mesoamerica from what it was in the regions of primary urbanism in the Old World, and such a distinction appears to be otiose.

NOTES AND REFERENCES

238. Gordon R. Willey, *Prehistoric settlement patterns in the Virú valley, Peru*. Bulletin no.155 of the Bureau of American Ethnology, Smithsonian Institution. Washington, DC 1953.

239. Richard P. Schaedel, 'Major ceremonial and population centers in northern Peru', in Sol Tax (ed.), *The civilizations of ancient America*. Selected Papers of the 29th International Congress of Americanists, New York 1949. University of Chicago Press 1951, p.240.

240. Cf. John Howland Rowe, 'Inca culture at the time of the Spanish conquest', in Julian H. Steward (ed.), *Handbook of South American Indians*. Bulletin no.143 of the Bureau of American Ethnology, Smithsonian Institution, vol.2 : *The Andean civilizations*. Washington, DC 1946, pp.210–11.

241. Adams, 'Early civilizations, subsistence, and environment', in *City invincible*, p.284.

242. John Howland Rowe, 'Urban settlements in ancient Peru', *Ñawpa Pacha*, vol.1 (1963), p.20. Rowe's definition of a 'city', which differs from that used in this book, is discussed on pp.395–7 below.

243. Dows Dunham, 'The biographical inscriptions of Nekhebu in Boston and Cairo', *Journal of Egyptian archeology*, vol.24 (1938), pp.1–8.

244. James H. Breasted, *Ancient records of Egypt*, vol.1. University of Chicago Press 1906, pp.146 *et seq.*

245. J. E. Quibell, *Hierakonpolis*, vol.1. London 1900, plate XXVI C.

246. Ludwig Borchardt, 'Ein Königserlass aus Dahschur', *Zeitschrift für ägyptische Sprache und Altertumskunde*, vol.42 (1905), pp.6 and 9.

247. Adams, 'Early civilizations, subsistence and environment', p.282.

248. For references see note 101 above; also Victor Goloubew, 'L'hydraulique urbaine et agricole à l'époque des rois d'Angkor', *Bulletin Economique de l'Indochine*, 1941, fasc.1 (1941), pp.9–18 [cf. p.10 : 'On peut dire des souverains d'Angkor qu'ils avaient poussé jusqu'à leurs extrêmes limites l'amour et le culte de l'eau']; and Bernard-Philippe Groslier, *Angkor et le Cambodge au XVIe siècle d'après les sources portugaises et espagnoles*. Annales du Musée Guimet : Bibliothèque d'Etudes, vol.63. Presses Universitaires de France, Paris 1958, pp.108–12.

249. P.[ierre] Paris, 'Anciens canaux reconnus sur photographies aériennes dans les provinces de Tà Kèv et de Châu-đôc', *Bulletin de l'Ecole Française d'Extrême-Orient*, vol.31 (1931), pp.221 4; 'Notes et mélanges : anciens canaux reconnus sur photographies aériennes dans les provinces de Takeo, Châu-Đôc, Long-Xuyên et Rach-giá', *op. cit.*, vol.41 (1941), pp.365–70; and 'Autre canaux reconnus à l'Est du Mékong par examen d'autres photographies aériennes', *loc. cit.*, pp.371–3.

250. Malleret, *L'archéologie du delta du Mékong*, vol.1, pp.117–24.

251. Malleret, *op. cit.*, vol.1, p.200.

252. Bernard-Philippe Groslier, *The art of Indochina*. Crown Publishers Inc.,

New York 1962, p.56: 'It therefore seems likely that the canal network was so arranged by skilful adjustments of the gradients that it both carried the water of the Bassac to the sea, and washed the salt out of the ground, making possible intensive cultivation of floating rice.'

253. Madeleine Colani, *Emploi de la pierre en des temps reculés. Annam – Indonésie – Assam*. Publication des Amis du Vieux Hué. Hanoi 1940.

254. For the argument that these sacro-economic systems were of prehistoric origin see Wheatley, 'Agricultural terracing. Discursive scholia on recent papers on agricultural terracing and on related matters pertaining to northern Indochina and neighbouring areas', *Pacific Viewpoint*, vol.6, no.2 (1965), pp.137–9.

255. E. R. Leach, 'Hydraulic society in Ceylon', *Past and Present*, vol.15 (1959), pp.2–25.

256. Cf. M.B.Ariyapala, *Society in medieval Ceylon*. Colombo 1956, Chapter 3; and S.Paranavitana, 'Glimpses of the political and social conditions of medieval Ceylon', in *Sir Paul Pieris Presentation Volume*. Colombo 1956, p.72.

257. B. H. Farmer, *Pioneer peasant colonisation in Ceylon*. London 1955, p.188.

258. Cf. Weber's definition of urbanism on p.371 below, and Werner Sombart [*Der Moderne Kapitalismus*. München 1902–27, vol.2, pt.2 and vol.3, Chapter 25], whose theory of urban origins, although devised in relation to the European city, has sometimes been taken as a generalized model of urban genesis.

259. For an attempt to extend this terminology to all regions of nuclear urbanism see Steward, *Irrigation civilizations*, pp.68–9.

260. In, for example, the received periodization of the Middle East.

261. E.g., Bennett, *Andean culture history*, and Mason, *The ancient civilizations of Peru*.

262. Henri Frankfort, *Cylinder seals*. Macmillan, London 1939, p.23.

263. Burrows, *Archaic texts*, no.371.

264. Falkenstein, 'La cité-temple sumérienne', p.810.

265. *Liang-Shu*, chüan 54, f.7 recto; repeated in *Nan-Shih*, chüan 78, f.6 verso.

266. *Ibid.*

267. Adams, *The evolution of urban society*, p.132.

268. Cf. Jane Holden, 'The Post-Classic stage in Mesoamerica', *The Kroeber Anthropological Society Papers*, no.17 (1957), pp.75–108; Pedro Armillas, 'Fortalezas Mexicanas', *Cuadernos Americanos*, vol.41 (1948), pp.143–63, and 'Mesoamerican fortifications', *Antiquity*, no.96 (1951), pp.77–86; Ángel Palerm, 'Notas sobre las construcciones militares y la guerra en Mesoamérica', *Ciencias Sociales*, vol.7. Pan American Union, Washington, DC 1956, pp.189–202; Robert Rands, *Some evidence of warfare*

NOTES AND REFERENCES

in classic Maya art. University of Michigan Microfilm Publication no.4233. Ann Arbor 1952. The shift from open to fortified hill-top sites has been documented by A. Ledyard Smith, *Archaeological reconnaissance in Central Guatemala.* Publication no.608 of the Carnegie Institute of Washington. Washington, DC 1955.

269. The México derived the toponym *Tollán* from *tollin* = reed; hence the interpretation 'Place of Reeds'. If this is the correct definition, which is by no means certain, the prestige of this particular city was such that the name eventually became synonymous with 'metropolis', a usage preserved in the present-day Otomí name for Tula : *Mamenhi*. Eric Wolf discusses the implications of the name, and expresses doubts as to the validity of the identification of Tollán with Tula, in *Sons of the Shaking Earth.* Phoenix Book P90, University of Chicago Press 1962, p.275.

270. K. Ruppert, J. Eric Thompson, and Tatiana Proskouriakoff, *Bonampak, Chiapas, Mexico.* Publication no.602 of the Carnegie Institute of Washington. Washington, DC 1955.

271. Adrián Recinos, Delia Goetz, and Sylvanus G. Morley, *Popol Vuh.* Hodge & Co., London 1951, p.114, note 6.

272. As mentioned above, there is a confusing diversity in the periodization of Peruvian prehistory, but the period under consideration is roughly that of the *Middle Horizon* of John Rowe ['Cultural unity and diversification in Peruvian archaeology', *Men and cultures; selected papers of the Fifth International Congress of Anthropological and Ethnological Sciences, Philadelphia, September 1–9, 1956.* Philadelphia 1960, pp.627–31; 'Tiempo, estilo y proceso cultural en la arqueología peruana'. Segunda edición, corregida. *Tawantinsuyu K'uzkiy Paqarichisqa – Instituto de Estudios Andinos.* Institute of Andean Studies, Berkeley 1960; 'Stages and periods in archaeological interpretation', *Southwestern Journal of Anthropology*, vol.18, no.1 (1962), pp.40–54]; of the *Master Craftsmen* of Bennett and Bird [*Andean culture history*, pp.82–3], of the *Florescent* of Mason [*The ancient civilizations of Peru*, pp.16–17], of the *Late Formative* and *Classic* of Bushnell [*Peru*, pp.26–7], and of the *Classic* of Collier [in Braidwood and Willey, *Courses toward urban life*, p.167].

273. Cf. Schaedel, 'Urban growth and ekistics', p.5.

274. Numa Denis Fustel de Coulanges, *La cité antique.* Librairie Hachette, Paris 1864. English translation under the title *The ancient city.* Doubleday Anchor Book no.A76, New York n.d.

275. *loc. cit.*, p.166.

276. *Vide* Braidwood and Willey, *Courses toward urban life*, p.350.

277. Fairservis, 'The Harappan civilization – new evidence and more theory', *American Museum Novitates*, no.2055 (1961), pp.29 and 32. See also p.319 below.

278. Adams, *The evolution of urban society*, pp.122 et seq.

THE NATURE OF THE CEREMONIAL CENTER

279. Thorkild Jacobsen, 'Early political development in Mesopotamia', *Zeitschrift für Assyriologie und Vorderasiatische Archäologie*, vol.18, (1957), p.108, note 32, and 'Ancient Mesopotamian religion : the central concerns', *Proceedings of the American Philosophical Society*, vol.107 (1963), pp.473–484.

280. Adams, *The evolution of urban society*, p.122, quoting a personal communication from Miguel Civil.

281. A. R. Radcliffe-Brown, 'On social structure', *Journal of the Royal Anthropological Institute*, vol.70 (1940), p.5. Reprinted in Radcliffe-Brown, *Structure and function in primitive society. Essays and addresses*. The Free Press, Glencoe 1952, where the reference is to p.193.

282. Frankfort's estimate is based on the area of extant ruins at Ur, Eshnunnak (Tell Asmar), and the much later site at Khafājah. The average of the densities thus computed is 160 per acre. On this basis Ur and Assur would each have housed some 24,000 people in the Assyrian period, while in an earlier age Lagash would have had a population of 19,000, Umma 16,000, Eshnunnak 9,000, and Khafājah 12,000 [*Kingship and the gods*. University of Chicago Press 1948, p.396, note 23]. For the unreliability of population figures in ancient Mesopotamian literature see A. Poebel, 'Der Konflikt zwischen Lagaš und Umma zur Zeit Enannatums I und Entemenas', in *Paul Haupt Anniversary Volume*. Baltimore 1926, p.234, note 4.

283. Wigberto Jiménez Moreno, 'Síntesis de la historia precolonial del Valle de México', *Revista Méxicana de Estudios Antropológicos*, vol.14. Mexico 1954–5, pp.219–36, and *Historia antigua de México*. Escuela Nacional de Antropología e Historia. Mimeographed, Mexico 1953.

284. O. G. Ricketson, Jr and E. B. Ricketson, *Uaxactun, Guatemala. Group E – 1926–1931*. Carnegie Institute of Washington Publication no.477. Washington, DC 1937. If all the house mounds investigated by the Ricketsons were occupied simultaneously, the density of population would have been of the order of 1,000 persons per square mile; if, as seems more likely, only one in four was inhabited at any one time, then the density would have been nearer 270 per square mile. Cf. Robert Wauchope, *House mounds of Uaxactun. Guatemala. Contributions to American Archaeology*, vol.2, no.7. Carnegie Institute of Washington Publication no.436. Washington, DC 1934.

285. Gordon R. Willey, 'Problems concerning prehistoric settlement patterns in the Maya lowlands', in Willey (ed.), *Prehistoric settlement patterns in the New World*. Viking Fund Publications in Anthropology no.23. New York 1956, p.110; Willey and W. R. Bullard, Jr, 'The Melhado site; a prehistoric Maya house mound group near El Cayo, British Honduras', *American Antiquity*, vol.22, no.1 (1956), pp.29–44; Willey, Bullard and J. B. Glass, 'The Maya community of prehistoric times', *Archaeology*, vol.8, no.1. Brattleboro, Vermont 1955, pp.18–25.

286. Ricketsons, *Uaxactun*.

NOTES AND REFERENCES

287. S. W. Miles 'Maya settlement patterns : a problem for ethnology and archaeology', *Southwestern Journal of Anthropology*, vol.13. Albuquerque, New Mexico 1957, pp.239–48.

288. George C. Vaillant, *The Aztecs of Mexico*. Pelican Book A200, Harmondsworth, Middlesex 1950, p.70.

289. William T. Sanders, 'The Central Mexican symbiotic region. A study in prehistoric settlement patterns', in Gordon R. Willey (ed.), *Prehistoric settlement patterns in the New World*. Viking Fund Publications in Anthropology no.23. New York 1953, pp.125–6.

290. Seton Lloyd and Fuad Safar, 'Tell Uqair. Excavations by the Iraq Government Directorate General of Antiquities in 1943 and 1944', *Journal of Near Eastern Studies*, vol.2, no.2 (1943), pp.131–58; 'Excavations at Eridu', *Sumer*, vol.3. Directorate-General of Antiquities, Baghdad 1947, pp.85–111; 'Eridu. A preliminary communication on the second season's excavations, 1947–48', *Sumer*, vol.4, no.2 (1948), pp.115–25; Pinhas Delougaz and Seton Lloyd, *Pre-Sargonid temples in the Diyala Region*. University of Chicago Oriental Institute Publications, vol.58. University of Chicago Press 1942; Ann Louise Perkins, *The comparative archaeology of early Mesopotamia*. University of Chicago Oriental Institute. Studies in ancient Oriental civilization, no.25. University of Chicago Press 1949, Chapter IV.

291. Pedro Armillas, 'Teotihuacan, Tula, y los Toltecas : las culturas post-Arcaicas, y pre-Aztecas del Centro de Mexico : excavaciones y estudios, 1922–1950', *Runa*, vol.3. Buenos Aires 1950, pp.37–70; René F. Millon, 'New data on Teotihuacan 1 in Teotihuacan', *Boletin del Centro de Investigaciones Antropologicas de Mexico*, no.4 (1957), pp.12–17.

292. G. R. Sharma, *The excavations at Kauśāmbī, 1957–1959*. University of Allahābād 1960.

293. *The History of Thukydides*, written in the last decades of the 5th century. The translation is that of the Modern Library edition. Random House, Inc., New York 1951, pp.93–4, somewhat modified in accordance with the Greek text and literal translation of C. Foster Smith, *Thucydides*. The Loeb Classical Library, London 1919, pp.288–91.

294. Translation based on the works cited in note 293. The role of the religio-administrative core of the Greek city has been well summarized in recent times by J. Hatzfeld, *La Grèce et son héritage*. Aubier, Editions Montaigne, Paris 1945, pp.14–16 : 'La cité est avant tout une association morale qui peut, comme on le verra pendant la deuxième guerre médique, survivre à la destruction de la ville, et dont l'unité a pour symbole visible, le Prytanée, la Maison des Premiers de la cité, où brule le feu sacré qui ne doit jamais s'éteindre, et les sanctuaires où résident les dieux protecteurs de la ville : association qui a pour base, non seulement la communauté d'origine, mais aussi l'identité de lois, la similitude des moeurs et des façons de penser.'

295. *Thukydides*, Book II, para.6. Cf. the grumbling of the peasants forced to move within the shelter of the Athenian walls in Aristophanes's plays *The Acharnians* and *Peace*.

296. *Thukydides*, Book I, para.1. An example of forced synoecism in later times is provided by Megalopolis, the extensive city designed as a headquarters for the Arkadian League. It was created out of forty Arkadian villages after the victory of Epaminondas over the Spartans at Leuctra in 371 BC.

297. The Aventine seems eventually to have attracted its own peasant population, for it was here that the temple of the agrarian deities Ceres, Liber, and Libera was built in 493 BC, while the temple of Mercury, god of trade, was raised close by at the Porta Capena in 495. The tradition of the sacred kingship which held sway from the walled city that extended over the Palatine and Esquiline Hills has been partially confirmed by the discovery of fragments of terracotta antefixes and friezes that clearly once belonged to richly adorned sacred buildings.

298. The feast of the Septimontium, a yearly religious ceremony celebrated in spring during the classical period of Rome, commemorated the federation of the villages that were by tradition Latin (those on the Cermalus, Palatium, Velia, Fagutal, Cispius, Oppius, and Caelius Hills), probably in the 7th century. Cf. also note 62 above.

299. A. Grenier, *L'Aventin dans l'Antiquité*. Paris 1906, pp.80–92.

300. Pe Maung Tin and G. H. Luce (transl.), *The Glass Palace Chronicle of the Kings of Burma*. Oxford University Press 1923, pp.28–9. [Reprinted with identical pagination for the Burma Research Society, Rangoon 1960], and *Mahā Yazawin Gyi*, Burma Research Society Publication, series no.5. Rangoon 1926, I, 163. For comments on this legend see J. S. F. (John Sydenham Furnivall), 'The foundation of Pagan', *Journal of the Burma Research Society*, vol.1, pt.2. Rangoon 1911, pp.6–9; Maung Maung, 'A history of Lower Burma', *loc. cit.*, vol.11, pt.2 (1921), p.83; Maung Htin Aung, 'The Lord of the Great Mountain', *loc. cit.*, vol.38, pt.1 (1955), pp.75–82.

301. The operation of a process of synoecism in the formation of the Sumerian city-states has already been suggested by Henri Frankfort, *Kingship and the Gods. A study of ancient Near Eastern religion and the integration of society*. University of Chicago Press 1948, p.223; Adam Falkenstein, 'La cité-temple sumérienne', *Cahiers d'Histoire Mondiale*, vol.1 (1954), p.790; Adams, in Kraeling and Adams, *City invincible*, p.34.

302. Adams, *The origins of urban society*, p.140.

303. These terms are defined in Emile Durkheim, *De la division du travail social*. Alcan, Paris 1893. See also pp.390–1 below.

304. Louis Wirth, 'Urbanism as a way of life', *American Journal of Sociology*, vol.44 (1938), pp.1–24. In recent years the validity of this alleged dichotomy has been called in question, and there is a succinct summary of the argument

NOTES AND REFERENCES

in Oscar Lewis, 'The folk-urban ideal types', in Philip M. Hauser and Leo F. Schnore, *The study of urbanization*. John Wiley & Sons, Inc., New York 1965, pp.491–503. Lewis is certainly correct in his criticisms in so far as they relate to Tepoztlan and similar cities, but Wirth's concept of urbanization as essentially a disruptive process would still seem to have considerable relevance to the great industrial cities of the West during the 19th and earlier 20th centuries.

305. For the implications of this term see Robert Redfield and Milton B. Singer, 'The cultural role of cities', *Economic Development and Cultural Change*, vol.3 (1954), pp.53–73.

306. Ban Th'at inscription (11th century AD); transl. George Groslier, mod.

307. Jacobsen, 'Early political development in Mesopotamia', *passim*, and 'Primitive democracy in ancient Mesopotamia', *Journal of Near Eastern Studies*, vol.2, no.3 (1943), pp.159–72.

308. Dietz O. Edzard, 'Die frühdynastische Zeit', in Elena Cassin, Jean Bottéro and Jean Vercoutter, *Fischer Weltgeschichte*, vol.2 : *Die altorientalischen Reiche, Pt.I*. Fischer Bücherei, Frankfurt-am-Main 1965, pp.74–5. It is not without relevance to the arguments put forward in this chapter that, in Uruk at any rate, the *en*'s official residence was also the *giparu*, the sacred storehouse where the crops were kept. In the words of Thorkild Jacobsen, 'the *en* is the human embodiment of the generative power, Dumuzi or Amaushumgalannak, which produces and informs them [the crops]' : 'Early political development', p.109.

309. It is usually said that the earliest occurrence of the term *lugal* in the sense of 'king' is in tablets dating from Early Dynastic I found at Ur : *vide* Burrows, *Archaic Texts*, UET II sign no.236, ref. for *lú-gal*, and p.16 (24). A single mention of the word in a text from the end of the Protoliterate period is thought by Igor Diakonoff to bear the more generic meaning of 'master' [*Vide* Adams, *The origins of urban society*, p.137].

310. The title *ensik* (Akkadian *iššakkum*) occurs but rarely in myth and epic, but when it does it seems to denote the leader who mustered and organized the temple community for work in the fields. By the time of the earliest historical texts it had come to refer specifically to the ruler of a major city and its dependent territory. Cf. Jacobsen, 'Early political development', p.123, note 71.

311. Sumerian=*abba* (father) and *abba uru* (city fathers). Jacobsen has aptly compared the assembled elders to 'an aggregate of the *patria potestas* in the community', and the assembly to the Roman *comitia* ['Primitive democracy', p.166, note 44].

312. Jacobsen, 'Primitive democracy', p.165.

313. *loc. cit.*, p.166.

314. *loc. cit.*, p.170, and Thorkild Jacobsen in Henri and H. A. Frankfort, John A. Wilson, Jacobsen, and W. A. Irwin, *The intellectual adventure of*

ancient man. University of Chicago Press 1946, p.177 [abridged as Pelican Book A198 under the title *Before Philosophy.* Harmondsworth, Middlesex 1949].

315. Adams, *The origins of urban society*, pp.133–45.

316. Cp., for example, the mercenary captains from the arid north who entered into service with Toltec garrisons during the 12th century AD, and who, under the name Chichimec, as Toltec power declined began to usurp the right to rule by force of arms [*Vide* Pedro Armillas, 'Tecnologia, formaciones socio-economicas y religion en Mesoamerica', in Sol Tax (ed.), *Selected Papers, XXIXth International Congress of Americanists.* University of Chicago Press 1949, pp.19–30].

317. Paul Kirchhoff, 'Quetzalcoatl, Huemac, y el fin de Tule', *Cuadernos Americanos*, vol.14 (1955), pp.163–96. But see also Pedro Armillas, 'Tecnologia, formaciones socio-economicas y religion en Mesoamerica', in Sol Tax, *The civilizations of ancient America. Selected Papers, XXIXth International Congress of Americanists*, vol.1. University of Chicago Press 1951, pp.19–30; Armillas, 'Teotihuacan, Tula, y los Toltecas : las culturas post-Arcaicus, y pre-Aztecas del Centro de Mexico : excavaciones y estudios, 1922–50', *Runa*, vol.3 (1950), pp.37–70; and Wigberto Jiménez-Moreno, *Historia antigua de Mexico.* Escuela Nacional de Antropología e Historia, Mexico, D.F; third edition 1958. Mimeographed. I.M. Diakonoff has postulated an analogous conflict in Lagash towards the end of the Ur-Nanshe dynasty, when priests and aristocracy leagued together to resist the encroachments of the Ensik on the autonomy of the temple estates : 'Some remarks on the "Reforms" of Uru-kagina', *Revue d'Assyriologie*, vol.52 (1958), p.12.

318. Alonso de Zurita, 'Breve y sumaria relación de los Señores de la Nueva España', in J. García Icazbalceta (ed.), *Nueva colección de documentos para la historia de México*, vol.3. Editorial Salvador Chávez Hayhoe, Mexico, D.F. 1941. English translation by Adams, *The origins of urban society*, p.141.

319. Adams, *The origins of urban society*, pp.141–2.

320. Miguel León Portilla, 'The concept of the state among the ancient Aztecs', *Alpha Kappa Deltan*, vol.30 (1959), p.11.

321. Cf. Frankfort, *Kingship and the Gods*, Chapter 2; Wilson, *The burden of Egypt*, Chapter 3.

322. Paul Kirchhoff, 'The social and political organization of the Andean peoples', in Julian H. Steward, *Handbook of South American Indians.* Bulletin no.143 of the Bureau of American Ethnology, Smithsonian Institution, vol.2 : *The Andean civilizations.* Washington, DC 1949, p.308.

323. J. Ph. Vogel, 'The yupa inscriptions of King Mulavarman from Koetei (East Borneo)', *Bijdragen tot de Taal-, Land- en Volkenkunde van Nederlandsch-Indië*, vol.74 (1918), pp.167–232; Bijan Raj Chatterjee, *India and Java*, pt.2. Calcutta 1933, pp.8–19; B.Ch. Chhabra, 'Three more yupa inscrip-

NOTES AND REFERENCES

tions of King Mulavarman from Koetei (E. Borneo)', *Journal of the Greater India Society*, vol.12 (1945), pp.14–17, and 'Note on Kundunga', *Journal of the Malayan Branch of the Royal Asiatic Society*, vol.15, pt.3 (1937), pp.118–19.

324. H. Kern, 'De Sanskrit-inscriptie van Canggal (Keḍu) uit 654 Cāka', *Verspreide Geschriften onder zijn Toesicht Verzameld*, vol.7. The Hague 1917, pp.115–28; Chatterjee, *India and Java*, pp.29–34; Chhabra, 'Expansion of Indo-Aryan culture during Pallava rule, as evidenced by inscriptions', *Journal of the Asiatic Society of Bengal, Letters*, vol.1 (1935), p.37.

325. C. L. [later Sir Leonard] Woolley, *Ur excavations, II : The royal cemetery*. London 1934.

326. Diego Durán, *Historia de las Indias de Nueva-España y islas de tierra firma*, vol.1. Impr. de J.M. Andrade y F. Escalante, Mexico, D.F., 1867, pp.253–4. English translation by Adams, *The origins of urban society*, p.145.

327. The grounds of Professor John Rowe's dissent from this conclusion are discussed on pp.395–7 below.

328. Otis Dudley Duncan and Leo F. Schnore, 'Cultural, behavioral, and ecological perspectives in the study of social organization', *American Journal of Sociology*, vol.65 (1959), pp.132–46; Duncan, 'Human ecology and population studies', in Philip M. Hauser and Duncan (eds.), *The study of population*. University of Chicago Press 1959, pp.678–716; Leo F. Schnore, 'Social morphology and human ecology', *American Journal of Sociology*, vol.63 (1958), pp.620–34. But see also Sidney M. Willhelm, 'The concept of the "ecological complex" : a critique', *American Journal of Economics and Sociology*, vol.23 (1964), pp.241–8.

329. Gideon Sjoberg, 'Theory and research in urban sociology', in Philip M. Hauser and Leo F. Schnore (eds.), *The study of urbanization*. John Wiley & Sons, Inc., New York, London and Sydney 1965, p.166.

330. Sidney M. Willhelm, *Urban zoning and land-use theory*. Free Press of Glencoe, New York 1962, pp.25–6.

331. S. N. Eisenstadt, 'Social change, differentiation and evolution', *American Sociological Review*, vol.29 (1964), pp.375–86.

332. Studies of such asymmetrical change, chiefly in colonial societies, are incorporated in Shmuel N. Eisenstadt, *Essays on sociological aspects of political and economic development*. Mouton, The Hague 1961.

333. It is true, of course, that urban forms did not crystallize out in hunting and gathering societies so that, to that extent, it can be claimed that there were preconditions of resource exploitation, settlement pattern, and social organization (if not possibly demographic considerations as well), but in no instance can they be shown to have been other than single components in a functionally interdependent network of factors.

334. Robert N. Bellah, 'Religious evolution', *American Sociological Review*, vol.29, no.3 (1964), p.359.

335. Eisenstadt, 'Social change, differentiation and evolution', p.377.

336. Cf. Raffaele Pettazzoni, *The all-knowing god*. Methuen & Co. Ltd, London 1956. In this paragraph I am following the general exposition of Robert Bellah, 'Religious evolution', pp.364–6.

337. Cf. Henri Hubert and Marcel Mauss, 'Essai sur la nature et la fonction du sacrifice', *L'Année Sociologique*, vol.2 (1897–8), pp.29–138.

338. Bellah, 'Religious evolution', p.365.

339. Julian H. Steward, 'Towards understanding cultural evolution' (A review of Robert Adams, *The evolution of urban society*) in *Science*, vol.153 (1966), p.730. Adams himself did not carry the argument this far.

340. Bellah, 'Religious evolution', p.367.

341. Frankfort, *The birth of civilization in the Near East*, p.16.

342. This interpretation is implicit both in the argument of the several publications cited in note 181 on p.352 and in his use of the term 'Urban Revolution'.

343. Braidwood and Willey, *Courses toward urban life*, pp.351–2.

344. *Ibid*.

345. Adams, *The evolution of urban society*, p.173. The diametrically opposed conclusions of Adams and Willey with regard to the applicability of the 'step' and 'ramp' metaphors to Mesoamerica illustrate succinctly the manner in which different categories of investigation, in this case sectors of social activity *versus* the morphology of shrines and ceremonial centers, are likely to lead to variant inferences.

346. Abdul Jalil Jawad, *The advent of the era of townships in northern Mesopotamia*. E.J. Brill, Leiden 1965.

347. *Op. cit.*, pp.3, 74, and 106.

348. *Op. cit.*, p.7.

349. *Op. cit.*, p.6. Jalil Jawad also uses the term 'township', by which he denotes 'a self-sufficient political territory; it is considered an intermediate form between village and city, a transition between rural and urban life' : *vide* p.70, note 1.

350. M.E. Mallowan, 'Excavations at Brak and Chagar Bazar', *Iraq*, vol.9 (1947), pt.1, pp.1–87 and pt.2, pp.89–259. Cf. also A. Tobler, *Excavations at Tepe Gawra*, vol.2, levels IX–XX. University of Pennsylvania Press 1950.

351. Walter Andrae, *Die Archäischen Ischtar-Tempel in Assur. Wissenschaftliche Veröffentlichungen der deutschen Orientgesellschaft*, vol.39. J.C. Heinrichs, Leipzig 1922, and *Das Wiedererstandene Assur*. Leipzig 1938; R.C. Thompson and R.W. Hamilton, 'The British Museum excavations on the temple of Ishtar at Nineveh, 1930–31', *Annals of Archaeology and Anthropology*, vol.19 (1932), pp.55–117; Mallowan, 'Excavations at Brak and Chagar Bazar [see note 10], and 'Excavations in the Bali*h* valley', *Iraq*, vol.5 (1938), pp.111–59; C.J. Gadd, 'Tablets from Chagar Bazar, 1936', *Iraq*, vol.4 (1937),

NOTES AND REFERENCES

and 'Tablets from Chagar Bazar and Tell Brak, 1937–1938', *Iraq*, vol.7 (1940); S. Lloyd, 'Iraq Government soundings at Sinjar', *Iraq*, vol.7 (1940), pp.13–21; T. Meek, *Old Akkadian, Sumerian, and Cappadocian texts from Nuzi* (1935); R. Starr, *Nuzi*. Harvard University Press, Cambridge, Mass. 1937; E. A. Speiser, *Excavations at Tepe Gawra I*. University of Pennsylvania Press, Philadelphia 1935, and 'Reports from our expeditions in Iraq, Tell Billa', *Bulletin of the American Schools of Oriental Research*, no.41 (1931).

352. Only for Gasur is there a textual basis adequate for the reconstruction of the organization of particular social units. There the existence of an organized political leadership can be discerned, with a governor at its head, an administrative staff (and, impliedly, personal retainers), a council of elders, and specialized craftsmen. The mention in several texts of settlements tributary to Gasur implies that it was a regional administrative center, perhaps something on the lines of the early *hsien* capitals discussed on pp.179–82. In the adjacent countryside a manorial-type institution, under the direction of élite lineages and worked by both serfs and slaves, was the unit of resource exploitation, and apparently included within its purview cereal cultivation, horticulture, and grazing, as well as hunting and fishing.

4

The Urban Character of the Ceremonial Complex

In the preceding pages I have, whenever possible, avoided using the unqualified term 'city'[1] in connection with the ceremonial complex, and have endeavored either to furnish it with some such epithet as 'ceremonial' or 'cult' or to find a less specific expression. However, the question inevitably arises as to whether this settlement form can legitimately be classed as urban. This in turn requires that we attempt a definition of urbanism.

Western classical sociology, which established the temper of urban studies in general, restricted its purview virtually to the more impressive manifestations of contemporary urbanism as they occurred in Europe and North America. It was in this context that, nearly half a century ago, Max Weber established the criteria of urbanism that have been endorsed by almost all subsequent investigators.

> 'Denn dazu gehörte, daß es sich um Siedelungen mindestens relativ stark gewerblich-händlerischen Charakters handelte, auf welche folgende Merkmale zutrafen: 1. die Befestigung, – 2. der Markt, – 3. eigenes Gericht und mindestens teilweise eigenes Recht, – 4. Verbandscharakter und damit verbunden, – 5. mindestens teilweise Autonomie und Autokephalie, also auch Verwaltung durch Behörden, an deren Bestellung die Bürger als solche irgendwie beteiligt waren.'[2]

Weber himself realized that the inclusion of autonomy and autocephaly among these criteria disqualified from full urban status a very high proportion of those settlements of the traditional world which have customarily been designated as cities or towns. Complete autonomy has been rare in the history of urbanism and, city-states apart,[3] has usually fallen to a city accidentally and temporarily during periods of political disruption. Outside Europe truly privileged cities, in the form of enclaves of urban law islanded in territories subject to the common law of the state, have occurred, as far as I have been able to ascertain, only in 14th-century Japan, in the Nile delta during the interludes between the Kingdoms, and from time to time during, and in various parts of, the Hellenistic empires.[4] Weber was quite prepared to accept the far-reaching implications arising from his adoption of these criteria of urbanism: namely, those settlements which failed to incorporate the salient features of the European city failed in a greater or lesser measure to qualify for urban status. 'Eine Stadtgemeinde im vollen Sinn des Wortes,' he wrote in 1921, 'hat als Massenerscheinung vielmehr nur der Okzident gekannt. Daneben ein Teil des vorderasiatischen Orients (Syrien und Phönizien, vielleicht Mesopotamien) und dieser nur zeitweisse und sonst in Ansätzen.'[5] In other words, in order to forge a construct capable of subsuming the partial formulations of the 19th century Weber was prepared to exclude not only the extra-European city in recent times (a sacrifice of which he was aware) but also the morphologically variable, though functionally homologous, forms from which urban life had developed (a concession of which he was almost certainly not cognizant).

Weber did not explain specifically the type of market which he had in mind when formulating his definition of urbanism, but presumably it was the autonomous price-fixing market of the Western classical economists, which we now know to have been something of a rarity in the traditional world.[6] Nor did Weber explicitly distinguish between market and trade, and he would doubtless have been surprised to learn of the volume of exchange which was conducted in some ancient ceremonial centers without the aid of a formal marketing system. The risk-free and marketless trading which Professor Oppenheim has investigated in ancient Assyria[7] would also have seemed anomalous in his schema, as would the apparent absence of a physical market place, even though, on other grounds, he would not have hestitated to deny the major settlements of that kingdom urban status. As to fortifications, in both Nuclear America and Asia these were often much less important than in the West-European city. In fact, not infrequently those constructions which the modern mind is predisposed to interpret as fortifications, and which may indeed have been pressed into service as such during emergencies, were in reality symbolic representations of the bounds of the cosmos. It is quite certain, for example, that the laterite wall surrounding Jayavarman VII's capital at present-day Aṅkor Thom in Cambodia contributed more to the welfare of the city in its symbolic role as the Cakravāla mountain range delimiting the Buddhist cosmos than ever it did as an instrument of defense (the symbolism of which this wall was a manifestation is discussed in the next chapter).

In America William Bennett Munro's adoption of Weber's definition of city status more or less in its entirety established criteria of urbanism that were virtually unchallenged for a quarter of a century.

> 'Off hand one might say that it [the city] is a large body of people living in a relatively small area. That, however, would be a very inadequate definition, for it would convey no intimation of the fact that the city has a peculiar legal status, a distinct governmental organization, a highly complicated economic structure, and a host of special problems which do not arise when an equal

number of people live less compactly together. A comprehensive definition of the modern city must indicate that it is a legal, political, economic, and social unit all rolled into one.'[8]

With the rapid expansion of urban studies after World War II, definitions of urbanism became almost as numerous as authors. Perhaps the most influential, and certainly the most widely quoted, of those definitions relating to the earliest cities is that of V. Gordon Childe, who proposed ten criteria of urbanism.[9] In the order in which Childe expounded them, these were:

1. The concentration of relatively large numbers of people in a restricted area.
2. Craft specialization.
3. The redistributive mode of economic integration (characterized by Childe as the appropriation by a central authority of an – alleged – peasant surplus).
4. Monumental public architecture symbolizing, as Childe put it, 'the concentration of the social surplus'.
5. Developed social stratification.
6. The use of writing.
7. The emergence of exact and predictive sciences.
8. Naturalistic art.
9. Foreign trade, which, by definition, had to be conducted over reasonably long distances.
10. Group membership based on residence rather than kinship.

It is at once apparent that these criteria of urbanism are explicitly delineatory rather than explanatory. They were evidently chosen to constitute an assemblage of supposedly easily recognizable indices whose occurrence would signify the advent of urban form into the world. Thus, although Professor Childe was attempting to analyze a particular *process* – that one to which he gave the name of the Urban Revolution – he has, in fact, furnished us with a set of traits purportedly diagnostic of a *stage* of social development. Consequently, it is not surprising that he failed to establish functional interactions between these criteria. In fact, some appear to be of minimal functional significance in urban development. It is difficult, for example, to relate the emergence of representational (Childe's 'naturalistic') art specifically to the appearance of urban forms. In its anthropomorphic manifestations it may have been a result either of the crystallization of social stratification or of the elaboration of a religious tradition. The former would appear to have been true of early Mesopotamia, where gods – or, at least, recognizably anthropomorphized deities – were portrayed at a somewhat later date than human figures.[10] In the mural art of Teotihuacán, by contrast, gods appear to have been portrayed at least as early as, and probably prior to, the representation of men. In Shang China animal forms seem, on present evidence, to have taken precedence over the portrayal of men, and there are no recognizable depictions of deities. Generally speaking, rather than an index of urbanism, representational art would seem, like urbanism itself, to be one specific characteristic within the inclusive category of civilization. In any case, the significance of representational art in relation to urban genesis is progressively declining as excavations at Jericho, Çatal Hüyük, and even Lepenski Vir, reveal sophisticated likenesses of gods, humans, and animals up to four millennia before the emergence of the earliest urban forms. Furthermore, not all of Childe's criteria occur in all cities, so that it is to be presumed that he himself regarded them less as indices of urbanism than as elements in a composite or ideal-type city.[11] Yet still other of the ten characteristics are not specific to cities. Monumental architecture, for instance, is to be found in both non-urban and pre-urban societies.

Let us for the moment, nevertheless, accept these criteria as indices of a particular stage in the evolution of society in the way that Lewis Henry Morgan might have done, and measure the social and economic institutions of the ceremonial center against them. Craft specialization, the redistributive mode of economic integration, monumental architecture, and varying degrees of social stratification are certainly associated with the phase of the ceremonial complex in each of its major cultural manifestations, and have been adequately discussed in the preceding pages. Representational art is also usually reckoned to be a significant feature of civilization, if not specifically related to urban development. The concentration of population in a compact settlement, however, is a characteristic of, at most, only two or three of the realms of nuclear urbanism, and possibly even there is an illusion which will be dispelled by future archeological research. Nor, as we have seen, was foreign trade equally strongly developed in all the nuclear regions. For instance, apart from symbiotic exchanges between upland and lowland, coast and interior, it is not easily demonstrated in ancient Peru, and is only inferentially evident in Shang China.

THE ROLE OF CORPORATE KIN GROUPS

As to the association of group identification with residence rather than with kinship, Childe appears to have argued inferentially that, as centralized control over production became institutionalized, so kin groups became economically disenfranchised and eventually replaced by a politically structured society. This was an oversimplified view, which may have owed something to the ideas of Franz Oppenheimer in the early years of this century.[12] Robert Adams, in one of the most insightful chapters of his book, has recently demonstrated that, at least in Mesopotamia and Mesoamerica, the transition from ethnically to territorially defined communities, from ascriptively to politically organized units based on residence, was not a matter of simple replacement. Kin-based institutions were not immediately rejected in favor of patron-client relationships. Rather the old gentile groupings persisted side by side with incipient politized structures, and the two articulated through institutions such as the army, corporate craft organizations, labor management on estate projects, and various forms of clientage. In the process the kin groups gradually became modified and absorbed, as specialized dependent elements, into a new socio-economic fabric. Far from being uniformly and entirely disenfranchised, some of the kin groups came to monopolize certain sectors of the new concentrations of power, whose material manifestations were the cult and ceremonial centers. This is not an altogether surprising development in the light of our earlier discussion of the role of conical clans, those basically kin units which yet incorporate elements of class in the form of unequal access to the means of production. We have shown that in Shang China an individual's rank within his clan was determined by his consanguineal proximity to the main line of descent, so that the so-called Shang lineages were something very close to conical clans. Robert Adams has discerned similar tendencies to internal stratification, based on the degree of relationship to a real or fictive ancestor, in the kin groups which constituted the elementary units of which the states of Early Dynastic Mesopotamia were composed. Summarizing the implications of materials recently reinterpreted by Igor Diakonoff, Adams writes, 'Clearly, there were groupings of nuclear families into ascriptive units organized at least in part along lines of descent. Such groups in some (and perhaps in most) cases corporately held title to agricultural lands. They also played a role in the organization of the crafts, of corvée labor called up by the state for certain purposes, and probably of the army. Such widely manifested functions suggest that lineage groupings had not become merely vestigial by late Early Dynastic and Akkadian times but, instead, were still both powerful and important.'[13]

In Mexico a succession of anthropologists have discussed the nature and role of the 'Big Houses' or *Calpulli*, strongly stratified, localized, endogamous lineages which held corporate title to agricultural land and constituted the basic units of organization in numerous crafts and professions. It has long been recognized that, although the fundamental ties uniting the calpullis were those of kinship, yet these lineages were also transected by relatively well-developed social and economic distinctions approximating closely to classes, and Eric Wolf is undoubtedly correct in describing the calpullis as conical clans.[14] Paul Kirchhoff, in proposing this term, had already pointed to the flexibility of these stratified kin groups in the face of change, and their potentialities for the evolution of socially and economically differentiated hierarchies.[15] In both Mesopotamia and the Valley of Mexico the available sources are just adequate to permit a reconstruction of the manner in which such reconstitutions of society did occur. The process was not identical in the two regions. Whereas in Mesopotamia it took the form of an organically induced stratification, in Mexico it was more in the nature of a politically superimposed stratification,

375

THE CEREMONIAL COMPLEX

but the final outcome was not significantly different in the two culture realms. Professor Adams has summarized it as follows:

> 'From the viewpoint of stratification, it is not too much to describe early Mesopotamia and central Mexico as slightly variant patterns of a single, fundamental course of development in which corporate kin groups, originally preponderating in the control of land, were gradually supplemented by the growth of private estates in the hands of urban élites. And, while such corporate kin groups still remained active and viable in many respects at the termination points in our two sequences, it is only fair to conclude that they had by then become encapsulated in a stratified pattern of social organization that was rigidly divided along class lines.'[16]

The information relating to kinship in the earlier phases of urban development in the other realms of nuclear urbanism is too exiguous to permit an analysis on the pattern of that undertaken by Robert Adams for Mesopotamia and Mesoamerica, but the semi-autonomous, patriarchal *uji* of Yamato Japan would seem to have exhibited some of the characteristics of conical clans. The members of the so-called imperial clan, about which Japanese tradition is most explicit, are known to have traced their descent to a common ancestor, and to have ascribed social, economic, and political privileges in accordance with consanguineal relationship to the main line of descent. There is reason to suppose that in these respects the imperial clan, which was simply the most powerful of the lineages, was not dissimilar from other *uji*. It is evident, too, that the lineages of the Quraysh tribe discussed above (p.286) were similarly constituted, as were some of those Yoruba kin groups which operated as landholding corporations, with positions of prestige distributed unequally among share-holding males. In any case it is evident that these stratified kin groups played an extremely important role in several of the realms of nuclear urbanism, and would repay more extended study. Adams appears to assume that, in Mexico at any rate, such kin groups 'were of high antiquity, considerably antedating the onset of civilized life by any definition'.[17] If this were indeed so, then it might plausibly be suspected that the places and times of urban genesis were causally related to the existence of such internal tendencies to stratification within kin groups, and further research directed accordingly. However, there is no real evidence for the high antiquity of conical clans, even in Mesoamerica. In the nature of things such evidence is, and probably always will be, irrecoverable, depending as it does on the written word. It is difficult to conceive of archeological evidence in the strict sense providing the sort of information relating to both kin and class which would prove the existence of such clans, and future investigations along these lines will presumably be forced to focus on the role of conical clans subsequent, rather than prior, to the emergence of urban forms. At the moment there is no way of telling if conical clans, even in those realms where they are known to have existed, were a precondition for the initiation of urban development or simply a manifestation of the process in operation. Presumably their formation was a possibility from the very first moment when egalitarian first began to be transformed into rank societies.[18] Nevertheless, a relationship of this type between kin and class surely lies at the heart of that process of social transformation which is commonly called the Urban Revolution, and its further investigation is a problem both obvious and exigent.

THE SIGNIFICANCE OF WRITING

Writing has proved a popular index of urban status among investigators of city origins since Lewis Morgan first drew attention to it in this context in 1910. Professor Childe, in a recent paper, has designated writing as the specifically distinguishing feature of urban society,[19] and Gideon Sjoberg has called it 'the single firm criterion for distinguishing the city, the nucleus of civilization, from other types of early settlements.'[20] Apparently these authors have envisaged writing as a medium of communication which, more than any other factor, has tended to promote the homogeneity of the ruling classes, as prime instrument in the consolidation and maintenance of their power, and as the principal disseminator of their value systems. Quite apart from the fact that the very small literate groups in most of the areas of nuclear urbanism, and particularly in Mesopotamia, Egypt and Nuclear America, were by no means identical with the corresponding political élites, this emphasis on literacy as a promoter of cohesion among the ruling classes fails to take account of the probable roles of different types of script. Very little work has been done on this problem, but it would seem likely that logographic scripts, for example, would be more liable to contribute to the consolidation of power among élites than would alphabetic systems, for they are more difficult to master and therefore preserve their arcane, often sacred, import the more effectively. Moreover, because they tend to reify concepts relating to the natural and social order, it would seem likely that they would tend to promote the stability of an existing social and ideological condition. In any case, the insistence on writing as a criterion of urbanism would force us to exclude from that category both the large but compact Central Andean settlements of Inca times, foci of the only true empire in pre-Columbian America (as well as the earlier Peruvian ceremonial complexes), and the dense aggregations of people in the Yoruba territories.

Of the seven original and fully evolved systems of writing which developed in the Old World only five need concern us here: Sumerian, Egyptian, Cretan, Proto-Indic, and of course Chinese (the other two being Proto-Elamite and Hittite). Of these five, Proto-Indic is undeciphered and Cretan only partially deciphered, so that our remarks on the *principles* of early writing must be restricted to the Sumerian, Egyptian, and Chinese systems. Ignace Gelb, to whom we owe much of the information in the following paragraphs, has pointed out that the unifying characteristic of these systems resides in their all having been phonographic from their earliest development, and in their all making use of logograms, syllabic signs, and auxiliary signs.[21]

The earliest extant Sumerian written records were discovered at Uruk, in the stratum known as Uruk IV, which should probably be dated to the closing centuries of the fourth millennium BC. The simplest forms of records were nothing more than tags, bearing impressions of cylinder seals, which were used to identify both commodities and their owners. The patent inadequacies of this method of recording soon induced the substitution of sketched signs for objects and of written signs for the seals. The earliest Uruk writing was, therefore, logographic in character, but phonetization was introduced well before the end of the Protoliterate period, in response to the need for a more precise representation of proper names, and spread rapidly as a solution to the ever more pressing problem in an expanding and diversifying culture of expressing words and sounds which could not be adequately signified by pictures or combinations of pictures. Henceforth the way was open for the expression of all linguistic forms, even the most abstract, by means of written symbols, and the necessary conventionalization of forms and principles proceeded rapidly. The development of Sumerian syllabic writing, consisting of signs which usually represented monosyllables (or more rarely dissyllables) ending in a vowel or consonant, resulted from the amalgamation of two processes, both subsumed in the notion to which Gelb has given the name Principle of Economy,[22] that is the tendency to express the totality of linguistic forms in any particular language by the smallest possible number of signs. In Sumerian one method, by far the most important, was to indicate the vowel correctly but not the consonant (voiced, voiceless, and emphatic consonants in signs ending in a consonant not being distinguished); the other was to indicate the consonant correctly but not the vowel. The overwhelmingly predominant material on which the Sumerians chose to write was clay and, as the rounded forms characteristic of early Sumerian logography could not easily be incised on clay with a stylus, in the course of time the signs came to assume an angular form, at the same time as the natural pressure of the scribe's hand on the stylus imparted a wedge-like appearance to individual strokes. Hence the descriptive term 'cuneiform', which is customarily applied to this system of writing.

The origins of writing in Egypt are somewhat more obscure than in the case of Sumer. On a number of slate palettes from Hierakonpolis, events are recorded by means of a descriptive-representational device (with no attempt to reproduce the word order of language), supplemented by the use of the rebus principle for the representation of proper names. By about the beginning of the third millennium BC, the rebus device, which on the palettes had been subordinate to the identifying-mnemonic representation, was elaborated into a full phonetic system of writing, perhaps as a result of Sumerian stimulus. For the rest of their history the Egyptians used a word-syllabic writing, expressed for purposes of public display in hieroglyphics, but in everyday life in two forms of cursive script, first hieratic, and subsequently demotic. The syllabary[23] devised by the Egyptians consisted of some twenty-four signs, each with an initial consonant plus any vowel, and of a further eighty signs each denoting two consonants together with any vowel or vowels. Unlike the Sumerian script, which made use of two economizing devices, Egyptian writing, probably in response to the relative stability of consonants but prevailing variability of vowels in Semitic languages, employed a syllabary based on signs which indicated consonants correctly but made no attempt to render vowels accurately, a procedure analogous to the second Sumerian method mentioned above. Vowels were never indicated in the actual writing, a legacy which Egyptian bequeathed to derivative Semitic languages.

Writing was certainly a prominent feature of Shang culture, but the place and manner of its origin are unknown. A Chinese tradition preserved in the *Appended Judgments* to the *I-Ching* tells us that, 'In the earliest times [prior to the invention of writing] government was achieved with the help of knotted cords', presumably some sort of mnemonic device similar to that known in K'ichuwa (Quechua) as *khipu* (*quipu*).[24] There is no archeological confirmation of this use in ancient China, but it is difficult to imagine that such a remark would have been incorporated in the *I-Ching* if the device had been wholly unknown in the area. As a matter of fact, the *khipu* was until recently used by at least one group of Miao tribesmen in southwest China and in the Liu Ch'iu islands, as well as in Prehispanic Peru, where its use is best known.[25] Consequently it would appear at one time to have had a natural circum-Pacific distribution, with which an occurrence in ancient China would not have been inconsistent. On balance there seems a fair likelihood that a remembrance of an actual item of material culture of high antiquity had been caught up among the omen texts preserved in the *I-Ching*. However, in no sense could the *khipu* be construed as a system of writing. In Chinese mythology the invention of this was attributed to an official of the fifth millennium BC,[26] but so far no sign of writing, no hint even of semasiography, has been discerned in Lungshanoid cultural assemblages. When writing first appeared on Shang oracle bones – or, at least, on those discovered so far – it was already a developed, though still evolving, instrument of visual communication, in constant use both as an adjunct of the patrimonial mode of government and for private purposes. But it did not possess a full syllabary comparable to those of the Sumerians and Egyptians. As the words of the language were regularly expressed in word signs, it was necessary to accord such signs a syllabic function only when representing foreign words and names. Even then specific syllables were not accorded standardized word signs. Not until the 5th or 6th century AD was a syllabic writing devised, based on the *fan-ch'ieh* principle, to assist in the reading of rare and difficult word signs.

So far as extant inscriptions allow an opinion, the chief use of writing was as a record of questions and answers in connection with the practice of scapulimancy. The topics on which advice was sought were virtually restricted to the propriety of sacrifice at certain times, the possibility of occurrence of various natural phenomena, the prognosis for harvests, the outcome of military expeditions, and the welfare of the king in both his private and public activities (though these two roles were not always easily distinguishable). More than 2,500 characters have been listed in the oracle records so far, the majority being logograms conventionalized well beyond the pictographic (primary sign) stage, but it is not impossible that others, which have not survived or so far been discovered, may have been devised for use in secular contexts where a terse and dignified style was not demanded. Even among the 1,500 or so that have been identified, there occur all six classes of character formation – pictographs, indirect symbols, associative compounds, mutually interpretative symbols, phonetic loan characters, and determinative-phonetics [27] – which were recognized in the analytical dictionary *Shuo-wen Chieh-tzŭ*, compiled in the 2nd century A D. Tung Tso-pin has proposed that two scripts, both logographic, may have been in use: one, simpler and restrained in style, being restricted to the oracle-bones, the other, more ornamental in character, being represented by inscriptions on bronze ritual vessels.[28] Tung has also discerned five phases in the evolution of the Shang oracle script, each characterized by a relatively distinctive style of writing.[29]

The oracle inscriptions were carved after they had been drawn with a brush,[30] and similar brushed characters have cropped up on pottery sherds at Cheng-Chou and other Shang sites. Not infrequently the standard of calligraphy of the potters falls considerably short of that achieved by the oracle scribes. Inscriptions also occur on bronzes, on various bone and horn articles (including a skull believed to be that of a tribal chieftain offered in sacrifice to the royal ancestor **Tso-·i̯et [Tsu-i]), on stone and jade artifacts, and on three bronze seals.[31] This would seem to imply that literacy in its broadest sense was not restricted to court ritualists, diviners, and other government officials, but also reached down, in somewhat debased form, to the artisan class. The fact that some inscriptions appear on circumstantial grounds to have been engraved in distant provinces but subsequently filed in the archives at the capital only serves to emphasize the centripetal tendencies of the patrimonial organization discussed in Chapter One.

Herrlee Creel, perhaps influenced by the frequency with which questions recorded on oracle bones were addressed to ancestors, has plausibly suggested that writing in the Chinese culture realm was in origin largely a response to a need to communicate with the dead,[32] an interpretation which he can support with certain etymological evidence. The Chinese scholar T'ang Lan has recently claimed to have discovered an alternative script to that of the oracle bones and the bronzes.[33] If such did exist, it may have been more closely related to mundane activities, particularly those usually considered inseparable from a redistributive economy. It might even be considered strange that so few records of this type have come to light. Moreover, the recognition in the oracle texts of the graph ***ts'ĕk*, denoting writing slips tied together or, in modern terms 'book', may imply that some perishable material such as wood was also used as a medium for writing, and it is just possible that such slips were employed for secular purposes and inscribed with a lost script different from that on the oracle bones. Against this it must be pointed out that, if such a system of writing did exist, it was not used by the potters or the craftsmen in bone mentioned above. In any case T'ang's evidence is ambiguous in the extreme and, in my opinion, he is unlikely to be able to sustain his thesis. In any case, there can be no shadow of doubt that the Shang script as it appears on tens of thousands of oracle bones was an indigenous development, and there is no need in the second half of the 20th century to offer refutations of the old idea that it was borrowed from southwestern Asia or Egypt. However, the possibility of stimulus diffusion having operated is not thereby ruled out, and is considered subsequently.

It is impossible to discuss the principles of the Proto-Indic writing system, for neither has the script itself been deciphered nor has the language it represented been identified. At least from the formal point of view the writing, which exhibits no recognizable evolution of form in the centuries of its existence, appears to have been a fully developed system, using conventionalized logographs of great clarity, often ingeniously modified by the addition of strokes or accents, and sometimes combined one with another in the form of conjuncts. Nearly four hundred distinct signs have been listed so far. It is believed that the script was primarily phonetic, with most of the signs representing open or closed syllables, and the remainder functioning as determinatives or logograms. The inscriptions, mainly on seals, are characteristically brief, averaging perhaps six lines, and the direction of writing is usually boustrophedon.[34]

Although Cretan writing is only partially deciphered, its evolution is somewhat better understood. Seals bearing representations of objects and living creatures appear at the beginning of the Early Minoan period, and a pictorial style of writing early in Middle Minoan I (*c.* 2000–1900 BC). To this form of writing Sir Arthur Evans, the excavator of Knossos, gave the name of *Hieroglyphic Class A*, to distinguish it from *Hieroglyphic Class B* which developed in Middle Minoan II (*c.* 1900–1700 BC).[35] During the next four or five centuries, in response to an increasing complexity in the economic basis of society, there evolved first a cursive writing known as *Linear A* (used until about 1450 BC), and then, subsequent to the Mykenaian conquest, a cursive *Linear B*, which continued in use up to about 1200 BC. Linear B has been deciphered and identified as a representation of the Greek language.[36] Linear A, however, has thus far not been deciphered, though it is extremely probable that it was used to express a non-Greek language. It consists of eighty or so syllabic signs, about half of which correspond formally to signs in Linear B, together with a relatively small number of logograms.

When we turn to the New World we find no developed systems of writing. In the Central Andean culture realm no system at all emerged, and in Mesoamerica only limited systems. Although incipient phonetization can be discerned among both Aztecs and Mayas (the earliest examples in the whole of Middle America coming from the stage known as Monte Albán II, at about the beginning of the Christian era), there can be no question of either of those languages ever having attained to a fully phonetized writing system. In principle Aztec records are not so very different from the identifying-mnemonic devices formerly employed by several North American Indian tribes. Phonetization is restricted almost exclusively to the representation of proper names, which could not be rendered otherwise. The Mayan writing has not so far been deciphered (claims to the contrary notwithstanding), and this in spite of the fact that the Maya languages are well known – a sure indication that Mayan writing, apart from a few signs for divinities, was not phonetic. Many attempts at decipherment of this writing have so far progressed no further than demonstrating its preoccupation with mathematical and astronomical matters.[37]

It is clear from what has been said about these several developed and limited systems of writing which emerged in the realms of nuclear urbanism that, although they doubtless did function as instruments for the promotion of cohesion among élites, they operated in different ways, at different levels, and in the interests of diverse categories of élites. Whereas the Egyptian and Chinese developed systems and the Mayan limited system seem in their earlier stages to have been used predominantly in broadly religious contexts, the Sumerian, and perhaps the Proto-Indic, appear to have been used for secular ends, although – demonstrably in the case of the former and probably in the case of the latter – in the service of religious institutions. The earliest use of writing in Mesopotamia was in the construction of economic schedules within temples, and only secondarily was it adapted to the preparation of lexical lists. However, these different contextual emphases do not appear to have influenced the mode of expression adopted, for, of those writing systems that we have described, Sumerian, Egyptian, Chinese, and presumably Proto-Indic, all employed a predominantly word-syllabic form of representation, while Cretan alone developed a syllabic system. It is possible, though, that the actual signs used in the systems may have reflected to some extent the purposes for which they were devised. The mechanical production of cuneiform with the help of a stylus, for example, was perhaps more consonant with the level of skill and conditions of work of a comparatively humble Sumerian scribe, a cog in the machine of public economy and administration, than would have been the elaborate drafting of early Egyptian hieroglyphs or Shang oracle characters, to say nothing of the involuted Maya signs. Against this, nevertheless, must be balanced the fact that tablets of clay, the only readily available medium in Lower Mesopotamia, were inimical, or at least offered no incentive, to sign elaboration. In any case there can be little doubt that even the technically primitive writing of Protoliterate times would have been capable of increasing the efficiency, and consequently of consolidating the managerial functions, of the temple hierarchs. Equally surely it would have contributed to the social status of those specialists who employed more elaborate and arcane scripts in the pursuit of specifically ritualistic aims.

These remarks inevitably raise the question of the monogenesis or polygenesis of writing, using that term in the sense of a system of inter-communication by means of conventional, visible, phonetized signs (picture communication is, of course, as universal as art forms). The clear chronological priority of Sumerian over the other six systems does nothing to establish it as a prototype, and the morphology of signs is an unreliable, though in the past not infrequently invoked, index of derivation. It is, after all, not surprising that a large number of objects in the environment which maintain a high degree of constancy of form in all parts of the world should be represented by basically similar signs. Even structural characteristics such as phonetization or vocalization might well have followed parallel courses of development, a process illustrated by the similarities in evolution exhibited by several writing systems created in recent times by primitive societies under the stimulus of Western influences. It is observable, however, that, in so far as the imperfect nature of the archeological record allows an opinion, the period of development of the fully phonetized Sumerian system was considerably longer than that of any of the other six systems. Either six long protohistories of writing have been wholly lost to archeology, or unknown factors rendered the Sumerian rate of progress especially slow, or – more probably – foreign influence in the nature of stimulus diffusion accelerated the process in several instances. Such an argument is strengthened when generalized evidence of cultural contact is supported by spatial proximity, as, for example, in the case of Sumerian, Proto-Elamite, and Proto-Indic, or of Hittite, Cretan, and possibly Egyptian. It is clearly less convincing when applied to Shang China. All in all, it is difficult not to agree with Ignace Gelb when he concludes that the arguments advanced in favor of the monogenesis of writing 'are neither stronger nor weaker than those advanced in favor of the dependency of Greek astronomy on Babylonian prototypes.'[38]

THE EMERGENCE OF EXACT AND PREDICTIVE SCIENCES

The stage of advancement of the sciences also varied from region to region, but it is safe to say that calendrical calculation took the foremost place in the early

THE CEREMONIAL COMPLEX

phases, though the evidence for this is often only inferential from subsequent developments. For Peru the evidence is especially meager, though the figures laid out in stone on the open *pampa* around Nazca, and dated to about AD 500, are usually interpreted as aids to astronomical observations for calendrical purposes.[39] It was in the northern realms of Nuclear America, by contrast, that the most complex and accurate of all calendrical systems were devised. There, a curiously distinctive conception of time as multidimensional and eternally recurrent led to the creation of two intermeshing time counts, which in combination permitted the numbering of years in terms of a cycle of fifty-two. The first of these counts (Nahuatl : *tonalpohualli* = 'count of the days'; Maya : *tzolkin* = 'wheel of the days'; Zapotec : *pije*; Matlazincas : *nitzihiabe*) took the form of a divinatory almanac, in which thirteen numbers and twenty signs were combined into a religiously conceived cycle of 260 days, the whole operating on a pattern analogous to that of the ten celestial stems and twelve terrestrial branches in China. It is evident that this count was used in very early times by the priests of Teotihuacán and Monte Albán,[40] but the circumstances of its origin are completely unknown. The number 260 has no astronomical significance. By the Nahuatl-speaking groups and by the Mixtec, Otomí, Huastec, Totonac, and Maya this calendar was integrated with the count of a solar year of 365 days (Nahuatl : *xihuitl*; Maya : *haab*), made up of eighteen months each of twenty days, and an intermission of five nameless and uncounted days (Nahuatl : *nemontemi*; Maya : *uayeb*) which were regarded as outside the flow of time, and therefore evil. In Mexico the months in this calendar were named after farming activities, and the days of the month were distinguished by numbers. The passage of time was charted by intermeshing the 260-day *tonalpohualli* year with the 365-day solar year. Any particular day in the 260-day cycle could coincide for a second time with the same day in the 365-day cycle only after a lapse of seventy-three revolutions of the former cycle and fifty-two of the latter. The least common multiple of 260 and 365 is 18,980 days, or fifty-two years, the period which constituted the sacred cycle or *xiuhmolpilli* (= year bundle), whose close signified a cosmic crisis in the Mesoamerican world. In the southern reaches of the Puebla valley and in the Maya culture realm another count subsumed both the *xiuhmolpilli* and a Venus year of 584 days, the *tonalpohualli*, the solar year, and the Venus year coinciding every 104 years, that is after two *xiuhmolpilli*.

Among the lowland Maya these calendrical calculations were extended even farther to encompass truly astronomical periods of time. The great cycle of the Maya was a period of 1,872,000 days or 5,125 solar years, which encompassed all time counts and within which known history was believed to occupy thirteen periods of 7,200 days (*katun*) each. This was the basis of the so-called Maya 'Long Count', which was held to have been initiated at a date in the past defined as *13.0.0.0.0 4 Ahau 8 Cumhu* (13 was the number of *baktun* and the zeroes denoted four other time counts that need not be specified). It has been calculated as having referred to various dates in the 32nd century BC, of which 3133 BC may be the most accurate. What transcendentally awesome event the Maya envisaged as having taken place on that date is unknown, but it is certain that the calendar itself originated much later, probably in the 3rd or 4th century BC. Because they counted by days rather than by years the Maya priests never lost a single day of elapsed time, and the Long Count was exact to within one day in 250,000. As a result, calculations of the dates on hundreds of Maya Long-Count stelae, without exception, lead back to 4 *Ahau* 8 *Cumhu*, that is to that climacteric day of the tonalpohualli which occupies the ninth position of the month Cumhu in the Haab year when the count was inaugurated.

About Sumerian astronomy and calendrics nothing is known directly,[41] but the comparatively advanced level of the earliest extant Babylonian astronomical texts affords grounds for believing that calendrical calculations were probably undertaken by the beginning of the third millennium BC or earlier. In Egypt the 365-day calendar was an invention of the early dynasties. It was a device of the administrators which, although presumably based on an average of observations of the dates of the Nile flood, bore little relation to daily life. The year was, in fact, an arbitrary period, anchored at first to an annual occurrence, the heliacal rising of Sirius, which was designed solely to ensure precision in record keeping. Of calendars which may have been devised in the Indus valley nothing is known.

So far as China is concerned, it is certain that the system of *hsiu*, or lunar mansions, was evolving during the middle centuries of the Shang dynasty, and there are implications in the oracle inscriptions that the equatorially based division of the heavens into four main 'palaces' had already been devised by the time of **M$\mathrm{\underline{i}}$wo-Tieng (Wu-Ting), who reigned, according to Tung Tso-pin's computations, from 1339 to 1281. In fact Chu K'o-chen would attribute the origin of the *hsiu* to some time in the third millennium.[42] The implications of surviving substantive literary records, as opposed to those archetyped texts which attribute a high civilization to remotest antiquity, are wholly antagonistic to such an early date for the beginnings of Chinese astronomy, and the archeological evidence is equivocal on this point, though it is not impossible that the earlier phases of the Cheng-Chou settlement may eventually be shown to have derived from the third millennium BC. Moreover, it would seem that astronomical observations were not restricted to the Shang capital, for several of the lunar eclipses recorded on the oracle bones had been observable only in fairly remote benefices. Tung Tso-pin's study of the Shang calendar over a period of one hundred and fifty-two years has shown that the Chinese had even at this early date been successful in solving the problem that confronts all users of a lunisolar calendar, namely the need to relate the synodic month to the solar year. But, like all the other early calendars, the Shang year count bears the impress of officialdom. It was not concerned with the needs of the farmer – who continued to regulate his activities by the onset of the floods, the coming of the rains, the heliacal rising of a star, or some similar phenomenon – but rather was one of a set of accounting devices fashioned to facilitate the ritualistic and managerial functions of sacrally oriented élites.

* * * * *

Subsequently some authors have taken these or similar characteristics – as probably did Childe himself – to be also criteria of civilization. This I believe to be a gratuitous source of confusion. The etymological link between the words 'city' and 'civilization' is wholly inadequate as a guarantee of their synonymity, and the attempt to combine them in a conjoint definition only engenders unnecessary difficulties. This, of course, is not to deny the very real broad correspondence that commonsense establishes between urban life on the one hand and civilization in any of its multitudinous manifestations on the other, but this is no ground for an *a priori* assumption that cities and civilization developed contemporaneously.[43] Here we shall be concerned solely with the definition of urbanism, and shall leave others to decide whether or not it accords with their concept of civilization.

It is evident from the foregoing remarks that many urbanists, certainly those who have adopted Childe's criteria, would exclude the ceremonial complexes of Shang China, classical Cambodia, Śrī Vijayan Java, Old and Middle Kingdom Egypt, pre-classical Greece and Rome, the classical Maya, and pre-Chimú Peru from the category of city on the grounds that they lacked one or more of these characteristics. But then again, these same criteria would also exclude some compact agglomerations such as Chanchan, the Inca cities, Teotihuacán, and Old Ọyọ, whose rulers were preliterate. In fact, applied strictly, such criteria would also exclude populous settlements such as Tenochtitlán, which never passed beyond a proto- or oligo-literate stage. The truth of the matter is that the relationship between political, social, and economic institutions on the one hand and their material expression in the landscape on the other is nothing like so direct as these indices of urban development would seem to imply, and the search for a single indispensable criterion of city life, as for a suite of physical features diagnostic through all cultural contexts, betrays a misunderstanding of what the city is and does. The core of functionally related institutions which are compositely designated by terms appositely rendered into English as 'city' – *pura, uru, alum, happira, asty, urbs, burgh, ville, Stadt, ciudad, città, gorod, qaṣaba, madīna, ch'eng, shi, balig, mu'ang, t'inh, ilu,* and the like – exhibits certain functional regularities irrespective of its cultural setting, but the particular *forms* of service it provides are appropriate to a specific cultural context. The ordering of social institutions at all times, and that series of structural relationships which constitutes the city in particular, are to a very great extent independent of cultural form, and, existing in a wide range of different cultures, may be symbolized in correspondingly diverse ways. In the Hellenistic world, for example, those services regarded as distinctively urban were reflected in the presence of a prytaneion, a gymnasion, and a theater.[44] For the medieval Muslim these elements were at the same time both deficient and excessive, for the chief features predicated of his city were a *jāmi'* (mosque for the Friday service),[45] a *sūq* (permanent market), and an *ḥammām* (public bath),[46] all of which served generalized social, as well as specialist, purposes. It was not fortuitous that a government office was omitted from these criteria, for autonomy under executive officials chosen from among full citizens was not a characteristic of the medieval Muslim city, which was merely an administratively convenient term for a functionally unified, reasonably populous, and relatively permanent settlement. To a Mesopotamian of the Jemdet Naṣr period city life was probably symbolized by the presence of a single feature, the temple. In the Kambujadeśa of Jayavarman VII probably a temple-mountain sufficed to define a city. A Carolingian, by contrast, could hardly have envisaged a city without a keep, a church, and a market. In Mauryan India, temple, palace, and market were the *sine qua non* of a city; and in China of the Spring-and-Autumn period an altar to the god of the soil, a temple to the ruler's ancestors, and a wall. It is clearly not in localized idioms of urban form that cross-cultural regularities are to be sought, but rather at the operational level, where social, political, and economic processes can be reduced to functional terms. And it is this underlying structural pattern, rather than its surficial cultural overlay, that is of primary concern to us in the present instance. From this point of view, Professor Childe's criteria of urban status can be seen to comprise one primary and several secondary variables; and he leaves us in no doubt that he regarded the progress of technology, resulting in the availability of augmented food surpluses, as the dependent variable in the process. Exactly how this newly acquired, deployable capital generated concurrent social and political differentiation he did not specify.

It is equally evident that Childe adopted as his standard of urbanism the cities of ancient Mesopotamia, Egypt, the Indus valley, and Mesoamerica, with the teleological implication that they were the first in a series of landscape features which, from that time to the present, had approximated more and more closely to the form of the contemporary city. This is a procedure which inevitably raises semantic problems as the initial constellation of material features is traced towards the present. The problems stem from two main causes. In the first place there can be no *a priori* certainty that these early congeries of features were indeed the forerunners of those of the modern city, and, secondly, the physical expression in the landscape of any particular institution will have changed from age to age and from cultural milieu to cultural milieu. It follows that any serviceable definition of urban form must be couched in functional terms, and must derive from the functionally interrelated nexus of institutions which is *currently* recognized as a city.

Not all contemporary urbanists subscribe to the same definition of urbanism. Some, while rejecting a definition based on architectural and spatial morphology, have yet adopted one based on social morphology. As would be expected, this has been the favored approach of sociologists, of whom Louis Wirth is perhaps the most representative. For him the city was minimally a 'relatively large, dense, and permanent settlement of socially heterogeneous individuals' (and when he used the phrase 'socially heterogeneous' he was thinking less of class differentiation than of ethnic variation: in fact he was not primarily concerned with class distinctions at all, but rather with the manner in which social groups in a city were subjected to processes of disruption).[47] The adequacy of this definition for the study of the contemporary city has been called in question on numerous occasions during the past thirty years, and again recently by Oscar Lewis,[48] but, whatever merits it may yet retain, it ultimately reduces the city to a Western and relatively recent phenomenon.[49] In this it is as constricting for the student of the pre-industrial or traditional city as is Max Weber's definition, already cited on p. 371; and, like Weber's criteria of urbanism, it excludes a large number of settlement types which have customarily been ascribed city status. Much the same argument can be urged against the economic bases of urbanism which have been propounded from time to time, notably by Henri Pirenne,[50] and, more recently, by Shigeto Tsuru.[51] Like the sociological – and for that matter the political, administrative, religious, and ekistical indices of urbanism – the economic definition of urbanism in practice turns out to be based on a combination of morphological and functional criteria, with, generally speaking, a preponderance of the former. I don't mean by this that these definitions depend on the form and spatial organization of the material expressions of social or economic or political institutions, but that they are cast in terms of abstract morphologies of urban society, of urban economics, or of urban politics. One of the few formally sustained approaches to the definition of urbanism in purely functional terms is that of the geographers who, in accordance with the powerful Theory of Central Place,[52] tend to look upon the city as an instrument for the organization of dependent territory. In other words, they define the city as a principle of regional integration, as a generator of effective space. John Friedmann (who, incidentally, is not a geographer) has stated this concept in the following terms: '... the hierarchy of urban places represents the ultimate means for organizing a geographic area into its component social, political-administrative and economic spaces ... urban institutions extend their influences outward, binding the surrounding regions to the central city and introducing to them urban ways of thought and action.'[53] In this context 'organization' implies a reorientation of the social, political, and economic activities of a tract of territory, not merely its exploitation, the utilization of its biological and mineral resources, by the inhabitants in daily sorties from a centrally located settlement. By this yardstick the ceremonial complexes which have constituted the focus of our discussion in previous pages qualify as urban forms, for the transformation that they symbolized from a primarily reciprocative to a dominantly superordinate redistributive mode of economic integration did indeed result in the generation of effective economic space. And, as economic processes were mediated by essentially non-economic institutions, the economic space generated by the ceremonial city was at the same time effective social, political, and administrative space. Above all, it was sacred space, the sanctified *habitabilis* of a group integrated politically, socially and economically by the reallocative functions of the central shrine.[54]

From the point of view of the contemporary urban geographer, then, the ceremonial complex would appear to qualify functionally as an urban settlement. But it is only fair to acknowledge that the concentration of population in a restricted area is a supremely important attribute of the present-day city, and should, in fact, be regarded as characteristic of the representative city in both modern and pre-industrial times.[55] John Wilson, working in ancient Egypt, felt that the ceremonial centers of the Nile valley prior to the advent of the New Kingdom were vaguely incongruous as urban forms, and contrived the formula 'civilization without cities' to take account of the anomaly.[56] Gordon Willey and S. W. Miles were both confronted with similar problems of terminology in their studies of Mayan settlement patterns,[57] as indeed were Kwang-chih Chang in early China,[58] John Rowe in Peru,[59] and Michael Coe in classical Cambodia,[60] and each felt the need to qualify the degree of urbanism involved. Rowe coined the term 'synchoritic', and Miles subsequently proposed 'extended boundary town' as a designation for the settlement that consisted of a focally situated complex of public and religious buildings serving a population scattered through the surrounding countryside.[61] But the real significance of such forms is that they lacked boundaries altogether – apart, of course, from the frontiers of the territory that they controlled. The inhabitants of the countryside did not feel themselves to be disenfranchised, underprivileged, or in any way different from those who farmed close under the walls of the ceremonial center, or even from those who practised their skills within the enceinte. All, at appropriate seasons, contributed a proportion of the dividends that they had drawn from the cycle of plant and animal life towards the maintenance of the ritual specialists who dwelt within the confines of the ceremonial complex, and who alone were able both to ascertain the will of the gods and to remind these remote arbiters of human destiny of their responsibilities to their chosen people. And, by their presence at the ceremonial center during the great festivals of the year, countrymen, no less than dwellers within the complex, played their parts in ensuring the effectiveness of those rituals designed to regulate the cycle of time and to ensure the fertility of the earth. All, by sanctioning the appropriational demands of religious *authority*, brought themselves equally within the social, political and economic *power* of the ceremonial center and, consequently, subject to corvée, boon days, tribute, levies, tithes, censuses, tax farming, auctions, markets by decree, and all the other techniques that have been devised at various times to mobilize resources in redistributive economies.

In a recent paper Michael Coe[62] pointed out that the ceremonial cities of both classical *Kambujadeśa* and the classical Maya realm fell within Durkheim's category of societies of mechanical solidarity.[63] Both constituted relatively undifferentiated societies made up of segments that tended to repetitive similarity. All individuals were brought within a unitary moral system which Durkheim called 'the collective conscience', and which was expressed through laws of a primarily penal and repressive character. Each of these societies exhibited a high degree of political centralization, under which its constituent territories were organized unilaterally for the support of a cult center by means of the techniques of resource mobilization mentioned above. But, despite this centripetality, mechanical societies proved extremely brittle when subjected to the forces of political or social change, and were relatively easily overthrown from within or without. This is an accurate characterization not only of those societies that constituted the classical Khmer and Mayan cities, but also of ceremonial cities in any culture, including that of Shang China, and to all Professor Coe denies urban status on the grounds that they lacked adequate social differentiation. I have no methodological quarrel with this *modus operandi*, which has the sanction of Western sociological practice, and is in the tradition established by Max Weber (cf. p.371 above). But it is also implicit in Professor Coe's argument that those cult centers which accommodated compact populations exemplified Durkheim's second polar ideal-type society, namely that of organic solidarity, characterized by a differentiation of its constituent parts that had now become functionally dependent organs. In Durkheim's own words, there has been a breakdown of internal segmentation within communities and a reduction of isolation between them.[64] The collective conscience is both less categorical and less pervasive than in societies of mechanical solidarity, and law tends to be restitutive rather than repressive. Durkheim also demonstrated that the division of labor characteristic of societies of organic solidarity arose as a means of resolving various forms of competition. But the mere fact of agglomerating people in compact cities does not, as Spencer believed,[65] necessarily generate competition between communities or differentiation within society. In fact society is not necessarily more highly differentiated in a compact temple-city than in a dispersed ceremonial complex, and I am unable to follow Coe when he contrasts an alleged organic solidarity of early Mesopotamian urban society with the very real and well-attested mechanical solidarity of Egyptian cities prior to the New Kingdom. Social differentiation develops with an increase in what Durkheim termed 'moral' or 'dynamic density', by which he meant opportunity for social interaction.[66] This certainly implies the introduction of new modes of communication and perhaps new forms of transportation, but it is not necessarily going to be affected significantly by the difference between a population grouped within a ceremonial enclave and that same population spread over a dozen or so square miles outside the enceinte. The almost perfectly pyramidal societies of the compact Sumerian city-states exhibited no higher degree of social differentiation, were no less brittle, no less centralized politically, and were governed by laws no less repressive than were the ceremonial cities of early Egypt, or for that matter of Shang China, classical Cambodia, or the Classic Maya. The same holds true for Teotihuacán and the cities of the pre-Khmer state of B'įu-nậm, both of which Coe also regards as societies of organic solidarity, in his terminology true cities.[67] Admittedly the evidence on which to base a conclusion is exiguous in the extreme, and in these matters archeology often hides more than it reveals, but the published accounts of the excavations at both Teotihuacán and the B'įu-nậm site at Oc-èo [68] seem to me to reflect the imprint of societies that were structured primarily on a mechanical rather than an organic pattern. In the case of B'įu-nậm the archeological evidence can be supplemented by meager gleanings from various Chinese annals and encyclopedias. These have been evaluated by a succession of scholars, notably by Paul Pelliot [69] and I find no clear indication in them of an organically structured society. Possibly Professor Coe was impressed by the evidence marshalled by Louis Malleret for commercial activity in the port-city at Oc-èo,[70] but this is no guarantee of an organic society. It is the nature of the instruments of exchange and the manner in which they intermesh with society as a whole, rather than the aggregate volume of commercial transactions, which is of consequence in the structuring of society.

I think that restriction of urban status to those compact societies which exhibit a high degree of differentiation, which – in Durkheim's phrase – are characterized by organic solidarity, has been a major factor in prolonging the debate about the true nature of the large, dense, permanent Yoruba population clusters which we have described in Chapter Three. Whereas Bascom, for example, regarded them as urban on the grounds that their inhabitants were economically independent, socially stratified, and politically unified,[71] W. Schwab wrote of a representative example that 'viewed on the level of form, it was an urban community; if viewed in terms of social organization and process, it was folk.'[72] In the geographers' functional definition of urbanism proposed above, that is as a principle of regional integration, a generator of effective space, the degree of differentiation and solidarity of society is relegated to the status of a secondary classificatory characteristic: important certainly for an understanding of the evolution of contemporary urban society, but not an essential criterion of urbanism. From this point of view, I have little hesitation in ascribing urban status to at least the regional capitals of Yorubaland in, say, the middle of the 19th century.

Durkheim's distinction between mechanical and organic societies was based solely on societal characteristics. Couched in formal morphological terms, it took little account of the precise role assigned to exchange in particular societies. Marcel Mauss, Durkheim's pupil and subsequently his collaborator, extended the theory to explain how exchange functioned as the cement binding individually non-viable, functionally differentiated parts into coherent and viable organic wholes,[73] but it was left to Robert Redfield and Milton Singer, a decade or so ago, to formulate a typology of urban forms that took cognizance of the changing place occupied by economies in society as a whole.[74] At one pole of their classification were those cities in which economic institutions were subordinated to the religious and moral norms of society, and which were mostly administrative and political foci diffusing traditional culture. At the other end of the spectrum were those cities in which the market system was autonomous and self-regulating, cities of the entrepreneur where the values of society were structured about expediential norms that manifested themselves in a consensus appropriate to the technical, rather than the moral, order.[75] In the first type of city, characterized by a rigid social stratification, change was mediated by literati according to the mores of a classical tradition, and was consequently felt to be an inevitable outgrowth from the past, whereas in the second type of city change was generated by conflict and dissent, cultures disintegrated, and an intelligentsia propagated heterodoxies that not infrequently assumed the complexion of heresy. Rootlessness and anomie were prevalent in such cities and, as new cultural integrations were forged, there developed marked and often painful discontinuities between past and future. On the basis of the manner in which these two types of city mediated change Redfield and Singer classified them as cities of, respectively, orthogenetic and heterogenetic transformation.[76]

It must be emphasized that these are 'ideal' polar types which represent developmental trends rather than immutable conditions. A particular city, for example, founded as a national capital primarily for administrative and religious purposes, may subsequently acquire commercial functions, which are perhaps elaborated when its role as a capital is abandoned, at the same time as the authority of the scriptures yields to the expediential mores of the bazaar, the one being expounded by literati, the other codified by an intelligentsia. Simultaneously, authority based on the validation of absolutes and implemented by ritually qualified experts is superseded by the sanction of power based on stratagem and force. Still later the same city, if reconstituted as a political and religious capital, may reactivate some of its original instruments of orthogenesis, and this sequence of changes may be repeated several times over. Of course, it goes without saying that in such a city at least some of the institutions of orthogenetic change persist through the heterogenetic phases, and vice-versa.

The port-city of Malaka affords a good illustration of such a change of role from mediator of orthogenetic change to instrument of heterogenetic transformation. Founded at the very beginning of the 15th century as the capital of a renegade Hindu nobleman,[77] its orthogenetic role was, within a quarter of a century, subordinated to heterogenetic functions induced by its status as the premier entrepôt of Southeast Asia. Yet, even in its heyday as a bustling emporium of trade, its preserved a bureaucratic hierarchy permeated with Indian cosmological concepts, and a rigorous system of court ceremonial[78] more consonant with protocol in a religio-administrative city than with the expediential values of a bazaar port. Moreover, it is possible to interpret Malakan history during the century of the Sultanate in terms of a conflict between social groups representing respectively the moral order and the technical order, namely a homogeneous and traditionalistic Malay élite and a cosmopolitan commercial community sharing only commonalities in economic motivation.[79]

The Chinese city of Hang-Chou underwent somewhat similar transformations. Founded in the 7th century as a *hsien* city, that is as a seat of administration and, by definition, assigned an orthogenetic role, the accident of its location on a sheltered but accessible estuary at the southern edge of the Yang-tzŭ delta, during a period when the trade of the South China coast was approaching its apogee, resulted in its assumption of many functions appropriate to the technical order.[80] The volume of its commerce with the *Nan-Hai*, for example, resulted in the establishment of a Superintendency of Merchant Shipping as early as 989. But when in 1136 the city was chosen as the capital of the Southern Sung, the presence of the imperial government, together with an influx of literati and officials, resuscitated its virtually moribund orthogenetic functions, though by no means eradicating, or even suppressing, its commercial role. There is no need to multiply examples of such modulations between orthogenesis and heterogenesis. For most of their life-histories most cities probably exhibit characteristics of both trends simultaneously, but nevertheless Redfield and Singer's typology does provide us with a perspective within which to view their structures and functions. Occasionally a trend in one direction is sufficiently pronounced to allow the characterization of a particular city, or class of cities, or phase of city development, as orthogenetic or heterogenetic. One such instance is the ceremonial city which, by definition, lies far over towards the pole of orthogenesis. From the point of view put forward by Redfield and Singer, the corollary to the exclusion of such settlement forms from urban status is the exclusion of a large proportion of the compact agglomerations of population which have customarily been described as cities.

It has recently been alleged that urban forms of much earlier date than any discussed in the preceding pages existed in the Levant and in Anatolia. The first of these was revealed by excavations in the Tell es-Sultan, close to present-day Jericho.[81] Its origins go back at least to 7000 BC, and in its maturity it extended over more than eight acres. Miss Kathleen Kenyon, its excavator, accorded it urban status by virtue of its enclosing wall. 'The settlement,' she said, 'is quite clearly on the scale, not of a village but of a town. Its claim to a true civic status is established by the discovery ... that it possessed a massive defensive wall.'[82] Her terminology has been adopted by most subsequent commentators,[83] and has become the authoritative interpretation of the semi-official *History of Mankind*, sponsored by UNESCO.[84] We have argued in the preceding paragraphs that no specific morphological feature, or even assemblage of features, is an adequate index of urban status, which can be defined only in terms of function. Perhaps a wall, even though massive and surrounding a compact settlement, is the least satisfactory of all criteria of urbanism, for it would lead to the classification of, say, a representative Lung-shan village, huddled within its *hang-t'u* defences, as an urban form. The truth is that not enough of the earliest walled settlement at Jericho has been excavated for it to be possible to say much about its function. Whether it was simply a largely undifferentiated aggregation of cultivators and part-time hunters, or whether it was an instrument for the organization of the surrounding territory (in the sense defined above), cannot be decided on the present evidence, but it may be significant that Jean Perrot, in a recent summary of present knowledge, concludes that, 'The "threshold of urbanization" ("urbanism" in our terminology) was reached later in Palestine than in lower Mesopotamia',[85] and thus implicitly excludes early Jericho from the category of city. If Miss Kenyon's assertion that pre-Pottery Neolithic Jericho was 'a culture with all the attributes of civilization, except that of a written language',[86] is satisfying to archeologists, then in the opinion of at least one social scientist she has not provided adequate evidence for that conclusion.

A similar set of terminological problems has also arisen in connection with another early Near Eastern compact settlement that has recently been partially excavated by Dr James Mellaart at Çatal Hüyük, thirty-two miles southeast of Konya on the Anatolian Plateau. This settlement, dated to the seventh millennium BC, covers some thirty-two acres and, although his projected excavations are still incomplete, Dr Mellaart has categorized it as deserving the name of city, because 'it was a community with an extensive economic development, specialized crafts, a rich religious life, a surprising attainment in art and an impressive social organization.'[87] I have read the reports published so far with great care but I can find no proof, on the evidence available, of functional urbanism as defined in the present work. It appears that excavation has so far been restricted to what Mellaart calls the religious quarter. Until the excavation of the site has been carried farther, it will be profitless for a layman to try to define the precise status of this site in the spectrum of settlement forms, but it is interesting that, even at this early stage of the investigation, Dr Mellaart

THE NATURE OF URBANISM

has suggested that only priests could have been bearers of authority. At Jericho, too, the first event seems to have been the establishment of a shrine by hunters of Lower Natufian culture. There can be no doubt that the evidence from both Çatal Hüyük and Jericho strengthens the probability, which has long approached certainty, of a primarily religious focus to social life prior to, and during, the earlier phases of urban generation. The excavations at these two sites have certainly contributed nothing to weaken the propositions and formulations put forward in Chapter Three of this work.

Finally, reference should also be made to an extensive pre-ceramic habitation site at Haldas, just south of Casma on the Peruvian coastal plain. Here, in a Primary Village Farming context, pre-ceramic occupation refuse covers an area of some two kilometers by one and averages 50 centimeters in thickness.[88] There is also a complex temple structure, part of which was built before the introduction of pottery. Canes used to wrap stones laid in the floor of this temple have yielded a radiocarbon date of 1631 BC ± 130.[89] The inhabitants still relied for sustenance primarily on the hunting of sea mammals, fishing, and the gathering of shellfish, supplemented by a little primitive root cultivation. Cotton was already of long-standing use as a textile fiber, but maize was not yet known. It would appear that, notwithstanding a preponderant reliance on maritime and littoral resources at Haldas, the implications of this site are not greatly dissimilar from those of Jericho. In both regions specialized and highly localized resources permitted, perhaps even induced, the congregation in restricted localities in predominantly arid environments of compact populations essentially alien to the prevailing level of technology. In other words, specially favorable environments in these instances appear to have compensated to some extent for a low level of technological advancement in allowing the formation of compact aggregations of farmers in a society lacking instruments for the structuring of such populations. But, as has been emphasized repeatedly in previous pages, the simple fact of agglomeration, particularly in the circumstances with which we are concerned here, does not necessarily imply differentiation of function or the ascription of organizational power to a settlement.

Professor John Rowe has intimated that he is inclined to regard the Haldas settlement as a 'pre-ceramic city', but he is able to do this only at the price of a somewhat idiosyncratic definition of urbanism:

'For the purpose of the present argument, an urban settlement is an area of human habitation in which many dwellings are grouped closely together. The dwellings must be close enough together to leave insufficient space between them for subsistence farming, although space for gardens may be present. In the case of a site where the foundations of the dwellings have not been excavated, an extensive area of thick and continuous habitation refuse provides a basis for supposing that the settlement was an urban one.

The intent of this definition is to exclude clusters of dwellings so small

THE CEREMONIAL COMPLEX [409

that they could be interpreted as belonging to the members of a single extended family. Twenty dwellings is perhaps the minimum number which would provide this exclusion.'[90]

Rowe goes on further to classify urban forms as *pueblos* and *cities*, using the former 'to designate an urban settlement in which all the residents are engaged in hunting, fishing, farming or herding at least part of the time,' and city 'to designate one which includes residents engaged in other activities (manufacturing, trade, services, administration, defence, etc.)'.[91] This definition of urbanism is based on criteria differing so markedly from those that we have employed, and is directed to such markedly different ends, that it is difficult to compare Rowe's conclusions with our own. It appears that, while Rowe's criteria for 'city' status are partially congruent with our category of 'urban', his advent of 'urbanism', by contrast, is analogous to the development of permanent *village* settlement in our schema. This is less important in a discussion of the Haldas site which in any case, by our definition, cannot qualify for urban status, than in a consideration of the implications of Professor Rowe's comprehensive survey of Prehispanic Peruvian cities for urban theory in general. By way of example let us take the following paragraph from Rowe's paper.

'... the Peruvian data throw some light on the relationship between cities and ceremonial centers. Except for the late and somewhat peculiar case of Cuzco, there is no example in our Peruvian data of large cities developing out of ceremonial centers. When large cities replaced or were added to ceremonial centers, as occurred on the north coast, the cities represent the intrusion of foreign ideas coming from another area where the urban tradition was much older. The ceremonial center, therefore, is not a necessary stage in the development of the city.'[92]

In evaluating these remarks there are, I think, three points to be borne in mind. First, translated into our terms, the urban tradition to which Professor Rowe refers was a tradition of fortified villages. The second point is slightly more subtle. It is not suggested – at least not in this work – that the ceremonial center is a necessary stage in the development of a city, but rather that it is likely to prove to have been a functional and developmental phase in the evolution of urban forms in general. This does not imply that any or every particular ceremonial center was transformed into a compact, secularly oriented city, but only that a phase when a mechanically organized society and a superordinate, predominantly redistributive economy, both structured centripetally about a cult center and directed to the achievement of traditional, sacrally sanctioned goals, was – if the process continued for long enough – succeeded by one in which both society and economy were subject to increasing differentiation, and in which both new and old institutions were concerned with patently secular achievements. There is no question here of individual cities necessarily assuming new roles (though that was by no means uncommon), but rather of entirely new patterns of settlement emerging to meet the demands of transformed societies. 'Jede Frühzeit einer Kultur ist zugleich die Frühzeit eines neuen Städtewesens'[93] is true whether cast in the pseudo-mystical idiom of Oswald Spengler or in more conventional sociological terms.

The third point which must be taken into account in any attempt to compare Professor Rowe's conclusions with our own is that in his terminology the term 'ceremonial center' is implicitly restricted to synchoritic urban settlements, 'extended boundary towns' in Miles's phraseology, 'dispersed ceremonial centers' in ours. In the present work, by contrast, the existence of compact ceremonial centers is not only envisaged but illustrated from the archeological record.

None of this is meant to imply that Professor Rowe's perspicacious evaluation of the Peruvian evidence is at fault, but simply that its integration into our schema will require a transmutation of categories, not merely a semantic transposition. The raw material from which his categories have been educed is not familiar to me at first hand, but my attempts at the required transmutation have led me to conclude that the Peruvian evidence is not inconsistent with the general position set forth in this chapter.

It is perhaps appropriate at this point also to mention one or two of those instances where the evolution of ceremonial centers appears to have been truncated at an incipient stage of development, before superordinate redistributive economies had been fully established. Such would seem to have been the case, for example, in the Hopewellian and Mississippian traditions of North America[94] and in the Tairona culture of northern Colombia.[95] Each of these societies affords evidence of a concentration of social and political power on a considerable scale, but each apparently failed to develop adequate instruments for the institutionalization of that increasing differentiation which is associated with the emergence of urban form. A third society, and one which seems to have progressed somewhat farther along the road to urbanism than any of the three just mentioned, is that of the builders in stone in Iron-Age Rhodesia. The most spectacular, but by no means the only, complex of structures still extant is that at Zimbabwe, a name which means literally 'the place where chiefs are buried'.[96] It is thought that an elliptical structure comprising a free-standing outer wall enclosing a second smaller and incomplete wall, two towers, and a mass of fallen stonework, are probably the remains of the residence of a god-chief, his wives, and his immediate entourage, together with an audience hall and the building which housed the sacred relics and palladia of the tribe. Soapstone birds set up on walls, pillars, and platforms may have been in the nature of charms against lightning or, as others think, memorials to departed chiefs. A quarter of a mile to the northward, beyond a wooded valley, is a fortified granite kopje, popularly known today as the Acropolis, whither the whole population probably retired in times of danger. In the valley between these two nodes of settlement were the dwellings and cattle kraals of the populace, presently represented by a confused mass of fallen walls and small stone enclosures going under the appropriate name of 'the Valley Ruins'. In principle, this layout was not significantly different from that of the fortified capital of King Kaśyapa on the Sīgiriya, of Monte Albán in Oaxaca, or of the Inca city of Acarí as described by Dorothy Menzel (Note 56 to Chapter Three), and Zimbabwe would seem to have reached the very threshold of urban status. Over three hundred stone ruins of Zimbabwe type have been located, chiefly in Rhodesia, but most are quite small. Only those at Khami, Dhlo-Dhlo, Nalatali, all in Rhodesia (but rather later than Zimbabwe), and Mapungubwe in the Limpopo valley sector of the Transvaal (which in its earlier stages was contemporary with Zimbabwe) appear to have approached the threshold at all closely. It is usually accepted that these ruins represent the chief settlements of the loosely structured, and often internally feuding, Monomatapa federation, which engaged in fairly extensive trade with the east coast at the time of the Portuguese incursion into the Indian Ocean. It is believed to have been established in the 14th or 15th century.

One final point merits discussion before we leave the topic of definitions. It follows from the functional criterion of urbanism adopted in this work that city and state were coeval, indeed the city was the organizing principle of the state, and all generated cities were in their earlier phases city-states. As emphasized above, this definition of urbanism in terms of the generation of effective space is not the only one which is possible or which may prove analytically profitable. In a perspicacious discussion of the diverse and protean categories which are customarily implicit in the rubric of 'urbanism', Donald McTaggart has warned us against the assumption that all so-called urban phenomena can be subsumed within one logically coherent structural field.[97] 'What is urbanism?' he points out, is a metaphysical rather than a scientific question, and as such is not likely to be answered satisfactorily by the empirical methods of the social sciences. This is substantially the point of view adopted in the present work. While we recognize that the concept of the city is compounded of a series of sets of ideal-type social, political and economic institutions which have combined in different ways in different cultures and at different times, we have directed our attention to the genesis of that instrument for the creation of effective space, that organizing and regionalizing principle, which contemporary *geographers* recognize as constituting the essence of urbanism. This leads us to the conclusion stated above, namely that the process of crystallization of urban forms at the same time brought into being the earliest state institutions. Search for the genesis of either more or less comprehensively defined levels of urban integration will, of course, be likely to lead to the resolution of different problems at different levels of abstraction, and, possibly, the attribution of urban genesis to a variety of different periods and places. One such verdict is that arrived at by Eric Wolf, who defined the city, more narrowly than we have, as 'a settlement in which a combination of functions are exercised, and which becomes useful because in time greater efficiency is obtained by having these functions concentrated in one site.'[98] Starting from these criteria, and restricting his investigations to the compact city, to the exclusion of the dispersed ceremonial center, Wolf was inevitably constrained to distinguish between the genesis of the city and the genesis of the state. 'The city', he says, 'is ... a likely, but not an inevitable, product of the increasing complexity of society',[99] and, like John Wilson who coined the phrase 'civilization without cities' (cf. p.389 above), Wolf is prepared to accede to the notion of cityless statehood. What is important in the present context is that many such apparently conflicting interpretations of urban evolution are less the expression of fundamental disagreements as to the nature of the process than the result of the adoption of varying definitions of urbanism, designed for the investigation of a whole range of social, economic, political, and cultural institutions.

Notes and References

1. For the implications of the term 'city' as used in this volume, see the note on Definitions on p.xviii.
2. Max Weber, *Archiv für Sozialwissenschaft und Sozialpolitik*, vol.47 (1921), pp.621 *et seq.* Reprinted in *Grundriss der Sozialökonomik*, III. Abteilung: *Wirtschaft und Gesellschaft*, 2. Halbband. J.C.B.Mohr (Paul Siebeck), Tübingen 1925. The reference is to p.523 of this reprint. For Louis Wirth's minimal, but nonetheless influential, definition which is subsumed by Weber's statement see p.388.
3. The city-state appears to represent a developmental phase of socio-political organization in which, it is true, the city exercises the sovereign powers of a state government. But this type of city constitutes a special case, coming as it does at that extremity of the spectrum of political dependence at which the territory of the city is coincident with that of the state. The German *Freistädte* and some Italian cities towards the end of the Middle Ages (when the authority of the German Emperor had become merely nominal in Italy) have sometimes been classed as quasi-sovereign, but such clearly do not represent a developmental phase, and should more properly be classed among those cities to which some degree of autonomy has fallen accidentally.
4. Vols.6 and 8 of the *Recueils de la Société Jean Bodin* (Editions de la Librairie Encyclopédique, Bruxelles) contain an extended discussion of the political, administrative and legal bases of urbanism. The three instances of wholly privileged cities mentioned in the text are discussed in André Gonthier, Les villes japonaises. Histoire des institutions administratives et judiciaires', vol.6 (1954), pp.241–48, and 'Le droit privé urbain au Japon', vol.8 (1957), pp.111–14; Jacques Pirenne, 'Les institutions urbaines dans l'ancienne Egypte et dans le pays de Sumer', vol.6, pp.27–48, and 'Le droit privé urbain dans l'ancienne Egypte', vol.8, pp.25–44; and Claire Préaux, 'Les villes hellénistiques, principalement en Orient. Leurs institutions administratives et judiciaires', vol.6. Concerning the status of the Hellenistic city see also Arnold H.M.Jones, *The Greek city from Alexander to Justinian*. Oxford University Press 1940.
5. Weber, *Wirtschaft und Gesellschaft*, p.523.
6. Cf. p.282 above.
7. *Ibid.*
8. William Bennett Munro, *The government of American cities*. Macmillan

NOTES AND REFERENCES

& Co., New York 1926, p.13.

9. V. Gordon Childe, 'The urban revolution', *Town Planning Review*, vol.21, no.1. Department of Civic Design, University of Liverpool 1950, pp.9–16. The process as Childe envisaged it in Mesopotamia is treated in more detail in *New light on the most ancient East*. Routledge and Kegan Paul, London 1952, Chapter 7.

10. Adams, *The evolution of urban society*, p.124.

11. Or, for that matter, in the 'real-type' city of Arthur Spiethoff's conceptualization : cf. 'Pure theory and economic gestalt theory : ideal types and real types', in F. C. Lane and Jelle C. Riemersma (eds.), *Enterprise and secular change*. Homewood, Illinois 1953, pp.444–63.

12. Franz Oppenheimer, *The State*. Bobbs-Merrill Co., Indianapolis 1914.

13. Adams, *The evolution of urban society*, p.86. A summary in English of Igor M. Diakonoff's studies of corporate landholding groups is available in 'Sale of land in pre-Sargonic Sumer', *Papers presented by the Soviet Delegation at the XXIII International Congress of Orientalists, Assyriology Section*. Publishing House of the USSR Academy of Sciences, Moscow 1954.

14. Eric Wolf, *Sons of the Shaking Earth*. Phoenix Book no.90, University of Chicago Press 1962, pp.135–6.

15. Paul Kirchhoff, 'The principles of clanship in human society', in Morton H. Fried (ed.), *Readings in Anthropology*, vol.2. Thomas Y. Crowell Co., New York 1959, p.268.

16. Adams, *The evolution of urban society*, p.119.

17. Adams, *op. cit.*, p.94.

18. These terms are defined on p.25 above.

19. V. Gordon Childe, 'Civilization, cities, and towns', *Antiquity*, vol.31 (1957), pp.36–8.

20. Gideon Sjoberg, *The preindustrial city*. The Free Press of Glencoe, Illinois 1960, p.33. Sjoberg is reporting Childe's views when he uses these phrases.

21. Ignace J. Gelb, *A study of writing*. University of Chicago Press, second edition 1963, p.195.

22. Gelb, *A study of writing*, p.251.

23. For Gelb's classification of the Egyptian non-semantic signs as syllabic, in opposition to Kurt Sethe [*Das hieroglyphische Schriftsystem*. Leipziger Ägyptologische Studien, no.3. Glückstadt and Hamburg 1935] and almost all modern Egyptologists who regard them, whether uniconsonantal or multiconsonantal, as consonantal writing, see *A study of writing*, pp.72–81. There is a useful set of references for the study of Egyptian hieroglyphic writing on pp.259–60 of this work.

24. *I-Ching, Hsi-Tz'ŭ* to Hexagram **Kwad* (*Kuai*). Joseph Needham has reproduced a 2nd-century AD tomb-shrine relief showing the culture-hero

THE CEREMONIAL COMPLEX

Fu-Hsi (**B'i̯ŭk-χia) and his sister consort Nü-Kua (**Ni̯o-Kwa) jointly holding a carpenter's square and a personified *khipu* as symbols of construction and order [*Science and civilisation in China*, vol.1 : *Introductory Orientations*. Cambridge, at the University Press 1954, p.164].

25. Cf. E. Simon, 'Über Knotenschriften und ähnliche Knotenschnüre der Riukiuinseln', *Asia Major*, vol.1 (1924), pp.657–67; Carl Whiting Bishop, in Herrlee Glessner Creel, *Studies in early Chinese culture*. Kegan Paul, Trench, Trübner & Co., Ltd, London 1938, p.33, note 24; L. Leland Locke, *The ancient quipu, a Peruvian knot-record*. New York 1923, and *Supplementary notes on the quipus in the American Museum of Natural History. American Museum of Natural History Anthropological Papers*, vol.30, pt.2. American Museum of Natural History, New York 1938, pp.39–74; André Eckardt, 'Das Geheimnis der Knotenschriften', *Forschungen und Fortschritte*, vol.32 (1958), pp.340–2; Porfirio Miranda Rivera, 'Quipus y jeroglíficos', *Zeitschrift für Ethnologie*, vol.83 (1958), pp.118–32; and [to be used with caution] Baron Erland Nordenskiöld, *The secret of the Peruvian quipus. Comparative Ethnographical Studies, Gothenburg [Göteborg] Museum*, vol.6, pt.1. Göteborg 1925, and [very dubiously] *Calculations with years and months in the Peruvian quipus*, idem., vol.6, pt.2. The famous Inca *khipu* had clearly been adapted for special purposes (about which there is still some dispute), and there is no reason to assume that those of ancient China would have taken that precise form. Those Peruvian examples which are still in existence are recording and mnemonic devices, and it is difficult to see how the principle of knotted strings could have anywhere been employed as an effective instrument for calculation. Certainly all known examples of *khipus* require verbal interpretations to render their stored information intelligible.

26. *Lü-shih Ch'un-Ch'iu*, chüan 17, f.7 verso. The attribution of a divine origin to writing is common to virtually all the Great Traditions of the Old World. For examples see Gelb, *A study of writing*, p.231.

27. In Chinese respectively *hsiang-hsing* (pictographs), *chih-shih* (indirect symbols), *hui-i* (associative compounds), *chuan-chu* (mutually interpretative symbols), *chia-chieh* (phonetic loan-characters), *hsing-sheng* (determinative-phonetics).

28. Tung Tso-pin, 'Chung-Kuo wen-tzŭ-ti ch'i-yüan', *Ta-lu Tsa-chih* vol.5, no.10 (1952), pp.28–38.

29. *Vide* note 124 to Chapter I.

30. T'eng Ku, *Chung-Kuo I-shu Lun-ts'ung*. Ch'ang-sha 1938, pp.78–80.

31. These Shang writings other than the oracle archives are conveniently enumerated by Cheng Te-k'un, *Archaeology in China*, vol.2 : *Shang China*. W. Heffer & Sons Ltd, Cambridge 1960, pp.185–91.

32. Creel, *Studies in early Chinese culture*, pp.36 *et seq*.

33. T'ang Lan, 'Tsai chia-ku chin-wen-chung so-chien-ti i-chung i-ching

NOTES AND REFERENCES

i-shih-ti Chung-Kuo ku-tai wen-tzŭ', *K'ao-ku Hsüeh-pao*, no.2 (1957), pp.33–6.

34. G. R. Hunter, *The script of Harappa and Mohenjodaro and its connection with other scripts*. London 1934; P. Meriggi, 'Zur Indus-Schrift', *Zeitschrift der Deutschen Morgenländischen Gesellschaft*, vol.87 (1934), pp.198–241; H. Heras, 'La escritura proto-Indica y su desciframiento', *Ampurias*, vol.1 (1939), pp.5–81; B. Hrozný, 'Inschriften und Kultur der Proto-Inder', *Archiv Orientální*, vol.12 (1941), pp.192–259, and vol.13 (1942), pp.1–102.

35. Arthur J. [later Sir Arthur] Evans, *Scripta Minoa*, 2 vols. Oxford University Press 1909, 1952.

36. John Chadwick, *The decipherment of Linear B*. Cambridge at the University Press 1958.

37. Cf., *int. al.*, Eduard Seler, *Gesammelte Abhandlungen zur amerikanischen Sprach- und Alterthumskunde*, 5 vols. Berlin 1902–23; Benjamin L. Whorf 'Maya writing and its decipherment', *Maya Research*, vol.2 (1935), pp.367–82, and 'Decipherment of the linguistic portion of the Maya hieroglyphs', *Annual Report of the Smithsonian Institution* (1941), pp.479–502; J. Eric S. Thompson, *Maya hieroglyphic writing*. Washington, DC 1950; and 'Systems of hieroglyphic writing in Middle American and methods of deciphering them' *American Antiquity*, vol.24 (1959), pp.349–64; Yuriy V. Knorozov, 'Drevnyaya pis'mennost' Centralnoy Ameriki', *Sovetskaya Etnografiya*, pt.3 (1952), pp.100–18; 'Pis'mennost' drevnikh Maiya, Opyt rasshifrovki', *loc. cit.*, pt.1 (1955), pp.94–125; and 'The problem of the study of the Maya hieroglyphic writing', *American Antiquity*, vol.23 (1958), pp.284–91; Tor Ulving, 'Russian decipherment of the Maya glyphs', *International Journal of American Linguistics*, vol.22 (1956), pp.184 *et seq.*, and 'A new decipherment of the Maya glyphs', *Ethnos*, vol.20 (1955), pp.152–8; T. S. Barthel, 'Die gegenwärtige Situation in der Erforschung der Maya-Schrift', *Journal de la Société des Américanistes*, new series, vol.45 (1956), pp.219–27. Knorozov has also provided a critique of attempts by Evreynov, Kosarev, and Ustinov to decipher the Mayan hieroglyphs with the aid of a computer in 'Mashinnaya deshifrovka pis'ma Maiya', *Voprosy yazykoznaniya*, vol.11, pt.1 (1962), pp.91–9.

38. Gelb, *A study of writing*, p.220.

39. María Reiche, *Mystery of the desert*. Lima 1949; Paul Kosok and María Reiche, 'The mysterious markings of Nazca', *Natural History*, vol.56, no.5. New York 1947, pp.200–7 and 237–8; Kosok, 'Ancient drawings on the desert of Peru', *Archaeology*, vol.2 (1949), pp.206–15.

40. *Vide* Alfonso Caso, '¿Ténian los Teotihuanacos conocimiento del Tonalpohualli?' *El México Antiguo*, vol.4, nos.3–4 (1937), pp.131–43; 'Calendario y escritura de la antiguas culturas de Monte Albán', in Miguel Othón de Mendizábel, *Obras completas*, vol.1. Talleres Gráficos de la Nación, México 1946, pp.113–45.

41. Unless, of course, the deification of heavenly bodies be called astronomy, which, as Neugebauer once remarked, would be analogous to counting as hydrodynamics a belief in a storm deity or the personification of a river.

42. Chu K'o-chen, 'Erh-shih-pa hsiu ch'i-yüan-chih ti-tien yü shih-chien', *Ch'i-hsiang Hsüeh-pao*, vol.18 (1944), pp.1 *et seq.* For a critical discussion of the origin of the *hsiu* system see Joseph Needham, *Science and civilisation in China*, vol.3. Cambridge University Press 1959, pp.252–9.

43. Robert J. Braidwood and Robert M. Adams have both been more circumspect in relating urbanism to civilization, and have postulated urbanism as one specific characteristic within the inclusive category of civilization. Braidwood defines civilization as a preponderance of the following : fully efficient food production (a technical term used by the author to denote a particular developmental phase of farming), urbanization, a formal political state, formal laws associated with a new sense of moral order, formal projects and works, classes and hierarchies, writing, and monumentality in art [*The Near East and the foundations for civilization*. Condon Lectures, Oregon State System of Higher Education, Eugene, Oregon 1952, p.2]. Adams writes of civilization as 'a functionally interrelated set of social institutions : class stratification, marked by highly different degrees of ownership or control of the main productive resources; political and religious hierarchies complementing each other in the administration of territorially organized states; a complex division of labor, with full-time craftsmen, servants, soldiers, and officials alongside the great mass of primary peasant producers. Each [civilization] was a complex, deeply rooted cultural tradition displaying most or all of V. G. Childe's more inclusive civilizational criteria as well : monumental public works, the imposition of tribute or taxation, "urban" settlements, naturalistic art, the beginning of exact and predictive sciences, a system of writing suitable at least for rudimentary records and accounts' [in Carl H. Kraeling and Robert M. Adams, *City invincible*. University of Chicago Press 1960, pp.270–1].

44. Cp. the remarks with which Pausanias the Periegete denigrated the Phokian city of Panopeus : 'Panopeis, einer phokischen Stadt, wenn man auch einen solchen Ort eine Stadt nennen darf weder Amtsgebäude, noch ein Gymnasion, noch ein Theater, noch einen Markt besitz, nicht einmal Wasser, dass in einen Brunnen fliesst . . .' [Ernst Meyer, *Pausanias : Beschreibung Griechenlands*. Zürich 1954, p.479. Greek text in W. H. S. Jones, *Pausanias' Description of Greece*. London 1935, Book x, iv, 1].

45. The social, as contrasted with the religious, function of the mosque is evident from Idrīs al-Khaulānī's phrase *al-masājid majālis al-kirām* (mosques are the salons of the noble) [Quoted by Ibn Qutaiba, '*Uyūn al-Akhbār*, vol.1. Cairo 1925, p.306]. For a perceptive study of these matters in general see G. E. von Grünebaum, 'Die islamische Stadt', *Saeculum*, vol.6, pt.2 (1955), pp.138–153.

NOTES AND REFERENCES

46. The 'greater ablution' (*ghusl*) prescribes a complete washing of the body after major pollution. Cf. von Grünebaum, *op. cit.* : 'Medieval authors are fond of indicating the size of a town by giving the number of its mosques and its (public and private) baths.'

47. Louis Wirth, 'Urbanism as a way of life', *American Journal of Sociology*, vol.44 (1938), pp.1–24, but especially the subsection entitled 'A sociological definition of the city'. Reprinted in Wirth's posthumous *Community life and social policy*. University of Chicago Press 1956, pp.110–32, and in Albert J. Reiss, Jr, *On cities and social life*. Phoenix Book no.172, University of Chicago Press 1964, pp.60–83. It should also be remarked that both social and ethnic heterogeneity, but particularly the former, are at best relative criteria and difficult to apply cross-culturally.

48. Oscar Lewis, 'The folk-urban ideal types', in Philip M. Hauser and Leo F. Schnore, *The study of urbanization*. John Wiley & Sons, Inc., New York, London and Sydney 1965, pp.491–517.

49. Wirth himself appears to have accepted this limitation on his definition when he wrote, 'A serviceable definition of urbanism should not only denote the essential characteristics which all cities – at least those in our culture – have in common . . . ' [*On cities and social life*, p.65].

50. Henri Pirenne, *Medieval cities*. Princeton University Press, Princeton, New Jersey 1925.

51. Shigeto Tsuru, 'The economic significance of cities', in Oscar Handlin and John Burchard, *The historian and the city*. Massachusetts Institute of Technology Press and Harvard University Press 1963, pp.44–55.

52. Walter Christaller, *Die zentralen Orte in Süddeutschland : eine ökonomisch-geographische Untersuchung über die Gesetzmässigkeit der Verbreitung und Entwicklung der Siedlungen mit städtischen Funktionen*. Gustav Fischer Verlag, Jena 1933. A statement of the simplest model of a hierarchy of cities in mathematical form is provided by Martin J. Beckmann, 'City hierarchies and the distribution of city size', *Economic Development and Cultural Change*, vol.6 (1958), pp.243–8. Bibliography by Brian J. L. Berry and Allen [Allan] Pred, *Central Place studies : a bibliography of theory and applications*. Regional Science Research Institute, Philadelphia 1961.

53. John Friedmann, 'Cities in social transformation', *Comparative Studies in Society and History*, vol.4, no.1. The Hague 1961, p.92. See also the same author's 'L'influence de l'intégration du système social sur le développement économique', *Diogène*, vol.33 (1961), pp.80–104.

54. In view of the merely incidental significance of size, whether expressed in terms of areal extent or volume of population, as an independent variable in a functional definition of urbanism, I can find little to say for V. Gordon Childe's advocacy of 'town' as a generic term for settlements midway between village and city ['Civilization, cities, and towns', *Antiquity*, vol.31 (1957),

pp.36–8]. Cf. Kingsley Davis, 'The origin and growth of urbanization in the world', *American Journal of Sociology*, vol.60, no.5 (1955), p.429. After enthusing over 'the clear-cut distinction' between town and city as a tool of urban analysis, the late Sir Leonard Woolley was unable to demonstrate its significance when writing what was clearly intended to be the definitive account of 'The urbanization of society', in *The beginnings of civilization. History of Mankind : Cultural and Scientific Development*, vol.1, pt.2. George Allen and Unwin, Ltd, under the auspices of UNESCO 1963, p.360 and Chapter 2.

55. The 'concentration in one place of people who do not grow their own food' has been raised to the level of a *sine qua non* of urban status by, among others, V. Gordon Childe [cf. p.373 above, and 'Civilization, cities and towns', *Antiquity*, vol.31 (1957), p.37] and Kingsley Davis ['The origin and growth of urbanization in the world', *The American Journal of Sociology*, vol.60, no.5 (1955), p.430].

56. John A. Wilson, *The burden of Egypt*. University of Chicago Press 1951, Chapter II. Reprinted as Phoenix Paperback no.11, University of Chicago Press, under the title *The culture of ancient Egypt*.

57. Gordon R. Willey, 'Problems concerning prehistoric settlement patterns in the Maya lowlands', in Willey (ed.), *Prehistoric settlement patterns in the New World*. Viking Fund Publications in Anthropology no.23. New York 1956, pp.109–12; S.W. Miles, 'Maya settlement patterns : a problem for ethnology and archaeology', *Southwestern Journal of Anthropology*, vol.13 (1957), pp.239–48.

58. Kwang-chih Chang, *The archaeology of ancient China*. Yale University Press, New Haven and London 1963, pp.165–6.

59. John Howland Rowe, 'Urban settlements in ancient Peru', *Ñawpa Pacha*, vol.1 (1963), p.3.

60. Michael D. Coe, 'Social typology and the tropical forest civilizations', *Comparative Studies in Society and History*, vol.4, no.1 (1961), pp.65–85.

61. Miles, 'Maya settlement patterns', and 'An urban type : extended boundary towns', *Southwestern Journal of Anthropology*, vol.14, no.4 (1958), pp.339–51.

62. Coe, 'Social typology'.

63. Emile Durkheim, *De la division du travail social : étude sur l'organisation des sociétés supérieures*. Alcan, Paris 1893, especially Chapters II and III. Coe prefers to use the term *unilateral* (an alternative proposed by Durkheim) rather than mechanical, but I have here retained the latter in order to avoid introducing unnecessary complications into the following discussion.

64. Durkheim was careful to point out that these are polar modes of solidarity, that 'mechanical solidarity persists even in the most elevated societies', and that both forms of integration can be found in every society.

NOTES AND REFERENCES

65. Herbert Spencer, *Principles of Sociology*, vol.1. D. Appleton & Co., New York 1892, p.459.

66. 'The division of labor develops ... as there are more individuals sufficiently in contact to be able to act and react upon one another. If we agree to call this relation and the active commerce resulting from it dynamic or moral density, we can say that the progress of the division of labor is in direct ratio to the moral or dynamic density of society [English translation of *De la division du travail social* by George Simpson. Published under the title *The division of labor in society*. Macmillan & Co., New York 1933, p.261].

67. Coe, 'Social typology', p.82.

68. Cf. notes 38 and 98 to Chapter III.

69. Paul Pelliot, 'Le Fou-nan', *Bulletin de l'Ecole Française d'Extrême-Orient*, vol.3 (1903), pp.248–303.

70. Professor Coe relies heavily on the account of B'ịu-nậm in Lawrence Palmer Briggs, *The ancient Khmer empire*. Transactions of the American Philosophical Society, new series, vol.41, pt.1. Philadelphia 1951, which was published before Malleret's final reports on his excavations at Oc-èo were available.

71. William Bascom, 'Urbanization among the Yoruba', *The American Journal of Sociology*, vol.60, no.5 (1955), pp.446–54.

72. Quoted from an unpublished MS. by Bascom, *op. cit.*, p.446.

73. Marcel Mauss, *The gift. Forms and functions of exchange in archaic societies*. [English transl. of *Essai sur le don* by Ian Cunnison. The Free Press, Glencoe, Illinois 1954].

74. Robert Redfield and Milton B. Singer, 'The cultural role of cities', *Economic Development and Cultural Change*, vol.3 (1954), pp.53–73.

75. The term 'moral order' was first used in this sense by C. H. Cooley [*Social organization*. Charles Scribner's Sons, New York 1909, p.54] and revived by Robert Ezra Park [*Human communities*. Free Press, Glencoe, Illinois 1952, pp.22–32, 35].

76. V. Gordon Childe had already used Durkheim's analysis of societies in his investigation of urban functions, but had considered the earliest cities of Mesopotamia, by reason of their compactness and concentration of population, as vehicles of organic solidarity. In other words, all urban forms were for Childe, by definition, societies of organic solidarity, whereas in actual fact early urban societies, whether compact cities or dispersed ceremonial cities (in the sense proposed above), appear to have been organized unilaterally and to have constituted societies of mechanical solidarity. Cf. Childe, *Prehistoric migrations in Europe*. Aschehoug, Oslo and Harvard University Press, Cambridge, Mass. 1950, p.16: '[The earliest cities] illustrate a first approximation to an organic solidarity based upon functional complementarity and interdependence between all its members such as subsist between the constituent cells of an organism.'

77. Sir Richard Winstedt, 'The Malay founder of medieval Malacca' *Bulletin of the School of Oriental and African Studies*, vol.12 nos.3 and 4. London 1948, pp.726–9.

78. *Sĕjarah Mĕlayu*, Sir Richard Winstedt's *rumi* transcription of *Raffles MS. no.18*, *Journal of the Malayan Branch of the Royal Asiatic Society*, vol.16, pt.3. Singapore 1938, pp.114–15.

79. For a synopsis of the history of the Malaka Sultanate in which this conflict is implicit see Paul Wheatley, *Impressions of the Malay Peninsula in Ancient Times*. Eastern Universities Press, Singapore 1964, Chapter 9.

80. Ch'üan Han-sheng, 'Nan-Sung Hang-Chou-ti wai-lai shih-liao yü shih-fa', *Shih-huo*, vol.2, pt.2 (1935), pp.42–4, and 'Nan-Sung Hang-Chou-ti hsiao-fei yü wai-ti shang-p'in-chih shu-ju', *Kuo-li Chung-yang Yen-Chiu-Yüan Li-shih Yü-Yen Yen-Chiu-so Chi-k'an*, vol.7, pt.1 (1936), pp.91–119.

81. Kathleen M. Kenyon, 'Jericho and its setting in Near Eastern history', *Antiquity*, vol.30 (1956), pp.184–95; 'Earliest Jericho', *loc. cit.*, vol.33 (1959), pp.5–9; 'Some observations on the beginnings of settlement in the Near East', *Journal of the Royal Anthropological Institute*, vol.89. London 1959, pp.35–43; *Digging up Jericho : the results of the Jericho excavations 1952–1956*. Frederick A. Praeger, New York 1957; F. E. Zeuner, 'The radiocarbon age of Jericho', *Antiquity*, vol.30 (1956), pp.195–7.

82. Kenyon, *Digging up Jericho*, pp.65–6.

83. E.g., Sir Mortimer Wheeler, 'The first towns', *Antiquity*, vol.30 (1956), pp.132–6.

84. Jacquetta Hawkes, *History of Mankind. Cultural and Scientific Development*, vol.1, pt.1 : *Prehistory*. Mentor edition, MQ632. Under the auspices of UNESCO, p.310 : 'This earliest full Neolithic settlement at Jericho has quite properly been called a town.'

85. Jean Perrot, 'Palestine – Syria – Cilicia', in Robert J. Braidwood and Gordon R. Willey, *Courses toward urban life*. Viking Fund Publications in Anthropology. Aldine Publishing Company, Chicago 1962.

86. Kenyon, *Digging up Jericho*, p.76.

87. James Mellaart, 'A Neolithic city in Turkey', *Scientific American*, vol.210, no.4. New York 1964, pp.94–104. The official reports of the Çatal Hüyük excavations published so far, all authored by Mellaart, are : 'Excavations at Çatal Hüyük, 1961. First preliminary report', *Anatolian Studies*, vol.12 (1962), pp.41–65; 'Excavations at Çatal Hüyük, 1962. Second preliminary report', *idem*, vol.13 (1963), pp.43–103; 'Excavations at Çatal Hüyük, 1963. Third preliminary report', *idem*, vol.14 (1964), pp.39–119; 'Excavations at Çatal Hüyük, 1965. Fourth preliminary report', *idem*, vol.16 (1966), pp.165–91. *Vide* also Mellaart's popular exposition, *Çatal Hüyük. A Neolithic town in Anatolia*. Thames and Hudson, London 1967.

NOTES AND REFERENCES

88. Edward P. Lanning, reported by Rowe, 'Urban settlements in ancient Peru', p.5.

89. Kigoshi Kunihiko *et al.*, 'Gakushuin natural radiocarbon measurements I', *Radiocarbon*, vol.4 (1962), pp.84–94.

90. Rowe, 'Urban settlements in ancient Peru', p.3.

91. *Ibid.*

92. Rowe, *loc. cit.*, p.20.

93. Oswald Spengler, *Der Untergang des Abendlandes*, vol.2. Oskar Beck, München 1922, p.107.

94. Summary in Joseph R. Caldwell, 'Eastern North America', in Braidwood and Willey, *Courses toward urban life*, pp.288–308. See also A. L. Kroeber, *Cultural and natural areas of native North America*. University of California Publications in American Archaeology and Ethnology, vol.38 (1939); Richard S. MacNeish, 'A speculative framework of northern North American prehistory as of April, 1959', *Anthropologica*, vol.1 (1959), pp.7–21; Philip Phillips, James A. Ford, and James B. Griffin, *Archaeological survey in the lower Mississippi alluvial valley*. Peabody Museum of American Archaeology and Ethnology, no.25 (1951); Antonio J. Waring and Preston Holder, 'A prehistoric ceremonial complex in the southeastern United States', *American Anthropologist*, vol.47 (1945).

95. Gerardo Reichel-Dolmatoff, 'Recientes investigaciones arqueológicas en el norte de Colombia', *Miscellanea Paul Rivet, octagenario dicata*. Universidad Nacional Autónoma de México, México City 1958, pp.471–86; and *Ancient peoples and places. Colombia*. Thames and Hudson, London 1965, Chapter 8.

96. G. Caton-Thompson, *The Zimbabwe culture*. Oxford University Press 1931; H. A. Wieschoff, *The Zimbabwe-Monomotapa culture in Southeast Africa*. General Series in Anthropology no.8. George Banta, Wisconsin 1941; J. Desmond Clark, *The prehistory of southern Africa*. Pelican Book A458, Harmondsworth, Middlesex 1959, pp.281–313.

97. W. Donald McTaggart, 'The reality of urbanism', *Pacific Viewpoint*, vol.6, no.2 (1965), pp.220–4.

98. Eric R. Wolf, *Peasants*. Foundations of Modern Anthropology Series, Prentice-Hall, Englewood Cliffs, New Jersey 1966, p.11.

99. *Op. cit.*, pp.10–11.

5

The Ancient Chinese City as a Cosmo-magical Symbol[†]

THE COSMO-MAGICAL BASIS OF THE TRADITIONAL CITY

The cosmo-magical symbolism of the Chinese city in classical times is a topic which has been touched upon by numerous authors, but which has never been the subject of a full-scale exposition. Nor is the present work the appropriate place at which to undertake such a study, so that the following notes are designed, in keeping with the purpose of the rest of this part of the investigation, only to draw attention to those symbolic features which link the early Chinese city – and indeed its successors[1] – to the general course of world urbanism.

The *locus classicus* for the layout of Chinese capitals was the *K'ao-kung Chi*, a document with some claim to antiquity which was substituted for a lost section of the *Chou-Li* by Liu-Hsiang during the second half of the 1st century BC. The relevant passage reads as follows [Chüan 12, f. 14 recto of the 1886 edition]:

> 'The artificers [lit. carpenters][2] demarcated the [Royal Chou] capital as a square with sides of 9 *li*, each side having 3 gateways. Within the capital there were 9 meridional and 9 latitudinal avenues, each of the former being 9 chariot-tracks in width.'

It will be remarked at once that this idealized urban plan relied on the same principle of subdivision as the old well-field system of land settlement which we have discussed in Chapter Two. However, whereas the latter resulted in eight units arranged about a central tract, the layout advocated in the *K'ao-kung Chi* was a more complicated affair of sixteen quarters or wards. There was, moreover, no central unit, only a group of four fulfilling that role, and occupying not a ninth, but a quarter, of the total area. It was also possible to space the nine internal avenues regularly only by allowing two of them to run along the outer walls of the city.[2a] In Ch'ang-an, the T'ang capital which approximated most closely of all Chinese cities to the canonical prescription, no attempt was made to achieve an equidistant spacing of the meridional arteries. Instead the

---

[†] A few paragraphs in this chapter were incorporated in an inaugural lecture, entitled *City as symbol*, which was delivered at University College London on November 20, 1967, and published in January 1970.

THE CITY AS A COSMO-MAGICAL SYMBOL

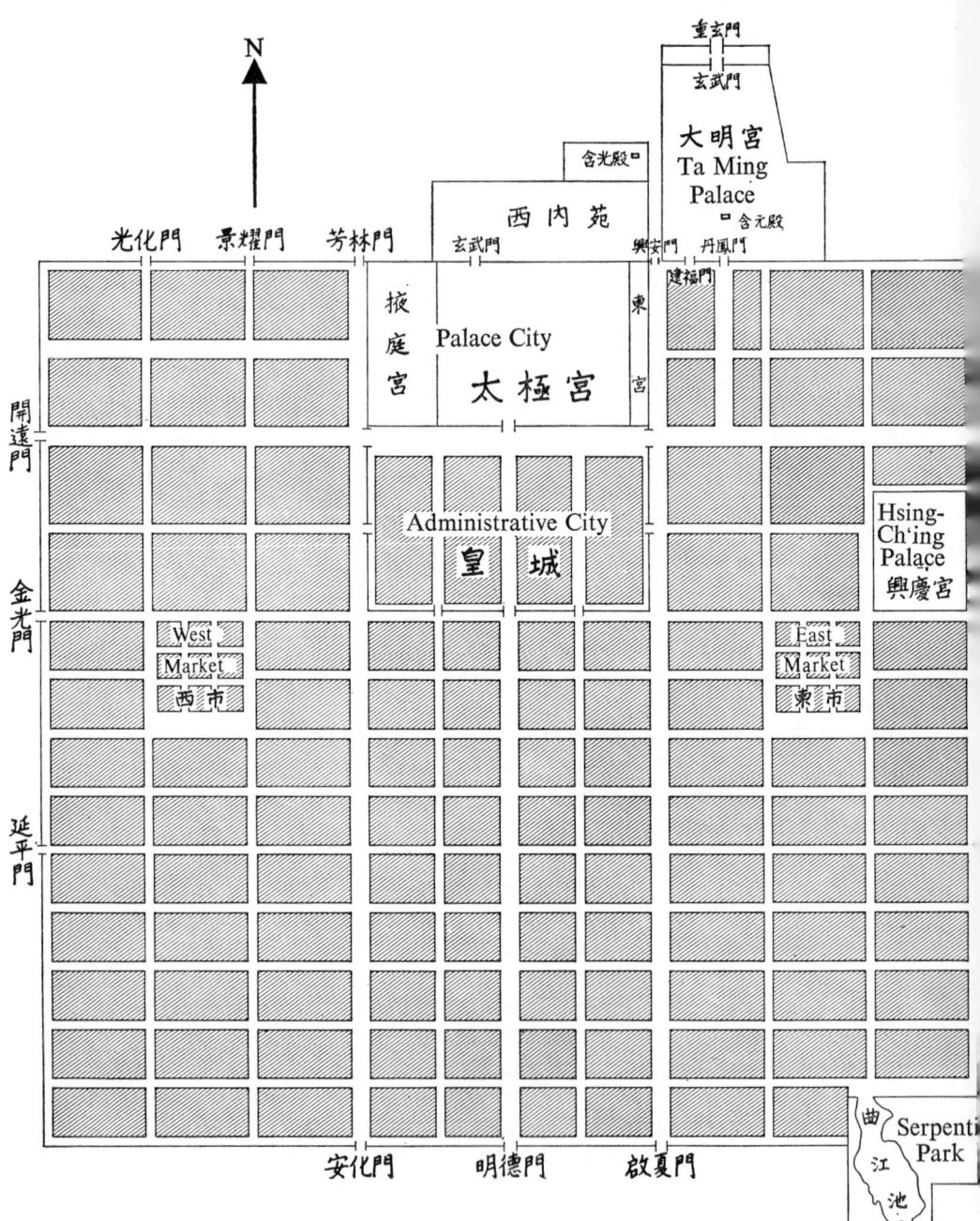

THE COSMO-MAGICAL BASIS

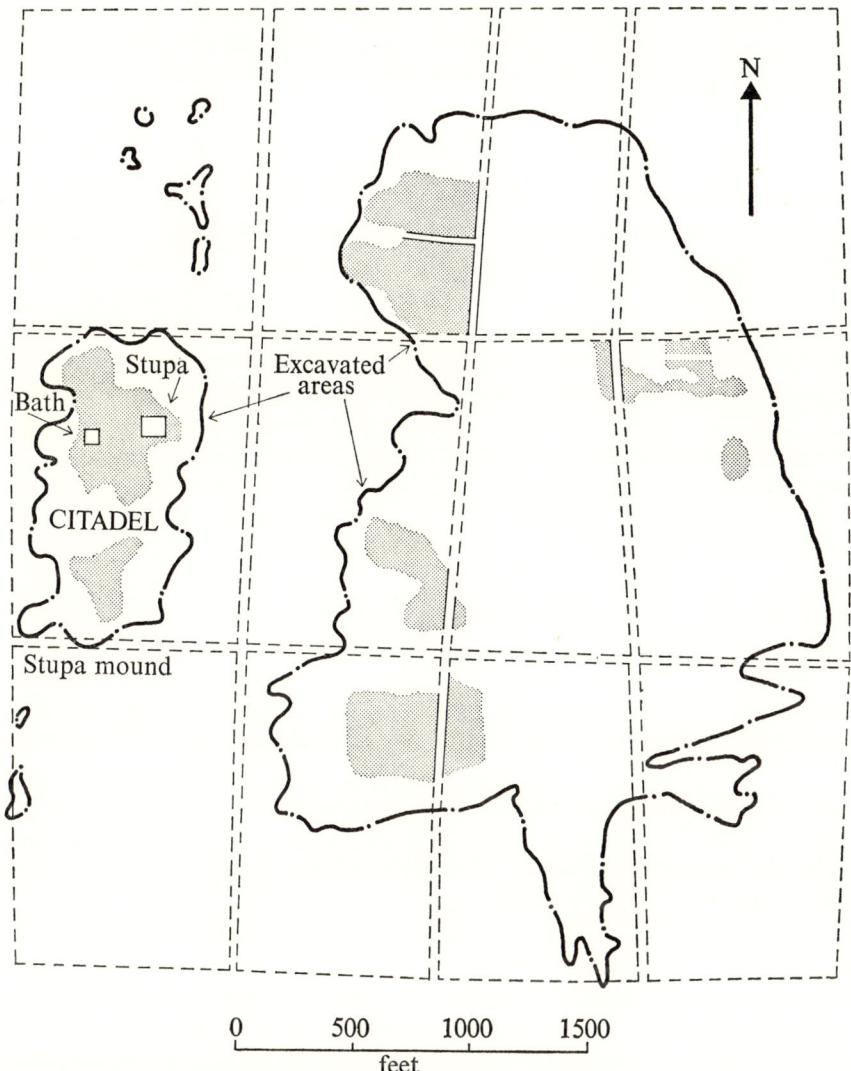

[22] A reconstruction of the probable ground plan of Mohenjo-daro. Redrawn from Stuart Piggott, *Some ancient cities of India* (Oxford University Press, 1945), p. 14.

[21 opposite] T'ang Ch'ang-an. Based on a plan in Ma Te-chih, 'T'ang-tai Ch'ang-an Ch'eng k'ao-ku chi-lüeh,' *K'ao-ku*, no. 11 (1963), plate 2.

arrangement depicted in Fig. 21 was adopted. Even though this schema was subsequently employed, sometimes in much modified form, in the layout of all the great capitals, and is particularly evident in Ch'ang-an (whence it was copied first at Nara [Heijō-kyō], and subsequently at Kyōtō [Heian-kyō]), Lo-yang, K'ai-feng, Nan-ching, Hang-chou, and, of course, Pei-ching, I had suspected that the text of the *K'ao-kung Chi* might have incorporated a confusion between the postulated nine meridional and nine latitudinal *avenues* of the city and the nine *units* of the well-field system. It was tempting to suppose that the ideal-type city should have originally comprised a regular nonary layout of eight sectors, pivoted about a central unit consisting of one-ninth of the total area. Nor was it difficult to imagine how the vicissitudes of transmission would have facilitated such a corruption of the text. That this may not have been the case is implied by the fact that the canonically sanctioned urban form prescribed for the Indian culture realm by the *Arthaśāstra*[3] is identical with that enjoined by the *K'ao-kung Chi*. Although the *Arthaśāstra* has traditionally been attributed to Kauṭilya, chief minister to Candragupta Maurya, modern views as to the date of this work differ widely. What is perhaps the best opinion holds that it was an immediately pre-Guptan elaboration of an original Mauryan compilation. But, although the *Arthaśāstra* may have been roughly contemporary with the *K'ao-kung Chi*, the urban form which it prescribed was certainly much older. A rather similar layout appears to have been used in the construction of the Indus city of Mohenjo-daro.[4] Subsequently, however, Indian city planners seem to have preferred the 'well-field' layout, such as is exemplified in the ground plan of Śiśupālgarh in Orissa, a city which has been dated to the 1st and 2nd centuries AD, and numerous temple-cities of later times such as Śrīraṅgam, Madurai, and Tiruvannamalai. I am not sure what is the precise relationship between these two bases of city-planning, but clearly both were expressions of basically similar attitudes towards the ordering of urban space,[5] and it is this topic which we shall now take up.

Underpinning urban form not only in traditional China but also throughout most of the rest of Asia, and with somewhat modified aspect in the New World, was a complex of ideas to which René Berthelot has given the name of astro-biology.[6] Berthelot sees this mode of thought, which presupposes an intimate parallelism between the mathematically expressible régimes of the heavens and the biologically determined rhythms of life on earth (as manifested conjointly in the succession of the seasons and the annual cycles of plant regeneration), as characteristic of that phase of social and intellectual development intervening

---

[23] **Gi̯wang-di̯ĕng (Wang-Ch'eng) as it was traditionally supposed to have been laid out according to the canonical plan. Redrawn from the *Yung lo Ta-tien* (AD 1407). Gi̯wang-di̯ĕng as it has been revealed by archeological investigation is depicted on fig. 10.

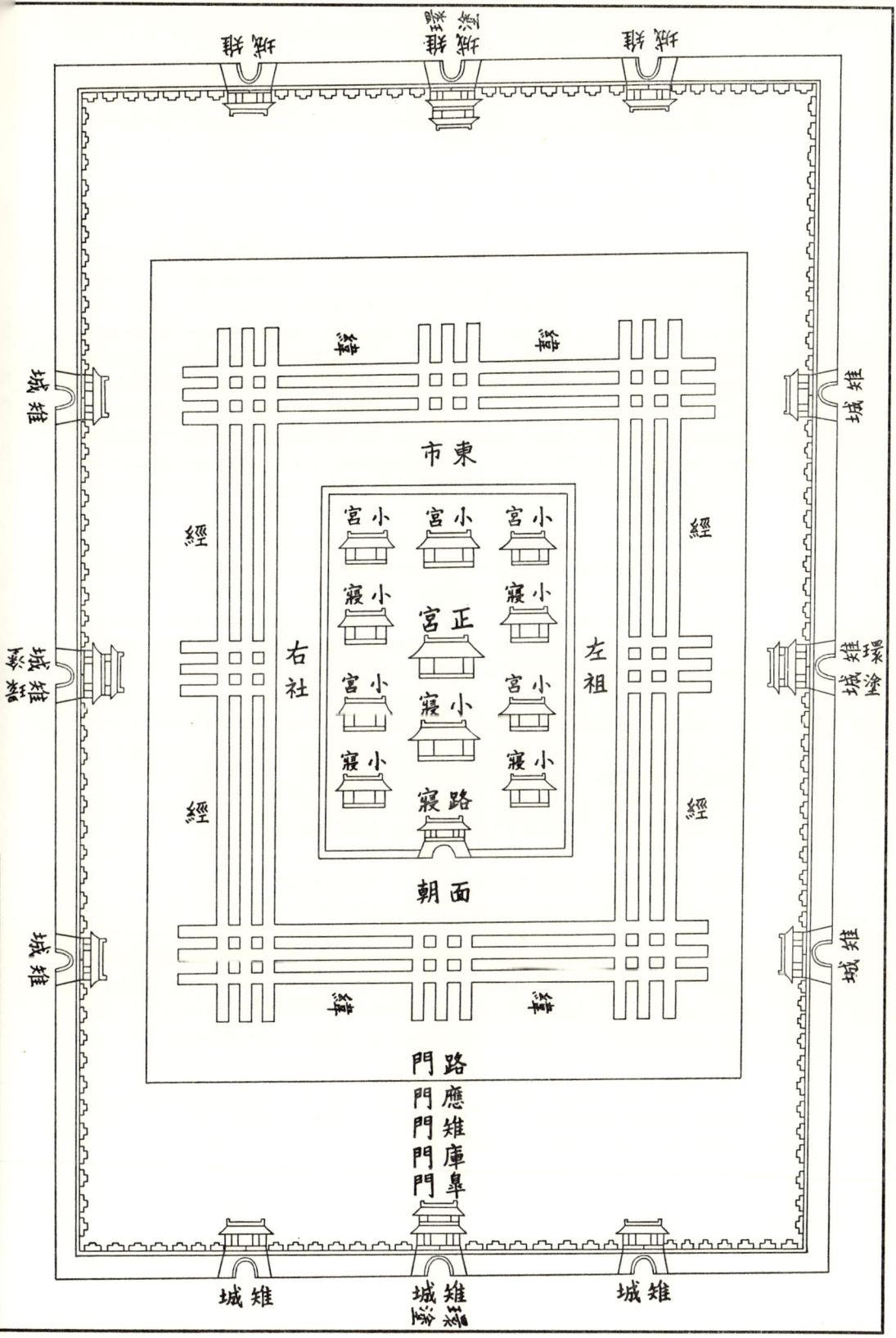

between the stages of pre-urban folk society, with its intensely personal participant apprehension of phenomena on the one hand, and, on the other, modern industrial society with its predilection for reducing individual events to types subject to universal laws.[7] It was, therefore, the style of thought associated with the phase of traditional urbanism. Some important elements in the system, particularly those associated with the delimitation of space, had been incorporated from a still earlier phase, which Berthelot subsumes under the term *bio-astrale*,[8] and some have persisted under various more or less deceptive guises into the modern world; but pre-eminently this was the mode of thought into which were fitted the new patterns of social and spatial organization which we associate with the Urban Revolution. Berthelot was almost certainly correct in looking to Mesopotamia for the earliest expression of these ideas, but I am less readily disposed to concur in his suggestion[9] that the conception of the parallelism of macrocosmos and microcosmos derived originally from the haruspicy practised in the ancient Near East.[10] I hold it to be at least as likely that haruspicy was itself but one manifestation of an already well-established and pervasive intellectual order. Moreover, some of these beliefs were as ancient as man himself; they were beliefs that had taken their rise coevally with the human mind, and had become so inextricably interwoven with the pattern of human thought that they were not consciously recognized as beliefs at all. Rather they inhered in the texture of life itself, so that symbolism was the natural and universal mode of thought. The divine, as Walter Otto phrased it in connection with another early civilization, was 'neither a justifying explanation of the natural course of the world nor an interruption and abolition of it; it was itself the natural course of the world.'[11] In any case, for present purposes we can restrict our remarks to those aspects of this system of beliefs which relate to the ordering of space. In general terms the rationale of this mode of thought was something as follows.

For the ancients, who conceived the natural world as an extension of their own personalities[12] and who consequently apprehended it in terms of human experience, the 'real' world transcended the pragmatic realm of textures and geometrical space, and was perceived schematically in terms of an extramundane, sacred experience. Only the sacred was 'real', and the 'purely secular – in so far as it could be granted to exist at all – was the purely trivial.'[13] By means of rites dramatizing the inception of the universal order, ritual specialists sought to establish an ontological link between the realm of the sacred and the realm of the profane. Although all religions dramatize their conceptions of world origins in this way, Erich Isaac, in a prescient discussion of the role of religion in ecological adaptation, has discerned a polarity in regard to their power of landscape transformation.[14] For those faiths which derive the meaning of human existence from revelation no site is, apart from a possible incidental soteriological sanctity, intrinsically more holy than another. The divine, in other words, is abstracted from the landscape, and those rites reactualizing the specific event which sanctioned human order have comparatively little direct effect on the landscape. On the other hand, those religions which hold that human order was brought into being at the creation of the world tend to dramatize the cosmogony by reproducing on earth a reduced version of the cosmos. Sacrality (which is synonymous with reality) is achieved through the imitation of a celestial archetype, as a result of which such religions can be powerful transformers of landscape, sometimes to an extreme degree. Throughout the continent of Asia, where this latter category of religious dramatization was strongly represented,[15] there was thus a tendency for kingdoms, capitals, temples, shrines, and so forth, to be constructed as replicas of the cosmos. Mircea Eliade has illustrated this point with a plethora of examples drawn primarily from the architecture, epigraphy, and literature of the ancient Near East and India,[16] and numerous others could be adduced from Southeast Asia[17] and Nuclear America.[18] In the astrobiological mode of thought, irregularities in the cosmic order could only be interpreted as misfortunes, so that, if a city were laid out as an *imago mundi* with the cosmogony as paradigmatic model, it became necessary to maintain this parallelism between macrocosmos and microcosmos by participation in the seasonal festivals that constituted man's contribution to the regulation of cyclic time,[19] and by incorporating in the planning a generous amount of symbolism.

Associated with this transcendental schema was the realization that, although the whole world was the handiwork of the gods, its maximum potential sacredness was realizable at only a few points. Before territory could be inhabited, it had to be sacralized, that is cosmicized. Its consecration signified its 'reality' and, therefore, sanctioned its habitation; but its establishment as an imitation of a celestial archetype required its delimitation and orientation as a sacred territory within the continuum of profane space. This could be effected only in relation to a fixed point, namely the village, city, or territory of the particular group, whence the sacred *habitabilis* necessarily took its birth (unsanctified, that is 'unreal' territory being uninhabitable), and whence it spread outwards in all directions. This central point, this focus of creative force, was thus quintessentially sacred, and as such the place where communication was likely to be effected most expeditiously between cosmic planes, between earth and heaven on the one hand, and between earth and the underworld on the other. And through this point of ontological transition passed the axis of the world, normally symbolized by a pillar (*universalis columna*), a tree, vine, or other plant (the Tree of Knowledge in both its Semitic and Mayan hierophanies; the *Chien-mu*; Yggdrasil; the shaman's sapling) or, most commonly of all, a mountain (Mount Meru of Indian mythology). This central axis of the universe, of the kingdom, the city, or the temple could be moved to a more propitious site or duplicated whenever circumstances rendered this desirable, for it was an attribute of existential rather than of geometrical space. From this point, the holy of holies at whichever hierarchical level it might occur, the four horizons were projected outwards to the cardinal points of the compass,[20] thus assimilating the group's territory, whether tribal land, kingdom, or city, to the cosmic order, and constructing a sanctified space or *habitabilis*. The sacred space delimited in this manner within the continuum of profane space provided the framework within which could be conducted the rituals necessary to ensure that intimate harmony between the macrocosmos and the microcosmos without which there could be no prosperity in the world of men. As the *Li-Chi* puts it, 'Rites obviate disorder as dikes prevent inundation.'

These basic modes of symbolism which are manifested in the ideal-type city of much of the traditional world, that is pre-eminently the capital city, and which are indicative of the cosmo-magical basis of that genre of urban forms, have been systematized by Mircea Eliade as follows:

1. Reality is a function of the Imitation of a Celestial Archetype.
2. The Parallelism between the Macrocosmos and the Microcosmos necessitates the practice of ritual ceremonies to maintain harmony between the world of the gods and the world of men.
3. Reality is achieved through participation in the Symbolism of the Center, as expressed by some form of *axis mundi*.
4. The techniques of orientation necessary to define sacred territory within the continuum of profane space involve an emphasis on the cardinal compass directions.[21]

Each of these modes of traditional symbolism is apparent to a greater or lesser degree in the planning of the Chinese city. Indeed, the astrobiological conceptual framework of which these ideas are an expression was structurally conformable to the associative or co-ordinative style of thinking of which the Chinese were perhaps the foremost exponents.[22] In fact, it might even be said that the pre-established harmony of the Chinese universe, which was achieved when all beings spontaneously followed the internal necessities of their own nature, and which led Chinese philosophers to seek reality in relation rather than in substance,[23] represented the most sophisticated expression of astrobiological concepts ever attained by any people. But this is by the way. What is beyond dispute is that the symbolic framework is clearly evident in those cities, Pei-ching pre-eminent among them, which, although laid out in traditional times, have persisted into the modern world, and is scarcely less visible in the archeological record relating to others. The evaluation of literary evidence, by contrast, is not infrequently a matter of extreme difficulty. It is not enough to know when a text containing references to cosmo-magical symbolism was composed : it is also necessary to know the filiation of the particular *chüan*, perhaps even of the particular paragraph, and, as has been emphasized in Chapter Two, our conclusion will often depend on the point of view which we adopt with regard to ancient Chinese texts. In any case, the worth of each text, and of each section of each text, must be assessed on its individual merits. And we would do well to remember that the point in time at which the symbolism was first recorded may not have been the period to which it refers. Furthermore, even when a conclusion has been reached on these points, it is still imperative that we be absolutely clear to which of the numerous groups in ancient China the text alludes. There were not one but many symbolisms in the Sinic culture realm, each undergoing subtle changes in emphasis through the centuries. Such is the intractable and equivocal nature of much of the evidence, however, definitive certainty on these matters is often unattainable and only too frequently we have to be content with a consensus of informed opinion.

The Cosmo-Magical Element in Chinese City Planning
Geomantic Precautions

Like architects in other realms of Asia, Chinese city planners were well aware that the fortunes of a city could be assured only if its site were adapted to the local currents of the cosmic breath (*ch'i*).[24] These local influences (*hsing-shih*), the dynamic powers of the *genius loci*, were modified from place to place by the morphology of terrain and from hour to hour by the dispositions and conjunctions of heavenly bodies. The analysis of the morphological and spatial expressions of *ch'i* in the surface features of the earth constituted the pseudo-science of *feng-shui*, the art of adjusting the features of the cultural landscape so as to minimize adverse influences and derive maximum advantage from favorable conjunctions of forms.[25] Expertise in this art, which was a prerogative of diviners known as *k'an-yü chia*,[26] was of crucial importance in siting the residences of the living and the tombs of the dead, so that no city was ever planned without the advice of a geomancer. A desirable site was one set among land forms generating auspicious, or at least benign, *feng-shui*, but such locations were not always readily available, so that only too frequently the geomancers were forced to concern themselves with the negative consideration of protection from evil influences or, if these could not be prevented from seeping into the city, allowing them to drain out of the area. However, not even unpropitious siting was wholly irremediable, for judicious excavation could both remove isolated boulders or hillocks, which were considered unlucky, and open new channels for the drainage of undesirable influences. At the same time, the selective planting of trees and shrubs could convert the contours of an inappropriately rounded eminence, a manifestation of superabundant *yin*, into an abrupt *yang*-denoting scarp face, or, of course, effect the reverse transformation. Continual modulations in the flow of *ch'i* naturally rendered it difficult to distinguish the results of poor initial siting from the misfortunes consequent upon subsequent oscillations of the natural currents circulating through the veins and vessels of the earth, and doubtless served to conceal not a few erroneous interpretations of *feng-shui*. A good example of the uncertainties in *feng-shui* interpretation is afforded by the movements of the capital of the Protectorate-General (Second Class) of the Pacified South [*An-nam Chung-tu Hu-fu*], that is present-day Tong-king, as preserved in certain Vietnamese sources.[27] Despite the fact that the capital of Đại-la (MSC = T'ai-lo) had been laid out on a cosmic plan as recently as the end of the 8th century AD, by 825 the geomancers had come to realize that the Bắc river, flowing to the northward of the city, was an unpropitious stream, an instrument through which evil influences of the north were being channelled into the district, where they bred revolt in the minds of the populace. The experts then chose a new site within the environs of present-day Hà-nội, but, some months after construction had recommenced, the geomancers announced that the desirable location was now on the opposite bank of the river, where the new capital was in fact eventually erected.

Because of the nature of the evidence on which we have to rely, there is no direct record of geomancy in the service of city planning in Shang times, but there are ample indications that the Chou chroniclers did not consider it anachronistic to attribute divinatory measures to Shang architects. Unfortunately this tells us little more than that the Chou themselves engaged in such practices. One such passage dealing with divination before the founding of a city occurs in a section of the *Shu-Ching*, the ***B'wân-kăng* (*P'an-keng*), which, although purporting to be of Shang date, was probably first composed late in the Western Chou period and revised under the Eastern Chou. It appears to have been prepared as a tract in defense of royal authority as against the power of the nobles, an interpretation which is in accord with its relatively late date. In the passage in question King B'wân-kăng attempts to justify the establishment of a new capital at An-yang. 'I have taken the [tortoise] oracle,' he says, 'and have enquired [about this matter], and the answer is as I say . . . I dare not disobey the oracle, and so I am undertaking [this enterprise] on a grand scale.'[28] Two passages in *Shih-Ching* are no less explicit in their implications. In the Ode ***Mi̯wən-Gi̯wang gi̯ŭg śi̯ĕng* [*Wen-Wang yu sheng* : Mao CCXLIV], which forms part of the *Shang-Sung* (cf. p.15 above), we read that:

> He who took the omens was the King [***Mi̯wo* (Wu)],[29]
> He took up his residence in the capital [called] ***G'og* (Hao);
> It was the tortoise[-shell] oracle which decided the matter.

Again in the Ode ***Mi̯an* [*Mien*: Mao CCXXXVII] there is an alleged recollection of the founding of the first Chou capital in the Wei valley by Duke ***Tân-B'i̯wo* (Tan-Fu) which incorporates a reference to divination.

> The plain of ***Ṯi̯ôg* (Chou) was wide and fertile,
> Even the **kɛn (*chin*) and ***d'o* (*t'u*)[30] plants were [sweet] as honey-cakes,

And so he set to work, and so he devised a scheme.
He notched our tortoise[-shells],
Which indicated that this was the place and time,
And that houses should be built here.

Finally, we may cite two passages in the *Shu-Ching* which describe the founding of **Glâk-dįang (Lo-yang) after the so-called 'second conquest of Shang'. We have seen above that there is reason to question the received version of the Chou conquest, including the role played by the Duke of Chou, but there is no reason at all to doubt that divination played a major part in site selection early in the Chou dynasty, and that, even if these passages are examples of Chou fiction, they are still true to the spirit of the times.

'In the third month, on the second [or third] day, **T̂įôg-Kung (Chou-Kung : the Duke of Chou)[31] began [to lay] the foundations and establish a new [and] important city at **Glâk (Lo) in the eastern state. The people of the four quarters concurred strongly and assembled [for the corvée][32] ... In the second month, the third quarter, on the sixth day *i-wei* in the morning the King walked from [the capital of] T̂įôg (Chou) and so reached **P'įông (Feng). The Great Protector preceded D̂įôg-Kung to inspect the site. When it came to the third month,[33] the day *ping-wu* was the third day of the month. On the third day, *mou-shen*, the Great Protector arrived at Glâk in the morning and took the [tortoise] oracle [as bearing] on the site. When he had obtained the oracle, he planned and laid out [the city]. On the third day, *keng-hsü*, the Great Protector and all the people of **·I̯ən (Yin) began work on the [public] emplacements in the loop of the Glâk [river] ...'[34]

[Transl. Karlgren, mod.].

A subsequent section of the *Shu-Ching* includes a memorial by T̂įôg-Kung on the results of the divinations undertaken at the site of the future city.[35]

'T̂įôg-Kung saluted and bowed his head, and said, I report to [You] my Son and Glorious Sovereign. As the King will not remain in [that place where] Heaven established the mandate and perpetuated it [i.e., in the western capital **G'og (Hao)], I have followed the Protector [i.e., **D̂įog-Kung (Shao-Kung)] and grandly surveyed the eastern lands, in order to found a [capital] where he will be the people's glorious sovereign. On the day *i-mao*, in the morning, I came to [the intended] capital Glâk. I took the oracle concerning the [region of the]**Liər (Li) river to the north of the **G'â (Ho); then I took the oracle concerning the [region] east of the **Kan (Chien) river and west of the **D'įan (Ch'an) river; but it was [the region of] Glâk that was commanded [sc. by the oracle]. Again I took the oracle about [the region] east of the **D'įan (Ch'an) river, but again it was [the region of] Glâk that was commanded. I have sent a messenger to come [to the King], to bring a plan and to present the oracles.' [Transl. Karlgren, mod.].

These are by no means the only references to divination in the service of site selection in ancient China. There are, in fact, others in the *Shih-Ching* itself, notably the mention of an auspicious tortoise oracle consulted prior to the construction of a new **Giwad (Wei) capital in 658 BC,[36] and in succeeding centuries the practice is recorded with ever-increasing frequency.[37] But enough has been said to demonstrate the degree to which ancient China shared in this widespread practice.

CARDINAL ORIENTATION AND AXIALITY

Prominent among the morphological features which the ideal-type Chinese city shared with a majority of the great capitals of Asia were cardinal orientation, cardinal axiality, and a more or less square perimeter delimited by a massive wall. In China this schema, glimpsed even in the plans of some of the earliest cities (pp. 135–150), was most apparent in the design of the imperial capitals,[38] but even the smaller *hsien* cities usually exhibited the rudiments of cardinal axiality and orientation. The *fang-chih* contain numerous plans and representations of cities whose spatial form was distorted by the need to adapt to exigencies of terrain, but invariably some attempt was made to preserve these two elements of cosmic symbolism. The development of extra-mural suburbs often brought radical change in the shape of a perimeter, but this was, as it were, the putting on of flesh by a healthy urban organism, and seldom obscured the structural skeleton established at the birth of the city. Perhaps the best example of an imperial capital where the full expression of the cosmic pattern was severely repressed by an intractable terrain is afforded by Hang-Chou.[39] During the 13th and 14th centuries this city was squeezed on to a neck of land, approximately half a mile in width, between the West Lake and the Che river, but even here, and although the rulers of the Southern Sung euphemistically referred to their adopted capital as Hsing-Tsai or the Temporary Abode, every effort was made to maintain the roughly rectangular form and approximate cardinal orientation that had characterized the original 7th-century ramparts; while the congestion and disorder of a century of rapid change that transformed this provincial town into the most populous city in the world failed to disrupt the axial predominance of the Imperial Way, the great thoroughfare that ran longitudinally through the city.[40]

Although the urban forms of China and of the other great culture realms of

---

[24] A late-Chʻing depiction of the Great Protector selecting the site of the future city of **Glâk-djang (Lo-yang), as described in *Shu-Ching*, *Shao-kao* section. The illustration is taken from the Imperial Illustrated Edition of the *Shu-Ching* (*Chʻin-ting Shu-ching tʻu-shuo*, 1905), which explains the egregious anachronism in the use of the magnetic compass a millennium and a half before it was in fact invented.

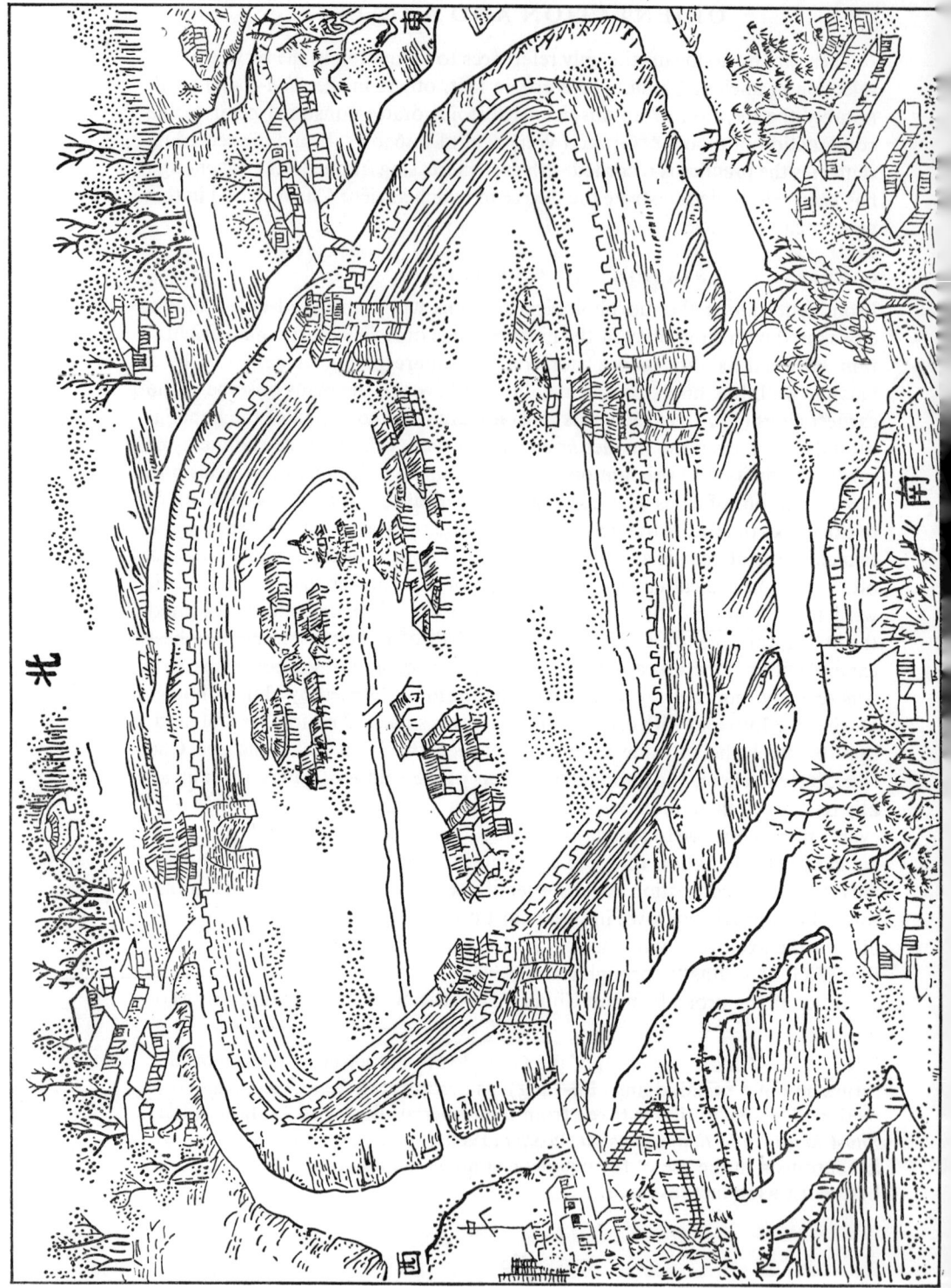

Asia were, even though mediated through very different cultural traditions, expressions of closely related attitudes towards the cosmological ordering of space, there was a difference of emphasis in one important feature of their plans. In the Chinese city the main processional axis running from south to north, 'the celestial meridian writ small', was of much greater significance than any avenue running from east to west. Along this axis were ranged the most important official buildings. Without exception, in the imperial capitals these faced south,[41] but, as would be expected, there were occasional deviations from this precept in cities of a lower order. The earliest archeological evidence for the emphasizing of this axis is the alignment of the four *hang-t'u* platforms in the western enceinte of the Chan-Kuo city of **G'ân-tân (Han-tan : p.142 above). It should be noted in passing that the function of the north-south axis in the Chinese city was quite different from that of the vista avenue in the Baroque city of Europe. Whereas the latter was designed to impress by the prospect it afforded of a distant architectural feature of central importance, the Chinese processional way was of symbolic rather than visual significance. In fact, its full sweep was never revealed at one time or from one point. It was not so much a vista as a succession of varied spaces integrated into an axial whole, in a manner that inevitably recalls the Chinese scroll painting. This axial design is superbly executed in Pei-ching, where the official visitor was formerly confronted in his progress along the processional way by a seemingly interminable succession of gates and towers and walls.

Cardinal orientation appeared very early in the arrangement of Chinese urban forms, and the *Chou-Li*, in its opening statement, preserved the fiction that it was the Emperor himself who determined the four cardinal points. It will be recalled that both the individual buildings at An-yang and the ceremonial complex as a whole were arranged about roughly north-south axes, and, furthermore, that the Shang kingdom itself was reputed – in its later phase at any rate – to have been divided into five regions : the capital and its environs at the center, surrounded by the Four Districts (***Si̯əd-t'o* : *Ssŭ-t'u*) named after the cardinal points of the compass. The suburbs of a Shang **·*i̯əp* in similar fashion were referred to the cardinal directions,[42] the whole arrangement and nomenclature illustrating a quincuncial pattern of organization widespread in Asia, but perhaps most fully developed in the radial geometry of the *pañcanāgara* that pervaded the cultural world of Southeast Asia proper.[43]

---

[25] Chin-T'ang *hsien*-city as depicted by Hsieh Wei-chieh in *Chin-T'ang Hsien Chih*, a topography in two volumes (of 10 and 8 chüan respectively), completed in 1810. The picture, which occupies pp. 3 and 4 of the first chüan of this edition, was omitted in subsequent editions in 1860 and 1921. I wish to thank Mr Joseph D. Lowe for the trouble he went to in locating this book in an uncatalogued section of the University of Washington Library.

The predominantly cardinal orientation of those Chou cities which have been located so far has been adequately emphasized in Chapter Two. However, it is noticeable that three of these cities, namely **·Ok (Wo), the Dz'iər (Ch'i) capital at Lin-tzŭ, and the city of ·Ian (Yen) known as the Lesser Capital, as well as numerous later foundations, were actually oriented a few degrees east of true north. In later times, certainly from the Han period onwards, this may have resulted from the use of 'the south-pointing [instrument]', a primitive form of compass, for declination was easterly until Sung times, after which the compass needle began to show a westerly declination.[44] In early times, however, such discrepancies were more likely to have arisen from the determination of the north-south axis of a city by reference to the celestial pole, which, as a result of precession, itself moves along the arc of a circle having the pole of the ecliptic for its center. Joseph Needham has already pointed out that the orientation of the Shang tombs at Hsi-pei Kang approximated fairly closely to the astronomical north of that time.[45] Nor should it be forgotten that the pole stars used by the Chinese in Chou times were a few degrees distant from the celestial pole,[46] a fact which may conceivably have contributed to the easterly orientation of some city plans. City walls that were oriented more or less accurately were probably laid out in conformity with a north-south axis determined by bisection of the angle between the directions of the rising and setting of the sun, a procedure that was, in fact, recommended in the *K'ao-kung Chi* section of the *Chou-Li*:

> 'They erected a post, took the plumb-line to it [to ensure its verticality], and then observed its shadow. They described a circle, and recorded the shadow of the sun at its rising and setting.'[47]

Presumably this was also the method of orientation referred to in the Ode ***D'ieng-t̂i̯əg pi̯wang-ti̯ông* (*Ting-chih fang-chung* : Mao L) from which we have quoted previously:

> When [the constellation] **D'ieng (Ting : = Pegasus)
>   had attained the zenith
> He began to build the **Tṣ'i̯o (Ch'u) palace.
> When he had calculated [its orientation] by the sun
> He began to build the Tṣ'i̯o mansion.

It is also interesting to discover the *Mānasāra-Śilpaśāstra* recommending what appears to have been an identical use of the gnomon (*Śaṅku-sthāpana-vidhāna*) in the cardinal orientation of Indian cities:[48]

> 'For the purpose of ascertaining the cardinal points, a gnomon of 12, 18, or 24 *aṅgulas* is erected from the center of a water surface (*salila-sthala*), and a circle is described with the bottom of the gnomon as its center and with a radius twice its length. Two points are marked where the shadow [of the gnomon] after and before noon meets the circumference of the circle. The

line joining these two points is the east-west line. From each of these east and west points a circle is drawn with their distance as radius. The two intersecting points, which are called the head and tail of the fish (*timi*), are the north and south points. The intermediate regions are found in the same way through the fish formed between the points of the determined quarters.'

Among pre-Sung Chinese cities whose plans have been preserved or reconstructed, a necessarily somewhat cursory survey of the evidence has revealed few with what must, in view of the preceding remarks, be regarded as anomalous orientations west of north. T'ang Ch'ang-an, it is true, was oriented 16' west of true north,[49] but this deviation from the ideal smacks of instrumental rather than methodological error. In earlier times Glâk-dịang, capital of the Royal Chou after 771 BC, had exhibited a more noticeable deviation in orientation. This city is still incompletely excavated and it is, in fact, only the exposed northern sectors of the eastern and western walls that exhibit a westerly orientation of about 4°. Other sections of wall in the extreme southwestern corner of the city are aligned respectively due north and south and due east and west (Figs. 10 and 12, IV). The remains of the twin cities in the New Fields also incorporate a westerly component. Those sectors of the walls of the settlement near the modern village of P'ing-wang imply that this city was oriented approximately 7° west of north, as indeed was the western wall of the Niu-Ts'un settlement. The eastern wall at Niu-Ts'un, however, ran due north and south (Fig. 12, III). A third city which I have found to show an anomalous westerly orientation was situated in a colonial context outside China proper. It is represented by ruins in the village of Lũng-khê in the *phu* of Thuận-thành in the Bắc-ninh Province of the People's Republic of Việt-Nâm. Claude Madrolle has identified these ruins with the former city of *Ljwiẹ-lịu (Sino-Việt. = Luy-lâu), seat of the Posterior Han administration in the Tong-king delta.[50] The sketch that accompanies Madrolle's paper shows a rectilinear enceinte oriented roughly 6° 30' west of north. Three alternative explanations of this deviation from true north suggest themselves. In the first place, Madrolle's plan may be inaccurate in this respect – it does, in fact, carry something of the flavor of a sketch map – but even so 6° is a large deviation to explain away in this manner. Second, the ruins may date from a much later period when declination was westerly : although Madrolle assumes that they represent the city under the governorship of *Dẓ'i-Siep (Sino-Việt. = Sĩ Nhiếp; AD 187–225), it should be remembered that Lũng-khê was also the site of a 10th-century Việt capital.[51] Or third – and this is perhaps the most likely interpretation – the geomancers who advised on the siting of the city were influenced knowingly by local topographical considerations or unwittingly by local magnetic variation, a phenomenon with which the Chinese probably became familiar only in the 15th century.

THE SYMBOLISM OF THE CENTER

The principle of symbolic centripetality was also clearly manifested in the traditional Chinese city, though the cosmo-magical basis was there transmuted in its expression through stylized, specifically Han-Chinese cultural forms. The essential Asian mode of urban design was, as it were, refracted through the lens of a Great Tradition whose primary concern was with the ordering of society in this world rather than with personal salvation in a future life. As a result the centrally situated temple of the archetypal South Indian and Southeast Asian city was replaced in the Chinese realm by the seat of secular authority. In the case of the *hsien* city this was often the *ya-men*, not infrequently a somewhat undistinguished building, but in the imperial capitals the symbolism of the center was more strongly developed, for it was at this quintessentially sacred spot that was raised the royal palace, which corresponded to the Pole Star (*Pei-Ch'en*), the residence (at the axis of the universe, be it noted) whence T'ai-i watched over the southerly world of men.[52] In the *Chou-Li* it is explained how the official known as the **D'âd-sịəg-d'o (*Ta-ssŭ-t'u*) calculated the precise position of this *axis mundi* (*ti-chung*), which is there characterized as 'the place where earth and sky meet, where the four seasons merge, where wind and rain are gathered in, and where *ying* and *yang* are in harmony'.[53] A gnomon erected there was held to cast no shadow at the summer solstice, a belief to which there were numerous parallels in other parts of the world. The Icelandic pilgrim Nicholas of Thverva, for example, in the 12th century reported that at Jerusalem (which was built on the rock that constituted the navel of the earth) 'on the day of the summer solstice the light of the sun falls perpendicularly from Heaven'.[54] Peter Comestor preserved an analogous tradition that the sun at the summer solstice cast no shadow on Jacob's Fountain, near Gerizim, as a result of which '*sunt qui dicunt locum illum esse umbilicum terrae nostrae habitabilis*'.[55] We may note in passing that the Pole Star is also situated directly above Meru, the sacred mountain that constitutes the *axis mundi* of Indian mythology,[56] as indeed it surmounts Sumbu, the holy axial mountain of the Uralo-Altaic peoples,[57] and Haraberezaiti (Elburz), sacred to the Iranians.[58]

A similar conception that first took form among the Western Semites in very ancient days was eventually absorbed into the traditions of Islam, for we find al-Kisā'ī of Kūfah, early in the 9th century, arguing that the Ka'bah constituted the culmination of terrestrial topography because, being below the Pole Star, it was consequently 'over against the center of Heaven'.[59] In this instance the concept of the *omphalos* had become fused with the idea that the axis of the world was the point where earth most nearly approached Heaven,[60] a belief which found expression in the Muslim tradition that prayer was likely to be more efficacious, because more easily heard, at Mecca, the center of the universe. The story of the people of 'Ād, who sent messengers to pray for rain in the holy city, as the place where their request was most likely to be heard, is wholly in accord with this tradition, as indeed was the advice they received on their arrival to ascend to the summit of Mount Abū Qubais, 'because never a repentant sinner had climbed it without being heard'.[61] In this same connection we may recall the tale of 'Abdallāh bin 'Abbās who, fearing that the unvoiced 'passing insinuations of the heart' (*khawāṭir al-qalb*) might yet be audible to Allah from a point in Mecca, prudently transferred his residence to Ṭā'if, where he would presumably be responsible only for his more overt actions and speech.[62] Furthermore, Mecca was not only the navel of the earth, *ṣurrat al-arḍ*: it was also the spot from which the creation of the world had been initiated.[63]

This feeling that an *omphalos* should be raised as near the heavens as possible seems to have been an almost universal concept in the traditional world, so much so in fact that the pyramid and the temple mountain became characteristic features in both the Old and the New Worlds. In ancient Mesopotamia with its ziggurats, in the Indian and Southeast Asian culture realms with their temple-mountains, in the Mexican, Mayan, and Andean territories with their pyramids, temples and shrines were raised towards the heavens, the better to facilitate communication with the divine. In not a few cases these *axes mundi* were also held to extend below the earth to establish contact with the underworld, and sundry symbolisms were devised to foster this illusion. The apparent exception to this tendency to raise the temple on a mound was the Egyptian pyramid, which was itself a tomb and not a means of elevating a temple. The analogous feature in the Nile valley was in fact the raised step at the entrance to an Egyptian temple. In ancient China the raising of important buildings on *hang-t'u* platforms is attested archeologically from Western Chou times onwards, and is confirmed by scenes incised on bronze vessels.[64] Such features are especially prominent in archeological remains of the old capitals of **Tsi̯ĕn (Chin) in the New Fields, in the Lesser Capital of ancient ·Ian (where there were more than fifty such platforms), in a former capital of **·I̯am (Yen), and in G'ân-tân, where they delineated the earliest known example of that dominance of the north-south axis which was to become an integral feature of later Chinese cities. I suspect that it may also have been this same concept of the omphalos reaching up to Heaven which the Taoist-inclined Emperor Wu of Han had in mind when he commanded young couples to dance on the summit of a high terrace within the precincts of his capital.[65]

Although this centripetalizing symbolism is not especially conspicuous in the exiguous and incomplete archeological remains of Chou times available to us, it is evident in at least one of the Odes. In the *Mi̯wən-Gi̯wang gi̯ŭg śi̯ĕng* already cited, we are reminded that the eponymous ruler

> Established his [sc. capital] city at P'i̯ông (Feng)
> . . .

> He constructed it so that it was surrounded
> And meted appropriately by a moat.66
> He retained the design [of his predecessors];
> And, mindful of the past, he came in filial piety.
>
> . . .
>
> The king's work was splendid,
> The walls of P'i̯ông
> *Were where the cardinal directions conjoined* [i.e.,
>   at the axis of the world],67
> The royal ruler was their support,
> The royal ruler was splendid indeed.
>   [Transl. Karlgren, mod.]

This symbolism of the center is perhaps even more explicit in an oration allegedly delivered by the Duke of Chou at the founding of the city of Glâk-di̯ang (as described above):

> 'May the King come and assume responsibility for the work of God on High and himself serve [in this capacity] at the center of the land. I, **Tân (Tan), say that, having constructed this great city and ruling from there, he shall be a counterpart to August Heaven.68 He shall scrupulously sacrifice to the upper and lower [spirits], and from there govern as the central pivot.'69
>   [Transl. Karlgren, mod.]

In the *Glâk-kôg* section of *Shu-Ching* the Duke of Chou addressed his sovereign in terms that again emphasized the centripetal symbolism of the royal presence, and of the capital city in which that symbolism could be made manifest : 'I say, if you rule from this central place, the myriad states will all enjoy peace and you, the King, will achieve complete success.' Later tradition, as represented by, among other works, a 2nd-century commentary on the *K'ao-kung Chi*, held that the Duke 'established **Glâk-·i̯əp (Lo-i : or Glâk-di̯ang : Lo-yang) in the center of the earth in order to govern the whole world', a statement which subsequently has often been understood by both Western and Oriental authors in a literal sense as signifying the center of the Chinese culture realm.70 There can be no doubt, however, that the centrality of the capital related to existential rather than to geometrical space. Finally, it will hardly be necessary to remind readers of the passage in the *Lun-Yü* in which Confucius is alleged to have remarked that, 'He who exercises government by means of his moral force may be compared to the Pole Star, which keeps its [central] position while all the [other] stars do homage to [that is revolve about] it.'71 What may be less appreciated is the added force which accrues to this simile from the equatorial character (that is concentrating attention on the Pole and circumpolar stars) of Chinese astronomy as opposed to the ecliptic-emphasizing nature of Greek and medieval European astronomy, and that based on azimuth and altitude as practised by the Arabs.[72] These passages are, of course, simply expressions of the doctrine which viewed the Emperor as the great mediator between Heaven and Earth, the Son of Heaven whose appropriate locale was at that axis of the universe which was also the axis of the kingdom and the only site for an imperial capital.[73] In the Mencian phrase, it was the Emperor's role 'To stand in the center of the earth and stabilize the people within the four seas . . .' [VII, A, xxi, 2].

Moreover, it can hardly have been other than this symbolism of the center which informed one of the famous paradoxes incorporated in the *Chuang-tzǔ*[74] as illustrative of the mode of thought of the 'dialecticians' during the 4th century BC, namely : '**·Iəng [Ying : capital of the state of Tṣ'i̯o] subsumes the whole world.'[75] In this mode of thought, as Marcel Granet expressed it more than thirty years ago:

> 'L'Autel du Sol . . . *représente la totalité de l'Empire*. On est pourvu d'un domaine dès qu'on s'est vu attribuer une motte de terre, empruntée à l'Autel du Sol . . . Mais que survienne, par exemple, une éclipse, et que les hommes s'en inquiètent comme d'une menace de destruction! Les vassaux accourent au centre de la patrie : pour la sauver, pour reconstituer, dans son intégrité, l'Espace détraqué (et le Temps comme lui), ils se groupent et forment le carré. Ils réussissent à écarter le danger si chacun d'eux se présente avec les insignes qui expriment, si je puis dire, sa nature spatiale et celle de son fief . . . L'Espace se trouve restauré dans toutes ses dimensions (et jusque dans le domaine des Astres), par la seule force des emblèmes correctement disposés dans le lieu saint des réunions fédérales.'[76]

Granet's remarks on the Altar of Earth and the Temple of the Ancestors conceived jointly as a microcosm of the empire are convincingly illustrated by an incident which has come to epitomize the idealized proprieties of military conflict in Chou times. In 547 BC the conqueror of **D'i̯ĕn (Ch'en) was met at the gate of the capital by the ruler and his chief of staff bearing in their arms the image of the God of the Soil and the ritual vessels used in the Temple of the Ancestors.[77] The event is probably apocryphal, and certainly archetyped, but the implication is clear enough. When the invader received these two symbols, the guarantees respectively of sustenance and government, it signified that the entire state had passed into his hands.[78]

The intense centripetality induced by the supreme sacredness of the *axis mundi* is probably also lurking behind Ssŭ-ma Ch'ien's remark that, whenever Ch'in Shih Huang-ti conquered a territory, he gave orders that the plan of the palace should be copied and the structure then recreated in the imperial capital at **G'ɛm-dḭang (Hsien-yang).[79] In this way he apparently sought to focus and concentrate at his own capital the vital forces that had previously been channelled through rival capitals.

Analogous instances of capital cities focusing the supernatural power of a kingdom within their enceintes, and therefore symbolizing whole states, are not difficult to find in the traditional world.[80] One of the most instructive examples is afforded by the ceremonial and administrative complex of Yaśodharapura, laid out by Jayavarman VII of Cambodia at the end of the 12th century AD. The centrally situated temple-mountain, known today as the Bàyon, consisted essentially of a central quincunx of towers, representing the five peaks of Mount Meru, axis of the world, surrounded by forty-nine smaller towers, each of which represented a province of the empire. According to Paul Mus's elucidation of the symbolism of this structure,[81] the chapels below the smaller towers housed statues of apotheosized princes and local gods connected with the provinces of the empire, so that the Bàyon as a whole constituted a pantheon of the personal and regional cults practised in the various parts of the kingdom. By thus assembling them at the sacred axis of Kambujadeśa, the point where it was possible to effect an ontological passage between the worlds so that the royal power was continually replenished by divine grace from on high, Jayavarman brought these potentially competitive forces under his own control.

In this same connection it is interesting to compare Jayavarman's efforts to concentrate the divine forces in his own capital with the ancient Roman, probably ultimately Etruscan, ritual known as the *evocatio*. Essentially this was an incantatory formula inviting the tutelary deities of a besieged city to migrate to Rome, where there would be greater scope for their powers. The Hittites had apparently practised an analogous rite in the second millennium BC.[82] In Italy the first recorded use of the *evocatio* in 496 BC brought Castor and Pollux, twin gods of Tusculum, into the Roman pantheon. In 386 BC Juno Regina was lured from Veii; in 264 BC Vertumnus forsook the Volsinii; and in 146 BC the gods of Carthage were all either ritually incapacitated or attracted away from the city.[83]

Another instance of this *pars pro toto* relationship between capital and empire is exemplified in the symbolism associated with the Roman *pomerium*. According to Latin tradition, the founding of Rome began with the excavation round what later became the Comitium of a trench, into which were thrown the first fruits of the fields and, significantly, handfuls of earth brought from each man's home locality. The ditch itself bore the name of *Mundus* (World), 'the same', so Plutarch phrases it 'as that of the universe'.[84] Subsequently Romulus was alleged to have marked out the compass of the future city by driving a furrow round it, carefully turning the clods inwards, 'not suffering any to remain outwards', thus cosmicizing and rendering habitable the quintessentially sacred pivot about which the *Orbis Terrarum* would revolve.[85] It was this ritually drawn line which was followed by the *pomerium*. In Republican times this was delimited by lines of stones and accounted holy, and, so far as the auspices were concerned, was adjudged the boundary between city and country.[86] Moreover, it seems originally to have enclosed only the politico-religious community of the Quirites, to the exclusion of the plebeian classes on the Aventine hill. What is of interest to us here is that Tacitus remarks in a passage in the *Annals* that an extension of the *pomerium* was admissible only on the grounds of an extension of the legal boundaries of the empire.87 In other words, the *Urbs*, whose foundations incorporated soil from dependent territories, symbolized the Roman imperium. The line of the *pomerium* did, in fact, remain unchanged until the time of Sulla.

It may also be remarked parenthetically that, as late as the reign of Augustus, the *Urbs* was still considered the material manifestation of the power of empire, as is witnessed by the erection of the *Milliarium Aureum* in the Forum to mark the center of the Roman ecumene, after the first map of the empire had been completed in AD 29.88 And it was not fortuitous that it was from this point that the legions set out on their campaigns, bearing on their banners the cosmic power generated at the axis of the world, just as the commander of a Chinese army received his commission in the ancestral temple of the ruling house in the capital of the state, and sacrificed at the altar of the state God of the Soil before undertaking a campaign.89

Qazwini's statement in his *Cosmography* that, 'when in any one year rain beats against one side of the Ka'bah, that year will witness fertility in the country on that side; when it beats on all sides, fertility will ensue on all sides', belongs to the same order of ideas.90

Stemming directly from the role of the capital city as the material manifestation of the concentrated power of the state is the widely diffused coronation rite in which the new king ceremonially circumambulates his capital.91 In Cambodia, for example, even in this century, the newly crowned king would take possession of Phnoṃ Penḥ by marching round its perimeter 'à l'imitation du monarque universal de la légende qui prit possession du monde en faisant une circumambulation le long du rivage de l'océan extérieur'.92 The cosmic symbolism of this royal circumambulation was further emphasized when the king changed both his mode of transport and his head-dress at each cardinal point of the compass, so as to conform with the *vāhana* and costume of the appropriate Lokapāla. In Thailand also the new king formerly undertook a Progress (*Liap Mo'aṅ*) round his capital, but the pious Buddhist monarch Rama IV transformed this circumambulation into a tour of the principal wats of Bangkok.93 The same rite of circumambulation was practised by Burmese kings, though Thibaw, the last king, chose to forego this part of his coronation for fear that a usurper might occupy his palace, the *axis mundi* of the Burmese ecumene, during his absence.94 These Southeast Asian practices derive from the ancient Hindu rite of *pradakṣiṇa*, or delimitation of sacred space, whether shrine or capital city. There is no evidence that this rite was known in Vedic times, but both the *Agni Purāṇa* and the *Mānasāra* depict the Indian coronation ceremony as concluding with the king riding round his city. The *cakravartin* also undertook a formal circuit of the *Dīpa*, a practice reminiscent of the quinquennial visitation inaugurated by the Chinese Emperor Shun (**Śi̯wən) to the four sacred mountains on the borders of his realm. Having thus delimited the bounds of the kingdom, in the intervening years the Emperor remained in his capital, symbolizing the axis of his ecumene.[95] By beginning his peregrination at the eastern mountain in the second month and following the march of the sun (the southern mountain in the fifth month, the western in the eighth, and the northern in the eleventh month), the Emperor integrated space and time, and thus co-ordinated the dispositions of his sanctified territory and the ordering of the calendar. Like the Khmer king, the Chinese emperor also emphasized the cosmo-magical character of his perambulation by changing his costume and carriage as he arrived at the different quarters of his realm.[96]

This ritual encompassing of the sacred enclave occurs far beyond the cultural realms of South and East Asia. In ancient Egypt, for example, each new Pharaoh came to Memphis to perform the Circuit of the White Wall, as it was alleged Menes had when he had first laid out this sacred city, known to ancient texts as the Fulcrum of the Two Lands. In the absence of this rite the ruler could not consider himself a true Pharaoh.[97] The circular rampart traced by Romulus's plough (*designat moenia sulco*)[98] was an expression of this same need to delimit sacred space, and it is not unlikely that the ritual race of the Luperci round the Palatine Hill on February 15th, which is usually categorized as a magic rite ensuring the safety of the settlement, was in fact derived from a ceremonial definition of the sacred enceinte, beyond which profane powers could not pass. Moreover, the fundamental conceptions manifested in the ceremonial progress of the Ark of the Lord round the city of Jericho, as decreed by Joshua, may have had their ultimate origin in the same desire to convert profane (hostile) space into sacred (propitious, habitable) space.[99]

There is, however, another aspect to this picture of centrality. The capital, the *axis mundi*, was also the point of ontological transition at which divine power entered the world and diffused outwards through the kingdom. When Jayavarman VII of Kambujadeśa had his own face, in the likeness of Vajradhara,[100] carved on each of the four sides of each of the fifty-four towers of the Bàyon, he was ensuring the projection of divine power, of which he was the transmitter, to the four quarters of his kingdom. Analogous in conception was the construction of the altar to the God of the Soil in the Chou capital – or rather the manner in which Han authors believed that altar to have been constructed. According to these relatively late sources, the tumulus which denoted the axis of the world was faced with earths of colors appropriate to the cardinal directions. On the east, the habitat of the Cerulean Dragon, the earth was blue-green, the symbol of the bursting vegetation of spring in the direction of the rising sun. On the south the earth was red, symbolizing the fire associated with the Red Phoenix of summer. On the west it was white, the color of the White

Tiger of what Nelson Wu calls 'The metallic autumn, symbolic of weapons, war, executions, and harvest; of fruitful conclusion and the calmness of twilight, of memory and regret, and unalterable past mistakes.' On the north, facing the realm of damp and darkness, the earth was black. Finally a capping of yellow earth was placed on the summit of the altar to symbolize the empyrean of Shang-Ti. At his investiture a noble carried a clod of earth from that side of the sacred altar facing the direction in which his benefice lay to the capital of his territory, where it formed the nucleus of his own altar to the God of the Soil.[101] In that way supernatural power reaching the earth at the sacred axis of the world was diffused to the four quarters through cosmo-magically sanctioned channels, so that the pre-ordained dispositions of symbolic space were maintained and harmony prevailed in the realm. It was not fortuitous that, according to one tradition, Shun inaugurated his reign by opening the four principal, that is cardinally oriented, gates of his capital.[102]

The city gates, where power generated at the *axis mundi* flowed out from the confines of the ceremonial complex towards the cardinal points of the compass, possessed a heightened symbolic significance which, in virtually all Asian urban traditions, was expressed in massive constructions whose size far exceeded that necessary for the performance of their mundane functions of granting access and affording defense. In the architectural canons of South and Southeast Asia the cosmo-magical reason for the extraordinary size of the city gates was often explicit, and, whereas the *Mānasāra-Śilpaśāstra* authorized the building of religious and residential edifices only up to twelve storeys in height, *gopuras* could be constructed up to sixteen or seventeen storeys (chaps. 20–30 and 33). In China, on the other hand, the cosmo-magical justification for the massiveness of these structures had apparently been long forgotten. Moreover, whereas in the representative South or Southeast Asian temple-city the *gopura* often reproduced, and not always on a much reduced scale, the temple or temple-mountain at the center of the city, the kingdom and the universe,[103] the Chinese gate-tower conformed to the same general architectural principles as did the imperial palace. Like so many other aspects of urban design, this feature is perhaps best illustrated from Pei-ching, where the Gate of Heavenly Peace at the entrance to the Imperial City overtops all buildings within the walls, and the Meridian Gate all those within the Forbidden City;[104] but the architectural prominence of the main gate-towers is a characteristic feature at all levels of the city hierarchy in China.[105] One contrast between the South Indian temple-city and the Chinese city lies in the fact that, whereas in the construction of the former the outer and higher walls and *gopuras* were raised last of all, in the Chinese city the walls were the first architectural features to be built. Such at least is the conclusion to be derived from the Ode *Mjan* [Mao CCXXXVII, *q.v.*] and from the practice of later times. This means that, whereas the Indian temple-city was easily extensible, the frame and internal ordering of the

435

Chinese city tended to be fixed, notwithstanding occasional irregular suburban development outside the walls. It also follows that all the interior space of a Chinese city was not always built over immediately after the walls had been raised, or perhaps ever.[106]

THE PARALLELISM OF MACROCOSMOS AND MICROCOSMOS

The need to maintain harmony between the world of the gods and the world of men – what A.J.L. Wensinck called the dramatic conception of nature[107] – required that man should participate in cosmic events by accompanying them with appropriate rituals. Such ceremonies, either actual or idealized, are well documented in China from Shang times onward, being epitomized in the saying of the *Li-Chi* that 'in ceremonies of the grandest form there is the same hierarchical relationship as that which exists between Heaven and Earth'.[108] But in many parts of the world the co-ordination of natural and social forces was expressed not only ceremonially but also plastically, by laying out the capital as a model of a celestial archetype. Wensinck, Eliade, Roscher, Soustelle,[109] and others have illustrated this theme with an abundance of examples from the early Middle East and Mesoamerica. All Babylonian cities, for example, had archetypes among the constellations: Sippara in Cancer, Nineveh in Ursa Major, Assur in Arcturus,[110] Babylon in Cetus-Aries,[111] and so forth. Nineveh, indeed, was explicitly constructed according to 'the plan delineated from distant times in the writing of the heaven of stars'.[112]

In South and Southeast Asia temple-cities were not infrequently laid out as chronograms symbolizing a sacred cosmography. Some of the more dramatic examples of capital cities designed in this way are to be found in ancient Kambujadeśa, 'diagrammes magiques tracés sur le parchemin de la plaine' as they have been called.[113] And one of the subtlest of these symbolic representations was built relatively early in the history of Khmer urban development. In 893 Yaśovarman I laid out a grandiose ceremonial capital which, according to Khmer principles of honorific nomenclature, received the title of *Yaśodharapura*. The city exhibited perfect cardinal orientation and axiality, and pivoted about the central hill of *Yaśodharagiri*, on which was erected the national temple now known as the Bǎkhèn. This temple, with its five terraces surmounted by a quincunx of towers, was a plastic representation both of cosmic space and of Mount Meru, home of the gods.[114] Basically a total of 108 towers were arranged symmetrically on the terraces round the one hundred and ninth, which occupied a central position on the summit; but, from a point opposite the middle of any side, only thirty-three towers were visible at any one time, these representing the abodes of the thirty-three gods of Indra's heaven. The parallelism was carried further in the construction of seven levels, corresponding to the seven heavens, this number being achieved by adding the ground level and the summit to the five terraces already mentioned. And, of the five towers soaring from the summit platform towards the clouds, to an observer posted at one of the cardinal points only three were visible, symbolizing the three particular peaks of Mount Meru on which were sited the heavenly cities of Viṣṇu, Brāhma, and Śiva. Moreover, the 108 towers considered in their entirety (4×27) represented the four phases of the moon and the twenty-seven lunar mansions. Finally, the sixty towers arranged in five sets of twelve, one set on each of the five terraces, represented the approximately twelve-year *Bṛhaspati-cakra* or Jupiter cycle which, in multiples of five, was used as a dating era from early in the 5th century AD. We can also be certain that in the present context the series of twelve towers served to recall the Cambodian version of the twelve-animal cycle.[115] Thus, while in elevation the Bǎkhèṅ was a plastic representation of Mount Meru, the axis of the universe, the kingdom, and the capital, in plan it constituted an astronomical calendar in stone, depicting from each of the four cardinal directions the positions and paths of the planets in the great Indian conception of cyclic time.

In subsequent centuries symbolism began to extend out beyond the precincts of the temple-mountain to embrace the whole of the ceremonial complex. By the beginning of the 13th century Jayavarman VII's capital, presently known as Aṅkor Thom, had been laid out as a representation in stone of a series of Indian cosmological myths extending over more than six square miles of ground. The symbolism of the centrally situated temple-mountain of the Bàyon has already been touched upon in our discussion of the principle of centripetality. Khmer monarchs have left us in no doubt as to the role of their temple-mountains in general. Udayādityavarman II, for example, on founding an earlier capital in the 11th century, erected at the foot of his sacred central temple-mountain, 'the jewel decorating the head [of his city]', a stele recording that, 'because he was aware that the center of the universe was distinguished by [Mount] Meru, he considered it appropriate that there should be a Meru in the center of his own capital'.[116] We have already seen that the Bàyon was something more than a simple Meru, that it was a pantheon of the personal and religious cults of the empire. And the austere stones of this temple-mountain were vitalized, transformed from a mere representation of a holy mountain into the very axis of the world itself, by the magic power of the images of gods, demons, apsarases, and all the other inhabitants of the slopes of Meru. But an *axis mundi* extends below the earth as well as above it, so the architects of the Bàyon arranged for the bas-reliefs at the base of the monument to depict gigantic fish, thus symbolizing the seas below which Meru reached into the nether world.[117] It has also been suggested that the simultaneous illumination from every direction of the faces on the towers of the Bàyon may have been designed as a representation of the great miracle of Śrāvastī, when the Buddha, in order to confound hostile magicians, rose into the air and multiplied himself ten thousand times.[118] Over the surrounding countryside Jayavarman raised a host of temples all redolent with the Mahāyāna mode of cosmic symbolism, including a representation of the legendary Anavatapta Lake in the Himālayas, whose water was a powerful apotropaion. His own palace was elevated on giant garuda caryatids with raised wings, indicating that it was a celestial construction floating above the earth, in a manner reminiscent of King Kaśyapa's palace on the Sīgiriya, which was described on p.301.

Equally dramatic are the symbolic representations on the outer boundaries of this great ceremonial and cult city. The symbolism of the wall and moat as physical expressions of the mountain range and the ocean bounding the cosmos have been mentioned previously. Even more impressive is the symbolism of the four entrance gates facing the cardinal compass points. On the outer side of each gate a file of fifty-four heavenly gods is locked in petrified contest with an equal number of gods of the underworld. It is clear from the disposition of these gods and demons that the serpent over which they are contending is twined symbolically around the temple-mountain of the Bàyon, so that the whole is in fact a representation of the myth in which the gods and demons churned the ocean to extract the liquor of immortality, using the cosmic serpent Vāsuki as a rope and Mount Meru as a churning stick.[119] Moreover, the *naga* or serpent in Indian cosmology was often used as a synonym for the rainbow, also called the bow of Indra, and interpreted as a bridge between earth and heaven. In conformity with this metaphor, twin statues of Indra seated on his three-headed elephant were placed in the angles of the *gopura* immediately behind the naga bridge, so that there could be no doubt in the mind of the pilgrim that, as he crossed over the bridge, he was indeed passing from the world of men into the realm of the gods,[120] a realm made both immortal and fruitful by the labors of the gods and demons in the churning of the cosmic ocean. For him all roads did quite literally lead to Heaven.

Although the Aṅkor complex is unusual in the quantity and explicitness of its symbolism, plastic representations are not rare in the design of such ceremonial centers both in Asia and in Nuclear America. Another splendid example is provided by Persepolis, the ritual capital of the Achaemenid dynasty.[121] Begun by Darius in 518 BC, construction continued through most of two centuries until the city was sacked by Alexander the Great in 330. Although this ceremonial city was of enormous size and unrivalled opulence in its day, it was little known outside Persia. There is no reference to it in the Old Testament, or in Babylonian, Assyrian, or Phoenician documents. Nor is it mentioned in any surviving fragment of the writings of Ktesias. This exclusivity stemmed from its role as the quintessentially sacred enclave of the Persian culture realm, a *Civitas Dei* modelled on the pattern of a celestial city, a *Civitas Coeli*. It was designed to be an appropriate setting for the hierophanies of Ahura Mazda himself, and, like Jayavarman's reproduction of Indra's capital in Cambodia, it was vitalized by a symbolism designed to invoke the co-operation of the gods.

MACROCOSMOS AND MICROCOSMOS

There is scarcely a foot of wall which does not bear the stamp of this grand essay in the establishment of a parallelism between the worlds. Processions of tribute bearers from twenty-three nations, arriving with gifts for the New Year festival, in one case occupy a thousand feet of wall. The *apadana* (audience hall) of Xerxes and the so-called Hall of a Hundred Columns are both transformed into sacred groves by the presence of columns in the form of palms, botanically incongruous symbols of the so-called Tree-of-Life. The bull, symbolizing with his horns the crescent moon, and thus the night, coolness, winter and moisture, is frequently depicted overcoming a lion, symbol of the sun at the height of its power in the constellation Leo, and so guaranteeing the return of the winter rains to replenish the parched earth. The Achaemenid King of Kings, his court officials, and even lesser folk are all depicted holding sacred lotuses as tokens of their common purpose, the glorification of Ahura Mazda, his earthly surrogates in the Achaemenid line, and the Persian nation. The rosettes which are a ubiquitous feature of the ornamentation of the buildings were probably stylized renderings of full-blown lotus blossoms seen affronted, potent symbols of fruitfulness. That they were not merely for decoration, but also served a symbolic purpose, is evident from their occurrence in situations where they could not have been seen by the casual observer. The pivot stones of the doors, for instance, all bear this *motif* on their underside where, although invisible, it is in direct contact with the earth. Equally prominent in the decoration is the mountain pictograph, in the form of a series of crenellations which, although suggesting themselves to the modern eye as battlements, are rather symbolic representations of the sacred mountain, where alone communication could be established with the gods. With its acres of buildings, including a reception hall open on all sides to symbolize the diffusion of divine authority to the four quarters, and its triple wall, itself symbolic but further strengthened by symbolic defensive signs and enormous supernatural figures standing guard before its gates, with its sacred groves in stone, its man-headed and lion-slaying bulls, sphinxes with paws uplifted in adoration before the Tree-of-Life, throne-room scenes, and all-pervading symbolic emblems, Persepolis constituted a magnificent demonstration of abundance, the contribution of the Persian people to the maintenance of harmony between the heavens and the earth, an unequivocal declaration that they were enacting their assigned roles in the cosmic process. Persepolis was the instrument by which this colossal effort was communicated to Ahura Mazda, an irresistible inducement to Him at the midwinter solstice to begin again his fructification of the earth.

In the Hindu realm the ideal-type city also conformed to a cosmo-magical pattern, and its founding was treated as the preparation of sacrificial ground, as the sanctifying of an *habitabilis*. The site was selected with care according to the ritualistic (and sanitary) prescriptions preserved in the traditions and treatises of the master-builders, and the city was laid out as a moated, rectangular enclosure exhibiting cardinal orientation and axiality. It was then divided into four wards by two axial avenues terminating in impressive *gopura*. It was also considered canonically desirable to provide four supplementary gates, one at each corner of the enceinte.[122] Round the outer edge of the city ran the *Maṅgalavīthī*, the Auspicious Way or Path of Blessings, along which was drawn the chariot of the presiding deity, and along which the population proceeded in the rite of *pradakṣiṇa*. Hence its alternative name of *Janavīthīkā*, or the Path of Men. The precise pattern of internal subdivision of the city depended on a variety of factors, including the status of its ruler and its position in the administrative hierarchy, its ethnic and caste composition (for the populace was segregated according to profession and social status), and the particular canonical plan to be followed. A *jayāṅga* or imperial headquarters, for example, was supposed to follow the stipulations of the *Arthaśāstra* (p.414 above), and with its nine east-west avenues crossed by nine from north to south, all enclosed within a cardinally oriented enceinte, approximated closely to the layout prescribed by the *K'ao-kung Chi*. *Dvārāvatī*, Kṛṣṇa's capital, by contrast, was held to have been laid out with only eight major highways crossing at right angles. However, despite differences in detail, it is certain that Indian cities were often planned according to the basic cosmo-magical traditions which we have been discussing. Even in relatively modern times Jaipur was constructed on these principles by a Bengali Brāhmaṇ, Vidyādhar Bhattācharyya, and as late as 1857 Mandalay, in the Theravāda Buddhist kingdom of Burma, was designed by five high officers of state according to the canonical prescription.

Binode Dutt has discerned indications in the prescriptive texts of differences in principle between a northern and a southern school of urban planning.[123] Whereas in the schemes propounded by Kauṭilya, Śukrācharyya, and in the *Agni Purāṇa* (all representing the northern school) the run of the streets is the main factor in the subdivision of the interior, the *Śilpaśāstras* tend to rely on various forms of *Padavinyāsa* to effect an internal structuring and disposition. It is also noticeable that the plastic symbolism tends to be more developed in the southern cities. It was ignorance of this symbolic framework which misled James Fergusson into uttering the egregiously ill-informed, indeed irrelevant, judgment that the South Indian temple-city was architecturally 'altogether detestable', with 'the bathos of decreasing size' of its walls and *gopuras* as one approached its center a feature to be deplored.[124] As Nelson Wu has pointed out, the pilgrim to the South Indian temple-city measured his proximity to ultimate truth by the depth to which he had penetrated into the heart of the sacred enceinte, not by the height of its *śikhara*.[125] And he would not expect this inner sanctum, the supremely sacred heart of reality, to be visible to the uninitiated. Only he who had purified his mind by meditation and rigorous ritual observance dare look on the face of God. As the pilgrim dragged weary feet across the plain, he would see, with the eyes of the unenlightened, one of the four magnificent outer *gopuras* marking the axis of the world and beckoning him from afar. As he passed through its portals and entered into the role of the neophyte, he would see plainly the next great barrier to enlightenment, and beyond that the next – and the next – and so on – a series of *gopuras* diminishing in height towards the center of the sacred enclave. Finally, at the very heart of the complex, at the point of ultimate reality, he would – if he were at, say, Madurai – at last look on the glowing gilded towers of the sanctuaries of Sundareśvar (Śiva) and his consort Minākṣi-devī (Parvātī). Here, at the heart of the eternal flux of creation and dissolution, architectural rhetoric would have been of no avail. Form here was subject to spirit, and there was at this ultimate stage of spiritual progress not the bathos imagined by Fergusson but what Westheim, with far deeper understanding of traditional spiritual values, has called 'The great pathos inherent in the solemn invocation of God.'

In the ceremonial centers of pre-Columbian Mesoamerica it is also possible to discern the plastic expression of a series of mythical or cosmic conceptions, although the implications of this symbolism have not yet been elucidated in all their complexity. Paul Westheim has drawn attention to the stepped fret (*xicalcoliuhqui*),[126] the most typical ornamental form of the valley of Mexico, which was the symbol of the fire serpent, the lightning that was an attribute of Tlàloc, god of the fire that will cause the third destruction of the world. More sibylline in its origin and signification is the snail emblem.[127] This is known to have been a symbol of birth and fecundity, but the whorl manifested in its shell appears to have had deeper implications. Westheim has gone a long way towards proving that asymmetrical distributions of form such as are exemplified in the stepped fret, the shell whorl, and the decorative volute were also exemplified in the plans of some Mesoamerican ceremonial centers. 'That dynamism manifested in the structure of the snail shell,' he suggests, 'the energy with which it is charged, the ordered asymmetry, the form that can only become Form in an incessant "becoming" by means of a discharge and struggle of forces held in an extremely complicated state of equilibrium' was in some way in harmony with pre-Cortesian thought patterns.[128] Within the grandiose unity of the axialized dispositions of the cult centers there was often a tendency to deflect the axis to one side. It has frequently been remarked, for instance, that the powerful integrating axis at Teotihuacán did not lead up to, or pass through, the Temple of Quetzalcóatl, which was instead set off to one side. In similar fashion the sanctuary dedicated to Tlàloc, the foremost deity in the Teotihuacán pantheon, was offset from, and at a lower level than, the main ceremonial avenue. This deflection of the axis, while yet conserving the geometric organization of the whole, is also evident in the layout of Monte Albán, Mitla, Cempoala, and Xochicalco, at Ixkún in Guatemala, and elsewhere. Although its significance is not fully understood, there can be no doubt that it was an important factor in the design of several Mesoamerican cult centers. In later times Aztec thought patterns showed a strong tendency to group creatures and things according to the cardinal compass directions, where they were ruled over respectively by Tezcatlipoca, Quetzalcóatl, Xipe Tótec, and Huitzilopochtli, the Aztec functional equivalents of the Lokapālas guarding the four cardinal points of the Brāhmaṇ cosmos.

In China, this aspect of city design concerned with the plastic representation of a cosmic prototype is less evident,[129] though elements of it are discernible in the layout of Han Ch'ang-an (*D'i̯ang-·ân). Because this city had been adapted from a pre-existing Ch'in temple complex, its perimeter was unusually irregular. Although an effort had been made to preserve the canonical desideratum of twelve gates, undulating terrain and the need to incorporate two already existing Ch'in palaces within the new city rendered a square enceinte impracticable. The resulting plan inspired subsequent speculation that the city had been laid out on the spatial pattern of the two constellations Ursa Major and Ursa Minor conjoined, with the imperial palace occupying the position of the Pole Star of the time, namely 4339 Camelopardi.[130] Moreover, certain remarks by Ssŭ-ma Ch'ien would seem to imply that the earlier Ch'in capital of **G'ɛm-di̯ang (Hsien-yang) may have incorporated analogous elements of symbolism.[131] Writing of a covered way [132] that connected the **·Â-b'i̯wang palace [133] to the city across the Wei river, Ssŭ-ma Ch'ien likened it to the gallery of **T'ien-g'i̯ək (T'ien-chi, i.e., the principal stars of Cassiopeia), which linked the Pole Star to the constellation of **Gi̯wĕng-śi̯ĕt (Ying-shih : αβ of Pegasus) on the far side of the Milky Way. This implies that the palace was in the position of the Pole Star relative to the constellations and the Milky Way, and suggests the possibility that other astral symbolism may have been incorporated in the layout of the city.

In Chinese Taoist lore there are also references to the **Kwən-lwən (K'un-lun) mountain as an urban archetype, a mode of symbolism which would seem to owe something to the Indian tradition of Indra's capital of Sudarsana on Mount Meru. The *Wu-Yüeh Ch'un-Ch'iu*, for example, preserves a claim by a 5th-century BC minister of the southern state of **Gi̯wăt (Yüeh) to have built a city that corresponded to the heavens and retained the likeness of the Kwən-lwən mountain.[134] The same symbolism occurs again in the poem **T'ien-Mi̯wən (T'ien-Wen) in the *Songs of Ch'u* (**Tṣ'i̯o-Dzi̯əg):

> Where is Kwən-lwən with its hanging garden?
> How many miles high are its ninefold walls?
> [Transl. Hawkes]

In early Chinese mythology this mountain lay vaguely in the frontier regions of northwest China, and became an appropriate locale for the domain of the Hsi-wang Mu. It seems to have been regarded as a nine-tiered *axis mundi*, an

MACROCOSMOS AND MICROCOSMOS

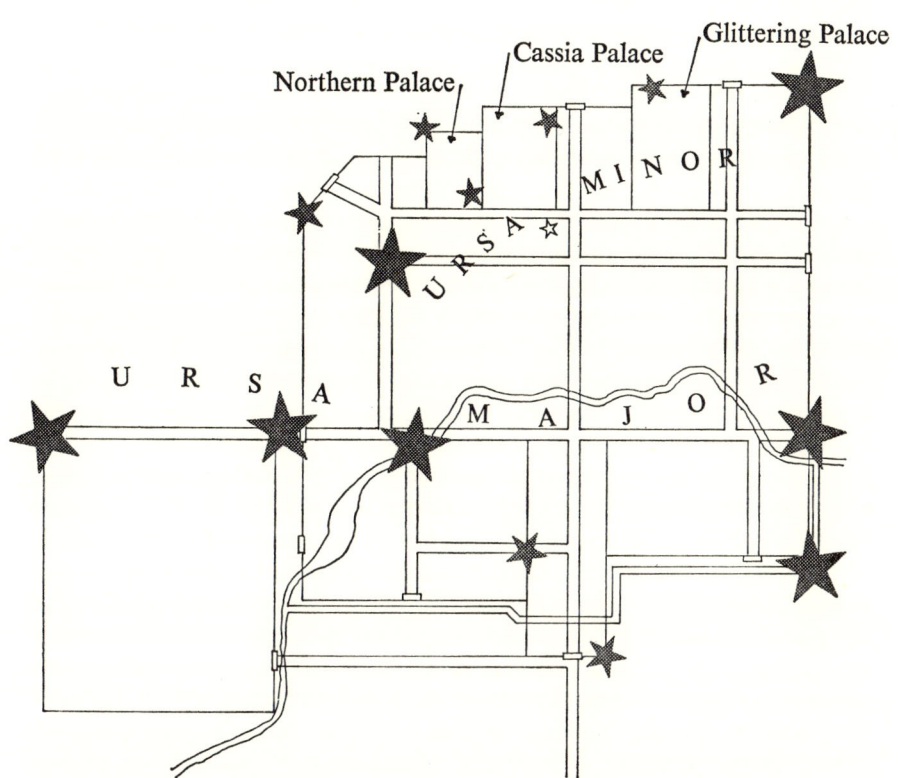

[26] The City of the Dipper. The constellations Ursa Major and Ursa Minor superimposed on the plan of Han Ch'ang-an. The popular belief of subsequent generations that the city was consciously designed to this pattern is unsupported by any independent evidence. Neither do the positions of the imperial palaces coincide with that of the Pole Star as was canonically prescribed, although it is probably true that they are closer to 4339 Camelopardi, the Pole Star of Han times (the white star on the plan), than to Polaris.

aspect which is equally explicit in a Lăc (Lo) tradition preserved in both Chinese and Viêtnamese annals.135 According to this tradition, Cô-loa, the City of the Conch, alleged capital of the Âu-lăc of Tong-king just prior to the beginning of the Christian era, was also constructed on the pattern of the Kwən-lwən mountain, with nine ramparts in the form of a conch shell. Rolf Stein has already drawn attention to the significance of the initials *k-* and *l-* in Tibeto-Chinese binoms denoting undulations, folds, or whorls such as those of the conch,136 and in this early Sino-Viêtnamese example the symbolism is reflected not only in the morphology of the city itself but also in the form of the name.

It is a truism that every ritual has a divine archetype, that it is an attempt to imitate what the gods did *in illo tempore*.137 By reactualizing the mythical moment when the cosmogonic act was first revealed, traditional man obtrudes a sacred instant into the flow of profane time, and in so doing initiates a new era in the cyclic regeneration of the world as he conceives it.138 As the construction rituals associated with capital [sc. sacred] cities were, in the traditional world, frequently simulations of the cosmogony, it is natural that the archetypes on which they were patterned should have been drawn from the past. Indeed, the past was normative and conformity with its precepts required no justification. Hence King **Mįwən (Wen), *mindful of the past,* 'retained the design of his predecessors' (p.430 above), and 'Heaven charged the corps of princes/To establish the capital where **Gįwo (Yü [the Great]) had wrought his works',139 just as Sennacherib constructed Nineveh according to 'the plan delineated from distant times', and Pharaoh could say of his temple-city, 'It was according to the ancient plan.' 140 It was the goddess Nanshe who revealed to Gudea of Lagash a plan of the temple he should build in honor of Ningirsuk.141 The city of Jerusalem seen by the prophet in the Syriac Apocalypse of Baruch II (chap. 4, verses 2–7) had been 'prepared beforehand here from the time when I took counsel to make Paradise'. 142 and Solomon's temple 'was prepared aforehand here from the beginning'. 143 When St John the Divine 'saw the Holy City, New Jerusalem, coming down from God out of Heaven, prepared as a bride adorned for her husband',144 his vision was one which had already had a long history among the Western Semites. Likewise, the traditional Indian urban form was modelled on that city where in the age of gold the Universal Sovereign had dwelt.

Although the plastic representation of cosmological concepts was less strongly developed in East than South Asia, yet there is abundant evidence that the location of the capital, that point of absolute reality about which the world revolved, was intimately connected with the welfare of the kingdom, so that its precise siting was a matter of extreme concern. The *Shu-Ching,* for example, records an alleged transcription of a speech by the Shang King B'wân-kăng vindicating the transference of his capital from a point norht of the Huang river to **·Iǝn (An-yang).¹⁴⁵ Apparently the populace had not welcomed the change, so Bʻwân-kăng reminded them that,

> 'When the former kings undertook affairs [of state], they were reverently attentive to the commands of Heaven, but even so they did not [always] ensure tranquillity [in the realm], they did not perpetuate their cities, [so that] up to the present there have been five city-states.¹⁴⁶ If we do not continue this ancient [practice, then it can only mean that] we are failing to recognize Heaven's abrogation of our mandate. How much less likely is it that we shall [then] be able to emulate the meritorious deeds of the former monarchs! Just as a fallen tree sends forth new shoots,¹⁴⁷ [so] Heaven will prolong our mandate in this new city, will renew and continue the great achievements of the former kings, and bring tranquillity to the four quarters.'
>
> [Trans. Karlgren, mod.]

Subsequently Bʻwân-kăng appealed to precedent in justification of his action:¹⁴⁸

> 'When there descended a plenitude¹⁴⁹ of great calamities the kings of former times did not cleave to the original site [of their capital, but] took account of the common weal and migrated. Why is it that you do not remember what is told of our ancient kings?' [Trans. Karlgren, mod.]

In relating the same events Ssŭ-ma Chʻien pointed out that Bʻwân-kăng was restoring the seat of government to the hallowed ground where **Tʻâng (Tʻang) the Successful had established his capital some centuries earlier,¹⁵⁰ and concluded with the following remarks:

> 'He crossed over to the south [side] of the river, established his government at **Bʻâk (Po) [and] practised Tʻâng's [style of] rule. That is why, subsequently, the populace was tranquil and the rule of the **·Iǝn (Yin) led to renewed prosperity. The feudal princes came to render homage at court because [Bʻwân-kăng] had practised the moral excellence of Tʻâng.'
>
> [Trans. Chavannes, eng. auct., mod.]

It is probably a similar conceptualization of the relationship between capital and kingdom which informs the political lament, **Miǝn-log (*Min-lao*), from the *Shih-Ching* (Mao CCLIII):

The people are indeed heavily burdened
And it is time for them to repose awhile.
Show favor to this central territory
So that tranquillity may come to the four quarters.
Do not indulge the wily and obsequious,
So that the wicked may be restrained.
Put down robbers and oppressors
Who have not feared the brightness [of the King].

THE CITY AS A COSMO-MAGICAL SYMBOL

Be gentle to those who are far off
And helpful to those who are near,
So that our King may be firmly established.

The people are indeed heavily burdened
And it is time for them to rest awhile.
Show favor to this central territory
So that people may congregate there.
Do not indulge the wily and obsequious,
So that the turbulent and obstreperous may be restrained.
Put down robbers and oppressors
So that the people are not made to suffer.
Do not desist from your labors,
So that our King may be at ease.

The people are indeed heavily burdened
And it is time for them to relax awhile.
Show favor to this capital city
So that tranquillity may come to the four quarters.
Do not indulge the wily and obsequious,
So that transgressors may be restrained.
Put down robbers and oppressors
So that they may do no evil.
Pay reverent attention to matters of decorum
So that you may associate with the virtuous.

The people are indeed heavily burdened
And it is time for them to pause awhile.
Show favor to this central territory
So that the sufferings of the people may be relieved.
Do not indulge the wily and obsequious,
So that the evil and the wicked may be restrained.
Put down robbers and oppressors
So that the upright be not corrupted.
Though you are as little children,
Your task is vast and great.

The people are indeed heavily burdened
And it is time for them to be tranquil awhile.
Show favor to this central territory
So that the kingdom may suffer no injury.
Do not indulge the wily and obsequious,
So that parasites may be restrained.
Put down robbers and oppressors
So that the straight be not deflected.

It is because the King wants you to be as jade
That I make this great remonstrance.

This ode is one of a number written at the very beginning of the Eastern Chou period, when nobility and commoners alike still harbored resentment at the transference of the capital to Glâk-dįang, and when in fact a former minister, **G'wâng-B'įwo (Huang-Fu), had apparently set up a rival capital at **Xįang (Hsiang), probably in the neighborhood of present-day K'ai-feng. It is more than probable that some lines of this ode as they have been transmitted to us are corrupt, but the role of the capital city as the instrument mediating the fortunes of the kingdom is evident enough in the refrain of the second couplet of each stanza.[151]

That belief in the magical harmonizing powers of construction according to a cosmic image persisted relatively late in Chinese history was attested by Ssŭ-ma Ch'ien when he observed of Erh-shih Huang-ti, son of Ch'in Shih Huang, that, 'He undertook the completion of the ·Â-b'įwang palace [left unfinished at his father's death, in order] to pacify the barbarians of the four quarters.'[152]

A remarkable parallel to Ssŭ-ma Ch'ien's statement has been preserved in the *Nan-Ch'i Shu*.[153] In 484 King Kauṇḍinya Jayavarman of *B'įu-nậm (Funan) sent the Indian Buddhist Nāgasena on an embassy to the Chinese court. We have already had occasion to cite one of this envoy's accounts of conditions in B'įu-nậm, and now is the time to quote the written report which he submitted:

> 'On the Mount of the Immortals called *Muâ-tậm (Mo-tan) auspicious trees flourish in great abundance [154] [so that] the divine Maheśvara regards it with favor [as a place on which] to send down his holy spirit. The princes of the country all receive this blessing and the people are all tranquil. It is because this grace is all-pervading that the subjects submit willingly to authority.'

It is probably unknowable to what extent the ideology of Nāgasena's report was transmuted in the minds of Chinese officials into a form congenial to their own preconceptions, so that we cannot be certain whether this text should be treated as evidence for the parallelism of the worlds in the thought-patterns of China or in those of B'įu-nậm. There is, however, independent testimony to the existence of such ideas in Cambodia in later centuries, and my own guess is that the Chinese officials recorded fairly accurately a concept which they had no difficulty in recognizing in their own cultural repertoire.

On the opposite side of Asia similar ideas were frequently expressed. Here, for example, inscribed on stone are the sentiments expounded by Esarhaddon (681–669 BC) of Assyria when he was restoring the temple of Assur that had originally been built by Shalmaneser V (728–722):

THE CITY AS A COSMO-MAGICAL SYMBOL [473

'... that temple, – the place of its site I did not change, but upon gold, silver, precious stones, herbs [and] cedar-oil I established its foundation walls [and] laid its brickwork. I built and completed it; I made it magnificent to the astonishment of the peoples. For life [lit. my life], for length of days, for the stability of my reign, for the welfare of my posterity, for the safety of my priestly throne, for the overthrow of my enemies, for the success of the harvest[s] of Assyria, for the welfare of Assyria I built it.'[155]

A close association of capital with dynasty was formerly common to most Asian political traditions. In some instances, indeed, the association was between capital and individual ruler. Each king of classical Kambujadeśa, for example, sought to construct a new capital, or at least a new temple-mountain, which after his death would become his mausoleum and the shrine for his personal cult. Not all rulers enjoyed long enough or peaceful enough reigns to achieve this aim, but the frequency with which temple-mountains and capitals were built is impressive testimony to the power of the idea : the Bàkoṅ at the center of Hariharālaya; Phnoṃ Bǎkhèṅ marking the axis of the first capital at Aṅkor; Koh Ker, briefly the capital of Jayavarman IV; the Phimeanakas that of Jayavarman V, and the Bàphuon that of Udayādityavarman II.[156] In Campā,[157] Java,[158] and Burma[159] it is possible to point to similar successions of capitals. In the last region, as late as 1857, Mindon Min abandoned the old capital of Amarapura, which had been associated with disastrous events during the reign of his elder brother, and established its population of 150,000 souls in a new city at Mandalay.[160] A similar impermanence was characteristic of some of the capitals of Peninsular India. The *Śilpaśāstras*, for example, prescribed that each new dynasty should found its own capital, and Bhoja went so far as to say that a king who resided in a city laid out by his enemy, or even by another king, would meet death in a very short time (*Yuktikalpataru*, verse 173). Other examples can be cited from the ancient Middle East. Khorsabad, for instance, was dedicated by Sargon in 706 BC, but abandoned by Sennacherib, his successor, a year later, despite the enormous amount of labor that had gone into its construction.[161] As a final example from among the hundreds that might be adduced we cite Sāmarrā, founded in AD 836 by al-Muʿtaṣim, eighth of the ʿAbbāsid caliphs, beautified by his son al-Mutawakkil and seven succeeding caliphs, but abandoned in 892 when al-Muʿtaḍid restored the seat of government to Baghdād.[162]

In China, capitals became relatively permanent foundations at an early date, but fairly reliable traditions record at least five movements of the capital under the Shang. Different scholars have accounted for these transfers in different ways. The 8th-century commentator Chang Shou-chieh, in his *Shih-Chi Cheng-i*, identified the changes as follows:

1. T'ang the Successful migrated from Southern **Bʿâk (Po) to Western Bʿâk [*Shih-Chi*, chüan 3, f. 2 verso];

2. **Dʻi̯ông-tieng (Chung-ting) moved to **Ngog (Ao) [f. 7 verso];
3. **Gʻâ-tân-kap (Ho-tan-chia) moved to **Si̯ang (Hsiang) [*ibid.*];
4. **Tso-·i̯ɛt (Tsu-i) established himself at **Gʻieng (Hsing) [*ibid.*];
5. Bʻwân-kăng returned to Western Bʻâk, where he founded the capital of ·I̯ən [f. 8 verso].

It is, however, possible to explain the five transfers in several different ways and, indeed, to discern more than five such migrations. In fact the preface to *Shu-Ching* [which is not accounted authentic] mentions eight changes of capital between the reigns of **Si̯at (Hsieh) and **Tʻâng the Successful, that is prior to the five discussed above.163 The *Chʻun-Chʻiu* and the *Tso-Chuan* also contain several references to multiple migrations of capitals. Particularly complex was the situation in the state of **Xi̯o (Hsü), where the seat of government was transferred from a site traditionally supposed to have been in present-day Hsü-Chou in Ho-nan province to **Śi̯ap (She), thence to **Di̯ər (I), and finally to **Di̯ung-Dʼi̯ĕng (Jung-Chʻeng). But, although the *Tso-Chuan* implies that these moves were initiated voluntarily by the ruler of Xi̯o, it is apparent from the context that this small state was a mere pawn in the power politics of its larger neighbor Tṣʻi̯o.164 The movements of Chou state capitals recorded elsewhere in the *Chʻun-Chʻiu* and the *Tso-Chuan* appear similarly to have been induced by political expediency or military constraint rather than by geomantic considerations.

As a colophon to this section we may appropriately quote a few lines from the **·I̯ən-Mi̯wo (*Yin-Wu* : Mao CCCV), which appear to epitomize the cosmomagical role of the ancient Chinese city. This ode forms part of the *Shang-Sung* section of the *Shih-Ching*, and as such may preserve the traditions of the **Sông (Sung) ruling house when it was still not fully assimilated to Chou culture.165

商邑翼翼
四方之極
赫赫厥聲
濯濯厥靈
壽考且寧
以保我後生

The capital of Śi̯ang (Shang)[166] was a city of cosmic order,[167]
The pivot[168] of the four quarters.
Glorious was its renown,
Purifying its divine power,
Manifested in longevity and tranquillity
And the protection of us who come after.

It is by no means established that the city referred to in these lines was the old capital of the Shang at An-yang. As the people of Sông (Sung) were regarded as descendants of that dynasty, so the term Shang became a literary honorific for the state of Sông, and the ode may have referred to a capital of the later kingdom. My own feeling, however, is that the eulogy was probably considered appropriate for any Sung or Shang capital, including the Great City Shang founded by B'wân-kăng at An-yang. I would suggest that a translation something after this fashion not only elicits a unity in the stanza which is less evident in previous versions, but also exhibits the chief modes of traditional urban symbolism which have been discussed in the preceding pages : namely, in the order in which they occur in the ode, the imitation of a supramundane archetype, the symbolism of the center and cardinal orientation, the role of the *omphalos* as a point of ontological transition where supernatural power enters the world, and the parallelism of the macrocosmos and microcosmos. In other words, the city functioned as an *axis mundi* about which the kingdom revolved, and was laid out as an *imago mundi* in order to ensure the protection and prosperity 'of us who come after'.

I am aware that the forms of Asian, and especially of Chinese, cities have sometimes been explained along other lines. In particular Nelson Wu, in what must surely be the most sensitive interpretation of Asian cities ever penned, has gone so far as to state categorically that, 'The Chinese walled city is not to be confused with the idealized Indian village or city plan of the *Mānasāra-Śilpaśāstra*. . . . They differ in every respect.'[169] Great as is my admiration for Professor Wu's insights into the cultural bases of these cities, I find myself compelled to differ from him on this point. Of course, it is not to be denied that to the casual visitor the traditional Chinese city presented a very different appearance from that of the Indian city. Nor is anyone likely to dispute the fact that there are vast differences between the regional traditions within the Chinese and Indian culture realms themselves. And even within those regional traditions the complex interplay of historical variables has induced a rich variety of urban forms. But in my reading of the evidence the ideal-type cities of India and China are affinal expressions of shared conceptions of the ordering of space, of a common 'astrobiological' mode of thought. Each was established only after an array of geomantic considerations had been satisfied. Each was constructed as an *axis mundi* incorporating a powerful impulse to centripetality. Each was laid out as a terrestrial image of the cosmos, in a schema which involved cardinal orientation and axiality and, as a corollary, strong architectural emphasis on the main gates. On the capitals in both traditions, at whatever level of the political and administrative hierarchy they occurred, devolved the maintenance of the prosperity of their respective territories, and, as such, they became paradigms for all other cities.

Of course, in each culture, as indeed in the cultures of the rest of Asia, the material forms through which this cosmo-magical symbolism was realized were highly distinctive. The palace of the Chinese emperor could hardly have been more different from the sanctuary at the heart of the South Indian temple-city, or both from the temple-mountain of 12th-century Kambujadeśa, but each symbolized an *axis mundi*, an *omphalos*, about which their respective kingdoms revolved. Similarly, whereas in these cultures cardinal orientation involved the positioning of the sides of a square or rectangle so as to face the cardinal points of the compass, in ancient Mesopotamia it was normally the corners of the enceinte which were directed in this manner. But in both instances the *principle* of cardinal orientation was strongly developed, the four compass directions were the reference points by which the sacred enceinte of the city was located in the continuum of profane space. Structural regularities in the traditional urban symbolism of Asia are to be sought not in the specific architectural units which make up the city, nor perhaps in their precise spatial inter-relationships, but rather in the manner in which the whole assemblage that we designate a city was believed to (not necessarily did) function. The classical city plan of China was not, as Wu claims, 'unnatural'[170]: it was a response to the basic need, which the Chinese shared with men elsewhere, to delimit and orient an *habitabilis* in space, and was achieved with the aid of the archetypally 'natural' ('bio-astrale' Berthelot would call it) progressions of the heavenly bodies. As those were regular and predictable, so the cosmicized territories, the ideal-type cities, of men everywhere tended to reflect this regularity. The 'Chinese world of walled cities' and 'the Indian world of holy places'[171] *in this respect* were not, as Wu stipulates, fundamentally opposed. That the value systems of these two Great Traditions were to a large extent opposed is a truism, but in the technical business of delimiting space both had been constrained to make use of the same astrobiological tool-kit. When and how these concepts were accepted into the Chinese intellectual universe is a difficult question, discussion – if not the resolution – of which can be left for another occasion. Suffice it to say here that, although Chinese pre-occupation with 'success and frustration in the arena of living', as contrasted with the Indian search for the metaphysical meaning of life, certainly caused these two civilizations to mediate the symbolism of urban form through widely different architectural designs, these latter never entirely obscured the shared astrobiological symbolism.

Notes and References

1. The broad outlines of the history of Chinese urbanism are fairly well established and have recently been summarized by Professor Sen-dou Chang, 'Some aspects of the urban geography of the Chinese hsien capital', *Annals of the Association of American Geographers*, vol.51, no.1 (1961), pp.23–45, and 'The historical trend of Chinese urbanization', *loc. cit.*, vol.53, no.2 (1963), pp.109–43. There is an extensive literature on various historical aspects of the Chinese city in both Chinese and Japanese, and a small part of that relating to Chou urbanism is cited in notes to this book. Wolfram Eberhard draws on both primary materials and secondary sources in his 'Data on the structure of the Chinese city in the pre-industrial period', *Economic development and cultural change*, vol.4, no.3. Chicago 1956, pp.253–68, and in 'The structure of the pre-industrial Chinese city', in Eberhard, *Collected Papers*, vol.1 : *Settlement and Social Change in Asia*. Hong Kong University Press 1967, pp.43–64, as does Etienne Balazs, 'Les villes chinoises. Histoire des institutions administratives et judiciaires', in *La ville*, part I : *Institutions administratives et judiciaires*. Recueils de la Société Jean Bodin, vol.6. Librairie Encyclopédique, Bruxelles 1954, pp.225–40 [Reprinted in English translation in Balazs, *Chinese civilization and bureaucracy. Variations on a theme*. Yale University Press, New Haven, and London 1964, pp.66–78]. The Han city has been studied by Miyazaki Ichisada in a paper entitled 'Les villes en Chine à l'époque des Han', *T'oung Pao*, vol.48 (1960), pp.376–92. See also the same author's *Chūgoku jōkaku no kigen isetsu* (1933). Reprinted in *Ajia-shi kenkyū*, vol.1 (1957). The majority of studies of Sung cities relate to the commercial functions of the ports of the south coast [a selection of references is incorporated in Wheatley, 'Geographical notes on some commodities involved in Sung maritime trade', *Journal of the Malayan Branch of the Royal Asiatic Society*, vol.32, pt.2. Singapore 1961, bibliography pp.132–7], but there is a more comprehensive approach by Katō Shigeshi in *Kuwabara Hakushi Kanreki Kinen Toyoshi Ronzo*. Kyōtō 1931, pp.93–140. Reprinted in *Studies in Chinese Economic History*, vol.1. Tōyō Bunko, Tōkyō 1952, pp.299–346. A recent study which takes account of the symbolism of the Chinese city is Nelson I. Wu [Wu No-sun], *Chinese and Indian Architecture. The city of man, the mountain of god, and the realm of the immortals*. George Braziller, New York 1963. See also Edward H. Schafer, 'The last years of Ch'ang-an', *Oriens Extremus*, vol.10, pt.2. Wiesbaden 1963, pp.133–79; Arthur F. Wright, 'Viewpoints on a

city. Changan (583–904) : Chinese capital and Asian cosmopolis', *Ventures, Magazine of the Yale Graduate School*, vol.5, no.1. Yale University 1965, pp.15–23, and 'Symbolism and function. Reflections on Changan and other great cities', *Journal of Asian Studies*, vol.24 no.4 (1965), pp.667–79.

2. The graph ***dz'i̯ang* (*chiang*) is compounded of two elements signifying 'box' and 'axe'. Does the use of this character imply that the primary defence of the city was a wooden palisade? Or had the graph already acquired the extended connotation of 'mechanic' or 'artificer' when the *K'ao-kung Chi* was compiled? I think that the latter interpretation is to be preferred.

2a. An 8th-century annotator did manage to circumvent this difficulty by assigning three avenues to each gate and allotting the right-hand one to men, the left-hand one to women, and the central one to carts and chariots. Within a sacred enclave in the heart of a city I suppose such a segregation of traffic might have been possible, but there is no doubt that, so far as Chou cities were concerned, it was a flight of fancy born of an excessive zeal for systematization. Which particular intimation in the ancient texts gave rise to this interpretation I have not been able to discover.

3. R. Shamasastry, *Kauṭilya's Arthaśāstra*. Sri Raghuveer Printing Press, Mysore 1956, Book II, Chapter 4. The apparently irreconcilable views of various scholars as to the date of the *Arthaśāstra* are summarized succinctly by H. C. Raychaudhuri in R. C. Mujumdar (ed.), *The History and Culture of the Indian People*, vol.2 : *The age of imperial unity*, Bharatiya Vidya Bhavan, Bombay; second edition 1953, pp.285–7. See also V. Kalyanov, 'Dating the Arthaśāstra', *Papers presented by the Soviet Delegation at the 23rd International Congress of Orientalists*. Cambridge 1954 [In Russian, with English abridgment].

4. Cf. the reconstruction of the ground-plan of Mohenjo-daro in Stuart Piggott, *Some ancient cities of India*. Oxford University Press 1945, p.14.

5. There is also reason to think that Chinese ritualists may themselves have been confused as to the implications of the two types of city plan, for in the ***Ngi̯wăt-Li̯ĕng* (*Yüeh-Ling*) section of the *Li-Chi* the last month of spring is prescribed as the time when animals should be dismembered before the *nine gates of the capital*, presumably to ward off disease in the ensuing year. A total of nine gates is consonant neither with the well-field plan nor with that prescribed by the *K'ao-kung Chi*. There was, moreover, another well-established tradition according to which the imperial capital was in the form of a square with sides of 12 *li*, while the seat of a prince of the first rank had a side of 9 *li*, of the second or third rank of 7 *li*, and of the fourth or fifth rank of 5 *li*. This led one commentator to infer that the *K'ao-kung Chi* was here referring to the customs of some dynasty other than the Chou, probably the Hsia or Shang.

It is not without interest that the urban design advocated in the *K'ao-kung Chi* and the *Arthaśāstra* is identical both with that prescribed by Ezekiel for

NOTES AND REFERENCES

the city of the Levites (Chapter 48) and with that envisioned by St John the Divine (*Revelation*, Chapter 21). In the 19th century the Mormons laid out Salt Lake City according to the plan delineated by Ezekiel.

6. René Berthelot, *La pensée de l'Asie et l'astrobiologie*. Payot, Paris 1949.

7. *loc. cit.*, p.7. Berthelot expresses this idea in somewhat different language: 'L'astrobiologie se situe entre les croyances des sauvages et la science moderne de la nature', p.65. Cf. also Mircea Eliade, 'Structures and changes in the history of religion', in Carl H. Kraeling and Robert M. Adams, *City invincible*. University of Chicago Press 1960, pp.351–66. The attraction of the regular movements of heavenly bodies to the primitive mind enveloped in an apparently order-less nature, unforeseeable and perpetually threatening, needs no emphasis.

8. *loc. cit.*, Chapter 2: 'Les antécédents de l'astrobiologie et son rôle dans la formation de la science', especially pp.54–5: 'Dans cette phase "bio-astrale", puis "bio-solaire", les hommes transportent aux objets célestes, aux astres, et, tout d'abord, à la lune comme au soleil, la vie et dans quelque mesure la conscience qu'ils attribuent aux êtres qui les entourent sur la terre. Ils s'en tiennent à la périodicité, conçue sans précision rigoureuse et numérique, que l'observation courante révèle, surtout en pays plus ou moins tempéré, dans la vie des plantes et les mouvements du soleil : naissance, croissance, floraison, fructification, mort et renaissance des plantes annuelles, cultivées par eux; rhythme quotidien selon lequel le soleil chaque jour se lève, monte à l'horizon, se couche et par lequel la nuit succède au jour, puis de nouveau le jour à la nuit; rhythme annuel, enfin, suivant lequel les saisons se succèdent conformément à la position du soleil dans le ciel.' According to Berthelot the bio-astral world view differed from the astrobiological chiefly in that the numerical regularities deduced from the motions of the heavenly bodies had not yet been adapted to the biological cycles of earth. Cf. p.62: 'A cet époque apparaît l'astrobiologie proprement dite : les hommes (c'est-à-dire d'abord les observateurs et calculateurs professionels) transportent aux événements terrestres l'idée des relations numériques précises et invariables, des lois mathématiques, qu'ils ont établies pour les mouvements célestes (astrologie et calendrier de plus en plus perfectionné) tout en conservant aux êtres célestes le caractère vivant et animé que leur prêtait l'époque antérieure et an attribuant éventuellement ce caractère au Ciel dans son ensemble ou même à l'univers entier, Ciel et Terre à la fois.' But, as Granet has demonstrated in the particular instance of China, in astrobiological formulations, 'Les nombres n'ont pas pour fonction d'exprimer des grandeurs : ils servent à ajuster les dimensions concrètes aux proportions de l'Univers' [*La Pensée chinoise*. Albin Michel, Paris 1934, p.273].

9. *loc. cit.*, pp.24, 41, 118, 163 and 343.

10. Cf. A. Bouché-Leclercq, *Histoire de divination dans l'antiquité*, 4 vols. Leroux, Paris 1879–82.

11. Walter F. Otto, *The Homeric gods : the spiritual significance of Greek religion*. New York 1954, p.287. This is a translation by Moses Hadas of *Die Götter Griechenlands : Das Bild des Göttlichen in Spiegel des Griechischen Geistes*, 2 vols. Frankfurt-am-Main 1947.

12. Cf., for example, A. E. Crawley, *The idea of the soul*. London 1909 : 'Primitive man has only one mode of thought, one mode of expression, one part of speech – the personal'.

13. Henri Frankfort, *Kingship and the gods*. University of Chicago Press 1948, p.3.

14. Erich Isaac, 'The act and the covenant : the impact of religion on the landscape', *Landscape*, vol.11, no.2 (1961–2), pp.12–17.

15. Cp. Berthelot's remark about the role of astrobiology : 'Et c'est cette manière de penser qui serait peut-être la plus caractéristique de la pensée de l'Asie, si celle-ci... n'était plus complexe et plus diverse, et si, au point de vue intellectuel comme au point de vue géographique, il ne valait mieux dire *les Asies*, plutôt que *l'Asie*' (p.66).

16. Mircea Eliade, *Le mythe de l'éternel retour : archétypes et répétition*. Librairie Gallimard, Paris 1949, Chapter 1. English translation under the title *The myth of the eternal return*. Pantheon Books 1954; reprinted under the title *Cosmos and History*. Harper Torchbook 50, New York 1959. Idem, *Das Heilige und das Profane*. Rowohlt Taschenbuch Verlag GmbH 1957, Chapter 1 English translation under the title *The Sacred and the Profane*. Harcourt, Brace & Co., Inc. 1959; reprinted as Harper Torchbook 81 (1961). Idem, *Traité d'histoire des religions*. Payot, Paris 1948, Chapter 10. English translation under the title *Patterns in comparative religion*. Sheed and Ward, Inc., New York 1958; reprinted as Meridian Book 155, The World Publishing Co., New York 1963; Idem, 'Centre du monde, temple, maison', *Le symbolisme cosmique des monuments religieux*. Serie Orientale Roma, XIV. Roma 1957, pp.57–82. The application of cosmo-magical principles specifically to urban construction was elaborated by Eliade in *Comentarii la legenda Meșterului Manole*. Bucharest 1943. Cf. also Th. H. Gaster, 'Myth and story', *Numen*, vol.1 (1954), pp.184–212, and especially p.191, where the author refers to 'earthly cities, temples or religious institutions [which] have their duplicates in some transcendental sphere, often identified with the heavens'; and Ernst Topitsche, *Vom Ursprung und Ende der Metaphysik* (1958). It was this same idea which was expressed by Māni in a passage in his long lost *Epistola Fundamenti* and which was subsequently quoted by St Augustin in *De Natura Boni* (Migne edition, col.570) : *In eadem* [*principis tenebrarum conjuge*] *enim construebantur et contexebantur omnium imagines, caelestium ac terrenarum virtutem, ut pleni videlicet orbis id quod formabatur similitudinem obtineret*.

I have also benefited in the preparation of this section from the analyses of pre-modern modes of thought contained in the following works : Ernst

NOTES AND REFERENCES

Cassirer, *Philosophie der symbolischen Formen, II : Das mythische Denken.* Berlin 1925; Lucien Lévy-Bruhl, *Le surnaturel et la nature dans la mentalité primitive.* Paris 1931, and *L'âme primitive.* Paris 1927 [Though dissociating myself from both his strictures on Chinese intellectual achievement (e.g. *Le surnaturel*, p.380) and those conceptualizations which produced them]; Rudolf Otto, *Das Heilige*, New edition, Munich 1947; and Henri and H. A. Frankfort, John Wilson, and Thorkild Jacobsen, *The intellectual adventure of ancient man.* University of Chicago Press 1946 : reprinted under the title *Before Philosophy* as Pelican Book 198, Harmondsworth 1949.

17. There is an introduction to this theme as it expressed itself in Southeast Asia in Robert von Heine-Geldern, 'Weltbild und Bauform in Südostasien', *Wiener Beiträge zur Kunst- und Kulturgeschichte Asiens*, vol.4. Wien 1930, pp.28–78.

18. Cf. Walter Krickeberg, 'Bauform und Weltbild im alten Mexico', *Mythe, Mensch und Umwelt.* Beiträge zur Religion, Mythologie und Kulturgeschichte. Bamberger Verlagshaus Meisenbach & Co., Bamberg 1950.

19. On early man's need to proclaim the knowledge that he shared with the gods, to dramatize the truth that had been revealed to him, see Frankfort, *Kingship and the Gods*, pp.3–4, and *The intellectual adventure of ancient man*, p.8; and Paul Westheim, *Arte Antiguo de México*. Fondo de Cultura Económica, México 1950. English translation, under the title *The art of ancient Mexico*. Doubleday Anchor Book 416, New York 1965, pp.19–21. Cf. also Eric Voegelin [*Order and history*, vol.1. Louisiana State University Press 1956, p.16] : 'To establish a government is an essay in world creation. When man creates the cosmion of political order, he analogically repeats the divine creation of the cosmos. The analogical repetition is not an act of futile imitation, for in repeating the cosmos man participates, in the measure allowed to his existential limitations, in the creation of cosmic order itself. Moreover, when participating in the creation of order, man experiences his consubstantiality with the being of which he is a creaturely part. Hence, in his creative endeavor man is a partner in the double sense of a creature and a rival of God.'

20. 'The bounds of space' as they are termed in the *Brāhmaṇa*. In another place in the same corpus the cardinal points of the compass are described as supporting horizontal space in the manner of a pelt suspended at its four corners.

21. Cf. note 16 above, but especially *Le mythe de l'éternel retour*, Chapter I.

22. For a discussion of the differences between Chinese co-ordinative thought-forms and European causal or nomothetic thinking see Joseph Needham, *Science and civilisation in China*, vol.2 : *History of scientific thought.* At the University Press, Cambridge 1956, pp.279–303.

23. This thesis is developed by Chang Tung-sun, 'Ssŭ-hsiang yen-lun yü wen-hua', *Sociological World*, vol.10 (1938).

24. The full implications of *ch'i* cannot be adequately ascribed to any single English word – or even series of words. Joseph Needham [*Science and civilisation in China*, vol.2. Cambridge University Press 1956, p.359 and vol.4 (1962), pp.xxiv, 131] employs such phrases as 'subtle matter', 'vital breath', 'emanation', 'matter-energy' and 'energy present in organized form', but expresses a preference, if synonyms must be found, for Greek πνεῦμα or Sanskrit *prāṇa*. Cf. p.369, note *d* : '. . . connotations similar to . . . our own conceptions of a vapour or a gas but which also has something of radiant energy about it, like a radioactive emanation'. The term 'cosmic breath' used here is inadequate as a translation but does subsume some of the more salient concepts implicit in the above phrases. In particular the use of 'cosmic' goes some way towards evoking the immanence of *ch'i*, at the same time that it reflects its pervasive operation through the material structure of the universe. 'Breath' possibly carries overtones of a passivity that is not inherent in *ch'i*, which is both active and passive, which both flows and stagnates, both surges and regresses Probably the term were best left untranslated.

25. A considerable number of *feng-shui* handbooks are still in existence and others now lost are known from bibliographies. In *Ch'ien-Han Shu* (compiled c. AD 100), for example, there are references to a *Golden Box of Geomancy* (*K'an-yü Chin-kuei*) and a *Terrestrial Morphology for [the siting of] Palaces and Mansions* (*Kung-chai Ti-hsing*), both of which are long since lost. It is possible that parts of a still extant work, *Mr Kuan's Geomantic Indicator* (*Kuan-shih Ti-li Chih-meng*), often attributed to Kuan-Lo, who lived from AD 209 to 256, may indeed have come from that author's brush. From the 5th century AD there has survived the *Yellow Emperor's Mansion[-siting] Classic* (*Huang-Ti Chai Ching*) by Wang-Wei; from the T'ang the *Mysterious principles of the Blue Bag* (*Ch'ing-nang Ao-chih*), ascribed to Yang Yün-sung; from the Ming the *K'an-yü Man-hsing* (which Dr Joseph Needham has felicitously translated as *Agreeable Geomantic Aphorisms*) by the mathematician Liu-Chi. Notable later geomantic textbooks include *Precious Tools of Geomancy* (*Ti-li Cho-yü-fu*) by Hsü Chih-mo, c. AD 1570; *Comprehensive Treatise on Mansion[-siting] according to the [influence of the] Yin and the Yang* (*Yin-Yang Erh-chai Ch'üan-shu*) by Yao Chan-ch'i, 1744; and *Five Mysteries of Geomancy* (*Ti-li Wu-chüeh*) by Chao Chiu-feng, 1786. Nineteenth-century Western accounts of *feng-shui* are to be found in the works of E. J. Eitel, *Feng-shui, principles of the natural science of the Chinese*. Hong Kong 1873; J. J. M. de Groot, *The religious system of China*, vols.2 and 3. Leiden 1892; and H. Hübrig, 'Fung Schui, oder chinesische Geomantie', *Sitzungsberichte d. berliner Gesellschaft f. Anthropol., Ethnol. und Urgeschichte* (1879), no.2. In this century L. C. Porter has written briefly on this topic ['Feng-Shui', *Chinese Recorder* (1920)], and E. J. Dukes has contributed an article to the *Encyclopaedia of Religion and Ethics* [ed. by Hastings], vol.5, p.833. Recently Joseph

NOTES AND REFERENCES

Needham has summarized our knowledge of this supremely important instrument in the creation of the Chinese landscape, both urban and rural, in *Science and civilisation in China*, vol.2 (1956), pp.359–63 and vol.4 (1962), pp.239–45.

26. This class of diviners is mentioned specifically perhaps as early as the beginning of the 1st century BC, the date when Ssŭ-ma Ch'ien wrote the *Shih Chi*. It should be noted, however, that some scholars have ascribed Chapter 127 of Ssŭ-ma Ch'ien's work, in which this reference occurs, to another and later hand.

27. Phạm Công-trứ, *Đại-Việt sử-kỉ toàn-thư* (1665) : *ngoại-kỉ toàn-thư*, Chapter 5, f.7 verso; Li Tê-xuyên, *Việt điện u linh tập* (1329), f.10a (here quoting *Giao-châu kí* of Master Triệu of the 9th century); *Tzŭ-ch'ih T'ung-chien*, Chapter 250, f.8 verso; *Man-Shu*, Chapter 10, p.49 (Ts'ung-shu Chi-ch'eng edition, comment of Wu-ying Tien editors).

28. *Shu-Ching*, ***B'wân-kăng* (*P'an-keng*) section. My translation is close to Karlgren's [*Bull. Mus. Far E. Antiquities* no.22 (1950), pp.20 and 26]. Legge's version of the second part runs : 'And you did not presumptuously oppose the decision of the tortoise : – and so we are *here* to enlarge our great inheritance' [*The Chinese Classics*, vol.3, p.246], which maintains the lofty tenor consonant with a royal pronouncement but (erroneously, I believe) reverses the general sense of the passage. However, the reference to divination would still stand even if Legge's version were to prove correct.

29. For textual comments on this line see Bernhard Karlgren, 'Glosses on the Ta Ya and Sung odes', *Bulletin of the Museum of Far Eastern Antiquities*, no.18. Stockholm 1946, p.60, gloss 862.

30. Legge [*The Chinese Classics*, vol.4, p.438] renders these plant names as violets and sowthistles; Waley [*The Book of Songs*. George Allen and Unwin, Ltd, London 1937, p.284] as celery and sowthistle, but identification of botanical species in the *Shih-Ching* is a hazardous business, and the names were perhaps best left untranslated. My rendering of the passage as a whole follows Karlgren's version closely ['The Book of Odes : Ta ya and Sung', *BMFEA*, no.17 (1945), p.67 : Glosses in *BMFEA*, no.18 (1946), pp.21–2].

31. Uncle of the Chou ruler Ch'eng-Wang (***Ḍi̯ĕng-gi̯wang*), and, in the canonical version of Chou history, both architect and consolidator of the Chou hegemony in North China.

32. These lines occur at the beginning of the ***K'âng-kôg* (*K'ang-kao*) section of the *Shu-Ching*, but Su-Shih has suggested (what seems most probable) that they have been abstracted in error from the **Glâk-kôg (*Lo-kao*) section. It may be added that they would not be inappropriate in the ***Ḍi̯og-kôg* (*Shao-kao*) section.

33. For the justification of this translation see Karlgren, 'Glosses', *BMFEA*, no.21, p.63.

34. This account is taken from the ***Ḍi̯og-kôg* (*Shao-kao*) section.

35. From the **Glâk-kôg (Lo-kao) section. For a commentary on this translation see Karlgren, 'Glosses', *BMFEA*, no.21, pp.74–5.

36. **D'ieng-t̂i̯əg pi̯wang-ti̯ông (Ting-chih fang-chung) : Mao L.

37. One such occasion must stand for all the rest, and I would suggest, as reasonably representative, the discussions and oracle-takings which preceded the founding of Sui Ch'ang-an : *vide Sui-Shu*, chüan 1, ff.17 verso–18 recto, and *Pei-Shih*, chüan 11, ff.12 verso–13 verso.

38. E.g. Ch'ang-an under the T'ang : Hang Te-chou, Lo Chung-ju, and T'ien Hsing-nung, 'T'ang Ch'ang-an Ch'eng ti-chi ch'u-pu t'an-ts'e', *K'ao-ku Hsüeh-pao*, no.3 (1958), pp.79–93; Ma Te-chih 'T'ang-tai Ch'ang-an Ch'eng k'ao-ku chi-lüeh', *K'ao-ku*, no.11 (1963), pp.595–611; Albert Herrmann, *Historical and commercial atlas of China*. Second edition, General editor : Norton Ginsburg. Aldine Publishing Company, Chicago 1966, p.13, IV and V; Ch'eng Kuang-yü and Hsü Sheng-mo (eds.), *Chung-Kuo Li-shih Ti-t'u-chi*, vol.1. T'ai-pei 1956, pp.56–7.

      Lo-yang : Herrmann, *op. cit.*, p.13; Ch'eng and Hsü, *op. cit.*, p.59.

      K'ai-feng : Herrmann. First edition, Harvard University Press 1935, p.48; Ch'eng and Hsü, *op. cit.*, p.64.

      Nan-ching : Herrmann. Second edition, p.45, V; Ch'eng and Hsü, *op. cit.*, p.61.

      Pei-ching : Herrmann, *op. cit.*, p.45, III; Ch'eng and Hsü, *op. cit.*, p.63.

39. Cf. A.C. Moule, *Quinsai, with other notes on Marco Polo*. Cambridge 1957, Fig.1; Herrmann (First edition), p.48; Ch'eng and Hsü, *op. cit.*, p.65.

40. For a vivid evocation of life in Hang-Chou at this time, based on the abundant primary records available, see Jacques Gernet, *La vie quotidienne en Chine à la veille de l'invasion mongole 1250–1276*. Hachette, Paris 1959. English translation by H.M. Wright under the title *Daily life in China on the eve of the Mongol invasion 1250–1276*. George Allen and Unwin, London 1962.

41. Chinese culture was permeated with the symbolism of an ominous threatening north as opposed to a benign, auspicious south : cf., for example, the *I-Ching : Shuo-Kua*, chüan 2 : 'That the holy sages turned their faces to the south while they gave ear to the meaning of the universe means that, in ruling, they turned towards what is light' [After Wilhelm]. Early Taoist authors were greatly intrigued by the fact that to the south of the Tropic of Cancer, for a variable number of days between the spring and autumn equinoxes, a gnomon cast a shadow towards the south. This was reflected in two names often applied to the poorly explored territories of South China in Chou and Ch'in times, namely **Ńi̯ĕt-nəm (*Ńźi̯ĕt-nậm : Jih-nan : = South of the Sun) and **Pək-[χi̯ang]-g'o (*Pək-[χi̯ang]-γuo, Pei-[Hsiang]-hu : = [Region of] North-facing Doors). As the Chinese acquired more substantive information about the southern regions, so they thrust these names farther and farther towards

the vaguely known frontier tracts, and Ńźi̯ĕt-nậm eventually became attached, for cosmo-magical reasons deriving from Taoist lore, to the territory lying between the Porte d'Annam and the Col des Nuages [R. A. Stein, 'Le Lin-yi', *Han Hiue*, vol.2, fasc.1–3. Peking 1947, pp.16–19]. In the earlier centuries of the Christian era, the supposedly north-facing doors of Tong-king (then known as *Kau-tśi) and North Annam (Ńźi̯ĕt-nậm) were a favorite theme of Chinese authors writing about the southern regions. Li Tao-yüan, for example, reported the manner in which Emperor Ming of Han (AD 58–75) interrogated a man from these regions as to the orientation of the houses in Tong-king [*Shui-Ching Chu*, Ssŭ-pu Ts'ung-k'an edition, Chapter 36, f.19 verso], and the Sung encyclopedia *T'ai-p'ing Yü-lan*, Chapter 78, f.5 recto, preserves a passage from a much earlier work stating that 'among the *Li̯əm- ·i̯əp (Lin-i) doors always opened to the north to face the sun'. It is noteworthy, though, that in the 3rd century AD the northern gate of the fortified commandery seat of *K'i̯u-si̯wok (Ch'ü-su), just south of the Hoành mountains, was kept permanently closed [*Shui-Ching Chu*, Chapter 36], presumably reflecting Chinese influence, and that in AD 819 An-nam La-thánh, capital of the Protectorate-General of the Pacified South, was constructed without a gate in the northern wall [*T'ang Hui-yao*, Chapter 73, f.17 verso; *An-nam chí-lược*, quan 9, ff.3 verso – 4 recto]. More surprising is the fact that T'ang Ch'ang-an, although provided with the canonically sanctioned three gates on each of its eastern, southern and western sides, had only one on the northern side. For innovations introduced into the planning of this city see Ch'en Yin-k'o, *Sui-T'ang Chih-tu Yüan-yüan Lüeh-lun-kao*. Ch'ung-ch'ing, 1944–5, pp.44–58, and Naba Toshisada, 'Shina shuto-keikakushijō yori Kōsatsushitaru Tō no Chōanjō', in *Kuwabara Hakushi Kanreki Kinen Toyoshi Ronzo*. Kyōtō 1931, pp.1203–69.

42. Ch'en Meng-chia, *Yin-hsü Pu-tz'ŭ Tsung-shu*. Pei-ching 1956, pp.249–332.

43. Cf. F. D. E. van Ossenbruggen, 'De oorsprong van het javaansche begrip Montjå-pat in verband met primitieve classificaties', *Verslagen en Mededeelingen der Koninklijke Akademie van Wetenschappen*, Afd. Letterkunde, 5de Reeks, deel 3 (1918), pp.6–44; A. W. Macdonald, 'Notes sur la claustration villageoise dans l'Asie du Sud-Est', *Journal asiatique*, vol.245, fasc.2 (1957), pp.185–210; H. L. Shorto, 'The 32 *myos* in the medieval Mon kingdom', *Bulletin of the School of Oriental and African Studies*, vol.26 (1963), pp.572–91. It is interesting to note that C. Hentze, on the evidence of character analysis alone, was led to conclude that Shang cities were laid out to a square design, with four towered gateways [*Tod, Auferstehung, Weltordnung*, 2 vols. Zürich 1956].

44. For a discussion of magnetic declination and the compass needle in China see Joseph Needham, *Science and civilisation in China*, vol.4, pt.1. Cambridge University Press 1962, pp.301–13. Declination seems not to have

been known in China much before the 9th century AD – but this was still earlier than Europeans were aware of polarity [L. de Saussure, 'L'origine de la rose des vents et l'invention de la boussole', *Archives des Sciences physiques et naturelles*, series 5, vol.5, nos.3 and 4. Paris 1923, p.31; and Needham, *loc. cit.*, p.309]. Needham has also pointed out that discrepancies in city alignments in later times may have derived from adherence to the theories of rival schools of geomancy (*ibid.*, pp.312–13).

45. *loc. cit.*, p.313. Cp. also the *T'an-Kung* section of the *Li-Chi* : 'To bury on the north side [of the city] and with the head [of the dead] turned towards the north, was the customary practice of the Three Dynasties, because the dead go to the region of darkness.'

46. *Vide* Joseph Needham, *Science and civilisation in China*, vol.3 (1959), Fig.97, p.260.

47. *Chou-Li, K'ao-kung Chi*, B, f.15 recto et verso.

48. Prasanna Kumar Acharya, *Indian architecture*. Oxford University Press 1928, p.37. Similar sets of instructions for the use of the gnomon are incorporated in the *Sūrya-śiddhānta*, the *Śiddhāntaśiromaṇi* and the *Līlāvatī*.

49. *Vide* 'T'ang Ch'ang-an-Cheng ti-chi ch'u-pu t'an-ts'e', *K'ao-ku Hsüeh-pao*, no.3 (1958), pp.79–94.

50. Claude Madrolle, 'Le Tonkin ancien', *Bulletin de l'Ecole française d'Extrême-Orient*, vol.37. Hanoi 1937, p.280.

51. *Đại-Việt sử-kỉ toàn-thư, ngoại-kỉ*, quan 1, ff.5 verso–6 recto; *Khâm-định Việt-su thông-giám Cương-mục*, Tiên biên, quan 1, ff.8–9.

52. Cf. Marcel Granet, *La pensée chinoise*. Albin Michel, Paris 1934, p.324.

53. *Chou-Li*, chüan 3, f.14 verso.

54. L.I. Ringbom, *Graltempel und Paradies*. Stockholm 1951, p.255.

55. Eliade, *Cosmos and history*, p.13. There is independent testimony that Gerizim was regarded as an *axis mundi* (*ṭabbūr ereṣ*) in *Judges*, IX, 37 : 'See there are people coming down by the Navel of the Earth . . .'

56. Willibald Kirfel, *Die Kosmographie der Inder*. Bonn and Lepizig 1920, p.15.

57. Uno Holmberg-Harva, 'Der Baum des Lebens', *Annales Academicae Scientiarum Fennicae*. Helsinki 1923, p.41.

58. Arthur Christensen, *Les types du premier homme et du premier roi dans l'histoire légendaire des Iraniens*, vol.2. Stockholm 1917, p.42.

59. al-Kisā'i, *'Ajā'ib al-Malakūt* (Leiden MS. Wanner 538), f.15 recto. Cf. A.J. Wensinck, 'The ideas of the Western Semites concerning the navel of the earth', *Verhandelingen der Koninklijke Akademie van Wetenschappen te Amsterdam*, Afdeeling Letterkunde, new series, vol.17, no.1 (1916), p.15.

60. Cf. Eliade, *Le mythe*, Chapter 1; *Das Heilige*, Chapter 1; and *Traité*, Chapter 10.

61. The story of the messengers of 'Ād is related by the Murcian Ibn

NOTES AND REFERENCES

Sabʿin (Quṭb al-Dīn, c.1217–69) in *al-Ajwibah ʿan al-Asʾilah al-Ṣiqillīyah*. This work is still unpublished, but see Wüstenfeld, *Die Chroniken der Stadt Mekka*, vol.3. Leipzig 1857, p.442. [Summarized in Wensinck, *loc. cit.*, p.25, and in G.E. von Grünebaum, 'The sacred character of Islamic cities', *Mélanges Ṭāhā Ḥusain*. Abdurrahman Badawī, Cairo 1962, p.33.]

62. Quoted in von Grünebaum, *op. cit.*, p.38.

63. Cf. Azraqī [on the authority of the converted Jew Kaʿb al-Aḥbār, a contemporary of Muḥammad], *Akhbār Makkah*. Wüstenfeld's edition. Leipzig 1858, p.1; Wensinck, 'The ideas of the Western Semites', p.18.

64. E.g., Ma Chʻeng-yüan, 'Man-tʻan Chan-Kuo chʻing-tʻung-chʻi-shang-ti hua-hsiang', *Wen-wu*, no.10 (1961), p.29.

65. *San-fu Huang Tʻu* (attributed to Miao Chʻang-yen, end of 3rd century AD), chüan 5, and *Shih-Chi*, chüan 24, f.2 verso.

66. Lit., 'The wall he built was moated, the [city] **$P'i\hat{o}ng$ he built matched it' [Karlgren, *BMFEA*, no.17, p.70].

67. Waley [*The Book of Songs*, p.263] renders these lines as, 'Within the walls of Feng [**$P'i\hat{o}ng$]/All the peoples came together'; Karlgren [*BMFEA*, no.17, p.70] as, 'the walls of Feng were where (the peoples of) the four quarters came together'. In view of the significance of the cardinal compass directions in the validation of sacred space and, consequently, in the construction of capital cities, I think that we can here assume that the text means what it says, namely that Pʻi̯ông was the point where the four quarters of the universe adjoined. Note that the same phrase occurs again in the following stanza: 'The river of Pʻi̯ông flowed to the east, [representing] an achievement of **$G_i wo$ (Yü) [the Great]; that was where the cardinal directions conjoined.'

68. For the basis of this translation see Karlgren, 'Glosses', *BMFEA*, no.21, p.70. Cp. also the Ode **$G'\check{a}-M_i wo$ [*Hsia-Wu* : Mao CCXLIII], where the following lines occur:

> The three rulers are in Heaven,
> The King is their counterpart in the capital.
> The King is their counterpart in the capital
> And actively seeks the hereditary virtue
> [Transl. Karlgren, mod.]

69. Cf. *ibid*.

70. Cf. also *I Chou-shu*, chüan 5, f.7 verso (Ssŭ-pu Pei-yao edition: in this edition the commentary explicitly advocates the literal interpretation).

71. *Lun-Yü*, II, 1.

72. For an exposition of this theme consult Needham, *Science and civilisation in China*, vol.3, especially pp.266–7.

73. For the evil consequences to be anticipated from a disruption of the ritual associated with the walling of **$\hat{D}i\check{e}ng-\hat{T}i\hat{o}g$ (Chʻeng-Chou) in 508 BC see *Tso-Chuan*, Duke **$D'ieng$ (Ting), 1st year, with which may be compared

THE CITY AS A COSMO-MAGICAL SYMBOL

Herodotus's terse remark that the city founded by the Spartan Dorieus without benefit of advice from the Delphic oracle survived for only three years (v, 42).

74. Chuang-Chou, *Chuang-tzŭ*, T'ien-hsia section: probably compiled at the beginning of the 3rd century BC. [see Hu Chih-hsin, 'Chuang-tzŭ K'ao-cheng', *Wen-hsüeh Nien-pao*, vol.3 (1937)]. The latest edition, with collated commentaries, is that of Liu Wen-tien, *Chuang-tzŭ Pu-cheng*. Shanghai 1947.

75. I prefer this interpretation to that of H. H. Dubs, who understands the paradox to imply that, compared with illimitable space, **Djěng and the whole of China are equally insignificant [*Hsüntze; the moulder of ancient Confucianism*. Probsthain, London 1927, p.219]. I am not certain but that this concept of centripetality may not underlie another famous paradox, this time attributed to Hui-Shih of the 4th century BC: 'I know the center of the world; it is north of the State of **·Ian (Yen: the northernmost of the feudal states) and south of the state of **Gi̯wăt (Yüeh: the southernmost state)' [Chuang-Chou, *op. cit.*]. Hu Shih [*The development of the logical method in ancient China*. Oriental Book Co., Shanghai 1922] believed that this paradox might have reflected the idea of the sphericity of the earth, but it seems at least as likely that it preserved some garbled reference, perhaps ill understood by Hui-Shih himself, to the location of the capital or other *axis mundi* in existential space. Possibly the Zen master who answered the question as to why Bodhidharma came to China with the famous response 'Ch'ang-an [a western capital of China] is in the east, Lo-yang [an eastern capital] is in the west' was influenced not only by the Zen predilection for 'answering west when asked about east', but also by Hui-Shih's paradox.

76. Granet, *La pensée chinoise*, p.91.

77. *Tso-Chuan*, Duke **Sni̯ang (Hsiang), 25th year.

78. Cf. also *Tso-Chuan*, Duke **Di̯og (Ch'ao), 27th year, where the sage **Ki̯wɛd-tsi̯əg (Chi-tzŭ) is reported as saying, 'He shall be my lord who does not permit the sacrifices to our former rulers to be neglected, which would deprive the people of government, and ensures that the Gods of the Soil and of Harvest receive their prescribed offerings so that the state shall not be overthrown.'

In this connection one is reminded of Jacques Soustelle's remark that, 'The Mexican city is above all the temple: the glyph that means "the fall of a town" s a symbolic temple half-overturned and burning. The very being of the city, the people, and the state is summed up in this "house of god", which is the literal meaning of the Aztec *teocalli*.' [*The daily life of the Aztecs*. Pelican Book A678, Harmondsworth 1964, p.28.]

79. *Shih-Chi*, chüan 6, f.13 verso. **G'ɛm-di̯ang (Hsien-yang), capital of the Ch'in dynasty, was some five miles east of the present-day subprefecture of the same name in Shen-hsi province. It became famous throughout southern and western Asia under its Arabic transcription of *Khumdān*. If

NOTES AND REFERENCES

the name had any semantic significance it meant 'united *yang*', a concept that Edouard Chavannes derived from the fact that the city was situated on the northern (or *yang*) side of the Wei river but to the south (or *yang*) side of the Chiu-tsung hills, thus producing as it were a double *yang* [*Les mémoires historiques de Se-ma Ts'ien*, vol.2. Ernest Leroux, Paris 1897, p.65, note 2]. To me this seems much like popular etymology, but I have no better theory to offer unless to suggest that the geomancers who laid out the city were perhaps influenced by the *t'uan* (or judgment) appended to the *Hsien* Hexagram (no. 31) in the *Book of Changes* (*I-Ching*) : '*Hsien* indicates that (on the fulfilment of the conditions implied in it), there will be free course and success. ... There will be good fortune' [Legge.] or

'Influence, success.
Perseverance furthers.
...'
[Wilhelm].

80. For pertinent remarks on *pars pro toto* as a figure of thought in the early world see Frankfort *et al.*, *The intellectual adventure of ancient man*, pp.12–13 : 'The primitive uses symbols as much as we do; but he can no more conceive them as signifying, yet separate from the gods or powers than he can consider a relationship established in his mind – such as resemblance – as connecting, and yet separate from the objects compared. Hence there is a coalescence of the symbol and what it signifies, as there is a coalescence of two objects compared so that one may stand for the other ... a name, a lock of hair, or a shadow may be felt by the primitive to be pregnant with the full significance of the man.' And, we may add, the capital may stand for the kingdom, though in this case there is the additional significance of a powerful cosmic centripetality to be considered.

81. Paul Mus, 'Symbolisme à Angkor Thom. Le "grand miracle" du Bayon', *Académie des Inscriptions et Belles-Lettres : Comptes-rendus des Séances* (1936), pp.57–68, and 'Angkor in the time of Jayavarman VII', *Indian Art and Letters*, new series, vol.11. London 1937, pp.65–75.

82. Cf. Macrobius, *Saturnalia*, III, 9.

83. *Vide* V. Basanoff, *Evocatio, étude d'un rituel militaire romain*. Paris 1947. On p.207 this author uses words that might well have come from the lips of a *purohita* in ancient *Kambujadeśa* : 'Evoquée, elle [la force divine] ne faisait qu'augmenter le potentiel divin de la cité victorieuse'.

84. Plutarch's *Parallel Lives*, 'Romulus', pp.119 and 120 of vol.1 of the Loeb edition.

85. *Ibid*. According to Varro the rites attributed to Romulus were not specifically 'Roman' but were common to all Latium and Etruria. Cato the Elder also observed that similar rites were carried out at the founding of all Italian cities [Cato, in Servius, v, 755; Varro, *L.L.*, v, 143; Festus, v. *Rituales*].

THE CITY AS A COSMO-MAGICAL SYMBOL

F. Altheim [in Werner Müller, *Kreis und Kreus*. Berlin 1938, pp.60 *et seq.*] has shown that similar concepts underlie the structure of numerous Germanic villages and cities.

86. Cf. Gellius, 13, 14, i : *pomerium est locus intra agrum effatum per totius urbis circuitum pone muros regionibus certis determinatus, qui facit finem urbani auspicii.* Cf. also, *int. al.*, Ovid, *Fasti*, Book IV. Cp. with the *pomerium* the Ancient Hebrew *migrach*, a zone *non aedificandi* which surrounded the ritual city of the tribe of Levi [*Ezekiel*, chap.48, v.17].

87. The *Annals* of Tacitus, Book XII, para.23 : pp.346 and 347 of vol.3 of the Loeb edition : . . . *more prisco, quo iis, qui protulere imperium, etiam terminos urbis propagare datur.*

88. The cosmo-magical role of the Milliarium may perhaps be compared to that of the *T'ien-Shu* or Axis of Heaven, a bronze pillar, 100 feet high and 5 feet 3 inches in diameter, which the Empress Wu of T'ang caused to be erected in front of her palace in AD 694.

89. *Tso-Chuan*, Duke **Mjwɛn (Min), 2nd year; the **Mjan (*Mien*) ode [Mao CCXXXVII] : 'They raised the grand altar to the God of the Soil (*tjung-t'o : chung-t'u*=the altar erected in the capital which represented the very axis, the quintessentially sacred point, of the kingdom)/From which the legions marched.' Note also that in a chapter of the *ku-wen*, and therefore historically suspect, version of the *Shu-Ching* (***T'âd-djad : T'ai-Shih*, pt.I), King **Mjwo (Wu) sacrificed both to Shang-Ti and at the grand altar to the God of the Soil (at the center of the world) before setting out on his campaign against the last ruler of Shang. This tradition is valueless as fact but it is in strict accord with Chou cosmo-magical symbolism.

90. F. Wüstenfeld, *Zakarija ben Muhammed ben Mahmud el-Cazwinis Kosmographie*, vol.1 : *Kitāb 'adjāib al-makhlūqat*. Göttingen 1848; Wensinck, *Navel*, p.31; von Grünebaum, 'The sacred character of Islamic cities', p.33.

91. On the *circumambulatio* as a cosmicizing of territory see P. Saintyves, 'Le tour de la ville et la chute de Jéricho', *Essais de folklore biblique*. Paris 1923, pp.177–204.

92. George Coedès, *Pour mieux comprendre Angkor*. Adrien Maisonneuve 1947, p.98. See also Jean Przyluski, 'Pradakshina et prasavya en Indochine', *Festschrift für M. Winternitz zum 70ten Geburtstag* (1933), p.320.

93. H.G. Quaritch Wales, *Siamese state ceremonies. Their history and function*. Bernard Quaritch, Ltd 1931, pp.106–7.

94. Robert von Heine-Geldern, 'Weltbild und Bauform in Südostasien', *Wiener Beiträge zur Kunst- und Kulturgeschichte Asiens*, vol.4 (1930), p.58.

95. *Shu-Ching*, Canon of Shun (*Śjwən*); *Li-Chi*, **Gjwang-Țjad (*Wang-Chih*); and *Shih-Chi*, chüan 1, f.18 recto.

96. In the **Ngjwăt-Ljěng (*Yüeh-Ling*) of the *Li-Chi* the building and repair of cities is also co-ordinated with this calendrical schedule. The raising of

NOTES AND REFERENCES

fortifications and walls, for example, was prohibited in the first month of spring, when the sun was in the *hsiu* (lunar mansion) of *Shih*, and earth work was similarly forbidden in the third month of summer. More positively, cities were to be established in the second month of autumn, and both **dįĕng (*ch'eng*) and **kwâk (*kuo*) walls, and their gates, repaired in the first month of winter. The *Tso-Chuan* also subscribes to these prescriptions: e.g., under the 9th year of Duke **·Įǝn (Yin) it is observed that the walling of **Lâng (*Lang*) in summer was unseasonable. In the case of ***T̂įông-k'įŭg* (Chung-ch'iu), which was also walled in summer, there is the additional explicit statement that the corvée interfered with agricultural work [Duke ·Įǝn (Yin), 7th year]. In fact, it cannot have been fortuitous that these urban tasks were integrated with those of the farming year so that, when performed in their proper seasons, the two sets of activities were not in conflict, but it was not unusual for the expression of astrobiological symbolism in the Chinese world to exhibit a high degree of functional rationality. Such was indeed implicit in the nature of its origin.

97. K. Sethe, *Beiträge zur ältesten Geschichte Ägyptens*. Leipzig 1903, pp.121–41; Henri Frankfort, *Kingship and the gods*, p.124.

98. Ovid, *Fasti*, Book IV, 11, 821–5.

99. *Joshua*, Chapter 6.

100. The aspect of Vajrapāṇi assumed by Lokeśvara when expounding the Law. *Vide* Coedès, *Pour mieux comprendre Angkor*, Chapter 6; and Jean Boisselier, 'Vajrapāṇi dans l'art du Bàyon', *Proceedings of the Twenty-second Congress of Orientalists*, vol.2. Leiden 1957, pp.324–32.

101. Cf. *int. al. I Chou-shu*, Chapter 48; *Tso-Lo*. According to a tradition first enunciated during the Sui dynasty this work, probably dating from the 3rd century BC, was among those found in a tomb in AD 281 (*vide* p.14 above), but the tradition is very suspect. In a splendid essay on the God of the Soil in classical China Edouard Chavannes has analyzed a number of other ancient texts dealing with the construction of the great altar to this deity in the capital, and with its relation to the altars of the benefice holders in the provinces [*Le T'ai chan; essai de monographie d'un culte chinois*. Bibliothèque d'Etudes, Annales du Musée Guimet, no.21. Paris 1910, Appendix: 'Le Dieu du Sol dans la Chine antique', part II]. *Vide* also Ssŭ-ma Ch'ien's account of the investiture of the three sons of Emperor Wu in 117 BC, when each received a clod of earth appropriate to the location of his new territory (*Shih-Chi*, chüan 60, f.3 recto).

102. *Shih-Chi*, chüan 1, f.24 recto.

103. This feature is exceptionally well developed in the complex now known as Aṅkor Thom: references in note 81 to this chapter. South Indian temple-cities in which the *gopura* were much more massive than the shrines in the quintessentially sacred heart of the consecrated site are illustrated in Percy Brown's *Indian architecture* (*Buddhist and Hindu periods*). D. B. Taraporevala

Sons & Co. Private Ltd., Bombay 1959, plates LXXIV (Tiravulur and Madura) and LXXV (Śrīraṅgam), and interpreted by Nelson I. Wu, *Chinese and Indian architecture*, pp.26–7.

104. Osvald Sirén, *The walls and gates of Peking*. John Lane, the Bodley Head 1924. Summaries in, *int. al.*, William Willetts, *Chinese art*, vol.2. Pelican Book 359, Harmondsworth 1958, pp.670–85, and Andrew Boyd, *Chinese architecture and town planning 1500 BC–AD 1911*. University of Chicago Press 1962, pp.60–72.

105. Cf. Ode *Mi̯an* (*Mien*) [Mao CCXXXVII]:
> And so they raised the outer gate;
> The outer gate soared high.
> And so they raised the inner gate,
> The inner gate was very grand.

Also the poem ***Tsʻieng-tsʻieng li̯ang-di̯ang păk* (*Chʻing-chʻing ling-shang pai*) in the collection *Ku-shih Shih-chiu-shou* : 'The two gate-towers [of Glâk-di̯ang] exceed a hundred feet'.

106. In the *Tso-Chuan*, for example, under Duke **Xi̯əg (Hsi), 18th year, and again under the 19th year, it is reported that the Duke of **Li̯ang (Liang) was given to walling cities which he had insufficient people to fill. As a result the skeleton populations were unable to maintain their defenses, lost heart, and eventually took to flight. For open spaces in *hsien* cities in later times see Chang, 'Some aspects of the urban geography of the Chinese hsien capital', p.36.

107. A. J. L. Wensinck, 'The Semitic New Year and the origin of eschatology', *Acta Orientalia*, vol.1 (1923).

108. For a discussion of the formulation in Han China of a fully phenomenalist doctrine in which socially and politically ethical lapses were associated with cosmic irregularities see Wolfram Eberhard, 'Beiträge zur kosmologischen Spekulation Chinas in der Han Zeit', *Baessler Archiv*, vol.16, pt.1 (1933), pp.1–100, and Needham, *Science and civilisation in China*, vol.2, pp.247–53, 378–82, 526–30. Cf. also *Huai-Nan-Tzŭ*, chüan 3, f.2 recto et verso; Tung Chung-shu, *Chʻun-Chʻiu Fan-lu*, chüan 44 : 'Wang-tao tʻung san', and chüan 64 : 'Wu-hsing wu-shih'. A similar view of the unity of the ethical and cosmic order among the ancient Greeks has been discerned by Cornford in a speech of Iamblichus : 'Themis in the realm of Zeus, and Dike in the world below, hold the same place and rank as Nomos in the cities of men; so that he who does not justly perform his appointed duty may appear as a violator of the whole order of the universe' [F. M. Cornford, *From religion to philosophy; a study in the origins of Western speculation*. Arnold, London 1912, p.55].

109. Cf. notes 16, 18, 19, and 107 to this chapter and additionally, W. H. Roscher, 'Neue Omphalosstudien', *Abhandlungen der Königlich Sächsischen Gesellschaft der Wissenschaft*, Phil.-hist. Klasse, vol.31, pt.1. Leipzig 1915;

NOTES AND REFERENCES

Raphael Patai, *Man and temple in ancient Jewish myth and ritual*. Nelson, London 1947; Jacques Soustelle, *La pensée cosmologique des anciens Mexicains*. Hermann, Paris 1940.

110. Eric Burrows, 'Some cosmological patterns in Babylonian religion', in S.H. Hooke (ed.), *The Labyrinth*. London 1935, pp.60 *et seq.*, and Mircea Eliade, *Cosmologie și alchimie babiloniană*. Bucharest 1937, p.22; E. Weidner, *Handbuch der Babylonischen Astronomie*. Assyriologische Bibliothek, no.23. Leipzig 1915, p.125.

111. François Thureau-Dangin, *Rituels accadiens*. E. Leroux, Paris 1921, p.136.

112. Bellino cylinder : B. Meissner and P. Rost, *Die bauinschriften Sanheribs*. Eduard Pfeiffer, Leipzig 1893, p.5. For evidence that Neo-Babylonian temples were oriented with reference to the constellations appropriate to their tutelary deities see G. Martigny, *Die Kultrichtung in Mesopotamien* (1932), pp.12 *et seq.* The astral affiliations of Mesopotamian temples are explicit in an ode composed for the dedication of the temple of Kish [*Vide* Langdon, *Oxford editions of cuneiform inscriptions*, vol.1. Oxford University Press 1923, p.53]. Cf. also the reply by the assembly of the *gurush* to Gilgamesh, in which the following lines occur:

> Uruk, the handiwork of the gods,
> Eannak, the temple descended from heaven,
> their various parts the great gods made;
> their great wall, resting on the ground like a cloud-bank,
> their exalted dwellings, founded by An
> . . .

[Transl. Samuel Noah Kramer, *American Journal of Archaeology*, vol.53 (1949), p.8].

113. Bernard-Philippe Groslier, *Angkor. Hommes et pierres*. Arthaud, Paris 1956, p.11.

114. Jean Filliozat, 'Le symbolisme du monument du Phnoṃ Bǎkheṅ', *Bulletin de l'Ecole Française d'Extrême-Orient*, vol.44, pt.2, 1954, pp.527-54.

115. Cf. George Coedès, 'L'origine du cycle des douze animaux au Cambodge', *T'oung Pao*, vol.31 (1935), pp.315-29.

116. Cf. also the statement on an inscription relating to the pyramidal temple now known as the Eastern Mebon, set like a jewel in the great lake of the Eastern Baray, that, 'In the middle of this sea, the sacred pool of Yaśodhara, [Rajendravarman] erected a mountain, with a summit like that of Meru . . .' For discussions of the symbolism of the Aṅkor complex see note 81 above.

117. Herodotus noted that the *ziggurat* of Babylon extended as far below the earth as it did above. On other occasions the Khmer architects masked basal reliefs depicting creatures from the subterranean slopes of Meru with an

overlay of reliefs illustrating scenes from the upper slopes, thus symbolizing the extension of the *axis mundi* below the surface of the earth. The same practice is found on some of the early Javanese monuments.

118. Bernard-Philippe Groslier, *The art of Indochina*. Crown Publishers, Inc., New York 1962, p.183.

119. Coedès interprets the *gopura* immediately behind the contending gods rather than the Bàyon as representing the churning stick [*Pour mieux comprendre Angkor*, p.101], but this does not affect the general concept of the symbolism.

120. Cp. the implications of the name which we know as Babylon : *Bab-ilani* = Gate of the Gods.

121. The official report of the excavations of the Oriental Institute at Persepolis is contained in two magnificent volumes by Erich F.Schmidt, *Persepolis*, vols.68 and 69 of the Publications of the Oriental Institute. University of Chicago Press 1953 and 1957, but for the elucidation of the symbolism of this cult center we are indebted to Arthur Upham Pope, 'Persepolis as a ritual city', *Archaeology*, vol.10, no.2 (1957), pp.123–30, and 'Persepolis – considered as a ritual city', Zeki Velidi Togan (ed.), *Proceedings of the Twenty-second Congress of Orientalists held in Istanbul, September 15th to 22nd, 1951*, vol.2. Leiden 1957, pp.58–66. For the ritual significance of the lion-and-bull combat which features prominently at Persepolis see Willy Hartner, 'The earliest history of the constellations in the Near East and the motif of the lion-bull combat', *Journal of Near Eastern Studies*, vol.24, nos.1 and 2 (1965), pp.1–16.

122. Binode Behari Dutt, *Town Planning in ancient India*. Thacker, Spink and Co., Calcutta and Simla 1925, p.6.

123. Dutt, *Town planning*, p.149.

124. James Fergusson, *History of Indian and Eastern Architecture*. John Murray, London 1876, p.847.

125. Wu, *Chinese and Indian architecture*, p.26.

126. Westheim, *The art of ancient Mexico*, p.144.

127. Westheim, *The art of ancient Mexico*, Chapter 7. See also Hermann Beyer, 'El origen, desarrollo y significado de la greca escalonada', in *El México Antiguo*, Book II, nos.3 and 4.

128. Westheim, *op. cit.*, pp.115–18; K.Th.Preuss, 'Kosmische Hieroglyphen der Mexikaner', *Zeitschrift für Ethnologie* (1901). There is an analysis of the functional relevance of cardinal axiality in Maya cities in late Pre-conquest times in Michael D.Coe, 'A model of ancient community structure in the Maya lowlands', *Southwestern Journal of Anthropology*, vol.21, no.2 (1965), pp.97–114.

129. The plastic expression of this astrobiological symbolism seems to have been most fully developed architecturally in China in the design of the half-

NOTES AND REFERENCES

legendary cosmological temple known as the *Ming-T'ang* or Hall of Brightness, the ritual residence where the Emperor performed the ceremonial acts, season by season, that were necessary to maintain the unity of heaven and earth. [*Vide* Hui Tung, *Ming-T'ang Ta-tao Lu* (c.AD 1736); W. E. Soothill, *The Hall of Light; a study of early Chinese kingship*. Lutterworth, London 1951; Henri Maspero, 'Le Ming-Tang et la crise religieuse chinoise avant les Han', *Mélanges Chinois et Bouddhiques*, vol.9 (1951); Marcel Granet, *La Pensée chinoise*, pp.177 et seq., and *Danses et légendes de la Chine ancienne*, vol.1. Alcan, Paris 1926, pp.116–19.

130. Or possibly, though less probably, 32²H. To the Chinese this star was known as *T'ien-Shu* (Celestial Pivot) or *Niu-Hsing* (Knot Star). *Vide* Needham, *Science and civilisation in China*, vol.3, p.261. For a description of the King as 'the counterpart of August Heaven' see p.463 above. The morphology of Han Ch'ang-an is discussed in Ku Yen-wu, *Li-tai Ti-wang Chai-ching-chi*, Chapter 4 : *Han Ch'ang-an Ku-ch'eng*. For excavations at this site see Wang Chung-shu, 'Han Ch'ang-an Ch'eng k'ao-ku kung-tso-ti ch'u-pu shou-huo', *K'ao-ku T'ung-hsün*, no.5 (1957), pp.102–10 and 'Han Ch'ang-an Ch'eng k'ao-ku kung-tso shou-huo hsü-chi', *K'ao-ku T'ung-hsün*, no.4 (1958), pp.23–32. The restoration of the ritual structures in the heart of this city has been discussed recently by Wang Shih-jen, 'Han Ch'ang-an Ch'eng nan-chiao li-chih-chien-chu (Ta-t'u-men-Ts'un i-chih) yüan-chuang-ti t'ui-ts'e', *K'ao-ku*, no.9 (1963), pp.501–15.

131. *Shih-Chi*, chüan 6, f.23 verso.

132. Chavannes's rendering of the phrase **$p\underset{.}{i}ôk$-$d'ôg$ (*fu-tao*) [*Les mémoires historiques*, vol.2, p.138].

133. Chang Shou-chieh, followed by the *K'ang-hsi Tzŭ-tien*, stated that the second element in the name of the palace (**$b'\underset{.}{i}wang$, now voiced as *fang* in MSC) was in Ch'in times pronounced as **$b'w\hat{a}ng$ (*p'ang* : = by the side of, adjacent to). Yen Shih-ku added that ** ·$\hat{a}$ also signified 'neighboring' or 'close to' (because the palace was close to G'ɛm-dįang). This is no better than folk etymology, but there can be no doubt that it was a misunderstanding of the significance of the second character in the name which in later centuries gave rise to the popular designation of 'Neighboring Palace'.

134. *Wu Yüeh Ch'un-Ch'iu*, chüan 5, f.2 verso. This work, the earliest extant example of the class of *Tsai-Chi* histories, was written by Chao-Yeh of the Posterior Han dynasty.

135. Shen Huai-yüan, *Nan-Yüeh Chi*, apud *T'ai-p'ing Huan-yü Chi*, chüan 165, f.5 verso; *Đại-Việt sử-kí toàn-thư*, quan.2, f.6 verso. Tradition located this city near Gia-làm, not far from Hà-nội : cf. *Đại-Việt*, ngoại-kỉ, quan.1, ff.5 verso–6 recto; *Khâm-định Việt-su thông-giám Cương-mục*, Tiên biên, quan.1, ff.8–9. This tale of Cô-loa forms part of a cycle of legends which attribute magnificent cities to the Tong-king lowland long before the Lạc tribes had been

THE CITY AS A COSMO-MAGICAL SYMBOL

incorporated in the kingdom of Southern Gi̯wăt (Nan-Yüeh), a quasi-autonomous territory ruled from **Pʻi̯wăn-ngi̯u (Pʻan-yü : = present-day Canton), in 208 B C. Subsequently a great deal of this legendary material was incorporated into official Vietnamese history, and until very recently formed the basis for most modern writing about the Tong-king delta in early times. A good example of this uncritical acceptance of ancient myth as historical fact is provided by the pamphlet entitled *Histoire des dix-huit règnes de Hung-vuong*, which was formerly distributed at the annual festival of the Hung-vuong Wat at Co-tich. Nor is the element of mythology entirely absent in the earlier chapters of Joseph Buttinger's *The Smaller Dragon*. Frederick A. Praeger, New York 1958. For *Cô-loa* itself see René Despierres, 'Cô-Loa, capitale du royaume Au-Lac', *Cahier de la Société de Géographie de Hanoi*, no.35. Ecole Française d'Extrême-Orient 1940, and Gustave Dumoutier, 'Etude historique et archéologique sur Cô-Loa, capitale de l'ancien royaume Au-Lac', *loc. cit.*

136. Rolf Stein, 'Jardins en miniature d'Extrême-Orient', *Bulletin de l'Ecole française d'Extrême-Orient*, vol.42 (1942), p.54.

137. Cf. Eliade, *Le mythe*, Chapter 2 and *Das Heilige*, Chapter 2.

138. In addition to Eliade, *vide* H. Hubert and M. Mauss, 'La représentation du temps dans la religion et la magie', in *Mélanges d'histoire des religions* (1909), pp.190–229; H. Reuter, *Die Zeit. Eine religionswissenschaftliche Untersuchung*. Bonn 1941; G. van der Leeuw, 'Ürzeit und Endzeit', *Eranos-Jahrbuch*, vol.17 (1950), pp.11–51.

139. *Shih-Ching*, Ode **·I̯ən-Mi̯wo (*Yin-Wu*), Mao CCCV.

140. James H. Breasted, *Ancient records of Egypt*, vol.2. University of Chicago Press 1906, para.339.

141. Gudea Cylinder A : translated by Thorkild Jacobsen; summarized by Frankfort, *Kingship*, pp.255–8.

142. R. H. Charles, *The Apocrypha and Pseudepigrapha of the Old Testament in English*, vol.2. Oxford University Press 1913, p.482.

143. *Wisdom of Solomon*, *loc. cit.*, vol.1, p.549.

144. *The Revelation of St John the Divine*, Chapter 21, v.2.

145. *Shu-Ching*, **Bʻwân-kăng (*Pʻan-keng*) section.

146. Karlgren [*Bull. Mus. Far. E. Ant.*, no.22 (1950), p.20] translates, 'at present (there have been) five capitals'; Legge [*The Chinese classics*, vol.3, p.223] renders the same phrase as, 'Up to this time *the capital has been in five regions*'. I am inclined to think that, for all its ungainliness, Legge's version conveys the implications of the original more accurately than does Karlgren's. **Păng (*pang*) did signify an extent of territory larger than that implicit in the term 'capital', and the text as it stands, intentionally or unintentionally, does preserve the connotation of 'city-state', which is what the political entities associated with ceremonial complexes essentially were. The parallel passage in

NOTES AND REFERENCES

Shih-Chi, chüan 3, f.8 recto avoids this difficulty by means of the phrasing, 'Thus there had been five changes without a fixed location [having been selected]'.

147. For comments on this phrase see Karlgren, 'Glosses on the Book of Documents', *Bull. Mus. Far E. Ant.*, no.20 (1948), p.178, para.1413.

148. *Shu-Ching*, loc. cit.

149. For an exposition of the fact that **·i̯ən (*yin*) should here be read as an adverbial phrase (as first suggested by Chuang Shu-tsu) rather than as the style of the dynasty (as understood by Cheng-Hsüan, the [Pseudo-]K'ung An-kuo, and Legge), see Karlgren, 'Glosses', *BMFEA*, no.20, p.192.

150. *Shih-Chi*, chüan 3, ff.8 recto et verso : 'Formerly the illustrious sovereign T'ang the Successful and your ancestors cooperated in the government of the realm and the rule of law prevailed. To dwell [in one place] and make no effort [to conform to the laws of Nature, i.e. to maintain the parallelism between the macrocosmos and microcosmos] – that is no way to ensure the triumph of virtue.'

151. Cf. Arthur Waley, 'The eclipse poem and its group', *T'ien-Hsia*, vol.3 (1936), pp.245–8.

152. *Shih-Chi*, chüan 6, f.32 recto. Chavannes [*Les mémoires historiques*, vol.2, p.203] translates **p'i̯wo as *en imposer à*, with the sense of physically 'overawing' the barbarians, presumably by size and splendor. I prefer to render this graph by 'pacify', thereby assuming, in conformity with what has been said above, a cosmic parallelism between earth and heaven. There could hardly have been harmony within or without the empire so long as the pivot of the universe was uncompleted.

153. *Nan-Chi'i Shu*, chüan 58, ff.10 verso–11 recto.

154. Or 'the Tree of Fortune bears an abundance of fine blossom'.

155. Quoted by Henri Frankfort, *Kingship and the gods. A study of ancient Near Eastern religion as the integration of society*. University of Chicago Press 1948, p.267.

156. The association of capital and sacred mountain in Indochina is certainly older than the beginnings of Kambujadeśa. In the kingdom known to the Chinese as *B'i̯u-nâm, a city now represented on the landscape of the Trans-Bassac only by the fitful shadows of fading sunlight, was laid out at the foot of Bnaṃ Ba-thê, while a subsequent capital seems to have been built below Bà Phnoṃ. Aṅkor Bórĕi, a capital of the state known to the Chinese under the orthography *Tśi̯ĕn-lâp (Chen-la), spread its cosmically oriented enceinte below Phnoṃ Da, and Śreṣthapura was sited beside the Liṅgaparvata. Farther south, where the isthmian tract of the Malay Peninsula broadens out, the same sort of relationship probably linked the city of Kaṭāha to Gunong Jĕrai [Wheatley, *The Golden Khersonese*, pp.273–81].

157. E.g. *Campāpura, Indrapura, Vijaya, Virapura*. Vide R.C. Majumdar,

Ancient Indian colonies in the Far East, vol.1 : *Champa*. The Punjab Sanskrit Book Depot, Lahore 1927.

158. Cf. notes 104–9 to Chapter Three. Vide N. J. Krom, *Hindoe-Javaansche Geschiedenis*. Second edition, Martinus Nijhoff, The Hague 1931.

159. E.g., *int. al.*, *Śrī Kṣetra, Sudhammapura, Haṃsāvatī, Arimaddanapura, Amarapura, Ava*, Mandalay.

160. V. C. Scott O'Connor, *Mandalay and other cities of the past in Burma*. New York 1908, pp.4–80.

161. Gordon Loud, *Khorsabad I, Excavations in the palace and at a city gate*; *II, The citadel and the town*. Oriental Institute Publications 38 and 40. University of Chicago Press 1936 and 1938. For a discussion of the still unelucidated symbolism of the gates of this city see Henri Frankfort, 'Town planning in ancient Mesopotamia', *The Town Planning Review*, vol.21, no.2 (1950), pp.104–7.

162. al-Ṭabari, *Ta'rīkh al-Rusul w'-al-Mulūk*, vol.3, ff.1179–81; al-Mas'ūdī, *Murūj*, vol.7, ff.118 *et seq.*, Yāqūt, *Buldān*, vol.3, ff.16–17; Ernst Herzfeld, *Der Wandschmuck der Bauten von Samarra*. Berlin 1923, and 'Geschichte der Stadt Samarra', *Ausgrabungen von Samarra*, vol.6 (1948).

Although the stimulus for the transference of these capitals, cities of orthogenetic change *par excellence*, invariably came from the royal court, not infrequently the move involved a large plebeian population which had been attracted to the outskirts of the royal enceinte. Sāmarrā itself was a case in point. When al-Mu'taḍid abandoned the city in 892 it housed an estimated population of about a million [Herzfeld, *Geschichte*, p.137]. Needless to say, not all the inhabitants of the former capital moved with the 'Abbāsid court, but the fact that the city rapidly fell into ruins indicates that, despite the presence of shrines which grew up among the decaying halls and which subsequently attracted a considerable pilgrim traffic, a large proportion of the populace either followed al-Mu'taḍid to Baghdād or drifted away into the surrounding region. It is also implicit in the Japanese chronicles that a substantial proportion of the population of Nara followed the Emperor when he moved his capital from that city to Nagaoka in AD 784 and during succeeding years. Rather better documented, although still possibly somewhat exaggerated, is the alleged migration of some 150,000 persons when Mindon Min transferred his capital from Amarapura to Mandalay in 1857. For several instances of the shifting of capital cities to new sites in the Indian subcontinent see Hugh Tinker, 'The city in Asia', in *Reorientations. Studies on Asia in transition*. Pall Mall Press, London 1965, pp.29–48. Cf. also Marco Polo's account of the transference of the inhabitants of *Cambaluc* to the new city of *Taidu* (<*Ta-tu*) for geomantic reasons in 1273–4 [A. C. Moule and Paul Pelliot, *Marco Polo. The Description of the World*, vol.1. George Routledge & Sons Ltd, London 1938, p.85.].

NOTES AND REFERENCES

163. Cf. *Shih-Chi*, chüan 3, f.2 verso.

164. *Vide Ch'un-Ch'iu* and *Tso-Chuan*, Duke **Ḏi̯ĕng (Ch'eng), 15th year, and Duke **Ḏi̯og (Ch'ao), 9th year; and *Ch'un-Ch'iu*, Duke **D'ieng (Ting), 4th year.

165. Cf. Herrlee Glessner Creel, *Studies in early Chinese culture*. Kegan Paul, Trench, Trübner & Co., Ltd, London 1938, pp.49–54.

166. Arthur Waley translated this stanza in the fashion of a poet as follows:
>Splendid was the capital of Shang,
>A pattern to the people on every side,
>Glorious was its fame,
>Great indeed its magic power,
>Giving long life and peace,
>And safety to us that have come after.
>
>[*The Book of Songs*. George Allen and Unwin Ltd,
>London 1937, p.280]

Bernhard Karlgren, by contrast, provided a literal translation to serve the purposes of the student of the technical aspects of sinology:

>The city of Shang was (orderly=) carefully laid out, it is the centre of the four quarters; majestic is its fame, bright is its divine power; in longevity and peace it protects us, the descendants.
>
>[*The Book of Odes*. The Museum of Far Eastern Antiquities, Stockholm, 1950: a reprint of papers in the *Bulletin of the Museum of Far Eastern Antiquities*, nos.16 and 17, p.266].

This particular ode has also been translated by, among others: James Legge, *The Chinese classics*, vol.IV: *The She King*. Lane Crawford, Hong Kong and Trübner, London 1871: reprints, with notes, by the Commercial Press, Shanghai, n.d., and Hong Kong University Press 1960, p.643.

William Jennings, *The Shi King, the old 'Poetry Classic' of the Chinese. A close metrical translation, with annotations*. Sir John Lubbock's Hundred Books Series. George Routledge & Sons, Ltd, London and New York 1891, p.382.

F.S. Couvreur, *Cheu King. Texte chinois avec une double traduction en français et en latin avec une introduction et un vocabulaire*. Imprimerie de la Mission Catholique, Ho Kien fou 1896, pp.467–9.

167. The basic meaning of ***gi̯ək-gi̯ək* (*i-i*) seems to have been 'to spread the wings over', that is 'to protect or shelter', but as early as the 12th century Chu-Hsi had adduced the additional implication of 'orderly'. This is also the rendering adopted by Karlgren (cf. above, and Ode no.238, p.190: *Tsâk mi̯og gi̯ək-gi̯ək*, 'they made the temple in careful order'). If this be a valid interpretation, then, in the contexts of these two odes, I am inclined to regard the doublet as implying a high-level order, an existential, ritual order rather than mere regularity of arrangement: in the present instance the cosmo-magical order proper for temples and capitals. Cf. also p.34 above.

168. ***G'i̯ək* (*chi*) was an ancient technical term for the astronomical pole vide Needham, *Science and civilisation in China*, vol.3, section 20e]. In Sung times the concept of the *t'ai-chi* came to play an important part in Neo-Confucian thought as expressive of 'the majesty of the universal design' (*T'ien-li-chih tsun*), an axis 'without form and existing only in existential space' [Jao Lu in *Hsing-li Ching-i*, chüan 1, f.5 recto. Cf. also Chu-Hsi in Li Kuang-ti (ed.), *Chu-tzŭ Ch'üan Shu*, chüan 49, *passim*, but especially f.13 recto where the *t'ai-chi* is compared to the longitudinal axis of a candlestick]. The axial implications of this graph are also evident in the *T'âi-g'i̯ək Ki̯ung (T'ai-chi Kung) of T'ang Ch'ang-an and in the name of the Great Hall of State in Heian-kyō : *Daigoku-den*, literally = the Great Pivot [or Pole] Hall. Today nothing remains of the original Daigoku-den, but it has been reproduced in the main hall of the modern Heian shrine at Kyōtō.

169. Wu, *Chinese and Indian architecture*, p.114, note 2.
170. Wu, *Chinese and Indian architecture*, p.30.
171. *loc. cit.*, p.11.

Conclusion

If the term 'city' be defined in accordance with the practice of contemporary urban geography, that is as an organizing and regionalizing principle, as a creator of effective space, then it is difficult to deny the existence of cities in Shang China. But this generic similarity between the Shang and the modern city extends only to a few of the more significant sets in the spectrum of urban characteristics. In fact, Shang cities exhibited a morphology and mode of social integration that would have led many Western urbanists to exclude them from the category of city. Nevertheless, the form that they assumed, namely that of the ceremonial center, has occurred so commonly in other regions of nuclear urbanism that it has a strong claim to be regarded as a functional and developmental stage in the process of urban genesis. Similar forms can be demonstrated at seemingly comparable phases of settlement evolution in Nuclear America, Mesopotamia, Egypt, South and Southeast Asia, in the Mediterranean realm, and in the Yoruba territories, and each is symptomatic of the emergence of a new and qualitatively distinct level of sociocultural complexity which, we have argued in Chapter Four, is essentially urban in character.

In seeking to explicate the manner in which these transformations came about we have been forced to the conclusion, not unwelcome on general theoretical grounds, that they were internally generated. An array of extra-cultural factors such as population pressure and the managerial imperatives of commerce, warfare, or large-scale irrigation – which have often been invoked as autonomous generative factors – proved on empirical examination to be no more than external parametric conditions, inextricably involved in the transformation of the ecotype, it is true, but in no way to be viewed as independent causative agents. Indeed, it is more than doubtful if primacy in this respect should be accorded to any one of the functionally interrelated components involved in the cumulative process of change that culminated in the crystallization of urban forms. But, validating the augmented autonomy resulting from each institutional adaptation, providing the expanded ethical framework capable of encompassing the transformation from ascriptive, kin-oriented groups to stratified, territorially based societies, and from reciprocative to superordinately redistributive economic integration, was a religious symbolization, which itself was becoming more highly differentiated and developing, in Weber's terms, more highly rationalized formulations.[1] The material expression of this symbolization of 'the general order of existence'[2] was the ceremonial

CONCLUSION

center, which afforded a ritual paradigm of the ordering of social interaction at the same time as it disseminated the values and inculcated the attitudes necessary to sustain it. In other words, it projected images of cosmic order on to the plane of human experience, where they could provide a framework for social action. It is, moreover, the evolution of the cult center, the material expression of focused sacredness, which can be most readily documented from the exiguous materials to hand. Whenever, through the murk of textual corruption or the technologically and stylistically biassed reports of archeological excavation, we catch a glimpse of the process of urban genesis, it is the integrative function of the shrine or cult center which attracts our attention. Cultivator and artisan alike, by submitting to the authority of the god who manifested himself in the shrine, placed themselves under the economic power of the ritual experts who both managed the earthly affairs of the deity and represented the interests of the populace before Him (or Her). And as administration of production came inexorably to assume the character, and develop the apparatus, of control, so the economic power of the shrine came to subsume social and political power as well. There had evolved a new and powerful instrument for the organization of economic, social, and political space, which was at the same time a symbol of cosmic, social, and moral order. Henceforward the continuity of culture was assured. Refined and distilled into a classical canon by a corps of literati versed in the technical skills of ritual service, it would develop into an urban-based Great Tradition, the repository of the values and aspirations of the group. These early urban forms, in Shang China no less than elsewhere, were in fact foci of orthogenesis, where the future was viewed as an endless repetition of the past, where moral and religious norms permeated all activities and manifested themselves in designs for political, social, economic, intellectual, and esthetic order. Perhaps the most significant conclusion to emerge from the comparative study of these proto-urban ceremonial centers is that such structural regularities as they exhibit – and these are by no means negligible – are to be discerned in certain shared trends of systemic change rather than in statically conceived formal categorizations.

In Shang ceremonial cities, and probably in those of the Western Chou, the great division between city and country had not yet appeared. It is true that the ceremonial city was the style center for Shang and early Chou civilization, the focus of every major creative effort in those cultures, but the tempo of life within the sacred enceintes – in so far as it can be reconstructed – was not significantly different from that in the countryside. The peasant doubtless found the ceremonial complex, with its glittering temples and palaces, an exciting place. He doubtless experienced feelings of awe when he saw the enormous size of the royal tombs at Hsi-pei Kang, or learnt from the gossip of neighbors of the solemn rituals that accompanied the interment of the Shang king. Equally certainly the ceremonial center was a reassuring feature of his landscape, for it was the *axis mundi*, the location of those hierophanies which guaranteed the continuation of the world as he knew it, the return of the seasons, the coming of the rains at appropriate times, the fructification of the earth, the springing up of crops, and the maintenance of the parallelism between nature and society which subsequently became symbolized in the harmony of *yin* and *yang*. Unlike the migrant to the modern city, the countryman summoned to the Shang capital for corvée, or bringing in his tithe or tribute, was not confronted with new and often alarming experiences. Nor was he confounded by an unfamiliar value system. Life in his village was more humdrum but no more bound to the rhythm of the seasons than was the annual cycle of events in the ceremonial center. Nor, apart from the presence of the royal lineages, nobility, and bureaucratic officials was there a significantly greater degree of social differentiation in the capital. Life there was far from being *zwecksrational* in the way that it is alleged to be in the modern city, and the mores of the ceremonial city were essentially those of the village in more refined form. Although Max Weber's dictum that *der antike Vollbürger ist 'Ackerbürger'*[3] was stated in the restricted context of early European urbanism, it is proving equally apposite in the wider context of city origins in general.

During the Ch'un-Ch'iu period in North China the dispersed ceremonial center was transformed into a compact city, in which a relatively dense population and divers industrial workshops were concentrated about a walled ceremonial center. However, the whole complex was now given definite limits by being brought within a second, outer wall. Yet it should be emphasized that, within this all-embracing outer wall, society was still one of predominantly mechanical solidarity. The mere fact of concentration did not of itself induce any significant shift towards organic solidarity. Moreover, these Ch'un-Ch'iu cities were still cities of the moral order, generators of orthogenetic change. In fact, they were religio-administrative foundations *par excellence*, and, as the seats of princes or government officials, were entirely devoid of aspirations towards civic unity or a specifically urban law. It may be inferred that some probably enjoyed a degree of administrative autonomy, particularly in regard to provisioning and transportation, but this was always exercised within the framework of the laws of the state. During the troublous times of the later centuries of the Chou dynasty, virtual autonomy probably fell to some cities accidentally, but it had no recognized political or legal basis and was, therefore, inevitably of a temporary character.

The forces which brought about the transformation from dispersion to compaction of city form are almost wholly obscure. The information relating to this process as it occurred in Chou China is so exiguous that there is little hope of its elucidation in the near future, and it were perhaps more profitable to search for clues in homotaxially equivalent situations in other realms. However, in none of the regions of nuclear urbanism is the situation sufficiently

CONCLUSION

explicit for the concentrative process to be explained with certainty, although in ancient Sumer, the Ægean, and parts of Mesoamerica, military considerations were certainly not unimportant. I have been unable to correlate the advent of the compact city with, for example, any change in political status such as the expansion from city-state to territorial empire, or with any mutation in the organization of government such as that from religious oligarchy to kingship. Nor does it seem invariably to be directly or clearly related to any specific methods of warfare, or, somewhat surprisingly, to specific advances in transportation technology. Possibly it may in some instances reflect the emergence of a new mode of economic exchange, but this topic is at present so obscure that it requires a study to itself.

It is, in fact, impossible at this stage of the enquiry to disentangle the several economic functions that must have been combined in the role of the Western Chou, or even the Ch'un-Ch'iu, city, mainly because of uncertainties as to the precise connotations of the graphs (particularly the Mencian $**djəg : shih$) which are customarily translated as 'market'. This is too broad a rendering for purposes of economic analysis : we need to know what type of two-way passing of goods is implied in each relevant context. It is, for example, not at all certain, given the societal and cultural context, that the markets mentioned in Chinese classical literature were invariably price-fixing, and not to be assumed that they were wholly autonomous and self-regulating, as witness the administrative intervention advocated in several sections of the *Kuan-tzŭ*. On *a priori* grounds it is to be anticipated that, in Western Chou times at least, non-economic factors played a significant role in price fixing. And if some markets were occasionally permitted to regulate themselves, it is still doubtful if in the aggregate they constituted a self-regulating system.

It is a truism that most of the formulations relating to urban life have been derived from recent European and American experience, so that it is not to be expected that all will be applicable in their entirety to the cities of the traditional world. It can be said at once, for example, that the early ceremonial cities, whether of dispersed or compact form, showed little tendency to absorb excess rural population; that the peasantry was not always, or even usually, free to migrate to the city; that the often cited negative relationship between degree of urbanization and density of agricultural population did not invariably obtain in the traditional world. More generally, it can be confidently asserted that not all types of traditional city equally generated socio-economic change or mediated it in the same manner, and that the expediential mores of the market-place did not always constitute the prevailing urban ethic. The role of traditional cities in the process of economic growth – which, though frequently treated as a phenomenon of the 20th century, was certainly not absent in the traditional world – has not been adequately explored, but certainly differed from that of the modern city. And it is evident from the preceding pages that,

CONCLUSION

although the pre-eminence of the central tract over the periphery is characteristic of both modern and traditional cities, whereas in the former it derives primarily from economic and technological considerations, in at least a substantial proportion of traditional cities it was induced by a principle that we may conveniently term proximity to the sacred. In the contemporary Western-style city high land-values in the central zones are associated with ease of intra-urban accessibility, savings in transport costs being set against higher rent payments for central locations. In the representative ceremonial city of the traditional world, by contrast, population densities did not necessarily decline as a negative exponential function of distance from the city center, and the supremely sacred central precinct, the *axis mundi*, was reserved as a theater for ritual and ceremony. Habitations in these zones were restricted to those of the gods themselves and of those élites who, in societies structured in the image of a hierarchical cosmic order, were either conceived as occupying status positions close to divinity or were experts in the technics of ceremonial and ritual service.

This mention of the sacred serves to introduce a final observation. The cosmic symbolism of the Chinese city has been the subject of frequent comment but seldom, if ever, has it been pointed out that the fundamental principles of this symbolism were not unique to China, or even to East Asia. Rather would it be true to say that they were all but ubiquitous in the high cultures of Asia, and in much of the traditional world besides. The Chinese city was established only after an array of geomantic considerations had been satisfied; it was constructed as an *axis mundi*, an *omphalos* incorporating the powerful centripetality of that symbol; and it was laid out as a terrestrial image of the cosmos, a schema involving cardinal axiality and orientation and, as a corollary, strong architectural emphasis on the main gates. On the capitals, at whatever level of the administrative hierarchy they occurred, devolved the burden of maintaining the prosperity of their respective territories, and as such they became paradigms for other cities. Not infrequently such cities of the moral order were surpassed in size and prosperity by rival foundations, often operating under a commercial ethic, but invariably it was the city of orthogenetic change which retained the greater prestige, which – in contrast to the viewpoint of our own culture – was considered the true or representative city. This is not to deny that in China the elements of this cosmo-magical symbolism were given a distinctive expression, just as in other civilizations they assumed characteristic cultural forms, but the structural basis of that symbolism was the heritage of the traditional world, not merely of China. It was this cosmo-magical role which underpinned the functional unity of the city everywhere until new bases for urban life began to develop in the Hellenistic world. Subsequently, in the Islamic world certain norms of Muslim culture were to some extent substituted for the cosmo-magical concepts, and finally there developed in medieval Europe an insistence on an essential, as opposed to an accidental,

CONCLUSION

civic unity as one of the criteria of true urbanism. This is now the accepted norm in urban studies, but in the evolution of world urbanism it has been the exception. This study of some neglected aspects of the early Chinese city is offered as a small contribution to the comprehensive investigation that will eventually correct the present Western bias in urban studies, and which will, paradoxically, be a prerequisite to a fuller understanding of the uniqueness of the present-day city.

NOTES TO CONCLUSION

1. On this point see Robert N. Bellah, 'Religious evolution', *American Sociological Review*, vol.29, no.3 (1964), p.360.

2. Clifford Geertz's phrase: *vide* 'Religion as a cultural symbol', in Michael Banton (ed.), *Anthropological approaches to the study of religion*. Association of Social Anthropologists Monograph no.3. Tavistock Publications, London 1965. Reprinted in abridged form in William A. Lessa and Evon Z. Vogt (eds.), *Reader in Comparative Religion. An Anthropological Approach*. Harper & Row, New York, Evanston, and London, second edition 1965, pp.204–16.

3. Max Weber, *Grundriss der Sozialökonomik*, III Abteilung : *Wirtschaft und Gesellschaft*, 2 Halbband [J.C.B. Mohr (Paul Siebeck), Tübingen 1925], p.518.

Glossary of Transcriptions of Foreign Names, Terms and Bibliographical References

Glossary of Transcriptions of Foreign Names, Terms and Bibliographical References

Compiled by Mrs T'ung Huang Yih

**·â (o) 阿
**·Â-bʻi̯wang (O-fang) 阿房
**·ăg (ya) 亞
   An-hui 安徽
   An-nam chí-lược (Việt.) 安南志略
   An-nam Chung-tu Hu-fu 安南中都護府
   An-nam La-thánh (Việt.) 安南羅城
   An-yang 安陽
   Âu-lạc (Việt.) 甌雒

   Bắc (Việt.) 北
**Bli̯əm-gʻi̯ung (Lin-chʻiung) 臨卬
**Bli̯əm-si̯ĕn (Lin-hsin) 廩辛
**Bʻâk (Po) 亳
**Bʻăk-Kiweg (Po-Kuei) 白圭

GLOSSARY

**Bʻi̯ĕng (Pʻing) 平

**Bʻi̯ĕng-di̯ang (Pʻing-yang) 平陽

**bʻi̯əng-bʻi̯əng (pʻing-pʻing) 馮馮

**bʻi̯u-di̯ung (fu-yung) 附庸

*Bʻi̯u-nậm (Fu-nan) 扶南

**bʻi̯ŭg (fu) 婦

**Bʻi̯ŭg-χôg (Fu-hao) 婦好

**bʻi̯ŭk (fu) 簏

**Bʻi̯wăm (Fan) 凡

*Bʻi̯wɒn Ṣi-mi̯wɒn (Fan Shih-man) 范師蔓

**Bʻi̯wăn (Fan) 繁 樊

**bʻi̯wang (fang) 房

**Bʻwân-kăng (Pʻan-keng) 盤庚

*bʻwâng (pʻang) 傍

**Bʻwo (Pʻu) 蒲

Chan-Kuo (**Tˆi̯an-Kwək) 戰國
Chan-Kuo Tsʻe 戰國策
Chang-chia-pʻo 張家坡
Chang-Chʻang 張敞
Chang-Hua, *Po-wu Chih* 張華 博物志
Chang-I, *Kuang-Ya* 張揖 廣雅
Chang Shou-chieh, *Shih-Chi Cheng-i* 張守節 史記正義

GLOSSARY

Chang-te Fu 彰德府

Chao Chiu-feng, *Ti-li Wu-chüeh* 趙九峯 地理五訣

Chao-k'ang Chen 趙康鎮

Chao-Yeh, *Wu Yüeh Ch'un-ch'iu* 趙曄 吳越春秋

Cheng-Chou 鄭州

Cheng-Hsüan 鄭玄

Cheng-i 正義

Chi 己

Chi-hsia (**Tsjək-g'å) 稷下

Chi-nan 濟南

chia 甲骨

chia-chieh 假借

chia-ku hsüeh 甲骨學

Chiang-Sheng 江生

Chiang-su 江蘇

chiao 窖

chieh-kao 桔槔

chien 建

Chien-ho 澗河

chih 觶

Chih-li 直隸

chih-shih 指事

chin 斤

GLOSSARY

Chin-p'en 金盆
chin-wen 今文
ching 鏡
Ching-Ts'un 荊村
chio 角
Chiu-tsung 九峻
Chou (**Ṭi̯ôg) 周
chou 冑
chou-chih 州志
Chou-k'ou Tien 周口店
Chou-Kuan 周官
Chou-Kung (**Ṭi̯ôg-Kung) 周公
Chou-Li 周禮
chu 箸
Chü-ho [Ch'eng] 巨合[城]
Chu-Hsi, *T'ung-chien Kang-mu* 朱熹 通鑑綱目
Chu-shu Chi-nien 竹書紀年
Chu-tzŭ Ch'üan-shu 朱子全書
Chu Yu-fu 朱右甫
Chu Yu-tseng 朱右曾
chuan 傳
chuan-chu 轉注
Chuan-Hsü (**T̂'i̯wan-Si̯u) 顓頊

488

GLOSSARY

Chuang-Chou, *Chuang-tzǔ* 莊周 莊子

chün 鈞

Chün-Hsien 濬縣

chung 鍾

Chung-Kuo K'e-hsüeh Yüan 中國科學院

Chung-yüan 中原

Ch'ang-an (*Ḍ'i̯ang-·ân) 長安

Ch'ang-Chou 常州

Ch'ao-ko 朝歌

Ch'en Meng-lei 陳夢雷

Ch'eng Kung-shuo, *Ch'un-Ch'iu fen-chi* 程公說 春秋分紀

Ch'eng-tzǔ Yai 城子崖

ch'i 氣 鏚

Ch'i-Ch'eng 齊乘

Ch'i-chia 齊家

Ch'i-li P'u 七里舖

Ch'ien-lung 乾隆

Ch'in-ting ku-chin t'u-shu chi-ch'eng 欽定古今圖書集成

Ch'ing-yüan 清苑

ch'ü 鑺

Ch'ü-fu 曲阜

Ch'u-Tz'ǔ (**Tṣ'i̯o-Dzi̯ǝg) 楚辭

Ch'ü-yang 曲陽

GLOSSARY

Ch'un-Ch'iu (**T̂'i̯wən-Ts'i̯ôg)　春秋

Ch'un-Ch'iu Tso-Chuan Cheng-i　春秋左傳正義

Daigoku-den (Jap.)　大極殿

**di̯å-ńi̯ĕn (yeh-jen)　野人

**Di̯ang (Yang)　陽　楊

**Di̯ang-b'i̯ĕng (Yang-p'ing)　楊[陽]平

**Di̯ang-d'i̯ĕn (Yang-ch'en)　楊[陽]陳

**Di̯ĕng (Ying)　郢

**Di̯ər (I)　夷

**Di̯o ·i̯ĕt-ńi̯ĕn (Yü i-jen)　余一人

**Di̯o-mi̯wo (Yü-wu)　余無

**Di̯ung-D̂i̯ĕng (Jung-Ch'eng)　容城

**Dzi̯o (Hsü)　徐

**Dzi̯ung (Sung)　訟

**Dzi̯wĕn (Hsün)　郇

**Dzwia (Sui)　隨

**D'âd- ·i̯əp (Ta-i)　大邑

***D'âd-Ngå (Ta-Ya)*　大雅

**d'âd-pi̯wo (tai-fu)　大夫

**D'âd-si̯əg-d'o (Ta-ssŭ-t'u)　大司徒

**D'âd-si̯əg-k'ung (Ta-ssŭ-k'ung)　大司空

***D'âd-Tung (Ta-Tung)*　大東

GLOSSARY

**D'əg (Tai) 代

**D'əm (T'an) 譚

**D'əng (T'eng) 鄧 滕

**D'i̯an (Ch'an) 澶

**D'i̯ang-d̑i̯ok (Ch'ang-shao) 長勺

**D'iek (Ti) 狄

**D'iek-dz'i̯wan (Ti-ch'üan) 狄泉

**D'ien (T'ien) 田

**d'ien (t'ien) 田

**D'i̯ĕn (Ch'en) 陳

**d'ien-di̯ǎ (t'ien-yeh) 田野

**D'ien-Śi̯ôk (T'ien-Shu) 田叔

**D'i̯ĕng (Cheng) 鄭

**D'i̯ĕng-D'i̯ĕng (Ch'eng-Cheng) 程鄭

**D'ieng-Kung (Ting-Kung) 定公

***D'ieng-ḟi̯əg pi̯wang-ti̯ông (Ting-chih fang-chung)* 定之方中

**d'i̯ər (chih) 雉

**D'i̯og (Chao) 趙

**D'i̯og-si̯an (Ch'ao-hsien) 朝鮮

**D'iok (Ti) 翟

**D'i̯ông-tieng (Chung-ting) 仲丁

**D'o (Tu) 杜

**d'o (t'u) 荼

GLOSSARY

**D'ôg (T'ao)　陶

*D'uo-γuâ-lâ-puâ-tiei (Tu-ho-lo-po-ti)　杜和羅鉢底

**Dz'ậg (Tsu)　昨

*Dẓ'i-Siep (Shih-Hsieh. Việt : Sĩ-Nhiêp)　士燮

**dz'i̯an (chien)　賤

**dz'i̯ang (chiang)　匠

**Dz'i̯ĕn (Ch'in)　秦

**Dz'i̯ĕn-Di̯ang (Ch'in-Yang)　秦陽

**dẓ'i̯əg (shih)　士

**Dẓ'i̯əg-Gwia (Shih-Wei)　士蔿

**Dz'iər (Ch'i)　齊

**Dz'ŏg (Ch'ao)　巢

**Dz'ôg (Ts'ao)　曹

Đại-la (Việt.)　大羅

**di̯ǎ (she)　社

**di̯ang (shang)　上

**Ḍi̯ang-Tieg (Shang-Ti)　上帝

**ḍi̯ĕg (shih)　氏

**ḍi̯ĕn (ch'en)　臣

**ḍi̯ĕng (ch'eng)　成　城 (Ch'eng)　郕

**Ḍi̯ĕng-Gi̯wang (Ch'eng-Wang)　成王

**Ḍi̯ĕng-Kung (Ch'eng-Kung)　成公

**Ḍi̯ĕng-Ṭi̯ôg (Ch'eng-Chou)　成周

GLOSSARY

**ḓi̯əg (shih) 市

**ḓi̯əg-tsi̯ĕng (shih-ching) 市井

**Ḓi̯og[-Kung] (Ch'ao[-Kung]) 昭[公]

**Ḓi̯og-kôg (Shao-kao) 召誥

**ḓi̯og-mi̯ôk (chao-mu) 昭穆

**Ḓi̯uk (Shu) 蜀

**ḓ'i̯ăg (she) 射

**Ḓ'i̯ĕn-Nông (Shen-Nung) 神農

Erh-li Kang 二里崗

Erh-shih Huang-ti 二世皇帝

erh-ts'eng t'ai 二層台

**·ər-Kung (Ai-Kung) 哀公

Fa-Fa (**pi̯wăp-pi̯wăp) 法法

fan-ch'ieh 反切

Fan-Ch'o, Man [*Mwan]-Shu 樊綽 蠻書

fang-chih 方志

Fang Hsüan-ling 房玄齡

Fen 汾

feng : Fr. fong (**pi̯ung) 封

Feng-chia An 馮家岸

feng-chien chih-tu 封建制度

GLOSSARY

Feng-huang T'ai 鳳凰台

feng-shui 風水

fu-chih 府志

Fu-Hsi (**B'i̯uk-χia) 伏羲

Fu-Hsüan 傅玄

Fu-Sheng 伏生

Fu-yüan 陣原

Giao-châu kí (Việt.) 交州記

**gi̯ək-gi̯ək (i-i) 翼翼

**Gi̯wad (Wei) 衛

**Gi̯wad-Pi̯ŭm (Wei-Feng) 衛風

**Gi̯wad Śi̯ad-kǎ (Wei Shih-chia) 衛世家

**gi̯wang (wang) 王

**Gi̯wang-Ḓi̯ĕng (Wang-Ch'eng) 王城

**gi̯wang-ńi̯ĕn (wang-jen) 王人

**Gi̯wang-Ṭi̯ad (Wang-Chih) 王制

**Gi̯wăt (Yüeh) 越

**Gi̯wĕng-śi̯ĕt (Ying-shih) 營室

**Gi̯wo-Kung (Yü-Kung) 禹貢

**Glâk (Lo) 洛

**Glâk-di̯ang (Lo-yang) 洛陽

**Glâk-·i̯əp (Lo-i) 洛邑

GLOSSARY

**Glâk-kôg (Lo-kao) 洛誥

**Gliok (Li) 櫟

**G'â (Ho) 河

**G'å-Mi̯wo (Hsia-Wu) 下武

**G'â-nəp (Ho-nei) 河內

**G'â-tân-kap (Ho-tan-chia) 河亶甲

**G'å-to (Hsia-tu) 下都

**G'ân (Han) 韓 邗

**G'ân-tân (Han-tan) 邯鄲

**G'ân-ts'i̯ĕg (Han-tz'ŭ) 寒餗

**G'ɛm-di̯ang (Hsien-yang) 咸陽

**G'ia (Ch'i) 錡

**g'ian d'âd-pi̯wo (hsien tai-fu) 縣大夫

**g'ian t̂i̯əg (hsien chih) 縣之

**G'i̯at (Chieh) 桀

**G'i̯ĕg (Chi) 薊

**G'i̯ĕg (Ch'i) 岐

**G'ieng (Hsing) 邢

**g'i̯əg (ch'i) 旗

**g'i̯ək (chi) 極

**G'i̯o-k'i̯ŭg (Ch'ü-ch'iu) 渠丘

**G'iweg (Hsi) 鄎

**g'iwen-tiôg (hsüan-niao) 玄鳥

GLOSSARY

**G'og (Hao) 鎬

**g'ǫng/ʔg'lông (hsiang) 降

**g'u (hou) 侯

**G'u-Tsi̯ǝk (Hou-Chi) 后稷

**G'ung-B'i̯wăm (Hung-Fan) 洪範

**g'wâd (hui) 會

**G'wân (Huan) 亘

**G'wân-Kung (Huan-Kung) 桓公

**G'wân-Pi̯wăt (Huan-Fa) 桓發

**G'wâng (Huang) 黃

**G'wâng-B'i̯wo (Huang-Fu) 皇父

**G'wâng Kwǝk-b'i̯wo (Huang Kuo-fu) 皇國父

**G'wâng-Tieg (Huang-Ti) 黃帝

**G'wěk (Hua) 畫

**G'wɛr (Huai) 淮

Han-Fei-tzǔ 韓非子

Han Wu-ti 漢武帝

Hang-chou 杭州

hang-t'u 硄土

Heian-kyō (Jap.) 平安京

Heijō-kyō (Jap.) 平城京

ho 盉

GLOSSARY

Ho-nan [Hsien] 河南[縣]

Ho-pei 河北

Hou-chia-chuang-nan-ti 侯家莊南地

Hou-kang 後崗

Hou-ma Chen 侯馬鎮

Hsi-an 西安

Hsi-ch'eng Chuang 西城莊

Hsi-kuan-wai 西關外

Hsi-pei Kang 西北崗

Hsi-Shan 西陝

Hsi-Tz'ŭ 繫辭

Hsi-wang Mu 西王母

Hsi-yin Ts'un 西陰村

Hsia (**G'å) 夏

Hsiang-fen 襄汾

hsiang-hsing 象形

hsiao 削

Hsiao Tzŭ-hsien, *Nan-Ch'i Shu* 蕭子顯 南齊書

Hsiao-T'un 小屯

hsien 咸 甗

hsien (**g'ian) 縣

hsien-chih 縣志

hsin 辛

GLOSSARY

Hsin-Hsiang 新鄉

Hsing-li Ching-i 性理精義

hsing-sheng 形聲

hsing-shih 形勢

Hsing-T'ai 邢台

Hsing-Tsai 行在

hsiu 宿

Hsü Chih-mo, *Ti-li Cho-yü-fu* 徐之鏌 地理琢玉斧

hsüeh 穴

Hsüeh-chia Chuang 薛家莊

hsün 塤/壎

Hsün-tzŭ 荀子

hu 壺

Hu An-kuo 胡安國

Hua-yin Hsien 華陰縣

Huai-nan-tzŭ 淮南子

Huan Ho 洹河

Huang-Chen 黃震

Huang Ho 黃河

Huang-niang-niang T'ai 皇娘娘台

Hui-Hsien 輝縣

hui-i 會意

Hui-Shih 惠施

GLOSSARY

Hung-an　紅安

Huo-Chih　貨殖

**Xi̯ăn-Kung (Hsien-Kung)　獻公

**Xi̯ang (Hsiang)　向

**Xi̯əg-Kung (Hsi-Kung)　僖公

**Xi̯o (Hsü)　許

**Xi̯og (Ao)　囂

**Xiwĕt (hsü)　溘

**Xmwəng-χmwəng (hung-hung)　薨薨

**Xŏg-Kung (Hsiao-Kung)　孝公

**Xwâk (Huo)　霍

**Xwâr (huo)　火

i　彝

I-chang shu Huang-Men　譯長屬黃門

I-Ching　易經

I-Ching, Ta-T'ang Hsi-yü Ch'iu-fa K'ao-seng Chuan　義淨 大唐西域求法高僧傳

I Chou-shu, Tso-Lo　逸周書 作雒

I Hou Nieh I　圛医矢彝

I-Hsien　易縣

I-Li　儀禮

i-mao　乙卯

GLOSSARY

i-wei 乙未

**·Ia-Twən (I-Tun) 猗頓

Ichisada Miyazaki (Jap.) 宮崎市定

**i̯uĕn (yin) 尹

**·I̯am (Yen) 奄

**·I̯an (Yen) 燕

*·i̯ĕn (yin) 印

**·I̯ɛr-i̯uĕn (I-yin) 伊尹

**·i̯ɛt (i) 乙

**·I̯əm-tsi̯ĕn (Yin-chin) 陰晉

**·I̯ən-Kung (Yin-Kung) 隱公

**·I̯ən-Mi̯wo (Yin-Wu) 殷武

**·I̯əng (Ying) 應

**·i̯əp (i) 邑

**·I̯ung (Yung) 雍

**·I̯ung Glåk-d̑i̯ĕng (Yung Lo-ch'eng) 雍樂成

**·I̯ung-Păk (Yung-Po) 雍伯

**·I̯wăd-g'lâk (Wei-ho) 穢貉

**·I̯wăn (Yüan) 宛

Jao Lu 饒魯

jen 壬

Jen-min Kung-yüan 人民公園

Jih-chao 日照

GLOSSARY

**Kăd-kən (Chieh-ken) 介根

**Kan (Chien) 澗

   Kan-su 甘肅

   Kao-liang 高梁

   Kao-Yu 高誘

**Kăp-ńjuk (Chia-ju) 郟鄏

**Kăn-D'iek (Chien-Ti) 簡狄

*Kân-t'â-lji (Kan-t'o-li) 干陀利

**Kăng-tieng (Keng-ting) 庚丁

*Kau-tśi (Chiao-chih) 交趾

   keng 庚

   keng-hsü 庚戌

**kɛn (chin) 堇

   Khâm-định Việt-sử thông-giám Cương-mục (Việt.)   欽定越史通鑑綱目

**Ki̯ĕng (Ching) 荊

**Ki̯əg (Chi) 姬

**Ki̯ər (Chi) 饑

**Ki̯ung (Kuŋg) 共

**Ki̯wɛd-Liek (Chi-Li) 季歷

**Ki̯wɛd-Ńjan (Chi-Jan) 季然

**Ki̯wɛd-tsi̯əg (Chi-tzŭ) 季子

**Ki̯wɛr (Kuei) 癸

**ki̯wən-tsi̯əg (chün-tzŭ) 君子

GLOSSARY

**Kiwər-piwang (Kuei-fang) 鬼方

**klâk-klâk (ko-ko) 閣閣

**Kliăng (Ching) 京

**Kliăng-Giwang (Ching-Wang) 景王

   ko 戈

   Ko-ta-wang 旭奋王 屹嵃王

**Kŏg (Chiao) 絞

**Kôg (Kao) 郜

**Kôg-piwang (Kao-fang) 告方

**Kộng (Chiang) 絳

**kộng/klộng (chiang) 降

   kou 鉤

**ku (kou) 溝

   ku 觚 鼓

   Ku-liang Chuan 穀梁傳

   Ku-shih Shih-chiu-shou 古詩十九首

   Ku Tung-kao, *Ch'un-Ch'iu Ta-shih Piao* (Wan-chüan-lou) 顧棟高 春秋大事表 (萬卷樓)

   ku-wen 古文

   kuan 罐

   Kuan-Lo, *Kuan-shih Ti-li Chih-meng* 管輅 管氏地理指蒙

   Kuan-lu 關盧

   Kuan-tzŭ 管子

GLOSSARY

kuei 鬹 圭 簋

kung 觥

**kung (kung) 工 公

**Kǔng (Chiang) 江

Kung-chai Ti-hsing 宮宅地形

**kung-dʻien (kung-tʻien) 公田

Kung-yang Chuan 公羊傳

Kung-yang Kao 公羊高

Kung-yang Shou 公羊壽

kuo 槨

Kuo-li Chung-yang Yen-chiu-yüan Li-shih Yü-yen Yen-chiu-so
國立中央研究院歷史語言研究所

Kuo-Yü 國語

**kwad (kuai) 夬

**Kwăk (Kuo) 虢

**kwâk (kuo) 郭

**Kwâk-Tsi̯ung (Kuo-Tsung) 郭縱

**Kwân (Kuan) 管

**Kwân-Dʻi̯ông (Kuan-Chung) 管仲

**Kwân-pi̯u (Kuan-fu) 官府

**kwək (kuo) 國

**Kwən-lwən (Kʻun-lun) 崑崙

Kyōtō (Jap.) 京都

503

GLOSSARY

K'ai-feng 開封

K'ai-jui Chuang 開瑞莊

k'an 坎

k'an-kuo 坩鍋

k'an-yü chia 堪輿家

K'an-yü Chin-kuei 堪輿金匱

K'ang (**K'âng) 康

K'ang-hsi Tzŭ-tien 康熙字典

**K'âng-kôg (K'ang-kao) 康誥

**K'âng-śiôk (K'ang-shu) 康叔

K'ao-kung Chi 考工記

**K'ât (Ko) 葛

K'e-tao 刻刀

k'eng 坑

**K'i̯ang (Ch'iang) 羌

**k'i̯ăng (ch'ing) 卿

**K'i̯əg (Ch'i) 杞

**K'i̯u-si̯wok (Ch'ü-su) 區粟

**K'i̯uk-·ok (Ch'ü-wo) 曲沃

**K'i̯uk-Śi̯ôk (Ch'ü-Shu) 曲叔

K'o (**K'ək) 克

k'uei 夔

**K'ung (K'ung) 孔

504

GLOSSARY

K'ung An-kuo 孔安國

K'ung Ying-ta 孔穎達

Lạc (Việt.) 雒

**Lâng (Lang) 郎

Lao-Lao T'ai 老姥台

**Ləg (Lai) 萊

li 里

Li Chi 李濟

Li-Chi 禮記

Li Kuang-ti 李光地

Li-K'uei 李悝

Li-Ssŭ (**Lịəg-Sịĕg) 李斯

Li Tao-yüan, *Shui-Ching Chu* 酈道元 水經注

Li Tê-xuyên, *Việt điện u linh tập* (Việt.) 李濟川 越甸幽靈集

**Lia-Sôg (*Li-Sao*) 離騷

liang 兩

**Lịang (Liaṅg) 梁

Liang-ch'eng Chen 兩城鎮

Liang Lü-sheng. *Tso-t'ung Pu-shih* (Wang Hsien-ch'ien, *Huang-Ch'ing Ching-chieh Hsü-pien*)
梁履繩 左通補釋（王先謙 皇清經解續編）

Liang-Shu 梁書

Liao-ning 遼寧

505

GLOSSARY

 Lieh-Chuan 列傳

**liei (li) 隸

 lien 鐮

**Lieng-Kung (Ling-Kung) 靈公

**Li̯ĕt (Li) 栗

**li̯əg (li) 吏

 *Li̯əm-·i̯əp (Lin-i) 林邑

**Li̯ər (Li) 黎

**li̯ər (li) 禮

**Li̯ər-ki̯wɛr (Lü-kuei) 履癸

 Lin-Li 林栗

 Lin-shan Chai 林山砦

 Lin-tzŭ 臨淄

 ling 鈴

 Ling-yüan 凌源

**Li̯ôg (Liu) 劉

 Liu-Chi, *K'an-yü Man-hsing* 劉基 堪輿漫興

 Liu-Hsiang, *Shuo-Yüan* 劉向 說苑

 Liu-Hsin 劉歆

 Liu-Hsü, *Chiu T'ang-Shu* 劉昫 舊唐書

 Liu-Shu, *T'ung-chien Wai-chi* 劉恕 通鑑外紀

**li̯uĕt (lieh) 乎

**Li̯ung (Lung) 隴

GLOSSARY

****Lji̯ung-pi̯wang (Lung-fang) 龍方

**li̯wər-dzi̯əg (lei-ssŭ) 耒耜

*Ljwiḙ-li̯u (Việt. Luy-lâu) 羸陵

**Lo (Lu) 魯

  Lo-ho 洛河

  Lo-Pi, *Lu-Shih* 羅泌 路史

  Lo-ta Miao 洛達廟

  Lu-wang Fen 潞王墳

  lui 罍

  Lun-Yü 論語

  Lũng-khê (Việt.) 隴溪

  Lung-shan Chen 龍山鎮

  Lung-T'ai 龍臺

  Lü Pu-wei 呂不韋

  Lü-shih Ch'un-Ch'iu 呂氏春秋

**mȧ (ma) 馬

  Ma-erh 馬耳

  Ma Tuan-lin, *Wen-hsien T'ung-k'ao* 馬端臨 文獻通考

  mao 矛

  Mao-Ch'ang 毛萇

  Mao-Heng 毛亨

  Mao-Kung 毛公

GLOSSARY

Mao Shih 毛詩

Meng-tzŭ 孟子

**Mi̯an (Mien) 縣

Miao-ti Kou 廟底溝

**mi̯at (mieh) 滅

Mien-ch'ih 澠池

**mi̯ən (min) 民

***Mi̯ən-log* (*Min-lao*) 民勞

**Mi̯ər (Mei) 郿

ming (**mi̯ăng) 命

Ming-kung Lu 銘功路

Ming-T'ang 明堂

**mi̯og (miao) 廟

**Mi̯ôk (Mu) 穆

**mi̯ôk (mu) 牧

**mi̯ôk-si̯ər (mu-shih) 牧師

**Mi̯wĕn-ti̯ôk (Min-chu) 敏竹

**Mi̯wɛn-Kung (Min-Kung) 閔公

**Mi̯wən[-Gi̯wang] (Wen[-Wang]) 文[王]

***Mi̯wən-Gi̯wang gi̯ŭg śi̯ĕng* (*Wen-Wang yu sheng*) 文王有聲

**Mi̯wo-Ḓi̯ĕng (Wu-Ch'eng) 武城

**Mi̯wo[-Gi̯wang] (Wu[-Wang]) 武[王]

**Mi̯wo-·i̯ɛt (Wu-i) 武乙

GLOSSARY

**Mi̯wo-Ti̯ĕg (Wu-Chih) 無知

**Mi̯wo-tieng (Wu-ting) 武丁

**Mlwan (*Mwan, Man) 蠻

Mo-Ti, *Mo-tzŭ* 墨翟 墨子

**Mog (Mao) 毛

**Môg (Mao) 茅

mou-shen 戊申

mu 墓

*Muâ-χiei-śi̯ə̯u-lâ (Mo-hsi-shou-lo) 摩醯首羅

*Muâ-tậm (Mo-tan) 摩眈

**Mwân-păk (Man-pe) 曼伯

*Nâ-ka-si̯än (Na-chia-hsien) 那伽仙

*Nậm-Tśi̯äu (Nan-Chao) 南詔

Nan-ching 南京

**Nan-Gi̯wang (Nan-Wang) 報王

Nan-kuan-wai 南關外

Nan-Shih 南史

Nan-yang 南陽

nao 饒

Nara (Jap.) 奈良

Nei-Chuan 內傳

Nei-yeh (**Nəp-ngi̯ăp) 內業

GLOSSARY

**nəm (nan) 男

**Nəm-Li̯əg (Nan-Li) 南里

**ngia (i) 義

**Ngi̯ən (Yin) 沂

**ngi̯o-sli̯əg (yü-shih) 御史

**Ngi̯wăn (Yüan) 原

**ngi̯wăn-d̯i̯ĕn (yüan-ch'en) 元臣

***Ngi̯wăt-Li̯ĕng* (*Yüeh-Ling*) 月令

**Ngi̯wər (Wei) 魏

***Ngi̯wər-Pi̯ŭm* (*Wei-Feng*) 魏風

**Ngi̯wo (Yü) 虞

**Nglŏk-χi̯əg (Yüeh-Hsi) 樂喜

**Ngo (Wu) 吳

**Ngo-ki̯əp (Wu-chi) 午汲

**Ngog (Ao) 隞

**ngwâd (wai) 外

  ni shui 逆水

**Ńi̯ak (Jo) 若

**ńi̯ĕn (jen) 人

  Nien-Piao 年表

**Ńi̯ĕn-pi̯wang (Jen-fang) 人方

**ńi̯əng-ńi̯əng (jeng-jeng) 陾陾

**Ńi̯ər-k'i̯wət (Erh-ch'ü) 二屈

510

GLOSSARY

**Nio-gʻwɛr-tsʻiĕng (Nü-huai-chʻing) 女懷清

**Ńiông (Jung) 戎 (Sung) 娀

   Niu-Chai 牛砦

   Niu-Hsing 紐星

   Niu-Tsʻun 牛村

   Nü-kua (**Nio-Kwa) 女媧

**Ńiĕt-nəm : *Ńźiĕt-nậm (Jih-nan) 日南

**ńźiuĕn (jun) 閏

**·O-gʻwân (Wu-huan) 烏桓

**·Ok (Wo) 沃

**·Ok-kwək (Wo-kuo) 沃國

   Ou-yang Hsiu, Sung-Chʻi, *Hsin Tʻang-Shu* 歐陽修 宋祁 新唐書

**På (Pa) 巴

**Păg (Pa) 霸

   Pai-chia Chuang 白家莊

**păk (po) 伯

   Pan-Ku, *Chʻien-Han Shu* 班固 前漢書

   Pan-pʻo Tsʻun 半坡村

   Pan-Shan 半山

   pang 榜

   Pao-chi 寶雞

GLOSSARY

Pei 淠

Pei-Ch'en 北辰

Pei-ching 北京

Pei-Shih 北史

pen 錛

Pen-Chi 本紀

**Pək-[χi̯ang]-g'o, *Pək-[χi̯ang]-γuo (Pei-[hsiang]-hu) 北[嚮]戶

Phạm Công-trứ, *Đại-Việt sử-ki toàn-thư, ngoại kỉ toàn-thư* (Việt.) 范公著 大越史記全書 外紀全書

pi 璧 匕

Pi-sha Kang 碧沙岡

**Pi̯ăng (Ping) 邴

pieh-chü 別居

Pieh-Shih 別史

**pi̯ĕk-ḓi̯ĕn (p'i-ch'en) 辟臣

**Pi̯ĕt (Pi) 畢

**pi̯əg (pi) 鄙

**Pi̯ən (Pin) 豳

Pin-Hsien 邠縣

ping 丙

ping-wu 丙午

**pi̯ôk-d'ôg (fu-tao) 複道

**Pi̯ŭg-Ḓi̯ən (Fu-Ch'en) 富辰

GLOSSARY

**pi̯wang (fang) 方

**pi̯wăp (fa) 法

**Pi̯wo-di̯o (Fu-yü) 夫餘

  Po-Hsien 亳縣

  Po-t'ing Ch'eng 博亭城

**Pôg-·i̯ɛt (Pao-i) 報乙

**Pôg-pi̯ăng (Pao-ping) 報丙

**Pôg-tieng (Pao-ting) 報丁

  pu 布

**puk (pu) 卜

**Pŭng (Pang) 邦

  p'an 盤

  P'an-ku (**B'wân-ko) 盤古

  p'ang 旁

  P'ei-Yin 裴駰

  p'en 盆

  P'ing-ling [Hsien/Ch'eng] 平陵[縣/城]

  P'ing-wang 平王

**P'i̯ông (Feng) 豐酆

**p'i̯ug (fu) 郛

**P'i̯wăn-ngi̯u (P'an-yü) 番禺

**p'i̯wo (fu) 撫

  p'ou 瓿

GLOSSARY

***Sâk-pi̯wang* (*Shuo-fang*)　朔方

San-Ch'i Chi　三齊記

San-fu Huang T'u　三輔黃圖

San-li T'un　三里墩

**Sĕng (*sheng*)　生

Shan-fu K'o (***Ḋi̯am-pi̯wo K'ək*)　善夫克

Shan-hsi　山西

Shan-Hsien　陝縣

Shan-tung　山東

Shang (***Śi̯ang*)　商

Shang-chieh　上街

Shang-Chou　商州

Shang-lo　商洛

shao　勺

Shen-hsi　陝西

Shen Huai-yüan, *Nan-Yüeh Chi*　沈懷遠　南越記

Shih　室

shih　杙

Shih-Chi: see Ssŭ-ma T'an

Shih-Chia　世家

Shih-Ching　詩經

Shih-li Miao　十里廟

Shih-li P'u　十里舖

514

GLOSSARY

Shu 書

Shu-Ching 書經

Shun (**Śi̯wən) 舜

Shuo-wen Chieh-tzŭ 說文解字

**Si̯ang (Hsiang) 相

**Si̯at (Hsieh) 契

**Si̯at (Hsüeh) 薛

**Si̯ĕg (Tz'ŭ) 賜

**Si̯ĕg-kân (Ssŭ-kan) 斯干

**Si̯ĕg-mi̯ăng (Tz'ŭ-ming) 賜命

**Siek-mi̯ăng (Hsi-ming) 錫命

**Si̯ĕn-d'ien (Hsin-t'ien) 新田

**si̯ĕng (hsing) 姓

**Si̯əd-t'o (Ssŭ-t'u) 四土

**Si̯ək (Hsi) 息

**si̯ər-d'ien (ssŭ-t'ien) 私田

**si̯og (hsiao) 小

**Siôg (Hsiao) 蕭

**si̯og-ḍi̯ĕn (hsiao-ch'en) 小臣

**Si̯og-·i̯et (Hsiao-i) 小乙

**si̯og-ńi̯ĕn (hsiao-jen) 小人

**Si̯og-si̯ĕn (Hsiao-hsin) 小辛

**Si̯wan-Kung (Hsüan-Kung) 宣公

GLOSSARY

**slı̯əg (shih) 史

**slı̯əg-śı̯u (shih-shu) 史戍

**Snı̯ang-Kung (Hsiang-Kung) 襄公

So-yin 索引

**Sông (Sung) 宋

    Ssŭ-ma Cheng 司馬貞

    Ssŭ-ma T'an, Ssŭ-ma Ch'ien, *Shih-Chi* 司馬談 司馬遷 史記

    Su-Ch'e 蘇轍

    Su-Shih 蘇軾

    Sui 隋

    Sui-Shu 隋書

    Sung-Shih 宋史

**Śia (Shih) 施

**śı̯ag-ńı̯ĕn (shu-jen) 庶人

**Śı̯ang-Dz'ı̯ung (*Shang-Sung*) 商頌

**Śı̯ap (She) 葉

**Śı̯ĕn (Shen) 申

**Śı̯ĕn Mı̯wo-gı̯wo (Shen Wu-yü) 申無宇

**Śı̯ĕng-tsı̯əg (Sheng-tzŭ) 聲子

**śı̯u-dzı̯əg tsı̯əg (shu-ssŭ tzŭ) 戍嗣子

**tâ-dı̯ĕn (to-ch'en) 多臣

. Ta-hsin Chuang 大辛莊

GLOSSARY

**Tâ-·i̯ĕn (To-yin) 多印

Ta-K'uang (**D'âd-K'i̯wang) 大匡

Ta-ssŭ-k'ung Ts'un 大司空村

Ta-tu 大都

Tai-Chen, *K'ao-kung Chi T'u* 戴震 考工記圖

**Tân (Tan) 旦

tan 擔

**Tân-B'i̯wo (Tan-Fu) 亶父

tao 刀

tao-te (Fr. tao-tö; **d'ôg-tək) 道德

Tao-te Ching 道德經

**tək (te; Fr. tö) 德

**tək-g'ăng (te-hsing) 德行

**təng-ńi̯ĕn (teng-jen) 登人

**təng-təng (teng-teng) 登登

**təng-t̑i̯ông ńi̯ĕn (teng-chung jen) 登眾人

ti-p'an 地盤

ti-chung 地中

**Ti̯ang (Chang) 張

**Ti̯ang-Li̯əg (Chang-Li) 張里

**Tieg/tieg (Ti/ti) 帝

**Tieg-·i̯ɛt (Ti-i) 帝乙

**Tieg-K'ôk (Ti-K'u) 帝嚳

GLOSSARY

**Tieg-sjĕn (Ti-hsin) 帝辛

**tieng (ting) 丁

**tjĕng-ńjĕn (chen-jen) 貞人

**Tiər (Ti) 氐

  ting 鼎

**tjôk (chu) 築

**tjông (chung) 中

**Tjông-Pjwən (Chung-Fen) 中分

**Tjông-Śjang (Chung-Shang) 中商

**tjông-to (chung-tu) 中都

**tjung-t'o (chung-t'u) 冢土

**to (tu) 都 堵

**Tŏk (Cho) 卓

  tou 寶 豆 斗

  Tsa-Shih 雜史

  Tsai-Chi 載記

**Tsâk mjog gjək-gjək (Tso miao i-i) 作廟翼翼

**tsâk-ts'ĕk (tso-ts'e) 作冊

  tseng 甑

**tsəg (tsai) 災

**Tsjang (Chiang) 蔣

**Tsjang-Kung (Chuang-Kung) 莊公

**Tsjĕn (Chin) 晉

518

GLOSSARY

  *Tśi̯ĕn-lâp (Chen-la) 真臘

  **Tsi̯ĕng (Ching) 井

  **tsi̯ĕng-dʻien (ching-tʻien) 井田

  **Tsi̯əg/tsi̯əg (Tzŭ/tzŭ) 子

  **Tsi̯əg-Di̯ôg (Tzŭ-Yu) 子游

  **Tsi̯og (Chiao) 焦

  **Tsi̯ok (Chʻüeh) 雀

  **tsi̯ok (chüeh) 爵

  tso 作

  Tso-chʻiu Ming : Tso Chʻiu-ming 左丘明

  Tso-Chuan 左傳

  **Tso-·i̯ɛt (Tsu-i) 祖乙

  **Tso-kăng (Tsu-keng) 祖庚

  **Tso-kap (Tsu-chia) 祖甲

  tsu 鏃 俎

  tsuan 鑽

  tsun 尊

  tsung 琮

  Tu-Lin 杜林

  Tu-Yu 杜佑

  *Tuən-suən (Tun-sun) 頓遜

  **Tŭk (Cho) 濁 涿

  Tung-Chai 董砦

GLOSSARY

Tung-Chi 龘季

Tung Chung-shu, *Ch'un-Ch'iu Fan-lu* 董仲舒 春秋繁露

Tzŭ-ching Shan 紫荊山

Tzŭ-Ch'eng 子城

Tzŭ-ch'ih T'ung-chien 資治通鑑

tzŭ-hsü 自序

***T'âd (T'ai)* 泰

***T'âd-Ḍi̯ad (T'ai-Shih)* 泰誓

***T'âd-·i̯ɛt (T'ai-i)* 大乙

***T'âd-tieng (T'ai-ting)* 太丁

***T'âd-Tsəg (T'ai-Tsai)* 大宰

T'ai-chi 太極

**T'âi-g'i̯ək Ki̯ung (T'ai-chi Kung)* 太極宮

T'ai-p'ing Huan-yü Chi 太平寰宇記

T'ai-p'ing Yü-lan 太平御覽

T'ai-shih Kung Shu 太史公書

**t'âk-t'âk (t'o-t'o) 橐橐

t'an 壇

T'an-kung 檀弓

***T'âng (T'ang)* 湯

T'ang Hui-yao 唐會要

***T'âng Ṭi̯ĕng (T'ang Cheng)* 湯征

T'ang-yin Hsien 湯陰縣

GLOSSARY

 t'ao-t'ieh 饕餮

 T'eng-Hsien 滕縣

 T'ien-chin 天津

**T'ien-gʻi̯ək (T'ien-chi) 天極

 T'ien-li-chih tsun 天理之尊

**T'ien-Mi̯wən (T'ien-Wen) 天問

 t'ien-p'an 天盤

 T'ien-Shu 天樞

**T'ien-tsi̯əg (T'ien-tzŭ) 天子

 T'ien-wang Kuei 天亡設

**T'nâm (T'an) 聃

**T'o (T'u) 土

**T'o-pi̯wang (T'u-fang) 土方

 t'uan 彖

 t'un-t'ien 屯田

 t'ung-chih 通志

**t̂i̯ad (chih) 制

**T̂i̯ang (Chang) 漳 鄣

**T̂i̯ĕd (Chih) 郅

**T̂i̯ĕn-p'i̯wăn (Chen-p'an) 真番

**t̂i̯ĕng (cheng) 正

**T̂i̯ək-pi̯wang-d̂i̯ĕg (Chih-fang-shih) 職方氏

**T̂i̯ən (Chen) 振

GLOSSARY

**t̑i̯o-gʻu (chu-hou) 諸侯

**T̑i̯ôg (Chou) 州

**T̑i̯ok (Chu) 祝

**T̑i̯ông-gʻi̯wɛr (Chung-kʻuei) 終葵

**T̑i̯ông-kʻi̯ŭg (Chung-chʻiu) 中丘

**t̑i̯ông-ńi̯ĕn (chung-jen) 象人

**T̑i̯ung (Chung) 種

**T̑ʻi̯ang (Chʻang) 昌

**Tsʻâd (Tsʻai) 蔡

   Tsʻai-Chuang 蔡莊

   Tsʻao-yen Chuang 曹演莊

**tsʻĕk (tsʻe) 冊

**Tsʻi̯am (Chʻien) 岍

**tsʻi̯an (chʻien) 遷

**tsʻi̯ap (chʻieh) 妾

**Tsʻi̯ĕng (Chʻing) 清

***Tsʻieng-tsʻieng li̯əng-d̑i̯ang păk (Chʻing-chʻing ling-shang pai)*
   青青陵上柏

**Tṣʻi̯o (Chʻu) 楚

**Tṣʻi̯o-kʻi̯ŭg (Chʻu-chʻiu) 楚丘

**Tsʻiôk (Chʻi) 戚

**tsʻi̯u (chʻü) 取

   Tsʻui Shu 崔述

GLOSSARY

Wai-Chuan 外傳

Wang An-shih 王安石

Wang I-yung 王懿榮

Wang-Mang 王莽

Wang Nien-sun 王念孫

Wang-Wan 王灣

Wang-Wei, *Huang-Ti Chai Ching* 王微 黃帝宅經

Wei 渭

Wei-Wang [Li] T'ai, *Kua-ti Chih* 魏王[李]泰 括地志

Wen-ting (**Mi̯wən-tieng) 文丁

wu 戊午

Wu-an Hsien 武安縣

Wu-kuan Ts'un 武官村

Wu-yüan 武原

ya-men 衙門

yang 陽

Yang-shao [Ts'un] 仰韶[村]

Yang-tzŭ 揚子

Yang Yün-sung, *Ch'ing-nang Ao-chih* 楊筠松 青囊奧旨

Yao (**Ngiog) 堯

Yao Chan-ch'i, *Yin-yang Erh-chai Ch'üan-shu* 姚瞻旂 陰陽二宅全書

yao-k'eng 腰坑

523

GLOSSARY

Yeh (**Di̯å) 埜

Yen (**·I̯ăn) 匽

Yen Shih-ku 顏師古

Yin (**·I̯ən) 殷

yin 陰

Yin-hsü 殷墟

Yin-kuo Ts'un 尹郭村

Yin Pen-chi 殷本紀

Yin-shih (**I̯uěn-ḓi̯ĕg) 尹氏

Ying-che 滎澤

Ying-Shao, *Feng-su T'ung-i* 應劭 風俗通義

yu 卣 酉

Yung 邟

Yung-lo Ta-tien 永樂大典

Yü (**Gi̯wo) 禹

Yü-Ch'in 于欽

yüeh 鉞

GLOSSARY

BIBLIOGRAPHICAL REFERENCES
Journals

Chung-Kuo K'ao-ku Hsüeh-pao
中國考古學報

Chung-Kuo She-hui Ching-chi-shih Chi-k'an
中國社會經濟史集刊

Chung-Kuo Wen-hua Yen-chiu Hui-k'an
中國文化研究彙刊

Chung-yang Yen-chiu-yüan : Min-ts'u-hsüeh Yen-chiu-so Chi-k'an
中央研究院民族學研究所集刊

Ch'i-hsiang Hsüeh-pao
氣象學報

Ch'ing-hua Hsüeh-pao
清華學報

Ch'ing-hua Ta-hsüeh She-hui K'o-hsüeh Chi-k'an
清華大學社會科學季刊

Hsüeh-shu Chi-k'an
學術季刊

Hsüeh-shu Hui-k'an
學術彙刊

Hua-hsi Hsieh-ho Ta-hsüeh Chung-Kuo Wen-hua Yen-chiu-so Chi-k'an
華西協合大學中國文化研究所集刊

Hua-hsi Ta-hsüeh Wen-shih Chi-k'an
華西大學文史集刊

K'an-tao Yüeh-k'an
康導月刊

K'ao-ku
考古

GLOSSARY

K'ao-ku Hsüeh-pao
考古學報

K'ao-ku T'ung-hsün
考古通訊

Kuo-li Chung-yang Yen-chiu-yüan Li-shih Yü-yen Yen-chiu-so Chi-k'an
國立中央研究院歷史語言研究所集刊

Kuo-li Chung-yang Yen-chiu-yüan Yüan-k'an
國立中央研究院院刊

Kuo-li Pei-ching Ta hsüeh Kuo-hsüeh Chi-k'an
國立北京大學國學季刊

Kuo-li T'ai-wan Ta-hsüeh K'ao-ku Jen-lei Hsüeh-k'an
國立臺灣大學考古人類學刊

Kuo-li T'ai-wan Ta-hsüeh Wen-shih-che Hsüeh-pao
國立臺灣大學文史哲學報

Ling-nan Hsüeh-pao
嶺南學報

Shih-huo [Pan-yüeh-k'an]
食貨[半月刊]

Ta-lu Tsa-chih
大陸雜誌

T'ien-yeh K'ao-ku Pao-kao
田野考古報告

Tung-fang Tsa-chih
東方雜誌

Wen-hsüeh Nien-pao
文學年報

Wen-wu
文物

Wen-wu Ts'an-k'ao Tzŭ-liao
文物參考資料

GLOSSARY

Yen-ching Hsüeh-pao
燕京學報

Yü-kung [Pan-yüeh-k'an]
禹貢[半月刊]

Authors, Books and Papers

An Chih-min, 'Cheng-Chou Shih Jen-min Kung-yüan fu-chin-ti Yin-tai i-ts'un'.
安志敏 鄭州市人民公園附近的殷代遺存

An Chih-min, 'Chung-Kuo Hsin-shih-ch'i shih-tai k'ao-ku-hsüeh-shang-ti chu-yao ch'eng-chiu'.
安志敏 中国新石器时代考古学上的主要成就

An Chih-min, 'Chung-Kuo ku-tai-ti shih-tao'.
安志敏 中國古代的石刀

An Chih-min, 'Ho-pei Ch'ü-yang tiao-ch'a-chi'.
安志敏 河北曲陽調查記

An Chih-min, 'I-chiu-wu-erh-nien ch'iu-chi Cheng-Chou Erh-li Kang fa-chüeh-chi'.
安志敏 一九五二年秋季鄭州二里岡發掘記

An Chih-min, 'I-chiu-wu-liu-nien-ch'iu Ho-nan Shan-Hsien fa-chüeh chien-pao'.
安志敏 一九五六年秋河南陝縣發掘簡報

An Chih-min, 'Kuan-yü An-yang Hou-kang hsün-tsang yüan-k'eng-ti shuo-ming'.
安志敏 關於安陽後岡殉葬圓坑的說明

An Chih-min, 'Shih-lun Huang-ho-liu-yü Hsin-shih-ch'i shih-tai wen-hua'.
安志敏 試論黃河流域新石器时代文化

An Chih-min, Cheng Nai-wu, Hsieh Tuan-chü, *Miao-ti Kou yü San-li Ch'iao*.
安志敏 郑乃武 謝端琚 廟底溝與三里橋

GLOSSARY

An Chih-min, Chiang Ping-hsin, Ch'en Chih-ta, '1958–1959-nien Yin-hsü fa-chüeh chien-pao'.
安志敏 江秉信 陈志达 1958–1959年殷墟发掘簡報

An Chih-min, Lin Shou-chin, 'I-chiu-wu-ssŭ-nien ch'iu-chi Lo-yang hsi-chiao fa-chüeh chien-pao'.
安志敏 林壽晋 一九五四年秋季洛陽西郊發掘簡報

An Chin-huai, 'Cheng-Chou Shih ku-i-chih, mu-tsang-ti chung-yao fa-hsien'
安金槐 鄭州市古遺址、墓葬的重要發現

An Chin-huai, 'Cheng-Chou ti-ch'ü-ti ku-tai i-ts'un chieh-shao'.
安金槐 郑州地区的古代遺存介紹

An Chin-huai, 'Shih-lun Cheng-Chou Shang-tai ch'eng-chih – Ao-tu'.
安金槐 試論郑州商代城址——隞都

An Chin-huai, 'T'ang-yin Ch'ao-ko Chen fa-hsien Lung-shan ho Shang-tai-teng wen-hua i-chih'.
安金槐 湯陰朝歌鎮發現龙山和商代等文化遺址

Ao Ch'eng-lung, 'Ho-pei Tz'ŭ-Hsien Chiang-wu Ch'eng tiao-ch'a chien-pao'.
敖承隆 河北磁縣講武城調查簡報

Chang Chien-chung, 'Cheng-Chou Shih Pai-chia Chuang Shang-tai mu-tsang fa-chüeh chien-pao'.
張建中 鄭州市白家莊商代墓葬發掘簡報

Chang Hsin-cheng, *Wei-shu T'ung-k'ao*.
張心澂 偽書通考

Chang Hsüeh-cheng, 'Wei-ho shang-yu T'ien-shui, K'an-ku liang-hsien k'ao-ku tiao-ch'a chien-pao'.
張學正 渭河上游天水、甘谷兩縣考古調查簡報

Chang Kuang-chih, 'Chung-Kuo Hsin-shih-ch'i shih-tai wen-hua tuan-tai'.
張光直 中國新石器時代文化斷代

Chang Kuang-chih, 'Chung-Kuo yüan-ku-shih-tai i-shih-sheng-huo-ti jo-kan tzŭ-liao'.
張光直 中國遠古時代儀式生活的若干資料

GLOSSARY

Chang Kuang-chih, 'Kuan-yü "Shang-wang miao-hao hsin-k'ao" i-wen-ti pu-ch'ung i-chien'.
張光直 關於"商王廟號新考"一文的補充意見

Chang Kuang-chih, 'Shang-Chou shen-hua-chih fen-lei'.
張光直 商周神話之分類

Chang Kuang-chih, 'Shang-wang miao-hao hsin-k'ao'.
張光直 商王廟號新考

Chang Shou-chung, '1959-nien Hou-ma "Niu-ts'un ku-ch'eng"-nan Tung-Chou i-chih fa-chüeh chien-pao'.
張守中 1959年侯馬"牛村古城"南東周遺址發掘簡報

Chang Tung-sun, 'Ssŭ-hsiang yen-lun yü wen-hua'.
張東蓀 思想言論與文化

Chang Yin-lin, 'Chou-tai-ti feng-chien she-hui'.
張蔭麟 周代的封建社會

Chao Ch'ing-fang, 'Nan-ching Shih Pei-yin-yang Ying ti-i, erh-tz'ŭ-ti fa-chüeh'.
趙青芳 南京市北陰陽營第一、二次的發掘

Chao Ch'ing-yün, '1957-nien Cheng-Chou hsi-chiao fa-chüeh chi-yao : 4 : Tung-Chai Shang-tai yü Chou-tai wen-hua i-chih-ti fa-chüeh'.
赵青云 1957年郑州西郊发掘记要 四 董砦商代与周代文化遗址的发掘

Chao Ch'ing-yün, Chao Shih-kang, Liu Hsiao-ch'un, Chang Ching-an, '1958-nien-ch'un Ho-nan An-yang Shih Ta-ssŭ-k'ung Ts'un Yin-tai mu-tsang fa-chüeh chien-pao'.
赵青云 赵世綱 刘笑春 张静安 1958年春河南安阳市大司空村殷代墓葬发掘簡报

Chao Ch'ing-yün, Liu Tung-ya, 'Cheng-Chou Ko-ta-wang Ts'un i-chih fa-chüeh pao-kao'.
趙青雲 劉東亞 鄭州旭畜王村遺址發掘報告

Chao Ch'üan-ku, Han Wei-chou, P'ei Ming-hsiang, An Chin-huai, 'Cheng-Chou Shang-tai i-chih-ti fa-chüeh.'
趙全古 韓維周 裴明相 安金槐 鄭州商代遺址的發掘

GLOSSARY

Chao Hsia-kuang, 'An-yang Shih hsi-chiao-ti Yin-tai wen-hua i-chih'.
赵霞光　安阳市西郊的殷代文化遗址

Chao Hsia-kuang, 'Cheng-Chou Nan-kuan-wai Shang-tai i-chih fa-chüeh chien-pao'.
趙霞光　鄭州南關外商代遺址發掘簡報

Chao I, 'Kai-yü ts'ung-k'ao,' Ou-pei Ch'üan-chi.
趙　翼　陔餘叢考　甌北全集

Cheng-Chou Shih Wen-wu Kung-tso-tsu, 'Cheng-Chou Shih Yin-Shang i-chih ti-ts'eng kuan-hsi chieh-shao'.
鄭州市文物工作組　鄭州市殷商遺址地層關係介紹

Chien Po-tsan, Chung-Kuo Shih-kang.
翦伯贊　中國史綱

Chou Chao-lin, Mou Yung-hang, 'Cheng-Chou fa-hsien-ti Shang-tai chih-t'ao i-chi'.
周兆麟　牟永杭　鄭州發現的商代製陶遺跡

Chou Hung-hsiang, Shang-Yin Ti-wang Pen-chi.
周鴻翔　商殷帝王本紀

Chou Tao, 'K'ao-ku Tung-t'ai : Ho-nan Hsin-hsiang Lung-shan wen-hua i-chih tiao-ch'a'.
周　到　考古動態：河南新乡龙山文化遺址調查

Chu K'o-chen, 'Erh-shih-pa hsiu ch'i-yüan-chih ti-tien yü shih-chien.'
竺可楨　二十八宿起源之地點與時間

Chuang Tung-ming, 'T'eng-Hsien Ku-Hsüeh-Ch'eng fa-hsien Chan-Kuo-shih-tai yeh-t'ieh i-chih'.
庄冬明　滕县古薛城發現战国时代冶铁遗址

Chuang Tung-ming, 'T'eng-Hsien Lin-Ch'eng ch'a-te ku-i-chih i-ch'u'.
庄冬明　滕县临城查得古遗址一处

Chung-Kuo K'e-hsüeh Yüan K'ao-ku Yen-chiu-so Lo-yang Fa-chüeh-tui, '1959-nien Yü-hsi liu-hsien tiao-ch'a chien-pao'.
中国科学院考古研究所洛阳發掘隊　1959年豫西六县調查簡报

GLOSSARY

Ch'ang Wen-chai, 'Hou-ma ti-ch'ü ku-ch'eng-chih-ti hsin-fa-hsien'.
暢文斋 侯馬地区古城址的新发现

Ch'ang Wen-chai, 'Shan-hsi Hsiang-fen Chao-k'ang fu-chin ku-ch'eng-chih tiao-ch'a'.
暢文斋 山西襄汾趙康附近古城址調查

Ch'ang Wen-chai, Chang Shou-chung, Yang Fu-tou, 'Hou-ma Pei-hsi Chuang Tung-Chou i-chih-ti ch'ing-li'.
暢文斋 张守中 楊富斗 侯馬北西庄东周遺址的清理

Ch'en Cheng-hsiang, *Chung-kuo Fang-chih-ti Ti-li-hsüeh Chia-chih*.
陳正祥 中國方志的地理學價值

Ch'en Chia-hsiang, 'Cheng-Chou Lo-ta Miao Shang-tai i-chih shih-chüeh chien-pao'.
陳嘉祥 鄭州洛達廟商代遺址試掘簡報

Ch'en Hui, 'Ho-pei Wu-an Hsien Wu-chi ku-ch'eng-ti Chou, Han mu-tsang fa-chüeh chien-pao'.
陳 惠 河北武安縣午汲古城的周、漢墓葬发掘簡報

Ch'en Hui, T'ang Yün-ming, Sun Te-hai, 'Ho-pei T'ang-shan Shih Ta-ch'eng-shan i-chih fa-chüeh pao-kao'.
陳 惠 唐雲明 孫德海 河北唐山市大城山遺址發掘報告

Ch'en Kung-jou, 'Lo-yang Chien-pin Tung-Chou ch'eng-chih fa-chüeh pao-kao'.
陳公柔 洛陽澗濱東周城址發掘報告

Ch'en Meng-chia, 'Shang-tai-ti shen-hua yü wu-shu'.
陳夢家 商代的神話與巫術

Ch'en Meng-chia, *Yin-hsü Pu-tz'ŭ Tsung-shu*.
陳夢家 殷墟卜辭綜述

Ch'en Meng-chia, 'Yin-tai t'ung-ch'i'.
陳夢家 殷代銅器

Ch'en P'an, 'Ch'un-Ch'iu Ta-shih-piao, Lieh-kuo chüeh-hsing chi ts'un-mieh-piao chuan-i'.
陳 槃 春秋大事表列國爵姓及存滅表譔異

GLOSSARY

Ch'en Yin-k'o, *Sui-T'ang Chih-tu Yüan-yüan Lüeh-lun-kao*.
陳寅恪　隋唐制度淵源略論稿

Ch'eng Kuang-yü, Hsü Sheng-mo, *Chung-Kuo Li-shih Ti-t'u-chi*.
程光裕　徐聖謨　中國歷史地圖集

Ch'i Ssŭ-ho, 'Chan-Kuo chih-tu k'ao'.
齊思和　戰國制度考

Ch'i Ssŭ-ho, 'Chan-Kuo Ts'e chu-tso shih-tai k'ao'.
齊思和　戰國策著作時代考

Ch'i Ssŭ-ho, 'Chou-tai hsi-ming-li k'ao'.
齊思和　周代錫命禮考

Ch'i Ssŭ-ho, 'Feng-chien-chih-tu yü Ju-chia ssŭ-hsiang'.
齊思和　封建制度與儒家思想

Ch'i Ssŭ-ho, 'Hsi-Chou ti-li-k'ao'.
齊思和　西周地理考

Ch'i Ssŭ-ho, 'Meng-tzŭ ching-t'ien shuo pien'.
齊思和　孟子井田說辨

Ch'i Ssŭ-ho, 'Yen Wu fei Chou feng-kuo shuo'.
齊思和　燕吳非周封國說

Ch'ien Po-ch'üan, '"Shuo T'ien-wang Kuei wei Wu-Wang mieh Shang i-ch'ien t'ung-ch'i" i-wen-ti chi-tien shang-ch'üeh'.
錢柏泉　"說天亡設為武王滅商以前銅器"一文的幾點商榷

Ch'üan Han-sheng, 'Nan-Sung Hang-Chou-ti hsiao-fei yü wai-ti shang-p'in-chih shu-ju'.
全漢昇　南宋杭州的消費與外地商品之輸入

Ch'üan Han-sheng, 'Nan-Sung Hang-Chou-ti wai-lai shih-liao yü shih-fa'.
全漢昇　南宋杭州的外來食料與食法

Fan Hsiang-yung, *Ku-pen Chu-shu Chi-nien Chi-chiao Ting-pu*.
范祥雍　古本竹書紀年輯校訂補

Fu Chen-lun, 'Yen-Hsia-tu fa-chüeh pao-kao'.
傅振倫　燕下都發掘報告

GLOSSARY

Fu Chen-lun, 'Yen-Hsia-tu fa-chüeh-p'in-ti ch'u-pu cheng-li yü yen-chiu'.
傅振倫 燕下都發掘品的初步整理与研究

Fu Ssŭ-nien, 'Shih-Ching Chiang-i-kao', *Fu Meng-chen Hsien-sheng Chi*.
傅斯年 詩經講義稿 傅孟真先生集

Han Wei-chou, Wang Ju-lin, 'Ho-nan Hsi-hsia Hsien chi Nan-yang Shih liang-ku-ch'eng tiao-ch'a-chi'.
韓維周 王儒林 河南西峽縣及南陽市兩古城調查記

Hang Te-chou, Lo Chung-ju, T'ien Hsing-nung, 'T'ang Ch'ang-an Ch'eng ti-chi ch'u-pu t'an-ts'e'.
杭德州 雒忠如 田醒農 唐長安城地基初步探測

Ho-nan Sheng Wen-hua-chü, *Cheng-Chou Erh-li Kang*.
河南省文化局 鄭州二里岡

Ho-nan Sheng Wen-hua-chü Wen-wu Kung-tso-tui, 'Cheng-Chou Shang-chieh Shang-tai i-chih-ti fa-chüeh'.
河南省文化局文物工作队 鄭州上街商代遺址的發掘

Ho-nan Wen-wu Kung-tso-tui Ti-erh-tui Sun-ch'i T'un Ch'ing-li Hsiao-tsu, 'Lo-yang Chien-hsi Sun-ch'i T'un ku-i-chih'.
河南文物工作隊第二隊孫旗屯清理小組 洛陽澗西孫旗屯古遺址

Ho-pei Sheng Wen-hua-chü Fa-chüeh-tsu, 'Hsing-T'ai Shih fa-hsien Shang-tai i-chih'.
河北省文化局發掘組 邢台市發現商代遺址

Hou Wai-lu, *Chung-Kuo Ku-tai She-hui-shih*.
侯外廬 中國古代社會史

Hsieh Ch'un-chu, 'Yen-Ch'eng fa-hsien Chan-Kuo-shih-ch'i-ti tu-mu-ch'uan'.
謝春祝 奄城发現战國時期的独木船

Hsieh Hsi-i, 'Yen-Hsia-tu i-chih so-chi'.
謝錫益 燕下都遺址瑣記

Hsieh Wei-chieh, *Chin-T'ang Hsien Chih*.
謝惟傑 金堂縣志

Hsü Chin-hsiung, 'Tui Chang Kuang-chih Hsien-sheng-ti "Shang-wang miao-hao hsin-k'ao"-ti chi-tien i-chien'.
許進雄 對張光直先生的"商王廟號新考"的幾點意見

GLOSSARY

Hsü Cho-yün, 'Kuan-yü "Shang-wang miao-hao hsin-k'ao" i-wen-ti chi-tien i-chien'.
許倬雲　關於"商王廟號新考"一文的幾點意見

Hsü Chung-shu, 'Ching-t'ien chih-tu t'an-yüan'.
徐中舒　井田制度探原

Hsü Chung-shu, 'Lei-ssŭ k'ao'.
徐中舒　耒耜考

Hsü I, ' "Yin-tai Ti-li Chien-lun" p'ing-chieh'.
許　藝　"殷代地理簡論"評介

Hu Chih-hsin, 'Chuang-tzŭ k'ao-cheng'.
胡芝薪　莊子攷證

Hu Hou-hsüan, *Chia-ku-hsüeh Shang-shih Lun-ts'ung*.
胡厚宣　甲骨學商史論叢

Hu Hou-hsüan, *Li-shih Yen-chiu*.
胡厚宣　歷史研究

Hu Hou-hsüan, *Wu-shih-nien Chia-ku-hsüeh Lun-chu-mu*.
胡厚宣　五十年甲骨學論著目

Hu Hou-hsüan, *Yin-hsü Fa-chüeh*.
胡厚宣　殷墟發掘

Hu Hou-hsüan, 'Yin-tai feng-chien-chih-tu k'ao', *Chia-ku-hsüeh Shang-shih Lun-ts'ung*.
胡厚宣　殷代封建制度考　甲骨學商史論叢

Hu Shih, 'Ching-t'ien pien', *Hu-Shih Wen-ts'un*.
胡　適　井田辨　胡適文存

Hu Yüeh-ch'ien, 'An-hui Hsin-shih-ch'i shih-tai i-chih-ti tiao-ch'a'.
胡悅謙　安徽新石器時代遺址的調查

Hua Chüeh-ming, Yang Ken, Liu En-chu, 'Chan-Kuo Liang-Han t'ieh-ch'i-ti chin-hsiang-hsüeh k'ao-ch'a ch'u-pu pao-kao'.
華覺民　楊　根　劉恩珠　戰國兩漢鐵器的金相學考查初步報告

Huang Chan-yüeh, 'Chin-nien ch'u-t'u-ti Chan-Kuo Liang-Han t'ieh-ch'i'.
黃展岳　近年出土的戰國兩漢鐵器

GLOSSARY

Huang Ching-lüeh, 'Yen-Hsia-tu ch'eng-chih tiao-ch'a pao-kao'.
黃景略 燕下都城址調查報告

Huang-ho Shui-k'u K'ao-ku-tui Hua-Hsien-tui, 'Shan-hsi [Shensi] Hua-Hsien Liu-tzǔ Chen k'ao-ku fa-chüeh chien-pao'.
黃河水庫考古隊華縣隊 陝西华县柳子鎮考古发掘簡报

Huang-ho Shui-k'u K'ao-ku-tui Hua-Hsien-tui, 'Shan-hsi [Shensi] Hua-Hsien Liu-tzǔ Chen ti-erh-tz'ǔ fa-chüeh-ti chu-yao shou-huo'.
黃河水庫考古队華縣队 陝西華縣柳子鎮第二次發掘的主要收獲

Hui Tung, *Ming-T'ang Ta-tao Lu*.
惠　棟　明堂大道錄

Hung Chün-p'ei, *Ch'un-Ch'iu Kuo-chi Kung-fa*.
洪鈞培　春秋國際公法

Hung Liang-chi, 'Ch'un-Ch'iu-shih i ta-i wei hsien shih-yü Ch'u lun', *Keng-sheng-chai Wen Chia-chi*.
洪亮吉　春秋時以大邑爲縣始于楚論　更生齋文甲集

Hung Yeh, Nieh Ch'ung-ch'i, Lee Shu-ch'un, Ma Hsi-yung, *Ch'un-Ch'iu Ching-chuan Yin-te*.
洪　業　聶崇岐　李書春　馬錫用　春秋經傳引得

Jao Tsung-i, *Yin-tai Chen-pu Jen-wu T'ung-k'ao*.
饒宗頤　殷代貞卜人物通考

Jen Pu-yün, 'Kan-su Ch'in-an Hsien Hsin-shih-ch'i shih-tai chü-chu i-chih'.
任步雲　甘肅秦安縣新石器時代居住遺址

Kao Ch'ü-hsün, 'Hsiao-ch'en Hsi shih-kuei-ti ts'an-p'ien yü ming-wen'.
高去尋　小臣艅石殷的殘片與銘文

Kao Yün-hui, 'Chou-tai t'u-ti-chih-tu yü ching-t'ien'.
高耘暉　周代土地制度與井田

Ku Chi-kuang, 'Chan-Kuo Ch'in-Han-chien chung-nung-ch'ing-shang-chih li-lun yü shih-chi'.
谷霽光　戰國秦漢間重農輕商之理論與實際

Ku Chieh-kang, 'Ch'un-Ch'iu-shih-tai-ti hsien'.
顧頡剛　春秋時代的縣

GLOSSARY

Ku Chieh-kang, *Han-tai Hsüeh-shu Shih-lüeh*.
顧頡剛　漢代學術史略

Ku Chieh-kang, 'Yü Ch'ien Hsüan-t'ung Hsien-sheng lun ku-shih-shu', *Ku-Shih Pien*.
顧頡剛　與錢玄同先生論古史書　古史辨

Ku Chieh-kang, Lo Ken-tse, *Ku-Shih Pien*.
顧頡剛　羅根澤　古史辨

Ku Yen-wu, *Li-tai Ti-wang Chai-ching-chi : Han Ch'ang-an Ku-ch'eng*.
顧炎武　歷代帝王宅京記　漢長安故城

Kuo Mo-jo, 'An-yang yüan-k'eng-mu-chung ting-ming k'ao-shih'.
郭沫若　安陽圓坑墓中鼎銘考釋

Kuo Mo-jo, *Ch'ing-t'ung Shih-tai*.
郭沫若　青銅時代

Kuo Mo-jo, *Chung-Kuo Ku-tai She-hui Yen-chiu*.
郭沫若　中國古代社會研究

Kuo Mo-jo, *Liang-Chou Chin-wen-tz'ŭ Ta-hsi K'ao-shih*.
郭沫若　兩周金文辭大系攷釋

Kuo Mo-jo, *Nu-li-chih Shih-tai*.
郭沫若　奴隸制時代

Kuo Mo-jo, *Pu-tz'ŭ T'ung-tsuan*.
郭沫若　卜辭通纂

Kuo Mo-jo, *Shih P'i-p'an Shu*.
郭沫若　十批判書

Kuo Pao-chün, 'I-chiu-wu-ling-nien-ch'un Yin-hsü fa-chüeh pao-kao'.
郭寶鈞　一九五〇年春殷墟發掘報告

Kuo Pao-chün, 'Lo-yang Chien-pin ku-wen-hua i-chih chi Han-mu'.
郭寶鈞　洛陽澗濱古文化遺址及漢墓

Kuo Pao-chün, 'Lo-yang ku-ch'eng k'an-ch'a chien-pao'.
郭寶鈞　洛陽古城勘察簡報

Kuo Pao-chün, Hsia Nai, *Hui-Hsien Fa-chüeh Pao-kao*.
郭寶鈞　夏鼐　輝縣發掘報告

GLOSSARY

Kuo Pao-chün, Lin Shou-chin, 'I-chiu-wu-erh-nien ch'iu-chi Lo-yang tung-chiao fa-chüeh pao-kao'.
郭寶鈞 林壽晉 一九五二年秋季洛陽东郊發掘報告

Kuo Te-yung, 'Kan-su Wei-ho shang-yu Wei-yüan, Lung-hsi, Wu-shan san-hsien k'ao-ku tiao-ch'a'.
郭德勇 甘肅渭河上游渭源、隴西、武山、三县考古調查

Kuo Te-yung, 'Kan-su Wu-wei Huang-niang-niang T'ai i-chih fa-chüeh pao-kao'.
郭德勇 甘肅武威皇娘娘台遺址發掘报告

K'ang Yu-wei, *Hsin-hsüeh Wei-ching K'ao*.
康有爲 新學僞經考

K'ao-ku-so Pao-chi Fa-chüeh-tui, 'Shan-hsi [Shensi] Pao-chi Hsin-shih-ch'i shih-tai i-chih fa-chüeh chi-yao'.
考古所宝雞發掘隊 陝西宝雞新石器时代遺址發掘記要

K'ao-ku Yen-chiu-so Hsi-an Pan-p'o Kung-tso-tui, 'Hsi-an Pan-p'o i-chih ti-erh-tz'ŭ fa-chüeh-ti chu-yao shou-huo'.
考古研究所西安半坡工作隊 西安半坡遺址第二次發掘的主要收穫

Lao Kan, 'Ch'un-Ch'iu Ta-shih-piao, Lieh-kuo chüeh-hsing chi ts'un-mieh-piao Chuan-i chung-p'ien Pa'.
勞 榦 春秋大事表 列國爵姓及存滅表 譔異中篇跋

Li Chi, *An-yang Fa-chüeh Pao-kao*.
李 濟 安陽發掘報告

Li Chi, *Ch'eng-tzŭ Yai*.
李 濟 城子崖

Li Chi, *Hsi-yin Ts'un shih-ch'ien-ti i-ts'un*.
李 濟 西陰村史前的遺存

Li Chi, 'Hsiao-T'un t'ao-ch'i chih-liao-chih hua-hsüeh fen-hsi', *Kuo-li T'ai-wan Ta-hsüeh Fu Ku-hsiao-chang Ssŭ-nien Hsien-sheng Chi-nien Lun-wen-chi*.
李 濟 小屯陶器質料之化學分析 國立臺灣大學傅故校長斯年先生紀念論文集

GLOSSARY

Li Chi, *Hsiao-T'un : Yin-hsü Ch'i-wu : T'ao-ch'i.*
李　濟　小屯　殷虛器物　陶器

Li Chi, 'Lun "Tao-sen-shih Hsiao-jen" an-chien chi yüan-shih tzǔ-liao-chih chien-ting yü ch'u-li'.
李　濟　論「道森氏、曉人」案件及原始資料之鑒定與處理

Li Chi, 'Yen-chiu Chung-Kuo ku-jü wen-t'i-ti hsin-tzǔ-liao'.
李　濟　研究中國古玉問題的新資料

Li Chi, 'Yin-hsü yu-jen shih-ch'i t'u-shuo'.
李　濟　殷墟有刃石器圖說

Li-Chi, 'Yu chi-hsing yen-pien so-k'an-chien-ti Hsiao-T'un i-chih yü Hou-chia Chuang mu-tsang-chih shih-tai kuan-hsi'.
李　濟　由笄形演變所看見的小屯遺址與侯家莊墓葬之時代關係

Li Chien-nung, 'Ch'e chu kung'.
李劍農　徹助貢

Li Chien-nung, *Chung-Kuo Ching-chi Shih-kao.*
李劍農　中國經濟史稿

Li Chien-yung, P'ei Ch'i, Chia Ngo [O], 'Lo-ning Hsien Lo-ho liang-an ku-i-chih tiao-ch'a chien-pao'.
李健永　裴琪　賈峨　洛寧縣洛河兩岸古遺址調查簡報

Li Ching-ch'ih 'Chou-I shih-tz'ǔ hsü-k'ao'.
李鏡池　周易筮辭續考

Li Chün-chih, 'Lü-Shih-Ch'un-Ch'iu-chung ku-shu chi-i', *Ku-Shih Pien.*
李峻之　呂氏春秋中古書輯佚　古史辨

Li Hsüeh-ch'in, *Yin-tai Ti-li Chien-lun.*
李學勤　殷代地理簡論

Li Pu-ch'ing, 'Chi-nan Ta-hsin Chuang i-chih shih-chüeh chien-pao'.
李步青　济南大辛庄遺址試掘簡報

Li Te-pao, 'Ho-nan Wei-ho chih-hung kung-ch'eng-chung-ti k'ao-ku tiao-ch'a chien-pao'.
李德寶　河南衛河滯洪工程中的考古調查簡報

GLOSSARY

Li Tung-fang, *Ch'un-Ch'iu Chan-Kuo P'ien* (*Chung-Kuo Li-shih T'ung-lun*).
黎東方　春秋戰國篇　中國歷史通論

Li Ya-nung, *Yin-tai She-hui Sheng-huo*.
李亞農　殷代社會生活

Li Yang-sung, 'Tui Wo-Kuo niang-chiu ch'i-yüan-ti t'an-t'ao'.
李仰松　对我国釀酒起源的探討

Li Yang-sung, Yen Wen-ming, 'Lo-yang Wang-wan i-chih fa-chüeh chien-pao'.
李仰松　严文明　洛阳王湾遗址发掘简报

Li Yü-ch'un, 'Shan-hsi [Shensi] Hua-yin Yüeh-Chen Chan-Kuo ku-ch'eng k'an-ch'a-chi'.
李遇春　陝西華陰岳鎮戰國古城勘查記

Liang Ssŭ-yung, 'Hsiao-T'un, Lung-shan yü Yang-shao', *Kuo-li Chung-yang Yen-chiu-yüan Li-shih Yü-yen Yen-chiu-so Ch'ing-chu Ts'ai Yüan-p'ei Hsien-sheng Liu-shih-wu-sui Lun-wen Chi*.
梁思永　小屯龍山與仰韶　國立中央研究院歷史語言研究所　慶祝蔡元培先生六十五歲論文集

Liang Ssŭ-yung, 'Hou-kang fa-chüeh hsiao-chi', *An-yang Fa-chüeh Pao-kao*.
梁思永　後岡發掘小記　安陽發掘報告

Liang Ssŭ-yung, 'Lung-shan Wen-hua – Chung-Kuo wen-ming-ti shih-ch'ien-ch'i-chih-i'.
梁思永　龍山文化—中國文明的史前期之一

Liang Ssŭ-yung, Kao Ch'ü-hsün, *Hou-chia Chuang*.
梁思永　高去尋　侯家莊

Liao Yung-min, 'Cheng-Chou Shih fa-hsien-ti i-ch'u Shang-tai chü-chu yü chu-tsao-t'ung-ch'i i-chih chien-chieh'.
廖永民　郑州市發現的一處商代居住与鑄造銅器遺址簡介

Lin Heng-li, 'P'ing Chang Kuang-chih "Shang-wang miao-hao hsin-k'ao"-chung-ti lun-cheng-fa'.
林衡立　評張光直"商王廟號新考"中的論證法

GLOSSARY

Ling Ch'un-sheng, 'Chung-Kuo tsu-miao-ti ch'i-yüan'.
凌純聲　中國祖廟的起源

Ling Chu'n-sheng, 'Pu-tz'ŭ-chung she-chih yen-chiu'.
凌純聲　卜辭中社之研究

Liu Chi-i, ' "Ao-tu" chih-i'.
刘启益　"隩都"质疑

Liu Chih-p'ing, Fu Hsi-nien, 'Lin-te Tien fu-yüan-ti ch'u-pu yen-chiu'.
刘致平　傅熹年　麟德殿复原的初步研究

Liu E, *T'ieh-yün Ts'ang-kuei*.
劉　鶚　鐵雲藏龜

Liu Hsiao-ch'un, 'I-chiu-wu-wu-nien-ch'iu An-yang Hsiao-T'un Yin-hsü-ti fa-chüeh'.
劉笑春　一九五五年秋安陽小屯殷墟的發掘

Liu Ju-lin, 'Lü-Shih-Ch'un-Ch'iu-chih fen-hsi', *Ku-Shih Pien*.
劉汝霖　呂氏春秋之分析　古史辨

Liu Pin-hsiung, 'Yin-Shang wang-shih shih-fen-tsu-chih shih-lun'.
劉斌雄　殷商王室十分組制試論

Liu Tung-ya, 'Ho-nan An-yang Hsüeh-chia Chuang Yin-tai i-chih, mu-tsang ho T'ang-mu fa-chüeh chien-pao'.
刘东亚　河南安阳薛家庄殷代遺址、墓葬和唐墓發掘簡報

Liu Wen-tien, *Chuang-tzŭ Pu-cheng*.
劉文典　莊子補正

Liu Yao, 'Ho-nan Chün-Hsien Ta-lai Tien shih-ch'ien i-chih'.
劉　耀　河南濬縣大賚店史前遺址

Liu Yao, 'Lung-shan Wen-hua yü Yang-shao Wen-hua-chih fen-hsi'.
劉　耀　龍山文化與仰韶文化之分析

Liu Yung-neng, ' "Miao-ti Kou yü San-li Ch'iao" wen-hua hsing-chih-ti chi-ko wen-t'i'.
柳用能　"庙底沟与三里桥"文化性質的几個問題

Lo Chen-yü, *Yin-hsü Shu-ch'i ch'ien-pien*.
羅振玉　殷虛書契前編

GLOSSARY

Lo Chen-yü, *Yin-hsü Shu-ch'i Ching-hua*.
羅振玉 殷虛書契菁華

Lo Ken-tse, *Kuan-tzǔ T'an-yüan*.
羅根澤 管子探源

Lü Chen-yü, *Chung-Kuo Cheng-chih Ssǔ-hsiang-shih*.
呂振羽 中國政治思想史

Lü Chen-yü, *Chung-Kuo She-hui Shih-kang*.
呂振羽 中國社會史綱

Ma Ch'eng-yüan, 'Man-t'an Chan-Kuo ch'ing-t'ung-ch'i-shang-ti hua-hsiang'.
馬承源 漫談戰國青銅器上的畫像

Ma Ch'üan, 'Cheng-Chou Shih Ming-kung Lu hsi-ts'e-ti Shang-tai i-ts'un'.
馬全 鄭州市銘功路西側的商代遺存

Ma Ch'üan, Mao Pao-liang, 'Cheng-Chou fa-hsien-ti chi-ko-shih-ch'i-ti ku-tai yao-chih'.
馬全 毛寶亮 鄭州發現的几個時期的古代窰址

Ma Te-chih, 'T'ang-tai Ch'ang-an Ch'eng k'ao-ku chi-lüeh'.
馬得志 唐代長安城考古紀略

Ma Te-chih, Chou Yung-chen, Chang Yün-p'eng, 'I-chiu-wu-san-nien An-yang Ta-ssǔ-k'ung Ts'un fa-chüeh pao-kao'.
馬得志 周永珍 張雲鵬 一九五三年安陽大司空村發掘報告

Mao Pao-liang, 'Cheng-Chou hsi-chiao Yang-shao wen-hua i-chih fa-chüeh chien-pao'.
毛寶亮 鄭州西郊仰韶文化遺址發掘簡報

Mao Tse-tung, *Chung-Kuo Ke-ming ho Chung-Kuo Kung-ch'an-tang*.
毛澤東 中國革命和中國共產黨

Mei Fu-ken, 'Hang-Chou Shui-t'ien Fan i-chih fa-chüeh pao-kao'.
梅福根 杭州水田畈遺址發掘報告

Meng Hao, 'Ho-pei Wu-an Hsien Wu-chi ku-ch'eng-chung-ti yao-chih'.
孟浩 河北武安縣午汲古城中的窰址

Meng Hao, Ch'en Hui, Liu Lai-ch'eng, 'Ho-pei Wu-an Wu-chi ku-ch'eng fa-chüeh-chi'.
孟浩 陳慧 劉來城 河北武安午汲古城發掘記

GLOSSARY

Ni Chen-kuei, 'Yen-Ch'eng ch'u-t'u-ti t'ung-ch'i'.
倪振逵 淹城出土的銅器

Pei-ching Ta-hsüeh, Ho-pei Sheng Wen-hua-chü Han-tan K'ao-ku Fa-chüeh-tui, '1957-nien Han-tan fa-chüeh chien-pao'.
北京大學,河北省文化局邯鄲考古發掘隊 1957年邯鄲發掘簡報

P'ei Wen-chung, *Chung-Kuo Shih-ch'ien-shih-ch'i-chih Yen-chiu*.
裴文中 中國史前時期之研究

Shan-hsi Sheng Wen-wu Kuan-li Wei-yüan-hui, 'Shan-hsi Sheng Wen-kuan-hui Hou-ma Kung-tso-chan kung-tso-ti tsung-shou-huo'.
山西省文物管理委員會 山西省文管会侯馬工作站工作的总收获

Shan-hsi [Shensi] Sheng Wen-wu Kuan-li Wei-yüan-hui, 'Ch'ang-an Chang-chia-p'o Ts'un Hsi-Chou i-chih-ti chung-yao fa-hsien'.
陝西省文物管理委員会 長安張家坡村西周遺址的重要發現

Shan-tung Sheng Wen-wu Kuan-li-ch'u, 'Shan-tung Lin-tzŭ Ch'i-ku-ch'eng shih-chüeh chien-pao'.
山東省文物管理处 山东临淄齐故城試掘簡报

Shang Ch'eng-tso, *Yin-hsü Wen-tzŭ Lei-pien*.
商承祚 殷虛文字類編

Shih Chang-ju, 'Chou-tu i-chi yü Ts'ai-tao i-ts'un'.
石璋如 周都遺跡與彩陶遺存

Shih Chang-ju, 'Hsiao-T'un C-ch'ü-ti mu-tsang-ch'ün'.
石璋如 小屯C區的墓葬群

Shih Chang-ju, *Hsiao-T'un : I-chih-ti Fa-hsien yü Fa-chüeh : Chien-chu I-ts'un*.
石璋如 小屯遺址的發現與發掘 建築遺存

Shih Chang-ju, 'Hsiao-T'un Yin-tai-ti chien-chu i-chi'.
石璋如 小屯殷代的建築遺蹟

Shih Chang-ju, 'Ho-nan An-yang Hou-Kang-ti Yin-mu'.
石璋如 河南安陽後岡的殷墓

Shih Chang-ju, 'Ku-pu yü kuei-pu t'an-yüan'.
石璋如 骨卜與龜卜探源

GLOSSARY

Shih Chang-ju, 'Kuan-chung k'ao-ku tiao-ch'a pao-kao'.
石璋如 關中考古調查報告

Shih Chang-ju, 'Yin-hsü fa-chüeh tui-yü Chung-Kuo ku-tai wen-hua-ti kung-hsien'.
石璋如 殷虛發掘對於中國古代文化的貢獻

Shih Chang-ju, 'Yin-hsü tsui-chin-chih chung-yao fa-hsien. Fu : Lun Hsiao-T'un ti-ts'eng'.
石璋如 殷墟最近之重要發現附論小屯地層

Shih Chang-ju, 'Yin-tai-ti chu-t'ung kung-i'.
石璋如 殷代的鑄銅工藝

Shih-Chang-ju, 'Yin-tai ti-shang-chien-chu fu-yüan-chih i-li'.
石璋如 殷代地上建築復原之一例

Shih Hsing-pang, 'Hsin-shih-ch'i shih-tai ts'un-lo i-chih-ti fa-hsien – Hsi-an Pan-p'o'.
石興邦 新石器時代村落遺址的發現──西安半坡

Shou T'ien, 'T'ai-yüan Kuan-she Hsin-shih-ch'i shih-tai i-chih-ti fa-hsien yü tsao-yü'.
壽 田 太原光社新石器時代遺址的發現与遭遇

Su Ping-chi, *Tou-chi T'ai Kou-tung-ch'ü Mu-tsang*.
蘇秉琦 鬥雞臺溝東區墓葬

Su Ping-chi, Wu Ju-tso, 'Hsi-an fu-chin ku-wen-hua i-ts'un-ti lei-hsing ho fen-pu'.
苏秉琦 吳汝祚 西安附近古文化遺存的類型和分佈

Sun Hai-po, *Chia-ku-wen Pien*.
孫海波 甲骨文編

Sun I-jang, *Ch'i-wen Chü-li*.
孫詒讓 契文舉例

Sun Tso-yün, 'Shuo "T'ien-wang Kuei" wei Wu-Wang mieh Shang i-ch'ien t'ung-ch'i'.
孙作云 說"天亡殷"为武王灭商以前銅器

GLOSSARY

Sun Tso-yün, 'Tsai lun "T'ien-wang Kuei" erh-san-shih'.
孫作云 再論"天亡毁"二三事

Sun Yao, *Ch'un-Ch'iu Shih-tai-chih Shih-tsu*.
孫 曜 春秋時代之世族

Ting Fu-pao, *Shuo-wen Chieh-tzǔ Ku-lin*.
丁福保 說文解字詁林

Ting Shan, *Chia-ku-wen so-chien Shih-tsu chi-ch'i Chih-tu*.
丁 山 甲骨文所見氏族及其制度

Ting Su, 'Hua-pei ti-hsing-shih yü Shang-Yin-ti li-shih'.
丁 驌 華北地形史與商殷的歷史

Ting Su, 'Lun Yin-wang-p'i shih-fa'.
丁 驌 論殷王妣謚法

Tjan Tjoe Som [Tseng Chu-sen], *Po-hu T'ung*.
曾珠森 白虎通

Tsang Li-ho, *Chung-Kuo Ku-chin Ti-ming Ta-tz'ǔ-tien*.
臧勵龢 中國古今地名大辭典

Tseng Chao-yü, Yin Huan-chang, 'Shih-lun Hu-shu wen-hua'.
曾昭燏 尹煥章 試論湖熟文化

Tsou Heng, 'Shih-lun Cheng-Chou hsin-fa-hsien-ti Yin-Shang wen-hua i-chih'.
鄒 衡 試論鄭州新發現的殷商文化遺址

Tung Hung, 'Cheng-Chou Pai-chia Chuang i-chih fa-chüeh chien-pao'.
東 紅 鄭州白家庄遺址發掘簡報

Tung Hung, 'Cheng-Chou Shih Jen-Min Kung-yüan ti-erh-shih-wu-hao Shang-tai mu-tsang ch'ing-li chien-pao'.
東 紅 鄭州市人民公園第二十五號商代墓葬清理簡報

Tung Tso-pin, 'An-yang Hou-chia Chuang ch'u-t'u-chih chia-ku wen-tzǔ'.
董作賓 安陽侯家莊出土之甲骨文字

Tung Tso-pin, 'Ch'eng-tzǔ Yai yü Lung-shan Chen', *Ch'eng-tzǔ Yai*.
董作賓 城子崖與龍山鎮 城子崖

Tung Tso-pin, *Chia-ku-hsüeh Wu-shih-nien*.
董作賓 甲骨學五十年

GLOSSARY

Tung Tso-pin, 'Chia-ku-wen tuan-tai yen-chiu-li', *Kuo-li Chung-yang Yen-chiu-yüan Li-shih Yü-yen Yen-chiu-so Ch'ing-chu Tsai Yüan-p'ei Hsien-sheng Liu-shih-wu-sui Lun-wen Chi.*
董作賓 甲骨文斷代研究例 國立中央研究院歷史語言研究所 慶祝蔡元培先生六十五歲論文集

Tung Tso-pin, 'Chung-Kuo shang-ku-shih nien-tai'.
董作賓 中國上古史年代

Tung Tso-pin, 'Chung-Kuo wen-tzŭ-ti ch'i-yüan'.
董作賓 中國文字的起原

Tung Tso-pin, *Hsiao T'un : Yin-hsü Wen-tzŭ.*
董作賓 小屯 殷虛文字

Tung Tso-pin, 'Kuan-yü ku-shih nien-tai-hsüeh-ti wen-t'i'.
董作賓 關於古史年代學的問題

Tung Tso-pin, 'T'an "T'an" '.
董作賓 譚譚

Tung Tso-pin, 'Tsai-t'an Yin-tai ch'i-hou'.
董作賓 再談殷代氣候

Tung Tso-pin, 'Wu-teng Chüeh tsai Yin-Shang'.
董作賓 五等爵在殷商

Tung Tso-pin, 'Wu-Wang fa Chou nien-yüeh-jih chin-kao'.
董作賓 武王伐紂年月日今考

Tung Tso-pin, 'Yin-hsü yen-ke'.
董作賓 殷墟沿革

Tung Tso-pin, *Yin Li P'u.*
董作賓 殷曆譜

Tung Tso-pin, 'Yin Li P'u hou-chi'.
董作賓 殷曆譜後記

Tung Tso-pin, 'Yin-tai-chih li-fa nung-yeh yü ch'i-hsiang'.
董作賓 殷代之曆法農業與氣象

GLOSSARY

Tung Tso-pin, 'Yin-tai li-chih-ti hsin-chiu liang-p'ai'.
董作賓 殷代禮制的新舊兩派

Tung Tso-pin, 'Yin-tai-ti niao-shu'.
董作賓 殷代的鳥書

T'ang Lan, 'Tsai chia-ku chin-wen-chung so-chien-ti i-chung i-ching i-shih-ti Chung-Kuo ku-tai wen-tzǔ'.
唐 蘭 在甲骨金文中所見的一種已經遺失的中國古代文字

T'ang Yün-ming, 'Hsing-T'ai Hsi-kuan-wai i-chih shih-chüeh'.
唐云明 邢台西关外遺址試掘

T'ang Yün-ming, 'Hsing-T'ai Nan-ta-kuo Ts'un Shang-tai i-chih t'an-chüeh chien-pao'.
唐云明 邢台南大郭村商代遺址探掘簡報

T'ang Yün-ming, 'Hsing-T'ai Ts'ao-yen Chuang i-chih fa-chüeh pao-kao'.
唐雲明 邢台曹演莊遺址發掘報告

T'ang Yün-ming, 'Hsing-T'ai Yin-kuo Ts'un Shang-tai i-chih chi Chan-Kuo mu-tsang shih-chüeh chien-pao'.
唐云明 邢台尹郭村商代遺址及战国墓葬試掘簡报

T'ang Yün-ming, 'K'ao-ku Tung-t'ai : Ho-pei Hsing-T'ai Tung-hsien-hsien Ts'un Shang-tai i-chih tiao-ch'a'.
唐云明 考古动态 河北邢台东先賢村商代遺址調查

T'ang Yün-ming, 'Lung-shan wen-hua yü Yin wen-hua t'ao-ch'i-chien-ti kuan-hsi'.
唐云明 龙山文化与殷文化陶器間的关系

[T'ang] Yün-ming, Lo P'ing, [Ch'eng] Ming-yüan, 'Hsing-T'ai Shang-tai i-chih-chung-ti t'ao-yao'.
[唐]云明 罗 平 [程]明远 邢台商代遺址中的陶窯

T'eng Ku, *Chung-Kuo I-shu Lun-ts'ung*.
滕 固 中國藝術論叢

T'ao Hsi-sheng, *Chung-Kuo She-hui-chih Shih-ti Fen-hsi*.
陶希聖 中國社會之史的分析

Ts'ui Shu, 'Chu-Ssǔ k'ao-hsin yü-lu', *Ts'ui Tung-pi I-shu*.
崔 述 洙泗考信餘錄 崔東壁遺書

GLOSSARY

Ts'ui Shu, 'Lun-Yü yü-shuo', *Ts'ui Tung-pi I-shu.*
崔述　論語餘說　崔東壁遺書

Wang Chen-to, 'Ssŭ-nan chih-nan-chen yü lo-ching-p'an'.
王振鐸　司南指南針與羅經盤

Wang Ching, 'Hu-pei Hung-an Chin-p'en i-chih-ti t'an-chüeh'.
王勁　湖北紅安金盆遺址的探掘

Wang Chung-shu, 'Han Ch'ang-an Ch'eng k'ao-ku kung-tso shou-huo hsü-chi'.
王仲殊　漢長安城考古工作收穫續記

Wang Chung-shu, 'Han Ch'ang-an Ch'eng k'ao-ku kung-tso-ti ch'u-pu shou-huo'.
王仲殊　漢長安城考古工作的初步收穫

Wang Han-yen, 'Chou-k'ou-tien Ch'ü Ts'ai-Chuang ku-ch'eng i-chih'.
王汉彦　周口店区蔡庄古城遺址

Wang Hsiang, *Fu-shih Yin-ch'i Lei-tsuan.*
王襄　簠室殷契類纂

Wang Hsien-ch'ien, *Han-Shu Pu-chu.*
王先謙　漢書補注

Wang Kuo-wei, *Hai-ning Wang Ching-an Hsien-sheng I-shu.*
王國維　海寧王靜安先生遺書

Wang Kuo-wei, 'Ku-pen Chu-shu Chi-nien chi-chiao', *Hai-ning Wang Chung-ch'io Kung I-shu.*
王國維　古本竹書紀年輯校　海寧王忠慤公遺書

Wang Kuo-wei, *Kuan-T'ang Chi-Lin.*
王國維　觀堂集林

Wang Kuo-wei, 'Yin pu-tz'ŭ-chung so-chien hsien-kung hsien-wang k'ao', *Hai-ning Wang Chung-ch'io Kung I-shu.*
王國維　殷卜辭中所見先公先王考　海寧王忠慤公遺書

Wang Ming-jui, Chin Shih-hsin, 'Ho-nan Hsin-hsiang Lu-wang Fen Shang-tai i-chih fa-chüeh pao-kao'.
王明瑞　靳世信　河南新鄉潞王坟商代遺址發掘报告

GLOSSARY

Wang Pao-hsin, *T'ung-chih T'iao-i*.
王葆心　通志條議

Wang Po-hung, Chung Shao-lin, Chang Ch'ang-shou, '1955–57-nien Shan-hsi [Shensi] Ch'ang-an Feng-hsi fa-chüeh chien-pao'.
王伯洪　钟少林　张长寿　1955-57年陕西长安沣西发掘简报

Wang Shih-jen, 'Han Ch'ang-an Ch'eng nan-chiao li-chih-chien-chu (Ta-t'u-men Ts'un i-chih) yüan-chuang-ti t'ui-ts'e'.
王世仁　汉长安城南郊礼制建筑(大土门村遗址)原状的推测

Wei Chü-hsien, *Chung-Kuo K'ao-ku-hsüeh-shih*.
衛聚賢　中國考古學史

Weng Wen-hao, 'Ku-tai kuan-kai kung-ch'eng fa-chan-shih-chih i-chieh', *Kuo-li Chung-yang Yen-chiu-yüan Li-shih Yü-yen Yen-chiu-so Ching-chu Ts'ai Yüan-p'ei Hsien-sheng Liu-shih-wu-sui Lun-wen Chi*.
翁文灝　古代灌溉工程發展史之一解　國立中央研究院歷史語言研究所　慶祝蔡元培先生六十五歲論文集

Wu Gin-ding [Wu Chin-ting], 'P'ing-ling fang-ku chi'.
吳金鼎　平陵訪古記

Wu Ju-tso, Yang Chi-ch'ang, 'Kuan-yü "Miao-ti Kou yü San-li Ch'iao" i-shu-chung-ti chi-ko wen-t'i'.
吳汝祚　陽吉昌　关于"庙底沟与三里桥"一書中的几个問題

Yang Chi-ch'ang, 'Ho-nan Shan-Hsien Ch'i-li P'u Shang-tai i-chih-ti fa-chüeh'.
陽吉昌　河南陝縣七里鋪商代遺址的發掘

Yang Ch'i-ch'eng, 'Cheng-Chou Ti-5-wen-wu-ch'ü Ti-1-hsiao-ch'ü fa-chüeh chien-pao'.
楊啟成　鄭州第5文物区第1小区發掘簡报

Yang Chien-fang, 'An-hui Tiao-yü T'ai ch'u-t'u hsiao-mai nien-tai shang-ch'üeh'.
楊建芳　安徽釣魚台出土小麦年代商榷

GLOSSARY

Yang Chien-fang, 'P'ing "Miao-ti Kou yü San-li Ch'iao"'.
楊建芳　評"庙底沟与三里桥"

Yang Fu-tou, 'Hou-ma-hsi hsin-fa-hsien i-tso ku-ch'eng i-chih'.
楊富斗　侯馬西新發現一座古城遺址

Yang Fu-tou, 'K'ao-ku Tung-t'ai : Shan-hsi Hsiang-fen Hsien fa-hsien-ti liang-ch'u i-chih : 2 : Chao-k'ang-Chen-ti Tung-Chou ku-ch'eng-chih'.
楊富斗　考古动态　山西襄汾县发现的两处遗址　二　赵康镇的东周古城址

Yang Tzŭ-fan, 'Chi-nan Ta-hsin Chuang Shang-tai i-chih k'an-ch'a chi-yao'.
楊子范　济南大辛庄商代遺址勘查紀要

Yao Nai, *Hsi-pao Hsüan Wen-chi*.
姚　鼐　惜抱軒文集

Yin Huan-chang, 'Pa-ko-yüeh-lai-ti Cheng-Chou wen-wu kung-tso kai-k'uang'.
尹煥章　八个月來的鄭州文物工作概況

Yin Huan-chang, Li Chung-i, 'Chiang-su Hsin-i Hsien San-li Tun ku-wen-hua i-chih ti-erh-tz'ŭ fa-chüeh chien-chieh'.
尹煥章　黎忠义　江蘇新沂縣三里墩古文化遺址第二次發掘簡介

Yin Ta, *Chung-Kuo Hsin-shih-ch'i Shih-tai*.
尹　達　中國新石器時代

Yin Ti-fei, 'Shih-lun "Ta-feng Kuei"-ti nien-tai'.
殷滌非　試論"大丰殷"的年代

Yu Ch'ing-han, 'K'ao-ku Tung-t'ai : Ho-nan Nan-yang Shih Shih-li Miao fa-hsien Shang-tai i-chih'.
游清汉　考古動態　河南南陽市十里廟發現商代遺址

Index

References to illustrations are in italic

Abęokuta, 239
ablution
   facilities: Baluchistan, 231, 232, 233; Indus valley, 232
   practices, Islamic, 405
   purposes of terraces and spillways, 296
Abydos, mortuary complex, 230
Academia Sinica, 3
Acarí, 238, 398
acropolis
   Athens, 309
   Copán, 260
   Indus valley, 232
   Zimbabwe, 397
Adams, Robert, 4, 262, 264-5, 266, 269-70, 272, 274, 276-7, 278, 279-80, 292, 293, 294, 295, 300, 304, 313, 314, 317, 320, 324, 328, 374-5, 376
administration
   of Chou state: bureaucracies of the Chan-Kuo, 118; oligarchic aristocracies of the Ch'un-Ch'iu, 117, 118; propertyless strata, 118
   of Shang state, 56-7
administrative
   enclaves: An-yang, *37*, 38; Cheng-Chou, 34, 35
   foundation, the city as, 176
   organization, in cities in realms of primary diffusion, 6
   staff: changes in personnel, 61; extension of, 57-8; owning means of administration, 118; separated from means of administration, 118
   structure, articulating with urban centers, 174
Aegean
   role of trade in urban origins, 288
   secondary diffusion in, 7
   secondary urban generation in, 9
   the question of compaction, 480
Afghanistan
   mother goddess cult, 232
   shrines, 326
afin(s)
   as sacred ceremonial enclaves, 240
   craftsmen of, 240
   defined, 238
   forms of, 239
   hierarchy of, 239
   inhabitants of, 240
   labor force for building, 261
   number of, 239
   plan of, 241, *243*
   sanctity of, 238-9, 240
   site of, 238-9
   size of, 239-40
   visitors to, 240
age
   prestige and, 25, 325
   sets, transformation of, 249
agriculture, agricultural
   centralization of, and the rise of ceremonial centers, 267

INDEX

agriculture, agricultural – *contd.*
  centralized control of: Cambodia, 264; Mesopotamia, 262, 264; Shang, 76, 262
  centralized control of produce: Cambodia, 265-6; Central Andes, 267; Crete, 267; Indus valley, 267; Mexico, 266; Shang, 255-7
  classes of land, 76, 262
  cropping patterns, 269
  crops: Chou, 130; Lung-shan, 26-7, 67, 272; Shang, 67-8, 102, 272; Yang-shao, 24, 87-8
  diversity, 129-30, 269
  ecological component and, 269
  entrepreneurs in, 127-8
  fertilization, 131
  functions of cities, 174
  harvests, storing of: Indus valley, 232, 267; Shang, 76
  hydraulic, 289, 290, 293
  implements: Chou, 130-1; hoes, 130, 131; iron, 130, 131; Lung-shan, 27, 67, 68, 76; ploughs, 131; Shang, 68, 69, 73-4; sickles, 130, 131; Yang-shao, 23-4, 87
  irrigated: Mayan, 293-4; productivity and, 297, 298
  officials in charge of, 56, 57
  pastoralism and settled: Lung-shan, 110; Mesopotamia, 270, 272; Shang, 272-3
  permanent field, 275, 352
  population density and, 110, 275
  ritual intercession for prosperity, 67
  royal concern for, 56-7, 75
  sectorial fallowing, 293
  significance of löss uplands, 128, 129
  swidden cultivation, 24, 26, 130, 275, 293
  technological innovation: and diversity, 269; in Shang period, absence of, 67-8, 74, 75; in Western Chou period, absence of, 130-1
  terraces, 260, 296
  yields, 131

Akkad, 329
Allāh, as protector of clients, 287
altar(s)
  Mesoamerica, 234
  Mesopotamia, 227
  roofing of, 175
  sacrificial, at Hsiao-T'un, 34, 40, 43
  to the god of the soil: as *axis mundi*, 434; as essential feature of Western Chou cities, 175; building of provincial, 175, 435; construction of, 434-5; divine power projected through, 434-5; investiture and, 197-8, 435; sacrifice at, before military campaigns, 433; symbolism of 431, 434-5
Amarapura, 307, 448
Amarāvatī, 253, 260
America
  Eastern North: chronology of urban genesis, *323*; truncated evolution of ceremonial centers, 397
  Nuclear, *see* Nuclear America
Amri, 231
Anatolia, urban forms in, 393, 394-5
ancestor(s)
  Chou ceremony and ritual for communication with, 123
  Chou sacrifices to Shang, 107
  cult: importance of, to Western Chou, 175; Lung-shan, 27-8
  supernatural powers of royal, 56
  tablets to agnatic, 175
  worship: at Hsiao-T'un, 40; calendar of ritual for, 56; role in urbanism, 179; the rulers and, 179
ancestral
  sacrifices, need to continue, 175
  temple: as focus of state functions, 175; Chou, 139, 144; Hsiao-T'un, 40; investiture ceremonies in, 121, 156, 200-1; symbolic role of Chou, 431
ancillary settlements
  An-yang, 3, *37*, 38

INDEX

ancillary settlements – *contd.*
  Cheng-Chou, 34-5
  Hsiao-T'un, 43-7
Andes, Central, *see* Central Andes
Aṅkor, hydraulic features at, 295
Aṅkor Bórĕi, 254, 259
Aṅkor Thom
  building of, 259, 265
  extent of, 437
  symbolism of, 437-8
  walls of, 372
Aṅkor Wat, 260
Anurādhapura
  hydraulic engineering at, 296-7
  labor force engaged at, 258
  ritual city of, 256
An-yang
  as an administrative center, 38
  as a ceremonial center, 37, 38, 47
  as an early urban form, 36-47
  bronze foundry at, 75
  evidence for climate, 21, 22
  founding of, 13, 420, 444-5
  history of excavations, 3-4, 15-16, 36
  oracle archive from, 3, 15-16, 19, 22, 39
  palace precinct, 316
  phase of Shang development at, 38
  significance of complex, 16-17
  situation of, 15
  spatial distribution of workshops, 74-5
  systematization of archeological evidence, *48-9*
  trade routes from, 283
  tombs of dynasty, 316
    see also Hsiao-T'un, Hsi-pei Kang
Arakan
  ceremonial centers of, 249, 250-1
  chronology of urban genesis, *323*
  enceinte, 250-1
  shrines, 251
  temple-cities of, 250
archeological
  evidence: available for study of urban genesis, 3; for morphology of Chou cities, 182; limitations of, 4
  record: Chou, 135-50; Shang, 15-19; Thai, 251
  research, deficiencies of Chinese, 18-19
archeology, progress of Chinese, 3-4, 15-18, 23
architectural, architecture
  assemblages: as instruments for creation of space, 225, 260; Cambodian examples of, 258-60; centralized direction of construction, 260-2; planned distribution of space and mass, 260; symbolism of, 225
  monumental: as criterion of urbanism, 373, 374; significance of, 325-6
areal extent, significance of, 183-4
Arimaddanapura
  ceremonial center at, 250
  founding of, 285
  synoecism in formation of, 250, 310
  walling of, 310
Aristotle, 178
art
  mural, of Teotihuacán, 373
  representational: as a criterion of urbanism, 373-4; association with ritual, 225; evidence of, 302, 303; Shang, 373-4
artisans
  emergence of class of, in Mesopotamia, 228
  in ancillary settlements, 47
  in compact cities, 305
  place in Chou society, 125
  place in Shang society, 66-7
  religious association with ceremonial centers, 478
  select group in ceremonial centers, 306
Asia
  Central, 7
  East, 189
  Minor, 323

INDEX

Asia – *contd.*
  Southeast, *see* Southeast Asia
  Western southeast, 7, 9
Assur
  plan, 436
  site, 329
  temple, 447-8
Assyria, trade and trading in, 282-3, 284, 372
astrobiology
  association with phase of traditional urbanism, 416
  defined, 414, 416
  in connection with Chinese cities, 418-9, 451-2
  in connection with Indian cities, 451-2
  relation between earth and heaven, 414, 416
  social and spatial organization and, 416
  symbolism of, 417, 418, 452
  the celestial archetype, 417, 418
  transforming the landscape, 416-17
astronomy
  Arab, 431
  Babylonian, 385
  Chinese, 385, 430-1
  Greek, 430
Athens
  morphology of, 307, 309
  role of the acropolis, 309
  synoecism under Theseus, 308-9
Australasia, 6
autonomy, as a criterion of urbanism, 371, 479
Ava, 307
avenues, 411, 414, 425
axis mundi
  as point of ontological transition, 434-6
  centripetality induced by supreme sacredness of, 431-2
  ceremonial centers as, 478-9, 480
  Chinese interpretation of, 431, 450, 451
  circumambulation of, 433-4
  communication between earth and heaven, 417
  extending below the earth, 417, 429, 437
  in Cambodia, 436, 8, 451
  movement or duplication of, 417-18
  Pole Star and, 428
  royal palace as, 428, 451
  summer solstice and, 428
  symbolism of the center expressed at, 418, 451
  symbols for, 417, 439
  temple as 428, 451
  temple-city as, 451
  temple-mountain, as 417, 451
Ayacucho, 236
Aztec
  distinction between king and nobility, 314
  documents bearing on urban origins, 5, 266
  élite traders, 284
  emergence of royalty, 313-14
  hereditary succession, 314
  hydraulic agriculture, 292-3
  independent economic bases, 314
  militarism of bureaucracies, 299-300
  patrimonial type of bureaucracy, 314
  tribute system, 284

Babylon
  astronomy, 385
  plan, 436
Bǎkhèṅ, the, 436-7
ball game, ritual, 235
Baluchistan
  ablution facilities, 231, 232
  ceremonial complex, 231, 277, 303, 304
  description of centers, 233
  drains, 233
  environmental deterioration, 237, 304
  evolutionary sequence of settlement forms, 231

INDEX

Baluchistan – *contd.*
  platforms with steps and ramps, 233
  population increases, 277, 304
  relation to Harappān culture, 231-2, 233
  religious function of centers, 304
  shrines, 231, 303, 326
  walled enceinte, 232
Bamboo Annals (*Chu-shu Chi-nien*), 14, 109, 151
Banteay Chhmar, 259
Banteay Kdei, 258-9
Banteay Samrè, 260
Barnard, Noel, 108, 111-12
Bascom, W., 391
Bau archives, 262, 264, 265, 270
Becán, 301
Bellah, R. N., 318-20, 321
benefices
  Chou: bestowed on ministers, 163; enumerated in *Shih-Chi*, 163; enumerated in *Tso-Chuan*, 162-4; established as garrison posts, 162; extent of, 128; holders, 112-13, 174, 176, 184; locating of 164; number of, 112; types of, 122; urban centers associated with, 162, 174
  investiture to: and altars to gods of the soil, 197-8, 435; in ancestral temples, 121, 156, 200-1
  Shang: association with defence, 109; Chou as holders of, 109; creation of, 57-8; duties of holders of, 58-9; feudal contracts and, 60-1; names and number of, 58; social distinction of holders, 61; women holding, 58
Beng Mealea, 260
Bennett, Wendell, 234
Berthelot, René, 414, 416, 451
Billa, 329
bio-astrale, 416, 451
*B'ju-nậm
  bibliography of, 344-5
  cosmo-magical symbolism, 447

cult role of city, 254, 447
federation of city states, 253
hydraulic works, 295-6
Indian and indigenous cultures, 253-4
location of, 253
palace, 254
palisaded and moated settlement, 254
political structure, 253
port of Oc-èo, 253, 254, 345, 391
sites on canal system, 254, 345
social structure, 391
bone
  carving, 36, 69
  oracle, *see* oracle archive
  workshops: at Cheng-Chou, 35, 74; at Hsiao-T'un, 43, 47; in Chou times, 138, 140; in precincts of ceremonial centers, 74-5; in Shang proto-cities, 50, 75; products of city and village, 176; spatial distribution of, 74-5
Book of Artificers, *see K'ao-kung Chi*
Book of Documents, *see Shu-Ching*
Book of Odes, *see Shih-Ching*
Borobudur, 256
Braidwood, R. J., 29, 279, 325
Brak, 329
brick
  -faced buildings, 250
  manufacture, 233, 267
bronze(s)
  arrowheads, 145
  artifacts in Shang proto-cities, 50
  association with ceremonial centers, 73, 74
  association with élite, 73, 74, 75-6
  casting: Chou, 131; Shang, 70-3; Western methods, 72, 73
  casting-on of accessories, 132
  classification of Shang, 104-5
  composition of alloy, 71-2
  foundries: at Cheng-Chou, 33, 36, 66, 71, 72, 74; at Hsiao-T'un, 43, 47, 74, 75; at other Shang sites, 47; Chou, 131-2, 139-40, 144;

555

bronze(s) – *contd.*
  relation to ceremonial centers, 74-5; spatial distribution of, 74-5
  funerary articles, 46, 64, 140
  inscriptions: Chou, 108, 111-12, 160-1; divinatory, 62-3, 111-12; giving liturgical benefices, 58; script used for, 380
  Mesopotamian objects, 280
  money, 134
  musical instruments, 73, 104
  prestige products used in cities, 176
  private demand for, 74
  technology: affinity between techniques of pottery and, 72-3, 281; appearance of, in China, 281; Shang, 69, 71-3, 104
  vessels: form of, 73; ritual, 43, 281; types of, 104
  weapons, 144
  workers' dwellings, 36, 66, 67
  working, Lung-shan, 27
Buddhism
  cosmic symbolism of Mahāyāna, 256, 437-8
  cosmos of, 372
  influence in Japanese building, 246
  monasteries, 250
bureaucracy
  and the *hsien*, 179-80
  Aztec patrimonial, 314
  Chan-Kuo, 118
  Chou, 117-18, 179-80
  erosion of political privileges of kin group by, 179-80
  evolution of Japanese, 245-6, 247
  hydraulic, 289, 290, 297
  increased vertical social mobility through, 128
  integration with kinship system, 245-6
  militaristic, of Mesoamerica, 299-300
  required for organization of labor force, 260
  rise of impersonal, 125, 179
  Western Chou proto-, 196

burial(s)
  animal, 40, 140
  class differentiation in, 64-5
  customs: at Cheng-Chou, 35; at Hsiao-T'un, 40, 44, 55; at other Shang sites, 47; evolution of, 47
  evolutionary sequence in élite, 64
  goods: manufacture of, 69-70, 74; types of, 64-5, 74
  mounds 144
  pits, 64
  sites, 40, *42*, 44
  see also cemeteries
Burma
  ceremonial centers of, 249, 250
  circumambulation of capitals, 433
  records of cities, 251
  succession of capitals, 448
  tradition of temple-cities, 251
  see also Pyū, Irawadi, Arakan

Cahuachi, 236
Cajamarquilla, 236, 237
Cakravāla range, 372
Calakmul, 235
calendrics
  advanced state of, 383-4
  astronomical calendar in stone, 437
  Babylonian, 385
  calendrical schedule for work, 466-7
  Chinese, 384, 385-6
  Egyptian, 385
  lowland Mayan, 384-5
  Mayan 'long count', 384-5
  Mexican, 384
  Peruvian, 384
  ritualistic and managerial needs of the élite, 385-6
  Sumerian, 385
  time counts, 384
Calpulli, 375-6
Cambodia
  agriculture: centralized control of, 264; control of produce, 265-6; dependability of production, 274; wet-padi cultivation, 269, 274

INDEX

Cambodia – *contd.*
  agro-architectural complexes, 296
  artificial lakes, 259
  canal system, 254, 295, 296, 345
  cardinal disposition of gates, 438
  carvings, 260
  ceremonial centers: areal extent of enceintes, 259; building of, 258-60; chronology of dispersed, *323*; description of, 258-60; dispersed settlement pattern around, 257, 306; Mekong valley, 249-50, 253-5, 258-60; numbers in service of, 266; plan and layout of, 241, 243, 259, 436-8
  circumambulation of capitals, 433
  cosmological layout of temple-cities, 295, 436-8
  cosmo-magical symbolism of canal system, 295, 296
  craftsmen employed, 260
  economy: appropriational movement of commodities, 265-6; as oblation to gods, 254-5; redistributive function of, 265-6
  gates, 438
  hospitals, 259
  hydraulic works: description of, 295-6; improving agronomy, 259; purpose of, 296; ritualistic aspects of, 295-6; symbolism of, 259, 295-6
  Indian and indigenous cultures, 253-4
  moats, 254, 259, 438
  palaces, 254
  palisaded and moated settlements, 254
  rest-houses, 259
  shrine-cities, 258-60
  social: differentiation, 288; solidarity, type of, 390-1
  statuary, 265-6
  symbolism: of hydraulic works, 259, 295-6; of the center, 432; parallelism of macrocosmos and microcosmos, 436-8; projection of divine power through *axis mundi*, 434; reciprocal relation of deity and state, 296
  temple, state: building of, 259, 437-8; sacred *liṅga*, 249
  temple-cities: cosmological layout of, 295, 436-8; description of, 254-5, 258-60; number of settlements supporting, 265; redistributive function of, 265-6
  temple-mountains: as *axes mundi*, 259, 451; centripetality of cosmic, 254; of Bàyon, 259, 432
  terraces, 259
  urbanism: criteria of, applied to, 386; genesis of, 326-7
  urban status, question of, 389
  walls, 254, 259, 372, 438
  see also *B'ịu-nậm
Campā
  appearance of name, 253, 344
  social differentiation in territories, 288
  succession of capitals, 448
canals
  Cambodian, 254, 295, 296, 345
  Central Andean, 294
  Egyptian, 297
  in Ceylon, 297
  of La Cumbre, 294
  system, Kalāwewa, 297
Caṇḍi Sari, 256
Caṇḍi Sewu, 256
canoes, remains of, 146
capital(s)
  areal extent, significance of, 183-4
  as point of ontological transition, 434-6
  association between dynasty and, 447-8
  avenues, 411, 414
  axes mundi, 428, 434
  basic modes of symbolism manifested in, 418

capital(s) – contd.
  cardinal orientation and axiality
    of, 423, 424
  ceremonial functions of Chou, 174,
    177, 178
  ceremonial, of Ceylon, 256-7, 260-1
  circumambulation of, 433-4
  divine power focused through, 434-6
  Eastern Chou state, *169*, 174
  focusing of powers of state through,
    431-3
  focusing of vital forces through,
    431-2
  hsien, 174, 179, 182, 423, *424*
  layout of: as celestial archetypes,
    417, 436-7; Cambodian, 436-8;
    Hindu, 439-41; Persepolis, 438-9;
    plan of, 411
  migration of: Burma, 448; Ceylon,
    257; Chou, 449
  modelled on constellations, 436-7
  pars pro toto relationship with
    territory, 431-3
  relation between kingdom and, 445-7
  shape of, 411
  siting of: Chinese, 444-5; geomantic
    precautions, 419-23
  sixteen quarters or wards, 411
  subdivisions of the well-field system
    and, 411, 414
carapaces, source of, 283
cardinal
  axiality: deflections from, 411-12;
    of Chinese cities, 432-5; of *hsien*
    cities, 423, *424*; of Javanese *candi*,
    256; of platforms, 142, 145, 185,
    425
  orientation: Central Andean com-
    plexes, 236; Chinese cities, 423-7,
    450, 451, 481; Chou, 138-9, 142,
    145, 146, 426; Hsi-pei Kang
    tombs, 426; Indian cities, 426-7,
    451; Mesopotamia, 451; observed
    in royal circumambulations, 433,
    434; of city walls, 426-7; of gates,
    435, 438; of platforms, 139, 142;

    required of sacred territory, 417,
      418; Shang, 425; Southeast Asia,
      451; Thai enceintes, 253; Vietna-
      mese, 427
    orientation and axiality: Cambodian
      cities, 436-7, 438; Indian cities,
      439-40
carving
  Cambodian, 260
  Shang, 69, 74
Casma valley complexes, 236
caste, occupational specialization and,
  249
Çatal Hüyük
  complexity of society, 326
  priesthood of, 394-5
  representational art, 374
  shrine at, 302-3, 395
  urban status of, 394-5
cemeteries
  Central Andean, 236
  Indus valley, 232
  royal, at Hsi-pei Kang, 16, 43-4
  sharing of common, Yang-shao,
    24-5
  see also burials
Cempoala
  deflected axis, 441
  plan, 241, *242*
censuses, 390
Central Andes
  amount of information on, 4
  as region of primary urban genera-
    tion, 9
  beginnings of religious ceremonial-
    ism, 235-6
  canals, 294
  cardinal orientation, 236
  ceremonial centers: description of,
    235-8; dispersed, *322*; early
    appearance of, 276; redistribu-
    tive function of, 267; spread of,
    236-7
  compaction: compact cities, *322*;
    of settlements, 236, 278
  courts, 236, 237

INDEX

Central Andes – *contd.*
  ecological: responses, 269; specialization, 271
  environmental diversity, 269
  gateways, 237
  geographical area comprising, 234
  geographical sections of, *322*
  Inca: centers, 238; domination, distortion of, 5; irrigation, 294; *see also* Inca
  insulation of civilization, 9
  irrigation system, 294
  morphology, 237
  mounds, 236
  omphalos concept in 429
  palaces, 238, 267
  platforms, 236
  plazas, 236
  public shrines, *322*
  pyramids, 236, 237, 429
  ramps, 236
  separation of dwellings and enclaves, 238
  stairways, 236, 237
  temples, 236, 238, 429
  terraces, 236, 237
  urban: evolution, rate of, 328; forms, earliest, 235-8; forms, regularity of, 237; genesis, chronology of, *322*; origins, evidence for, 5
  urbanism, bibliography of, 337-8
  Urbanist or City Builder phase, 237-8
  warfare and defence, 300-1
  see also Peru
centripetality
  centralized: control (of labor force 258, of social power 257-61); direction of construction, 260-2; resource exploitation, 262, 264
  circumambulation of capitals and kingdoms, 433-4
  function of the ceremonial center, 257-67
  induced by sacredness of *axis mundi*, 428-9, 431-2
  induced by sacred and cosmic mountains, 254
  movement of commodities, 264-7
  of Teotihuacán, 300
  of the Chinese ceremonial center, 429-31, 381
  ontological transition of divine power and, 434-6
  pars pro toto relationship and, 431-3
  political power exercised from center, 257-61
  redistributive systems, arranged from centers, 105
  relating to existential space, 418, 430
  religious function, 257
ceremonial
  activities, influence of lineage on, 52
  artifacts: jade, 69-70; manufacturing of, 69-70
  centers and complexes, *see below*
  crafts: emergence of, 27-8; Shang jade, 69-70
  enclaves: at Cheng-Chou, 32, 34, 47; at Hsiao-T'un, 34, *37*, 38, 39-40, *41*, 42, 43, 47; *hang-t'u* foundations of walls, 32, *33*, 34
  functions of cities and capitals, 174, 177
  investiture, 121
  of the Chou court, 112-13
  ritual and protocol of Chou, 114
ceremonial centers and complexes
  absence of, in Northern Mesopotamia, 329
  absence of role of, in European urban origins, 179
  appropriative role of, 264-5
  architectural assemblages of, 225
  areal extent of, 258, 259-60
  as a functional and developmental phase, 316, 396, 477
  as an ideal type, 316-30
  as centers of ritual and ceremony, 225
  as idealized structural models, 305
  as mirrors to society, 305

INDEX

ceremonial centers – *contd.*
  as origin of urban forms, 225-6, 316
  as reassurance of cosmic certainty, 311
  axis of the kingdom, 179
  building of, 258-60
  cases of truncated evolution of, 397-8
  centralized: control of labor, land, and produce, 258-60, 264, 267; direction of construction, 260-2; resource exploitation, 262, 264
  centripetalizing function of, 257-67
  China, abrupt emergence of, in North, 325-6
  Chou: dispersed Western, 479; encéinctes, 138-40, 144-6; supremacy of common ritual in, 122
  chronology of dispersed, *322-3*
  'classic' phase of, defined, 321
  conceptual intricacy of, 260-1
  Developed Village Farming as precondition of, 279
  dispersed: chronology of, *322-3*; forms becoming compact, 324; Old and New World, *326-7*; Shang, 479; Western Chou, 479
  early appearance of, in Mesoamerica and Central Andes, 276
  ecological: patterns, 317, 320-1; surplus employed in use of, 268; zones, integration of, and rise of, 273-4
  economic: functions of, 225-6; power of, 390
  'effective' space: controlled from and oriented to, 267; generated by, 389
  élite of, 226, 306, 321
  evolution of, 328
  genesis of the, 267-305
  in regions of primary urbanism: Central Andes, 235-8; Egypt, 229-30; Indus valley, 230-4; Mesoamerica, 234-5; Mesopotamia, 226-9; Southwestern Nigeria, 238-40
  in regions of secondary urbanism: Crete, 244; Etruria, 244-5; Japan, 245-8; Southeast Asia, 248-57, 258-60
  models of: Duncan and Schnore, 317; generalized, 316-17
  morphology of the, 305-11
  nature of the, 225-369
  on defensive sites, 300-1
  orthogenetic role of, 311, 324, 478, 479, 481
  palladium of the group in, 249, 257
  plans of, 241, *242-3*
  political power attested by erection of, 257-61
  population: density and 276-7, 305, 306, 307-8; social solidarity and compaction, 324
  reallocative role of, 265
  redistributive role of, 225-6, 264-7, 274, 317, 320, 389
  religious: function, 225; symbolism, 303
  secularization of the, 311-16
  Shang: allocative pressures, 75; bronze associated with, 73, 74; characters for, 99, 100; competing, 62-3; craftsmen within precincts of, 74-5; discovery of, 321; dispersed, 479; pottery associated with, 71, 74; redistributive role of, 266-7; spatial distribution of workshops in relation to, 74-5; technological advances demanded by needs of, 70, 71, 73, 74-5
  social: duality of, 321; order, sacrally sanctioned, 305; organization of, 318; power attested by erection of, 257-61; solidarity and compaction, 324; types of society, 310, 317, 390-1, 479
  symbolism: as symbolic statements, 305; of the center, 428-36; religious, 303

INDEX

ceremonial centers – *contd.*
  synoecic phase of, 308-9, 324
  temporary use of, 257
  the shrine and, 237, 267-8
  transience of institutions in, 321
  urban: character of the, 371-409; status of Egyptian, 389
Ceylon
  Aryanization in, 256
  ceremonial capitals, 256-7, 260-1
  ceremonial centers: defensive sites for, 301; description of, 256-7; plan of, 241, *243*; symbolism of, 301
  hydraulic engineering, 296-7
  irrigation systems, 295, 296-7
  migration of capitals, 257
  tanks, 297
  urban genesis: chronology of, *323*; course of, *326-7*
Chagar Bazar, 329
Cham
  chronology of dispersed ceremonial centers, *323*
  cult centers, 253, 307
Chanchan, 237, 386
Ch'ang-Chou
  areal extent of, 183
  circular enceinte, 183
  description of, 146
  moat, 146, 183
Chanhu-daro, 232
Chan-kuo Ts'e (Intrigues of the Contending States), 151, 155, 177, 190
Chao-k'ang Chen
  areal extent of, 183
  description of, 141
  gates, 141, 185
Chao Phraya river
  ceremonial centers, 249, 251
  dispersed settlements, *323*
  Mōn culture, 251
chao-mu system, 53
Chavín de Huántar, 236, 257
Cheng-Chou
  ancillary settlements, 34-5
  bone workshops, 35, 36, 74-5
  bronze foundries, *33*, 36, 66, 72, 73, 74
  brushed characters on pottery, 380
  burial customs, 35, 64
  ceremonial centers, 31, 32, *33*, 47
  Chou remains at, 108
  chronological sequence at, 17, 30-1
  circumvallation at, 302
  description of site, 17, 31-6
  distillery, *33*, 36, 75
  drainage, 35, 68
  dwellings, 35, 68
  extent of site, 31
  identification with **Ngog, 84
  labor force for building, rampart at, 76, 258
  Lungshanoid: influence at, 30, 31; settlement at, 31-2
  metal artifacts, 71
  oracle archive, 19, 35
  phase of Shang development at, 38
  pottery, 32, 35, 36, 74-5
  pottery-making, 35-6, 67, 70
  ring-footed vessels, 32
  significance of, 30-1
  sites in neighborhood of, 4, 17, *33*
  spatial: distribution of workshops, 74-5; specialization at, 35-6
  stratigraphical phases: Jen-min Kung-yüan, 31, 38; Lo-ta Miao, 31, 32, 71; Lower Erh-li Kang, 31, 32-3, 71, 108; Shang-chieh, 31-2; Upper Erh-li Kang, 31, 71, 108
  systematization of archeological evidence, *48-9*
  tripods, 32
  urban nucleus at, 32
  wall surrounding enceinte, 32, *33*, 34
ch'i, 458
Ch'eng-tzŭ Yai
  excavation at, 136
  drainage pattern and settlement, 208, *209*

INDEX

Chiapas, 300
Childe, V. Gordon, 278-9, 289, 325, 373-4, 377, 386, 387
China, North
  astronomy, 385
  calendrical calculations, 384, 385-6
  celestial stems and terrestrial branches, 384
  compaction of cities, 307, *323*
  conflict between herdsmen and farmers, 272-3
  dependability of production, 274-5
  ecological: history of North China Plain, 21-2; interdependencies, 272-3; physiographical variation, 269; range and diversity of zones, 268-9; specialized subsistence zones, 272
  economic integration, 273
  hsiu, 385
  pastoralism, 272-3
  phases of technological and urban development, 280-1
  Plain: arcuate zone of sites on, 4; as area of primary urban generation, 9; climate, 20; physiography of, 20-1, 269
  technology: absence of advance in agricultural, 280-1; class differentiation and production, 281
  urban: evolution, rate of, 328; genesis, chronology of, *323*; genesis, course of, *326-7*
China, Shang
  dispersed settlement patterns, 306
  hydraulic systems, 291-2
  kingship, 315
  representational art, 373-4
  trade: long-distance, 283, 374; treaty, 283
  tribute system, 129, 284
  Wittfogel's theory and, 291-2
China, South
  cities arising from secondary diffusion, 7
  urban imposition, 330

chinampas, 272, 293
Chinese
  city: as a cosmo-magical symbol, 411-76; astrobiological framework applied to, 450-1; cosmo-magical basis of traditional, 411-19; cosmo-magical element in city planning, 419-52; Indian and, compared, 450-1
  writing, 377, 379-81
Cholula
  hegemony of, 313
  pyramid of, 235
Chou
  agricultural associations of, 108, 110
  agricultural innovations under, 110, 130-1
  ancestral temples of, 139, 133
  annexes to urban enclaves, 142, 144, 145
  archeological record, 135-50
  as a barbarian people, 107
  as a unitary people, 108
  as holders of Shang benefices, 109
  as nomadic invaders, 109-10
  as semi-nomads, 109, 111
  as Shang territorial chieftains, 109
  Barnard's theory of origins, 108
  benefices, 112-13, 128, 162-4, 174, 176, 184
  bronze: foundries, 131-2, 139-40, 144; inscriptions, 108, 111-12, 160-1
  bronzes, 131-2
  burial mounds, 144
  cardinal orientation, 138-9, 142, 145, 146, 426
  Chief of Herdsmen, 109
  city: function of the, 173-82; plans of, *137*, *143*, 147, *148-9*; size of, 189-90
  coinage, 140
  coins, 144, 145
  colonia, 188
  commerce, 134-5
  conquest of Shang, 107-8, 421

INDEX

Chou – *contd.*
  crafts: dispersion of, 139-40; specialized production, 140
  cult centers, 108, 113, 162, 174
  culture: compared with Shang, 62-3, 110-12; development from Lung-shan, 135; heroes, 109
  diffusion of Shang cultural traits among, 109, 111
  Duke of, 107, 108, 109, 114, 191, 420-1, 430
  dwellings, 139, 141
  dynasty: charisma of rulers, 123, 202; chronology of, 107, 114; dating of, 10; debasement of royal style, 116; decline of power, 113-14, 123; descent from gods, 124; mandate from Heaven, 107, 116, 163, 175; powers assumed by nobles, 115-16; religion of Heaven, 116, 430-1; ritual and sovereignty, 123; Son of Heaven, 116, 123, 174, 175, 431; traditional account of rise of, 107-8; transference of power from Shang to, 107-8
  Eastern, *see below*
  economy, 128-35
  enceintes: irregular, 144; quadrangular, 138-9; rectangular, 140, 141, 145, 146; square, 138, 140, 145, 146
  environment, 128-30
  epigraphic evidence, 62-3, 108, 109
  ethnic: composition of, 108, 109-10; divisions and the *colonia*, 188; same group as Shang, 110; suprastratification, 120
  extent of sites, 138, 140, 142, 146
  gates, 141, 142, 146
  government, *see* government, Chou
  hang-t'u: constructions, 136, 138, 139, 141, 142, 144, 150; platforms, 139, 142, 144, 145
  iron: foundries, 144; technology, 130, 131
  irrigation, 131
  jade carving, 131-2
  knife money, 145
  land tenure, 132-4
  literary evidence, 109, 150-60
  martial qualities of, 107, 111, 175
  moats, 139, 145, 146, 150
  morphology of cities, 182-9
  origins of, 108-9
  parallel development with Shang, 111
  pastoral economy of pre-conquest, 109
  platforms: circular, 142; *hang-t'u*, 139, 142, 144, 145; oval, 145; square, 139, 142, 144; triple-terraced, 139; with ramps, 139; with stone pillars, 142
  political: consolidation, degree of, 115; organization, 63
  pottery, 131-2, 136
  pottery kilns, 136, 138, 140, 141
  pottery tiles, 138, 139, 141, 145
  pre-urban way of life, 109
  problem of food supplies, 175-6
  question of feudalism, 118-22
  reconstruction of Hsia history, 12-13
  relations with Shang and tribal folk, 175-6
  roadways, 139
  society: description of, 122-8; internally generated stratification, 120; suprastratification, 120
  state and government, 112-22
  storage pits, 139
  technology, 130-2
  territories, extent of, 128-9
  tribes, 108
  tribute system, 129-30
  urbanism, nature of, 173-80
  walls, 136, 138, 140, 141, 144, 145, 146
  water channels, 138
  Wei valley associations, 108, 109, 111, 128, 420-1
  Western, *see below*
  workshops: antler, 140; bone, 138, 140; stone, 138

INDEX

Chou, Eastern
  Chan-Kuo (Contending States):
    agriculture, 131; bureaucracies, 118; compaction of cities, 307; entrepreneurs and land tenure, 133-4; merchants, 134-5; period, 144, 117-18; sites, 141-50
  Ch'un-Ch'iu (Spring and Autumn):
    appearance of compact cities, 307, 479; groups of ruling houses, 123-4; merchants of, 134, 177-8; oligarchic aristocracies, 117, 118; period, 114, 116-17; sites, 136-41; taxes and rent replacing labor, 133; urban forms, 136-41; urban symbols, 387; walls, 387, 479; workshops, industrial, 479
  state capitals, 169, 174
  urbanism, spread of, 169-73
Chou, Western
  artifacts in Wei valley, 108, 111
  degree of political consolidation under, 115
  dispersed ceremonial centers, 479
  history of, 109
  origin and nature of polity, 110
  period of the, 114
  sites, 135-6
  spread of urbanism, 161-8
Chou-Li (Chou Ritual)
  evaluation of, as source, 156-7
  lost section of, 411
  nature of text, 151
  references to: buildings, 43; land tenure, 132, 176; orientation of cities, 425, 426; regional diversity, 130; symbolism, 428
Chuang-Tzŭ, 151, 158, 174
Ch'ü-fu, 146
Ch'un-Ch'iu
  commentaries on, 114
  compilation of, 153
  nature of the, 151
  references to: movement of capitals, 449; urbanism, 170, 171, 172
  traditions, 153

Chung-Kuo, 114, 129
Chu-shu Chi-nien (*Bamboo Annals*), 14, 61, 109, 151, 164, 166
Ch'ü-yang, 4, 70
circumambulation, 433-4
cities, city
  and state: as coeval, 398-9; *pars pro toto* relationship, 431-3; power of state concentrated in, 433-4
  as a core of functionally related institutions, 386-7, 388
  as a generator of effective space, 388-9, 391, 398-9, 477
  as a principle of regional integration, 388, 391, 398, 477
  as a series of structural relationships, 386-7
  characteristics symbolic of, 387
  Chou: annexes to, 142, 144; archeological record, 135-50; extent of, 138, 140, 142, 146; foundation of, 161, 162; function of, 173-82; morphology of, 182-9; plans of, *137, 143*, 17, *148-9*; urban density of, 189-90
  civilization: and, 386, 404; without, 389, 399
  extended boundary towns, 389, 397
  founding of, 19
  functional regularities regardless of culture, 386-7
  Jawad's definition of, 329
  localized idioms of, 387
  resulting from primary diffusion, 6
  Shang: genesis and morphology of, 20-52; persisting in Chou times, 161
  status of Western Chou, 110
  synchoritic, 389, 397
  use of term, 371
  see also urban, urbanism
city-planning
  astrobiological, 414, 416-19
  cardinal orientation and axiality, 423-7
  Chinese: canonically sanctioned

INDEX

city-planning – *contd.*
    forms, 411, 414; cosmo-magical element in, 419-52, 481-2; geomantic precautions, 419-23; plans, *412*
    concern with ordering of urban space, 414-19
    cosmicizing of territory, 372, 417-18, 439-40
    Hindu, 414, 439-40
    in accordance with ancient plans, **444**
    Japanese, 246-7
    siting of, 419-23
city-states
    as early phase of generated city, 398
    autonomy of, 371
    rise of, in Malaysia, 255
    survival of, 161
civilization
    and cities, 386, 404
    criteria of, 386
    without cities, 389, 399
civitas, societas to, 267
class
    differentiation: in burial customs, 64-5; in dwellings, 63-4; in grave goods, 64-5; in Shang society, 63-7; position of artisans and craftsmen, 66-7; position of peasantry, 65-6; proliferation of craft products in response to, 281; relation of kin and craft, 66-7; rise of, in Mesopotamia, 228; status differentiation in Lungshan, 63
    elements of, in Shang lineages, 53
    stratification, and redistribution, 266
    see also social, society
clientage
    Quraysh, 286, 287
    relationship, 374-5
climate of North China Plain, 21-2
Coe, Michael, 389, 390-1
coins
    finds of, 144, 145
    manufacture of, 140

collective conscience, 390
Colombia
    chronology of dispersed ceremonial centers in, *322*
    truncated evolution of ceremonial centers in, 397
Comestor, Peter, 428
commerce, commercial
    activity: commodities exchanged, 134; entrepreneurs and, 126-7, 177; extent of trading, 177-8; interdependence of natural products, 134; transforming urban society, 126
    level of development in cities, 176-7
    market: location of, 177; quarter, 178
    merchants: emergence of wealthy, 134, 177; political influence of urban, 126
    role of: in Chou urbanism, 177-8; in heterogenetic cities, 392-3; in manorial type economy, 134, 176-7, 178; *see also* market, trading
    toll stations, 134
compaction
    forces inducing, 479-80
    generation of competition and, 390
    in Chou cities, 189-90, 307, 479
    in Old and New World, *326-7*
    military considerations, 480
    of agriculturalists in Haldas, 395-6
    social differentiation and, 390, 391, 395
    urban: origins, 275-8, 281, 318; status, 281, 318, 390, 391, 395; *see also*, population
conclusion, 477-82
concordia to *justitia*, 267
Copán
    abandonment of, 300
    'acropolis', 260
    cult complex, 235
    plan, 241, *242*
corporations of Japanese workers, 245

INDEX

cosmic
  Mahāyāna Buddhist system, 256, 372, 437-8
  mountains, 254, 259, 417, 442
  order: ceremonial centers projecting image of, 478; symbols, 225
  temples, embodying Subtle-Self, 249
cosmicizing of territory, 372, 417-18, 439-40
cosmological
  certainty, reassured by ceremonial centers, 311
  crises, seasonal festivals and, 304, 311
  emphasis in Javanese temples, 256
  justification of roles of divine and natural, 319
  monism replaced by transcendental systems, 321
  role of Memphis, 229-30
  symbolism: Cambodian canal layout, 295; Cambodian temple-cities, 259-60; modes of, 418; of the center, 428-36, 481
  world view, 320
cosmo-magical
  axis mundi, 417-18, 434-6
  basis of the traditional city, 411-19
  cardinal orientation and axiality, 423-7
  element in Chinese city planning, 419-52
  geomantic precautions, 419-23, 481
  habitabilis, 417, 418, 439-40, 451
  Ode epitomizing role of Chinese city, 449-50
  parallelism of macrocosmos and microcosmos, 436-52, 481
  religions dramatizing the cosmogony, 417
  symbol, the ancient Chinese city as, 411-76
cosmos
  Buddhist, 256, 372
  earthly reproduction of, 417
  walls representing bounds of, 372

court(s)
  as part of ceremonial complex, 225
  Central Andean, 236, 237
  Mesoamerican, 234, 301
court chroniclers, Shang, 57
craft(s)
  centralized management of production, 273
  economic implications of distribution of, 75-6
  élite, production for, 176, 228, 280, 281
  for cult purposes, 228, 279-80
  kin groupings and, 66-7
  Mesopotamian, 228-9, 279-80
  organization by corporate kin groups, 375
  outer walls protecting, 180
  Shang, 69-70
  spatial distribution: Chou, 140, 176; Shang, 74-5
  specialization: as criterion of urbanism, 373, 374; ceremonial centers as foci of, 226; incipient regional, 130; of production, 140; stimulated by warfare, 228-9, 280, 281, 298-9
  technological: advances in, 281; changes in Shang, 68-75; demand affecting quantity rather than quality, 229, 280
  tools, 69, 105
  village, utility, 176
craftsmen
  absence of autonomous groups, 178
  decorating Cambodian temples, 260
  dwellings of, 66
  emergence of, as social group in Mesopotamia, 280
  in precincts of ceremonial centers, 74-5
  lineages and, 67
  living in ceremonial centers, 257, 311
  position in: Chou society, 125; Shang society, 66-7

INDEX

craftsmen – *contd.*
  selected group of, in ceremonial centers, 306
  Yoruba, 240
Creel, H. G., 272, 380-1
Crete, Cretan
  ceremonial centers, 244
  compact cities, 244
  economic redistribution in, 267
  palaces, 244, 307
  question of population density, 307
  sanctuaries, 244
  urban forms, earliest, 244
  urban genesis: chronology of, *322*; role of trade in, 288-9
  writing: hieroglyphic, 381; Linear A and B, 381-2; systems of, 377, 381-2
Cuicuilco, 234, 307
cult centers
  adapting to pressures of social differentiation, 321
  as religio-political foci of society, 319
  Chou: at Hsi-an, 108; culturally unifying influence of, 113; **G'og as, 174; in garrison towns for élite, 162
  closed high-status communities of, 319, 321
  Greek, 113
  integrative function of, 478
  Mayan, 235
  Memphis as, 229-30
  Mesoamerican, 234
  Mesopotamian, 113
  morphological distinction of, 319
  populace alienated from sacred and secular power, 319
  Southeast Asian, 254
  Yoruba, 113
cultural
  contacts, trans-Pacific, 8
  diffusion and political absorption, 176
  discontinuity between Old and New Worlds, 8-9

evolution, 317
imperialism, 7
milieu of Shang urban generation, 22-30
traits: borrowing of, 6; of Shang among Chou, 109, 111; of Shang diffused into peripheral areas, 17, 18, 50, 52, 62, 109; secondary diffusion of, 8; stimulating evolution of society, 7
culture
  aboriginal, 116
  Chou and Shang compared, 110-12
  Lung-shan, 26-30
  Yang-shao, 22-5
culture heroes
  Chou, 109, 117, 123
  **Gi̯wo, 129-30
  in literature, 14
  lineages traced back to, 123, 175
  rule of, 9
  Shang emergence under, 10
  synoecism attributed to, 310
Cuzco, 238, 396
cyclic time
  hierophanies guaranteeing seasonal renewal of, 311, 479
  man's part in regulating, 389-90, 417, 479
  plant regeneration, 304, 389-90, 414 479
  representations of Indian concept of, 437

dagobas, 258, 260
Dambadeniya, 257
Damb Sadaat, 232
deciphering of scripts, 5, 19, 20, 377, 381
demographic
  component, 275-8
  factor, 281, 318, 477
dependability of production, 274
Developed Village Farming
  as pre-condition of urbanism, 279
  at Cheng-Chou, 4, 6
  changes in society and ecotype in, 328

INDEX

Developed Village Farming – *contd.*
  course of urban genesis, *326-7*
  in Lung-shan culture, 29
  religious component in phase of, 302
  social differentiation in era of, 317, 326
Dhlo-Dhlo, 398
Diakonoff, Igor, 375
Dieng plateau
  absence of settlements, 257, 276
  monuments, 256
diffusion
  as a process, 7-8
  of urban life in ancient China, 107-90
  primary, defined, 6
  secondary: affecting regions of primary urban generation, 324; cities arising from, 7; cultural, 244, 324; defined, 6; of Shang culture, 50, 52, 109, 111, 135; planned city spreading by, 7
  similarity to evolution, 7-8, 81
  stimulus: affecting regions of primary urban generation, 324; defined, 6-7; inappropriate to early urban forms, 7; in writing, 379, 381, 383
distillery at Cheng-Chou, *33*, 36, 75
divination in siting of cities, 419, 420-1, 423
divine, the, as the real, 416-17
division of labor, 29-30
Diyālā plains
  large-scale canalization, 292
  settlements on, 226
domestic animals
  Lung-shan, 27, 68
  sacrifice of, 43, 46-7, 68, 272
  Shang, 68, 272
  Yang-shao, 24
Dong Lakhon, 253
Dong Si Maha Phot, 252
drainage
  at Cheng-Chou, 35, 68
  at Hsiao-T'un, 38, 40, 68

  imperfect, and soil salinization, 226
  patterns affected by physiography, 269
Duncan, Otis, and Leo Schnore, 317
Durkheim, Emile, 317, 390-2
Dutt, Binode, 440
Dvāravatī, 252
dwellings
  at Cheng-Chou, 34-5, 66
  at Hsiao-T'un, 16, 38, 40, 43, 63
  bronze workers', 36, 66
  class differentiation in, 63-4
  hang-t'u, 63-4, 186
  Inca, 238
  in Chou suburbs, 186
  Mesopotamian, 227, 228
  of: artisans, 66; élite, 43, *46*, 63-4; peasantry, 63-4; potters, 66; powerful families, 188-9
  pit, 16, *42*
  semi-subterranean, 34-5, 36, 63, 139, 141
  separation of enclave and, 238
  Southeast Asian, 254, 255
  thatched, 186
  tile-roofed, 139
Dzibilchaltún, 235, 258

earliest urban forms
  An-yang, 36-47
  Cheng-Chou, 30-6
  other sites, 47-52
Eberhard, Wolfram, 132, 175-6, 188, 292
ecological, ecology
  adaptations: evidence of, 22, 23; in Mesoamerica, 270; in Mesopotamia, 269-70; on löss uplands, 128, 129; role of, in socio-cultural integration, 320; role of religion in, 416-17
  climatic variation, 268, 269
  complex, elements in, 317
  component in urban genesis, 268-75, 317
  cropping patterns, 269

INDEX

ecological, ecology – *contd.*
  dependability of production, 274-5
  differences between Baluchistan and Indus valley, 231-2
  diversity: exploited by ceremonial centers, 274; reallocation and, 269, 273; redistribution and, 274
  effect of expanded environmental perception, 320-1
  factor, role of, 281
  history of the North China Plain, 21-2
  instability, 304
  interdependencies: Central Andes, 271; date of evidence for, 273; Egypt, 271; Indus valley, 271; in established cult centers, 273; Mesoamerica, 270; Mesopotamia, 269-70, 272; North China, 272-3; Yoruba, 270-1
  irrigation: and social surplus, 298; effects of, 298
  responses, 269
  soil: fertility, 268, 274; types, 269
  surplus, question of: absolute, 268; social, 268, 274, 298
  zones: centralized power and variety of, 273; exploitation of diversity of, 273-4; integration of disparate into socio-political units, 273; Mesopotamian, 269-70, 272; North Chinese, 268-9; rise of ceremonial centers and integration of, 273-4; specialized subsistence, 269-70, 272
eco-niches
  emergence of highly specialized, 269
  extended by permanent-field agriculture, 275
economic, economy
  activities of Yamato and kinship society, 245-6
  appropriational movement of commodities, 265-6
  appropriative role of ceremonial centers, 264-5
  change: accompanying urban development, 4; intensifying urbanism, 171
  Chou: agricultural technology, 130-1; change in urban society, 126; commerce, 134-5, 177-8; description of, 128-35; development in central states, 114; emergence of the merchant class, 134, 177-8; entrepreneurs, 126-7, 133-4; environment, 128-30; increased diversity of resource base, 128, 129-30, 134; iron technology, 131; landless peasants, 126, 133-4; land tenure, 132-4; markets, social consolidatory effect of, 176; regional diversity, 129-30; self-contained manorial system, 176-7; significance of löss uplands, 128-9; stratification and class distinction, 126, 128; taxes and rent replacing labor, 126, 133; technology, 130-2; toll stations, 134
  demand, effect on technology, 228-9
  exchange, ritualized, 265
  function of the ceremonial center, 225-6
  institutions subordinate to religious moral norms, 311, 390, 392-3
  integration: Mesopotamian, 272; Shang, 273
  interdependence, 265
  Lung-shan, 75
  power of the ceremonial centers, 390
  private and craft production, 280
  process embedded in non-economic institutions, 282
  reallocative, 265, 269, 274, 276, 304-5, 389-80
  reciprocity, 77, 105, 249
  redistribution, 77, 105, 186, 225-6, 249, 264-7, 274, 303, 317, 320, 373, 374, 389, 390
  Shang: allocative pressures, 75; appropriation, 266; centripetal

INDEX

economic, economy – *contd.*
    forces remoulding, 75, 105;
    coercion and exploitation, 30;
    dependence, 30; institutionalized integration, 77; integration, 75-7, 237; labor (centralized control of 76-7, 262; centralized management of 76, 262); organization of territories, 75-7; reciprocity, 77, 105; redistribution, 77, 105, 186, 225-6; transformation and urban life, 77; village, 75, 77
    space: instruments for creation of, 225; non-economic agencies generating, 389, 478
    specialization and caste in Southeast Asia, 249
    storage of produce in ceremonial centers, 76, 232, 264, 267
    stratification in Mesopotamia, 228
    urban: classification based on, 392-3; definitions and, 388
    Yang-shao, 75
    see also reallocation, redistribution
ecosystems
    generalized, 275, 351-2
    Mayan, 293-4
    small-scale irrigation modulating, 297
    specialized, 275, 352
    under permanent-field and swidden cultivation, 275
ecotypes
    changes in Primary Village Farming Efficiency, 328
    crop diversity and, 269
    large-scale irrigation reconstructing, 298
    relative rates of transformation, 328
    transformation of the, 477
Egypt
    amount of information on, 4
    archeological evidence for, 229, 280
    as area of primary urban generation, 9
    attention paid to urban origins, 3
    autonomy of cities, 371
    calendrics, 385
    canal construction, 294-5
    ceremonial centers, 229-30, *323*, 477
    compact cities, 307, *323*
    cult centers, migration of, 230
    dating of cities, 6
    earliest urban forms, 229-30
    ecological interdependencies, 271
    encompassing the sacred enclave, 434
    evidence for urban origins, 5, 20
    irrigation, 294-5
    kingship, 314
    linear settlements, 278
    local incarnations of universal deity, 229
    mortuary cities, 229, 230, 306
    omphalos concept, 429
    palaces, 230
    pyramids, 230, 235, 316, 429
    role of Memphis, 229-30
    secondary urban diffusion between Mesopotamia and, 8
    social: solidarity, 390; stratification, 229
    temples, 230, 429
    treaty trade, 283
    unification of, 229
    urban: evolution, rate of, 328; genesis, chronology of, *323*; genesis, course of, *326-7*; genesis, technological advance and, 280; status, question of, 386
    village: as basic unit of settlement, 229; walled, 229, 333
    warfare, 299
    writing, 377, 378-9, 382, 383
Eisenstadt, S.N., 317, 319
Elburz, 428
Eliade, Mircea, 417, 418
élite
    associated with irrigation, 289, 290-1
    Aztec traders, 73, 74, 75-6
    burials, evolutionary sequence of, 64
    calendar for ritualistic and managerial needs of, 385-6

INDEX

élite – *contd.*
  craft production for, 76, 176, 228, 280, 281
  cult centers in garrison towns, 142, 162
  diffusion of Shang cultural traits among Chou, 111
  dwellings, 43, 46, 63-4
  in dispersed ceremonial centers, 306
  religious and secular, 321
  sacerdotal, 226, 321
  Sanskritization of names of Southeast Asian, 316
  schism among cultural-religious and political-military, 321
  section of city for sacrally ordained, 186
  treaty trade and, 283-4
  writing and the, 377, 382
enceinte(s)
  accretions to, 184-5
  areal extent of: Cambodian, 259; Chou, 183-4; Japanese, 247; Mesopotamian, 228
  as focus of ceremonial centers, 305
  Baluchistan, 232
  Cambodia, 258-9
  cardinal orientation and axiality, 185, 253
  Central Andes, 238
  Chou, 138-46
  double or two, 186, 187, 188
  function of: administration, 186-7; ceremonial, 186
  Japan, 247, 248
  Mesoamerica, 306, 307
  Mesopotamia, 228
  of state capitals, 183
  relation to urban annexes, 188
  settlements in relation to, 238, 257
  Shang, 32, *33*, 34, 35, *37*, 38, 39-40, 41, 42, 43, 47
  shape of: circular, 183; irregular, 144; quadrangular, 138-9, 183; rectangular, 140, 141, 145, 146, 184; spear-head shaped, 252; square, 136, 140, 145, 183, 184; tendency to regularity, 184; trapezoidal, 252
  site of ruler's palace in, 188
  Southeast Asia, 250-3, 258-9
  Thai, 252-3
ensik, 312, 365
epigraphic, epigraphy
  evidence for: Chou origins, 109; ritual, 156, 160; transference of power to Chou, 108; value of evidence, 160-1
  secularization of, 161
  traditions, 62-3, 111-12
Eridug
  abandonment of, 226
  fish bones from temple, 265
  temples, 226-7, 265, 303
  tutelary deity of, 304
Eshnunnak, 226
ethnic
  composition of Chou, 108, 109-10
  division of cities, 188
  suprastratification, 120
  to territorial communities, 374-5
Etruria
  as region of secondary urban generation, 9
  ceremonial centers, 244-5
  cities arising from secondary diffusion, 7
  Etruscan origins, 340
  urban: forms, earliest, 244-5; genesis, chronology of, *322*
Evans, Sir Arthur, 381
evocatio, 432

Fairservis, Walter, 23, 232, 234, 277, 278, 288-9, 294, 303, 304
Falkenstein, Adam, 258, 264, 299
fauna of North China plain, 21
feasts, 56
feng-shui, 419-20, 458
Fergusson, James, 440
Fernea, Robert, 291

festivals
  Bẹẹrẹ, Yoruba, 261
  New Year, Persepolis, 439
  regulating cyclic time and fertility, 389-90, 417
  role of ritual specialists in, 389-90
  seasonal: need to participate in, 417; peasants' contact with ceremonial center at, 320, 389-90; persons visiting ceremonial center for, 257
  terrace to view Cambodian, 259
feudalism
  as an evolutionary process, 120
  Chou government and question of, 118-22
  coining of term, 197
  contrasted with Shang patrimonialism, 59-61
  date of emergence of, 120
  feng signifying enfeoffment, 198
  Hall's definition of feudal society, 121-2
  interpretations of, 118-19
  investiture, 121, 156, 197-8, 200-1
  landed aristocracy and, 120-1
  patrimonialism and Chou, 122, 201
  popular and press use of, 118
  resulting from supra-ethnic stratification, 120
  sacred family loyalties, 121
  sub-infeudation, 120
  weakness of contractual concept in China, 120-1, 122
  Western conception, 118-19
fire precautions, 186-7
fishing
  Lung-shan, 27, 272
  Mesopotamia: economic importance of, 273; numbers of Bau community engaged in, 270
  Shang, 68, 272, 273
  Yang-shao, 24
food
  collecting, terminal, *326-7*
  collection to food production, 277
foreign trade
  as criterion of urbanism, 373, 374
  Mesopotamian, 280
  Shang, 283, 374
Frankfort, Henri, 306, 314, 325
Friedmann, John, 288
fruit growing, 270, 272
Fujiwara-no-miya, 246-7
functions of the Chou city
  administrative role of, 176, 178-9
  agricultural, 174, 178
  agro-military role, 175-6, 178
  as agrarian labor force, 178
  ceremonial, 174, 177, 178
  commerce, 177-8
  composition of Chou settlements, 173-4
  economic role, 176-8
  essential features of Chou city, 175
  evolution of the representative Chou city, 175-8
  hierarchy of cities, 174
  industrial role, 176, 178
  instrument for exercise of central authority, 178-9
  military role, 174, 176, 178
  origin of the *hsien* city, 179-82
  problem of food supplies, 175-6
  spatially integrated hinterland organized from, 178
  ternions of cityhood, 175
  tertiary economic activity, 177-8
funeral ceremonies, 316
Fustel de Coulanges, N.D., 302

Gampola, 257
garden crops, 270, 272
Gasur, 329, 369
gates, gateways
  cardinal orientation of, 435, 438
  Central Andean carved monolithic, 237
  Chinese: arrangement of, 185; Chou 141, 142, 146; emphasis on, 481; number of, 185, 411, 442; season for repair of, 183; situation of, 185, 435

INDEX

gates, gateways – *contd.*
  cosmo-magical significance of, 435-6
  gopura, 435, 438, 440, 441
  height of, 435
  Indian, 440, 441
  Japanese, 246, 247;
  Pei-ching, 435
  reasons for massive, 435
  Southeast Asian, 250, 435, 438
  supplementary, 440
  -towers, 435
  visitors' quarters in Yoruba afins situated near, 240

***G'â-to*
  accretions to, 144, 184
  areal extent of, 144, 183
  description of site, 144-5
  Old Dame's Terrace, 144, 185
  plan of, 147, *148*
  platforms, 144, 185

gazetteers, 173, 216
Gelb, Ignace, 265, 377-8, 383
generalized integrative pattern, 316
generation, urban
  climacteric phase of, 19
  in Southeast Asia, 7
  primary: ceremonial centers in regions of, 226-43; cities of, 8; defined, 8; ecological component in, 268-9; regions of, 9
  secondary: ceremonial centers in regions of, 244-57; cities of, 8; defined, 8; ecological component in, 269; regions of, 7, 9; Shang, 50, 52

genesis
  and morphology of Shang cities: earliest urban forms, 30-52; pre-urban North China, 20-30
  of the ceremonial center: components (demographic 275-8, ecological 268-75, technological 278-81); factors inducing social differentiation (irrigation 289-98, religion 302-5, trade and marketing 281-9, warfare 298-302)

of the city in China: class differentiation in Shang society, 63-7; economic organization, 75-7; genesis and morphology of Shang dynasty, 9-13; introduction, 3-9; political structure of Shang state, 52-63; sources for study of Shang urbanism, 13-20; technological change, 67-75
  see also urban

geography
  early documents on, 129-30
  of Chou, territories, 128-9
  of North China plain, 20, 21
  view of geographers on urbanism, 388-9, 391, 389, 477

geomancers, 417-23, 481
geomantic precautions, 417-23, 451
Gilgamesh, 312, 313
Gio-Linh uplands, 296
Girshu, 226

**Giwo
  as a culture hero, 129-30
  bronze cauldrons of, 130, 136

Gizeh, 230, 316

***G'og*
  as apex of urban hierarchy, 174
  divisions of city, 188
  soil from the national altar, 175

government, Chou
  absorption of smaller polities, 115, 117
  administration, 117-18
  bureaucracy: and the *hsien*, 179-80; despotism and, 117-18; rise of impersonal, 125, 179
  cult centers, role of 113, 162, 174
  decline of central power, 113-14, 118
  divine sanction, 112-13
  familialistic: system of, 112-13; oligarchic aristocracy replacing, 117, 118
  feudalism, question of, 118-22
  foreign policy, 116
  garrisons, 112, 162

INDEX

government, Chou – *contd.*
  Han view of Chou government, 113
  Hegemon, the, 115-16
  kinship and, 112-13
  magnates: assumption of titles, 116-17; Ch'un-Ch'iu, 116-17; powers of, 115-16, 120-1
  ministers: grades of, 124; hereditary, 125
  patrimonialism, extension of, 112
  periods of, 114
  political consolidation under Western Chou, 115
  Royal Chou: ceremonial significance of, 114, 121; debasement of styles of, 116; ritual authority of, 112, 113, 114
  Shang benefice holders under, 112
  states: central, 114, 129, 166; conflict between, 115, 117-18; government within, 117-18; important, 114; independent, 114, 122; interstate relations, 114, 115-17; number of, 112, 114, 117
  traditional: authority replaced by rational-legal, 115-16; view of, 113
  tribal territories, 115, 175
  zones of influence, 114-15, 121, 129, 479
government, Shang
  as a patrimonial system, 56-7
  as a theocracy, 55-6
  benefices: and feudal contracts, 60-1; Chou as holders of, 109; creation of, 57-8; duties of holders, 58-9; military association of, 99, 109; names of, 58; number of, 58; social distinction of holders of, 61; women holders of, 58
  Chou as tribal chieftains under, 109
  elaboration of military force, 57-8
  extension of: administrative stage, 57; patrimonial authority, 57-9
  extent of dominion, 61-3
  military organization, 58-9
  officials of, 56-7
  outer zone of influence, 58-9
  proto-bureaucracies of Western Chou, 196
  territory of tribal chieftains, 58-9, 109
granaries
  Indus valley, 232, 267
  Mesopotamia, 227
Greece, Greek
  autonomy of cities, 371
  cult center at Delphi, 113
  economic and social functions of the *agora*, 178
  dispersion and compaction of cities, 308-9
  question of urban status in pre-classical, 386
  religion and urban origins, 302-5
  synoecism in urban development, 308-9
Gulf, 323

habitabilis, 389, 417, 418, 439-40, 451
Haldas, 326, 395-6
Halingyi, 250
Han
  anhistoricity of, 62
  distortion of reconstituted texts, 5, 14-15
  exegesis, 152, 159-9
  image of Chou era, 119-20
  reconstitution of 'classical' tests, 5, 13, 113
  traders, 284
  version of the past, 113
Han Ch'ang-an, 442, *443*
Hang-Chou
  cardinal orientation and axiality of, 423
  layout of, 414
  significance of, 393
hang-t'u
  absence of, in proto-cities, 50
  alternative terms for, 91
  at Cheng-Chou, 3, 39

INDEX

hang-t'u – contd.
  at Hsiao-T'un, 38, 40
  consecration of foundations and buildings, 65
  defined, 32, 34
  dwellings of nobility, 63-4
  foundations of dwellings of: bronze workers, 36; potters, 66
  in Chou cities, 136, 138, 139, 141, 142, 144, 150
  in systematization of archeological evidence, *48-9*
  Lung-shan: invention of, 69; ramparts, 26
  platforms, 139, 142, 144, 145, 185, 425, 429
  ramparts, 26, 32, 39-40, 302
  walls, 183, 302
Han-tan
  annexes, 142, 188
  description of, 142, 144
  plan of, *143*, 147, *148*
  platforms, *hang-t'u*: axial arrangement of, 142, 185, 425; *omphalos* concept and, 429; shape of, 142, 185; situation of, 185
  walls, height of, 142, 183
Harappā
  ablution facilities, 232
  absence of detail of mode of origin, 5
  'acropolis', 232
  areal extent of, 231
  cemetery, 232
  date of, 234
  dual form of city, 232
  granary, 232, 267
  problem of excavation, 230-1
  redistributive function of, 267
  situation of, 231
  tradition, 308
haruspicy, 416
Hassuna, 303
heaven, proximity to, 428-9
Hegemon, 115-16
Heian-kyō, 247-8
heterogenesis, 392-3

hierarchy of cities
  imperial capital at apex of, 174
  minor polities, 184
  pressures tending to upgrade settlements, 167
  provincial towns, 182
  ranks: areal extent and, 183-4; attempts to rationalize, 174; of *hsien* capitals, 179
  state capitals, 174, 182
  **to, **kwək and **·*i̯əp*, 167, 174
  types of settlements in, 174
hieroglyphics
  Cretan, 381
  Mesoamerican, 234
Ḥijāz
  Quraysh monopoly of trade, 286, 288
  transmutation from kin group to politized unit, 286-8
historicity of the Shang dynasty, 3-4, 9-13
Hmawza, 250
Hopewellian
  shrines, *323*
  truncated evolution, 397
hospitals, Cambodian, 259, 265
Hou-chia Chuang, 258
Hou-ma Chen
  areal extent, 138, 139, 183
  description of sites, 138-41
  omphalos concept, 429
  plan, 147, *148*
  workshop dispersion, 139-40, 185-6
  see also Niu-Ts'un, P'ing-wang
Hsia
  in traditional Chinese history, 9
  overthrown by Shang, 10
  relationship between Shang and, 12-13
Hsi-an, 108
Hsiao-T'un
  altar at, 34, 40, 43
  ancillary settlements, *37*, 43-7
  architectural features, 16
  as the last capital of Shang, 62
  bone workshops, 43, *45*

INDEX

Hsiao-T'un – *contd.*
 bronze: artifacts, 73; foundries, 43, 73; ritual vessels, 43, 73
 buildings, reconstruction of, 43, *45*, 46
 burial sites, *37*, 42
 ceremonial precinct, *37*, 38, 39-40, *41*, *42*, 43, *45*, 55, 241, *242*
 complex, 34, *37*
 description of excavations, 16
 drainage, 38, 40, 68
 dwelling sites, *37*
 hang-t'u: construction, 40, 43, 45; foundations, *42*, 43, 46, 65; phase, 38
 land use, *42*
 morphological classification of buildings, 40, 93-4
 palaces, 40, 44, 55, 74
 pits, *42*
 pottery kilns, 43
 residential area of the ruling élite, 40, 43, 46
 royal cemetery, *see* Hsi-pei Kang
 service areas, *42*, 43
 spatial arrangement, 40
 stratigraphical levels, 38
 systematization of archeological evidence, *48-9*
 temples, 40, 43, 55, 65, 74
 workshops, *37*, *45*, 74
hsien
 as a government instrument, 179-80, 181
 capital, 179
 diffusion of, 180
 earliest example of, 181
 graph for, 179
 heritable, 180, 181, 219-20
 in **Dz'jĕn, 179-80
 in **Tsjĕn, 180, 181-2
 in **Tṣ'jo, 180-1
 kin groups and, 180, 181
 non-hereditary officials, 179, 180-1
 origin of: Bodde's theory, 179-80; Creel's theory, 180-1
 situations giving rise to, 179

Hsing-T'ai
 description of site, 50
 secondary urban generation, 329
 spatial distribution of workshops, 75
 systematization of archeological evidence, *48-9*
Hsi-pei Kang
 cruciform pits, 316
 dualistic arrangement and lineage system, 55
 furnishing of tombs, 65
 impression given by, 478
 labor force required, 76-7, 258
 mausolea, 16, 44, 64, 65, 316
 orientation of, 426
 royal cemetery, 16, *37*, 43-4
 workshops, 74
Hsi-Shan Hsien, 150
hsiu, 385
Hsüeh-chia Chuang, 17
Hua-yin Hsien, 150
Hui-Hsien
 bronze artifacts, 73
 description of site, 47, 50
 pottery, 70
 systematization of archeological evidence, *48-9*
hunting
 Lung-shan, 27
 modes of, 68
 Shang, 68
 weapons, 73-4
 Yang-shao, 24
hydraulic
 agriculture, 289-90
 bureaucracy, 289, 290, 297
 engineering: Ceylon, 296-7; Chou, 131
 purposes: architecture, 295, 296; ritualistic, 295-6; transportation (Egypt 294-5, China 292)
 state, emergence of, 289-90
 system in the Mekong valley, 254, 345
 see also irrigation

INDEX

Ica valley
  compaction, 236
  irrigation, 294
I-Ching, 158, 167, 190, 215, 379
I Chou-shu, 188, 221
Ife
  afins, 239
  ecological zones, 271
Ijẹbu-Ode, 239
I-Li, 151, 157
imago mundi, 417, 450
Inca(s)
  ceremonial centers, 238, 307
  cities, 238, 386
  disintegration of empire, 238
  expansion, 238, 241
  irrigation, 294
  militarism, 238, 314
  palaces, 238
  settlement patterns, 307
  temples, 238
  terraces, 294
India, Indian
  axial avenues, 440
  capitals, migration of, 448
  cardinal orientation and axiality, 426-7, 439-40
  circumambulation, 433-4
  city: comparison of Chinese and, 450-1; planning, 439-41; schools of planning, 440-1
  compaction, 308, *323*
  dating of literary sources, 308
  entrepreneurs from Gupta, 285, 356
  gateways, 440, 441
  gopuras, 440, 441
  temple-city: as *axis mundi*, 451; building of walls of, 435-6; cosmo-magical significance of, 451; role of central temple, 428; symbolism of, 439-40
  tension between sacred and secular authority, 315
  urban forms: burgeoning of, on North Indian plain, 308; canonically sanctioned layout, 414

urban genesis, chronology of Ganges valley, *323*
Indianization
  accounts of, 341
  changing authority relationships, 249, 256
  changing cultural configuration, 249, 253-4
  of Indus valley culture, 231
  political model of divine kingship, 249, 256, 314-15
  religion in Southeast Asia, 249, 254, 256, 436-8
  Sanskritization of names, 255, 314-15
Indochina, ceremonial centers in, 253-5
Indus valley
  'acropolis', 232
  archeological evidence for, 229, 230-1
  as area of primary urban genesis, 9
  brick manufacture, 233, 267
  cemeteries, 232
  ceremonial centers: description of, 230-4; deterioration of habitat, 277, 304; Mohenjo-daro and Harappā, 231, 232; population density and, 277, 304
  cities: compaction, *323*; dual form of, 232
  cult centers: morphology, 307; settlements around, 257
  cultivation, 269, 271
  culture: dating of, 233; extent of, 231; Indianization of, 231; relation to Baluchistan culture, 231-2, 233
  deciphering of inscriptions, 5, 20
  diffusion from Mesopotamia, 7, 8, 233
  ecological interdependencies, 271
  fortification, 232
  granaries, 232, 267
  question of: irrigation, 294; religion, 303; warfare, 299
  redistributive function, 267

577

INDEX

Indus valley – *contd.*
  settlement patterns, 257, 278
  trade: links with Mesopotamia, 233; treaty, 283
  urban: evolution, rate of, 325-6, 328; forms, earliest, 230-4
  urban genesis: chronology of, *323*; course of, *326-7*; technological advance and, 280
  urban origins, evidence of, 5, 20
  village settlements, 233
inscriptions
  bronze, 58, 62-3, 108, 111-12, 160-1
  Chan-Kuo, 160-1
  Chou, 108, 111-12, 160-1
  Ch'un-Ch'iu, 160
  I Hou Nieh I, 108, 111-12, 122, 163
  script used for Shang, 380
  Shang, 62-3, 111-12
interdependencies, ecological, 269-73
intermarriage, Shang-Chou, 176
Irawadi
  ceremonial centers, 249, 251, *323*
  Mōn culture, 251
  temples on banks of, 250
  urban genesis, chronology of, *323*
iron
  agricultural implements, 130-1
  diffusion of technology in Chou times, 131
  -foundry, 131, 144
  -smelting, 126
  weapons, 131, 144
irrigation
  absence of evidence in Shang and Western Chou, 68, 110, 131, 292
  allocation of water, 292
  and advancement of science, 290
  and agriculture, 293-4, 297, 298
  as a factor in social differentiation, 289-98, 477 ff
  Aztec systems, 292-3
  Cambodia, 259, 295-6
  Central Andes, 294
  central government and, 291, 292
  Ceylon, 295, 296-7
  Eastern Chou, 131
  evidence for developed, 291
  flood control, 289, 290
  hydraulic: agriculture, 289-90; bureaucracy, 289, 290, 297; economy, role in state, 289-90; engineering, 131, 296-7
  Inca, 294
  Indus valley, 294
  labor force: control of, 294; deployment of, pre-supposing superordinate authority, 298; Mesopotamian temples directing, 292
  labor, preparatory role of, 289-90
  large-scale: reconstituting ecotypes, 297; resulting from state and urban organization, 297-8
  Maya, 293-4
  Mesoamerica, 292-4
  Mesopotamia, 292
  militarism and, 293, 298
  Old World, 294-5
  political power and, 289, 291, 292, 293
  population density and, 292-3
  productivity and, 297, 298
  small-scale: Cambodia, 296; Central Andes, 294; Maya, 293-4; Mesopotamia, 292; modulating ecosystems, 297; type of society required for, 297-8
  social surplus and, 297
  urban genesis and, 292-3, 297
  water control as a local matter, 292, 295
  Wittfogel's theory, 289-92
Isaac, Erich, 416-17
Islam
  cultural norms substituted for cosmo-magical, 481
  omphalos concept in, 428-9
Ixkún, 441

Jacobsen, Thorkild, 228, 311-12
jade
  artifacts, 46

jade – *contd.*
  carving: Chou, 131-2; Shang, 69
  for ceremonial purposes, 69-70
  funerary articles, 64, 69-70, 74, 140
  Lung-shan, 69
  ornaments, 69, 74, 140
  production for élite, 76, 176
  Shang, 36, 69-70, 74
Japan
  bibliography, 340
  bureaucracy, 245-6, 247
  ceremonial: centers, 245-8; halls, 246, 247; pavilions, 248
  cities: areal extent of, 247-8; autonomy, 371; compact, *323*; planning, 246-7; structure, 246
  corporate groups, 245, 376
  enceintes, 247
  gates, 246, 247
  hereditary associations of workers, 245
  hierarchy: of Yamato cult centers, 245; social, 245-6
  influence of Buddhism, 246
  kinship groups, 245-6, 376
  lineages and officials, 245-6
  migration of capitals, 246
  militarism, 245, 246
  moats, 247
  palaces, 246-7, 248
  religion: divorced from secular administration, 247; function of head of state, 245; sanction for government, 245-6
  semi-autonomous patriarchal units (*uji*), 245
  shrines, 246, 247, *323*
  slave class, 245
  taxation, 247
  temples, 246, 247-8
  trade, role of, 289
  urban forms, earliest, 245-8
  urban genesis: chronology of, *323*; course of, *326-7*
Jarmo, 303
Java
  Buddhist influence, 256
  caṇḍi, 256
  capitals, succession of, 448
  ceremonial centers: description of, 255-6; dispersed, *323*
  compaction, 307, *323*
  cosmo-magical significance, 256
  Dieng plateau, 255-6
  Kĕdu plain, 256, 260
  Śailendra dynasty, 256, 346
  Sanskritization, 256, 314-15
  settlement patterns, 306, 307
  shrines, 255, 256
  stupa, 256
  temple-cities, 256, 257
  terraces, 256
  urban: genesis, chronology of, *323*; status, question of, 386
Jawad, Abdul Jalil, 328-9
Jayavarman VII
  buildings erected by, 258-60, 265, 372
  symbolism of Yaśodharapura under, 432, 434, 437-8
Jericho
  complexity of society, 326
  progress of the Ark round, 434
  representational art, 374
  shrine, 302, 395
  urban status, question of, 394
Jerusalem
  omphalos concept, 428
  planning of, 444
Jidle, 329
justitia, concordia to, 267

Ka'bāh
  as an ancient shrine, 288
  omphalos concept, 428-9
  rain on, as indicative of fertility, 433
  trade, religion and social status, 286-7
K'ai-feng, 414
Kalat, 231
Kalibangan, 230, 232
Kambujadeśa
  capital of, as *axis mundi*, 434

Kambujadeśa – *contd.*
  building of new capitals, 448
  canal systems, 295
  conceptual intricacy of symbolism, 260, 295, 436-7
  dualistic structure of authority, 315
  erection of shrines, 258-9
  irrigation works, 295
  parallelism between macrocosmos and microcosmos, 436-7
  role of temple-city, 254
  social solidarity, 390, 391
  symbolism of the center, 295, 432, 436-7, 451
  see also Khmer empire
Kaminaljuyú, 234, 235, 300
Kampheng Sen, 252
Kanburi Kao, 252
Kandy, 257
K'ao-kung Chi (*Book of Artificers*)
  description of buildings, 43
  nature of text, 156
  plans for layout of Chinese cities, 411, 414, 426
  ritualized urban schema of, 177
Kauśāmbī, 308
Kauṭhāra, 253
Kĕḍu, 256, 260
Kenyon, Kathleen, 394
Khafājah, 227, 310
Khami, 398
khipu, 379, 402
Khmer empire
  agro-architectural complexes, 296
  cosmo-magical symbolism, 295, 296
  dispersed settlements, 307
  history of, 345
  social solidarity, 390-1
  territories of Mekong valley, 249-50
  see also Cambodia, Kambujadeśa
Khorsabad, 448
kin groups
  aims of kingship and, 315
  coexistence with politically organized units, 374-5
  conical clans, 53, 55, 375, 376-7
  corporate, role of, 374-7
  corvée organized by, 375
  craft production and organization, 66-7, 375
  decline of cohesiveness, 128
  disenfranchisement of, 287, 374-5
  dysfunctions introduced into, 286-7
  economic and social differentiation, 375-6
  erosion of political privileges of, 179-80
  Japanese, 245-6, 376
  landholding, corporate, 375, 376
  lineages and, 375
  Meccan, 286-8, 376
  Mesoamerican, 375-6
  Mesopotamian, 374, 375, 376
  Mexican, 375-6
  modification of, 375
  persistence of, 374-5
  relation between class and, 377
  Shang, 53, 55, 63, 375
  Southeast Asian, 288
  specialized technology as prerogative of, 67
  stratification, induced and superimposed, 375-6
  territorial concept, shift from, 286-7, 477
  transmutation of Arabian, 286, 288
  Yoruba, 376
kin, kinship
  as basis of Lung-shan society, 29-30
  corporate: defined, 194; extension of nomenclature, 112-13
  in Shang lineages, 53, 55
  under Chou, 112-13
  under Shang, 53, 55, 63, 375
king, kingship
  as a secular warrior, 311
  as vicegerent of deity, 315
  class differentiation and, 228
  craft production and, 280
  divine, 225-6, 249, 256, 288, 313, 314
  Dynastic phase of urbanism, 298

INDEX

king, kingship – *contd.*
  emergence of palaces and mausolea, 298, 315-16
  hereditary succession, 313, 314
  introduced to meet emergencies, 312
  in: Egypt, 314; Mesoamerica, 313-14; Mesopotamia, 228, 280, 311-13; Shang, 315; Southeast Asia, 314-15; South India, 314
  kinship and, 311, 315
  office focusing political power, 311, 315
  priest-kings of Knossos, 244
  prosperity of community and, 311
  rise of, 228, 280, 311-14
  secular sphere of government extended, 311, 315
  subscribing to religious norms, 315, 316
  warfare and, 298, 313
kingdoms
  as replicas of cosmos, 417
  powers of, focused in capitals, 431-3
  relation between capital and, 445-7
Kirchhoff, Paul, 234, 313, 375
Kish, 226
Knossos
  description of, 244
  Middle Minoan palace, 260
  redistributive function, 267
Ko-ta-wang, 31, 32
Kot Diji, 230, 231, 232, 233
Kotte, 257
Kuan-tzŭ, 157-8, 160, 174
Kuntur Wasi, 236
Kuo-Yü
  compilation of, 154-5
  nature of, 151, 152
  references to: commerce, 177; urbanism, 187
Kurunagala, 257
Kyōtō, 414

labor
  centralized control of: and rise of ceremonial centers, 267; by Cambodian temple-cities, 264, 265-6; by Mesopotamian temple officials, 262, 264; of agricultural, 76, 262, 264; resource exploitation, 262, 264
  corvée, 261, 262, 263, 375, 390, 479
  division of, 29-30
  force: for irrigation, 289-90, 292, 294, 298; means of procuring, 261; required for intensive construction, 258-60
  pools, 261
  preparatory, 289-90
  recruitment of: Malaysian, 261-2; Yoruba, 261
lacquer
  advances in Chou technology, 131
  use by nobility, 176
Lagash
  cult center at, 226, 264, 265
  planning, 444
  population associated with fishing, 270
  synoecism in development, 310
lakes, artificial, 259
land
  as a purchasable commodity, 133-4
  centralized control of, 267
  holding by corporate groups, 375
  -tenure: Chou system and manorial, 118-22, 132-3; impersonal relations in, 133-4; possession and ownership, 133; semi-military *colonia*, 132; taxes and rent, 133, 206; well-field system, 132-3, 176, 205
landscape
  geomancy and transformation of, 419-20
  religion transforming, 416-17
Las Bela, 231, 232
Lattimore, Owen, 120
Lavapura, 252
La Venta, 234
Leach, Edmund, 258, 296-7
Lepenski Vir, 374
Levant, The, 7
Lewis, Oscar, 388

INDEX

Li-Chi (*Record of Rituals*)
  nature of text, 151, 157;
  prescription for: ancestral temples, 55; investiture ceremonies, 156
  references to: altars, 175; rites, 418; wall-building, 182-3
lineage(s)
  class differentiation and, 63
  conical clans, 375, 376
  crafts and, 66-7
  groupings in Mesoamerica and Mesopotamia, 375-6
  Quraysh, 376
  ramage system, 53
  Shang: grand, 52-5; kinship and class, 53, 55; rank in society determined by, 375
  stratified, 53
  system: in Japan, 245-6, 376; in Nigeria, 239
liṅga, 249, 256
Lin-i, 253
Lin tzŭ
  areal extent of, 183
  description of, 145
  enceintes, 145, 183, 188
  plan of, 147, *149*
  platform, 145, 185
  population, 190
Li-Sao, 151
literary evidence
  Chou origins, 109
  Chou society, 122-3
literary sources
  archetyping of texts, 150-1
  books of ritual, 155-7
  for: Chou, 150-60; cosmo-magical symbolism, 418-19; Eastern Chou, 151, 152-3; Shang, 13-15; urban evolution, 152-60; Western Chou, 151
  free texts, 151-2, 157
  historiographical, 151, 159-60
  nature of early Chinese, 5, 13-20
  reconstituted, 4, 5
  systematizing texts, 151-2, 155-6

lithic
  artifacts, 69-70, 76
  decline of industry under Shang, 69
liturgical
  obligations of benefices, 58
  use of term, 99
**Lo, state of, 114, 133, 183, 187
long houses
  Lung-shan, 26
  Yang-shao, 24
Lopburi, 252
Loralai, 231
Lothal
  description of, 232
  redistributive function, 232, 267
Lo-yang
  altar, 175
  areal extent, 183
  Chou cities near, 136-8
  description of site, 47, 50
  layout of, 414
  pottery, 70
  removal of Chou capital to, 113
  Royal City, width of walls, 183
  selection of site of, *422*
  systematization of archeological evidence, *48-9*
lugal, 312, 365
Lung-shan, Lungshanoid
  agricultural: crops, 26-7, 67, 272; domestic animals, 27, 68; economy, 29, 67-8, 75, 76; implements, 27, 67, 68, 76
  Chou culture developed from, 108, 110, 135
  development and diffusion of culture, 26
  division of labor, 30
  ecological level, 317
  ecotype, 26, 29, 269, 272
  extent of culture, 26
  hunting and fishing, 27, 272
  influence at Cheng-Chou, 30, 31
  jade, 69
  kinship, 29-30
  occupational specialization, 28, 30

INDEX

Lung-shan, Lungshanoid – *contd.*
  political organization, 26, 28
  pottery, 27, 28, 32, 70, 71, 281
  ritualism, 27-8, 303
  scapulimancy, 303
  settlement: morphology, 233; permanence of, 26; situation of, 278; walled, 28, 69, 229, 233, 302, 394
  society, 26, 27-8, 229, 317
  status differentiation, 27-8, 63, 69
  stratification, social, 28-9
  technological advances, 27, 68, 69, 70, 71
  village economy, 75
  warfare, 28, 302
Lun-Yü, 133, 151, 158, 167, 174, 215, 430
Lü-Shih Ch'un-Ch'iu, 155, 174
lustrations, 244, 265, 296
Luzon, 260

macrocosmos and microcosmos
  harmony between, necessary for state, 254-5, 418, 436
  parallelism between: building in accordance with ancient plan, 444; Cambodian evidence, 296, 436-8; Chinese evidence, 442-7, 450; constellations, 442, *443*; Hindu cities, 439-41; Mesoamerica, 441-2; participation through ritual, 418, 436; Persepolis, 438-9
  question of haruspicy, 416
  religions reproducing terrestrial version of cosmos, 417
  symbolism of: gates, 438, 440, 441; moats, 438, 439-40; walls, 438
McTaggart, Donald, 398
Madagascar, Tanala of, 110, 192-3
Madrolle, Claude, 427
Madurai, 414, 441
Malaka, 261-2, 393
Malaya
  assemblage of labor force, 261-2
  ceremonial centers, 255
  élite, 393
  heterogenetic and orthogenetic change in, 393
  Indianization, 255
  Mōn culture in, 251, 255
  rise of city-states, 255
  social differentiation, 288
  urban life, 255, 345-6
Malleret, Louis, 295-6, 391
Mallia, 244
Mapungubwe, 398
Marango, 236
marble
  funerary articles, 64
  ornaments, 69
  sculptures, 74
Marimdah, 233
market(s), marketing
  absence of market-places, 228, 282-3, 372
  autonomous, price-fixing, 282, 372
  by decree, 390
  distinction between trade and, 282, 372
  risk-free marketless trading, 372
  self-regulating, 282, 353, 392-3
  social and political power and, 282
  type of Chinese, 480
Mauryas, 117
mausolea, 16, 44, 46, 47, 64, 65
Mauss, Marcel, 392
Maya, Mayan
  agriculture, 275, 293-4
  bibliography on cities, 336-7
  calendrics, 384-5
  ceremonial centers, 300
  chronology, 336
  Classic or Florescent period, 336
  cult centers, abandonment of, 307-8
  dependability of production, 274
  inscriptions, 5
  Lowland: cities, *322*, 330; dispersed settlements, 307-8; long count, 384-5; temples, 235
  number of architectural complexes, 235
omphalos concept, 429

INDEX

Maya, Mayan – *contd.*
  pyramids, 429
  settlements: affinity for *bajo* fringes, 306; dispersed, 307-8; grouping of house mounds, 306; round enceintes, 257
  shrines, 257, 429
  social solidarity, 390-1
  swidden ecosystem, 275, 293
  temples, 235, 429
  temple-cities, 308
  urban: imposition, 330; origins, documents for, 5; status, question of 386, 389
  urban genesis: chronology of, *322*; course of, *326-7*
  warfare, 300
  water-lily motif, 293
  writing 382, 383
Media Luna, 236
Mediterranean, urban genesis in, *322*
Mekong valley, 249-50, 253-5, 258-60, 295-6
Mellaart, James, 394-5
Memphis
  ceremonial center, 229-30
  Circuit of the White Wall, 434
  founding of, 333
  land drainage, 295
Memphite Theology, 229, 333
Mendut, 256
Menes, unifier of Egypt, 229, 295, 333, 434
Meng-tzŭ, 151, 158
Menzel, Dorothy, 238, 398
merchants
  absence of autonomous group, 178
  associated with artisans in urban sector of society, 321
  entrepreneurial, 133-4
  in Chou society, 125, 177
  in Ch'un-Ch'iu, 134, 177-8
  items of trade, 177-8
  rise of: class of wealthy, 134; Meccan oligarchy, 286-8; Mesopotamian oligarchy, 280

  role in urbanism, 177-8
  use of wealth to acquire political power, 126
Mersin, 299
Meru, Mount
  as *axis mundi* of Indian mythology, 428, 432
  Cambodian plastic representations of, 436, 438
  represented by Bàyon, 432, 437-8
Mesoamerica
  agriculture, 272, 275
  altars, 234
  amount of archeological evidence, 3
  architecture, 235
  as area of primary urban genesis, 9
  Aztec royalty, emergence of, 313-14
  carvings, 234
  ceremonial centers: areal extent of, 235; compaction of, 278, *322*, 480; decline of, 235; dispersed, *322*; early appearance of, 276; emergence of, 234-5; number of, 235; plan of, 241, *242*; redistributive function, 235, 266; size of, 235
  corporate kin groups, 374-5
  culturally related developments, 9
  decline of sacral authority, 313
  defined, 234
  ecological: instability, 304; interdependence, 270, 273
  militarism, 299-301, 313, 314, 480
  parallelism between macrocosmos and microcosmos, 441-2
  platform mounds, 234, 301
  population increase, 276
  religion, 304
  ritual ball game, 235, 300
  secularization of authority, 313-14
  shrines, *322*
  stairways, 234, 301
  temple(s): enclaves, 234; mounds, 234, 235; pyramids, 235, 301; raised near heaven, 301
  terraces, 234

INDEX

Mesoamerica – *contd.*
  tombs, 301
  trade: and tribute, 270, 284; treaty, 283
  urban: evolution, rate of, 328; forms, earliest, 234-5; life, post-Conquest evidence for, 5; population densities, 306
  urban genesis
    chronology of, *322-3*
    course of, *326-7*
  warfare and defence, 299-301
  writing, 382
Mesopotamia (Lower)
  agriculture, 269-70, 280
  as area of primary urban genesis, 9
  cardinal orientation, 451
  centralized control of land, labor and resources, 262, 264
  centralized management of craft production, 273
  ceremonial centers: description of, 226-30; dispersed, 299, *323*
  cities, compact, 299, *323*
  climatic change, 21
  craft production, 228-9, 273, 279-80
  cult centers, earliest, 226
  diffusion from, 7, 8
  ecology: instability, 304; interdependencies, 269-70, 272, 273; specialized subsistence zone, 269-70
  en, 311-12
  enceintes, 228
  ensik, 312
  fishing, 270, 273
  fruit and garden crops, 270
  irrigation, 292
  kin groups: corporate, 374-6; stratified, 375-6
  kingship in, 228, 311-13
  lugal, 312, 365
  metallurgy, 280
  omphalos concept, 429
  palace, 228
  pastoralism, 270, 272
  popular assembly, 312
  population: and urban genesis, 276-7; densities, urban, 306, 307
  Protoliterate: period, 226, 257, 262, 264, 273, 311, 312; texts, 4-5, 20
  reallocation, 265
  religion, 304
  representational art, 373
  secularization of authority, 311-13
  settlements: linear, 278; round enceintes, 257
  shrines, 303
  stratification, social and economic, 228
  synoecism, 310
  technological advances, 279-80
  temple: architecture, 227; evolution of, 226-7; reallocative role of, 265; role in irrigation, 292
  textiles, 280
  tombs, 228
  trade: demand for metals, 280; export, 280; links with Indus valley, 233; marketless trading, 282, 372; organized from temples, 283; treaty, 283
  urban: evolution, rate of, 328; forms, earliest, 226-30
  urban genesis: chronology of, *323*; course of, *326-7*; nature of, *325-6*; population and, 276-7; technology and, 279-80
  urban origins: attention paid to, 3; evidence of, 5, 9, 20
  walls, 228, 299
  warfare, 228, 299
Mesopotamia (Northern)
  diffusion in, 329
  urban development in, 328-9
  urban imposition, 330
metallurgy, 280
Mexico
  calendrics, 384
  Central, urban genesis in, *322*
  kin groups, corporate, 375-6
  omphalos concept, 429

INDEX

Mexico – *contd.*
  shrines, *322*, 429
  valley of: architectural complexes, 234-5, 260; irrigation, role of, 292-3; secularization of authority, 313-14; settlements round enceintes, 257; urban genesis, course of, *326-7*
militarism
  Aztec, 299-300
  characteristics of, 321
  differentiation of political and religious authority under, 321
  Inca, 238
  Japanese, 245-6
  Mayan, 300
  Mesoamerican, 299-301, 313, 314, 480
  Peruvian, 301
  phase of urban evolution, 298, 300-1
  reasons for, 321
  see also warfare
military
  archery, 126
  chariots, 59, 73, 126, 140
  command, men of ability rising to, 125-6
  conscription, 59, 126
  duties of benefice holders, 58
  equipment, demand for, 228, 280
  expeditions, 58, 59
  force, elaboration of, 57
  functions of cities, 174, 176
  garrison towns of Chou, 162, 174
  infantry, 59, 126
  motivation for compaction, 310, 480
  officials, Shang, 56, 57
  organization: Lung-shan, 28; Shang, 59
  prisoners of war: sacrifice of, 65, 66; use of, 76
  weapons: bronze, 104-5; iron, 131; Mesopotamian, 280; ritual, 281; stimulating technological advance, 73, 281
  see also warfare
Mĩ-sơn, 307

Miles, S. W., 389
Mississippi:
  dispersed ceremonial centers, *323*
  truncated evolution of ceremonial centers, 397
Mitla, 441
moats
  cosmo-magical significance of, 438
  defensive, 139, 145, 146, 150
  Hindu, 439-40
  Japanese, 247
  Mesoamerican, 300, 301
  Southeast Asian: Mekong valley, 254, 259, 438; Pyū, 250; Thai, 252, 253
  surrounding walls, 183
Moctezuma I, 316
Moctezuma II, 266, 314
Mohenjo-daro
  ablution facilities, 232
  'acropolis', 232
  areal extent, 231
  citadel, precincts of, 260
  dating of, 233, 234
  deforestation near, 233
  dual form of, 232
  economic decline of, 233-4
  granary, 232, 267
  lack of information on origins, 5
  layout, 414
  problem of excavation, 230-1
  reconstruction of ground plan, *413*
  redistributive function, 266
  role of, 232
Mōn culture, 249, 251, 288
monarchy, divine, *see* kingship
Monro, W. B., 372-3
Monte Albán
  calendrics, 384
  defensive advantages, 301
  deflection of axis, 441
  layout, 398
  mound architecture, 234
  platform and courtyard, 301
  monumental complexes, exclusive study of, 3

INDEX

moral order
  cities as symbols of, 225, 479
  in cities of orthogenetic transformation, 392, 478, 479, 481
Morgan, L. H., 374, 377
morphology
  compact: and society of mechanical solidarity, 310, 390-1; and society of organic solidarity, 310, 390-1; chronology of, *322-3*; economic change and, 310; Greek cities, 308-9; Indian cities, 308; Mesopotamia, 310; military motivation for, 310; population densities, 305, 306, 307-8; Rome, 309; social change and, 310, 390-1; synoecic phase in, 308-9; technological change and, 310
  dispersed: Cambodia, 306; Chou, 185-6, 188; chronology of, *322-3*; enceinte as focus of, 305; Maya, 306; population and, 305-6, 307; Shang, 306
  of ceremonial centers, 305-11
  of Chou city; annexes, 188; areal extent, 183-4; enceintes, 184-5; spatial and functional dichotomy, 187-8; suburbs, 186-7; walls, 182-3, 185-6
  of Shang city, 20-52, 477
mortuary complexes, Egyptian, 229-30
Mo-tzŭ, 151
mounds
  Central Andes, 236
  Mesoamerica, 234-5, 306
mountain(s)
  as *axis mundi*, 417, 451
  cosmic, 254, 259, 417, 442
  gods, 296
  in Chinese mythology, 442, 444
  sacred, 254, 434
  spirits, 256
  temple-, 259, 429, 432, 451
  visit of Chinese emperor to, 434
Mus, Paul, 432

musical instruments
  bronze, 73, 104
  pottery, 71, 74
Muslim, state structure, 287-8

Nagaoka, 248, 258
nāgara, 308
Nagas, 260
Nakhon Pathom, 252, 306
Nalatali, 398
Nan-ching, 414
Naniwa, 246
Nan-yang Hsien, 150
Nara, 414
navel of the earth, 428-9
  see also axis mundi, omphalos
Nazca, 384
Neak Pean, 259
Needham, Joseph, 426
Nepeña valley, 236
nephrite, 283
New Fields, *see* Niu Ts'un, P'ing-wang, Hou-ma Chen
**Ngog, *33*, 84
Nicholas of Thverva, 428
Nigeria, Southwestern
  afins, 238-9, 240
  as area of primary urban generation, 9
  bibliography of, 338-9
  ceremonial centers, 238-40, 477
  craftsmen, 240
  crops, 269, 270-1
  cult center, 113
  gateway, 240
  irrigation, question of, 294
  labor force, 261
  ọbas, 238, 239
  plan of Afin Ọyọ, 241, *243*
  swidden cultivation, 275
  synoecism, 239
  treaty trade, 283
  urban: forms, earliest, 238-40; genesis, chronology of, *322*; -rural relationships, 310-11; status, question of, 391-2
  warfare, 299

INDEX

Ninā, 226
Nineveh
  planning of, 444
  plan of, 436
  site at, 329
Nippur, 226
Niu-Ts'un
  areal extent, 183
  cardinal axiality, 185
  cardinal orientation, 138-9, 427
  moat, 139, 183
  platform, 139, 185
  quadrangular enciente, 138, 183
nobility, see élite
Non Phra, 252
North America, 6, *323*, 397
Nuclear America
  attention paid to urban origins, 3
  calendrics, 384-5
  ceremonial centers, 477
  defined, 78
  question of diffusion, 9
  technological advance and urban genesis, 280
  unfilled spaces within city walls, 189
  village shrines, 302

Oaxaca
  chronology of urban genesis, *322*
  layout of, 398
  mound architecture, 234, 301
ọbas, 238-9
occupational
  and social differentiation, 267-8
  specialization: and redistribution, 270; Lung-shan, 28, 30
Oc-èo
  city, 254, 391
  port, 253, 345, 391
**·Ok, 140-1, 183, 188, 221, 426
Old Ica, 236
omphalos
  axis mundi, and, 428-9
  Chinese concept, 450, 451, 481
  in other regions, 451
Oppenheimer, Franz, 374

oracle archives, bones
  association with court and priesthood, 43
  as source for Shang urban studies, 19-20
  characters on, 380
  deciphering of, 19-20
  extent of, 6
  interpretation of, 85-6
  method of inscribing, 380
  nature of information, 19, 46
  periodization based on, 10, 39
  Shang, 3-4, 15-16, 19-20, 21, 22, 35, 39, 43, 46, 50, 52, 56-9
  utility of, 4-5, 20
  writing on, 379-80
Orans, Martin, 277-8
organizational inputs, 279
oriental despotism
  definition of, 356-7
  Wittfogel's theory, 289-91
ornaments
  Chou, 140, 144
  proliferation of, 281
  Shang jade, 69, 74
orthogenesis, orthogenetic
  modulations between heterogenesis and, 392-3
  role of ceremonial centers, 311, 324, 478, 479, 481
Otto, Walter, 416
Ọwọ, *263*
Ọyọ
  afin of, 239, 361
  corvée for, 261, *263*
  ecological zones, 271
  élite traders, 284
  question of urban status, 382

Pachacámac, 236, 237
palaces
  as *axes mundi*, 428
  as part of ceremonial centers, 225
  Chou, 175
  Cretan, 244
  Egyptian, 230

INDEX

palaces – *contd.*
  emergence of, 315-16
  Inca, 238
  Japanese, 246-7, 248
  Mesopotamian, 228, 262, 264, 283
  Southeast Asian, 254-5
  Shang, 71
  symbolism of, 315
Palenque, 235
Palerm, Angel, 292-3
Palestine, urban genesis in, *323*
palladium of the group, 249, 257
Pāṇḍuraṅga, 253
Paris, Pierre, 295-6
pars pro toto relationship, 431-3
Patan-qotu, 236
patrimonialism, Shang
  effect of, 52
  extension of, 57-9
  feudalism and, 59-61
  nature of, 59-61
  state as, 56-7
Pawon, 256
Pearson, Harry, 278
peasantry
  and the ceremonial center, 226, 389-90, 478-9
  living in villages, 47, 65
  master-servant relationship, 133, 134
  nature of Shang, 65-6
  position in: Chou society, 124-5, 133-4; Shang society, 63
  rise of landless, 126, 133-4
  rural-urban distinction, 321, 331
Pegu, 251
Pei-ching
  axial design, 425
  gates, 435
  layout, 414
  symbolic framework 418, 435
Pelliot, Paul, 391
Perrot, Jean, 394
Persepolis, 438-9
Peru, Peruvian
  calendrics, 384-5
  compact settlements, 278
  Co-tradition: defined, 234; militarism, 300-1; urban status, 386
  early ceremonial centers, 276
  population densities of ceremonial centers, 307
  question of urban status, 395-7
  secularization of authority, 314
  symbiotic exchanges, 374
  urban genesis, course of, *326-7*
  use of the *khipu*, 379
Phaistos, 244, 267
Phanat, 252-3
Phetchaburi, 252
Phnoṃ Bǎkhèṅ, 448
Phnoṃ Peṅḥ, 433
Phong Tük, 252
Piedras Negras, 235
P'ing-wang
  cardinal orientation, 139, 427
  description of site, 139-40
  industries, 139-40
  triple-terraced platform, 139, 182
Pirenne, Henri, 388
pit(s)
  classification of, 93-4
  cruciform, 44, 316
  dwellings, 16, 40, *42*
  granaries, 26
platform(s)
  as part of ceremonial complex, 225
  Baluchistan mud-brick, 232, 233
  cardinal axiality, 142, 185, 425
  Central Andes, 236
  hang-t'u, 139, 142, 144, 145, 185, 429
  Japanese, 248
  Mesoamerican, 234, 235, 301
  Mesopotamian, 227
  omphalos concept and, 429
  purpose of, 185
  shape of: circular, 142, 185; irregular, 185; oval, 145, 185; square, 139, 142, 144, 185
  triple-terraced, 139, 145
  with ramps, 139, 185, 233
  with steps, 233
  with stone pillars, 142

INDEX

plazas
  Central Andes, 236
  Copán, 260
  Mesoamerica, 235
Polanyi, Karl, 264, 282, 283, 285
Pole Star, 428, 430, 442
political
  absorption and cultural diffusion, 176
  authority organizing labor force, 260
  forms, evolution of Chinese, 116-17
  organization, Lung-shan, 26, 28
  power: attested by erection of ceremonial centers, 257-61; marketing and, 284, 304
  space, creation of, 225
  structure and urban centers, 174
  structure of Shang state: extension of patrimonial authority, 57-9; extent of dominion, 61-3; grand lineage of Shang, 52-5; nature of patrimonialism, 59-61; practice of government, 55-61
  theory of the Chou, 176
  see also government
Polonnaruva
  buildings planned from 260-1
  ceremonial center, 256, 261
  hydraulic engineering, 296-7
  plan of, 241, *243*
pomerium, 432-3
population
  compaction, 236, 378, 374, 390-1
  density: assessment of, 189; changes in, 276-7, 307-8; Chou cities, 189-90; competition and, 390-1; deterioration of habitat and, 276, 277; irrigation and, 292-3; improved agricultural techniques and, 110, 275; Mesoamerica, 292-3; Mesopotamia, 306, 307-8; of ceremonial centers, 257, 305-6; social differentiation and, 390-1; superordinate redistribution and, 275-6; urban genesis and, 275
  increase and urban generation, 276, 277, 278
  sparse, reallocation among, 276, 277, 305-6
  see also morphology
pottery
  affinity with bronze casting, 72-3
  An-yang, 74
  associated with ceremonial centers, 71, 74
  brushed characters on, 38, 381;
  Cheng-Chou, 35, 66, 67, 74-5
  Chou, advances in, 131-2
  form and design of, 71
  houses of potters, 35, 36, 66
  kilns, 24, 32, 35-6, 43, 47, 50, 66, 70, 71, 74-5, 136, 138, 140, 141
  Lung-shan, 27, 28, 32, 71
  musical instruments, 71, 74
  private demand for, 74
  production for élite, 76, 176
  Shang: manufacture, 32, 50, 69; technological change, 70-1
  specialization in craft, 28
  tiles, 128, 139, 141, 145
  types of ware, 70-1
  uses of, 25, 27
  wheel used for, 70
  Yang-shao, 24
praetorian guards, 226, 306
Práḥ Khǎn, 259, 265-6
Preah Vihear, 260
pre-urban North China
  Lung-shan phase, 26-30
  Yang-shao phase, 22-5
priesthood
  association with ceremonial centers, 43, 47, 257, 306
  emergence of Mesopotamian, 227-8
  expertise in scapulimancy, 56
  inscription of names on oracle bones, 56
  liberation from subsistence labor, 303
  organized, 303-4
  participation in administration, 228

INDEX

priesthood – *contd.*
  priest-kings of Knossos, 244
  priestly augurs, 56
Primary Village Farming Efficiency, 23, *326-7*, 328, 395
proto-cities, Shang, 4, 50
Proto-Elamite writing, 377
Proto-Indic writing, 377, 381, 382
Pucara, 236
Pumpun, 238
pyramids
  as part of the ceremonial center, 225
  Central Andean: stone faced, 237; triple-terraced, 236
  Egyptian: as a tomb, 429; association with temples, 230; at Gizeh, 235, 316
  Mesoamerican: Pyramid of Cholula, 235; Pyramid of the Moon, 260; Pyramind of the Sun, 235, 258; temple-, 235, 301, 429
  omphalos concept and, 429
Pyū, 249-50, 288

Qotu-qotu, 236
Quetta valley, 231-3
Quirites, 309, 432-3
Quraysh, 286-8, 354-5, 376

Ratburi, 252
ration lists, 228, 265
reallocation
  by Mesopotamian temples, 265
  diversity of subsistence base and, 269
  in areas of sparse population, 276
  increase in craft production and, 280
  in folk societies, 274
  redistributive institutions and, 274, 389-90
  village shrine and, 304-5, 389
Redfield, Robert, 392, 393
redistribution, redistributive
  as function of ceremonial centers, 264-5, 317, 320, 389

centripetally arranged systems of, 105
ceremonial centers and: Cambodia, 265-6; Central Andes, 267; Crete, 267; Indus valley, 267; Mesoamerica, 270; Mesopotamia, 264-5, 273; Mexico, 266; Shang, 76, 186, 266-7; Southeast Asia, 249
change from reciprocative to, 389, 477
effect of: class differentiation, 266; rural-urban differences, 266
elaboration of, 225-6
fertility and, 274-5
flow of goods and services, 264-5
mode of integration as criterion of urbanism, 373, 374, 389
occupational specialization and, 270
Polanyi's model, 264-5
population density and, 275-6
priesthood's role in, 303
'surplus' and, 268
techniques for mobilizing resources, 268, 390
village shrine and, 304-5
religion, religious
  action, 319
  ancient Greek and Roman, 302
  as a factor in social differentiation, 302-5
  astrobiology and, 416
  authority: decline of, 311-12; of ceremonial center, 304-5, 389-90; reinforcing social action, 320, 428
  cosmic scheme, 305, 320
  Chou, 112-13, 116
  collectivities, failure to develop differentiated, 319-20
  cult and, 319
  defined, 319
  dramatizing the cosmogony, 417, 428-36
  ecological instability and, 304
  expression, stylized modes of, 225
  family loyalties and, 112-13

INDEX

religion, religious – *contd.*
  formalism, craft production and, 281
  gods, fertility, 281
  hierophanies guaranteeing renewal of cyclic time, 311, 479
  Japan, 245-6, 247
  Java, 256
  Lung-shan, 27-8
  Mesoamerica, 304
  Mesopotamia, 303, 304
  messianic expectations, 320
  monism: cosmological, 321; differentiated, 319
  need for communication, 319, 436
  need for worship and sacrifice, 319, 320
  norms, 315, 316
  North China, 303
  organization, 319-20
  parallelism between macrocosmos and microcosmos, 116
  political: aims, 315, 316; duties, 112-13
  revealed, 416-17
  ritual and ceremonies, 225, 305
  ritual and sovereignty, 123
  role in ecological adaptation, 416-17
  social implications of, 302-5, 320
  space, 304-5
  status differentiation and, 27-8
  symbolism, 305, 319, 428-36
  transcendental, 321, 428
  transforming landscape, 416-17
  tribal, 319
  village shrines, 302-5
  writing for, 382, 383
  Yang-shao, 24
Renfrew, Colin, 288
rest houses, 259
Rhodesia, *322*, 397-8
rice cultivation, 24, 27, 67-8, 129, 130, 272
ring-footed vessels, 27, 32, 71
ritual
  annointings and lustrations, 244, 265, 296
  aspects of Cambodian hydraulic system, 295-6
  Chou, 112-13
  craft production and, 43, 228, 279-80
  display, and techological advance, 74, 305
  ensuring the renewal of cylic time, 311, 389-90, 417, 479
  Lung-shan, 27
  representational art and, 225
  role of ceremonial centers in, 225, 305
  specialists, role of, 389-90, 410
  vessels, 43, 281
  weapons, 281
  writing and, 225
  Yang-shao, 25
roadways, 139, 185
Rome
  bibliography, 339-40
  capital, vital forces focused in, 432
  ceremonial center, 244
  evocatio, 432
  forum, role of, 178
  Icilian law, 309
  merchant community of Aventine hill, 309, 433
  Milliarium Aureum, 433
  morphology of Etruscan, 307
  pomerium, 432-3
  Romulus, 432, 434
  settlement pattern, 309, 364-5
  urban genesis, course of, *326-7*
  urban status, question of, 386
  walled enceinte, of Palatine hill, 309, 432-3, 434
Rowe, John, 236, 238, 294, 389, 395-7
ruler, function and role of, 175, 178-9, 188

sacrality, 417
sacred
  as the natural course of the world, 416
  link between profane and, 416

INDEX

sacred – *contd.*
  space: creation of, 225, 305; delimitation of, 417
sacrifice
  animal, 43, 46-7, 65, 68, 101, 272, 316
  breeding of animals for, 68, 272
  consecratory, 40, 43, 44, 65
  human, 43, 44, 46, 47, 64-5, 316
  Mesopotamia, 227
  of prisoners of war, 65, 66
  pits for, 44, 65
  schedule of, 123
  to Shang ancestors, Chou offering, 107
  vessels, 74
Sagaing, 307
Ṣagamu, 239
Śailendra dynasty, 256, 346
salt
  sale of, 134
  specialization, regional in, 130
  trade in, 126
Sāmarrā, 303, 448
sanctuaries, 244, 302-3
Sanders, W.T., 269, 293, 306, 307
scapulimancy
  evidence from, 303
  in Lung-shan, 27-8
  priesthood as experts in, 56
  role of, 19-20
  use of writing in, 380
Schwab, W., 391
sciences, exact and predictive
  development of, 226
  emergence of 373, 383-6
  varied stages of advancement, 383
secular
  authority, seat of, and *axis mundi*, 428
  dichotomy between sacred and, 247, 311
  subsumed in sacred, 225
  warriors, 311, 314, 315
secularization
  decline of sacerdotal hierarchy, 311-12

distinction between religious and secular élites, 321
emergence of the palace, 315-16
extension of sphere of government, 315
kingship and, 311-15
militaristic cults and leadership, 311, 312, 313, 314
of authority: Mesoamerica, 313-14; Mesopotamia, 311-13; Southeast Asia, 314-15
of ceremonial centers, 311-16
political aims, 315, 316
popular assemblies, 312, 313, 314
role of warfare in, 313, 314, 321
Shang
  agriculture and cultivation, 67-8, 73-5, 102, 272-3
  ancestors, 107
  artisans, 66-7
  benefices, 57-61, 109, 112
  bronze inscriptions, 58, 62-3, 111-12
  capitals, migration of, 448-9
  ceremonial centers: allocative pressures, 75; characters for, 99, 100; competing, 62-3; dispersed, 479; map of, *51*; redistributive function, 266-7; technological advance induced by, 70, 71, 73, 74-5
  cities, genesis and morphology of, 20-52, 477
  claims of descent, 52, 96-7, 124
  conquest of, 107-8, 421
  culture: diffusion of traits, 17, 18, 50, 52, 62, 109, 135; limits of developed, 50-2
  craft production, 74-5, 273
  dominion, extent of, 61-3
  dynasty: chronology of, 9; dating of, 9-10; historicity of, 3-4, 9-13; history of, 10-11
  economic organization, 30, 75-7, 105, 186, 262
  epigraphic tradition, 62-3, 111-12
  fishing, 68, 272, 273
  government, practice of, 55-61, 108-9

593

INDEX

Shang – *contd.*
 kin groups, 53, 55, 63, 375
 kings: named in oracle archives, 4, 12; nature of authority, 52; posthumous styles of, 52, 53, 55; succession, 53, *54*
 lineages: and rank, 375; grand, 52-5; groups, 12
 origin of, 10-11
 peasantry, 63, 65-6
 political structure, 52-63
 relations with: Chou, 175-6; Hsia, 12-13
 sites: number of, 18; phases and periodization of, 38-9; spatial significance of, 50, *51*, 52
 society: class differentiation in, 63-7; solidarity, 390-1; structure, 63
 state, political structure of, 52-63
 storage pits, 266-7
 technological change, 67-75
 urbanism: core area of, 50, *51*, 161; criteria applied to, 386; sources of (archeological 15-19, literary 13-15, oracle archive 19-20)
 use of term, 10
 workshops, dispersion of, 185-6
 writing, 379-80
Shang-Sung, 15
Shan-Hsien, 4
shells, inscribed, 3, 4
Shih-Chi
 authenticity of genealogies, 152
 Chou evidence from, 151
 commentaries of, 14-15
 content of, 14-15, 159-60
 list of benefices, 163
 miraculous birth of Shang ancestors, 52
 references to: hierarchy of cities, 174; *hsien*, 180; irrigation, 131; urbanism, 164, 166
 value of, 159-60
Shih-Ching (*Book of Odes*)
 Chou evidence from, 151
 commentaries on, 153-4
 description of, 15
 references to: benefices, 100; geomancy, 420, 423; wall building, 34
Shogunate, 115
shrine(s)
 antiquity of, 302-3
 as supramundane source of authority, 304
 Baluchistan, 231, 303
 Central Andes, 236, 429
 -cities of Cambodia, 258-60, 265
 evolution into temples, 225, 226-7
 integrative function of, 478
 Japanese, 246, 247
 Mesopotamian, 226-7, 303
 omphalos concept and, 429
 organizing economic, social and political space, 305, 478
 public, chronology of, *326-7*
 redistributive function of, 304-5
 Southeast Asian, 249, 251, 255, 256
Shu-Ching (*Book of Documents*)
 centripetal symbolism in, 430
 Chou evidence from, 151
 description of, 13-14
 references to: geomancy, 420, 421, 423; movement of capitals, 449; siting of capitals, 444-5; urban forms, 164, 166
Shuruppak, 226
sickle(s)
 cache of, 76, 262
 iron, 130, 131
 lien, 68, 69, 73-4
Sīgiriya, 301, 438
Singer, Milton, 392, 393
Sippara, 436
Śiśupālgarh, 414
Sitawaka, 257
Sjoberg, Gideon, 317, 377
slaves
 Chou, 125, 203
 Japanese, 245
 Mesopotamian, 228
 Shang, 66
 used in agriculture, 76

INDEX

social
- action, and religion, 320-1
- caste, occupational specialization hardening into, 126, 128, 249
- change: accompanying urban development, 4; intensifying urbanism, 171
- class, emergence of, and technological advance, 74-5
- component in socio-cultural complexity, 281
- development, traits characteristic of, 373
- differentiation: activities inducing, 318-19; as independent variable, 267, 218-19; compaction and, 290-1; craft production and, 280; cult center adapting to pressures of, 321; defined, 317; dynamic density and, 391; factors inducing 281-305; in era of Developed Village Farming, 326; in response to environmental resources 320; irrigation and, 289-98; kingship and, 288, 311; levels or stages, 318; Meccan, 286-8; occupational as concomitant with, 267-8; religion and, 302-5; rise of ceremonial centers, and, 267, 318-19; Shang and Western Chou, 479; Southeast Asian, 288; territorial differentiation and, 267-8, 317, 324; trade and marketing, 281-9; urban and rural, 310-11, 321, 479; warfare and, 298-302
- exchange, market as venue for, 178
- institutions and rise of ceremonial centers, 267
- interdependence, exploitation of environment and, 270
- life, religion as consensual focus of, 319
- milieu, of pre-urban North China, 22-30
- morphology, definitions based on, 388
- order: architectural assemblages as symbols of, 225; sacrally sanctioned, 305
- organization, 281, 318-21
- persons, 305
- power: and marketing, 282; attested by erection of ceremonial centers, 257-61
- prestige, technological advance and, 74
- solidarity: and improved agricultural techniques, 110; compaction and, 324; mechanical, 267, 300-1, 479; organic, 267, 390-1, 392
- space, creation of, 225, 389, 478
- stratification: as criterion of urbanism, 373-4; Egypt, 229; incipient, in Mecca, 286; Lung-shan, 229; Mesopotamia, 228; sanctioned by religious and moral norms, 311
- structure, factors changing, 281
- transformation in Ch'un-Ch'iu, 177

society
- absorption by another, 318
- ascriptive, 317, 374-5
- Chou: agro-military communities, 175-6; artisans and craftsmen, 125; bureaucratic institutions, 128; changes in, 125-6; classes of people, 122-3; closed aristocracy, 123; description of, 122-8; disintegration of higher strata, 125; effects of economic change, 126-8; emergence of élite, 128; emergence of rankless landowners, 126; entrepreneurs, 126-7, 133-4; gentlemen of good birth, 124; kin-based, decline of cohesiveness, 128; king, charisma of, 123; king's men, 122-3; magnates, 133; merchants, 125; ministers, 124; nobility, degrees of, 121, 122, 199-200; peasantry, 123, 124-5; political change affecting, 125-6; pyramidal form, 123; rise of individuals on merit, 125-6, 128;

595

INDEX

society, Chou – *contd.*
   spatial expression of dichotomy in, 186; state rulers, 123-4; story of Po-Kuei, 127; vertical mobility, 128
class differentiation in Shang, 63-7
differentiation as a classificatory concept, 317-18
egalitarian, 25, 249, 317, 377
Egyptian, 229
folk, 90-1
gentile to politized, 315
heterogeneity, 321
Japanese, 245
Lung-shan, 28-30, 229
moral norms of, 282
paternalistic, of the great traditions, 291
pyramidal, 63, 123, 226, 391
quadripartite division of, 321
rank, 25, 325, 377
Redfield's formulation, 29-30
Shang, 63-7
slave, 125, 245
Southeast Asian, 249
stratified, 28-9, 224
tribal, 249
Yang-shao
soil salinization, 226, 233
Southeast Asia
   canal system, 254, 345
   cardinal axiality and orientation, 253, 256
   centripetality, 254
   ceremonial centers: areal extent, 252-3; description, 248-57; dispersed, *323*; enceintes, 250-1, 252; phase, 477; plan of, 241, *243*
   Chinese literary sources relating to, 248, 250, 252, 253, 254, 255
   circumambulation, 433
   city-states, 253, 255
   cult centers, 253
   dwellings, 254, 255
   gates, 250, 435
   Indianization, 248-9, 253, 314-15, 341
   kingship, 249, 256, 314-15
   labor force, 261-2
   moats, 250, 252, 253, 254
   mountains, 254
   omphalos concept, 429
   palaces, 254, 255
   palisades, 254, 255
   parallelism between macrocosmos and microcosmos, 436-8
   ramparts, 252
   redistribution, 249
   regions of, 249-50
   shrines, 249, 251, 252, 255, 256
   society: changes in, 249; dysfunctions in, 288; thalassocratic, 253
   stupa, 256
   swidden cultivation, 275
   synoecism, 310
   temple-cities: as chronograms, 436; settlement patterns, 307, 310; traditions of, 257
   temples, 249, 250, 428
   tribute, 284
   urban: forms earliest, 248-57; genesis, chronology of, *323*; walls, 250, 252, 254, 255, 310
   warfare, 299
   see also Burma, Cambodia, etc.
space
   and mass, planned distribution of, 260
   architectural assemblages creating, 225
   cosmological ordering of, 416, 423, 425
   delimitation of, 417, 418, 433-4, 451-2
   economic, 225, 389, 478
   effective, 267, 389, 398-9, 477
   existential, 418, 430
   political, 225, 389, 478
   sacred, 225, 305, 389, 417, 418, 433-4, 478
   social, 225, 389, 478
   urban, ordering of, 414-19, 451
Sparta, 309
specialization, defined, 318

INDEX

Spencer, Herbert, 390
Spengler, Oswald, 397
Śrī Kṣetra, 250
Śrīraṅgam, 414
staircases, stairways, 225, 234, 235, 236, 237, 301
state(s)
  Chou, 114-16
  Shang, 55-9
  urban generation and foundation of, 8
Stein, Rolf, 444
stelae, 225, 234, 300
Steward, Julian, 281, 320
storage pits, 38, 40, *42*, 43, 76, 139, 226-7
storehouses, 227, 235
stupa, 256
suburbs, 186-8
Sudan, 7, 9
Sumbu, 428
Sumer, Sumerian
  archeological evidence, 3
  calendrics, 385
  civilization, shift of center of gravity of, 226
  compaction of urban forms, 480
  cult centers, 113, 194
  date of, 6
  irrigation, 292
  trade, 283, 284
  writing, 377, 378, 382, 383
summer solstice, 428
surplus
  concept of, 349-50
  social, nature and function of, 277-8
  technology and creation of, 278-9
swidden cultivation, 24, 26, 130, 275, 293
symbol(s), symbolism
  architectural, 225
  astrobiological, 417
  axes mundi, 259, 417-18, 431-2, 434-6
  centripetal, 438
  circumambulation, 433-4
  cosmo-magical: applied to Chinese city planning, 418-19; of Cambodia, 254, 259-60, 296, 372; of canal system, 259, 295; of Ceylon, 301; of Chinese, 411-76; participation in, 417, 418
  of: ceremonial centers, 477-8; Chou China, 429-31; gates, 435-6; the ancient temple, 431; the Chinese city, 411-76; walls, 372
  omphalos concept, 428-9
  pars pro toto relationship, 431-3
  spatial, 254, 259-60
synoecism
  as intermediate stage in compaction, 308-9, 324
  cities formed by, 250
  examples of, 308-10
  Yoruba, 239

Tabasco, urban genesis, *322*, *326-7*
Tagoung, 307
Tairona
  chronology of dispersed centers, *322*
  course of urban genesis, *326-7*
  truncated evolution, 397
Tajahuana, 236
Tambo Viejo, 236
T'ang Ch'ang-an
  influence on Japanese building, 247
  layout of, 411, 414
  orientation of, 427
  plan of, *412*
Ta Prohm, 258-9, 265
Tarquinia, 245
taxes, 258, 390
technical order, 392-3
technological, technology
  advance and change: archeologists' preoccupation with, 4; Chou, 114, 130-2; in agriculture, 67-8, 74, 75, 110, 130-1, 269, 280; in ceremonial centers, 70, 71, 73, 74, 279, 305; in crafts, 68-73, 228, 279-80, 281; military, 73, 280, 281; ritualism and, 74, 280, 305; royalty and élite and, 73, 74, 280, 281;

INDEX

technological, technology – *contd.*
  Shang, 67-75; social class and, 74-5, 280; surpluses and, 278-9; temporary fluctuations of power through, 304
  component in urban genesis, 278-81, 381
  development, phases of urban and, 279-81
  progress, Urban Revolution and acceleration of, 279

Tell Brak, 227, 329
Tell el-Amarna, 307
Tell es-Sultan, 393-4
Tell Khoshi, 329
Tell 'Uqair, 227

temple(s)
  agricultural control exercised by, 262, 264
  as part of the ceremonial complex, 225
  as replicas of the cosmos, 417
  axes mundi, 249, 259, 417-18, 428, 432, 451
  Cambodian, 249, 254-5, 258-60, 265-6, 295, 432, 436-8, 448, 451
  cardinal orientation of, 436, 451
  Central Andean, 236-8, 429
  Chinese: ancestral, 55, 121; at Hsiao-T'un, 40, 43, 55, 65; dedication of, 65; *omphalos* concept, 429; pottery associated with, 71
  -cities, 254-5, 258-60, 265-6, 279, 307-8, 436-8, 451
  Egyptian, 230, 429
  Japanese, 246, 247-8
  Mesoamerican, 234-5, 260, 301, 429
  Mesopotamian, 226-8, 262, 264, 279-80, 292, 331-2
  mounds, 234, 235, 429
  -mountains, 254, 259, 387, 429, 432, 437-8, 448, 451
  of Quetzalcóatl, 260, 441
  omphalos concept, 429
  orthogenetic role, 311
  -pyramids, 235, 301, 429
  Pyū, 250
  redistributive function, 262, 264, 292
  Southeast Asian, 249, 250-1, 254-7, 260, 307, 428, 429
  state, 249
  terraces, 436-7

T'eng-Hsien, 146, 183

Tenochtitlán
  as a compact settlement, 306
  Aztec city of, 266
  irrigation system, 293
  question of urban status, 386
  supply of vegetables to, 272

Teotihuacán
  axis, 441
  calendrics, 384
  centripetalizing power of, 300
  characteristics of Classic, 326
  extent of, 235
  irrigation, 293
  labor force, 258
  militarism, 300
  morphology of Tzacualli phase, 307
  mural art, 300, 373
  planned distribution of space and mass, 260
  plan of, 241, *242*
  population density, question of, 306-7
  previous settlements, 234-5
  Pyramid of the Moon, 260
  Pyramid of the Sun, 235, 258
  settlement round enceinte, 257
  Temple of Quetzalcóatl, 260, 441
  theocratic government, 313
  urban status, 386

Tepe Gawra, 299, 329

terraces
  agricultural, 260, 293, 296
  as part of ceremonial complex, 225
  Cambodian, 259, 296, 436
  Central Andean, 236, 237
  Javanese, 256
  Mesoamerican, 234, 293
  Terrace of the Elephants, 259

INDEX

textiles
  Lung-shan, 27
  Shang, 69
Thai, Thailand
  ceremonial centers: description of, 251-3; tradition of, 251, 257
  City of the Sacred Chariot, 252
Thatōn, 251
Theory of Central Place, 388
Theseus, King, 308-9
Thinis, 230
Tiahuanaco
  absence of settlement, 257, 276
  description of, 236-7
  impact of, 301
T'ien-Wen, 151
Tikal, 237
tin, 283
Tiruvannamalai, 414
tithes, 390, 479
Tlaloc, 304, 441
Tollán, 300, 361
Toltec, 300, 306, 308
tombs
  Egyptian royal, 230
  emergence of royal: as an architectural feature, 316; in Mesopotamia, 228
  geomantic precautions in siting, 419
  labor force required for building, 76-7
  Mesoamerican, 301
  'regular', 64
  royal Chinese, 64, 187
  see also mausolea
toponymy, problems of, 163-4, 166-7, 168
trade, trading
  administered, 226, 282, 283-4
  and marketing as factors in social differentiation, 281-9
  and tribute, 270
  Assyrian, 282-3, 372
  disparagement of small-scale, 285
  distinction between marketing and, 282, 372
  Eastern Chou, 177
  entrepreneurial, 285
  fluctuations in power arising from, 304
  gift, 226, 284
  importance of, 177-8
  in centers of secondary urban generation, 288-9
  items sold, 177-8
  long-distance, 283
  marketless, 282-3, 372
  Meccan, 286-8
  Mesoamerican, 270, 284
  Mesopotamian, 282-3
  peddling, 284-5
  role in urban genesis, 285-6
  Shang, 283
  size of cities and, 184
  treaty, 226, 282, 283-4, 285
  tribute, 282, 284
Transbassac, 253, 295-6
transportation
  degree of autonomy in, 479
  Egyptian canals used for, 295
  hydraulic systems in China designed for, 292
  technological advance and, 279
  technology and compaction of urban forms, 480
tribute
  brought to ceremonial centers, 479
  collection of, 58
  lists, 266
  organized as an economic system, 266, 390
  paid to Chou, 176
  Shang, 58, 284
  system, 129, 130, 284
  trade, 270, 282, 284
Tribute of **Gįwo (Yü), 129-30, 284
tripods, 27, 32, 35, 64, 71, 104
Ts'ai-Chuang, 145, 183
Tso-Chuan
  compilation of, 114, 151-2
  list of benefices, 162-4
  nature of text, 151-2

INDEX

Tso-Chuan – contd.
   references to: accretions to cities, 184-5; areal extent and rank of cities, 183-4; commerce, 177; discrete quarter of cities, 186; *hsien*, 181; movement of capitals, 449; tax, 133; urbanism, 170, 171, 172, 174; walling of suburbs, 187
   relation between kin and craft, 66-7
   value of, 153-4
Tula, 300, 313
Tumipampa, 238
turquoise, 283

Uaxactún, 235, 300, 306
uji, 245, 376
Umma, 226
Ur, 226, 316
urban
   character of the ceremonial complex, 225-6, 371-409
   forms: earliest, 225-57; imposition of, 8, 324; in Anatolia, 393, 394-5; in Levant, 393-4; in North China, 30-47; in regions of primary urban generation, 226-43; in regions of secondary urban generation, 244-57; pre-urban, in North China, 22-30; systematization of earlier phases, 48-9
   generation, *see* generation
   genesis: ceremonial centers as functional and developmental phase of, 316, 477; course of, *326-7*, 328; ecological component in, 268-75, 477; rates of evolution, 325-6; relative chronology, *322-3*; 'step' and 'ramp' metaphors, 325, 368; structural regularities in evolutionary process, 324
   life, diffusion of, in ancient China, 107-90
   origins, archeology and, 3-5
   Revolution: acceleration of technological progress and, 279; as a process, 277, 373; as a social transformation, 281, 315, 377; astrobiology and organization of space and society, 416; institutions of, 265; population increases and, 276; use of term, 281
urbanism
   Chou: areal extent, 168; Chan-Kuo, 172; Ch'un-Ch'iu, *169*, 170-2; city building activities, 172-3; Eastern, 169-75; nature of, 173-90; number of cities, 171, 173; pattern of distribution, 162-8; persisting Shang cities, 161, 164, 174; recorded settlements, *165*, 168, *169*; spatial pattern of, 161, *165*, 167-8; types of settlement, 167; urban settlement defined, 167-8; Western, 161-8
   city and state, 398-9
   criteria of, 371-4
   definitions of: Childe's, 373-4, 377, 378, 387; geographers', 388-9, 391, 398, 477; Monro's, 372-3; Rowe's, 396-7; Weber's, 371-2
   mechanical and organic social solidarity applied to, 390-2
   nature of, 386-99
   nuclear regions: Chinese, 50, *51*; Mesopotamian, 226-30
   orthogenesis and heterogenesis, 392-3
   predictive and exact sciences, 383-6
   qualifying degrees of, 389-90
   role of corporate kin group, 374-7
   settlements on threshold of, 393-6, 389-9
   Shang, sources for, 13-20
   truncated evolution of, 397-8
   writing, significance of, 377-83
Uruk
   cult center, 226
   population and areal extent, 228
   ration lists, 265
   seal from, 299
   synoecism in formation of, 310
   temples at, 227, 265
   writing from, 378

INDEX

U-Thong, 252
Uxmal, 235

Vaillant, G. C., 306
Vaiśālī, 250-1
Vasiliki, 244
Vat Nokor, 259
Vat Phu, 254
Vera Cruz, *322*, *326-7*
Vijaya, 253
village(s)
  artisans and peasantry living in ancillary, 47
  as basic unit of settlement, 229
  Egyptian, 229, 333
  fortified, 233, 390
  Lung-shan, 26, 229
  permanent, 26, 396
  walls, 299, 300
  Yang-shao, 24-5, 277
Virú, 236, 294
Vyādhapura, 254

walls
  as criterion of urbanism, 394
  Cambodia, 259, 372, 438
  characters for, 182, 186, 187
  Chou city, 136, 138, 140, 141, 144, 145, 146, 182-3
  cosmo-magical significance of, 378, 438
  Damb Sadaat enceinte, 232
  defensive, 228, 299, 300
  hang-tʻu, 183, 302
  height of, 183
  interpreted as fortifications, 372
  orientation of, 426, 427
  outer and inner, 186, 187, 479
  Persepolis, 438-9
  Rome, 309
  seasons for building and repair, 182-3, 435-6
  Southeast Asia, 250, 252-5, 310, 372
  South Indian temple-cities, 435-6
  village, 229, 300
  width of, 183

Wang-Chʻeng
  description of, 136, 138
  plan of, *137*, 147, *149*, *415*
warfare
  accompanying rise of city-state, 228
  chronic raiding and, 228, 298, 321
  compaction and, 299, 300, 310, 480
  defensive: sites, 300-1; walls, 299, 300
  economic demands of, 228
  endemic character of, 299, 302
  in: Mesoamerica, 299-300; Mesopotamia, 299; Peruvian Co-tradition, 300-1
  institutionalized, 298
  intensifying urban development, 298-9
  Lung-shan, 28
  role in social differentiation, 298-302
  tribal conflict, 301-2
  weapons of, 228, 298, 302
  see also military
Warqa, 227, 258, 307
water
  channels, 138
  -lifting devices, 131
Weber, Max, 371-2, 388, 390, 479
well-field system, 132-3, 176, 205, 411, 414
Wellhausen, Julius, 286, 287
Wensinck, A. J. L., 436
Westheim, P., 441
Wheeler, Sir Mortimer, 7
Willey, Gordon, 276, 277, 325, 389
Wilson, John, 389, 399
Wirth, Louis, 388
Wittfogel, Karl, 289-97
Wolf, Eric, 293, 375, 399
women, 58
workshops
  city, 176, 479
  dispersion of, 185-6
  near temples, 227
  village, 176
writing, significance of, 377-83
Wu, Nelson, 440, 450-1

INDEX

Wu-an, 183, 185
Wu-Ch'eng, 145, 147, *148*
Wu-chi, Chen, 141

Xochicalco
  deflection of axis, 441
  hegemony, 313
  site, 300

Yamato, 245-6
Yang-shao
  agriculture: crops, 24, 87-8; implements, 23-4, 87
  as egalitarian society, 25
  common cemetery, 24-5, 277
  description of culture, 22-5
  division of labor, 29-30
  fission of parent villages, 24-5, 277
  village economy, 75
Yaśodharapura
  ceremonial center, 241, *243*
  description of, 259, 436-8
  symbolism of, 432, 436-7
Yaxuná, 235
Yen, 185, 188, 426, 429
Yin, 10
Yoruba, *see* Nigeria, Southwestern

Zakro, 244
Zhob, 231
ziggurats, 227, 233, 258
Zimbabwe, 397-8

知我者其惟春秋乎
罪我者其惟春秋乎